D1261337

Shang Civilization

KWANG-CHIH CHANG

Shang Civilization

NEW HAVEN AND LONDON
YALE UNIVERSITY PRESS
1980

Set in Monophoto Apollo type by
Asco Trade Typesetting Ltd., Hong Kong.
Printed in the United States of America by
The Murray Printing Co., Westford, Mass.

Published in Great Britain, Europe, Africa, and Asia (except Japan) by Yale University Press, Ltd., London. Distributed in Australia and New Zealand by Book & Film Services, Artarmon, N.S.W., Australia; and in Japan by Harper & Row, Publishers, Tokyo Office.

Library of Congress Cataloging in Publication Data

Chang, Kwang-Chih.
Shang civilization.

Bibliography: p.
Includes index.
1. China—History—Shang dynasty, 1766-1122 B.C.
2. China—Antiquities. I. Title.
DS744.C383 931 79-19107
ISBN 0-300-02428-2

Dedicated to Professor Li Chi

(1896–1979)

Contents

Figures

Tables

Preface

This volume presents a brief but comprehensive history of the Shang civilization of ancient China (ca. eighteenth–twelfth century B.C.), drawing upon available sources of all kinds. There are many reasons why a book of this kind is now timely, but the following are foremost.

First, we need a book on Shang *history*, as well as on Shang *historical sources* (with the accent on the plural of the word sources). Because of the way Shang historiography has evolved (see the prolegomena, following), Shang scholars have been traditionally trained within individual disciplines that focus on particular sources—texts, oracle bone inscriptions, bronze inscriptions, or archaeological data. All of these source materials are important, but each discipline tends to emphasize only some particular aspect or aspects of the Shang civilization. There is need for a study that is to be based on all of these sources, resulting, it is hoped, in a more complete picture of the Shang history than can be achieved within each single discipline.

Second, archaeological discoveries in the last decade of Shang sites and Shang artifacts throughout China have, on the one hand, immensely enriched our knowledge of this particular civilization and its antecedents and called into question some of our cherished notions about the nature of Shang society and the characteristics of Shang history and, thus, on the other hand, are compelling us to rethink some of our fundamental premises about the Shang. A book at this time is more than a synthesis of the known and the familiar; it prompts us toward new ideas and new understandings at a crucial juncture of Shang studies.

Third, our understanding of the Shang civilization has now reached a point, qualitatively, where we are able to attempt to place Shang society in a comparative light, essential for us to understand it in a world context and for world historians (as well as comparative social historians and evolutionary anthropologists) to formulate, or at least to assess, evolutionary models that are purported to be universal. The Chinese civilization is an important component of human civilization, and its study must carry its own weight in the illumination of theoretical issues of universal interest. It is time, I believe, to take stock of the available data and studies to see where we stand with regard to such important issues as the origin of the state, the so-called Asiatic society, and universal evolutionary models. Let me add, finally, that placing China in a comparative context will also serve to better our understanding of China herself.

The fact that such a book ought to be written is not by itself sufficient to enable it to be written by any author. There are a couple of points about the writing of this book to which experts may take exception, and let me put in a word or two here about them by way of explanation. First of all, although I advocate a comprehensive—instead of a disciplinary—approach, I myself, like the rest of us, was trained within a single traditional discipline—archaeology—and the book will undoubtedly reflect that fact. Second, the sheer volume of first-hand data and important studies is simply overwhelming, and I have been forced to be highly selective with regard both to the use of data and to the description of various options. I have tried to write a book that can be read by more than the handful of experts on Shang history, and sometimes I have been rather subjective and arbitrary in not only what to include in the book but also how to describe and explain an issue. I hope my expert colleagues will excuse me for not writing a bibliographic essay under every footnote.

Finally, my reliance at many points on textual data to enrich and corroborate has resulted from a deliberate decision. It would have been ideal to use contemporary documents (i.e., oracle bone and bronze inscriptions) for every issue I discuss, but the contemporary documentation does not suffice to give life and spirit to the picture that can be painted. I use Chou and even later textual documents to help complete the Shang picture only under two conditions: First, when they alone are not the crucial data on which to base any critical point, and, second, when we have reason to believe or justify the essential continuity in that area of society and culture in which the pertinent documents are used.

March 8, 1978
Cambridge, Massachusetts

Acknowledgments

My thanks go first of all to Professors Li Chi 李濟, Shih Chang-ju 石璋如, and Kao Ch'ü-hsün 高去尋 and the late Professor Tung Tso-pin 董作賓, my college professors all, who taught me archaeology through teaching me about An-yang. An-yang has ever since occupied a special place in me, and that I have written a book on the Shang at all despite the great difficulties of such a task I owe to this emotional attachment to An-yang. The late Mr. P'an K'o 潘慤 and Messrs. Li Kuang-yü 李光宇 and Hu Chan-k'uei 胡占奎, also participants in the An-yang drama before the war, taught me their valuable experience in informal ways.

For information and first-hand accounts of post-war An-yang work I am indebted to the generous help of Dr. Hsia Nai 夏鼐 and Messrs. An Chih-min 安志敏, Wang Shih-min 王世民, Ch'en Chih-ta 陳志達, Yang Hsi-chang 楊錫璋, Yang Pao-ch'eng 楊寶成, Tai T'ung-hsing 戴同興, Hsü Ching-yüan 許景元, and Mmes. Cheng Chen-hsiang 鄭振香 and Liu Yi-man 劉一曼, whom I met and talked with in 1975 and/or 1977. I will always remember the two days and two nights of long and very fruitful conversations I had at An-yang in July 1977 with Yang Pao-ch'eng, Ch'en Chih-ta, and Cheng Chen-hsiang.

This work was made possible through the assistance of a research grant from the National Endowment for the Humanities. The findings and conclusions presented here do not necessarily represent the views of the Endowment.

The discussion here on Shang chronology was helped by two unpublished manuscripts by P'an Wu-su and Elizabeth Freund. Shao Cheng-yuan of the Astronomy Department of Harvard was helpful in astronomical material. David N. Keightley of the University of California at Berkeley has influenced my thinking about various issues of Shang historiography in more ways than can be enumerated.

I thank Mr. Lai Yung-hsiang at the Harvard-Yenching Library for his generous bibliographic help, Whitney Powell, Donna Pletcher, and Nancy Fernald for their artwork, Hillel Burger and Christopher Burnett for their assistance in photography, and Mary Clare Gubbins, who typed the manuscript.

At the Yale University Press, Sally Cobb Serafim, herself a China scholar, prepared the manuscript for publication with meticulous care and infinite patience.

Bibliographic Note

A full bibliography, arranged alphabetically according to the names of the authors, is given at the end of the book. In the footnotes only the names of the authors and the titles of the works are given.

All works are listed under the name of the author or authors when their names are given in the publications. When works are published anonymously or under the name of an institution, they are listed, alphabetically according to the first word of the title, under the journal or series in which they are published. The latter are abbreviated as follows:

CR	*China Reconstructs*
JH	*Jen-min Hua-pao* 人民畫報
KK	*K'ao-ku* 考古, *K'ao-ku t'ung-hsün* 考古通訊
KKHCK	*K'ao-ku-hsüeh chuan k'an* 考古學專刊
KKHP	*K'ao-ku hsüeh pao* 考古學報
	Chung-kuo k'ao-ku hsüeh pao 中國考古學報
	T'ien-yeh k'ao-ku pao-kao 田野考古報告
SS	*Scientia Sinica*
WW	*Wen-wu* 文物, *Wen-wu ts'an-k'ao tzu-liao* 文物參考資料

Periodicals are listed according to the standard Western practice by volume number, except for certain Chinese periodicals that use citation by year rather than by volume number.

Prolegomena: Five Doors to Shang

Shang 商 is the second of the Three Dynasties—Hsia 夏, Shang, Chou 周—of ancient China, the three dynasties that marked the end of Chinese prehistory and the beginning of Chinese civilization. But who were the Shang? Or, perhaps more appropriately, what does the name Shang mean? Shang is the name the Shang used to refer to their own ancestral capital town,[1] and the Chou people, who came after the Shang on China's political stage, called the dynastic rulers who resided in force in their walled capital towns the Shang.[2]

Shang, thus, is first the name of the royal house which was afforded a dynastic status in Chou literature. The term came to symbolize the state ruled by the Shang royal house, and it has further been extended to the civilization created by the people of the Shang state and the people of the other states contemporary with the Shang. Shang is also used to designate the period of Chinese history in which the Shang dynasty reigned.

Many of the above terms and concepts are tricky to use, but this will not become clear until later on in the course of our study. At the outset, we need only say enough to make clear who the people are whose history we are describing. In this volume we deal with the people in China during the Shang period, traditionally placed between 1766 and 1122 B.C. (The traditional chronology is, however, problematic; we discuss this later.) We are primarily concerned with the people within the Shang state, but we also touch upon some of those outside whose civilization was similar or almost identical.

Shang was a literate civilization, but after the fall of the dynasty the royal archives, if there were any that survived the wrecking of the capital, became gradually dissipated. By the time of Confucius, barely

1. See Ch'en Meng-chia 陳夢家, *Yin-hsü p'u-tz'u tsung-shu* 殷墟卜辭綜述, pp. 255–258; but see also chapter 4 below.

2. See, for example, the poem "Pi kung" in *Lu sung*: "Descendant of Hou Chi/Was the Great King/Who lived on the southern slopes of Mount Ch'i/And began to trim the Shang. . . . /In the field of Mu . . . /He overthrew the hosts of Shang." Arthur Waley, trans., *The Book of Songs*, p. 270.

six hundred years after the fall, the Master was known to have lamented the fact that,

> I could describe the ceremonies of the Yin 殷 [-Shang] dynasty, but Sung 宋 cannot sufficiently attest my words. (They cannot do so) because of the insufficiency of their records and wise men. If those were sufficient, I could adduce them in support of my words. [*Lun yü* 論語, section "Pa yi" 八佾; translated by James Legge]

In the first century B.C., when Ssu-ma Ch'ien 司馬遷 came to compile his *Shih chi* 史記, there were only a few documents he was able to use for the Shang history; the Shang (or Yin) chapter was only a bare outline, consisting of a royal genealogy and a few events. This meager amount of information about Shang was all we had to contend with during most of Chinese history, and Chinese scholars developed a long and detailed historiographic tradition dealing with the few surviving documents.

It was in the Northern Sung dynasty, around the twelfth century, that scholars of ancient China began to pay serious attention to the many bronze ritual vessels, known since the Han dynasty, that were regarded as being of the Three Dynasties. Most of the attention was given to the inscriptions that were cast on the bronzes. During the last century or so, these bronzes found their way into museum collections in Japan and the West, forming the focus of many significant studies by art historians.

Toward the end of the Ch'ing dynasty, another source of Shang history—inscribed cattle shoulder blades and turtle shells used by the Shang for divination—unexpectedly turned up in the antiquities market and eventually fell into the hands of ancient historians. The study of these inscribed shells and bones—*chia ku hsüeh* 甲骨學 —has become a primary source of much information on Shang society and religion, a source of great importance that was totally unknown to Confucius and to Ssu-ma Ch'ien.

Finally, beginning in 1928, the year when the Academia Sinica began scientific excavations in An-yang 安陽, the site of the last royal capital of the Shang, modern archaeology is providing a new and constantly increasing source for Shang history.

Thus, the major sources of Shang history did not become available at the same time; rather, they appeared on the historiographic scene successively, each becoming available a long interval after the appearance of the previous source, during which a long and sophisticated historiographic tradition had become established, with its peculiar body of literature, conventions, and defenders. For this reason, to this day Shang scholars are often trained as narrow specialists. This volume attempts to use all available sources to write the beginning of a comprehensive Shang history. It is, however, necessary to begin it with a brief description of the several historiographic traditions—the several doors to the same Shang history.

1. *TRADITIONAL HISTORICAL TEXTS*

The single most important traditional text pertaining to Shang is found in *Yin pen chi* 殷本紀, a chapter of *Shih chi*, by Ssu-ma Ch'ien. Ssu-ma served as an official historian-archivist under Emperor Wu Ti 武帝 (140–87 B.C.) of the Han dynasty; his writing of *Shih chi*, the first of China's official historical annals, began in 104 B.C., when he was forty-two years old. As court historian-archivist, Ssu-ma had access to the records preserved at the Han court, but even then the material available to him on the Shang dynasty was severely limited. For the Shang chapter, we know that his major sources consisted of *Shu ching* 書經 (including *Shu hsü* 書序), *Shih ching* 詩經, *Kuo yü* 國語, *Tso chuan* 左傳, *Shih pen* 世本, *Ta Tai li* 大戴禮 (section "Ti hsi" 帝繫), and other books.[3] Some of these books survive to this day, often in fragmentary form, while others have long since been lost.

In the next few pages, I will enumerate and describe the major events and principal categories of information contained in *Yin pen chi*, supplemented by other sources.

THE GENESIS OF THE CLAN

The royal house of the Shang dynasty came from the Tzu 子 clan, whose mythological founding ancestor was Hsieh 契. *Yin pen chi* begins with the story of Hsieh's birth:

> Yin's Hsieh, his mother was Chien Ti 簡狄, a daughter of Yu Jung shih 有娀氏 and second consort of Ti K'u 帝嚳. Three persons [including Chien Ti] went to take a bath. They saw that a black bird dropped an egg. Chien Ti took and devoured it, became impregnated, and gave birth to Hsieh 契. Hsieh grew up, assisted Yü 禹 in his work to control the flood, with success.

3. Ch'ü Wan-li 屈萬里, "'Shih-chi Yin pen-chi' chi ch'i-ta chi-lu chung so tsai Yin-Shang shih-tai ti shih shih" 史記殷本紀及其他紀錄中所載殷商時代的史事, 87; Chin Te-chien 金德建, *Ssu-ma Ch'ien so chien shu k'ao* 司馬遷所見書考.

> Ti Shun 帝舜 . . . enfeoffed Hsieh at Shang 商, and gave him the clan name Tzu 子. [Translated by author.*]

This ancestral myth of the Tzu clan, also seen in *Shih ching*,[4] has a theme of bird-egg birth, which is widely seen in the eastern coastal parts of China in early historical periods.[5]

THE ROYAL GENEALOGY AND CAPITALS

The genealogy of the Shang royal house consists of two segments as recorded by Ssu-ma Ch'ien: predynastic, from Hsieh to T'ang 湯, the dynasty's founder, and dynastic, from T'ang to Chòu 紂.[6] It was commonly believed that there were fourteen predynastic lords prior to the dynastic founding, belonging to fourteen successive generations.[7] The lords' names, in their various versions according to *Yin pen chi* and other sources, are as follows:

Hsieh 契
Chao-ming 昭明
Hsiang-t'u 相土
Ch'ang-jo 昌若
Ts'ao-yü 曹圉 (糧圉 in *Shih chi so yin* 史記索隱, quoting *Shih pen*; 根圉 in *Han shu ku chin jen piao* 漢書古今人表; 根國 in *Li chi Chi fa cheng yi* 禮記祭法正義, quoting *Shih pen*)
Min 冥 (季 in *T'ien wen* 天問, according to Wang Kuo-wei 王國維)
Chen 振 (王亥, according to Wang)
Wei 微 (上甲 in *Kuo yü Lu yü* 國語魯語)
Pao-ting 報丁
Pao-yi 報乙
Pao-ping 報丙

*Unless another translator is specifically mentioned, all translations of Chinese sources were made by the author.

4. See the poem "Hsüan niao" in *Shang sung*: "Heaven bade the dark bird/To come down and bear the Shang." Translation by Waley, *The Book of Songs*, p. 275.

5. Fu Ssu-nien 傅斯年, "Yi Hsia tung hsi shuo" 夷夏東西說.

6. The last Shang king was referred to by the Chou (first tone) people as Chou 紂 (fourth tone). In order to avoid possible confusion, Chou the people will be spelled without tone mark, but Chou the king will be spelled as Chòu.

7. *Kuo yü* 國語 ("Chou yü", hsia 周語下): "The Dark King was industrious for the cause of Shang, which rose in power after fourteen generations." *Hsün tzu* 荀子 ("Ch'eng hsiang" 成相): "Hsieh, the Dark King. . . . After fourteen generations there was T'ien Yi, who was Ch'eng T'ang."

Chu-jen 主壬
Chu-kuei 主癸
T'ien-yi 天乙 or Ch'eng T'ang 成湯

Some of these names have been found in the oracle bone inscriptions (to be described later), but in the latter are other names of possible predynastic Shang lords. Ssu-ma's selection of the fourteen listed above was based on grounds that are no longer clear. Both traditional texts and oracle bone incriptions, however, are clear on one point: From Wei, or Shang-chia, on, all the kings' names contain one or another of the ten "celestial stems": chia 甲, yi 乙, ping 丙, ting 丁, wu 戊, chi 己, keng 庚, hsin 辛, jen 壬, or kuei 癸. The Shang calendar uses the ten stems to mark the cyclical *hsün* 旬; each *hsün* consisted of ten days, beginning with the day *chia*. The traditional explanation of the naming practice has been that Shang children were named according to the days of the *hsün* on which they were born.[8] Other explanations have been proposed, including one by this author.[9] We will come back to this issue in due course.

The predynastic lords are thought to have ruled from a number of capital towns. The precise nature of the Shang state and its predynastic form are topics to be discussed at length later in the book, but it can be stated now that the predynastic Shang lords were probably overlords of a political entity of considerable magnitude, and that capital towns were essential ingredients of such an entity.

As stated above, Hsieh, Shang's founding ancestor, is said to be seated in Shang. Shang was placed by Cheng Hsüan 鄭玄 (d. 200) and Huang-fu Mi 皇甫謐 (late third c.), as quoted in *Shih chi chi chieh* 史記集解, in Shang Hsien 商縣 in east-central Shensi.[10] Wang Kuo-wei 王國維, however, has convincingly demonstrated that Shang was located in eastern Honan, near the present city Shang-ch'iu 商丘.[11] Wang's view is widely accepted by modern historians.[12]

According to *Shu hsü* 書序, from Hsieh to T'ang, the political seat of power of Shang had moved eight times. Wang Kuo-wei made an

8. *Pai hu t'ung* ("Hsing ming p'ien"): "The Yin people named their sons according to the day of birth." See Tung Tso-pin 董作賓, "Lun Shang jen yi shih jih wei ming" 論商人以十日爲名, and Ch'ü Wan-li 屈萬里, "Shih fa lan-shang yü Yin tai lun" 謚法濫觴於殷代論.

9. "Shang wang miao hao hsin k'ao" 商王廟號新考.

10. Ch'ü Wan-li 屈萬里, "Shih chi Yin pen-chi chi ch'i-ta chi-lu chung so tsai Yin-Shang shih-tai ti shih shih" 史記殷本紀及其他記錄中所載殷商時代的史事, 105–106.

11. Wang Kuo-wei 王國維, "Shuo Shang" 說商.

12. Ch'ü Wan-li 屈萬里, *op. cit.*, 106.

attempt to name all eight capitals according to miscellaneous references scattered in various texts, and they seem to be concentrated in the eastern and northern Honan and the western Shantung area,[13] but he admits to the highly uncertain nature of his identification.

The precise number of Shang kings from T'ang to Chòu is somewhat uncertain, and the generational relationships of the kings are not always clear. The following lists the kings given in *Yin pen chi*:

1. Ch'eng T'ang 成湯
   [T'ai Ting 太丁: Crown prince, son of Ch'eng T'ang. Died before ascension.]
2. Wai Ping 外丙, younger brother of T'ai Ting
3. Chung Jen 仲壬, younger brother of Wai Ping
4. T'ai Chia 太甲, son of T'ai Ting
5. Wo Ting 沃丁, son of T'ai Chia
6. T'ai Keng 太庚, younger brother of Wo Ting
7. Hsiao Chia 小甲, son of T'ai Keng
8. Yung Chi 雍己, younger brother of Hsiao Chia
9. T'ai Wu 太戊, younger brother of Yung Chi
10. Chung Ting 仲丁, son of T'ai Wu
11. Wai Jen 外壬, younger brother of Chung Ting
12. Ho T'an Chia 河亶甲, younger brother of Wai Jen
13. Tsu Yi 祖乙, son of Ho T'an Chia
14. Tsu Hsin 祖辛, son of Tsu Yi
15. Wo Chia 沃甲, younger brother of Tsu Hsin
16. Tsu Ting 祖丁, son of Tsu Hsin
17. Nan Keng 南庚, son of Wo Chia
18. Yang Chia 陽甲, son of Tsu Ting
19. P'an Keng 盤庚, younger brother of Yang Chia
20. Hsiao Hsin 小辛, younger brother of P'an Keng
21. Hsiao Yi 小乙, younger brother of Hsiao Hsin
22. Wu Ting 武丁, son of Hsiao Yi
23. Tsu Keng 祖庚, son of Wu Ting
24. Tsu Chia 祖甲, younger brother of Tsu Keng
25. Lin Hsin 廩辛, son of Tsu Chia
26. Keng Ting 庚丁, younger brother of Lin Hsin
27. Wu Yi 武乙, son of Keng Ting
28. T'ai Ting 太丁, son of Wu Yi
29. Ti Yi 帝乙, son of T'ai Ting
30. Ti Hsin 帝辛, son of Ti Yi

13. Wang Kuo-wei 王國維, "Shuo tzu Hsieh chih Ch'eng T'ang pa ch'ien" 說自契至成湯八遷. See also Chao T'ieh-han 趙鐵寒, *Ku shih k'ao shu* 古史考述.

Most of the thirty names recorded here have been identified in the oracle bone inscriptions, but there are a few discrepancies and a few corrections to be made, which will be described in chapter 3.

Seven dynastic capitals are generally attributed to the dynasty's thirty kings. T'ang is long known to have had his capital in Po 亳, believed by a number of historians to be located near Po Hsien 亳縣 in Anhwei.[14] P'an Keng, the nineteenth king, is known to have moved his capital to Yin 殷. Before his move, the book *P'an keng* in *Shu ching* speaks of "five moves," presumably five moves since the first capital, Po. Yang Shu-ta 楊樹達[15] lists them as follows:

Po 亳, old capital under T'ang (no. 1)
Hsiao 囂 (or Ao 隞), moved under Chung Ting (no. 10)
Hsiang 相, moved under Ho T'an Chia (no. 12)
Keng 耿 or Hsing 邢, moved under Tsu Yi (no. 13)
Pi 庇, moved under Tsu Yi when Keng was destroyed by a flood
Yen 奄, moved under Nan Keng (no. 17)
Yin 殷, moved under P'an Keng (no. 19)

These seven towns are all thought to be located in the eastern and northern parts of Honan, western Shantung, and northern Anhwei.[16] Or, in other words, they are in the same general area as the one in which the capitals of the predynastic lords are believed to be located (fig. 1). Yin, near the modern city of An-yang, remained the dynastic capital until Shang's fall. *Ku pen Chu shu chi nien* 古本竹書紀年 stated that "from P'an Keng's move to Yin through to the fall under Chòu, for 273 years[17] [they] had not moved [their] capitals."

MAJOR PERSONALITIES AND EVENTS

Textual records pertaining to each of the 44 Shang lords and kings vary greatly in amount and detail. Many are mere names to us, while others are known as personalities and doers of events. I will give

14. Wang Kuo-wei 王國維, "Shuo Po" 說亳; Tung Tso-pin 董作賓, "P'u tz'u chung ti Po yü Shang" 卜辭中的亳與商; Chao T'ieh-han 趙鐵寒, *op. cit.*

15. *Chi Wei Chü tu-shu chi* 積微居讀書記, p. 1.

16. T'ang Lan 唐蘭, "Ts'ung Ho-nan Cheng-chou ch'u-t'u ti Shang tai ch'ien ch'i ch'ing-t'ung-ch'i shuo ch'i" 從河南鄭州出土的商代前期青銅器說起; Ch'ü Wan-li 屈萬里, *op. cit.*; Chao T'ieh-han 趙鐵寒, *Ku shih k'ao shu* 古史考述.

17. 773 years in another version.

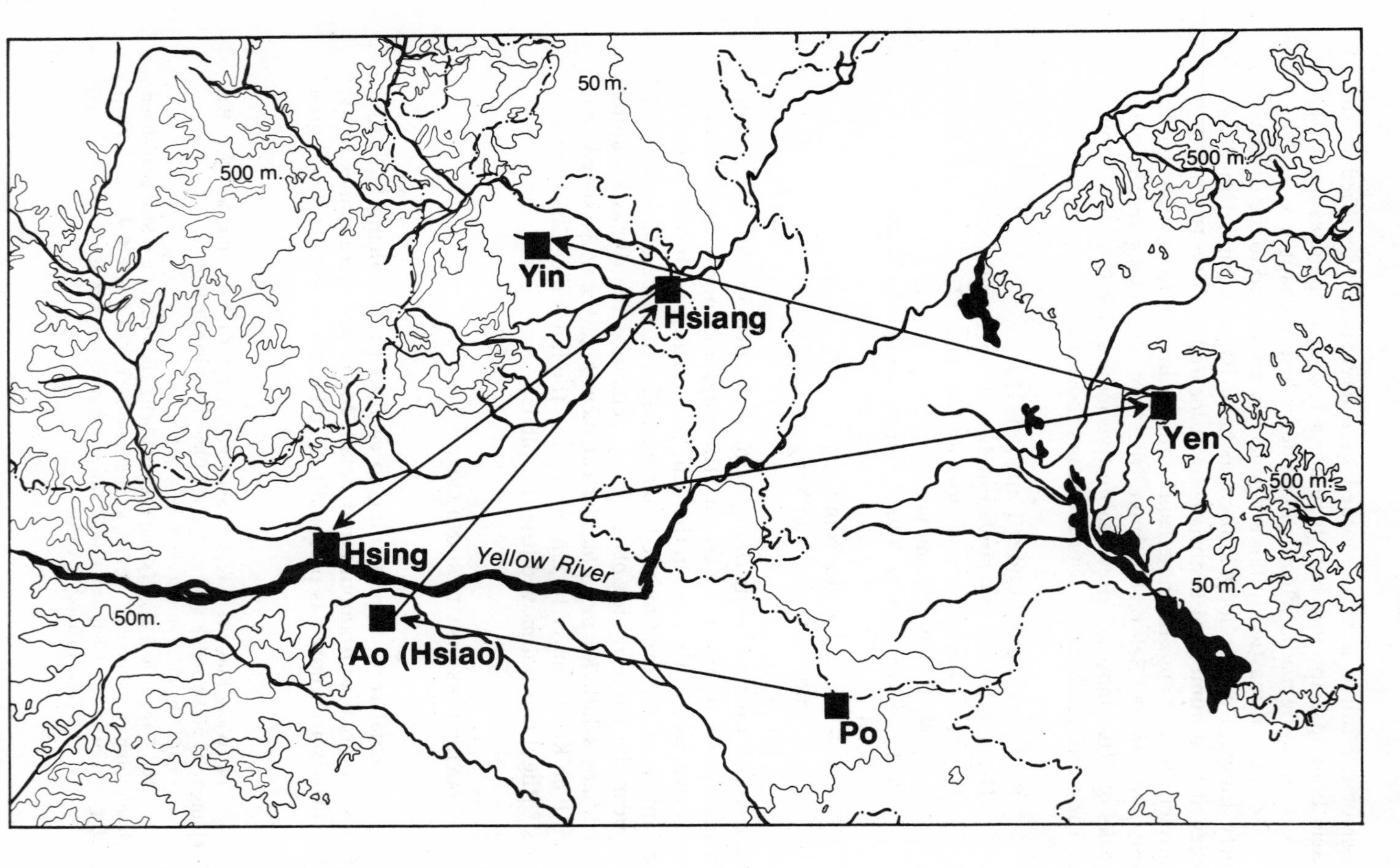

1. Possible locations of the capital cities of the Shang dynasty.

below a brief account of the major personalities, based on *Yin pen chi* but supplemented by other sources.[18]

Predynastic Lords. Other than Hsieh, the founder, the predynastic lords are not at all well known. Hsiang T'u is in some accounts (*Shih pen* as quoted in various texts) credited with the use of horses, and he is called a "glorious" king whose rule was extended to the seacoast (*Shih ching*, "Ch'ang fa"). Another lord, Chen (= Wang Hai in the oracle bone inscription, after Wang,[19]) is credited with the first use of cattle (*Shih pen*) and he apparently led the Shang to significant hostilities with an alien group (Yu yi 有易) in the Yi River area of Hopei.[20] The story concerning the latter had it that Chen, while a guest of Yu yi, had committed moral indiscretions and was killed by King Mien Ch'en 緜臣 of Yu Yi. Four years later, Chen's son, Wei, took revenge and killed Mien Ch'en after a raid.

T'ang (*Ch'eng T'ang, T'ien Yi*). *Mencius* claimed that T'ang's initial territory was only 70 *li* 里 across ("Liang Hui Wang, hsia") and that from that small beginning he reached political preëminence after a series of eleven conquests, starting with conquering his neighboring lord of Ko 葛. In addition to Ko, T'ang's successful conquests aimed at Wei 韋, Ku 顧, and K'un-wu 昆吾. Both *Yin pen chi* and *Mencius* (*Meng-tzu* 孟子) attributed his success to his moral superiority over his adversaries. The initial conquest of Ko, for example, was carried out only because the lord of Ko refused to worship his ancestors even after repeated pleadings and offers of assistance by T'ang and, also, because he killed a boy who was bringing food to farmers in the field (but see chapter 4 for more on the story). His final triumph at the ruins of Yu Jung, over King Chieh 桀 of the Hsia dynasty, was because Chieh was a hated despot. His conquests were eagerly awaited by the people of the conquered states: people in the west were heard to complain, when T'ang directed his troops eastward, "Why later for us?" Those in the north said the same when his troops headed toward the south. He even treated birds and beasts fair and square: he once had a hunting net open on three sides so that only willing victims would get caught!

18. This accounting is restricted to the most important events, based on sources that are somewhat reliable. For a more detailed account, see Chou Hung-hsiang 周鴻翔, *Shang Yin ti wang pen chi* 商殷帝王本紀.

19. Wang Kuo-wei 王國維, "Yin p'u-tz'u chung so chien hsien kung hsien wang k'ao" 殷卜辭中所見先公先王考.

20. Ku Chieh-kang 顧頡剛, "Chou Yi kua yao tz'u chung ti ku-shih" 周易卦爻辭中的故事.

When this story became widely known, thirty-six states voluntarily submitted themselves to T'ang as his subordinates! Another story concerning T'ang's moral leadership relates to a long drought and T'ang's offer of himself as sacrifice in a rain-praying ritual in a grove of mulberries. (Rain came and put out the ritual fire before T'ang was roasted.) These stories undoubtedly reflect the prevailing principle of benevolent rule in the late Chou period, but very possibly the same principle constituted one of the factors for the maintenance or change of the world order during earlier times as well. We will discuss this again later on.

During his reign T'ang was aided by Yi Yin 伊尹, his most important official. *Yin pen chi* records two versions of how Yi Yin came to his post. One had Yi Yin serve as a dowry-servant from Yu Hsin Shih 有莘氏 and bring himself to T'ang's favor by his extraordinary cooking skills. The other had Yi Yin as a farmer well known for his wisdom, who finally succumbed to T'ang's repeated invitations to serve in his court. Some texts claim that Yi Yin had once left T'ang to become an official of Hsia, but he came back to T'ang because he didn't like what he saw at Hsia. Many of these stories, mostly based on late Chou accounts, are undoubtedly conflicting and unreliable, but that Yi Yin and T'ang acted sometimes in opposition and sometimes in concert seems to be a common theme. This becomes clear after T'ang's death. T'ai Ting, who was crown prince under T'ang, predeceased him. After T'ang's death, the throne was assumed by T'ai Ting's younger brothers Wai Ping and Chung Jen, successively. They ruled only three and four years respectively. After Chung Jen died, Yi Yin brought T'ai Chia (T'ai Ting's son, or T'ang's grandson) to the throne. But within three years T'ai Chia is said to have begun to rule contrary to T'ang's traditions, and Yi Yin had him exiled at the T'ung 桐 palace, assuming himself the power of regent. After that, the accounts differ. *Yin pen chi* says that within three more years, Yi Yin brought T'ai Chia, now repentant, back to the throne, where he later became a good ruler. But *Ku pen Chu shu chi nien* says differently: T'ai Chia escaped from T'ung palace and assassinated Yi Yin, making Yi Yin's sons Yi Chih 伊陟 and Yi Fen 伊奮 succeed to his office and divide up his land and houses between them. We will seek to reconcile these different stories later, with a new interpretation.

T'ai Chia to Yang Chia. No significant stories are known for the period from T'ai Chia (no. 4) through Yang Chia (no. 18). *Yen pen shi* speaks of Shang's ups and downs. When they were down, "the state lords did not come," and when they came up again, "the lords came to pay homage." A significant period of low prestige was, according to

Yin pen chi, the nine reigns beginning with Chung Ting (no. 10–no. 18). There is, however, a significant discrepancy in the records. According to *Wu yi* 無逸, in *Shu ching*, Chung Tsung 中宗 was considered a good king, and he enjoyed his reign for seventy-five years. *Yin pen chi* identifies Chung Tsung as T'ai Wu, Chung Ting's father, but Wang Kuo-wei has convincingly shown that this good king was really Tsu Yi.

P'an Keng and Wu Ting Renovations. In traditional texts P'an Keng and Wu Ting are the best-known kings following T'ang. The major contribution P'an Keng made to his own fame was the removal of the royal capital from Yen to Yin, crossing the Yellow River. The event was immortalized by the three documents called *P'an keng* in *Shu ching*, in which P'an Keng admonished his officials and his people, whose inertia did not favor the move, about the compelling reasons behind his decision, beginning with these words:

> Our king Tsu Yi came and fixed on Keng for his capital. He did so from a deep concern for our people, because he would not have them all die where they cannot help one another to preserve their lives. I have consulted the tortoise shell and obtained the reply: "This is no place for us." When the former kings had any important business they gave reverent heed to the commands of Heaven. In a case like this especially they did not indulge the wish for constant repose; they did not abide ever in the same city. Up to this time the capital has been in five regions. If we do not follow the example of these old times, we shall be refusing to acknowledge that Heaven is making an end of our dynasty here. How little can it be said of us that we are following the meritorious course of the former kings! As from the stump of a felled tree there are sprouts and shoots, Heaven will perpetuate its decree in our favour in this new city. The great inheritance of the former kings will be continued and renewed. [Translated by James Legge and Clae Waltham]

His persuasion was apparently successful, for the move was made and Yin remained the Shang capital until the end of the dynasty. *P'an keng* is considered one of the most important texts pertaining to the Shang, because it is believed to contain many genuinely Shang elements and because, made up of words that are both pleading and threatening, it reveals some of the essence of the governing art of the Shang dynasty.

After his death, P'an Keng was succeeded by two younger brothers before the throne went to a nephew, King Wu Ting. In *Wu-yi*, a *Shu ching* document, we find:

> If we come to the time of Wu Ting, he toiled at first away from the court and among the lower people. When he came to the throne and occupied the mourning shed, it may be said that he did not speak for three years. Afterwards he was still inclined not to speak; but when he did speak, his words were full of harmonious wisdom. He did not dare to indulge in useless ease but admirably and tranquilly presided over the regions of Yin until throughout them all, small and great, there was not a single murmur. It was thus that he enjoyed the throne fifty and nine years. [Translated by Legge and Waltham]

According to *Yin pen chi* and a few other late Chou texts Wu Ting was effectively aided by Fu Yüeh 傅說 in his rule. In a dream, Wu Ting met a sage whose name was Yüeh. Undertaking a search Wu Ting found the same man at Fu-hsien 傅險, where he was a pisé (版築 *pan chu*, "rammed earth") builder at a labor camp. He talked to the man, was pleased by what he said, gave him the name Fu Yüeh, and made him prime minister. All this diligence and ability to use the right people apparently served Wu Ting well. He undertook some major military campaigns; an important campaign, referred to in *Yi ching* (*The Book of Changes*), was with Kuei Fang 鬼方 in the northwest, whom he eventually subdued after three years. As the result of his conquests, Wu Ting is depicted in the poem *Hsüan niao* in *The Book of Songs* (*Shih ching*) as presiding over a vast state.

> Even their inner domain was a thousand leagues;
> In them the people found sure support.
> They opened up new lands as far as the four seas.
> Men from the four seas came in homage,
> Came in homage, crowd on crowd;
> Their frontier was the river.
> Yin received a charge that was all good;
> Many blessings Yin bore.
>
> [Translated by Arthur Waley]

And *Mencius* ("Kung-sun Ch'ou, shang") says of him, "Wu Ting commanded the homage of the feudal lords and maintained the possession of the Empire as easily as rolling it on his palm" (translated by D. C. Lau).

The End of the Shang Dynasty. After Wu Ting, not much is said about the kings until Chòu in the traditional texts, but one or two references are of interest. Tsu Chia (no. 24) is said by *Yin pen chi* to be one who indulged in moral improprieties (*yin luan* 淫亂) and led the dynasty into another decline. *Kuo yü* also talks about his interference with tradition, resulting in the dynasty's demise after seven additional reigns. But *Wu yi* in *Shu ching* refers to him as another exemplary Shang king.

> In the case of Tsu Chia, he refused to be king unrighteously, and was at first one of the lower people. When he came to the throne, he knew on what they must depend for their support and was able to exercise a protecting kindness toward their masses. He did not dare to treat with contempt wifeless men and widows. Thus it was that he enjoyed the throne thirty and three years. [Translated by Legge and Waltham]

This conflict in the textual accounts is important, as Tung Tso-pin's oracle bone inscription studies have revealed that Tsu Chia was in fact a significant reformer. We will discuss this point in chapter 3.

After Tsu Chia, the dynasty is seen in the traditional texts as undergoing a steady decline that climaxed in the Chou conquest. *Wu yi* says:

> The kings that arose after these from their birth enjoyed ease. Enjoying ease from their birth, they did not know the painful toil of sowing and reaping, and had not heard of the hard labors of the lower people. They sought for nothing but excessive pleasure; and so not one of them had long life. They reigned for ten years, for seven or eight, for five or six, or perhaps only for three or four.

The most morally defunct king, in this telling, was, of course, Chòu. The section of *Yin pen chi* dealing with Chòu deserves to be translated in full, below:

> Ti Chòu had a quick intelligence and discriminating powers, and was fast in his hearing and eyesight, and had unusual physical strength, [and was known] to have fought with strong beasts with his bare hands. He was intelligent enough to resist criticism and had enough verbal faculty to cover up his wrongdoings. Dazzling his subordinates with his ability and towering over all under Heaven with his talk, he believed that all were beneath himself. He enjoyed wine and music and was fond of women. He loved Ta Chi 妲己, followed Ta Chi's every word. Thus he asked musician Chüan 涓 to compose new erotic lyrics, North Precinct's dances, and degenerate music. He

increased tributes and taxes to fatten his treasury on the Deer Platform and his granaries at Giant Bridge. He collected more dogs, horses, and exotic objects to fill the palace rooms. He expanded his gardens and platforms at Sand Dunes and placed in them more wild beasts and flying birds. He was negligent to ghosts and deities. He presided over orgies at Sand Dunes, pouring wine into a pond and hanging meats like trees in a forest. He had men and women undressed and chasing one another among them, drinking into the night.

The commoners [began to] complain and some of the subordinate lords tore themselves away. Thereupon Chòu used heavy penalties, inventing the Grill Roast Technique. He made Hsi Po Ch'ang 西伯昌, Chiu Hou 九侯, and Eh Hou 鄂侯 his Three Senior Lords. Chiu Hou had a pretty woman and presented her to Chòu. The Chiu Hou girl was not fond of sensual pleasures. Angry, Chòu killed her and made Chiu Hou into meat sauce. Eh Hou expressed his disagreement strongly and argued violently. And Chòu had Eh Hou made into dried meat. Hsi Po Ch'ang heard about this, and sighed in private. Ch'ung Hou Hu 崇侯虎 heard about his sigh and informed Chòu on him. Chòu had Hsi Po imprisoned at Yu Li 羑里. Hsi Po's official, Hung Yao 閎夭, and others gathered beautiful women, exotic objects, and good horses to present to Chòu, who then released Hsi Po. After he was out, Hsi Po presented the land west of River Lo [to Chòu] and asked him to eliminate the use of the Grill Roast penalty. Chòu agreed, giving him a gift of [ceremonial] bows, arrows, adzes, and axes so that Hsi Po was [again] enabled to make conquests and to act like Hsi Po ["Duke of the West"]. He employed Fei Chung 費中 as an administrator. Fei Chung was good at flattery and fond of greed, and the Yin people could not be close to him. Chòu also employed Eh Lai 惡來. Eh Lai was good at saying bad things, and the subordinate lords drifted away.

Hsi Po returned (to Chou), and discreetly built merits and did good things. Many subordinate lords turned against Chòu and drifted toward Hsi Po. Hsi Po spread [his powers], and Chòu gradually lost authority and weight. Prince Pi Kan 比干 gave him critical advice, but he did not accept. Shang Jung 商容 was a wise man. The commoners loved him, but Chòu removed him [from his office].... After Hsi Po died, Chou Wu Wang 周武王 led an eastern expedition to Meng Chin 孟津. Eight hundred subordinate lords left Yin to meet Chòu. The lords said, "it is time to conquer Chòu." Wu Wang said, "You do not know the Heaven's Mandate," and returned.

> Chòu continued his indulgence in inappropriate behavior without cease. Wei Tzu 微子 critically advised him several times without him listening. After discussing it with the Senior Ritualist and Junior Ritualist, he went [into exile]. Pi Kan said, "As an official I must register my disapproval at the risk of death," and went to advise Chòu against his behavior in very strong terms. Angry, Chòu said, "I hear sages' hearts have seven holes," and had Pi Kan cut open in order to observe his heart. Afraid, Chi Tzu feigned madness to join the rank of the slaves, and Chòu had him imprisoned in any event. The Senior and Junior Ritualists of Yin went to Chou, carrying their ritual and musical paraphernalia. Thereupon Chou Wu Wang 周武王 came to lead his subordinate lords in a conquest of Chòu. Chòu sent his troops to resist them at Mu Yeh 牧野. On day *chia-tzu*, Chòu's troops were defeated. Chòu went in, climbed the Deer Platform, put on his precious jade clothing, and went into a fire to his death. Chou Wu Wang cut off Chòu's head, hanging it at the top of a large white flag pole. He killed Ta Chi, released Chi Tzu from prison, marked Pi Kan's tomb, put up a sign of honor at the gate to Shang Jung's precinct, and gave Chòu's son, Wu Keng Lu Fu 武庚祿父, an office to continue Yin's rites, asking him to administer in the tradition of P'an Keng. Yin's people were greatly pleased. . . . After Chou Wu Wang's death, Wu Keng, in collusion with Kuan Shu 管叔 and Ts'ai Shu 蔡叔, rebelled. Ch'eng Wang 成王 ordered Chou Kung 周公 to have him exterminated, and placed Wei Tzu at Sung to continue Yin's descent.

SHANG CHRONOLOGY

In traditional texts, the first year of the Kung Ho 共和 regency during the Western Chou dynasty, the year 841 B.C., is of especial import. *Shih chi* gives yearly accounts of events after this year, but before it Ssu-ma Ch'ien was only able to place the kings in relative sequential order, without being able to assign a precise number of years to each reign. In various states of the Chou and Shang dynasties good genealogical records were apparently kept in the royal and noble houses for the sake of ancestral worship, but undoubtedly many were lost before Ssu-ma's time, and the materials that he had perhaps were not adequate or mutually consistent.

There will be occasions later on to discuss some of the more important chronological problems pertaining to Shang, using a variety of non-textual methods and sources. But here we will describe a few of the chronological issues wholly within the textual domain. These include: (a) the year of the Wu Wang conquest of Shang; (b) the total number of years of Shang's dynastic reign, which, when added to the conquest year, would also give the initial year of T'ang's dynastic founding; and (c) the years of each of the thirty reigns.

In the traditional texts there are basically four items that have a direct bearing on the dating of the Wu Wang conquest. They are as follows:

1. *Kuo yü Chou yü* 國語周語："昔武王伐殷，歲在鶉火"("When Wu Wang attacked Yin, the year[-star] [Jupiter] was at the Cancer-Leo station.")
2. *Shu ching Wu ch'eng* 書經武成 (as quoted by *Shih ching* 世經 in *Han shu Lü li chih* 漢書律曆志): "惟一月壬辰旁死霸。若翌日癸巳，武王迺朝步自周于征伐紂。粵若來三月既死霸，粵五日甲子，咸劉商王紂。唯四月既望，旁生霸，粵六日庚戌，武王燎于周廟，翌日辛亥，祀于天位。粵五日乙卯，乃以庶國祀馘于周廟。" (The above passage can be approximately translated as: "In the first moon, day *jen-ch'en,* the moon was at the *p'ang ssu pa* position. The following day, *kuei-ssu,* Wu Wang left Chou in the morning on a journey of conquest of Chòu. In the following third moon, the moon was at the *chi ssu pa* position, and five days later, on day *chia-tzu,* [the Chou] exterminated Shang king Chòu. In the fourth moon, the moon was at the *chi wang* and *p'ang sheng pa* positions. Six days later on day *keng-hsü* Wu Wang performed the *liao* ceremony at the Chou temple. The following day, *hsin-hai,* ritual was performed to Heaven. Five days later on day *yi-mou* the junior states participated in the sacrifice of the Shang head(s) at the Chou temple.")
3. *Ku pen Chu shu chi nien* 古本竹書紀年 (as quoted in *Hsin T'ang shu li chih* 新唐書曆志): "(武王)十一年庚寅，周始伐商" ("The 11th Year [of Wu Wang], the year keng-yin, the Chou began their conquest of Shang").
4. *Ku pen Chu shu chi nien* (as quoted in *Shih chi* 史記 *Yin pen chi chi chieh* 殷本紀集解): "自武王滅殷以至幽王凡二百五十七年" ("From the time when Wu Wang extinguished Yin to King Yu, 257 years [had passed].")

Several hypotheses concerning the year of the conquest have been proposed on the basis of these passages, supplemented by other, more indirect, sources. The most influential has been the one advanced by Liu Hsin 劉歆 (46 B.C.–A.D. 23), who based his calculations on the first and second items, above. The first refers to the position of Jupiter in its twelve-year cycle through the stars, and the second includes information pertaining to the *kan-chih* names of several dates in the first, third, and fourth months in the lunar calendar. According to Liu Hsin's calculations, the only year that fits both items is "142,109 years after the primeval year." We know from Liu's system that the year 206 B.C. (the first year of the Han emperor Kao Tsu) was 143,025 years from the primeval year and, therefore, that the primeval year was 143,231 B.C. Take 142,109 years from 143,231 B.C. and we get 1122 B.C. This 1122 B.C. date of the Wu Wang conquest is the so-called orthodox chronology.

The calendrical system which Liu Hsin used to reconstruct the late Shang–early Chou calendar to match the lunar month divisions and the *kan-chih* dates according to the information contained in *Wu-ch'eng* has, however, long been considered less than accurate. In the year A.D. 721, a Buddhist monk, Yi Hsing 一行, recalculated the pieces of information in *Wu-ch'eng* according to an improved calendrical system, resulting in the year 1111 B.C. This new date, which is seen in *T'ang shu* ("Li chih"), would still fit the same Jupiter station, with its short, twelve-year cycle, and it would also fit item (3); namely, that the year 1111 was a *keng-yin* year. However, *kan-chih* is not known to be used for recording years until late in the Later Han period, so this piece of information must represent an extrapolation long postdating the original *Chu shu* passage. Therefore, this 1111 B.C. date does not represent a vast advance from the 1122 B.C. orthodox date, but its having been embraced by Tung Tso-pin has given it greater weight.

The final piece of textual information on the year of the conquest stands mainly by itself, giving no support to the two schemes above, nor deriving any support from them. Since we know the final year of Yu Wang is 771 B.C., we can simply add 257 years to 770 and arrive at 1027 B.C. This is the year adopted by Lei Hai-tsung,[21] Ch'en Meng-chia,[22] Bernhard Karlgren,[23] and other contemporary scholars.[24]

These three dates, 1122, 1111, and 1027 B.C., are the most influential, but none can stand on its own on textual evidence alone. There are other hypotheses that are more or less problematic.[25] We will

21. Lei Hai-tsung 雷海宗, "Yin Chou nien-tai k'ao" 殷周年代考.
22. Ch'en Meng-chia 陳夢家, *Hsi Chou nien-tai k'ao* 西周年代考.
23. Bernhard Karlgren, "Some Weapons and Tools of the Yin Dynasty."
24. Ho Ping-ti 何炳棣, "Chou ch'u nien-tai p'ing yi" 周初年代平議.
25. See Tung Tso-pin 董作賓, "Wu Wang fa Chòu nien yüeh jih chin k'ao" 武王伐紂年月日今考; Ting Su 丁驌, "Sui tsai Ch'un-huo yü Wu Wang fa Chòu" 歲在鶉火與武王伐紂; Chou Fa-kao 周法高, "Certain Dates of the Shang Period," and "Hsi Chou nien-tai k'ao" 西周年代考; Wang Pao-tê 王保德, "Wu Wang fa Chòu tu yü Meng-chin ti nien-tai k'ao" 武王伐紂渡于孟津的年代考; Lao Kan 勞榦, "Chou ch'u

come back to this issue later on when new kinds of evidence are added to the discussion. It should be noted here that all of the above textual information represents knowledge of people of Eastern Chou period, several hundred years after the conquest. Its seeming inconsistency may suggest that by Eastern Chou times there already were different versions of the event; some may represent an accurate surviving text, while others had seen corruption. We surely need contemporary records before we can date the conquest with conviction.

The second chronological issue has to do with the dynasty's length. Chou texts contain three references to this, as follows:

> *Tso chuan*, 3rd year of Hsüan Kung: "Chieh had bad virtue, and the ritual vessel was moved to Shang, where rituals were performed for six hundred years" 桀有昏德，鼎遷于商．載祀六百．
>
> *Mencius*, "Chin hsin, hsia": "From T'ang to Wen Wang, more than five hundred years [had passed]" 由湯至於文王，五百有餘歲．
>
> *Ku pen Chu shu chi nien*: "From T'ang's overthrow of Hsia to Shou, [there were altogether] twenty-nine Kings and 496 years" 湯滅夏以至於受，二十九王，用歲四百九十六年．

The first two items are approximations, but they are quite consistent with each other. Mencius mentions the period through Wen Wang only; Wen Wang is known to have reigned a long time (fifty years, according to *Wu yi*, in *Shu ching*), and when the years of his reign are added to the "more than 500 years" mentioned by Mencius, the total could come close to the 600-year figure in *Tso chuan*. Add 600 to 1122 B.C., and we have the founding year of T'ang in the eighteenth century B.C., but the exact year is unknown.[26] The 496-year figure of *Chu shu* is probably wrong, being on the too-brief side.

Since the beginning year of the Shang dynasty cannot be exact, the reign years of the 30 kings cannot be known in all cases, and

nien-tai wen-t'i yü yüeh hsiang wen-t'i ti hsin k'an-fa" 周初年代問題與月相問題的新看法. In a recent study of the mention of Halley's comet in Chinese historical records ("Ha-lei hui-hsing ti kuei-tao yen-pien ti ch'ü-shih ho ta ti ku-tai li-shih" 哈雷慧星的軌道演變的趨勢和它的古代歷史), Chang Yü-chê 張鈺哲, the astronomer at the Purple Mountain Observatory in Nanking, citing a record in *Huai-nan tzu* 淮南子 ("Ping Lüeh hsün" 兵略訓) about a comet in the sky at the time of Wu Wang's conquest, maintains that the event could be placed in 1057–1056 B.C., a year when Halley's comet could be seen in North China. There are too many uncertainties for us to accept this view at this time.

26. Liu Hsin placed the conquest of Hsia (in T'ang's own sixteenth year of reign) in 1751 B.C.

the exact figures given in many studies[27] can only be a game of allotments. The only textually exact reign years contained in Chou literature were the following:

1. T'ang	?	
2. Wai Ping	2 years	(*Mencius*)
3. Chung Jen	4 years	(*Mencius*)
4. T'ai Chia	12 years	(*Chu shu*, quoted by *Shih chi Lu shih-chia So-yin* 史記魯世家索隱)
5. Wo Ting		
6. T'ai Keng	25 years	(*Shih chi* as quoted by *T'ai-ping yü lan* 太平御覽, vol. 8)
7. Hsiao Chia	17 years	(*Shih chi* as quoted by *T'ai-ping yü lan* 太平御覽, vol. 8)
8. Yung Chi		
9. T'ai Wu		
10. Chung Ting		
11. Wai Jen		
12. Ho T'an Chia		
13. Tsu Yi	75 years	(*Wu yi*)
14. Tsu Hsin		
15. Wo Chia		
16. Tsu Ting		
17. Nan Keng		
18. Yang Chia		
19. P'an Keng	(From P'an Keng to Chòu, 773, 275, or 273 years, according to different references in *Chu shu*).	
20. Hsiao Hsin		
21. Hsiao Yi		
22. Wu Ting	59 years	(*Wu yi*)
23. Tsu Keng		
24. Tsu Chia	33 years	(*Wu yi*)
25. Lin Hsin	(10 years, 7 or 8 years, 4 or 3 years	
26. Keng Ting	[*Wu yi*] but *Chu shu*, as quoted in *Hou*	
27. Wu Yi	*Han shu* ["Hsi Ch'iang Chuan"], mentions	
28. T'ai Ting	the 35th year of Wu Yi and 11th year of	
29. Ti Yi	T'ai Ting)	
30. Ti Hsin		

27. Such as the figures given in *Chin pen Chu shu chi nien* 今本竹書紀年; see Chou Hung-hsiang 周鴻翔, *Shang Yin ti wang pen chi* 商殷帝王本紀.

2. *BRONZES*

Ritual bronze vessels have long been known as common Shang artifacts; *Yin pen chi* records a ritual event during the reign of Wu Ting in which a pheasant landed on top of the handle of a bronze cauldron. *Kuo yü* (chapter "Chin yü") even includes an essay supposedly inscribed on a bronze vessel dating from the declining years of the Shang. Ever since at least Han times, ancient Chinese bronzes have been an important part of the antiquarian collections in the royal houses and of private individuals, and the earliest extant catalogue (*K'ao ku t'u* 考古圖) was published in 1092 (or shortly thereafter) by Lü Ta-lin 呂大臨.

This catalogue, *K'ao ku t'u*, initiated the field of study of ancient Chinese bronzes in important ways. Drawing its data from the Imperial (Sung dynasty) Collection and from thirty-seven private collections, it includes drawings and descriptions (as to size, capacity, weight, and place of origin of each piece) of 148 Shang and Chou artifacts, 63 Ch'in and Han artifacts, and 13 jade objects. Each artifact is given a type designation according to the ancient Chinese terminology in use in the classics, and Shang objects are distinguished from Chou objects largely on the basis of inscriptions—those that contain names with a *t'ien kan* compound (Father Chia, Mother Yi, Ancestor Ping, Brother Ting, and so forth), in the manner of the names of the Shang kings, are usually classified as Shang. These practices of *K'ao ku t'u* are repeated in other, later catalogues; among the latter the most famous include *Po ku t'u* 博古圖 (revised after 1123), *Hsi Ch'ing ku chien* 西清古鑑 (1755), *Ning Shou chien ku* 寧壽鑑古 (between 1755 and 1795), *Hsi Ch'ing hsü chien* 西清續鑑 (1793), *T'ao Chai chi chin lu* 陶齋吉金錄 (1908), and many, many others. The collections that these catalogues record do not always survive (of the more than six hundred pieces recorded in Sung catalogues, only 2 are extant).[28] These catalogues constitute important firsthand source material for archaeological study pertaining to the Shang and Chou civilizations before modern archaeology brought about the discovery of not only archaeological remains but also additional bronzes with true provenances. In a very recent catalogue of Shang and Chou bronze inscriptions,[29] 4,835 bronze artifacts are listed as having inscriptions, and they have been taken from 192 titles in Chinese, Japanese, and Western languages. Most of these titles record bronzes of unknown provenance, including uninscribed as well as inscribed pieces. The oldest catalogue included therein is *K'ao ku t'u*, previously mentioned, and the most recent ones were published in the nineteen seventies.

28. Jung Keng 容庚, *Shang Chou yi-ch'i t'ung k'ao* 商周彝器通考, p. 257.

29. Chou Fa-kao 周法高, *San Tai chi chin wen ts'un chu lu piao* 三代吉金文存著錄表.

These catalogues are the basic sources for all types of contemporary studies of the Shang and Chou civilizations using bronze artifacts.

In what ways can bronzes be studied to illuminate Shang history, culture, and society? Those that have been excavated scientifically serve as a part of the total archaeological assemblage and can be studied in the same manner as all other classes of archaeological artifacts are studied. These scientific archaeological methods and results we will take up later. Here we concentrate on bronzes per se, that is, bronzes found in art collections, without precise archaeological provenance. Scholars of Shang and Chou bronzes have focused on four areas of research: inscription, typological classification, decorative art, and manufacture. We will briefly describe the main results of studies in each area.

Before we proceed with these descriptions, a word must be said here about the issue of separating Shang bronzes from Chou bronzes. Traditionally, bronzes were referred to as "of the Three Dynasties," and it is not always possible to separate them. But the phrase "Three Dynasties" can have two meanings: it marks three successive chronological periods, and it also designates three overlapping political entities. There are bronzes apparently of Shang date that have been found in Chou territory. Traditionally, these would have been classified as Shang bronzes, since the successive chronological sense of the Three Dynasties was stressed. However, the political transition from Shang to Chou dynasties is not clearly marked in art, and early Western Chou bronzes cannot always be separated from late Shang bronzes. We shall refer in the following to the methods and results of research that are applicable to bronzes of all periods and shall specify Shang only when necessary to do so.

INSCRIPTIONS

Inscriptions, which are present on only a small portion of the extant Shang and Chou bronzes artifacts, were usually cast as intaglios in the process of making the whole artifact. The shortest inscription consists of a single character, and the longest known is that cast on *Mao Kung ting* 毛公鼎, a Western Chou piece, numbering 497 characters.[30] All the inscriptions can be classified into two groups: signs and statements.

A sign consists of one or more of the following elements: (a) One

30. *Mao Kung ting* 毛公鼎 is a controversial piece as regards its authenticity. See Noel Barnard, "Chou China: A Review of the Third Volume of Cheng Te-k'un's *Archaeology in China*"; Chang Kuang-yüan 張光遠, "Hsi Chou chung ch'i Mao Kung ting" 西周重器毛公鼎.

of a number of characters (mostly pictographic) that are considered as family or clan emblems; (b) a kin term such as *tsu* 祖 (ancestor), *p'i* 妣 (ancestress), *fu* 父 (father), *mu* 母 (mother), *hsiung* 兄 (elder brother), *fu* 婦 (royal consort), and *tzu* 子 (prince); and (c) one of the ten celestial stems (*chia, yi, ping, ting, wu, chi, keng, hsin, jen, kuei*). The usual interpretation of the signs is that they identify the ancestral group and person to whom the artifact was dedicated or by whom it was used. A sign consisting of *emblem-Father-Chia*, for example, is usually interpreted as follows: Father Chia (an individual ancestor) of the clan represented by that emblem. I have suggested a modified interpretation: instead of a specific individual, Father Chia refers to the generation (father's) and the lineage unit (Chia) for which the ritual object was made.[31] But in any event, signs contain no statements of any kind and were cast simply to mark the social position of the object.

Scholars have studied these signs with a number of objectives. The emblems and the other marks have been studied for sociological information pertaining to the users.[32] They have been used for chronological studies; usually most emblems are considered as Shang rather than Chou markers,[33] and the use of ancestral signs has been regarded as a late Shang institution.[34] Since the emblems are often pictographic, they are sometimes regarded as representing an archaic stage of Chinese writing and thus are used in the study of the history of writing in China.[35]

Inscriptions that contain statements also often include signs, but they contain statements mostly about the circumstances that led to the casting of the vessel. Most of the statements had to do with the making of the bronze as the result of a royal gift, and often mentioned the amount of money that formed part of the gift, but some pertained to other matters such as a military campaign or a royal journey. These statements, though not historical in intent, very often incidentally record pieces of information that are highly significant, and much of our knowledge pertaining to Western Chou history must derive from this source. Among bronzes

31. Chang Kwang-chih 張光直, "Shang Chou ch'ing-t'ung-ch'i ch'i-hsing chuang-shih hua-wen yü ming-wen tsung-ho yen-chiu ch'u-pu pao-kao" 商周青銅器器形裝飾花紋與銘文綜合研究初步報告.

32. Kuo Mo-jo 郭沫若, "Yin yi chung t'u-hsing wen-tzu chih yi chieh" 殷彝中圖形文字之一解; Hayashi Minao 林巳奈夫, "In Shū jidai no zushō kigō" 殷周時代の図象記号.

33. Jung Keng 容庚, *Shang Chou yi-ch'i t'ung k'ao* 商周彝器通考, p. 67; Karlgren, "Yin and Chou in Chinese Bronzes."

34. Virginia Kane, "The Chronological Significance of the Inscribed Ancestor Dedication in the Bronze Vessels." But see *KKHP*, "An-yang Yin hsü wu-hao mu ti fa-chüeh" 安陽殷墟五號墓的發掘.

35. Tung Tso-pin 董作賓, "Chung-kuo wen-tzu chih ch'i-yüan" 中國文字之起源.

that are regarded as being Shang, only a few contain statements, and they are relatively short, numbering at most fifty characters.[36] However, since they are contemporary records, these inscriptions are exceedingly valuable "literary texts" for a period of Chinese history with few reliable contemporary literary texts of other kinds. Akatsuka in a 1959 collection of Shang bronzes texts[37] collected sixty inscriptions with statements, classified under the following headings: recording the years, conquests, gifts, agricultural rites, ancestral rites, feasts, women, and miscellaneous. But a far more comprehensive concordance has been compiled by Chou Fa-kao and others where one finds detailed entries on occurrences of specific names, terms, phrases, and the like.[38]

TYPOLOGY

Shang and Chou bronzes may be classified according to either a contemporary or an archaeological terminology. Names of classes of bronze artifacts appear in the classics and sometimes in the inscriptions themselves; in fact, in the Sung catalogues, artifacts were fitted into categories with names from classical sources. This practice, if successful, would probably be the best for the purpose of Shang and Chou cultural reconstruction, but it cannot in fact be universally applied. The names that appear in inscriptions do not include all the types and they are of various levels of inclusiveness. The names that appear in the classics are not always reliably identifiable with actual artifacts. For these reasons practically all scholars of bronzes adopt one or another kind of archaeological classification, using the traditional names when possible and other, newly coined names when traditional names are lacking or uncertainly applicable.

The most widely adopted classification system of Shang and Chou bronzes is one based on the known or conjectured uses of the objects. The following classification by Ch'en Meng-chia[39] is a good example:

1. Food Vessels
   a. Cooking vessels
      (1) *Ting* 鼎, *Li* 鬲, *Yen* 甗
      (2) *Lu* 鏀, *Chao* 盄
      (3) *Lu* 鑪, *Li* 鬲, *Tsao* 竈

36. Jung Keng 容庚, *Shang Chou yi-ch'i t'ung k'ao* 商用彝器通考, p. 82.
37. Akatsuka Kiyoshi 赤塚忠, *In kinbun kōshaku* 般金文考釋.
38. Chou Fa-kao 周法高 et al., *Chin wen ku lin* 金文詁林.
39. *Hai wai Chung-kuo t'ung-ch'i t'u lu* 海外中國銅器圖錄.

b. Food-containers: *Kuei* 毁, *Hsü* 盨, *Fu* 簠, *Tou* 豆
c. Serving Instruments: *Ssu* 匕
2. Drinking Vessels
a. Wine-warming Vessels: *Chia* 斝, *Ho* 盉, *Chüeh* 爵, *Chiao* 角, *Chiao Tsun* 鐎尊
b. Wine-containers:
(1) *Tsun*-family: *Tsun* 尊, *Ku* 觚, *Kuang* 觥
(2) *P'ing*-family: *Lei* 罍, *Chan* 罎, *Cheng* 盨, *P'en* 盆
(3) *Hu*-family: *Yü* 盂, *Hu* 壺
c. Serving Instruments: *Shao* 勺
3. Vessel Supports
4. Water Vessels
5. Musical Instruments
6. Weapons
7. Chariot and Horse Fittings
8. Measurements and Weights
9. Farming and Crafts Implements
10. Garment and Toilet Articles
11. Miscellaneous Articles

The major classes (1–11) are based on presumed use, and so are the secondary classes. Specific varieties of each type are then named according to the traditional terminology. These are principles that are almost universally followed at the present time in classifying both bronze objects in museum collections and freshly excavated pieces, but the precise classes and terminologies for them vary greatly,[40] primarily because the classificatory criteria, based upon uses that are mostly guessed at, cannot be precise (fig. 2).

Reacting, in part, to the imprecision of classification systems like the one just mentioned, Li Chi 李濟, using the ritual vessels excavated from the Shang sites in An-yang, proposed a new system in which the primary classes are based exclusively upon the form of the vessels.[41]

1. Round-based Vessels
2. Flat-bottomed Vessels
3. Ring-foot (Pedestal) Vessels

40. See Hayashi Minao 林巳奈夫, "In Shu seidō iki no meishō to yotō" 殷周青銅彝器の名称と用途; Umehara Sueji 梅原末治, "Kodōki keitai no kōkogakuteki kenkyū" 古銅器形態の考古学的研究; Jung Keng 容庚, *Shang Chou yi-ch'i t'ung k'ao* 商周彝器通考.

41. Li Chi 李濟, "Chi Hsiao-t'un ch'u-t'u chih ch'ing-t'ung ch'i, Shang pien" 記小屯出土之青銅器, 上篇; and his "Yin hsü ch'u-t'u ch'ing-t'ung li-ch'i chih tsung chien-tao" 殷虛出土青銅禮器之總檢討, 789–795, 806–807.

2. Principal types of Shang and Chou bronze vessels (after K. C. Chang, *The Archaeology of Ancient China,* fig. 174).

4. Tripods
5. Quatropods
6. Animal-form Vessels
7. Lids Separated from Vessels

Under each class, more specific types of vessels are named according to the traditional terms, but these terms are suffixed by the words "-shaped vessels." Under "4. Tripods," for example, is a major type, *ting*-shaped vessels. In order words, Li Chi is saying, whether or not this was indeed something called *ting*, it is definitely something that is shaped like what people referred to as a *ting*. The difference between this system and calling it a *ting* may be quite fine; it does indicate a degree of caution. Many contemporary Chinese archaeologists have adopted this "-shaped vessel" practice, although Li's primary classification according to base and foot forms is not always being used in ways that he had intended.

There is much room for theoretical refinement in the classification of Shang bronzes; in fact, this is so in the whole area of artifact classification in Chinese archaeology. As J. O. Brew stated more than thirty years ago;

> A group of objects to be studied must be classified in a number of different ways, depending upon the information the student wishes to obtain, and generally the classes will not coincide.[42]

Depending upon the information we wish to obtain, our bronzes could be classified in a number of ways. They may be classified into types and modes,[43] which can be shown to be distributed in time and space for the purpose of tracing the histories of individual types of artifacts, both within a single cultural tradition and among diverse cultural traditions. Examples are Li Chi's studies of the histories of individual types of bronze vessels and weapons.[44] The histories of individual bronze artifacts, arrived at in the manner described above, may be used to suggest the interrelationship of diverse cultures.[45] Typological changes of individual artifact classes give rise to diagnostic features of those artifact classes of each period, and distinctive artifacts may, thus, be used for the purpose

42. "Archaeology of Alkali Ridge, Southeastern Utah," 46.

43. In the definitions of Irving Rouse, *Prehistory in Haiti*.

44. Li Chi 李濟, "Chi Hsiao-t'un ch'u-t'u chih ch'ing-t'ung ch'i, shang, chung" 記小屯出土之青銅器, 上、中.

45. An example is Li Chi 李濟, "Yin hsü ch'u-t'u t'ung-ch'i wu chung chi ch'i hsiang-kuan chih wen-t'i" 殷虛出土銅器五種及其相關之問題.

of dating whole assemblages in which they occur.[46] Bronze artifacts in an assemblage may be classified simply for descriptive purpose. For this any classificatory system that is efficient and economical would be useful, but to facilitate comparative study archaeologists constantly seek to devise systems that are widely applicable.[47] Bronze artifacts may be classed, along with artifacts of other materials, into types that, when interarticulated, indicate the organization of the culture in question. Examples are the classification of Shang and Chou vessels for food and drink.[48] Finally, bronze artifacts may be grouped (most likely hierarchically) according to their internal terminological system. Such a grouping will coincide to a larger or lesser extent with the Shang people's own classification system. Some of the above ways to classify Shang bronzes have not yet even been attempted.

DECORATIVE ART

The decorative art applied to Shang bronzes is characterized as an animal style,[49] featuring mythicized motifs taken from the animal world. Traditional Chinese antiquarianism does not emphasize the study of the ornamental art, and when ornaments are mentioned they are taken as symbols having a moralistic implication.[50] This symbolic approach continues into modern scholarship: animal motifs in Shang and Chou bronze art are identified with mythological and legendary themes contained in the classics, and their significance in the rituals is ascertained.[51]

The decorative patterns of the bronzes can surely be treated in the same manner as the forms of the bronzes for the typological purposes mentioned above. Although a number of studies have been undertaken by Shang scholars, mostly historians of art, on this aspect of the bronzes, those of Karlgren and Loehr are the most influential.

46. An example is Li Chi 李濟, "Yü pei ch'u-t'u ch'ing-t'ung kou-ping fen-lei t'u-chieh" 豫北出土青銅勾兵分類圖解.

47. Chang Kwang-chih 張光直 et al., *Shang Chou ch'ing-t'ung-ch'i yü ming-wen ti tsung-ho yen-chiu* 商周青銅器與銘文的綜合研究; Vadime Elisseeff, "Possibilités du scalogramme dans l'étude des bronzes Chinois archaïques," and *Bronzes archaïques Chinois au Musée Gernuschi*.

48. K. C. Chang, "Food and Food Vessels in Ancient China."

49. Karlgren, "Some Characteristics of the Yin Art"; Li Chi 李濟, "Hunting Records, Faunistic Remains and Decorative Patterns from the Archaeological Site of Anyang"; Cheng Te-k'un 鄭德坤, "Animal Styles in Prehistoric and Shang China."

50. Jung Keng 容庚, *Shang Chou yi-ch'i t'ung k'ao* 商周彝器通考, p. 99.

51. Phyllis Ackerman, *Ritual Bronzes of Ancient China*; Florance Waterbury, *Early Chinese Symbols and Literature: Vestiges and Speculations*.

In a series of articles published in the 1930s[52] Bernhard Karlgren grouped Shang and Chou bronze vessels into three periods: Archaic (Yin and early Chou prior to 950 B.C.), middle Chou (c. 950–650 B.C.) and Huai (c. 650–200 B.C.), and he divided the decorative elements of the Archaic period bronzes into three groups: A, B, and C. These elements are:

A elements: mask t'ao t'ieh 饕餮, bodied t'ao t'ieh, bovine t'ao t'ieh, cicada, vertical dragon, uni-decor

B elements: dissolved t'ao t'ieh, animal triple band, de-tailed bird, eyed spiral band, eyed band with diagonals, circle band, square with crescents, compound lozenges, spikes, interlocked Ts, vertical ribs

C elements: deformed t'ao t'ieh, dragonized t'ao t'ieh, trunked dragon, beaked dragon, jawed dragon, turning dragon, feathered dragon, winged dragon, S dragon, deformed dragon, bird, snake, whorl circle, blade, eyed blade, spiral band

These elements of design are combined on Shang and earliest Chou vessels in a patterned manner, ascertained Karlgren, on the basis of these elements' distribution in more than five hundred samples. The pattern is this: in general A elements and B elements are not combinable in one and the same vessel, although either can combine with C elements. Karlgren interpreted this to mean that in Shang bronze art there were two contending styles, A style and B style (fig. 3). He saw A as the primary style and B the secondary style derived from A, perhaps "the achievement of newly started *rival houses* of casters to create a new style, the B style, on the basis of and yet radically deviating from the earlier A style."[53]

Karlgren's was the first systematic analysis of the bronze art of the Shang, resulting in an internal division that may be chronologically derived. More recent work along his lines has included an attempt to show that his A and B styles may be manifest not only on individual bronze vessels but also in whole archaeological assemblages, a pattern of occurrence that may be sociologically rather than chronologically derived,[54] and a new statistical study, using a new comprehensive catalogue arranged in numerical code of more than four thousand

52. "The Exhibition of Early Chinese Bronzes"; "Yin and Chou in Chinese Bronzes"; "New Studies on Chinese Bronzes."

53. Karlgren, "New Studies on Chinese Bronzes," p. 91.

54. K. C. Chang, "Some Dualistic Phenomena in Shang Society."

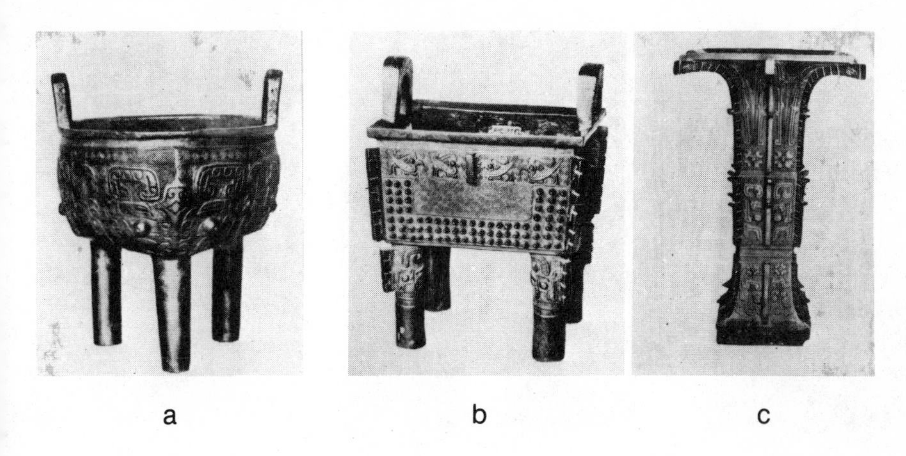

3. Bronze vessels of Karlgren's Style A (*a*) and Style B (*b, c*) (from Jung Keng, *Wu-ying-tien yi-ch'i t'u-lu*).

inscribed Shang and Chou bronzes,[55] of Karlgren's A, B, and C elements, has resulted in the conclusion that "the data provide no evidence that Karlgren's hypothesis is false," although "the data also do not dismiss the possibility of other clusters identical in behavior to Karlgren's A, B, and C groups but composed of different motifs."[56]

Max Loehr's grouping of bronze styles is applicable wholly within Karlgren's archaic period and has in fact been based on bronze vessels selected on the basis of their being of probable Shang date and from the site at An-yang, but his analysis has been based, not on isolated elements or motifs but on "the total effect of the vessels . . . : the shape of a vessel; the decoration (comprising motifs, form of the motifs, and arrangement of these motifs); and technical characteristics."[57] A brief summary of the five styles is given by Loehr as follows:[58]

Style I : Thin relief lines; simple forms; light, airy effect
Style II : Relief ribbons; harsh, heavy forms; incised appearance
Style III: Dense, fluent, more curvilinear figurations developed from the preceeding style
Style IV: First separation of motifs proper from spirals, which now becomes small and function as ground pattern. Motifs and spirals are flush

55. Chang Kwang-chih et al., *Shang Chou ch'ing-t'ung-ch'i yü ming-wen ti tsung-ho yen-chiu* 商周青銅器與銘文的綜合研究.

56. Bruce Spencer, "Archaic Chinese Bronzes: A Statistical Study of Motif Co-occurrence," p. 12.

57. Loehr, "The Bronze Styles of the Anyang Period (1300–1028 B.C.)," 42.

58. *Ritual Vessels of Bronze Age China*, p. 13.

4. Bronzes of Loehr's Styles I–V: *a*, I; *b*, II; *c*, III; *d*, IV; *e*, V. (*a* and *b*, The Arthur M. Sackler Collections, New York, accession nos. V59 and V108; *c*, Asian Art Museum of San Francisco, The Avery Brundage Collection; *d*, William Rockwell Nelson Gallery of Art, Kansas City, Mo.; *e*, The Cincinnati Art Museum—given in honor of Mr. and Mrs. Charles F. Williams by their children.)

Style V : First appearance of motifs in relief; the motifs rise above the ground spirals, which may be eliminated altogether

Two conclusions are reached by Loehr from his five styles (fig. 4). The first is that these styles form an evolutionary sequence of development.

The second is that the ornaments came into being as sheer design and they had no ascertainable meaning—religious, cosmological, or mythological. The first of these conclusions, in any event, has been basically borne out by archaeological excavations during the 1950s, as will be described presently.[59]

MANUFACTURE

In traditional scholarship the manufacture of Shang bronzes was not a topic of great interest. In a few early works ancient bronzes are described as being manufactured by *cire-perdue* techniques,[60] now known to be a very late introduction into China. For really serious study in this area we had to wait until the introduction of modern science into China, and such study has focused on three areas of inquiry: physical and chemical analysis and reconstruction of the Shang technology;[61] the sources of the metals used and the information they provide on Shang economy;[62] and the interrelationship of manufacturing technology and decorative art.[63] Although some of these inquiries were made on museum specimens, all of them evidently must depend upon excavated materials. The significant issues pertaining to some of these topics will be pursued later.

3. *ORACLE BONES*

The Chou people had long been known to have practiced divination with the aid of turtles. In the *Shih ching* the poem "Mien" describes how the ancestors of the Chou house used turtles to help them build their capital near Ch'i-shan in Shensi:

> The plain of Chou was very fertile,
> Its celery and sowthistle sweet as rice-cakes.
> "Here we will make a start; here take counsel,

59. See A. C. Soper, "Early, Middle and Late Shang: A Note."
60. Jung Keng 容庚, *Shang Chou yi-ch'i t'ung k'ao* 商周彝器通考, p. 157.
61. Noel Barnard and Satō Tamotsu, *Metallurgical Remains of Ancient China*; Noel Barnard, *Bronze Casting and Bronze Alloys in Ancient China*; R. J. Gettens, *The Freer Chinese Bronzes: II, Technical Studies.*
62. Shih Chang-ju 石璋如, "Yin tai ti chu t'ung kung-yi" 殷代的鑄銅工藝; Amano Motonosuke 天野元之助, "Indai sangyō ni kansuru jakkan no mondai" 殷代產業に関する若干の問題.
63. Wilma Fairbank, "Piece-Mold Craftsmanship and Shang Bronze Design"; Li Chi 李濟, "Yin hsü ch'u-t'u ch'ing-t'ung li-ch'i chih tsung chien-t'ao" 殷虛出土青銅禮器之總檢討.

Here notch our [turtle]."
It says, "Stop", it says, "Halt.
Build houses here."

[Translated by Arthur Waley]

Remains of the turtles used for taking such counsel were found at a Chou site near Ch'i-shan in late 1977,[64] but until then scholars were not aware of the fact that some of the Chou turtle shells were inscribed! Nor did they know that oracle taking was in fact also a Shang custom, but they learned about this fact—plus the knowledge about their inscriptions—much earlier than 1977. The inscribed oracle bones of the Shang people became known toward the end of the nineteenth century, and their discovery drastically transformed our knowledge about Shang history.

The Shang oracle bones are close to being a product of modern archaeology; unlike bronzes, which had been studied throughout a good part of China's period of written history, initial discovery of the oracle bones happened less than thirty years before their archaeological excavation. But the oracle bones are described here in a separate section from the Shang archaeology because of their inscriptions, whose study required more textual than archaeological knowledge.

Let me first briefly describe the essential features of these inscribed oracle bones.[65] Inheriting the practice of divination by interpreting cracks produced by heat on a piece of bone, the Shang diviners at An-yang nevertheless developed the art to new heights. First they prepared for their act by selecting the bones, polishing them, and making rows of grooves and pits on each piece. The bones they used were of two kinds. The first were bones of domestic cattle (*Bos exiqus*), water buffalo (*Bubalus mephistopheles*), and a few other animals,[66] mostly shoulder blades. (Hence the terms scapulimancy and pyroscapulimancy.) The second were plastrons and (rarely) carapaces of turtles, which, used for this purpose only with the Shang, have been identified as belonging to the following species: *Ocadia sinensis*, *Chinemys reevesi*, *Mauremys mutica*, *Cuora* sp., and *Testudo emys*.[67] Other than

64. According to a news dispatch of Hsin Hua She in the 1 November 1977 *Mei-chou Hua Ch'iao Jih Pao* 美洲華僑日報.

65. Two comprehensive studies of the oracle bone inscriptions as historical sources appeared in 1978: David N. Keightley, *Sources of Shang History*, and Yen Yi-p'ing 嚴一萍, *Chia ku hsüeh* 甲骨學. Too recent to be cited extensively in this volume, both works should be consulted thoroughly by any serious student of Shang history.

66. Pierre Teilhard de Chardin and C. C. Young, *On the Mammalian Remains from the Archaeological Site of An-yang*, pp. 45, 56, 58.

67. Keightley, *Sources of Shang History*, appendix 1.

Chinemys reevesi, none of the other turtles now inhabit North China, and their shells could have been imported during the Shang period as well.

In preparation, the shoulder blades were polished to remove any residual flesh and to render the surfaces smooth. The turtle shells were sawn at the bridge to separate the plastrons and the carapaces (leaving the bridges with the plastrons, on which notations were often inscribed to record the source of the shells and the number in the batch) and then smoothed to polish. Both bones and shells were possibly soaked in a liquid substance at some point as part of the preparation in order to soften them to facilitate hollowing, fire-cracking, and inscribing, but details are not yet clear.[68]

The rows of hollows on one side of the bone or shell were produced to make the bone or shell thinner and easier to crack and to position the cracks that would appear on the other side upon the application of some heat source. These hollows had been scooped out on some of the neolithic oracle bones, but only with the Shang people had the hollows become regularly spaced and sophisticatedly bored and chiselled. Many of the hollows consist of two overlapping depressions, one circular with a flat or rounded bottom and the other lentoid with a chiseled V-shaped cross-section. When the heat was applied, usually two cracks would appear on the reverse side, one vertical along the axis of the lentoid groove and the other transverse, joining and perpendicular to the vertical crack at one end, along the diameter of the circular pit. Usually the groove and the pit overlap with the pit toward the median line of the shell so that the transverse crack would point toward the median axis of the shell, and with the pit on the same side of the bone so that the transverse cracks of all the crack patterns would point toward the same direction.

At the time of divination, heat was applied at the bottom of the hollow, cracks appeared on the reverse surface and were then interpreted for an answer to the question put to the ancestors. For a discussion of the whole institution of Shang divination we shall wait for the right moment, later in this book; but here, to explain the oracle bone inscriptions as a source material, an account of the relevant points must be given.

Oracle taking may have been widespread among the various segments of Shang society, but since virtually all of the inscribed oracle bones were left from the kings' inquiries we confine our description to the practice at the royal court. Apparently several people were involved in the process of divining and its aftermath: The king himself,

68. Chou Hung-hsiang, personal communication.

who sometimes initiated an inquiry but in whose name all inquiries were made in any event; the *chen-jen* 貞人, or the person who made the inquiry (*chen*) as the king's official representative; the *p'u-jen* 卜人 or person who carried out the divining act (*p'u* 卜); the prognosticator or *chan-jen* 占人, who specialized in the interpretation of the cracks; and the *shih* 史 or archivist who inscribed the notations pertaining to the whole inquiry.[69] These, however, were basically roles that could be performed by as many individual persons, or by fewer persons who combined some of the functions. In the royal court, divination was an important activity that presumably played an important part in decisions pertaining to the royal persons and to the state. Inscribed records pertained to the following matters: sacrificial rituals, military campaigns, hunting expeditions, comings-and-goings, well-being during the following "week" (*hsün*), well-being during the forthcoming night or day, weather, harvest, sickness, life or death, birth, dream, building, and others.[70] Some of these inquiries were undertaken on a fixed schedule (e.g., pertaining to some rituals, the coming week, day, or night, etc.), but others were dictated by a need that had arisen. To make an inquiry within any of these categories, the inquirer would ask the diviner to divine, he would do it, and the prognosticator would receive the answer from the ancestral deities with whom the diviner had just made contact. Then the archivist would on occasion record the query, the prognostication, and, rarely, the verification. It is from these records that we have learned about the divining process.

Each act of divination in a single inquiry may comprise several scorchings and crackings on different parts of the bone or shell. Chang Ping-ch'üan[71] has found that, insofar as the plastral divinations are concerned, these repeated scorchings-and-crackings followed one of five possible orders: from upper end to lower end, from center to outer edges and from upper to lower ends, from outer edges to center and from upper to lower ends, from lower end to upper end, and irregular. These repeated inquiries were phrased both positively and negatively: Is it going to be this or do this? Is it not going to? When more than one row of scorchings were made, it often happened that positive inquiries and negative inquiries were located on opposite halves of the shell. After the crackings were made, the diviner would sometimes incise

69. Here I follow the traditional interpretation of these roles as elaborated by Jao Tsung-yi 饒宗頤, in *Yin tai chen p'u jen-wu t'ung k'ao* 殷代貞卜人物通考. David Keightley has a new definition of the word *chen*; see his 1972 manuscript," Shih Chen: A New Hypothesis about the Nature of Shang Divination."

70. Chang Ping-ch'üan 張秉權, "Chia-ku-wen ti fa-hsien yü ku p'u hsi-kuan ti k'ao-cheng" 甲骨文的發現與骨卜習慣的考證, 857.

71. "P'u kuei fu chia ti hsü shu" 卜龜腹甲的序數, 231–236.

along the cracks to make them clear and permanent, put numbers near each crack to indicate the proper order, and to write down, next to each crack, a prognosticative code. Exactly how the prognosticator interpreted the cracks is impossible to say. Chang Ping-ch'üan[72] suggested that some angles at which the transverse crack joins the vertical crack (blunt angles higher than seventy degrees) are more frequently associated with auspicious prognostications than others, but that other factors must also be taken into account, since different prognosticatory codes were found associated with the same angles. He suggested, therefore, that possibly the diviner had, in some cases, entered into an ad hoc agreement with the ancestral deity as to the cracking patterns.[73]

After the divining act, the archivist then sometimes proceeded to enter the act into a record on the bone or shell used during the act. Most of them were incised, with a knife;[74] occasionally they were brushed on and then incised or first incised and then filled with red, black, or brown pigments. Each record would typically consist of the following parts:

1. *Preface:* This part usually consists of two segments: The cyclical date of the divining (□□卜) and the name of the inquirer (□貞).
2. *The Inquiry:* The question that was put to the ancestor(s).
3. *The Prognostication:* This part usually consists of short notations on the reverse side, but occasionally (when the king himself was the prognosticator) it constitutes a part of the record following the inquiry.
4. *The Verification:* This was put in after the event that proved the correctness of the prognostication.

These four parts are not always present in every record; (3) and (4) are usually omitted. When inquiries were made repeatedly, the record would be repeated on the bone or shell, but in its second and subsequent occurrences it usually appeared in abbreviated form. Moreover, the inquiry often appeared in both positive and negative forms, placed on opposite sides of the shell.[75] The records would thus constitute a whole

72. "Yin hsü p'u kuei chih p'u chao chi ch'i yu-kuan wen-t'i" 殷虛卜龜之卜兆及其有關問題.

73. "Chia-ku wen ti fa-hsien yü ku p'u hsi-kuan ti k'ao-cheng" 甲骨文的發現與骨卜習慣的考証, 859–860.

74. Chou Hung-hsiang 周鴻翔, "Yin tai k'e tzu tao ti t'ui-ts'e" 殷代刻字刀的推測.

75. Chou Hung-hsiang 周鴻翔, *P'u-tz'u tui chen shu li* 卜辭對貞述例.

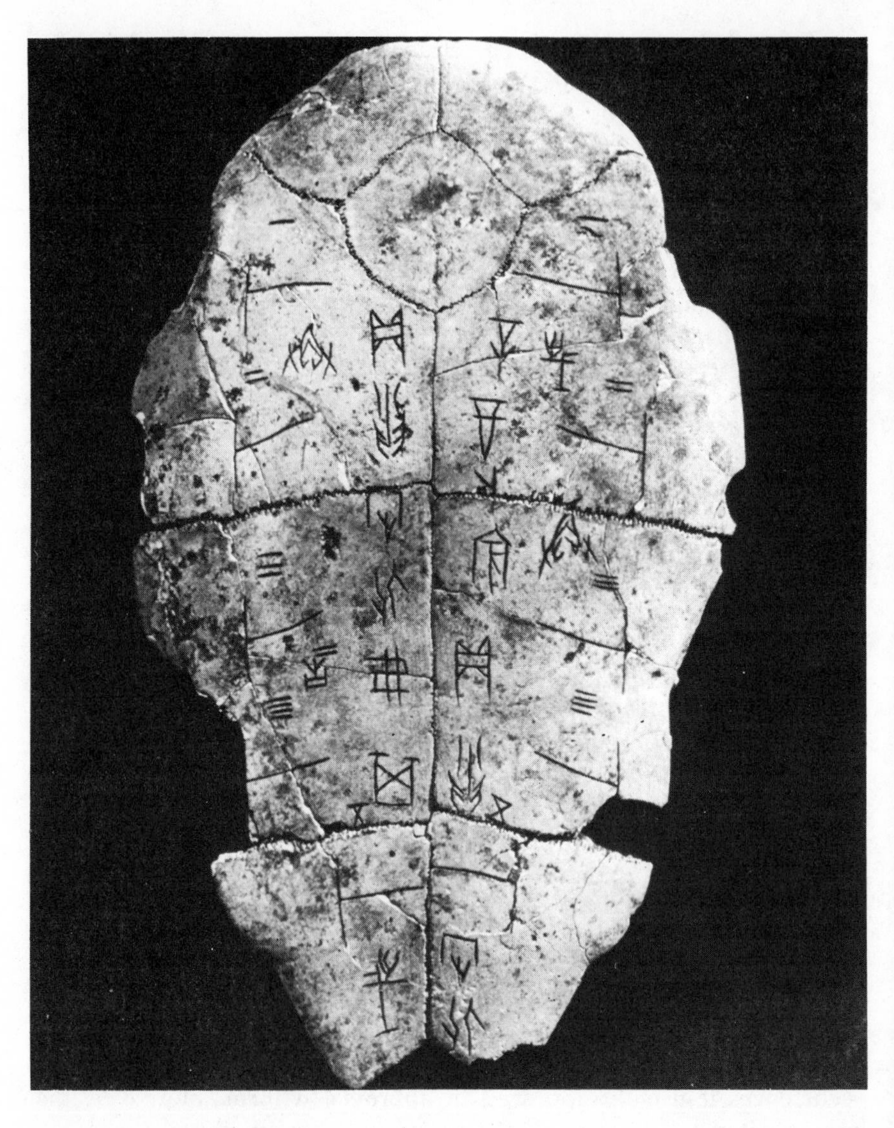

5. An inscribed turtle shell in the collection of Academia Sinica (Taipei) (after Smith and Weng, *China, A History in Art,* p. 26).

6. An inscribed shoulder blade in the collection of Academia Sinica (photo supplied by *Life*).

"set".[76] Since the inscribed bones or shells are often found broken, record sets in complete condition are the exception rather than the rule, and many efforts have been made and are being made to piece scattered fragments of a set back together,[77] sometimes with the aid of a computer.[78]

These records, in fragments or in original or restored sets, provide an exceedingly important new source of Shang history that was not available until the end of the nineteenth century. The Shang court apparently had an archives office, which housed the shells (fig. 5) and bones (fig. 6) on which such records were inscribed. After the fall of the dynasty, these archives became part of the Ruins of Yin (Yin hsü 殷墟) and lay buried and unknown. Archaeological excavations of the Ruins of Yin undertaken after 1978 disclosed the fact that during the period of Sui (581–618) and T'ang (618–907) dynasties many dead persons were buried in An-yang, and in the process of burial inscribed bone and shell fragments were disturbed and then reburied. If the fragments were seen by the gravediggers they didn't pay enough attention to them to make this a widely known fact. But beginning some time later, these ancient shells and bones began to be collected for medicinal use as a kind of "dragon bones," long a traditional medicinal ingredient now known to be ancient (often fossilized) animal bones. Some of these dragon bones came into the attention of Western paleontologists, and efforts to trace their origins eventually led to the discovery of Peking man, a story that is now quite well known.[79]

The dragon bones also led to the discovery of the oracle bone inscriptions. A widely circulated story has it that in the year 1899 a Peking scholar of some note, Wang Yi-Jung 王懿榮, was sick with malaria and had been taking a medicinal prescription that contained dragon bones. A house guest, Liu Eh 劉鶚, another scholar and famed author of the novel *Lao Ts'an's Travels*, happened to have seen the medicine and caught sight of some inscribed fragments. After Liu brought his find to his host, the two men were both astonished at these hitherto unknown archaic characters and began to launch an effort to trace the origins of these pieces.[80] After considerable meandering,

76. Chang Ping-ch'üan 張秉權, "Lun ch'eng t'ao p'u-tz'u" 論成套卜辭.

77. Examples are: Kuo Jo-yü 郭若愚 et al., *Yin hsü wen-tzu chui ho* 殷墟文字綴合; Chang Ping-ch'üan 張秉權, *Yin hsü wen-tzu Ping pien* 殷虛文字丙編.

78. H. H. Chou, "Computer matching of oracle bone fragments"; T'ung En-cheng 童恩正, Chang Sheng-k'ai 張陞楷, and Ch'en Ching-ch'un 陳景春, "Kuan-yü shih-yung tien-tzu chi-suan-chi chui-ho Shang tai p'u chia sui-p'ien ti ch'u-pu pao-kao" 關於使用電子計算機綴合商代卜甲碎片的初步報告.

79. Harry Shapiro, *Peking Man*.

80. Tung Tso-pin 董作賓, "Chia ku nien piao" 甲骨年表.

their and other scholars' efforts were successful, leading to the discovery of the archaeological sites in An-yang, Honan, where these inscribed dragon bones had been harvested. Scholars and dealers alike immediately began intense collecting activities, leading to further extensive damage to the site. Finally, in 1928, scientific archaeological excavation began at An-yang, resulting, for the first time, in inscribed shells and bones that were found *in situ*. In his new book, *Anyang*, Li Chi gives a detailed account of the collecting activities and of the excavations there that centered on the oracle bones, and readers are referred to it for more information and anecdotes than can be given here.

According to Tung Tso-pin,[81] there are altogether some one hundred thousand pieces of inscribed bones, all presumably from An-yang. These pieces vary in size, ranging from whole shells and shoulder blades to tiny nail-size pieces that came from broken shells and bones. Of these hundred thousand, only two lots were listed by Tung as having come from excavations:

24,918 pieces,	excavated by the Institute of History and Philology, Academia Sinica, 1928–1937.
3,656 pieces,	excavated by Honan Provincial Museum in 1929 and 1930.

Additional pieces have been excavated from An-yang since Tung wrote; the most important being the some 5,000 pieces excavated in 1973.[82] Thus, about 33,500 pieces have been excavated since 1928, while the rest of the hundred thousand plus was collected without the benefit of archaeological provenance, mostly before 1928. These are now housed in various public and private institutions in China and abroad. According to the account by Ch'en Meng-chia in 1956,[83] their distribution was as follows:

In China, public collections:	c. 51,000 pieces
In China, in private hands:	c. 4,000 pieces
In Taiwan province:	c. 26,000 pieces
In Europe and North America:	c. 7,000 pieces
In Japan:	c. 10,000 pieces

Scholars of Shang history do not, however, always have to use the original pieces for research; in fact, most research topics can

81. *Chia ku hsüeh liu-shih nien* 甲骨學六十年, pp. 11–13.

82. *KK*, "1973-nien An-yang Hsiao-t'un nan-ti fa-chüeh chien pao" 1973年安陽小屯南地發掘簡報.

83. *Yin hsü p'u-tz'u tsung-shu* 殷墟卜辭綜述, p. 47.

be satisfactorily handled by using the catalogues of oracle bone inscriptions in the form of rubbings, photographs, or tracings. The most important of these catalogues are in the table below (only those catalogues that include more than 500 pieces are listed, except for the third item, important because it includes several whole blades):

	Date	*No. of pieces*
T'ieh-yün ts'ang kuei 鐵雲藏龜		
by Liu Eh 劉鶚	1903	1058
Yin hsü shu ch'i ch'ien pien 殷虛書契前編		
by Lo Chen-yü 羅振玉	1913	2229
Yin hsü shu ch'i ch'ing hua 殷虛書契菁華		
by Lo Chen-yü 羅振玉	1914	68
Yin hsü shu ch'i hou pien 殷虛書契後編		
by Lo Chen-yü 羅振玉	1916	1104
Chien-shou-t'ang so ts'ang Yin hsü wen-tzu 戩壽堂所藏殷虛文字		
by Chi Fo-t'o 姬佛陀	1917	655
Yin hsü p'u tz'u 殷墟卜辭		
by Ming Yi-shih 明義士 (James Menzies)	1917	2369
Kikō jūkotsu moji 龜甲獸骨文字		
by Hayashi Taisuke 林泰輔	1921	1023
P'u-shih Yin ch'i cheng wen 簠室殷契徵文		
by Wang Hsiang 王襄	1925	1125
Yin ch'i p'u tz'u 殷契卜辭		
by Jung Keng 容庚 and Ch'ü Jun-min 瞿潤緡	1933	874
P'u tz'u t'ung ts'uan 卜辭通纂		
by Kuo Mo-jo 郭沫若	1933	929
Yin hsü shu ch'i hsü pien 殷虛書契續編		
by Lo Chen-yü 羅振玉	1933	2016
Yin ch'i yi ts'un 殷契佚存		
by Shang Ch'eng-tso 商承祚	1933	1000
K'u Fang erh shih ts'ang chia ku p'u-tz'u 庫方二氏藏甲骨卜辭 by Fang Fa-lien 方法斂 (Frank F. Chalfant)	1935	1687
Yin ch'i ts'ui pien 殷契粹編		
by Kuo Mo-jo 郭沫若	1937	1595
Chia ku wen lu 甲骨文錄		
by Sun Hai-po 孫海波	1937	930

Seven Collections of Inscribed Oracle Bone by Fang Fa-lien 方法斂 (Frank F. Chalfant) and R. S. Britton	1938	527
Yin ch'i yi chu 殷契遺珠 by Chin Tsu-t'ung 金祖同	1939	1459
Ch'eng-chai Yin hsü wen-tzu 誠齋殷墟文字 by Sun Hai-po 孫海波	1940	500
Chia ku liu lu 甲骨六錄 by Hu Hou-hsüan 胡厚宣	1945	659
Chan hou P'ing Chin hsin huo chia ku chi 戰後平津新獲甲骨集 by Hu Hou-hsüan 胡厚宣	1946	538
Yin hsü wen-tzu chia pien 殷墟文字甲編 by Tung Tso-pin 董作賓	1948	3942
Yin hsü wen-tzu yi pien 殷墟文字乙編 by Tung Tso-pin 董作賓	1948,1949	6272
Chan hou Ching Chin hsin huo chia ku chi 戰後京津新獲甲骨集 by Hu Hou-hsüan 胡厚宣	1949	854
Chan hou Ning Hu hsin huo chia ku chi 戰後寧滬新獲甲骨集 by Hu Hou-hsüan 胡厚宣	1951	1143
Chan hou Nan Pei hsin huo chia ku lu 戰後南北新獲甲骨錄 by Hu Hou-hsüan 胡厚宣	1951	3276
Yin ch'i shih tuo 殷契拾掇 by Kuo Jo-yü 郭若愚	1951–53	550
Kyōto Daigaku Jinbun Kagaku Kenkyujo Shozo Kokotsu Moji 京都大學人文科學研究所所藏甲骨文字 by Kaizuka Shigeki 貝塚茂樹	1959	3446
The Menzies Collection of Shang Dynasty Oracle Bones, Vol. I by Hsü Chin-hsiung 許進雄	1972	3176

An ambitious project is being launched in Peking, under the direction of Hu Hou-hsüan, to collate all the inscribed pieces, both published and unpublished, and to make them available between two covers (under the title *Chia ku wen ho chi* 甲骨文合集). The best aids for scholarly research in this field are a collection of studies on individual characters by Li Hsiao-ting[84] and a concordance keyed to both characters and common names and terms by Shima Kunio.[85]

84. Li Hsiao-ting 李孝定, *Chia ku wen-tzu chi shih* 甲骨文字集釋.
85. Shima Kunio 島邦男, *Inkyo bokuji sōrui* 殷墟卜辞綜類.

Because the oracle bones were inscribed about religious matters, the information they contain pertains primarily to Shang religion, but Shang scholars have used them in ingenious ways to poke into almost all areas of Shang culture and society. One of the first studies of oracle bone inscriptions by Lo Chen-yü[86] discusses the following topics: the capital, kings and names of personages, place names, the script, divination, inscriptions and rituals, and divination methods. Kuo Mo-jo, whose vision was both broad and penetrating, initiated oracle bone inscription studies concerning Shang society and such aspects of Shang culture as the cyclical signs, numerals, genealogy, astronomy and meteorology, economy, war, hunting, and so on.[87] Since the publication of these pioneer works, numerous studies have appeared that touch upon every aspect of Shang civilization, and the results are indispensable for the present volume or for any study of Shang history.[88]

4. *ARCHAEOLOGY*

The quality of Shang historiography was radically changed with the appearance of the oracle bone inscriptions, in two ways. First, these inscriptions for the first time provided a direct approach to Shang history through their own writings. Second, the oracle bones eventually led to the archaeological site at An-yang and to its scientific excavation. When the inscribed oracle bones first came on the market, the merchants maintained that they came from both T'ang-yin 湯陰 and An-yang in Honan. By 1910, Lo Chen-yü was able to track down the source of the oracle bones at the Hsiao-t'un 小屯 village, northwest of An-yang, and to eliminate T'ang-yin as a diversion put up by the merchants to protect their source. Oracle bone scholars then came to Hsiao-t'un to look at the sites themselves: Menzies in 1914, Lo Chen-yü in 1915, and Hayashi Taisuke in 1918. These scholars, however, were merely interested in the writings, and, besides, they lacked the modern archaeological training necessary to undertake the excavation of the cultural remains at the Shang sites in An-yang, which was to be the next logical step.

Modern archaeology was introduced into China at just about this time. For Western sinologists, archaeological explorations of China must date at the latest from the expeditions of Sven Hedin, Le Coq, and

86. Lo Chen-yü, *Yin hsü shu ch'i k'ao shih* 殷虛書契考釋.

87. *Chung-kuo ku-tai she-hui yen-chiu* 中國古代社會研究; *P'u-tz'u t'ung ts'uan* 卜辭通纂.

88. For a brief history of oracle bone inscription studies, see J. A. Lefeuvre, "Les inscriptions des Shang sur carapaces de tortue et sur os."

Aurel Stein in the very late nineteenth and early twentieth century in Chinese Turkistan and Kansu, which led to the discovery, among other finds, of the famous site of Tun-huang 敦煌. For Japanese archaeologists their early explorations date to the late nineteenth century in Manchuria. But for Chinese scholars, whose attention was focused primarily upon the Chung Yüan, the Central Plains, the area of China—Honan, Shensi, Shansi, Hopei, and Shantung—that, to them, cradled the legendary ancestors of all Chinese, the Three Sovereigns, the Five Emperors (including the famed Yellow Emperor), and the Three Dynasties, the idea of digging into the ground to find the remains of the ancients did not begin to make a deep impression until around 1920, with the discoveries at Chou-kou-t'ien 周口店, home of Peking man, and Yang-shao-ts'un 仰韶村, location of the first Neolithic site of China. The 1920s also witnessed the rise of the so-called *yi ku p'ai* 疑古派, the "Doubting Antiquity" school, of ancient Chinese historiography. A rising generation of young Chinese historians, led by Ku Chieh-kang 顧頡剛, called into question the historicity of not only the Three Sovereigns and the Five Emperors but also of much about the first two of the Three Dynasties.[89]

The 1920s were, thus, a crucial decade in the ancient historiography of China. All ancient textual history, hitherto the orthodox genesis of the Chinese civilization, was now open to question, but the newly appearing oracle bone inscriptions provided a strong shot in the arm, and the new science of field archaeology appeared to be the only cure-all that was going to settle the whole issue once and for all. In 1928, therefore, the year the Nationalist government under Chiang Kai-shek established itself in Nanking, and the year a Central Academy of Science and, under it, a National Research Institute of History and Philology were founded in Canton, one of the first acts of the young director of the new institute, Fu Ssu-nien 傅斯年, a comrade-in-arms of Ku Chieh-kang during the 1918 May Fourth Movement of Peking, was to dispatch Tung Tso-pin 董作賓 to An-yang to see if there was anything left by way of inscribed oracle bones that might still be worth excavating.

Tung, then thirty-three, a scholar of Chinese and native of Honan, the province in which An-yang is located—a fact not unrelated to his assignment—was in An-yang from August twelfth to fourteenth, 1928. The following is a translation of his own report of the trip:

> It was August twelfth that I arrived in An-yang. After getting off the train, I went to call upon Mr. Chang T'ien-chi, principal of the Provincial Number 11 Middle School of Honan.

89. Ku Chieh-kang 顧頡剛, *Ku shih pien* 古史辨.

Upon learning the purpose of my trip to An-yang, Mr. Chang told me about his own investigations in 1925. He said that the inscribed oracle bones were uncovered in the village of Hsiao-t'un, five *lis* to the northwest of town. The River Huan 洹 flows by about a *li* or a little more north of the village, and all the farming fields along the banks of the river have yielded oracle bones. He brought some of his pupils on a trip there; they saw many uninscribed oracle bones throughout the fields. When they dug into the ground with a stick, inscribed bones were encountered in a depth of a *ch'ih* or so. He also stated that it was easy to buy them in the village. If you announced your intention to purchase, women and children would gather. He purchased more than a handful of small pieces for a silver dollar. . . . Mr. Chang further stated that they continued to appear in recent years and that a Mr. So-and-so had acquired a complete shell.

On the thirteenth it was rainy and it was not possible to go to Hsiao-t'un. I went instead to the antique shops in town in search of oracle bones. . . . At [another] Mr. Chang's shop inside the West Gate, there were several fragments of oracle bones as large as fingernails. I asked him where those had been found and, also, the recent conditions of the discoveries, but he pleaded ignorance to most of my questions. It proved to be the same with other antique dealers also. . . . Finally I went to the Tsun-ku-chai shop in the Bell Tower Alley. The owner, [yet another] Mr. Chang, was more forthcoming. He told me that many oracle bones were uncovered in the early years of the Republic, but that recent years such as 1920, 1925, and 1928 also saw the discoveries of large batches. Some of these finds had not yet been sold, and he promised to search for me. He showed the few dozen pieces he had, but they were small, the largest ones only a *ts'un* long. . . .

The next day was somewhat clear. I went to Number 11 Middle School to fetch my friend Hsü Chao-chieh as my guide and we headed toward Hsiao-t'un. . . .

At Hsiao-t'un I purchased several batches of oracle bones, more than a hundred fragments altogether at three silver dollars, brought by women and children, just as Mr. Chang had said. Occasionally there were pieces two or three *ts'un* long, but the asking price was high, about four or five silver dollars each, and these I didn't buy. But all this goes to show that many oracle bones are still being turned up, and every household in the village had some. According to the villagers, antique dealers come regularly to purchase inscribed oracle bones, but they were not interested in tiny fragments, and the villagers in their diggings simply threw tiny fragments away, which were then collected by women and children. My purchase thus came from the latter. The tiny pieces sometimes have only a stroke or half a character, but my purpose in purchasing them was not to acquire a large quantity of good pieces but was, rather, to learn about the condition of the discoveries and to obtain souvenirs for this trip.

We hired a small child to take us to the north of the village in search of find spots of oracle bones. The child pointed to a sand heap and stated that oracle bones came from underneath it. I was rather surprised, because Lo Chen-yü was there himself in 1915 and he stated that "the oracle bones came from cotton and wheat fields," and Mr. Chang also referred to farming fields. Could it be that they had come to a different spot? Or that they came to a spot nearby? After carefully examining the western side of the sand heap, in an area near the cotton field, I found ten newly dug and refilled pits. Near one of the pits I picked up an inscribed bone, which was in fact an oracle bone. It appeared that the child was in fact telling the truth. The sand heap was several *ch'ih* above the fields, its eastern slope sliding down to the bank of the Huan River. The heap-top was not arable, but over-grown with yellow grass and paved with white sands.

So much for our investigation. What we have learned from this investigation is the fact that the oracle bones have not been excavated to exhaustion. The oracle bones from Yin hsü were first known in 1899, but it was not until 1910 that Lo Chen-yü began an extensive search, and during the following several years tens of thousands of them have been found. Lo Chen-yü's opinion was that "the treasure trove has now been emptied." However, since the founding of the Republic (in 1912), according to the antique merchants, several times have excavations taken place and proven productive. Mr. Chang's 1925 investigation also showed that they occurred throughout the farming fields. All of these are proof that the Yin hsü oracle bones have not yet been exhausted. The only thing we can say about the find spots is that they are located in the sand heap area and in the farm fields along the Huan River. . . . Scientific excavation by national scholarly institutions must be undertaken without delay.[90]

90. Tung Tso-pin, "Min-kuo shih-ch'i nien shih yüeh shih chüeh An-yang Hsiao-t'un pao-kao shu" 民國十七年十月試掘安陽小屯報告書, 3–6.

7. Major archaeologists who excavated the Yin hsü from 1928–37 (*a*, Li Chi; *b*, Liang Ssu-yung; *c*, Tung Tso-pin; *d*, Shih Chang-ju; *e*, Kao Ch'ü-hsün).

Tung's recommendation was immediately accepted, and the first field season at Shang site in An-yang took place in October of the same year. Thus began a series of 15 seasons of archaeological excavation in An-yang by archaeologists (headed by Li Chi beginning with the second season) (fig. 7) of the Institute of History and Philology, Academia Sinica, which ended in 1937 shortly before the July Seventh Incident that triggered the full-fledged Sino-Japanese War (fig. 8). The 1928–37 archaeological data from An-yang are described in Academia Sinica

8. A scene of Yin hsü excavations in the 1930s (after Shih Chang-ju, *Yi ch'ü chi-chih shang hsia ti mu-tsang,* pl. 3).

publications dating from the 1920s and 1930s in Peking, from the late 1930s and 1940s in the Southwest, from the late 1940s in Nanking, and from the 1950s to date in Taiwan, successive locations of the Institute as it moved with the migrating seat of the Nationalist government.[91]

91. For the principal literature on the An-yang excavations 1928–1937, see *An-yang fa-chüeh pao-kao* 安陽發掘報告, nos. 1–4, 1929–1933; *Chung-kuo k'ao-ku pao-kao chi chih erh Hsiao-t'un* 中國考古報告集之二, 小屯, 1948–1976; *Chung-kuo k'ao-ku*

After 1949, the year the People's Republic of China was founded, the An-yang Shang sites continued to be the focus of much archaeological activity. The following is a brief chronicle of the archaeological work at An-yang, with the available published sources:

1928 First season of the excavation by the Institute of History and Philology (IHP), October 13–30. Excavated foci at Hsiao-t'un, Hsiao-t'un North, Hsiao-t'un Northeast.[92]

1929 IHP's second season. March 7–May 10, at Hsiao-t'un, Hsiao-t'un North, and Hsiao-t'un South.[93] IHP's third season. October 7–21 and November 15–December 12, at Hsiao-t'un North and Pa-t'ai 壩台 to the northwest of Hsiao-t'un.[94]

1931 IHP's fourth season, March 21–May 11, at Hsiao-t'un North,[95] April 16–30, at Ssu-p'an-mo 四盤磨,[96] and April 16–May 12 at Hou-kang 後岡.[97] IHP's fifth season, November 7–December 19, at Hsiao-t'un North, and November 10–December 4, at Hou-kang.[98]

1932 IHP's sixth season. April 1–May 31, at Hsiao-t'un

pao-kao chi chih san Hou-chia-chuang, 中國考古報告集之三, 侯家莊, 1962–1976; *Chung-kuo k'ao-ku pao-kao chi hsin pien* 中國考古報告集新編, 1964–1972. (All of the above published by the Institute of History and Philology, Academia Sinica.) Li Chi, *Anyang*; Hu Hou-hsüan 胡厚宣, *Yin hsü fa-chüeh* 殷墟發掘; Shih Chang-ju 石璋如, *K'ao-ku nien piao* 考古年表; Chang Kwang-chih 張光直, "Yin hsü fa-chüeh wu-shih nien" 殷墟發掘五十年.

92. Tung Tso-pin 董作賓, "Min-kuo shih-ch'i nien shih yüeh shih chüeh An-yang Hsiao-t'un pao-kao shu" 民國十七年十月試掘安陽小屯報告書.

93. Li Chi 李濟, "Hsiao-t'un ti-mien hsia ch'ing-hsing fen-hsi ch'u-pu" 小屯地面下情形分析初步; "Yin Shang t'ao-ch'i ch'u-lun" 殷商陶器初論.

94. Li Chi 李濟, "Min-kuo shih-pa nien ch'iu-chi fa-chüeh Yin hsü chih ching-kuo chi ch'i chung-yao fa-hsien" 民國十八年秋季發掘殷墟之經過及其重要發現; "Hsiao-t'un yü Yang-shao" 小屯與仰韶; "Fu shen tsang" 俯身葬.

95. Li Chi 李濟, "An-yang tsui-chin fa-chüeh pao-kao chi liu tz'u kung-tso chih tsung ku-chi" 安陽最近發掘報告及六次工作之總估計; Kuo Pao-chün 郭寶鈞, "B-ch'ü fa-chüeh chi chih yi" B區發掘記之一.

96. Li chi 李濟, "An-yang tsui-chin fa-chüeh pao-kao chih liu tz'u kung-tso chih tsung ku-chi" 安陽最近發掘報告及六次工作之總估計; Wu Chin-ting 吳金鼎, "Chai chi Hsiao-t'un yi hsi chih san ch'u hsiao fa-chüeh" 摘記小屯迤西之三處小發掘.

97. Liang Ssu-yung 梁思永, "Hou-kang fa-chüeh hsiao chi" 後岡發掘小記; "Hsiao-t'un Lung-shan yü Yang-shao" 小屯龍山與仰韶.

98. Li Chi 李濟, "An-yang tsui-chin fa-chüeh pao-kao chi liu tz'u kung-tso chih tsung ku-chi" 安陽最近發掘報告及六次工作之總估計; Kuo Pao-chün 郭寶鈞, "B-ch'ü fa-chüeh chi chih erh" B區發掘記之二; Liang Ssu-yung 梁思永 (see note 97 above).

North, April 8–16, at Kao-ching-t'ai-tzu 高台井子, April 15 at Ssu-mien-pei 四面碑, and April 14–May 10 at Wang-yü-k'ou 王裕口 and Ho-chia-hsiao-chuang 霍家小莊.[99]

IHP's seventh season, at Hsiao-t'un North.[100]

1933 IHP's eighth season. October 20–December 25, at Hsiao-t'un North,[101] November 15–December 21 at Ssu-p'an-mo, and November 15–January 3, January 15–24 at Hou-kang.[102]

1934 IHP's nineth season. March 9–April 1 at Hsiao-t'un North, March 15–April 1, April 10–20 at Hou-kang, April 30–May 22 at Nan-pa-t'ai 南壩台, and April 2–May 31 at Hou-chia-chuang 侯家莊 South.[103]

IHP's tenth season. October 3–December 30 at Hsi-pei-kang 西北岡 near Hou-chia-chuang and October 29–December 5 at T'ung-lo-chai 同樂寨.[104]

1935 IHP's eleventh season. March 10–June 15, at Hsi-pei-kang.[105]

IHP's twelfth season. September 5–December 16 at Hsi-pei-kang, October 20–December 5, at Ta-ssu-k'ung-ts'un 大司空村 South, and October 20–November 7, at Fan-chia-chuang 范家莊 North.[106]

1936 IHP's thirteenth season. March 18–June 24, at Hsiao-t'un North.[107]

IHP's fourteenth season. September 20–December 31,

99. See note 96 above.

100. Shih Chang-ju, 石璋如, "Ti ch'i tz'u Yin hsü fa-chüeh: E-ch'ü kung-tso pao-kao" 第七次殷墟發掘：E區工作報告.

101. Shih Chang-ju 石璋如, "Yin hsü tsui-chin chih chung-yao fa-hsien fu lun Hsiao-t'un ti-ts'eng" 殷墟最近之重要發現附論小屯地層; "Hsiao-t'un ti wen-hua ts'eng" 小屯的文化層.

102. Shih Chang-ju 石璋如, "Ho-nan An-yang Hou-kang ti Yin mu" 河南安陽後岡的殷墓.

103. See note 101 above.

104. Shih Chang-ju 石璋如, "Hsiao-t'un ti wen-hua ts'eng" 小屯的文化層.

105. Liang Ssu-yung 梁思永 and Kao Ch'ü-hsün 高去尋, *Hou-chia-chuang 1001-hao ta mu* 侯家莊1001號大墓, *1002-hao ta mu* 1002號大墓, *1003-hao ta mu* 1003號大墓, *1004-hao ta mu* 1004號大墓.

106. Shih Chang-ju 石璋如, "Yin-hsü tsui-chin chih chung-yao fa-hsien fu lun Hsiao-t'un ti-ts'eng" 殷墟最近之重要發現附論小屯地層; Liang Ssu-yung 梁思永 and Kao Ch'ü-hsün 高去尋, *Hou-chia-chuang 1217-hao ta mu* 侯家莊1217號大墓; *1500-hao ta mu* 1500號大墓; *1550-hao ta mu* 1550號大墓; Kao Ch'ü-hsün 高去尋, "The Royal Cemetery of the Yin Dynasty of An-yang"; Paul Pelliot, "The Royal Tombs of An-yang," 1937 and 1938.

107. Shih Chang-ju 石璋如, "Yin hsü tsui-chin chih chung-yao fa-hsien fu lun Hsiao-t'un ti-ts'eng" 殷墟最近之重要發現附論小屯地層.

at Hsiao-t'un North, and October 24–December 10 at Ta-ssu-k'ung-ts'un South.[108]

1937 IHP's fifteenth (final) season. March 16–June 19, at Hsiao-t'un North.[109]

1937–45 During the war years Japanese archaeologists of Keio and Tokyo universities undertook excavations in An-yang in 1938 and 1940–41.[110] In 1939, S. H. Hansford made a brief visit there and made a report of conditions at the time.[111]

1950 The first excavation after the founding of the People's Republic of China was undertaken by the Institute of Archaeology of the Academia Sinica, April 12–June 10 at Hsi-pei-kang (renamed Wu-kuan-ts'un 武官村 North) and at several localities south of the River Huan to the west of Hsiao-t'un.[112]

1953–54 Excavation by the Institute of Archaeology at Ta-ssu-k'ung-ts'un Southeast in March–April, June–July, and January.[113]

1955 Excavation by the First Cultural Relics Work Team of the Bureau of Culture, Honan Province, in August 18–October 23, at Hsiao-t'un South.[114]

1957 Excavation by Cultural Relics Work Team of the Bureau of Culture, Honan Province, in August–September at Hsüeh-chia-chuang 薛家莊 South.[115] Excavation by same team in early November at Hsüeh-chia-chuang North.[116]

108. *Ibid.*; Shih Chang-ju 石璋如, "Yin hsü tsui-chin . . . hou chi" 殷墟最近…後記.

109. See note 108 above.

110. Hu Hou-hsüan 胡厚宣, *Yin hsü fa-chüeh* 殷墟發掘, pp. 117–118.

111. "A Visit to An-yang."

112. Kuo Pao-chün 郭寶鈞, "Yi-chiu-wu-ling nien ch'un Yin hsü fa-chüeh pao-kao" 一九五〇年春殷墟發掘報告.

113. Ma Te-chih 馬得志, Chou Yung-chen 周永珍, Chang Yün-p'eng 張雲鵬, "Yi-chiu-wu-san nien An-yang Ta-ssu-k'ung ts'un fa-chüeh pao-kao" 一九五三年安陽大司空村發掘報告.

114. *KKHP*, "1955 nien ch'iu An-yang Hsiao-t'un Yin hsü ti fa-chüeh" 1955年秋安陽小屯殷墟的發掘.

115. Chao Hsia-kuang 趙霞光, "An-yang shih hsi chiao ti Yin tai wen-hua yi-chih" 安陽市西郊的殷代文化遺址; Chou Tao 周到 and Liu Tung-ya 劉東亞, "Yi-chiu-wu-ch'i nien ch'iu An-yang Kao-lou-chuang Yin tai yi-chih fa-chüeh" 一九五七年秋安陽高樓莊殷代遺址發掘.

116. *KK*, "Ho-nan An-yang Hsüeh-chia-chuang Yin tai yi-chih mu-tsang ho T'ang mu fa-chüeh chien pao" 河南安陽薛家莊殷代遺址墓葬和唐墓發掘簡報.

1958 Excavation by above team in February and March at Ta-ssu-k'ung-ts'un South.[117]
Beginning that year, continual excavations in An-yang by the Institute of Archaeology (IA). Localities excavated in 1958–59 included Hsiao-t'un West, Miao-p'u 苗圃 North, Chang-chia-fen 張家墳, Pai-chia-fen 白家墳, Mei-yüan-chuang 梅園莊, Hsiao-min-t'un 孝民屯, Pei-hsin-chuang 北辛莊, Fan-chia-chuang 范家莊, Hou-kang, Ta-ssu-k'ung-ts'un, and Wu-kuan North.[118]

1959 IA's work continued. A field station and museum were constructed just west of the village of Hsiao-t'un.[119]

1962 IA's excavations in autumn at Ta-ssu-k'ung-ts'un Southeast.[120]
IA's investigations of Huan River sites outside the immediate perimeter of Yin hsü.

1963 Continued investigations of Huan River sites outside Yin Hsü.[121]

1969 IA excavated in spring at Wu-kuan-ts'un North (Hsi-pei-kang).[122]

1971 IA and the Culture and Education Bureau of An-yang City excavated in Hou-kang.[123]
IA excavated on December 8 at an oracle bone locality at Hsiao-t'un West. This excavation continued intermittently until May 1973.[124]

117. *KK*, "Yi-chiu-wu-pa nien ch'un Ho-nan An-yang shih Ta-ssu-k'ung ts'un Yin tai mu-tsang fa-chüeh chien pao" 一九五八年春河南安陽市大司空村殷代墓葬發掘簡報.

118. *KK*, "1958–1959 nien Yin hsü fa-chüeh chien pao" 1958-1959年殷墟發掘簡報; Kuo Mo-jo 郭沫若, "An-yang yüan k'eng mu chung ting ming k'ao-shih" 安陽圓坑墓中鼎銘考釋; Chao P'ei-hsin 趙佩馨, "An-yang Hou-kang yüan-hsing k'eng hsing-chih ti t'ao-lun" 安陽後岡圓形坑性質的討論.

119. *KK*, "1958–1959 nien Yin hsü fa-chüeh chien pao" 1958-1959年殷墟發掘簡報.

120. *KK*, "1962 nien An-yang Ta-ssu-k'ung ts'un fa-chüeh chien pao" 1962年安陽大司空村發掘簡報.

121. *KK*, "An-yang Huan ho liu-yü chi ko yi-chih ti shih chüeh" 安陽洹河流域幾個遺址的試掘.

122. *KK*, "An-yang Yin hsü nu-li chi-ssu k'eng ti fa-chüeh" 安陽殷墟奴隸祭祀坑的發掘.

123. *KK*, "1971 nien An-yang Hou-kang fa-chüeh chien pao" 1971年安陽後岡發掘簡報.

124. Kuo Mo-jo 郭沫若, "An-yang hsin ch'u-t'u chih niu chia-ku chi ch'i k'o tz'u" 安陽新出土之牛胛骨及其刻辭.

1972 IA excavated in January 28–March 30 at Hou-kang.[125] IA excavated in March–April at Hsiao-min-t'un South.[126]

1973 IA excavated at Hsiao-t'un South in March–August 10 and October 4–December 4.[127]

1975 IA excavated in winter at Hsiao-t'un North.[128]

1976 IA excavated in April 16–June 30 at Wu-kuan-ts'un North.[129]
IA excavated in July in Hsiao-t'un North.[130]

It has now been fifty years since Tung's initial digging at An-yang, and the An-yang work is continuing. The archaeological data from the sites there, as well as the textual information provided by the oracle bone records that have been found in An-yang almost exclusively,[131] constitute the bulk of our basic sources on Shang civilization and are the principal basis of the present volume.

Outside An-yang, archaeology has disclosed a large number of sites with a civilization similar or evidently related to that at An-yang, but only at Cheng-chou 鄭州 has there been extensive archaeological work with detailed stratigraphic information. To summarize work that has been done, I give the following list of the Shang archaeological work at Cheng-chou and elsewhere.

SHANG ARCHAEOLOGY AT CHENG-CHOU

The first Shang remains in the Cheng-chou area were found in 1950 on the Erh-li-kang 二里岡 hill, southeast of the city, by a school

125. *KK*, "1972 nien ch'un An-yang Hou-kang fa-chüeh chien pao" 1972年春安陽後岡發掘簡報.

126. *KK*, "An-yang hsin fa-hsien ti Yin tai ch'e-ma k'eng" 安陽新發現的殷代車馬坑.

127. *KK*, "1973 nien An-yang Hsiao-t'un nan-ti fa-chüeh chien pao" 1973年安陽小屯南地發掘簡報.

128. *KK*, "1975 nien An-yang Yin hsü ti hsin fa-hsien" 1975年安陽殷墟的新發現.

129. *KK*, "An-yang Yin hsü nu-li chi-ssu k'eng ti fa-chüeh" 安陽殷墟奴隸祭祀坑的發掘; Yang Hsi-chang 楊錫璋 and Yang Pao-ch'eng 楊寶成, "Ts'ung Shang tai chi-ssu k'eng k'an Shang tai nu-li she-hui ti jen sheng" 從商代祭祀坑看商代奴隸社會的人牲; *KK*, "An-yang Yin tai chi-ssu k'eng jen ku ti hsing-pieh nien-ling chien-ting" 安陽殷代祭祀坑人骨的性別年齡鑒定.

130. *KKHP*, "An-yang Yin-hsü wu-hao mu ti fa-chüeh" 安陽殷墟五號墓的發掘; *KK*, "Yin hsü k'ao-ku fa-chüeh ti yu yi chung-yao shou-hu—Hsiao-t'un fa-hsien yi-tso pao-ts'un wan-cheng ti Yin tai wang-shih mu-tsang" 殷墟考古發掘的又一重要收穫—小屯發現一座保存完整的殷代王室墓葬.

131. For oracle bone records found outside An-yang, see Ch'en Meng-chia, *Yin hsü p'u-tz'u tsung-shu* 殷墟卜辭綜述, p. 27, and Li Hsüeh-ch'in 李學勤, "T'an An-yang Hsiao-t'un yi-wai ch'u-t'u ti yu tzu chia-ku" 談安陽小屯以外出土的有字甲骨.

teacher.[132] Erh-li-kang was then investigated by staff members of the Honan Provincial Commission for the Preservation of Cultural Relics[133] and of the Institute of Archaeology, Academia Sinica, in 1951.[134] In 1952 and 1953 the site was the location for a Short Term Archaeological Training Institute field program sponsored jointly by the Ministry of Culture, Peking University, and the Institute of Archaeology.[135] These investigations revealed that Erh-li-kang, together with a few other localities in the Cheng-chou area, was the site of a Shang settlement of considerable magnitude and, further, that the Shang remains there included those left from a cultural phase seemingly earlier than the remains at Yin hsü in An-yang.[136] Intensive investigations then began to be undertaken, in 1953, by staff members of the Cultural Relics Work Team of Cheng-chou City (later the Cultural Bureau of the city, the City Museum, and Honan Provincial Museum). The following is a listing of all known excavations and the published accounts of them:

1953 Beginning of continual investigations, in conjunction with the urban constructive programs, by the city of Cheng-chou. The initial locus was at Erh-li-kang, site of the 1952 excavations.[137]

1954 Four major sites were excavated in this year: Jen-min 人民 (People's) Park,[138] Pai-chia-chuang 白家莊,[139] Tzu-ching-shan 紫荆山 North,[140] and Nan-kuan-wai 南關外.[141]

1955 The Pai-chia-chuang excavation begun the previous year

132. *KKHCK, Cheng-chou Erh-li-kang* 鄭州二里岡, p. 1.

133. Chao Ch'üan-ku 趙全嘏, "Ho-nan chi ko hsin-shih-ch'i shih-tai yi-chih" 河南幾個新石器時代遺址.

134. Hsia Nai 夏鼐, "Ho-nan Ch'eng-kao Kuang-wu ch'ü k'ao-ku chi lüeh" 河南成皐廣武區考古紀略.

135. An Chih-min 安志敏, "Yi-chiu-wu-erh nien ch'iu chi Cheng-chou Erh-li-kang fa-chüeh chi" 一九五二年秋季鄭州二里岡發掘記.

136. *WW*, "Cheng-chou shih Yin Shang yi-chih ti-ts'eng kuan-hsi chieh-shao" 鄭州市殷商遺址地層關係介紹.

137. *WW*, "Yi nien lai Cheng-chou shih ti wen-wu tiao-ch'a fa-chüeh kung-tso 一年來鄭州市的文物調查發掘工作; *KKHCK, Cheng-chou Erh-li-kang* 鄭州二里岡.

138. An Chih-min 安志敏, "Cheng-chou shih Jen-min kung-yüan fu-chin ti Yin tai yi-ts'un" 鄭州市人民公園附近的殷代遺存; *WW*, "Cheng-chou shih Jen-min kung-yüan ti erh-shih-wu hao Shang tai mu-tsang ch'ing-li chien pao" 鄭州市人民公園第二十五號商代墓葬清理簡報.

139. *WW*, "Cheng-chou shih Pai-chia-chuang Shang tai mu-tsang fa-chüeh chien pao" 鄭州市白家莊商代墓葬發掘簡報; *WW*, "Cheng-chou Pai-chia-chuang yi-chih fa-chüeh chien pao" 鄭州白家莊遺址發掘簡報.

140. *KKHP*, "Cheng-chou Shang tai yi-chih ti fa-chüeh" 鄭州商代遺址的發掘, 56.

141. *Ibid.*

continued. Additional excavations took place at Ming-kung-lu 銘功路 West,[142] Erh-li-kang,[143] and Nan-kuan-wai.[144]

1956 Excavations took place this year on a broad front, at the following sites: Ming-kung-lu West,[145] Tzu-ching-shan North,[146] Lo-ta-miao 洛達廟,[147] Nan-kuan-wai,[148] and Ko-la-wang 旭奋王.[149] Also beginning this year was an extensive effort to trace and map the Shang town wall, an undertaking that persisted until 1973.[150]

1957 After 1956, insofar as published accounts are concerned, archaeological work at the Shang sites in Cheng-chou became less intensive though still persistent. The only accounts have dealt with excavations at Shang-chieh 上街 in 1957–59,[151] Ming-kung-lu West in 1965,[152] a palace foundation site in 1973 and 1974,[153] and Chang-chai-nan-chieh 張寨南街 in 1974.[154]

142. *WW*, "Cheng-chou fa-hsien ti Shang tai chih t'ao yi-chi" 鄭州發現的商代製陶遺跡.

143. *WW*, "Cheng-chou ti wu wen-wu ch'ü ti yi hsiao ch'ü fa-chüeh chien pao" 鄭州第五文物區第一小區發掘簡報.

144. *KKHP*, "Cheng-chou Nan-kuan-wai Shang tai yi-chih ti fa-chüeh 鄭州南關外商代遺址的發掘."

145. Ma Ch'üan 馬全, "Cheng-chou shih Ming-kung-lu hsi ts'e ti Shang tai yi-ts'un" 鄭州市銘功路西側的商代遺存.

146. Liao Yung-min 廖永民, "Cheng-chou shih fa-hsien ti yi ch'u Shang tai chü-chu yü chu-tsao t'ung-ch'i yi-chih chien chieh" 鄭州市發現的一處商代居住與鑄製造銅器遺址簡介.

147. *WW*, "Cheng-chou Lo-ta-miao Shang tai yi-chih shih chüeh chien pao" 鄭州洛達廟商代遺址試掘簡報.

148. *KK*, "Cheng-chou Nan-kuan-wai Shang tai yi-chih fa-chüeh chien pao" 鄭州南關外商代遺址發掘簡報.

149. *KKHP*, "Cheng-chou Ko-la-wang ts'un yi-chih fa-chüeh pao-kao" 鄭州旭奋王村遺址發掘報告.

150. *WW*, "Cheng-chou Shang tai ch'eng chih shih chüeh chien pao" 鄭州商代城址試掘簡報.

151. *KK*, "Cheng-chou Shang-chieh Shang tai yi-chih ti fa-chüeh" 鄭州上街商代遺址的發掘; *KK*, "Ho-nan Cheng-chou Shang-chieh Shang tai yi-chih fa-chüeh pao-kao" 河南鄭州上街商代遺址發掘報告.

152. *KK*, "Cheng-chou shih Ming-kung-lu hsi ts'e ti liang tso Shang tai mu" 鄭州市銘功路西側的兩座商代墓.

153. *WW*, "Cheng-chou Shang ch'eng yi-chih nei fa-hsien Shang tai hang-t'u t'ai chi ho nu-lu t'ou ku" 鄭州商城遺址內發現商代夯土台基和奴隸頭骨.

154. *WW*, "Cheng-chou hsin ch'u-t'u ti Shang tai ch'ien ch'i ta t'ung ting" 鄭州新出土的商代前期大銅鼎.

The archaeological work at Cheng-chou, like that at An-yang, is still continuing, and the work there has been much less intensive, in part because of the coincidence of the center of the Shang town with the present city site. But from what has been learned so far,[155] the Shang archaeology there is of extreme importance in providing data on a Shang settlement which is in all likelihood earlier than An-yang and is, therefore, an ancestral form of the latter capital.

SHANG ARCHAEOLOGY ELSEWHERE

In the last thirty years archaeological sites with remains similar to those of An-yang and/or Cheng-chou and, thus, designated as of a Shang date have been brought to light throughout China, from Liaoning in the north to south of the Yangtze River in the south. None of these sites have been excavated to the degree seen at An-yang and Cheng-chou, but quite likely other sites will be shown by future investigations to be as important or in some ways even more so. A brief summary of available information is given below in each of the major areas of distribution.

Northwest Honan and Southern Shansi. This is the area of distribution of the Erh-li-t'ou 二里頭 type of sites, usually referred to as Early Shang in the archaeological literature.[156] In view of more recent research on the Erh-li-t'ou type of culture and on the origin question of the Shang civilization,[157] aspects that will be discussed in detail later in this volume, we will remove this culture from the domain of the Shang. Deprived of the Erh-li-t'ou sites, the area has relatively few Shang sites

155. The following syntheses of the Cheng-chou site may be consulted: *WW*, "Cheng-chou shih Yin Shang yi-chih ti-ts'eng kuan-hsi chieh-shao" 鄭州市殷商遺址地層關係介紹; *KK*, "Cheng-chou shih ku yi-chih mu-tsang ti chung-yao fa-hsien" 鄭州市古遺址墓葬的重要發現; Tsou Heng 鄒衡, "Shih lun Cheng-chou hsin fa-hsien ti Yin Shang wen-hua yi-chih" 試論鄭州新發現的殷商文化遺址; *KKHP*, "Cheng-chou Shang tai yi-chih ti fa-chüeh" 鄭州商代遺址的發掘; An Chin-huai 安金槐 "Cheng-chou ti-ch'ü ti ku-tai yi-ts'un chieh-shao 鄭州地區的古代遺存介紹; An Chin-huai 安金槐, "Shih lun Cheng-chou Shang tai ch'eng chih—Ao tu" 試論鄭州商代城址—隞都; An Chih-min 安志敏, "Kuan-yü Cheng-chou 'Shang ch'eng' ti chi-ko wen-t'i" 關于鄭州'商城'的幾個問題; Liu Ch'i-yi 劉啓益, "'Ao tu' chih yi" '隞都'質疑; T'ang Lan 唐蘭, "Ts'ung Ho-nan Cheng-chou ch'u-t'u ti Shang tai ch'ien-ch'i ch'ing-t'ung-ch'i shuo ch'i" 從河南鄭州出土的商代前期青銅器說起; *WW*, "Cheng-chou Shang tai yi-chih" 鄭州商代遺址.

156. K. C. Chang, *The Archaeology of Ancient China*, pp. 258–259.

157. Chang Kwang-chih 張光直, "Yin Shang wen-ming ch'i-yüan yen-chiu shang ti yi-ko kuan-chien wen-t'i" 殷商文明起源研究上的一個關鍵問題; Chang Kwang-chih 張光直, "Ts'ung Hsia Shang Chou san-tai k'ao-ku lun san-tai kuan-hsi yü Chung-kuo ku-tai kuo-chia ti hsing-ch'eng" 從夏商周三代考古論三代關係與中國古代國家的形成.

(of the Cheng-chou or An-yang varieties) other than those in the Cheng-chou region, at the eastern margin of it. They include sites found in Ch'i-li-p'u 七里鋪 in Shan Hsien,[158] Lu-ssu 鹿寺 in Mien-ch'ih,[159] Chien-hsi 澗溪 in Meng Hsien,[160] Hsiao-nan-chang 小南張 in Wen Hsien,[161] a series of sites in the neighborhood of Lo-yang,[162] Shao-ch'ai 稍柴 in Kung Hsien,[163] and Mei-shan 煤山 in Lin-ju.[164]

Central Shansi and Shensi. Shang style bronzes are said to have been found in Shih-lou 石樓, in central-western Shansi in the Huang Ho valley before 1949. Assemblages of these finds, mostly chance discoveries, have now been reported all along the Yellow River valley as north as Pao-te 保德, and important finds are now available from several localities (Erh-lang-p'o 二郎坡,[165] T'ao-hua-chuang 桃花莊,[166] Hou-lan-chia-kou 後蘭家溝,[167] Yi-tieh 義牒,[168] and others[169]) in Shih-lou, Pao-te,[170] and also Sui-te 綏德 in Shensi, across the river from Pao-te.[171]

158. *KKHP*, "Ho-nan Shan Hsien Ch'i-li-p'u Shang tai yi-chih ti fa-chüeh" 河南陝縣七里鋪商代遺址的發掘.

159. *KK*, "Ho-nan Mien-ch'ih Lu-ssu Shang tai yi-chih shih chüeh chien pao" 河南澠池鹿寺商代遺址試掘簡報.

160. *KK*, "Ho-nan Meng Hsien Chien-hsi yi-chih fa-chüeh" 河南孟縣澗溪遺址發掘.

161. *WW*, "Wen Hsien ch'u-t'u ti Shang tai t'ung-ch'i" 溫縣出土的商代銅器.

162. Kuo Pao-chün 郭寶鈞 and Lin Shou-chin 林壽晉, "1952 nien ch'iu-chi Lo-yang tung chiao fa-chüeh pao-kao" 1952年秋季洛陽東郊發掘報告; *KKHP*, "Lo-yang Chien pin ku wen-hua yi-chih chi Han mu" 洛陽澗濱古文化遺址及漢墓; *KK*, "Yi-chiu-wu-ssu nien ch'iu-chi Lo-yang hsi chiao fa-chüeh chien pao" 一九五四年秋季洛陽西郊發掘簡報; *KK*, "1958 nien Lo-yang Tung-kan-kou yi-chih fa-chüeh chien pao" 1958年洛陽東乾溝遺址發掘簡報.

163. T'ung Chu-ch'en 佟柱臣, "Ts'ung Erh-li-t'ou lei-hsing wen-hua shih t'an Chung-kuo ti kuo-chia ch'i-yüan wen-t'i" 從二里頭類型文化試談中國的國家起源問題, 29.

164. *KK*, "Ho-nan Lin-ju Mei-shan yi-chih tiao-ch'a yü shih chüeh" 河南臨汝煤山遺址調查與試掘.

165. *WW*, "Shan-hsi Shih-lou hsien Erh-lang-p'o ch'u-t'u Shang Chou ch'ing-t'ung-ch'i" 山西石樓縣二郎坡出土商周青銅器.

166. Hsieh Ch'ing-shan 謝青山 and Yang Shao-shun 楊紹舜, "Shan-hsi Lü-liang hsien Shih-lou chen yu fa-hsien t'ung-ch'i" 山西呂梁縣石樓鎮又發現銅器.

167. Kuo Yung 郭勇, "Shih-lou Hou-lan-chia-kou fa-hsien Shang tai ch'ing-t'ung-ch'i chien pao" 石樓後蘭家溝發現商代青銅器簡報.

168. *KK*, "Shan-hsi Shih-lou Yi-tieh fa-hsien Shang tai t'ung-ch'i" 山西石樓義牒發現商代銅器; *WW*, "Shan-hsi Shih-lou Yi-tieh Hui-p'ing fa-hsien Shang tai ping-ch'i" 山西石樓義牒會坪發現商代兵器.

169. *WW*, "Shan-hsi Shih-lou hsin cheng-chi tao ti chi-chien Shang tai ch'ing-t'ung-ch'i" 山西石樓新徵集到的幾件商代青銅器.

170. Wu Chen-lu 吳振彔, "Pao-te hsien hsin fa-hsien ti Yin tai ch'ing-t'ung-ch'i" 保德縣新發現的殷代青銅器.

171. *WW*, "Shan-hsi Sui-te Yen-t'ou ts'un fa-hsien yi-p'i chiao-ts'ang Shang tai t'ung-ch'i" 陝西綏德墕頭村發現一批窖藏商代銅器.

Isolated finds of Shang-like remains have also been identified in the Fen Ho valley of Central Shansi, such as T'ai-yüan 太原 and Hsin Hsien 忻縣,[172] and in Ch'i-shan 岐山 in Central Shensi.[173]

Northern Honan and Southern Hopei. This is the plains area of the lower Yellow River with An-yang as its center, extending northward along the eastern side of the T'ai-hang Mountains. Known sites in this area include Lu-wang-fen 潞王墳 in Hsin-hsiang,[174] several sites in Hui Hsien,[175] Ch'ao-ko 朝歌 in T'ang-yin,[176] Chieh-tuan-ying 界段營 in Tz'u Hsien,[177] Chien-kou-ts'un 澗溝村 in Han-tan,[178] several sites in Hsing-t'ai,[179] T'ai-hsi-ts'un 台西村 in Kao-ch'eng,[180] Pei-chai-ts'un 北宅村 in Ling-shou,[181] Feng-chia-an 馮家岸 in Chü-yang,[182] and Liu-chia-ho

172. *WW*, "Shan-hsi sheng shih nien lai ti wen-wu k'ao-ku hsin shou-hu" 山西省十年來的文物考古新收穫, 2. Shen Chen-chung 沈振中, "Hsin hsien Lien-ssu-kou ch'u-t'u ti ch'ing-t'ung-ch'i"忻縣連寺溝出土的青銅器.

173. *WW*, "Shan-hsi sheng Ch'i-shan hsien fa-hsien Shang tai t'ung-ch'i," 陝西省岐山縣發現商代銅器.

174. *KKHP*, "Ho-nan Hsin-hsiang Lu-wang-fen Shang tai yi-chih fa-chüeh pao-kao" 河南新鄉潞王墳商代遺址發掘報告.

175. Kuo Pao-chün 郭寶鈞, Hsia Nai 夏鼐, et al., *Hui Hsien fa-chüeh pao-kao* 輝縣發掘報告; *KK*, "Ho-nan Wei-ho chih-hung kung-ch'eng chung ti k'ao-ku tiao-ch'a chien pao" 河南衛河滯洪工程中的考古調查簡報; *KK*, "Ho-nan Hui hsien Ch'u-ch'iu ch'u-t'u ti Shang tai t'ung-ch'i" 河南輝縣褚丘出土的商代銅器.

176. An Chin-huai 安金槐, "T'ang-yin Ch'ao-ko-chen fa-hsien Lung-shan ho Shang tai teng wen-hua yi-chih" 湯陰朝歌鎮發現龍山和商代等文化遺址.

177. *KK*, "Tz'u Hsien Chieh-tuan-ying fa-chüeh chien pao" 磁縣界段營發掘簡報.

178. *KK*, "1957 nien Han-tan fa-chüeh chien pao" 1957年邯鄲發掘簡報; *KK*, "Ho-pei Han-tan Chien-kou ts'un ku yi-chih fa-chüeh chien pao" 河北邯鄲澗溝村古遺址發掘簡報.

179. *KK*, "Ho-pei Hsing-t'ai Tung-hsien-hsien ts'un Shang tai yi-chih tiao-ch'a" 河北邢台東先賢村商代遺址調查; *KKHP*, "Hsing-t'ai Ts'ao-yen-chuang yi-chih fa-chüeh pao-kao" 邢台曹演莊遺址發掘報告; *WW*, "Hsing-t'ai shih fa-hsien Shang tai yi-chih" 邢台市發現商代遺址; *WW*, "Hsing-t'ai Shang tai yi-chih chung ti t'ao yao" 邢台商代遺址中的陶窰; T'ang Yün-ming 唐雲明, "Hsing-t'ai Nan-ta-kuo ts'un Shang tai yi-chih t'an-chüeh chien pao" 邢台南大郭村商代遺址探掘簡報; *WW*, "Hsing-t'ai Chia ts'un Shang tai yi-chih shih chüeh chien pao" 邢台賈村商代遺址試掘簡報; *WW*, "Hsing-t'ai Yin-kuo-ts'un Shang tai yi-chih chi Chan-kuo mu-tsang shih chüeh chien pao" 邢台尹郭村商代遺址及戰國墓葬試掘簡報.

180. *KK*, "Ho-pei Kao-ch'eng hsien Shang tai yi-chih ho mu-tsang ti tiao-ch'a" 河北藁城縣商代遺址和墓葬的調查; *KK*, "Ho-pei Kao-ch'eng T'ai-hsi ts'un ti Shang tai yi-chih" 河北藁城台西村的商代遺址; *WW*, "Ho-pei Kao-ch'eng hsien T'ai-hsi ts'un Shang tai yi-chih 1973 nien ti chung-yao fa-hsien" 河北藁城縣台西村商代遺址1973年的重要發現.

181. *KK*, "Ho-pei Ling-shou hsien Pei-chai ts'un Shang tai yi-chih tiao-ch'a" 河北靈壽縣北宅村商代遺址調查.

182. An Chih-min 安志敏, "Ho-pei Ch'ü-yang tiao-ch'a chi" 河北曲陽調查記.

劉家河 in Peking.[183] An assemblage of bronze vessels found in Liaoning, much farther to the north, has also been described as Shang.[184]

Shantung. According to survey data up to 1972, Shang remains are said to have been reported from the entire province except for the district of Te-chou in northernmost Shantung.[185] The best known of the Shang sites, however, are two that were discovered many years ago and where new investigations have revealed important data. These are Ta-hsin-chuang 大辛莊, in the eastern suburb of Chi-nan,[186] and Su-fu-t'un 蘇埠屯, northeast of Yi-tu.[187]

Huai Ho Plain in Honan, N. Kiangsu, and Anhwei. The Huai Ho plain in eastern Honan, southwestern Shantung, and northern Kiangsu and Anhwei is potentially a crucial area for Shang archaeology because most historians (as shown earlier) have placed Po—T'ang's capital—in the environs of Shang-ch'iu. But despite the fact that the Huai Ho area was an early target of Shang archaeologists,[188] Shang sites here are not yet very many. Shang remains have been reported at Fu-kou 扶溝 in Yen-ling, central Honan;[189] several sites in the Hsü-chou area of northern Kiangsu, especially Kao-huang-miao 高皇廟[190] and Ch'iu-wan

183. *WW*, "Pei-ching shih P'ing-ku hsien fa-hsien Shang tai mu-tsang" 北京市平谷縣發現商代墓葬.

184. *KK*, "Liao-ning K'o-tso hsien Pei-tung-ts'un fa-hsien Yin tai ch'ing-t'ung-ch'i" 遼寧喀左縣北洞村發現殷代青銅器; *KK*, "Liao-ning K'o-tso hsien Pei-tung ts'un ch'u-t'u ti Yin Chou ch'ing-t'ung-ch'i" 遼寧喀左縣北洞村出土的殷周青銅器; Yen Wan 晏琬, "Pei-ching Liao-ning ch'u-t'u t'ung-ch'i yü Chou ch'u ti Yen" 北京遼寧出土銅器與周初的燕.

185. Ch'i Wen-t'ao 齊文濤, "Kai shu chin-nien lai Shan-tung ch'u-t'u ti Shang Chou ch'ing-t'ung-ch'i" 概述近年來山東出土的商周青銅器; see also *KK*, "Shan-tung P'ing-yin hsien Chu-chia-ch'iao Yin tai yi-chih" 山東平陰縣朱家橋殷代遺址.

186. F. S. Drake, "Shang Dynasty Find at Ta-hsin-chuang, Shantung"; F. S. Drake, "Ta-hsin-chuang Again"; *WW*, "Chi-nan Ta-hsin-chuang Shang tai yi-chih k'an-ch'a chi yao" 濟南大辛莊商代遺址勘察紀要; Ch'i Wen-t'ao 齊文濤, "Kai shu chin-nien lai Shan-tung ch'u-t'u ti Shang Chou ch'ing-t'ung-ch'i" 概述近年來山東出土的商周青銅器; *KK*, "Chi-nan Ta-hsin-chuang yi-chih shih chüeh chien pao" 濟南大辛莊遺址試掘簡報; Ts'ai Feng-shu 蔡鳳書, "Chi-nan Ta-hsin-chuang Shang tai yi-chih ti tiao-ch'a" 濟南大辛莊商代遺址的調查.

187. Ch'i Yen-p'ei 祁延霈, "Shan-tung Yi-tu Su-fu-t'un ch'u-t'u t'ung-ch'i tiao-ch'a chi" 山東益都蘇埠屯出土銅器調查記; *WW*, "Shan-tung Yi-tu Su-fu-t'un ti-yi-hao nu-li hsün-tsang mu" 山東益都蘇埠屯第一號奴隸殉葬墓.

188. Li Ching-tan 李景聃, "Yü tung Shang-ch'iu Yung-ch'eng tiao-ch'a chi Tsao-lü-t'ai Hei-ku-tui Ts'ao-ch'iao san ch'u hsiao fa-chüeh" 豫東商邱永城調查及造律台黑孤堆曹橋三處小發掘.

189. *KK*, "Ho-nan Yen-ling Fu-kou Shang-shui chi ch'u ku wen-hua yi-chih ti tiao-ch'a" 河南鄢陵扶溝商水幾處古文化遺址的調查.

190. *KKHP*, "Hsü-chou Kao-huang-miao yi-chih ch'ing-li pao-kao" 徐州高皇

丘灣;[191] sites in Fu-nan,[192] Shou Hsien,[193] and Chia-shan[194] in northern Anhwei, and even in Fei-hsi in central Anhwei at the Yangtze drainage.[195]

The Hanshui and Middle Yangtze Valleys. This area represents the Shang civilization's southern extent, brought to light archaeologically most recently. To begin, in southwestern Honan in the upper Hanshui Shang sites are known at Shih-li-miao 十里廟 in Nan-yang[196] and at Hsia-wang-kang 下王崗 in Hsi-ch'uan.[197] Further down the Hanshui, a series of important Shang sites have been found in the district of Huang-p'i.[198] South of the Yangtzu River, Shang remains occurred in Ch'ung-yang in Hupei,[199] Shih-men,[200] Li-ling,[201] Ning-hsiang, and

---

廟遺址清理報告; *KK*, "1959 nien Hsü-chou ti-ch'ü k'ao-ku tiao-ch'a" 1959年徐州地區考古調查.

191. *KK*, "Chiang-su T'ung-shan Ch'iu-wan ku yi-chih ti fa-chüeh" 江蘇銅山丘灣古遺址的發掘; Yü Wei-ch'ao 俞偉超, "T'ung-shan Ch'iu-wan Shang tai she ssu yi-chi ti t'ui-ting" 銅山丘灣商代社祀遺迹的推定; Wang Yü-hsin 王宇信 and Ch'en Shao-ti 陳紹棣, "Kuan-yü Chiang-su T'ung-shan Ch'iu-wan Shang tai chi-ssu yi-chih" 關于江蘇銅山丘灣商代祭祀遺址.

192. Ko Chieh-p'ing 葛介屏, "An-hui Fu-nan fa-hsien Yin Shang shih-tai ti ch'ing-t'ung-ch'i" 安徽阜南發現殷商時代的青銅器; Shih Chih-lien 石志廉, "T'an-t'an lung hu tsun ti chi-ko wen-t'i" 談談龍虎尊的幾個問題.

193. Wang Hsiang 王湘, "An-hui Shou hsien shih-ch'ien yi-chih tiao-ch'a pao-kao" 安徽壽縣史前遺址調查報告; Li Chi 李濟, "Yin hsü yu jen shih-ch'i t'u-shuo" 殷虛有刄石器圖說, 612.

194. *WW*, "An-hui Chia-shan hsien Po-kang-yin-ho ch'u-t'u ti ssu-chien Shang tai t'ung-ch'i" 安徽嘉山縣泊崗引河出土的四件商代銅器.

195. The Committee of the Exhibition of the Archaeological Finds of the People's Republic of China, *The Exhibition of Archaeological Finds in the People's Republic of China*, p. 18.

196. *KK*, "Ho-nan Nan-yang shih Shih-li-miao fa-hsien Shang tai yi-chih" 河南南陽市十里廟發現商代遺址.

197. *WW*, "Ho-nan Hsi-ch'uan Hsia-wang-kang yi-chih ti shih chüeh" 河南淅川下王崗遺址的試掘.

198. *WW*, "Yi-chiu-liu-san nien Hu-pei Huang-p'i P'an-lung-ch'eng Shang tai yi-chih ti fa-chüeh" 一九六三年湖北黄陂盤龍城商代遺址的發掘; *WW*, "P'an-lung-ch'eng yi-chiu-ch'i-ssu nien tu t'ien-yeh k'ao-ku chi yao" 盤龍城一九七四年度田野考古紀要; *WW*, "P'an-lung-ch'eng Shang tai Erh-li-kang ch'i ti ch'ing-t'ung-ch'i" 盤龍城商代二里岡期的青銅器; Kuo Ping-lien 郭冰廉, "Hu-pei Huang-p'i Yang-chia-wan ti ku yi-chih tiao-ch'a" 湖北黄陂楊家灣的古遺址調查; *KK*, "Hu-pei Huang-p'i K'uang-shan shui-k'u kung-ti fa-hsien liao ch'ing-t'ung-ch'i" 湖北黄陂礦山水庫工地發現了青銅器; Kuo Te-wei 郭德維 and Ch'en Hsien-yi 陳賢一, "Hu-pei Huang-p'i P'an-lung-ch'eng Shang tai yi-chih ho mu-tsang" 湖北黄陂盤龍城商代遺址和墓葬.

199. *WW*, "Hu-pei Ch'ung-yang ch'u-t'u yi-chien t'ung ku" 湖北崇陽出土一件銅鼓.

200. Chou Shih-jung 周世榮, "Hu-nan Shih-men hsien Tsao-shih fa-hsien Shang Yin yi-chih" 湖南石門縣皂市發現商殷遺址.

201. Hsiung Ch'uan-hsin 熊傳新, "Hu-nan Li-ling fa-hsien Shang tai t'ung hsiang tsun" 湖南醴陵發現商代銅象尊.

Ch'ang-ning[202] in Hunan, and in Ch'ing-Chiang[203] and Tu-ch'ang[204] in Kiangsi.

Most of the Shang sites and remains enumerated above have been found only recently, and the data are still meager. But the geographical expanse of a civilization so widely indicated by these finds has already had very vast implications for Shang history. Some of these implications will be explored later in the volume.

5. *THEORETICAL MODELS*

In Shang historiography in China two basic attitudes toward explicit theory have prevailed: Dataism and Marxism.

"Dataism" is an attempted translation of the Chinese word, *Shih-liao-hsüeh* 史料學, the study of historical data. The equation of *Shih-liao-hsüeh* with *shih-hsüeh* 史學, historiography, may be said to be the fundamental philosophy of the Institute of History and Philology, Academia Sinica, from its founding in 1928 in Canton up to its present life on Taiwan. Because of the important role the Institute has played in the An-yang excavations, Chinese Shang historiography, either that generated from within the Institute or that practiced outside it but deeply affected by it, has to a large extent focused upon the procurement of new historical sources and their piecemeal study.

A dataistic proclamation appears in the "Introductory Remarks" in the first issue of the *Bulletin of the Institute of History and Philology, Academia Sinica*, written by Fu Ssu-nien, the Institute's director from 1928 until his death in 1950:

> Modern historiography is merely the study of historical data, using all the tools provided us by natural sciences to put into order all the available historical data. . . .
>
> The reason that in China philology and historiography had a glorious past was precisely because they were able to expand and develop the data they used. And the reason that

202. Kao Chih-hsi 高至喜, "Hu-nan Ning-hsiang Huang-ts'ai fa-hsien Shang tai t'ung-ch'i ho yi-chih" 湖南寧鄉黃材發現商代銅器和遺址; Kao Chih-hsi 高至喜, "Shang tai jen mien fang ting" 商代人面方鼎; *WW*, "Chieh-shao chi chien ts'ung fei-t'ung chung chien hsüan ch'u-lai ti chung-yao wen-wu" 介紹幾件從廢銅中揀選出來的重要文物.

203. *WW*, "Chiang-hsi Ch'ing-chiang Wu-ch'eng Shang tai yi-chih fa-chüeh pao-kao" 江西清江吳城商代遺址發掘報告.

204. T'ang Ch'ang-p'u 唐昌朴, "Chiang-hsi Tu-ch'ang ch'u-t'u Shang tai t'ung-ch'i" 江西都昌出土商代銅器.

> they came to a decline later on was exactly because their subject matter became stagnant, their data did not much expand, and their tools were not renewed. Nevertheless, within the area of China there is a good deal of philological and historical data, data that Europeans sought with difficulty but we sat on our hands to see destroyed and lost. We are mighty dissatisfied with this state of affairs, mighty resentful that not only material resources but also scholarly resources must be moved away or even stolen away by the Europeans. We very much would like to borrow a few tools that are not old to deal with some newly procured data, and this is the reason for the establishment of the Institute of History and Philology. . . .
>
> What we pay the most attention to is the acquisition of new data. The first step in our plans is to go up along the Peking–Hankow Railroad for An-yang and Yi-chou. In An-yang the plundered materials from Yin hsü were not thoroughly excavated, and Yi-chou and Han-tan were the old capitals of Yen and Chao, and this whole area was, besides, the old territory of Wei and Pei. . . . The second step is to go to Lo-yang and its environs. In the future we will move westward step by step, toward Central Asia . . . In short, we are not book readers. We go all the way to Heaven above and to the Yellow Spring below, using our hands and feet, to look for things![205]

Thus, the An-yang excavations were undertaken under the auspices of the Institute of History and Philology with the explicit objectives of data acquisition: When new data are procured, new problems arise and are solved, and Shang history is enriched and expanded. The scholars who were involved in the An-yang work were involved with bodies of data: "Tung [Tso-pin] was to study the written records while [Li Chi] was to take care of all other artifacts,"[206] and Woo Ting-liang, the physical anthropologist, was to be given the human remains.[207] The planned official report of the An-yang excavations was to be organized by data categories:[208]

1. An Account of the Excavations
2. Architectural Sites

205. Fu Ssu-nien, "Li-shih Yü-yen Yen-chiu So kung-tso chih chih-ch'ü" 歷史語言研究所工作之旨趣

206. Li Chi, *Anyang*, p. 59.

207. *Ibid.*, p. 122.

208. Li Chi 李濟, "Pien hou yü" 編後語; see also his "An-yang fa-chüeh yü Chung-kuo ku shih wen-t'i" 安陽發掘與中國古史問題.

3. Scapulimancy, Plastromancy, and Oracle Bone Inscriptions
4. Bronze Metallurgy and Bronze and Other Metal Objects
5. Pottery
6. Stone Objects, Bone Objects, Shell Objects, etc.
7. Animal Bones
8. Archaeological Sites Nearby
9. Burials
10. Religion, Art, and Social Organization

There is no question, on the positive side, that our knowledge concerning Shang history *has* been vastly enriched and expanded by the new data that have been procured from An-yang. The question is, rather, do facts really speak for themselves? The data categories represent a system of categorization of the ancient civilization. Is this the system that best reveals the internal order of the civilization in question? In other words, dataism itself is a theory. Is it the best theory for ancient historiography?

No, say the Marxists, the only group of scholars who have studied the Shang society with explicit theory. To Kuo Mo-jo 郭沫若, the most effective and one of the earliest advocates of Marxist interpretation of Chinese history, dataistic scholars such as Li Chi and Tung Tso-pin were "beggars holding a golden rice-bowl."[209] As early as 1930, just as the Institute of History and Philology scholars had begun to procure new data, Kuo Mo-jo, in a ground-breaking book, *Chung-kuo ku-tai she-hui yen-chiu* (*Studies of Ancient Chinese Society*),[210] for the first time attempted "to study and interpret history according to a scientific historical viewpoint," a viewpoint represented by Frederick Engels's *Der Ursprung der Familie, des Privateigentums und des Staats* (1884). In this book by Kuo, after briefly characterizing the evolutionary stages of human society according to Marx and Engels—primitive society, slave society, feudal society, and capitalist society—Kuo proceeded to analyze the available historical data, including oracle bone inscriptions and bronzes inscriptions, and reached the conclusion that Shang society represented a terminal stage of the primitive society, wherein clan institutions survived, but a class system was already beginning. Ironically, as new data began to accumulate from the field, Kuo was forced to modify his conclusions concerning the evolutionary status of Shang society. As he stated in 1954, "the mastery of correct, scientific historical viewpoint is very important; this is the primary issue. But, [even] given

209. Kuo Mo-jo 郭沫若, *Nu-li-chih shih-tai* 奴隸制時代. (Quotation was written in 1950).

210. 1964 edition.

the correct historical viewpoint, if there are no adequate correct data, or if the data are incorrectly dated, there cannot be correct conclusions either".[211] On the basis of more recent data, Kuo has modified his view and now regards the Shang society as being squarely within the slave society stage of social evolution.[212] This classification of the Shang society is today the established view of Chinese Marxist historians.[213]

Later on we will have much to say about the status of the Shang society in evolutionary perspective. Here we are merely interested in Marxist evolutionary theory—as interpreted by Chinese Marxist historians—as an explicit theoretical model for the articulation of Shang historical data: cultural and social elements are aligned in ordered structures in each of the evolutionary stages; these structures are qualitatively transformed from one stage to another; the cultural and social elements are accordingly realigned. Once we have correctly classified a society—e.g., the Shang—as to its evolutionary status, we are in a position to do two things: to place our data in a structurally meaningful manner, as to order and hierarchy, to help us understand the system they thus constitute, and to fill in gaps where available data are absent. This interpretive methodology is a powerful tool of not only Marxist historians but also the new evolutionists who are on the rise among contemporary archaeologists studying the beginning of civilizations everywhere. The evolutionary stages of Elman Service,[214] for example—band, tribe, chiefdom, and state—serve precisely the same purpose for the articulation of our data and have the added advantage of characterizing the primitive society at three separate levels instead of only one.

While both data and broad evolutionary theories are necessary for any effective and valid understanding of the Shang civilization—or of any civilization—we also need middle-level theoretical models to help bring data and theory together. Dataism, as has just been stated, is not devoid of theory; only its theory is undisciplined, implicit, and untestable. On the other hand, before we state that our data can be interpreted by universal theory, we had better make sure that the theory, hitherto based upon data from other regions of the world, is indeed universal, and to do this we must demonstrate its applicability to our data by putting the data together, independent of the theory, on internal evidence.

211. *Chung-kuo ku-tai she-hui yen-chiu* 中國古代社會研究, 1954 ed., preface.

212. *Nu-li-chih shih-tai* 奴隸制時代, 1952, 1954, 1972 eds.

213. Shih Hsing 史星, *Nu-li she-hui* 奴隸社會; Chang Ching-hsien 張景賢, *Chung-kuo nu-li she-hui* 中國奴隸社會.

214. Elman Service, *Primitive Social Organization: An Evolutionary Perspective.*

What is "internal evidence"? By this I do not refer to the intrinsic qualities of the data themselves: the dataists have already seen to the value of them. Rather I refer to the interrelationships of empirical data; it is the interrelationships that must constitute the building plans of any structure. In a structure any element articulates with other elements in all directions, some horizontal, some diagonal, some stratigraphical, and some all or most of the above in a truly complex manner. They then organize into a complex, dynamic whole. After the civilization's passing, these elements have all fallen apart and some of them are lost. Our job is to put them back together again. For this we need good, solid data, and the more the better. We also need correct overall theoretical control, confident of the general plans of all human society. But we also need concrete, specific, and reliable devices to restore the complex interrelationships of our data at specific levels. Some of these devices are self-evident: the archaeological context that defines the interrelationships spatially, and the textual description. But others are not as obvious: in other words, the middle-level theoretical models.

Middle-level theoretical models are laws that govern the interaction among discrete elements of culture—discrete in the sense of being capable of standing alone in the historical record. They are laws because cultural elements covary and discrete elements must be placed together in accordance with definite and specifiable rules. Historians (and archaeologists) employ these rules in reconstructing past societies and restoring their missing elements.

Where do we get the rules? I believe there is only one way we can work out useful rules that help restore the whole system—or at least the essential structure of it—from fragmentary material, and that is to employ theoretical models, i.e., blueprints of working systems or subsystems of culture and society derived from studies of contemporary situations or from historical periods where detailed documentation is available. Let me at once make one thing clear. This is not to try to fit or even tailor our facts to any preconceived theories. Our theories are blueprints of known situations, and if our pieces cannot fit into any of them, it simply means either that this is a new situation completely, or that we do not yet have enough pieces. There can never be any "cutting the foot to fit the shoe," as the Chinese saying goes. If we have a few pieces from an engine, we have to have the blueprints of all the engines there have been before we can try to match them with one that fits. Conceivably the engine from which these pieces came could be one whose mechanisms are lost to man's knowledge forever. In that event either we can put together a new engine or we can put together nothing at all. This analogy is not necessarily an apt one, for human institutions, with which historians have often had to deal, certainly are not engines, and their workings, though potentially more complex, are based on simpler principles.

Ethnological laws of cultural and social behavior can be cross-culturally derived. "In recent years a number of cross-cultural studies have been reported . . . studies which seek to establish relationships between certain variables in human existence through cross-cultural comparisons."[215] The number of cultures involved in the comparison need not be large, but the purpose is to seek a statistical concomitance of the variables and a satisfactory explanation of this concomitance.[216]

215. C. S. Ford, "On the Ananlysis of Behavior for Cross-Cultural Comparisons."

216. S. F. Nadel, "Witchcraft in Four African Societies: An Essay in Comparison"; Fred Eggan, "Social Anthropology and the Method of Controlled Comparison."

PART I THE SHANG SOCIETY FROM AN-YANG

1 An-yang and the Royal Capital

1. *THE ROYAL CAPITAL AND THE AN-YANG CORE*

Most Shang texts agree that P'an Keng, the dynasty's nineteenth king, moved his capital to Yin, where he and his descendants stayed until the dynasty's fall.[1] From the oracle bone inscriptions it appears that divination records attributable to Shang kings from Wu Ting (twenty-second king, P'an Keng's nephew) to Ti Hsin (thirtieth and last king) have been found kept in the storage pits at Hsiao-t'un.[2] Thus, both new and old textual data testify to the capital status of Yin. However, the name Yin is seen only in Chou texts, whereas in Shang texts and some of the Chou texts, as well as in the oracle records, the name Shang is often seen as the Shang's own designation of their capital city. Shima Kunio's *Concordance of Oracle Records* lists numerous occurrences of the word Shang 商 or 商, including twelve references to Ta yi Shang 大邑商 ("Great City Shang").[3] However, there are differing opinions on the location of this name in present geographical terms, and only a few scholars see it located in the An-yang area where the oracle records were found.[4] This is a question we will come back to in discussing the Shang political order.

In any event, it was at Yin that the last Shang king, Chòu, met his end. Very shortly thereafter, Chi Tzu, King Chòu's uncle (or cousin), who was said to have disapproved of Chòu's evil ways and have gone into voluntary exile, became an honored guest of the Chou, the conqueror. *Shih chi* (section "Sung shih-chia") records him as having made a journey of homage to Chou.

1. *Ku pen Chu shu chi nien* 古本竹書紀年: "From P'an Keng's removal to Yin to the fall of Chòu, for [2]73 years [they] did not move the capital" 自盤庚徙殷至紂之滅[二]百七十三年更不徙都.

2. Shima Kunio 島邦男, *Inkyo bokuji kenkyū* 殷墟卜辞研究, pp. 35–49.

3. Shima Kunio 島邦男, *Inkyo bokuji sōrui* 殷墟卜辞綜類, p. 279.

4. Shima Kunio 島邦男, *Inkyo bokuji kenkyū* 殷墟卜辞研究, pp. 360–361; Ch'en Meng-chia 陳夢家, *Yin hsü p'u-tz'u tsung-shu* 殷墟卜辭綜述, pp. 255–258.

> [On the trip] Chi Tzu went by the old Yin hsü [Yin Ruins]. Struck by the fact that the palaces had gone to ruin and millet had grown over them, Chi Tzu was saddened.

It thus appears that soon as the dynasty fell (or at least after the short-lived rebellion by Chòu's son was crushed), the last Shang capital had become Yin hsü 殷墟 (or Shang hsü 商墟). *Shih chi* refers to both names in its accounts of events that took place in the former capital area. In section "Hsiang Yü pen-chi," Ssu-ma Ch'ien states that Hsiang Yü (d. 202 B.C.) led his troops to "Yin hsü, south of the Huan River," and in "Wei Shih-chia," he describes how Chou Kung, regent and brother of the late Wu Wang, enfeoffed his younger brother K'ang Shu 康叔 at "the old Shang Ruins, between the Ho 河 (Yellow River) and the Ch'i 淇." Thus, at least as late as early Han times the old ruins of the last Shang capital were known to be in an area south of the river Huan and between the former course of the Yellow and the Ch'i Rivers, in the northern part of what is now Honan Province.

Since the finding of Shang ruins in An-yang in 1928, scholars have had reason to suppose that Yin hsü is located northwest of the modern An-yang city, "south of the River Huan," outlined by the archaeological sites of the area. But Miyazaki Ichisada, citing the reference to Shang hsü that places it "between the Ho and the Ch'i," believes that Yin hsü (or Shang hsü) should really be located way to the south at the site of the founding of the statelet of Wei, and he thinks that the archaeological sites at An-yang are merely the royal mausoleums.[5]

Although the location of Yin in northern Honan is unquestionable, it need not be identified merely with a relatively small locus. In fact, the name Yin may have encompassed a royal domain of considerable dimensions. One version of *Ku pen Chu shu* states that "at the time of Chòu he slightly enlarged his city. South from Ch'ao-ko and north to Han-tan and Sha-ch'iu 沙丘 the area was full of [his] resort palaces and secondary residences." Ch'ao-ko is usually identified with the present town of Ch'i Hsien; Han-tan, the present city of Han-tan; and Sha-ch'iu, near the present city of Hsing-t'ai or Chü-lu.[6] From Hsing-t'ai to Chi Hsien is a north-south distance of about 165 kilometers. *Han-shu Ti-li-chih* also states that after the conquest the Chou divided the Shang capital city into three states: Pei 邶, Yung 鄘, and Wei 衛. Pei and Wei were near Ch'i Hsien, and Yung was located in Hsin-hsiang, another

5. Miyazaki Ichisada 宮崎市定, "Chūgoku jōdai no toshi kokka to sono bochi—Shōyū wa doko ni atta ka" 中国上代の都市国家とその墓地一商邑は何処にあったか; "Hoi" 補遺.

6. See *Shih chi chi chieh* 史記集解 and *Shih chi cheng yi* 史記正義.

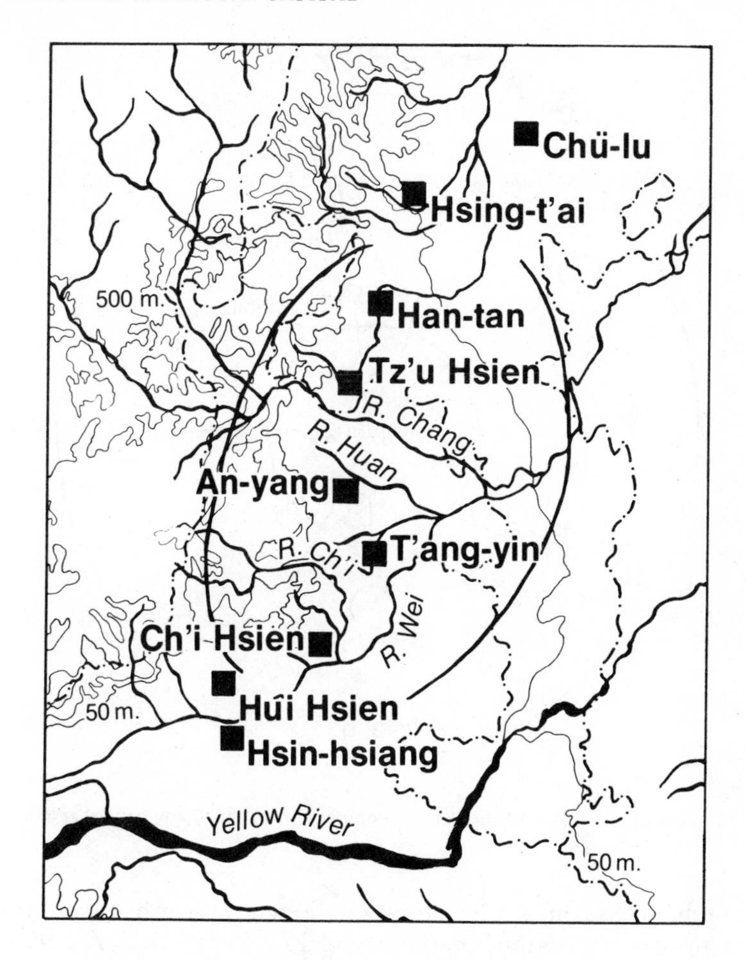

9. Possible areal scope of the Shang capital at Yin.

forty kilometers further to the south.[7] Within this area have been found scattered remains of Shang types. Possibly all of them were in Ssu-ma Ch'ien's day considered part of Yin hsü[8] (fig. 9), but there is no question that the Shang sites near An-yang had a special significance by virture of their oracle bones and their enormously rich finds. One may construe a settlement pattern of the royal capital, Yin, as in fig. 10. Perhaps even

7. For this version of the locations of Pei, Yung, and Wei, see Ch'eng Fa-jen 程發軔, *Ch'un-ch'iu Tso-shih-chuan ti ming t'u k'ao* 春秋左氏傳地名圖考, pp. 105, 213.

8. Ch'en Meng-chia 陳夢家, *Yin hsü p'u-tz'u tsung shu* 殷墟卜辭綜述, pp. 20–34.

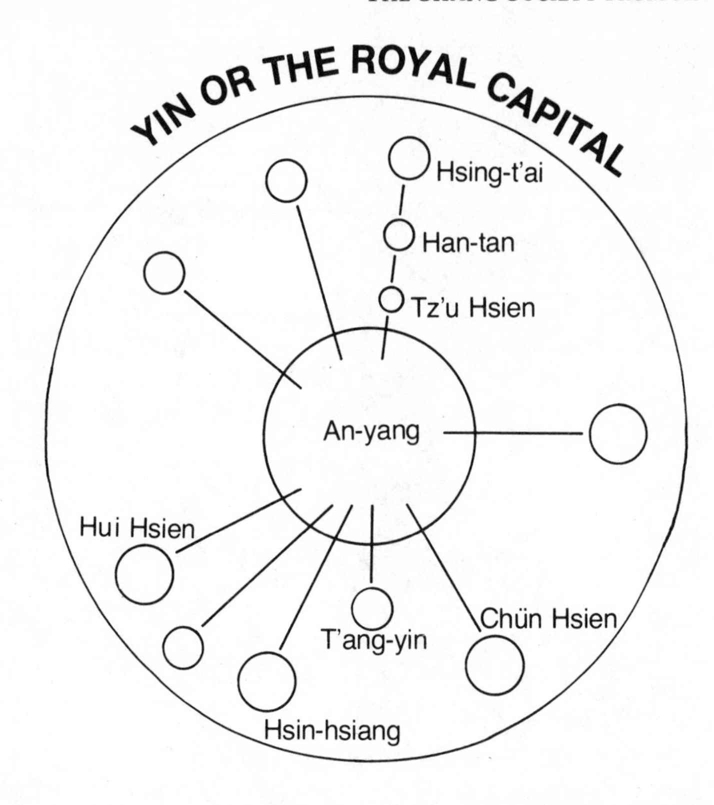

10. Possible structure of the various components of the Shang capital at Yin.

at the time of Ssu-ma Ch'ien, the exact extent of Yin hsü was already becoming obscure, although there was knowledge that Yin ruins or Shang ruins were located "south of the River Huan" or "between the Ho and the Ch'i rivers." But whatever traces above ground that still existed must have soon become completely obliterated and the vast Yin area turned into a covered archaeological site.

The uncovering of the Yin hsü remains began at, and has remained focused on, the An-yang area. As stated earlier, bronze vessels uncovered in the An-yang area began to be recorded in the literature by the Sung dynasty; the earliest such find occurred in 1079.[9] But scientific excavations had to wait until 1928, following the discovery of inscribed oracle bones in 1899. During the last fifty years, a number of archaeological loci have been excavated and described in the An-yang area. Other sites are also known outside An-yang but within the probable

9. *Ibid.*, pp. 39–40.

territory of the royal capital, but in this chapter our material pertains almost exclusively to the An-yang sites. I shall refer to the area within which the An-yang sites cluster as the *An-yang core*, and the larger area of Shang sites in northern Honan, of which the An-yang core was only a part, as the *Royal Capital*.

Archaeological sites in the An-yang core are distributed along the River Huan, on both banks, in an area approximately six kilometers along the river and 4 kilometers deep, to the northwest of the present city of An-yang (fig. 11). The predominant site on the south bank is Hsiao-t'un, principal depository of inscribed oracle bones in a palace-temple complex. The conspicuous site to the north of the river is the royal cemetery at Hsi-pei-kang. The following description of the Shang sites in the An-yang core will, thus, be divided into three sections: Hsiao-t'un, Hsi-pei-kang, and other sites.

2. *HSIAO-T'UN* 小屯

Hsiao-t'un ("small hamlet") is a small village about 3 kilometers northwest of the town wall of An-yang. The Huan River flows from west to east about 600 meters to the north of Hsiao-t'un, but turns south and flows about 160 meters to the east of the village. Shang remains have been found north and northeast of the village all the way to the river (Locus North), in the southern half of the village and to its south (Locus South), and west of the village (Locus West).

Locus North of Hsiao-t'un is the best-excavated area of the An-yang core, having undergone archaeological excavations in 1928, 1929, 1931, 1932, 1933, 1934, 1936, 1937, 1975, and 1976. From this locus have come remains of foundations, ditches, sacrificial burials, dwelling and storage pits, workshops, and several richly furnished tombs. Many artifacts have been brought to light from these architectural features and burials, and practically all of the inscribed oracle bones have come from the Hsiao-t'un loci, especially Locus North. Unfortunately, to this date the excavations here have yet to be reported in full. The very abundant, but incomplete, material on the architecture of the site, in the context of which we must describe and discuss its artifacts and inscribed oracle bones, has come largely from the writings of one man, Professor Shih Chang-ju 石璋如, which have been coming out over a period of over forty years. The following description of the Hsiao-t'un Locus North—including stratigraphy, architectural layout during each cultural stratum, and major artifact categories—must be based on data of very uneven completeness and, therefore, contain significant elements of conjecture and uncertainty.

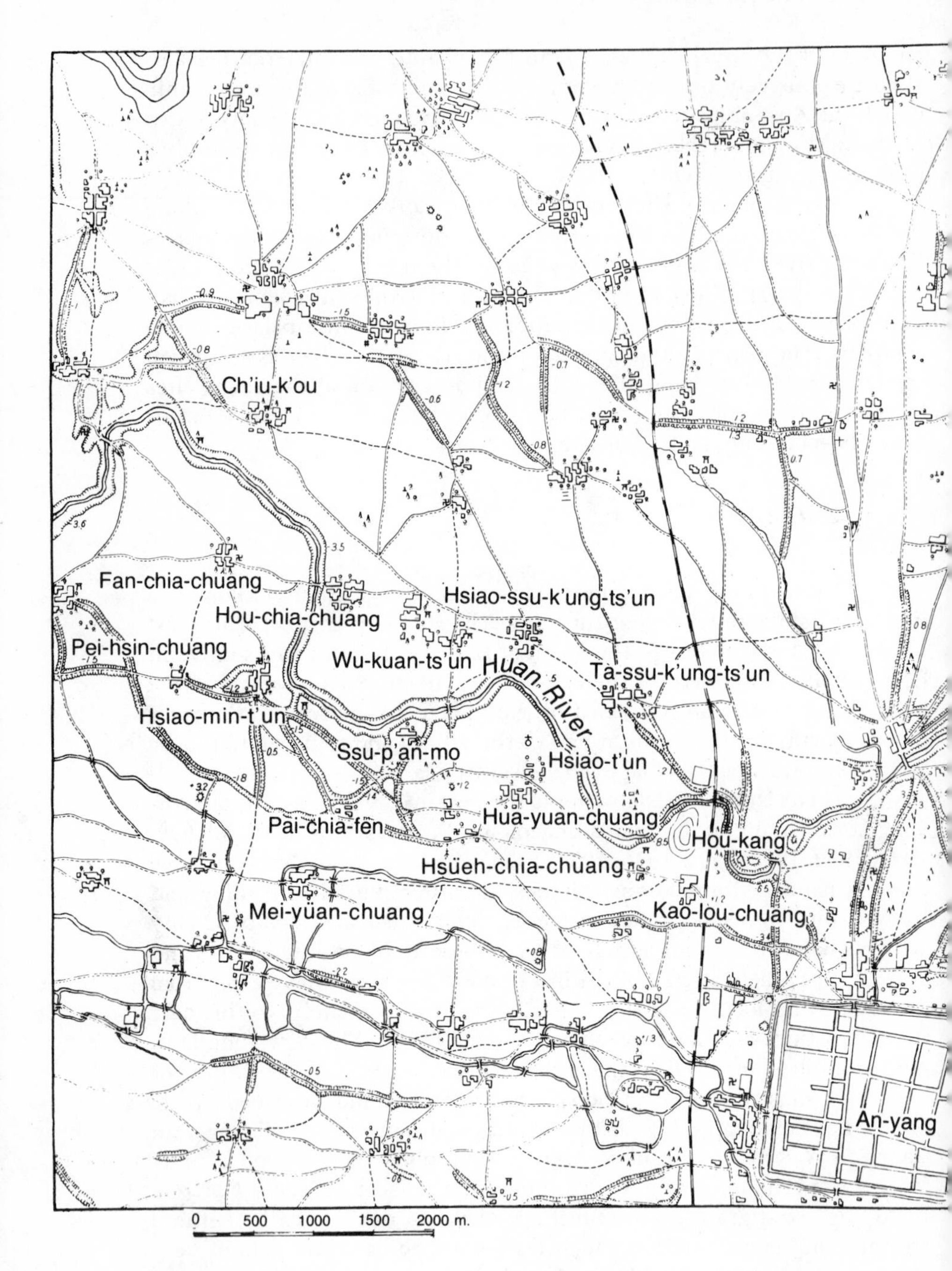

11. Locations of archaeological loci near An-yang (after Umehara Sueji, *Kanan Anyō ihō*, p. 13).

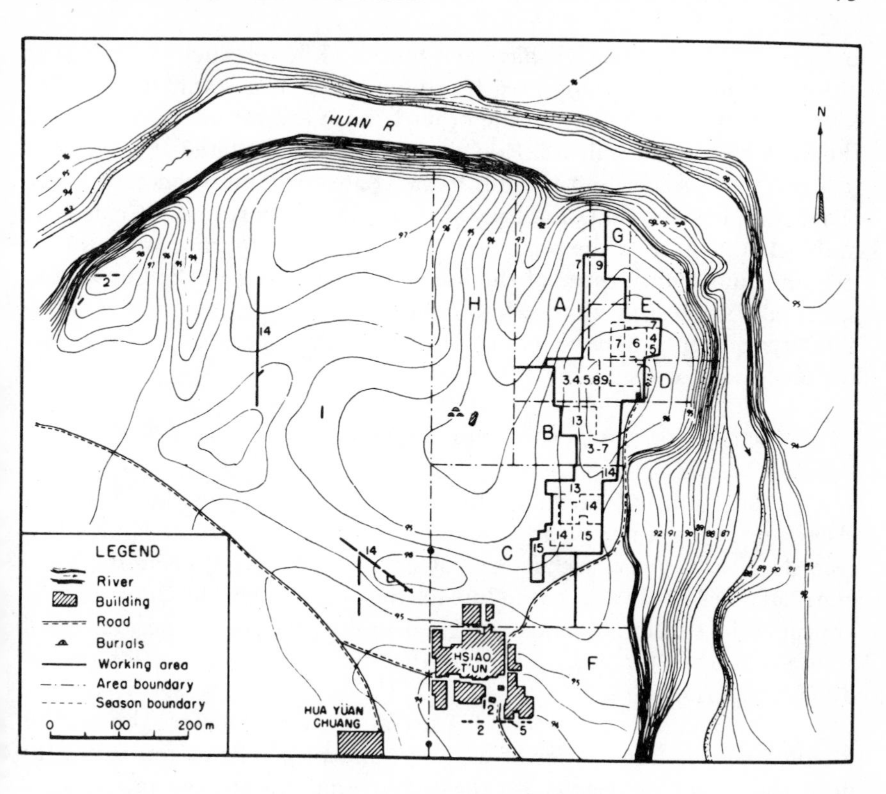

12. Grid divisions of the archaeological site at Hsiao-t'un Locus North. (After Li Chi, *Anyang*, fig. 6. Map originally published by Academia Sinica, Institute of History and Philology. By permission of University of Washington Press.)

Locus North was divided by the Academia Sinica excavations into 9 excavation grids: A, B, C, D, E, F, G, H, I (fig. 12). Description of all features will be referred to according to this grid system. In stratigraphy, Locus North may be divided into four major phases: prehistoric period, predynastic Shang (prior to P'an Keng's removal of the capital to Yin), dynastic Shang (P'an Keng to Ti Hsin), and post-Shang. The last phase will be omitted from our discussion here.

As to the prehistoric phase of Hsiao-t'un, Locus North, only a brief mention is necessary. A single piece of painted pottery sherd, of the Yang-shao style of northern Honan, was found at Hsiao-t'un in 1929,[10] but no occupation layer of the Yang-shao culture, now dated from

10. Li Chi 李濟, "Hsiao-t'un yü Yang-shao" 小屯與仰韶, 337–347.

before 5000 to 3000 B.C.,[11] has been found, although such layers occur elsewhere in the An-yang area (prominently at Hou-kang and Ta-ssu-k'ung-ts'un).[12] There are, on the other hand, very extensive remains of the next prehistoric culture, Honan Lung-shan, now dated at from 2800 to 2300 B.C.[13] According to Shih,[14] the center of Lung-shan remains at Hsiao-t'un lies in Grid D and they also extend into portions of Grids B, C, and E. Li Chi studied the remains of forty pairs of superimposed storage pits and found only three of the lower pits to belong to the Lung-shan stratum,[15] suggesting that, while Hsiao-t'un had a Lung-shan occupation, it represents merely a relatively small village dwarfed by the massive settlement of the Shang culture.

PREDYNASTIC SHANG OCCUPATION AT LOCUS NORTH

The cultural stratigraphy of the Shang occupation here, as elsewhere in the An-yang area, is not altogether clear from the published records. I will use the archaeological assemblage of Tomb Number Five, excavated in 1976, as a starting line for the dynastic period. Remains that appear to be earlier are, thus, assigned to the predynastic period. I will state the reasons for this decision at the beginning of the section on the dynastic period.

The major architectural feature at Hsiao-t'un before the time of P'an Keng is "a large series of underground pits, cellars, and subterranean dwellings";[16] related to these dwelling and storage pits were a large system of drainage ditches and, probably, a number of graves, some of which contained ritual bronzes.

Reports on some of the archaeological material excavated before the war have now been published, but the underground pits have not yet been fully described. We lack a detailed plan of such pits throughout the site and a detailed description of all the remains in each pit. If, as Shih Chang-ju now concludes,[17] the water-ditches served as a drainage

11. Hsia Nai 夏鼐, "T'an-14 ts'e-ting nien-tai ho Chung-kuo shih-ch'ien k'ao-ku hsüeh" 碳-14測定年代和中國史前考古學, 222.

12. *KK*, "1958–1959 nien Yin hsü fa-chüeh chien pao" 1958-1959年殷墟發掘簡報, p. 63.

13. See note 11 above.

14. "Yin hsü tsui-chin chih chung-yao fa-hsien fu lun Hsiao-t'un ti-ts'eng" 殷墟最近之重要發現附論小屯地層.

15. "Studies of the Hsiao-t'un Pottery: Yin and Pre-Yin," 113.

16. Li Chi, *Anyang*, p. 104.

17. Shih Chang-ju 石璋如, *Yin hsü chien-chu yi-ts'un* 殷虛建築遺存, p. 268; "Yin tai ti hang-t'u pan-chu yü yi-pan chien-chu" 殷代的夯土版築與一般建築, 139–141.

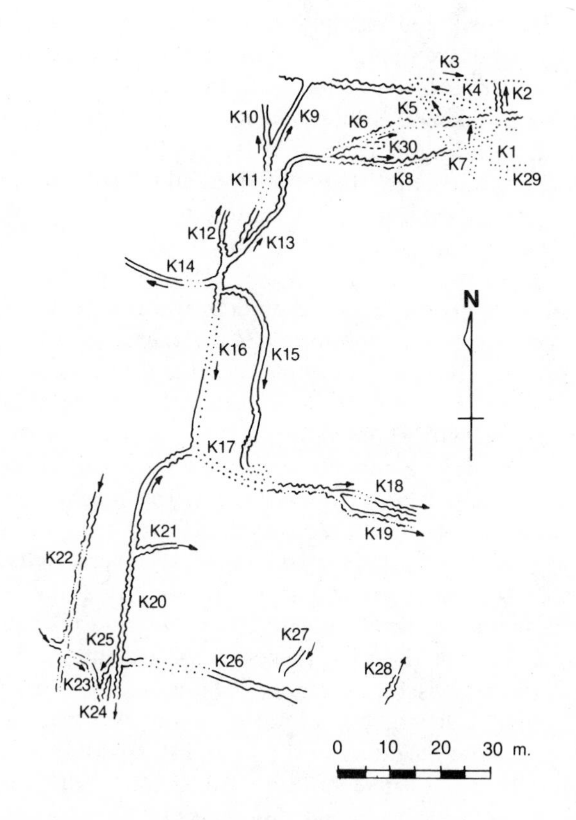

13. The water-ditches at Hsiao-t'un (after Shih Chang-ju, *Yin hsü chien-chu yi-ts'un,* p. 140).

system for the semi-subterranean dwellings at Hsiao-t'un, then the predynastic occupation here must have been quite extensive. The area covered by the ditches stretches about 170 meters north-south and almost 90 meters east-west,[18] and we are told that underground pits cluster densely along the ditches.[19] The ditches thus outline a predynastic settlement of considerable size (fig. 13). Within the settlement, there are indications that pit dwellings clustered in groups. Shih Chang-ju has published the layout of the pits at the southwest corner of Grid C of the site (fig. 14). Here in an area 20 meters north-south and 18 meters east-west there were forty-seven pits, divided into five groups, each consisting of a large and semi-subterranean dwelling pit and several small storage pits surrounding it. If the density of pits was relatively uniform throughout the settlement, then the area filled by the ditches could accommodate about two hundred dwelling pits.

These dwelling pits "are for the most part large and shallow structures, with rather straight walls . . . and ramps or stairs for going up and down. If we compare the diameter and the depth of the pits, in most cases the diameter is greater than the depth. Sometimes they are about equal, but only rarely is depth greater than diameter. Six types may be distinguished according to the exterior shape and the position of the stairs : circular, with stairs along the wall; circular, with stairs in the middle; oval, with stairs along one wall; oval, with stairs along two walls; oval, with stairs in the middle; and square, with stairs along the wall. . . . On top of each of these pits there was probably a roof or cover. At the center of the smaller pits there was often a large rock, which may have supported a central post. For larger pits, not only was there a large rock at the center, smaller rocks often ringed the pit along the upper edge of the pit. . . . In some of the pits, pieces of wattle-and-daub were found among the deposits, possibly remains of fallen roofs"[20] (fig. 15).

Since the archaeology of the dwelling pits has not been systematically published, we have no usable information on the contents of these pits. In his *Corpus of Yin Hsü Pottery*,[21] Li Chi illustrated pottery samples as type specimens of his classification system, and among the samples are nine complete vessels that are marked as coming from some of the forty-seven pits of five groups shown just above. These include a *li*-tripod (from pit YH 190), a *kuei*-bowl (from YH 302), a *yu*-bowl (from YH 285), and a flat-bottom *kuan* (from YH 272) that are

18. Shih Chang-ju 石璋如, *Yin hsü chien-chu yi-ts'un* 殷虛建築遺存, p. 203.

19. *Ibid.*, p. 268.

20. Shih Chang-ju 石璋如, "Hsiao-t'un Yin tai ti chien-chu yi-chi" 小屯殷代的建築遺蹟, 131–136.

21. Li Chi 李濟, *Hsiao-t'un t'ao-ch'i* 小屯陶器.

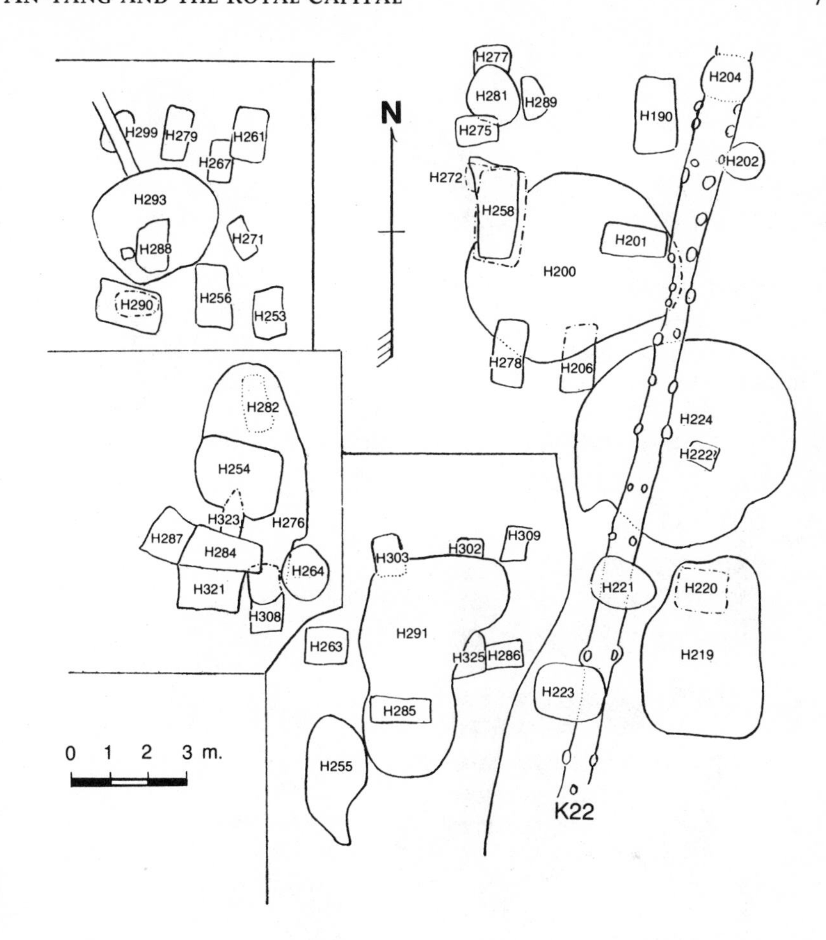

14. Clusters of pit dwellings in predynastic Hsiao-t'un (after Shih Chang-ju, "Hsiao-t'un Yin tai ti chien-chu yi-chi", 168).

typologically characteristic of the Period I pottery of Miao-p'u-pei-ti[22] or the Early Period of Hsiao-t'un Locus South.[23] The chronology of ceramic types from Hsiao-t'un will be discussed in some detail presently. Suffice it to say here that the typology of this group of pottery shows clearly that these pits are indeed early, and that the first period of the

22. Labels and exhibitions at the exhibition hall at the An-yang Field Station, Institute of Archaeology, Chinese Academy of Social Sciences.

23. *KK*, "1973 nien An-yang Hsiao-t'un nan-ti fa-chüeh chien pao" 1973年安陽小屯南地發掘簡報.

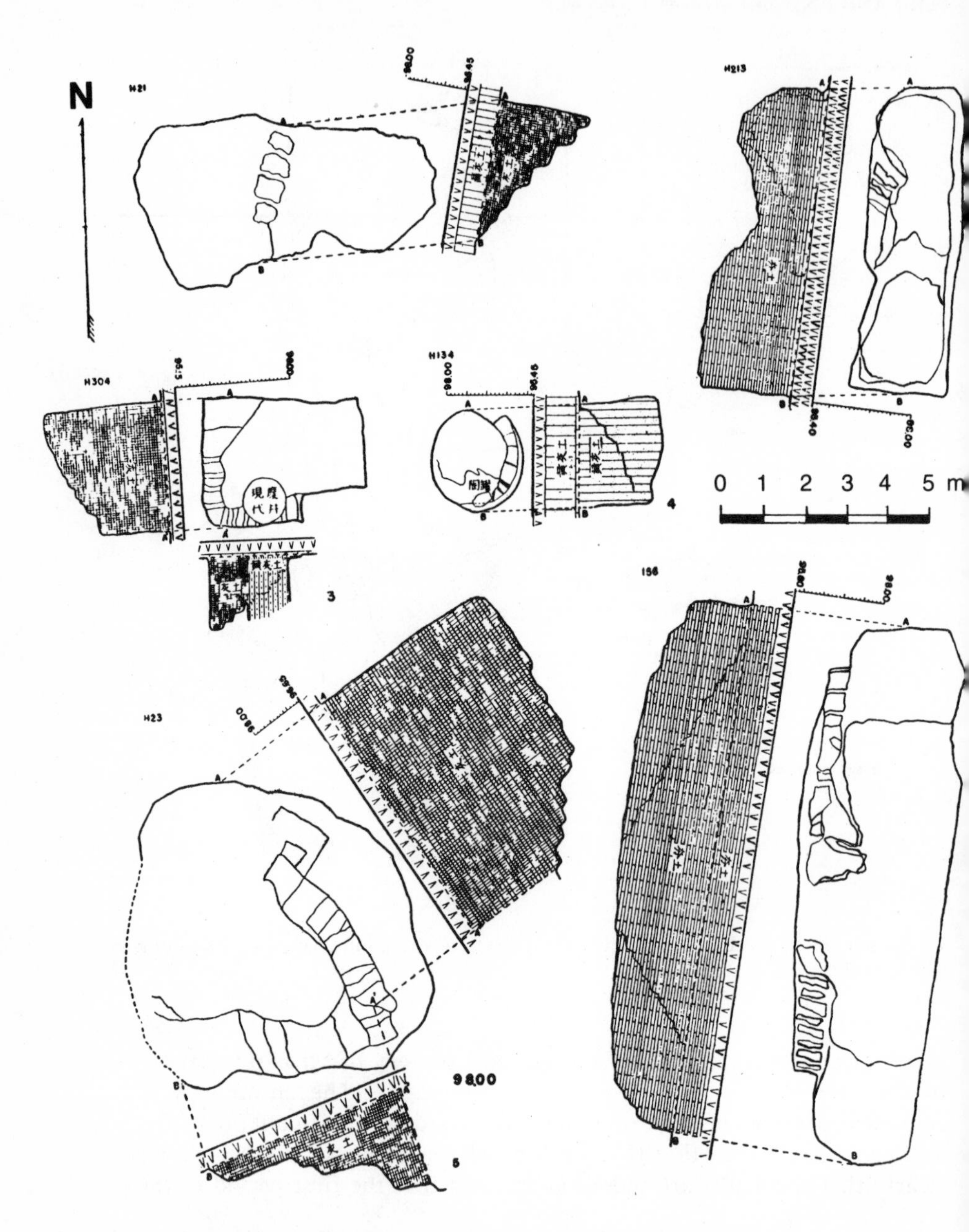

15. Cross-sections and plans of major types of predynastic pit dwellings at Hsiao-t'un (after Shih Chang-ju, ''Hsiao-t'un Yin tai ti chien-chu yi-chi,'' 134).

prevalent four-stage system of Yin hsü ceramics is probably equivalent, at least in part, to the predynastic period.

At the Hsiao-t'un site there were a large number of graves evidently of the Shang period. These graves have often been described in conjunction with the ground structures of the dynastic period, as will be mentioned below. There are other graves, however, that are, spatially speaking, free-standing, and their dating must be based more on artifact typology than on stratigraphy. If Tomb Number Five is taken to initiate the dynastic period, then all Hsiao-t'un tombs containing artifacts typologically antecedent to Tomb Number Five artifacts could be predynastic.

Here Max Loehr's five styles of An-yang bronze vessels may be helpful. The bronze vessels from Tomb Number Five, at least those that have been published so far,[24] clearly fall within Loehr's styles IV and V. This recent discovery is, thus, of the utmost importance in bronze dating, since it means that the latest of Loehr's styles had already appeared by Wu Ting's reign, very close to the beginning years of the An-yang royal capital instead of belonging to the latest period of Yin, as is sometimes thought. It also suggests that the bronze vessels from Hsiao-t'un that are classifiable in Loehr's styles I–III, if not accompanied by vessels of a later style, have the potential of being predynastic in origin. According to Virginia Kane's analysis of the bronze vessels from these tombs,[25] the following Hsiao-t'un tombs so qualify: M 188, M 222, M 232, M 333, and M 388. Among them, M 232 and M 333 are grouped by Tsou Heng into his earliest segment and M 388 and M 188 into his second earliest.[26]

On the basis of Shih Chang-ju's detailed description of M 222, we know that it contains late features and should not be included with the predynastic group.[27] Among the remaining four, two are located within the middle (*yi*) group of house foundations (M 188, M 232), and two (M 333 and M 388) are within the southern (*ping*) group. Shih Chang-

24. *KKHP*, "An-yang Yin hsü wu-hao mu ti fa-chüeh" 安陽殷墟五號墓的發掘.

25. "A Re-examination of An-yang Archaeology," 108.

26. See his "Shih lun Yin hsü wen-hua fen-ch'i" 試論殷墟文化分期.

27. M 222 is a rectangular pit-grave, oriented east-west, 2.2 meters long east-west, 1.05 meter wide north-south, 0.31 meter deep, filled with yellow and gray earth. Three human skeletons were found inside. One was in the western half, heading north, bent at the waist, lying face-down. The two others lie stretched in the eastern half, heading west, the northern skeleton lying face-up and the southern one face-down. Grave goods included four bronze vessels (two *ku*-beakers and two *chüeh*-tripods), three pottery vessels, and a deer antler. (See Shih Chang-ju 石璋如, *Yi-ch'ü chi-chih shang hsia ti mu-tsang* 乙區基址上下的墓葬, pp. 159–166). The pottery vessels, including a round-base *kuan* and two flat-base *lei* with shoulder handles, resemble the type

ju[28] regards them as accessory graves to the house foundations, perhaps laid there as ritual sacrifices relating to the construction of the houses, but this is merely based on their location and has no stratigraphical foundation, since M 188, M 232, M 333, and M 388 are all free-standing. Available description of these four graves is as follows:

M 188. M 188 is a rectangular pit grave, oriented east-west, 1.8 meters long east-west and 1.08 meters wide north-south, 0.55 meters deep, filled with yellow earth that is not compressed. Two human skeletons were inside. One was located in the eastern half heading north and facing east, kneeling, with arms folded in front, and the other was in the western half, heading north but facing west, probably also kneeling with arms folded behind the back. Grave furnishings include eight ritual vessels, most placed on top of the person on the west, which consist of a *ting*-tripod, a *hsien*-tripod, a *p'o*-container, two *chia*-tripods, a *pien*- (or *kuei*) container, and a *ku*-tripod (figs. 16, 17). Shih believes that the two persons (perhaps a man and a woman, judging by the way that their arms were tied behind and in front) were ritual attendants who had taken care of the vessel set.[29]

M 232. This was the largest grave found in Hsiao-t'un before Tomb Number Five was discovered in 1976. It is again a pit grave, but in it there were a wooden chamber (3.10 meters by 2.15 meters by 1.35 meters being the exterior dimensions) and a wooden coffin (painted in red lacquer, 2.10 meters from north to south, 0.9 meter from east to west, and 0.8 meter deep). The master of the grave was presumably buried in the coffin, but his skeleton no longer exists, due to an early plundering. Eight sacrificial victims were placed within the wooden chamber, and the skeletons of four dogs were also found, one at the bottom of the pit and the other three near the upper end of the grave pit. Grave goods (fig. 18), most found within the wooden chamber, include 10 bronze vessels (2 *ku*, 2 *chüeh*, 2 *chia*, 2 *p'o*, 1 *ting*, and 1 *p'an*), 9 weapons (6 bronze *ko*, 2 stone *ko*, and 1 stone ax), 9 sets of head ornaments (of jade, turquoise, shell, stone, bronze, and bone), and a stone mortar.[30]

M 333. M 333 is a pit grave, 0.95–1.75 meters from ground surface, in which there are four human skeletons, three of them probably sacrificial victims, and a dog burial at the center of the bottom. Grave

---

specimens of the Middle group of the pottery of Hsiao-t'un Locus South (see *KK*, "1973 nien An-yang Hsiao-t'un nan-ti fa-chüeh chien pao" 1973年安陽小屯南地發掘簡報, pp. 35–36), and stratigraphically the tomb intruded into a house foundation (Shih Chang-ju 石璋如, *op. cit.*, p. 160). For these reasons M 222 should not be included in the pre-dynastic group despite the stylistic characteristics of its bronze vessels.

28. Shih Chang-ju 石璋如, *Yin hsü chien-chu yi-ts'un* 殷墟建築遺存.
29. Shih Chang-ju 石璋如, *Pei tsu mu-tsang* 北組墓葬, pp. 343–350.
30. Shih Chang-ju 石璋如, *Nan tsu mu-tsang* 南組墓葬.

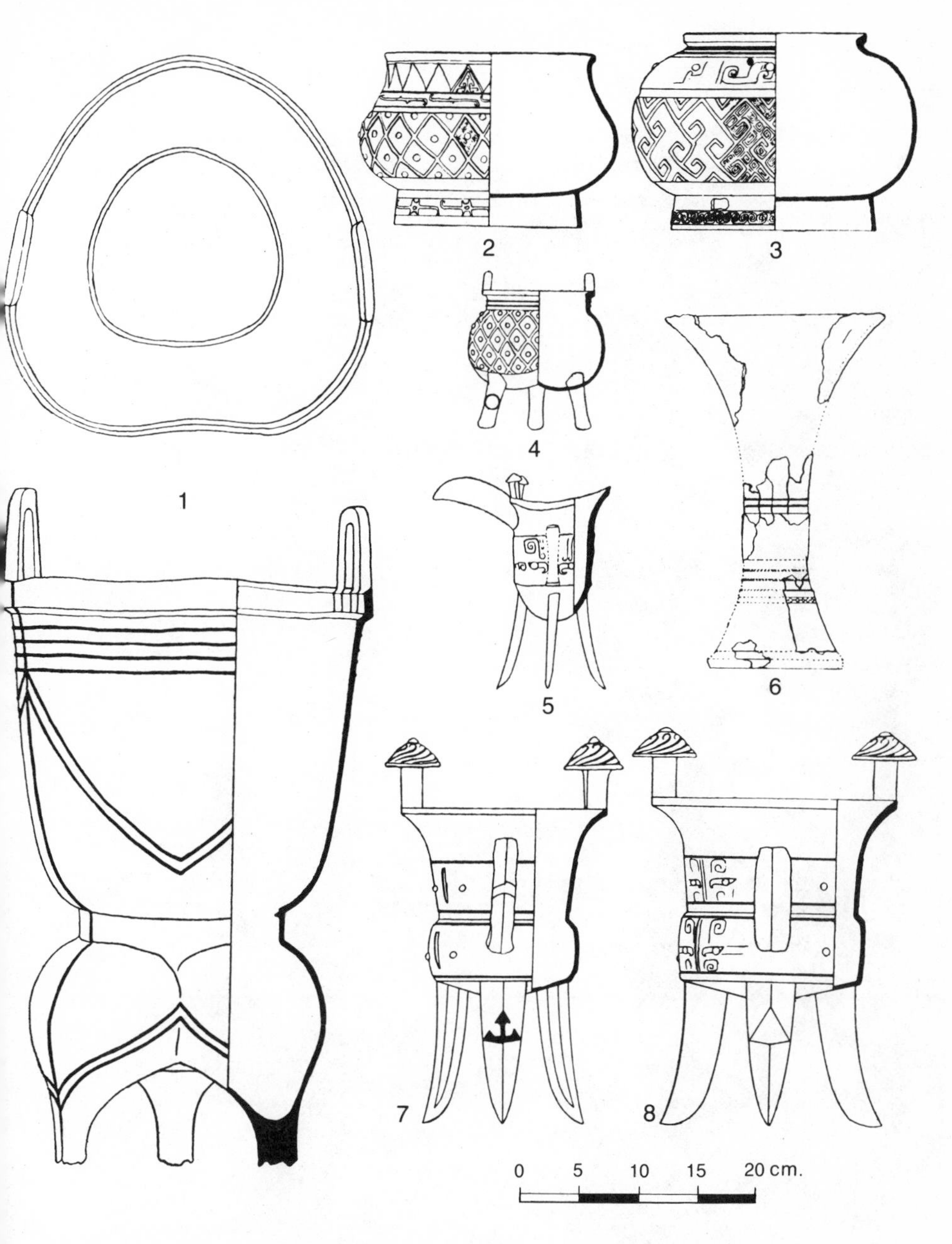

16. Artifacts from grave M 188 at predynastic Hsiao-t'un (after Shih Chang-ju, *Pei tsu mu-tsang*, fig. 105).

17. Artifacts from grave M 188 at time of excavation (after Shih Chang-ju, *Pei tsu mu-tsang,* pl. 242).

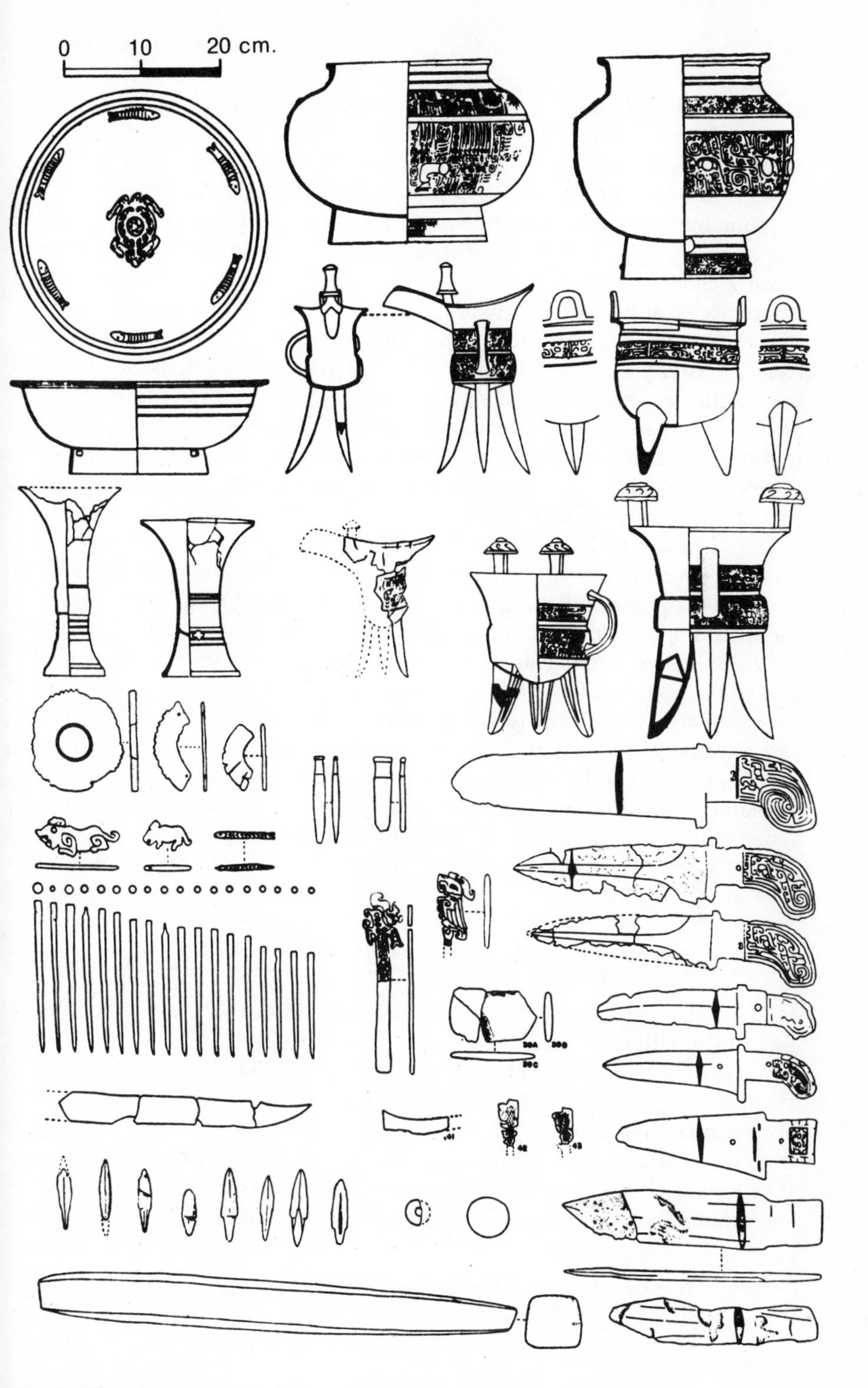

18. Artifacts from grave M 232 at predynastic Hsiao-t'un (after Shih Chang-ju, *Nan tsu mu-tsang*, p. 67).

goods found there include 10 bronze vessels (2 *ku*, 2 *chüeh*, 2 *ting*, 2 *chia*, 2 *p'o*), 1 bronze knife, 12 pieces of jade ornaments and stone artifacts, 29 bone and shell artifacts, and 2 pottery objects.[31]

M 388 is a pit grave, 0.95–2.06 meters from the surface, containing four human skeletons, three of which were probably victims, and a dog at the center of the bottom. Grave goods include 10 bronze vessels (2 *ku*, 2 *chüeh*, 1 *ting*, 2 *chia*, 2 *p'o*, 1 *p'ing-yü*), 5 bronze *ko*, 33 jade and stone pieces, and 2 pottery *tou*.[32]

Summing up the above data that are known or presumed to be from the predynastic occupation period at Hsiao-t'un Locus North, we see a settlement measuring at least 170 meters from north to south and 90 meters from east to west. Within the area were possibly as many as two hundred dwelling houses that formed clusters. A drainage system of water ditches was built amid the houses. Among the remains found in these houses were pottery (of Period I in the Yin hsü ceramic chronology), stones, uninscribed oracle bones, and possibly bronzes, although an accurate inventory is impossible to compile on the basis of available data. Four graves possibly belong to this period, two in a group southwest of the dwelling area and the other two at the center of the settlement area outlined by the ditch system. These graves indicate a level of Shang art and technology similar to the late Cheng-chou period (see chapter 5) and a level of society not drastically different from the dynastic period. It is not possible to say whether the graves were all contemporary with the dwellings, or whether the dwellings included any that were those of noblemen (those buried as masters in the graves). But it is clear that Hsiao-t'un, though small, was densely inhabited prior to its assuming capital status, and that its inhabitants included people of high political station.

DYNASTIC SHANG OCCUPATION AT LOCUS NORTH

The dynastic period at Hsiao-t'un (and elsewhere in An-yang) saw the qualitative transformation of the site from a moderate-sized settlement into a royal capital featuring the archaeological appearance of three new phenomena: house foundations of major proportions ("palace foundations"), inscribed oracle bones, and tombs so large and rich as to warrant a "royal" designation. According to textual records, it was P'an Keng, who, in his fourteenth year of reign (according to *Ku pen Chu shu chi nien*), moved his capital to Yin, and died fourteen years later. His

31. Shih Chang-ju 石璋如, "Hsiao-t'un Yin tai Ping tsu chi-chih chi ch'i yu-kuan hsien-hsiang" 小屯殷代丙組基址及其有關現象, 795–798.

32. *Ibid.*

two brothers, who succeeded him one after another, accounted for another thirty or so years.[33] This initial period, of about thirty-five years, still cannot be specifically identified with certainty in the archaeological records. The next king, Wu Ting, however, who reigned fifty-nine years according to all textual records, was extremely active and left a conspicuous record. Tomb Number Five, excavated in 1976, is generally believed to be the tomb of one of his major wives, Fu Hao 婦好 ("Lady Hao" or "the Lady Who Came from the Tzu Clan"), also known as Hou Hsin 后辛 ("Queen Hsin"). This grave is a very rich find, and it has been well preserved. I propose, therefore, to use this grave to represent the Wu Ting period. The pre–Wu Ting dynastic period of thirty-five years may for the time being be regarded as a prefatory appendage of the Wu Ting period until proven otherwise by future archaeological finds.

The Fu Hao Tomb. Shang remains came to light during agricultural work in the winter of 1975 on a piece of land of slightly higher elevation than the surrounding fields, northwest of the village of Hsiao-t'un, approximately 200 meters west of the southern edge of Grid C. In the summer of 1976, the site was excavated by members of the An-yang Archaeological Team of the Institute of Archaeology, Academia Sinica. More than a dozen Shang house foundations, eighty pits, and more than a dozen Shang tombs were disclosed. Of the tombs, Tomb Number Five is the largest and the most important.[34]

The construction of the grave was largely in the same tradition as M 232 described above from the predynastic period, but Tomb Number Five was more elaborate and much richer. Again it was a rectangular pit grave, oriented largely from north to south. The opening of the grave pit was only half a meter below the ground surface, but an aboveground house foundation 5.5 by 5 meters was built exactly on top of it, possibly a sacrificial structure for the burial underneath. The grave pit opening was 5.6 meters north-south and 4 meters east-west, and the pit was 7.5 meters deep, the pit walls sloping slightly inward. About 6.2 meters down from the pit opening, a ledge 0.3 meter wide and 1.3 meter tall was built along all four walls. Just above the ledge on the east and west walls, a long niche (less than 2 meters in length) was excavated on each wall in which sacrificial victims were buried. A chamber constructed of timber filled the pit within the ledge, and a coffin was placed inside the chamber. At the bottom of the pit a small pit was excavated south of the

33. Tung Tso-pin 董作賓, *Yin li p'u* 殷曆譜, part I, vol. 4, pp. 9–11.

34. *KKHP*, "An-yang Yin hsü wu-hao mu ti fa-chüeh" 安陽殷墟五號墓的發掘; *KK*, "Yin hsü k'ao-ku fa-chüeh ti yu yi chung-yao shou-hu 殷墟考古發掘的又一重要收穫; *CR*, "Best-preserved Yin Dynasty Tomb"; *JH*, "Yin hsü k'ao-ku ti hsin fa-hsien" 殷墟考古的新發現.

center for a sacrificial human victim and a dog. The mistress of the grave was presumably placed in the coffin, and she was accompanied by sixteen sacrificed humans (four on top of the chamber, two inside under the eastern wall niche, one inside the western wall niche, one in a pit dug in the floor of the chamber, and the remaining eight taken out of underground water with their original positions unknown but presumably within the chamber) and six sacrificed dogs (one in the pit below bottom and the other on top of the chamber). Among the sixteen humans, four were men, one of them young; two were women, two were children; the sexes and ages of the rest were unclear. At least one was killed; one other was cut in half at the waist.

Enormous quantities of grave goods were placed in various parts of the grave, inside the coffin, inside the chamber, and in the fill of the grave pit all the way to within a meter of the opening. Altogether there were more than 1,600 objects, plus about 7,000 cowrie shells. Among the objects there were more than 440 bronzes, more than 590 jades, over 560 bone objects, in excess of 70 stone objects, several ivory carvings, several pottery objects, more than a dozen shell objects, and three seashells (fig. 19). These were placed in the grave and in the pit fill as the pit was filled with stamped earth layer by layer (each layer was 10–11 centimeters deep).

Tomb Number Five is a discovery of the first magnitude in the history of Shang archaeology because of its richness, accounted for by the fact that since its construction the tomb has never been plundered, unlike the overwhelming majority of Shang graves in an area where grave plunderers had been active for at least eight hundred years. The combined total of bronze vessels from all the excavations between 1928 and 1937 in An-yang is only 176, much smaller than the number of bronze vessels from this one tomb! The tomb thus gives us a much truer measure about both the range and the attainment of Shang art and technology at the beginning of the Yin period.

Moreover, the name of the tomb mistress is known, and she is a historical personage well known from previous research on oracle bone inscriptions. Many of the bronze vessels and weapons and a few jade and stone pieces were inscribed, and the bulk of the inscriptions contain seven names or emblems. The name Fu Hao appears on more than sixty objects; Hou Hsin appears on at least five objects, including two large square cauldrons; Hou T'u appears on some twenty objects; the three ya-names and the seventh name, an emblem, appear on a relatively few pieces. Fu Hao, or Lady Hao (Lady from the Tzu clan), was, in addition to being one of Wu Ting's sixty-four known wives, a prominent personage whose name and activities appear often in oracle bone inscriptions of of the Wu Ting period. She is known from the inscriptions to have been

19. Selected artifacts from the Fu Hao tomb (after *Jen-min Hua-pao,* 1977:6, 1978:1).

a leader of military campaigns; she was made mistress of a landed estate outside the royal capital; she was sometimes in charge of specific rituals; and she was the subject of Wu Ting's divinations concerning her illnesses, child births, and general well-being. She died during Wu Ting's long reign.[35] The name Hou Hsin (Queen Hsin) is also significant: In the ritual calendar of later Shang kings (to be described later), Wu Ting was shown to have been paired with three official wives: Hsin 辛, Kuei 癸, and Wu 戊. Since these are believed to be posthumous names, Queen Hsin was evidently the posthumous name of the wife who was known in her lifetime as Fu Hao. The fact that in this tomb in the same bronze assemblage the names Fu Hao and Hou Hsin occur together is reasonable proof that these names referred to the same person, the person known as Fu Hao in Wu Ting period inscriptions (fig. 20). This is the first time in Shang history that an archaeological find can be identified with a historical individual.[36]

Palace Foundations. The most prominent archaeological feature at Hsiao-t'un for the dynastic period is the *hang-t'u* 夯土 ("stamped or rammed earth") foundations of above-ground houses, known in Chinese archaeological terminology as *chi chih* 基址 ("foundation sites"). Strictly speaking, *chi chih* may be built on solid and level ground without any *hang-t'u*, but most of the above-ground houses at Hsiao-t'un were built on at least some thin *hang-t'u* foundations and some of them were constructed on thick foundations as deep as 3 meters, consisting of as many as 30 layers of stamped earth (fig. 21). Most of the foundations are square or rectangular, although some may be irregular. On the foundations a timber structure was built, sometimes with posts rested on boulders or bronze disks as supports, and then wattle-and-daub walls and thatched roofs were built. Extant archaeological remains consist of the foundations, post holes and some boulder or bronze post supports, and wattle-and-daub fragments presumably fallen from walls.[37] Some of the post holes and boulders show evidence of fire, suggesting that these

35. Wang Yü-hsin 王宇信, Chang Yung-shan 張永山, and Yang Sheng-nan 楊升南, "Shih lun Yin hsü wu-hao mu ti 'Fu Hao'" 試論殷墟五號墓的'婦好'.

36. There is another Fu Hao in the oracle bone inscriptions of a later period, and some scholars are inclined to identify Tomb Number Five with the later Fu Hao; see *KK*, "An-yang Yin hsü wu-hao mu tso-t'an chi-yao" 安陽殷墟五號墓座談紀要. But the combination of Fu Hao and Hou Hsin strongly favors the earlier identification, and the art style as a whole of the Fu Hao tomb assemblage also points to an earlier rather than later dating.

37. Shih Chang-ju 石璋如, "Hsiao-t'un Yin tai ti chien-chu yi-chi" 小屯殷代的建築遺蹟; *Yin hsü chien-chu yi-ts'un* 殷虛建築遺存; "Yin tai ti hang-t'u pan-chu yü yi-pan chien-chu" 殷代的夯土版築與一般建築.

38. Shih Chang-ju 石璋如, *Yin hsü chien-chu yi-ts'un* 殷虛建築遺存, pp. 49–50.

20. Fu Hao (*left*) and Hou Hsin (*right*) in the bronze inscriptions from the Fu Hao tomb (from *KKHP*, "An-yang Yin hsü wu-hao mu ti fa-chüeh").

21. A house foundation made of rammed earth (after Shih Chang-ju, *Yin hsü chien-chu yi-ts'un*).

buildings were burnt down.[38] On the basis of posthole and boulder patterns, Shih Chang-yu has reconstructed three houses from the Dynastic Shang period at Hsiao-t'un[39] (fig. 22).

Fifty-three *hang-t'u* foundations were excavated by the Institute of History and Philology before the war at Hsiao-t'un Locus North. The longest foundation is 85 meters long and 14.5 meters wide and the largest is at least 70 meters long and 40 m wide. Shih Chang-ju groups these into three clusters, the Northern Group (or *chia* 甲-group), consisting of 15 foundations; the Middle Group (or *yi* 乙-group), 21 foundations; and the Southern Group (or *ping* 丙-group), 17 foundations[40] (fig. 23). In view of their sometimes massive size, their regular arrangement, and the many sacrificial burials that appear to be associated with some of the houses (to be described below), these houses have been described as palaces or temples, and Hsiao-t'un Locus North is generally believed to be the center of the An-yang core.

The fifteen foundations of the *Northern Group*, located in Grids D and E in an area about 100 meters from north to south and 90 meters from east to west, are for the most part arranged parallel to one another, running lengthwise north-south. The larger houses had their doors facing east, but the smaller ones faced south. No human or animal sacrificial burials were found in this area. Shih believes that these buildings were residential. On the basis of stratigraphy and associated materials, Shih believes, further, that the Northern Group of houses was the earliest to be built, perhaps during the reign of Wu Ting, although the houses continued to be occupied until the end of Yin. If he is right, the settlement layout at Hsiao-t'un during the earliest segment of the Dynastic period consisted of a residential area in the north and a burial area (where the Fu Hao tomb is located) about 300 meters to the southwest.

The Middle Group, consisting of twenty-one house foundations in an elevated area about 200 meters north-south by 100 meters east-west, largely within excavation grids B and C, is regarded by Shih to be the next group to be constructed, possibly begun by Tsu Chia's reign. Here most (sixteen) houses had their doors facing south, and only a few (four) faced east. Many of the massive houses seem to have been placed in relation to one another in accordance with an overall plan. The layout began in the north, with Foundation *yi*-1, a square platform of pure yellow earth. Other houses then ran south, possibly in two rows

39. Shih Chang-ju 石璋如, "Yin tai ti-shang chien-chu fu-yüan chih yi li" 殷代地上建築復原之一例; "Yin tai ti-shang chien-chu fu-yüan ti ti-erh li" 殷代地上建築復原的第二例; "Yin tai ti-shang chien-chu fu-yüan ti ti-san li" 殷代地上建築復原的第三例.

40. Shih Chang-ju 石璋如, *Yin hsü chien-chu yi-ts'un* 殷虛建築遺存.

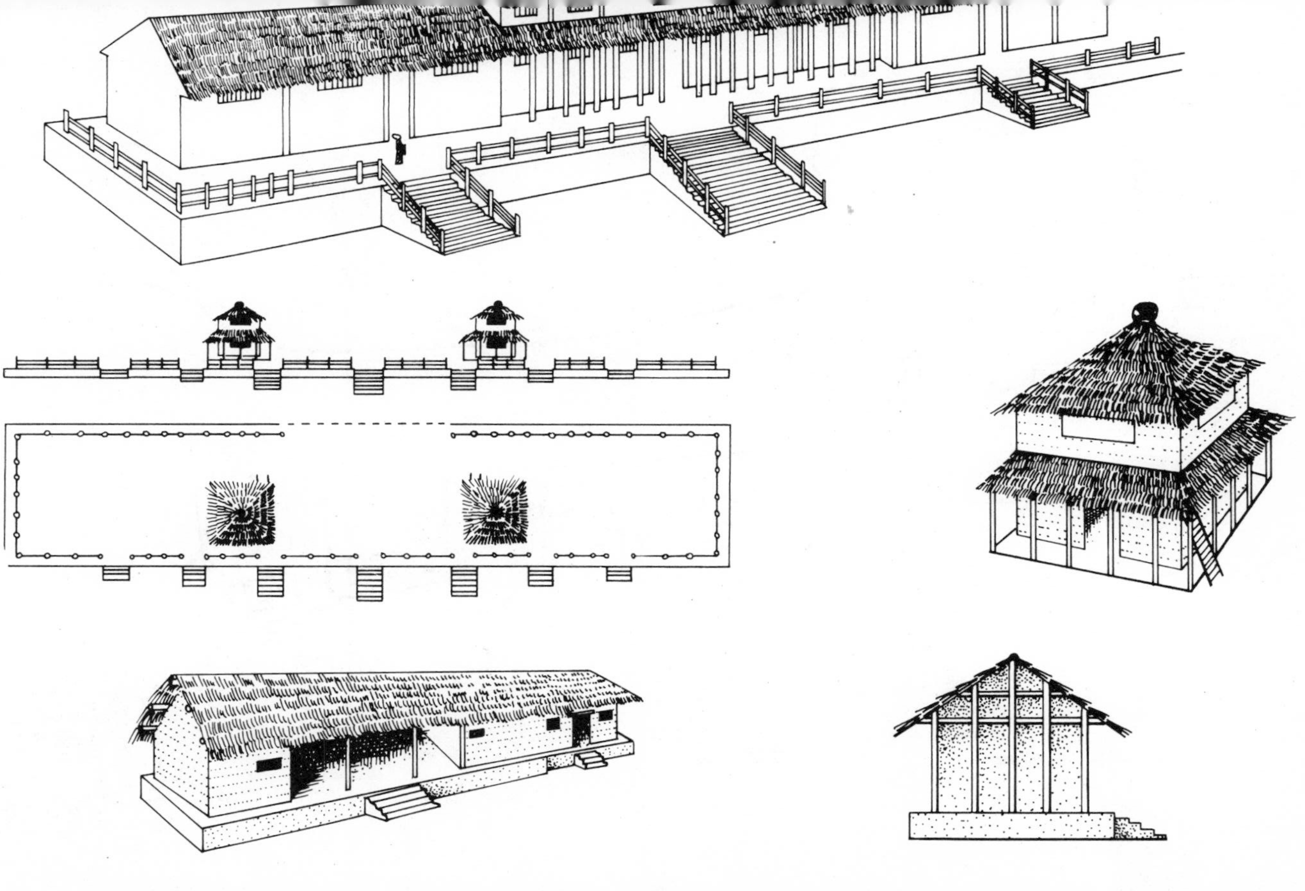

22. Three reconstructions of ground houses at Hsiao-t'un (*bottom*, after Shih Chang-ju, "Yin tai ti-shang chien-chu fu-yüan chih yi li"; *middle*, after his "Yin tai ti-shang chien-chu fu-yüan ti ti erh li"; *top*, after his "Yin tai ti-shang chien-chu fu-yüan ti ti-san li").

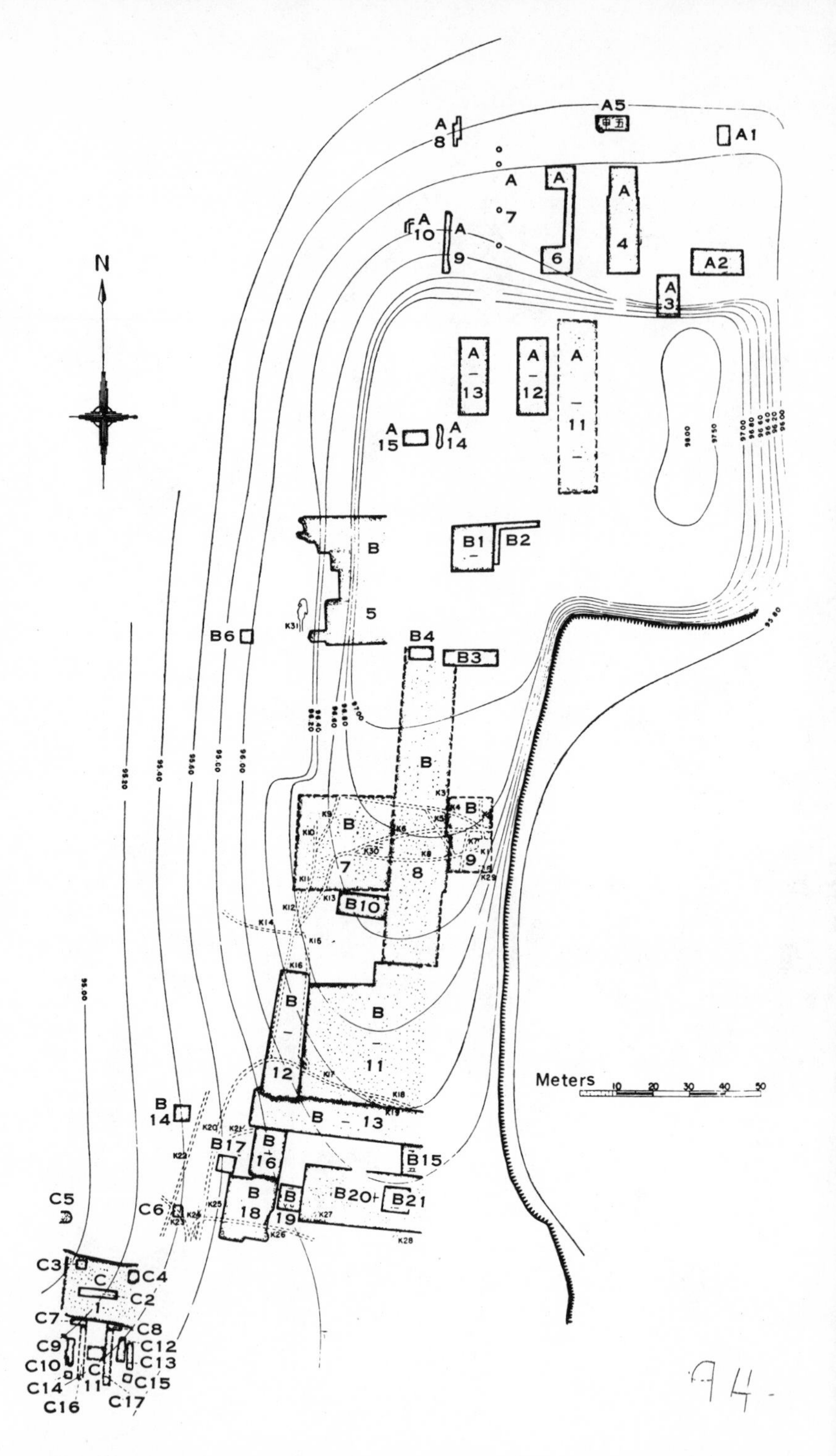

23. Ground plan of the three groups of house floors at Hsiao-t'un (after Shih Chang-ju, *Yin hsü chieh-chu yi-ts'un*, fig. 4). (A—Northern Group; B—Middle Group; C—Southern Group.)

symmetrically on the east and the west. In the middle, south of the platform, were three houses (*yi*-3, *yi*-9, and *yi*-11) and a series of five gates (three on *yi*-3, one on *yi*-9, and one on *yi*-11) pointing south. Furthermore, in this area were a number of sacrificial burials of humans, animals, and chariots (fig. 24). Shih believes that these burials, especially those near foundation *yi*-7 (fig. 25), were a part of the construction process of some of the houses, offered as sacrifices during the foundation laying, post erecting, door installing, and completing processes.[41] Associating all the burials with the construction process may be tenuous, and some were possible sacrificial burials independent of the construction. But these sacrificial burials indicate the ritual nature of these houses, which may thus be described tentatively as temples.

The Southern Group, consisting of seventeen small foundations, is the strangest. In an area only 50 by 35 meters, the houses were dominated by the largest foundation of the group, *ping*-1, in the north, facing south, and then small houses were arranged north to south in two groups in the east and the west. A number of sacrificial burials, humans on the right and animals on the left, also accompanied the foundations, which seem to have constituted a separate quarter for specific ritual uses.[42] Shih believes that this group was constructed the latest, possibly toward the end of the Yin period.

Accessory Buildings. Other than the ever-expanding block of above-ground houses and the burial ground for important people as represented by the Fu Hao Tomb (use of which may have been discontinued after Wu Ting because of the expansion of the palatial block, while the royal burials became concentrated in Hsi-pei-kang, north of the Huan River), the Shang settlement at Hsiao-t'un included other buildings and their associated activities. At least three major categories of such buildings, which were all semi-subterranean or underground, can be distinguished : dwellings, storage pits, and workshops.

The pit houses in essence carried on the predynastic tradition, with their roundish shape, an occasional stair, and low walls in some cases. "The contents of these pit houses were mostly animal bones and potsherds, all necessities of daily life."[43] Numerous such pit houses have been found at Hsiao-t'un; some were underneath the above-ground house foundations, some were built beside and amidst them, and others

41. Shih Chang-ju 石璋如, "Hsiao-t'un C-ch'ü ti mu-tsang ch'ün" 小屯C區的墓葬羣.

42. Shih Chang-ju 石璋如, "Hsiao-t'un Yin tai Ping tsu chi-chih chi ch'i yu-kuan hsien-hsiang" 小屯殷代丙組基址及其有關現象.

43. Kuo Pao-chün 郭寶鈞, "B-ch'ü fa-chüeh chi chih erh" B區發掘記之二, 603.

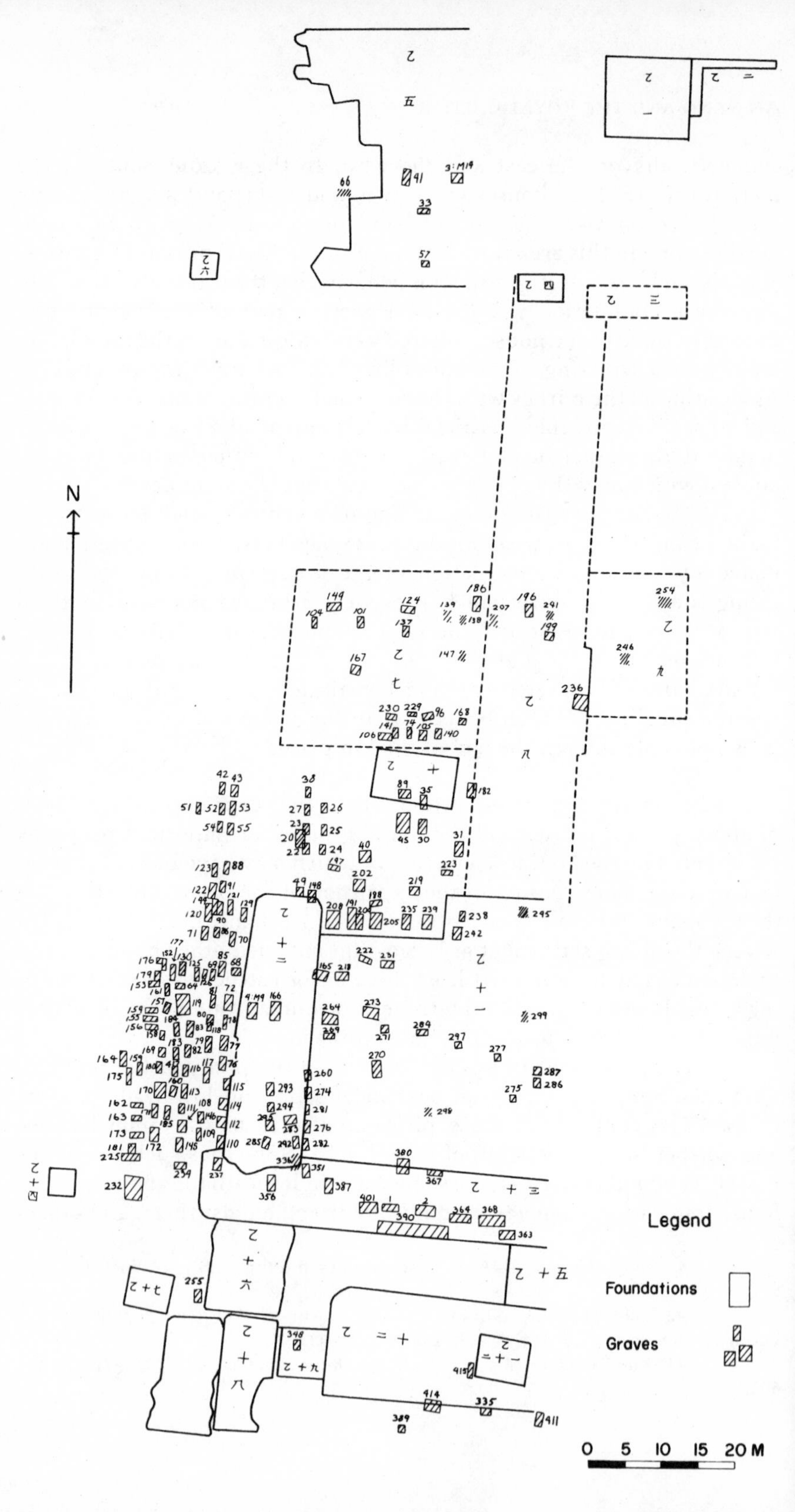

24. Ground plan of the house floors and associated graves in the Middle Group at Hsiao-t'un (after Shih Chang-ju, *Pei tsu mu-tsang*, fig. 2).

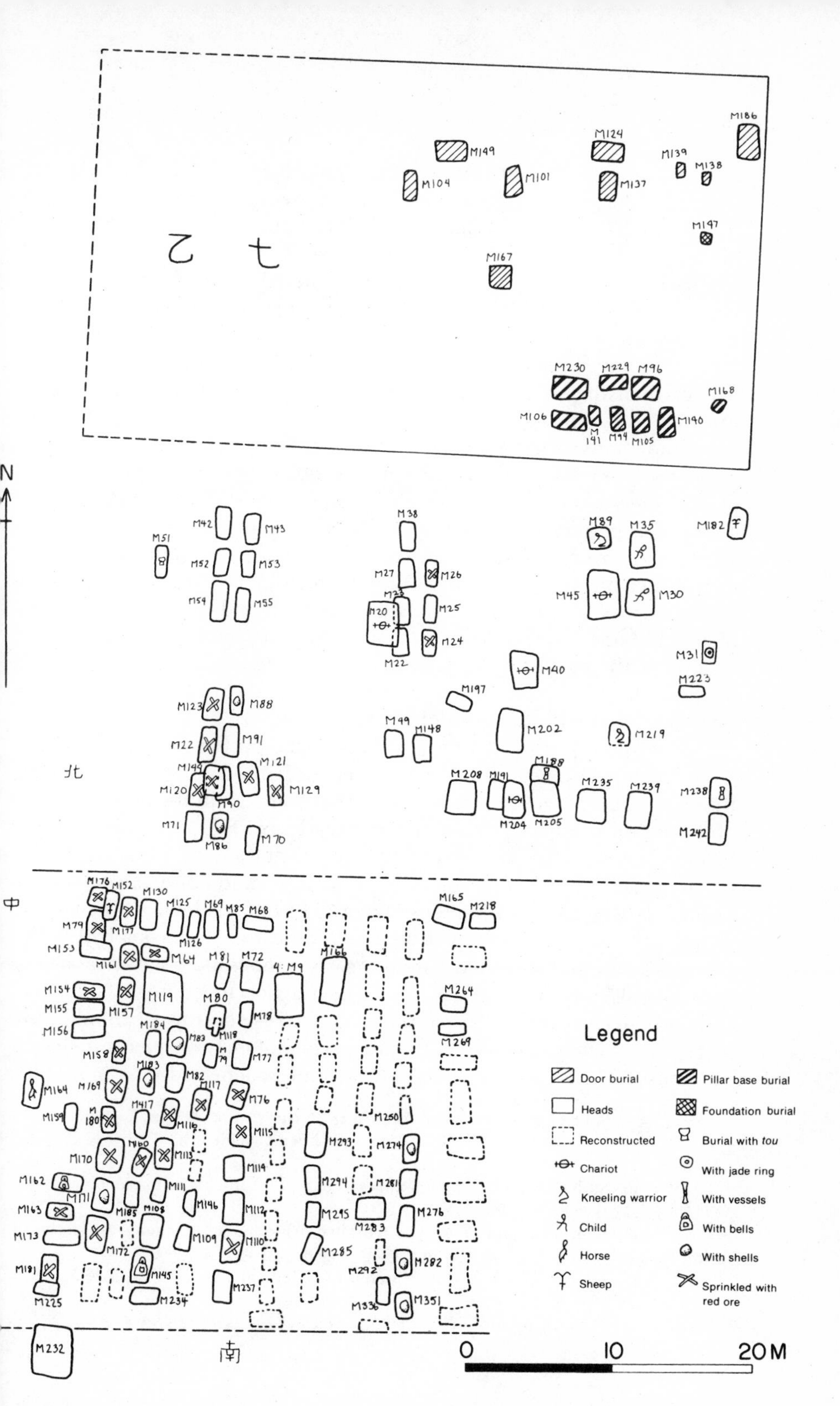

25. House floor *yi*-7 in the Middle Group at Hsiao-t'un and the burials believed to be associated with its construction (after Shih Chang-ju, *Pei tsu mu-tsang*, fig. 3).

intruded into them, testifying to their long history of use but varying lengths of individual occupation.[44] If the above-ground houses included the dwellings of the royal family and other important people, then these pit houses were probably domiciles of the support, maintenance, and service personnel, although the absence of detailed reporting about these pits makes it impossible to study the precise relationship of specific pit houses with specific ground houses.

Storage pits were rectangular or round in ground plan and often deeper than they were wide. Many such storage pits contained pure, greenish soil, and were apparently granaries.[45] Others have yielded important finds:[46] large numbers of bronze weapons, oracle bones, and white pottery from pit H-16, near ground house *chia*-2; large numbers of oracle bones and fragmented musical stones from H-20 near *chia*-6; a set of thirteen pottery *tou*-dishes and pottery jars from H-196 near *yi*-17; several dozen burned spaculae from H-001 near *yi*-5; and the spectacular H-127 pit near *yi*-7 and *yi*-12, in which more than three hundred whole turtle plastrons and more than ten thousand pieces of fragments of oracle bones were found in 1936.[47] Apparently a large part of the wealth of the royal house, including grains, precious objects, and the oracle archives, formed the content of many of the underground storage pits associated with the ground houses.

From the scattered descriptions of the pit houses it is clear that the residents of some of them engaged in specialized industrial activities. Kuo Pao-chün observed a major industrial complex in the northern part of the middle group of ground houses as early as 1933: "Several hundred bronze-casting molds and several tens of crucibles were found near B-15 (in the northern end of the middle group of ground houses), probably a bronze-casting area; several tens of worked stones, jades, and shells, and nearly a thousand stone knives were found near or to the north of B-14, perhaps a jade and stone workshop; nearly a thousand bone arrowheads and several hundred pieces of bone materials occurred near B-12, possibly a bone-working area".[48] Another bronze-working area, indicated by as many as ten pit houses containing clay molds (1,610 pieces in one of the houses),[49] with two of them possibly interconnected into an under-

44. Shih Chang-ju 石璋如, *Yin hsü chien-chu yi-ts'un* 殷虛建築遺存.

45. Kuo Pao-chün 郭寶鈞, "B-ch'ü fa-chüeh chi chih erh" B區發掘記之二, 605–606.

46. Shih Chang-ju 石璋如, "Yin tai ti hang-t'u pan-chu yü yi-pan chien-chu" 殷代的夯土版築與一般建築, 133.

47. Shih Chang-ju 石璋如, "Yin hsü tsui-chin chih chung-yao fa-hsien fu lun Hsiao-t'un ti-ts'eng" 殷墟最近之重要發現附論小屯地層, 7–8.

48. Kuo Pao-chün 郭寶鈞, "B-ch'ü fa-chüeh chi chih yi" B區發掘記之一, 594.

49. Shih Chang-ju 石璋如, *Yin hsü chien-chu yi-ts'un* 殷虛建築遺存, p. 75.

ground molten-metal pouring system,[50] only slightly to the northwest of the bronze workshop near B-15, is possibly an extension of it.

Outside this major industrial area, at least two other workshops have been found in Hsiao-t'un Locus North, one in the northeastern part of the site and the other in the southwestern extremity. The former is represented by storage pit E-181, in which were found, other than potsherds, 760 pieces of animal bones, 102 bone objects, 535 molluscan shells, 78 shell object pieces, 89 pieces of stone, 444 stone knives, various stone objects, 1,179 turtle shell places, 163 cowrie shells, and various and sundry other objects.[51] The other workshop was brought to light in 1975, including a complex of pit houses, a storage pit, and large numbers of grinding stones, unfinished stone artifacts, and stone blanks.[52]

CHRONOLOGICAL SUBDIVISIONS OF THE DYNASTIC PERIOD

The dynastic period at Hsiao-t'un, according to *Ku pen Chu shu chi nien* and other sources, lasted for 273 years and included the reigns of twelve kings. The issue of dating an artifact, a house, or an event archaeologically within this not too brief segment is of considerable importance to Shang archaeology and history. Stratigraphy is only useful in isolated circumstances since a Hsiao-t'un-wide stratigraphy has never been worked out by the excavators.[53] The ground houses did not overlap, so that their chronological interrelationship can only be conjectured at from their stratigraphical relationships with other structures and their artifactual association. Good chronological sequence, however, is available by using the changing characteristics of two categories of archaeological finds: oracle bone inscriptions and pottery. Bone hairpins provide a third potentially useful chronological yardstick.

Dating the Oracle Bone Inscriptions. No oracle bone inscriptions dating from the first three kings in Yin (P'an Keng, Hsiao Hsin, Hsiao Yi) have yet been identified.[54] Therefore, all oracle bone inscriptions that

50. Shih Chang-ju 石璋如, "Yin tai ti chu t'ung kung-yi" 殷代的鑄銅工藝, 124–125.

51. Shih Chang-ju 石璋如, "Ti-ch'i-tz'u Yin hsü fa-chüeh: E-ch'ü kung-tso pao-kao" 第七次殷墟發掘：E區工作報告, 722–723.

52. *KK*, "1975 nien An-yang Yin hsü ti hsin fa-hsien" 1975年安陽殷墟的新發現.

53. Tsou Heng 鄒衡, "Shih lun Yin hsü wen-hua fen-ch'i" 試論殷墟文化分期 is a noble attempt but cannot be used as the definitive source because he had to cull his information from incompletely published materials.

54. Ch'en Meng-chia 陳夢家, *Yin hsü p'u-tz'u tsung shu* 殷墟卜辭綜述, p. 139.

have been found so far in Hsiao-t'un (and elsewhere within An-yang) belong to the period in Shang history covered by nine kings: Wu Ting, Tsu Keng, Tsu Chia, Lin Hsin, K'ang Ting, Wu Yi, Wen Wu Ting, Ti Yi, and Ti Hsin. (The names are given here according a modified genealogy not identical with that of *Yen pen chi*; see chapter 3 for details.) Dating the oracle bone inscriptions is in fact to date them to the individual reigns of the nine kings. This, however, is not an easy operation, because none of of the inscriptions was marked by a reign name. But, since almost all of the inscriptions pertained to activities within the royal family, deceased kings were referred to by their posthumous cyclical signs, together with kin terms. The kings referred to, however, often cannot be specifically identified, because many of them had the same cyclical signs, and the father and his brothers were indistinguishably referred to by the same term, *fu* 父. A Fu Yi 父乙, for example, referred to in an oracle record, could have been Hsiao Yi, father of Wu Ting, or Wu Yi, father of Wen Wu Ting, or Ti Yi, father of Ti Hsin. A Fu Ting 父丁 could have been Wu Ting, father of both Tsu Keng and Tsu Chia, or K'ang Ting, father of Wu Yi, or Wen Wu Ting, father of Ti Yi.

The identity of an ancestor referred to in the oracle record can be narrowed down further when some of the less commonly used signs appear and when several fathers were mentioned together. A piece with the name Father Hsin on it is likely of either Wu Ting's period or else Wu Yi's, and a piece with the names of all four fathers, Father Chia, Father Keng, Father Hsin, and Father Yi, can only be of Wu Ting's period, and so forth. This method of dating was the earliest used,[55] but it is far from precise in most cases, not only because many kings used the same cyclical signs but also because the names of many of the kings' other deceased ancestors besides those who were earlier kings also appear in the inscriptions, vastly confusing the identity problem.[56]

The most important criterion for dating, to supplement that based on the ancestral names when they are clearly known and to supercede them when they are not, is the name of the inquirer. Tung Tso-pin was the first scholar to recognize the character in the oracle bone inscriptions before the character *chen* 貞 (to ask, inquire) as the name of the inquirer and to discover that the fact that their names sometime occur together on the same bone or shell provides a sound basis for grouping them into "inquirers' groups" that served at the courts of individual kings.[57] The first such group that Tung worked out, in large

55. Wang Kuo-wei 王國維, "Tsu mou fu mou hsiung mou" 祖某父某兄某.

56. Ch'en Meng-chia 陳夢家, "Shang wang miao-hao k'ao 商王廟號考, 5. Kaizuka Shigeki 貝塚茂樹, *Kyōto Daigaku Jinbun Kagaku Kenkyūjo shozō kōkotsu moji* 京都大学人文科学研究所所藏甲骨文字, pp. 106–109.

57. Tung Tso-pin 董作賓, "Ta kuei ssu pan k'ao shih" 大龜四版考釋.

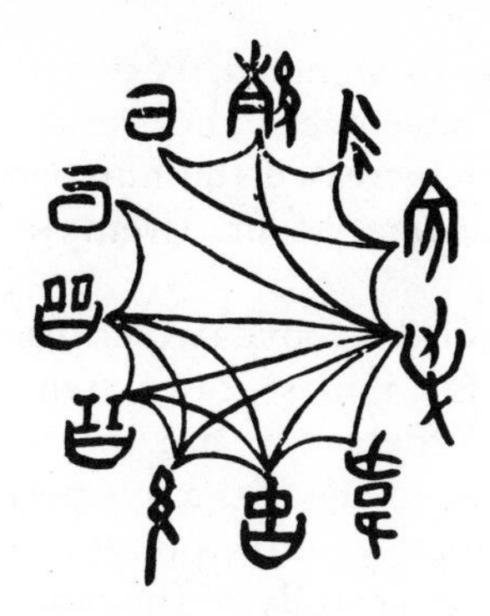

26. Tung Tso-pin's first group of *chen-jen*, who served at King Wu Ting's court (after Tung Tso-pin, "Ta kuei ssu pan k'ao shih").

part based on two turtle plastrons with concurrent inquirers' signatures,[58] was one consisting of the names in fig. 26. This group can be firmly dated to King Wu Ting's reign because over the signatures of some of them, rituals having to do with "Father Yi" and "Mother Keng" were divined about.[59] Since the only King Yi with a wife named Keng was Hsiao Yi, we know that the inquirers must have served on Wu Ting's court. The same process can then be repeated, taking into account an ever-increasing data base. In 1933, when Tung Tso-pin published his ground-breaking "Chia-ku-wen tuan-tan yen-chiu li",[60] he was able to group the nine kings into five periods, on the basis of the inquirers' groups and other criteria:

Period I	Wu Ting (and his three predecessors)	11 inquirers
Period II	Tsu Keng, Tsu Chia	6 inquirers
Period III	Lin Hsin, K'ang T'ing	8 inquirers
Period IV	Wu Yi, Wen Wu Ting	0 inquirers
Period V	Ti Yi, Ti Hsin	1 inquirers

Subsequent research by Tung himself and by several other scholars following his lead has substantially increased the numbers of inquirers who can be identified within each period, and in many cases has enabled scholars to make finer subdivisions within some of the periods. Tung's latest work increased the number of known Period I inquirers to twenty

58. *Ibid.*, p. 440.

59. Tung Tso-pin 董作賓, "Chia ku wen tuan-tai yen-chiu li" 甲骨文斷代研究例, 347.

60. *Ibid.*

five, Period II inquirers to eighteen, Period III inquirers to thirteen, Period IV inquirers to seventeen, and Period V inquirers to four.[61] Shima Kunio has further increased the numbers in the five periods to thirty-six, twenty-four, twenty-four, twenty-four, and seven, respectively[62] (fig. 27).

The application of the above two criteria—ancestral names and inquirers' signatures—is in most cases, where these two items of information, or at least the latter, are included in the inscriptions, sufficient to date the piece to one of the five periods or even to the reign of a single king. Unfortunately, at the present time there is a major controversy in the chronological study of the oracle bone inscriptions that involves the assignment of a few important inquirers to Period I or Period IV. This concerns in the main two groups of inquirers, one comprising of [oracle bone graphs] and other associated names (often including [oracle bone graph], the king himself), and the other of [oracle bone graphs] and their associated names. The first group is referred to as the [oracle bone graph] group by Ch'en Meng-chia[63] but as the "Royal Family" group of inquirers by Kaizuka Shigeki,[64] and the second is referred to as the [oracle bone graph] group by Ch'en and as the "Groups of Princes" inquirers by Kaizuka. Both Ch'en and Kaizuka place these two groups in Wu Ting's reign and, thus, as part of Period I, although Ch'en specified that they belonged to a later subperiod. He believed that these groups of inquirers probably served groups of noblemen only overlapping with or outside the royal family, but Kaizuka thinks that the Royal Family inquirers served the kings' private lineage interests (as against the Court's public interests served by the other Wu Ting period inquirers) and that the Groups of Princes inquirers served the Groups of Princes, a speculated paramilitary organization of the royal princes. Tung Tso-pin, on the other hand, put them both together into his Period IV (the reigns of Wu Yi and Wen Tu Ting).[65] Tung readily concedes that in significant ways the secondary characteristics of his Period IV inscriptions are similar to Period I inscriptions, but he uses this point as a principal basis for his theory of "Old School" and "New

61. *Chia ku hsüeh liu-shih nien* 甲骨學六十年, pp. 79–86.

62. *Inkyo bokuji kenkyū* 般墟卜辭研究, p. 34.

63. Ch'en Meng-chia 陳夢家, "Chia ku tuan-tai yü k'eng wei—Chia-ku tuan-tai hsüeh ting p'ien" 甲骨斷代與坑位—甲骨斷代學丁篇; *Yin hsü p'u-tz'u tsung shu* 般墟卜辭綜述, pp. 145–155, 158–161.

64. Kaizuka Shigeki 貝塚茂樹, *Chūgoku kodai shigaku no hatten* 中国古代史学の発展; Kaizuka Shigeki 貝塚茂樹 and Itō Michiharu 伊藤道治, "Kōkotsubun dandaihō no saikentō—Tōshi no Bunbutei jidai bokuji o chūshin to shite" 甲骨文断代法の再検討—董氏の文武丁時代卜辞を中心として; Kaizuka Shigeki 貝塚茂樹, *Kyōto Daigaku Jinbun kagaku kenkyūjo shozō kōkotsu moji* 京都大学人文科学研究所所藏甲骨文字.

65. *Yin li p'u* 般曆譜; *Yin hsü wen-tzu yi pien hsü* 般虛文字乙編序.

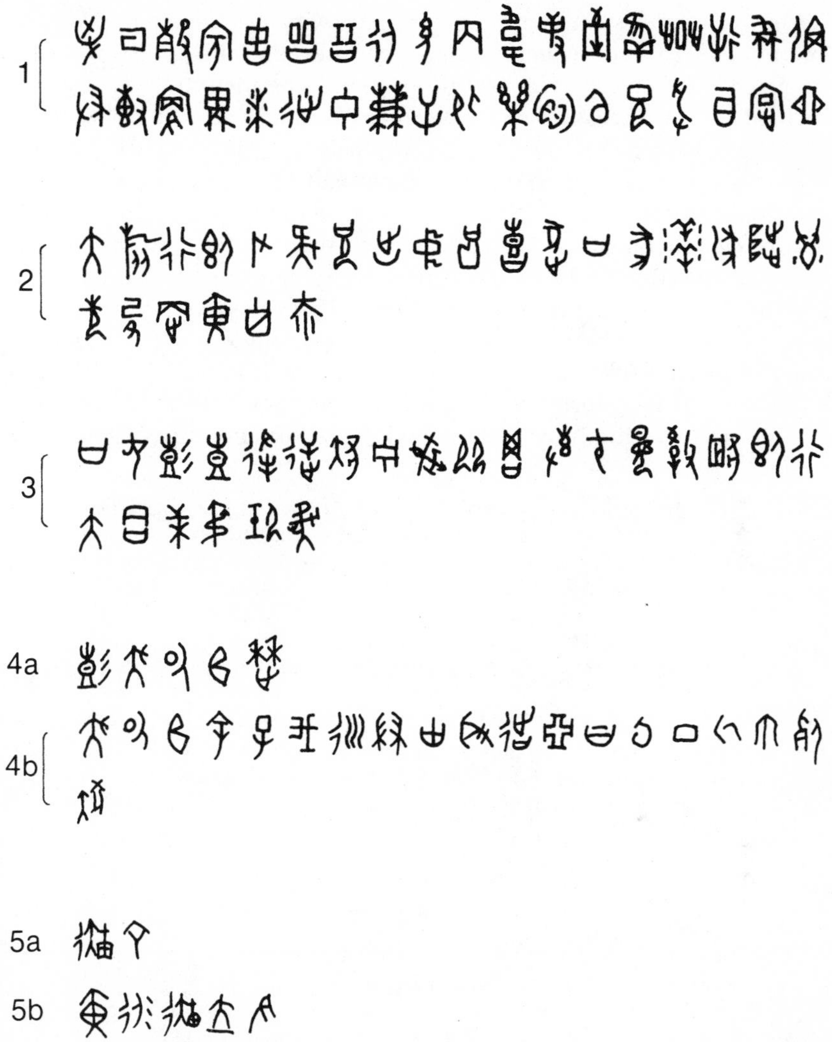

1

2

3

4a

4b

5a

5b

27. The *chen-jen* of five periods according to Shima Kunio. *4a* are *chen-jen* he has assigned to Wu Yi, *4b* to Wen Wu Ting, *5a* to Ti Yi, *5b* to Ti Hsin (after his *Inkyo bokuji kenkyū*).

School'' oppositions during the Yin period—Old School Wu Ting, Period II (mainly Tsu Chia) innovation, Period IV Return to Old School, and Period V Return to Reformation. (This point will be returned to in chapter 3.)

On the basis of the two main criteria for dating oracle bone inscriptions—ancestral names and inquirers' names concurrent on the same bones—this controversy cannot be resolved. The ancestral names associated with these two groups of inquirers include, but are not confined to, the ancestral names of both Wu Ting and Wu Yi-Wen Wu Ting, and are, therefore, not conclusive evidence. These names, further, are not found associated with any of established Period I names;[66] Ch'en and Kaizuka's explanation is that it is because they belonged to separate divining establishments, but it appears clear that on this point the burden of proof—that there *were* separate divining establishments—is on them. Most of the assignments on both sides relate to relatively secondary issues or stand on the strength of this or that single piece of evidence which is often itself subject to varying interpretations.[67] Two recent studies on this issue brought forward weighty new evidence; however one favors the Period I assignment[68] while the other adds real substance

66. The oracle record Chia-2361 (In *Chia pien* 甲編) has characters for Pin (Period I inquirer) and Fu (Period IV inquirer), but the context there is not clear, and it is far from certain that they are used as inquirers' names. See Hsü Chin-hsiung 許進雄, *P'u ku shang ti tsao tsuan hsing-t'ai* 卜骨上的鑿鑽形態, p. 4.

67. *On Tung's side*:

Shima Kunio 島邦男, *Inkyo bokuji kenkyū* 殷墟卜辞研究.

Li Hsüeh-ch'in 李學勤, "P'ing Ch'en Meng-chia *Yin hsü p'u-tz'u tsung shu*" 評陳夢家殷墟卜辭綜述.

Yen Yi-p'ing 嚴一萍, "Chia ku wen tuan-tai yen-chiu hsin li" 甲骨文斷代研究新例.

Yen Yi-p'ing 嚴一萍, *Chia ku hsüeh* 甲骨學.

Hsü Chin-hsiung 許進雄, *The Menzies Collection of Shang Dynasty Oracle Bones*.

On Ch'en's and Kaizuka's side:

Hu Hou-hsüan 胡厚宣, *Chia ku hsü ts'un* 甲骨續存.

Ikeda Suetoshi 池田末利, "Shima shi *Inkyo bokuji kenkyū* o yomu" 島氏殷墟卜辞研究を讀む.

Jao Tsung-yi 饒宗頤, *Yin tai chen p'u jen-wu t'ung k'ao* 殷代貞卜人物通考.

Ch'ü Wan-li 屈萬里, *Yin hsü wen-tzu Chia pien k'ao shih* 殷虛文字甲編考釋.

68. *KK*, "1973 nien Hsiao-t'un nan-ti fa-chüeh chien pao" 1973年小屯南地發掘簡報; Hsiao Nan 肖楠, "An-yang Hsiao-t'un nan-ti fa-hsien ti 'Shih tsu p'u chia'—chien lun 'Shih tsu p'u tz'u' ti shih-tai chi ch'i hsiang-kuan wen-t'i" 安陽小屯南地發現的'自組卜甲'—兼論'自組卜辭'的時代及其相關問題.

The archaeological association ("pit location" in Tung's ten criteria of dating) of inscribed oracle bones is very tricky as a practical yardstick. Many Period I and Period IV pieces were found in the same pits (see Shih Chang-ju 石璋如, *Yin hsü chien-chu yi-ts'un* 殷墟建築遺存), but the dating of the pit depends on dating of the inscriptions, but not, in most cases, vice versa. In fact, the association of these two groups of oracle bones favors Tung's "Old School" theory (archives of the same school being housed together) rather than Ch'en and Kaizuka's theory of contemporary but separate divining establishments (which could demand separate storage facilities). As for the Hsiao-t'un Locus South association of Shih (自)-group pieces together with Early Period pottery, it is certainly highly significant, but the stratum where the pieces in question were found

to Period IV classification.[69] I am persuaded by the latter study as well as by the intellectual force of Tung Tso-pin's original presentation. In the absence of clinching evidence (such as indisputable and recurrent new finds of the concurrence of inquirers' names), I prefer the simpler scheme of Tung to the more complex but non-corroborated schemes of Ch'en and Kaizuka.

With this controversial issue decided upon (but not yet resolved) for the time being, it is possible to date many inscribed oracle bone pieces when information about inquirers is available thereon. But all oracle bone fragments do not necessarily give this information, and thus supplementary criteria—all derived from the characteristics of already firmly dated pieces—must be employed. Tung Tso-pin in his 1933 study listed ten criteria for dating oracle bone inscriptions, as follows: royal genalogy, modes of address, names of inquirers, pit location, tribes and states referred to, personalities, kinds of events inquired about, grammar, structure of characters, and style of writing.[70] Tung's subsequent studies have further elaborated upon some of these latter, secondary, criteria,[71] and the last two—structure of characters and style of writing—actually play important parts in the controversy just described. Hsü Chin-hsiung's recent studies of the chiseled hollows on the backs of shoulder blades add the construction of the hollows as another dating criterion.[72]

Dating the Pottery Vessels. In the pre-war excavations pottery constituted the bulk of the archaeological remains from Hsiao-t'un:[73] 247,565 pieces of potsherds and more than 1,500 complete or nearly complete pieces.[74] Li Chi's descriptive study of this group of pottery has long been available,[75] and his *Corpus of Yin Hsü Pottery* has exerted a profound influence upon the field of Chinese archaeology in providing a standard terminology of classification for vessels of whatever material. Unfortunately, the stratigraphical data for the pottery are not yet available. In a general paper on Yin pottery, Li mentioned that he already

---

had a complicated multiple intrusive stratigraphy, and secondary deposition of either oracle bones or (more likely) potsherds cannot be ruled out. See also Chin Hsiang-heng's 金祥恒 critique in his "Lun Chen-jen Fu ti fen ch'i wen-t'i" 論貞人扶的分期問題, 90–91.

69. Hsü Chin-hsiung 許進雄, *P'u ku shang ti tsao tsuan hsing-t'ai* 卜骨上的鑿鑽形態.

70. "Chia ku wen tuan-tai yen-chiu li" 甲骨文斷代研究例.

71. *Chia ku hsüeh liu-shih nien* 甲骨學六十年.

72. Hsü Chin-hsiung 許進雄, *P'u ku shang ti tsao tsuan hsing-t'ai* 卜骨上的鑿鑽形態.

73. Li Chi, "Studies of the Hsiao-t'un Pottery: Yin and Pre-Yin," p. 104.

74. Li Chi, *Hsiao-t'un t'ao ch'i* 小屯陶器, p. 36.

75. *Ibid.*

had data on the ceramic content of forty pairs of superimposed pits, and that, as mentioned earlier, only three of the lower pits were datable to the Lung-shan culture.[76] This must mean that he already has data on thirty-seven pairs of superimposed pits showing ceramic changes within the Shang period. Such data have not, as far as I know, been published, not even in Li Chi's latest synthesis of the An-yang excavations.[77]

Archaeologists who are currently working at the Shang sites in An-yang, including Hsiao-t'un, employ a fourfold ceramic chronology, which has been based upon Shang sites in Tu-ssu-k'ung-ts'un,[78] Miao-p'u-pei-ti[79] (fig. 28), as well as Locus South of Hsiao-t'un[80] (fig. 29). This chronology is best expressed through the changes in shape of a few diagnostic vessel types. The vessel *tou* began as a shallow, low-pedestalled form with a sharp, inverted V-shape rim (Period I), and changed to one with a roundish rim (Period II), later to one with a higher and thinner pedestal and in-turned rim (rare, Period III), and then to small, toy-like things, rare if not absent altogether (Period IV). As for *li*, the mouth widens and the legs shorten from earlier to later periods. The *ku* did not appear until Period II, in squat and low form, and in Period III it got taller and thinner. As for *kuei*, the rim was a sharp and inverted V in Period I, and incised triangles on the exterior reached a peak in Period IV. It has been mentioned before that Period I is probably predynastic, and Periods II–IV cover the dynastic period. The data so far published on ceramic typology are still sketchy and insufficient, but they already provide a chronological perspective for studying Li Chi's *Corpus*.

Dating the Bone Hairpins. Another category of artifact whose typological change within the Shang period at Hsiao-t'un may serve chronological purposes is the bone hairpin, which has the added advantage of being relatively simple and valueless so that even in plundered tombs hairpins have often survived to provide a chronological indicator for the site. In an excellently written essay on the bone hairpins,[81] Li Chi

76. *Ibid.*, p. 113.

77. *Anyang*.

78. *KK*, "1958–1959 nien Yin hsü fa-chüeh chien pao" 1958-1959年殷墟發掘簡報; *KK*, "1962 nien An-yang Ta-ssu-k'ung ts'un fa-chüeh chien pao" 1962年安陽大司空村發掘簡報.

79. According to the exhibition cases at the museum at Yin hsü, studied by the author in July 1977. Mr. Yang Pao-ch'eng, Mr. Ch'en Chih-ta, and Miss Cheng Chen-hsiang provided explanations.

80. *KK*, "1973 nien An-yang Hsiao-t'un nan-ti fa-chüeh chien pao" 1973年安陽小屯南地發掘簡報.

81. "Pien hsing pa lei chi ch'i wen-shih chih yen-pien" 笄形八類及其文飾之演變.

28. The four phases of Yin hsü pottery as illustrated by burial finds at Miao-p'u-pei-ti. M 248: Period I; M 17: Period II; M 237: Period III; M 105: Period IV (photo taken by author at the exhibition room at Yin hsü, 1977).

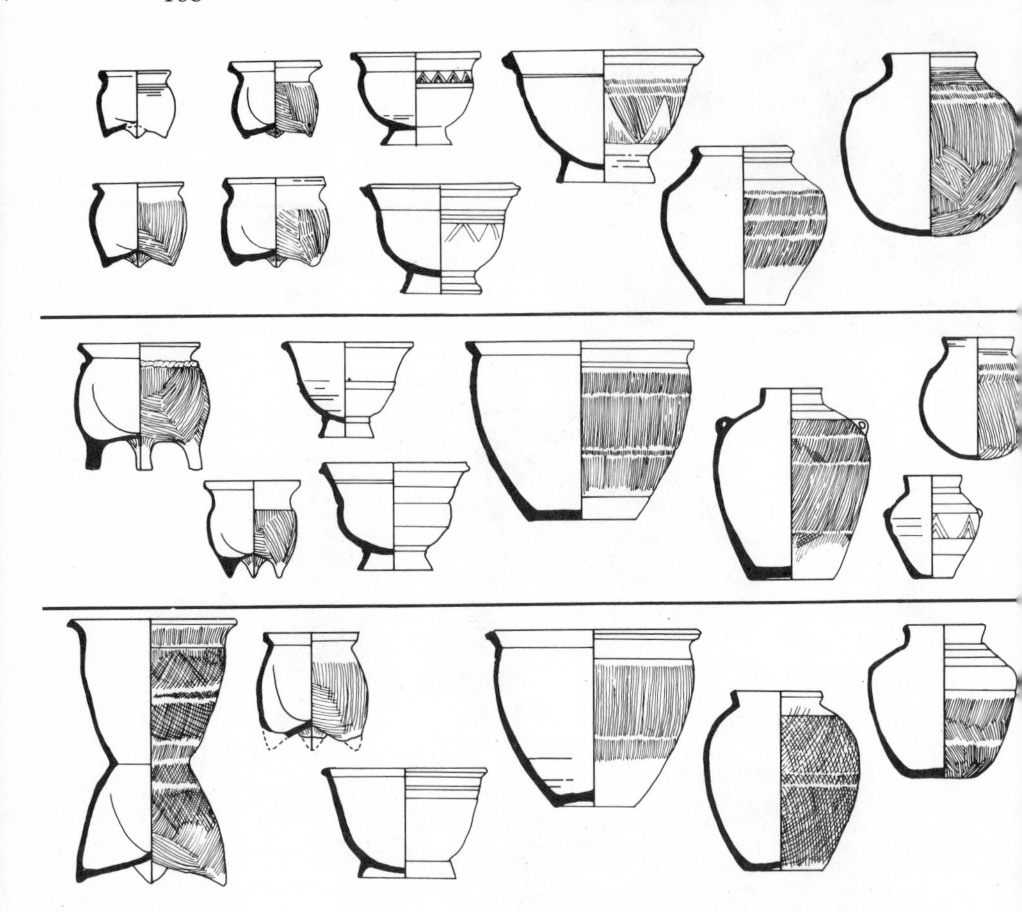

29. Three phases of ceramics at Hsiao-t'un Locus South (*Lower row:* Early; *middle row:* Middle; *upper row:* Late) (from *KK*, "1973 nien An-yang Hsiao-t'un nan-ti fa-chüeh chien pao").

described the 388 hairpins found in An-yang (mostly from Hsiao-t'un, Hsi-pei-kang, Wang-yü-k'ou, and Ta-ssu-k'ung-ts'un) under eight types distinguished according to the shape of the top: plain, incised, capped, tag-shaped, sheep-character-shaped, geometric, bird-shaped, and animal-shaped. Each type he subdivided into various varieties. On the basis of stratigraphy and other chronological indicators, Li Chi was able to work out some typological evolutionary patterns of the hairpins, which he then amplified and elaborated on a typological basis for further chronological use. The chronological arrangement of a few type loci and their hairpin samples in fig. 30 serve as a useful guide for dating on the basis of the hairpins.

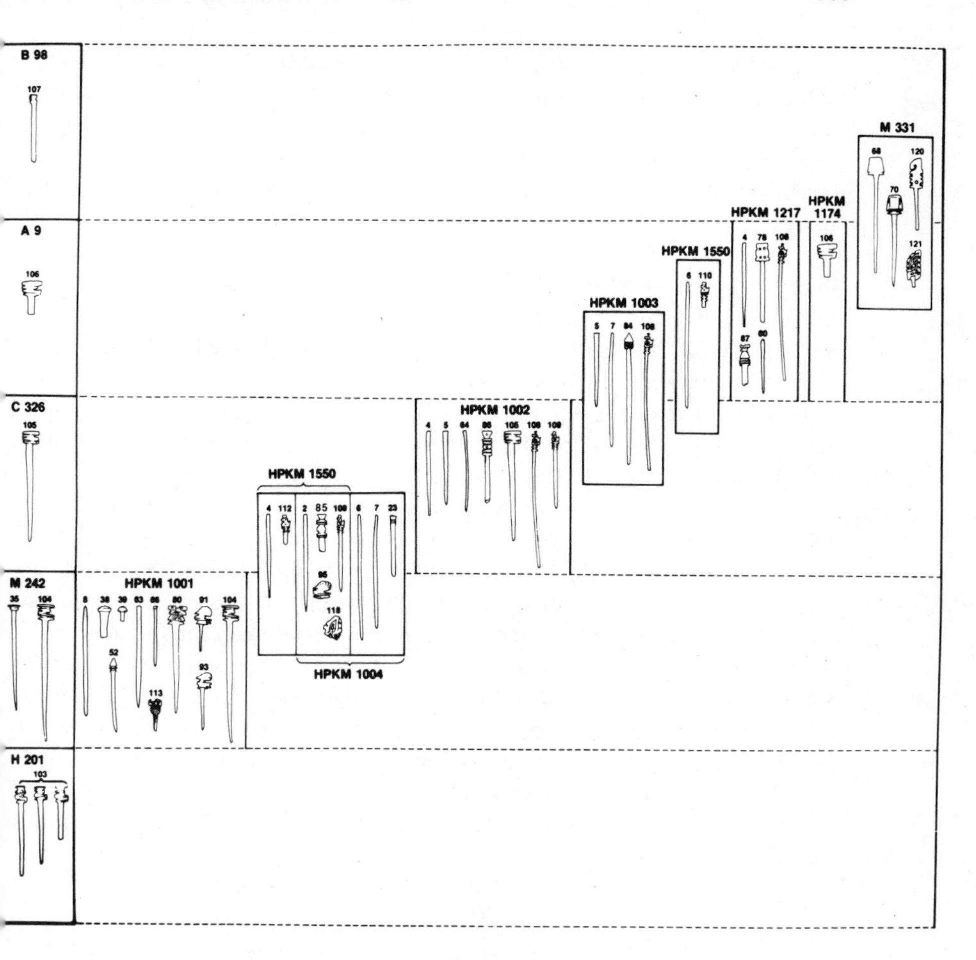

30. An-yang stratigraphy according to typological changes of bone hairpins (based on Li Chi, "Pien hsing pa lei chi ch'i wen-shih chih yen-pien").

OTHER ARCHAEOLOGICAL LOCI AT HSIAO-T'UN VILLAGE

Although archaeological excavations in Hsiao-t'un have so far concentrated in the area north of the village (Locus North), the precise perimeter of the Shang settlement there has not been clearly delineated. The river Huan flows along the northern and western borders of the archaeological locus, but the ancient course of the river has not been precisely determined; its southward turn after flowing past the village to its north was a post-Shang event, since it obviously cut into the heart of the Middle Group of ground houses and eroded away their eastern portions.

Little work has been done to the west of the village. In 1929 a few test pits were opened on the small mound northwest of Hsiao-t'un (locally known as a *pa-t'ai* 壩台), west of Grid I, but only burials and ash pits were encountered.[82] It does not look as though the palace area extended this far to the west. The area immediately west of Hsiao-t'un, however, is another story. Since Fu Hao's tomb is situated immediately to the northwest of the village there is no reason to suppose that the Shang occupation stopped right there. In 1958–59, a section of a large ditch, full of ashes 7–21 meters wide and 5–10 meters deep, was discovered about 200 meters west of Hsiao-t'un, and nearby was a section of a road paved with potsherds and pebbles. Some archaeologists believe that the ditch remained from a moat-like defensive work around the palace area.[83] A cache of twenty-one whole shoulder blades of cattle, ten of them inscribed, was brought to light in 1971 in Locus West.[84]

The area south of the village, now mainly covered by a road separating Hsiao-t'un from its neighboring village to the south, Hua-yüan-chuang, was excavated in 1929, 1955, and 1973. Ground house foundations have been brought to light here, and the 1973 season saw the recovery of a human sacrificial pit (with the skeletons of five adult humans—one carrying a bronze arrowhead imbedded in his left leg bone—two children, and a horse) and also more than four thousand pieces of inscribed oracle bones dating from Periods I, III, IV, and V.[85] It appears that the palace area characterized by ground houses, human sacrifice, and inscribed oracle bones extended both west and south of Hsiao-t'un village, although it is doubtful that it extended very much farther.

3. *HSI-PEI-KANG* 西北岡

Toward the end of 1933, during the eighth season of the An-yang excavations by the Academia Sinica, a large tomb with ramps was uncovered at Hou-kang, a low mound only about 1.3 kilometers due east of Hsiao-t'un.[86] This alerted the archaeologists to the possibility of a royal

82. Li Chi 李濟, "An-yang tsui-chin fa-chüeh pao-kao chi liu tz'u kung-tso chih tsung ku-chi" 安陽最近發掘報告及六次工作之總估計.

83. *KK*, "1958–1959 nien Yin hsü fa-chüeh chien pao" 1958-1959年殷墟發掘簡報, 66.

84. Kuo Mo-jo 郭沫若, "An-yang hsin ch'u-t'u chih niu chia-ku chi ch'i k'o tz'u" 安陽新出土之牛胛骨及其刻辭.

85. *KKHP*, "Yi-chiu-wu-wu nien ch'iu An-yang Hsiao-t'un Yin hsü chih fa-chüeh" 一九五五年秋安陽小屯殷墟之發掘; *KK*, "1973 nien An-yang Hsiao-t'un nan-ti fa-chüeh chien pao" 1973年安陽小屯南地發掘簡報.

86. Shih Chang-ju 石璋如, "Ho-nan An-yang Hou-kang ti Yin mu" 河南安陽後岡的殷墓.

burial area outside Hsiao-t'un, and Shih Chang-ju and Liu Yao 劉耀 (now known as Yin Ta 尹達) were given the assignment of surveying the whole An-yang area to determine the most likely spot. After an extensive search in 1934, their attention was directed toward a formation of higher land less than 3 kilometers northwest of Hsiao-t'un (hence the archaeological name for the site, Hsi-pei-kang, "the Northwestern High-ground") on the other side of the river, whence freshly plundered bronze vessels were rumored to have come. Liang Ssu-yung 梁思永, then field director of the An-yang project, agreed with them, and from 3 October to 30 December 1934 they concentrated their efforts at the site northeast of Hou-chia-chuang and north of Wu-kuan-ts'un. (The site is, therefore, variously referred to as *Hou-chia chuang Hsi-pei-kang* or *Wu-Kuan-ts'un pei ti*), and found large graves in the first try.[87] Excavations continued there throughout 1935, bringing to light an enormously rich burial and ritual area, with no residential remains.[88] Additional excavations took place there in 1950,[89] and intermittently since 1958.[90]

The 1934–35 excavations are masterfully summarized by Kao Ch'ü-hsün 高去尋 in a paper published in 1959.[91] His summary will be paraphrased below, supplemented here and there with additional data that has since become available.

Large Royal Tombs. The royal cemetery was divided into a western and an eastern part, separated by a hundred meters. In the 1934–35 excavations the archaeologists located the western, northern, and eastern perimeters of the western part of the cemetery, and, although the southern perimeter was not similarly delineated, Kao was confident that to the south of the excavated area there were no more large royal tombs. Within the western section thus defined, seven large tombs (M 1001, M 1002, M 1003, M 1004, M 1217, M 1500, M 1550) and a large rectangular pit (M 1567) (perhaps an unfinished and unused eighth tomb) were found. In the eastern part of the cemetery about fifteen thousand square meters of field were turned over in 1934–35 and the

87. Shih Chang-ju 石璋如, "Yin hsü tsui-chin chih chung-yao fa-hsien fu lun Hsiao-t'un ti-ts'eng" 殷墟最近之重要發現附論小屯地層, 2.

88. Liang Ssu-yung 梁思永 and Kao Ch'ü-hsün 高去尋, *Hou-chia-chuang* 侯家莊 Nos. 2–8 (concerning large graves numbered M 1001, M 1002, M 1003, M 1004, M 1217, M 1500, M 1550).

89. Kuo Pao-chün 郭寶鈞, "Yi-chiu-wu-ling nien ch'un Yin hsü fa-chüeh pao-kao" 一九五〇年春殷墟發掘報告.

90. *KK*, "1958–1959 nien Yin hsü fa-chüeh chien pao" 1958-1959年殷墟發掘簡報; *KK*, "An-yang Yin hsü nu-li chi-ssu k'eng ti fa-chüeh" 安陽殷墟奴隸祭祀坑的發掘; Yang Hsi-chang 楊錫璋 and Yang Pao-ch'eng 楊寶成, "Ts'ung Shang tai chi-ssu k'eng k'an Shang tai nu-li she-hui ti jen sheng" 從商代祭祀坑看商代奴隸社會的人牲.

91. "The Royal Cemetery of the Yin Dynasty at An-yang."

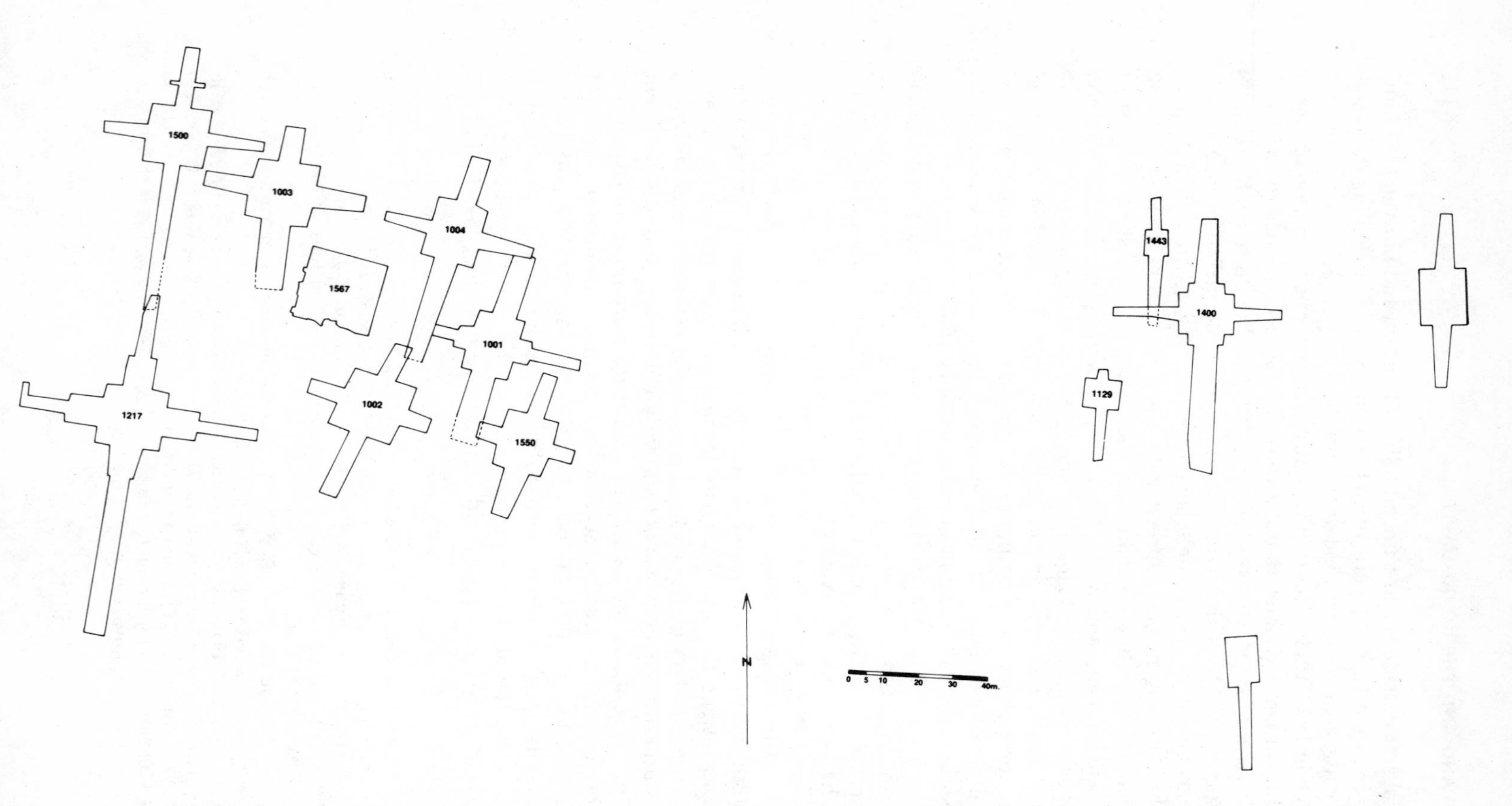

31. Ground plan of the large royal graves at Hsi-pei-kang (based on K. C. Chang, *The Archaeology of Ancient China*, fig. 121. Eastern section augmented according to Yang Hsi-chang and Yang Pao-ch'eng, "Ts'ung Shang tai chi-ssu k'eng k'an Shang tai nu-li she-hui ti jen sheng," 13).

32. Royal grave M 1001 at Hsi-pei-kang (after Liang Ssu-yung and Kao Ch'ü-hsün, *Hou-chia-chuang 1001-hao ta mu*).

northern and western perimeters of the area were located, disclosing an estimated quarter of the whole burial part and three large royal tombs (M 1129, M 1400, M 1443). The 1950 season added a fourth tomb just 40 meters to the east of M 1400 excavated in 1935, and another pit, in which a large square bronze cauldron was reportedly found in the 1940s, was identified in 1959 (fig. 31).

All the large tombs were oriented north-south, the northern end inclining toward the east by a few degrees (fig. 32). According to the number and position of the ramps, constructed to facilitate descending into the pit, the tombs were of two kinds: those with four ramps and those with two. The tombs with two ramps were all rectangular pits, and from the northern and southern walls of the bottom of the pits two ramps extended upward to the ground level. The tombs with four ramps were rectangular or shaped like a cross, and one ramp extended from the bottom of each wall. The dimensions of the large tombs varied. M 1004, for example, was 17.9 meters long (north-south), 15.9 meters wide at the mouth of the pit, and 13.2 meters by 10.8 meters at the bottom. It was 12 meters deep. The four ramps were 31.4 meters, 14.1 meters, 15.2 meters and 13.8 meters long in the north, south, east, and west, respectively.

The construction process of the large tombs can be reconstructed as follows. First the tomb pit was excavated, and a number of smallish pits were dug in the floor for the placement of sacrificial human victims. In one tomb, M 1001, there were nine such small graves, in each of which were buried a human, a *ko*-halberd, and a dog. In all other tombs where the floor was reached, there was only one such pit in each tomb, in which human skeletons and weapons were found.

A wooden chamber was then built at the center of the floor of the tomb pit. It was cross-shaped in those tombs with four ramps or rectangular in those with two ramps. Kao believes that the cross-shaped wooden chamber was a symbolic imitation of the ancestral temple of the Shang, although none of the ground houses found at Hsiao-t'un was of that shape.[92] The floor of the chamber was first built of long wooden beams, 20 or 30 centimeters in diameter, then the side-walls were erected, and, later on after the chamber was filled, the roof would be put in place. The cross-shaped chambers were about 3 meters high, and the rectangular ones were somewhat lower. For the rectangular chamber, after the walls were erected, earth was poured into the space between the chamber and the walls to the level of the chamber roof and was beaten solid layer by layer to form the so-called *shu-t'u erh-ts'eng-t'ai* 熟土二層台 ("the second-level platform built on turned-over earth") for the placement of grave goods and sacrificial burials outside the chamber. The coffin and grave goods were then placed inside the chamber before the roof was put up. For the cross-shaped chambers, the process was the same, but a door seems to have been created on the south wall. For the dimensions of the chamber, M 1004 may again serve as an example : the basic rectangle was 5.75 meters long north-south and from 3 to 9 meters wide east-west, and a small wing about 2 by 2 meters in size extended out from each wall. Since the chamber was the resting place of the master of the tomb, it was presumably the most richly furnished part of the tomb; unfortunately all the large Hsi-pei-kang tombs had been repeatedly robbed and we can only guess at the original opulence from the little that has survived (figs. 33, 34).

Outside the wooden chamber, in the tomb pit and in the ramps, additional goods were placed to accompany the burial. In some tombs a level surface was made on the beaten earth that surrounds the top of the wooden chamber—the second-level platform—and on it were placed a variety of artifacts and human victims. On the platform in M 1001 were found fragments of wooden implements and eleven human skeletons; the wood had long since decayed, but on the earth were left impressions

92. Kao Ch'ü-hsün 高去尋, "Yin tai ta mu ti mu shih chi ch'i han-yi chih t'ui-ts'e" 殷代大墓的墓室及其涵義之推測.

33. Stone sculptures from royal grave M 1001 at Hsi-pei-kang (after Liang Ssu-yung and Kao Ch'ü-hsün, *Hou-chia-chuang 1001-hao ta mu*).

34. Impressions on clay of wooden sculpture from royal grave at Hsi-pei-kang (after Umehara Sueji, *Inbo hatsugen mokki in'ei zuroku*).

of decorative designs, color pigments, and inlaid objects (fig. 34). In M 1400 and M 1500, only human skulls (29 and 111 of them respectively) were found in the beaten earth surrounding the chamber. As for the ramps, these were furnished variously. In M 1001, for example, a human sacrificial burial was found in the northern ramp and one in the western. In the southern ramp were 11 rows of 59 headless skeletons, and one such skeleton was found in the eastern ramp. In all four ramps were found rows of human skulls, which were grouped in 27 sets and totalled 73. In M 1004, there were four layers of grave goods at the northern end of the southern ramp. The lowest layer consisted of chariot fittings, leather armor, and traces of shields; the second layer from the bottom consisted of over 100 helmets and some 360 bronze halberds, the next layer consisted of 36 bronze spearheads, and the top layer a musical stone, a jade stick, and 2 square bronze cauldrons.

Other than their structural features and grave-furnishings, these large "royal" tombs at Hsi-pei-kang are of interest in two important respects. The first is because of their relative chronological position in relation to one another and the chronological correspondence between the Hsi-pei-kang and the Hsiao-t'un sequences. The other issue, which is related to the first, is the question of the sociology of the tombs: whose tombs they were and the significance of their sequence and layout in the study of the Shang royal house. The second question will be left for a later discussion, but this much is clear: these were tombs of people at the very top of the Shang society, namely the kings and, possibly, their queens.

On the chronology of the tombs, the stratigraphical interrelationship of those tombs that touched on each other makes it clear that the following three segments (shown in the table below) are established:[93]

M 1500——(earlier than)——→ M 1217
M 1001——————→M 1004——→M 1002
  └——→M 1550
M 1443 ——→M 1400

Further placement of these segments and other individual tombs chronologically must then be based on typological studies of artifacts, since no oracle bones, inscribed or not, have been found in the cemetery. But because these tombs have been repeatedly robbed, such typological studies must be based on a very small and skewed sample and are, thus, highly tentative. On the basis of the occurrence pattern of various types

93. Li Chi 李濟, "Yin hsü pai t'ao fa-chan chih ch'eng-hsü" 殷墟白陶發展之程序, 861.

TABLE 1 Chronological Correlation of Hsiao-t'un and Hsi-pei-kang According to Hairpin Types

Hairpin types	*Hsiao-t'un*	*Hsi-pei-kang*
I	Some pit houses	Before large graves
II	*Yi*-7 house floor	M 1001
III	*Ping*-1 house floor	M 1002
IV	Upper ash layers	M 1174
V	Disturbed surface layer	—

of bone hairpins, Li Chi has arranged the large tombs in the western section at Hsi-pei-kang into the following chronological sequence: M 1001–M 1550–M 1004–M 1002–M 1003–M 1500–M 1217–M 1174.[94] Furthermore, according to the occurrence pattern of one type of bone hairpin in Hsi-pei-kang and Hsiao-t'un, Li Chi has attempted the correlation in table 1.[95] In this view, the Middle Group house floors at Hsiao-t'un were contemporaneous with the earliest Hsi-pei-kang tombs in the western section. Since Li Chi follows Shih's sequence of North-Middle-South house groups at Hsiao-t'un, his conclusion is that the Hsi-pei-kang royal cemetery was not begun to be built until the middle of the dynastic period. But the recent discovery of the Fu Hao tomb may force a reconsideration of this view. Commentators are fairly well in agreement that the Fu Hao tomb and the Hsi-pei-kang M 1001 are so similar in their artifact typology that they were most likely contemporary.[96] In that case, it seems necessary either to push up the date of at least some of the *yi*-group house floors to the Wu Ting period or to push up the date of M 1001 to immediately following the Wu Ting period. Either is permissible under the current available evidence.

The status of being the earliest tomb acquired by M 1001 because of its similarity to the Fu Hao tomb may be viewed in connection with Alexander Soper's suggestion that M 1001 was the tomb of none other than Wu Ting himself: "1001 is older than any of the other three (1002, 1004, 1550). Again, its position in relation to the others seems meaningful; it stands roughly at a center, with 1550 hemming it in on the

94. Li Chi 李濟, "Pien hsing pa lei chi ch'i wen-shih chih yen-pien" 笄形八類及其文飾之演變, 68.

95. "Yu pien hsing yen-pien so k'an-chien ti Hsiao-t'un yi-chih yü Hou-chia-chuang mu-tsang chih shih-tai kuan-hsi" 由笄形演變所看見的小屯遺址與侯家莊墓葬之時代關係.

96. *KKHP*, "An-yang Yin hsü wu-hao mu ti fa-chüeh" 安陽殷墟五號墓的發掘, 94; *KK*, "An-yang Yin-hsü wu-hao mu tso-t'an chi-yao" 安陽殷墟五號墓座談紀要, 341, 344, 345, 350, with comments by Cheng Chen-hsiang 鄭振香, Li Hsüeh-ch'in 李學勤, Hu Hou-hsüan 胡厚宣, and Wang Shih-min 王世民.

southeast, while 1002 and 1004 close off the diagonal axes on the southwest and northwest respectively. I suggest that this situation points to two adjacent generations in a royal family, a father and his three sons. Such a pattern is satisfied in the An-yang period only once. The father was Wu Ting."[97] Objection to this view on stylistic grounds (that the square cauldrons of M 1004 cannot be as early as the generation after Wu Ting)[98] can now be removed with the findings of the Fu Hao tomb, but demurrers may be raised on sociological grounds, namely, the question of whether or not father and sons belonged to the same moiety,[99] a question that we must defer until later.

As to the eastern section, in a recent analysis of the royal tombs and their adjacent small graves, Yang Hsi-chang and Yang Pao-ch'eng place M 1400, the grave that yielded the large square Ssu Mu Wu cauldron, and the Wu-kuan-ts'un North tomb excavated in 1950, all in the Early Period or Period II, contemporary with M 1001.[100]

Small Graves. The 1934–35 excavations at Hsi-pei-kang yielded, in addition to the 10 large tombs and the single unused pit, 1,221 small graves, 1,117 of them in the eastern section (fig. 35) and only 104 in the western section. Among these, only 643 are available for classificatory purposes. By Kao's count, 131 were single burials, 57 were multiple burials (from 2 to 11 skeletons to each grave), 72 were burials (single to multiple up to 10) with the skull separated from the rest of the skeleton, 209 (all in the eastern section) were skulls only (from 3 to 39 skulls to each pit), 192 were body skeletons only (from 1 to 10 to each), 9 (all in the western section) were infants buried between layers of potsherds, 20 were horse burials (1–37 horses in each), 2 were elephants, 20 burials of other animals, 1 chariot pit, and 1 pit with bronze vessels. Most of these small graves were arranged in parallel rows, running from east to west and located beside or near the large graves. These rows then clustered in well-defined groups: one such group in the western section and nine in the eastern.

In 1950, with the excavation of the fourth large tomb in the eastern section, 18 small graves to its south were unearthed.[101] Another

97. "Early, Middle, and Late Shang: A Note," 26.

98. V. Kane, "A Re-examination of An-yang Archaeology," 105–106.

99. K. C. Chang, "Some Dualistic Phenomena in Shang Society."

100. Kane, *op. cit.*, and Yang Hsi-chang 楊錫璋 and Yang Pao-ch'eng 楊寶成 "Ts'ung Shang tai chi-ssu k'eng k'an Shang tai nu-li she-hui ti jen sheng" 從商代祭祀坑看商代奴隸社會的人牲, 14.

101. Kuo Pao-chün 郭寶鈞, "Yi-chiu-wu-ling nien ch'un Yin hsü fa-chüeh pao-kao" 一九五〇年春殷墟發掘報告.

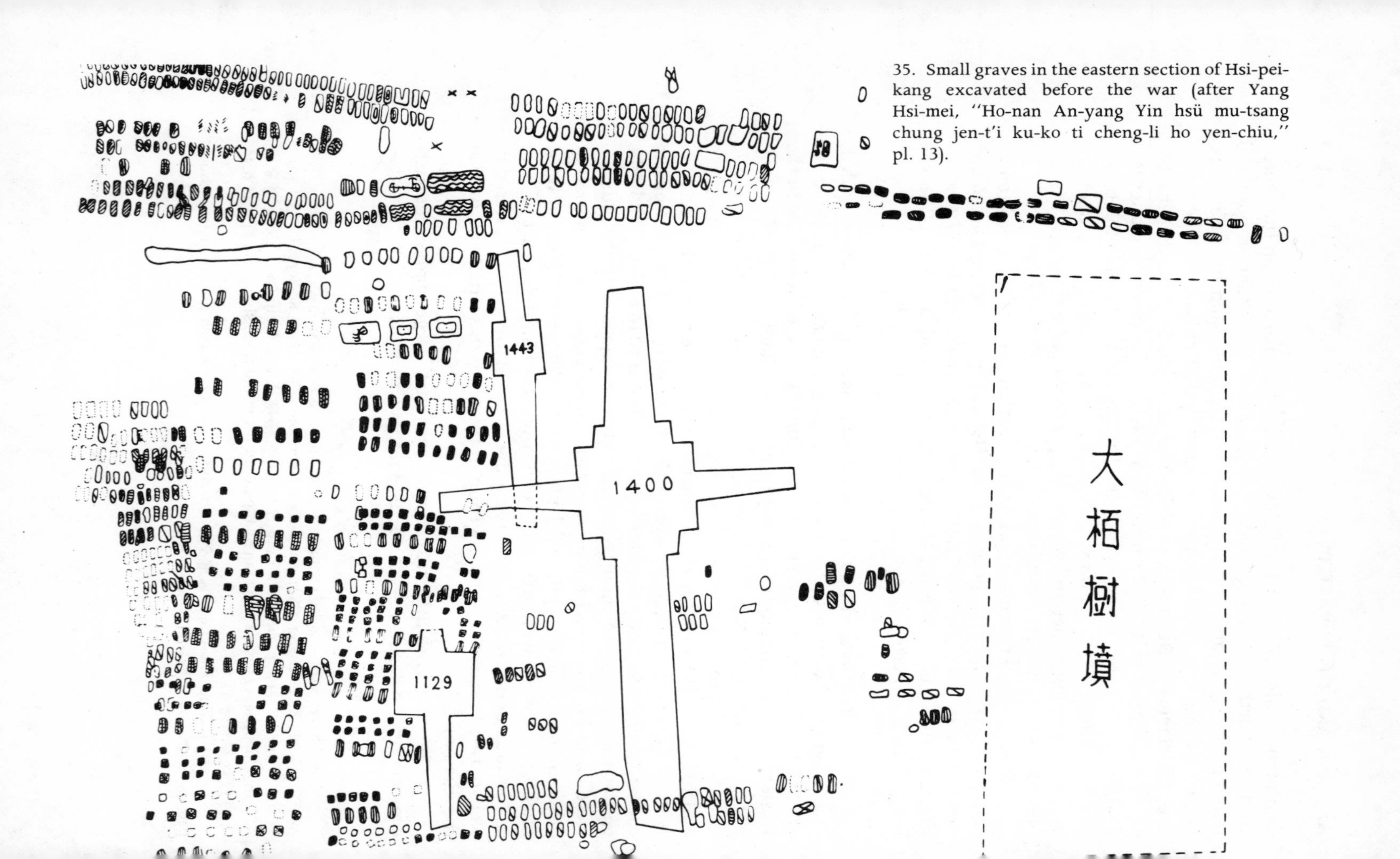

35. Small graves in the eastern section of Hsi-pei-kang excavated before the war (after Yang Hsi-mei, "Ho-nan An-yang Yin hsü mu-tsang chung jen-t'i ku-ko ti cheng-li ho yen-chiu," pl. 13).

group of 10 was excavated in 1958–59.[102] In 1969 and 1976, additional excavations took place in the area east of the 1934–35 excavations and west of the small graves area of 1950; 250 such graves were located, but only 191 were excavated. They were similarly clustered, and the excavators recognized 22 groups, ranging in their size from 1 to 47 graves (fig. 36). The burial patterns are again similar to Kao's description, but the 1976 excavators explicitly stated that many skeletons were dismembered or mutilated and many were bound.[103] Of the 1,178 skeletons and skulls that were found, 715 to 718 individual skeletons have been studied with regard to sex and age. Of these, 339 were believed to be males, 35 famales, the rest undetermined. Other than 19, which were probably children under age fourteen, all were young adults: averaging 20–35 years old for women, and 15–25 for men. Men and women tended to be buried in the same pits.[104] Chronologically, the excavators observed that from stratigraphical indications the graves that were oriented north-south were earlier than those oriented east-west, but that the whole group excavated in 1969 and 1976 belonged to the Early Periods (but essentially Period II).

Kao Ch'ü-hsün believes that all the small graves "must be related to the ten big tombs in one way or another," although he is not yet certain about "the question of to which big tombs the nine groups of small graves were dedicated as sacrifices" in the eastern section of the cemetery.[105] But since the small graves were clustered in the eastern section (into at least thirty-six groups, including Kao's nine, the four groups of 1950, one group in 1958–59, and the twenty-two excavated in 1976), and if each group represents a single ritual act, the ritual events represented there cannot have been confined to mere sacrificial burials that were made in coordination with the construction and use of the large royal tombs. Yang Hsi-chang and Yang Pao-ch'eng's interpretation—namely that although some of the small graves could be related to the royal burial rites, these graves largely represent the sacrificial use of human victims in rituals as abundantly recorded in oracle bone inscriptions—is certainly consistent with the facts (fig. 37).

The human victims may include members of more than a single social stratum. Grave goods were found among some of the graves, but the nature and amount of such goods varied with the type of burial. In the

102. *KK*, "1958–1959 nien Yin hsü fa-chüeh chien pao" 1958-1959年殷墟發掘簡報, 70–72.

103. *KK*, "An-yang Yin hsü nu-li chi-ssu k'eng ti fa-chüeh" 安陽殷墟奴隸祭祀坑的發掘.

104. *KK*, "An-yang Yin tai chi-ssu k'eng jen ku ti hsing-pieh nien-ling chien-ting" 安陽殷代祭祀坑人骨的性別年齡鑒定.

105. "The Royal Cemetery of the Yin Dynasty at An-yang," 9.

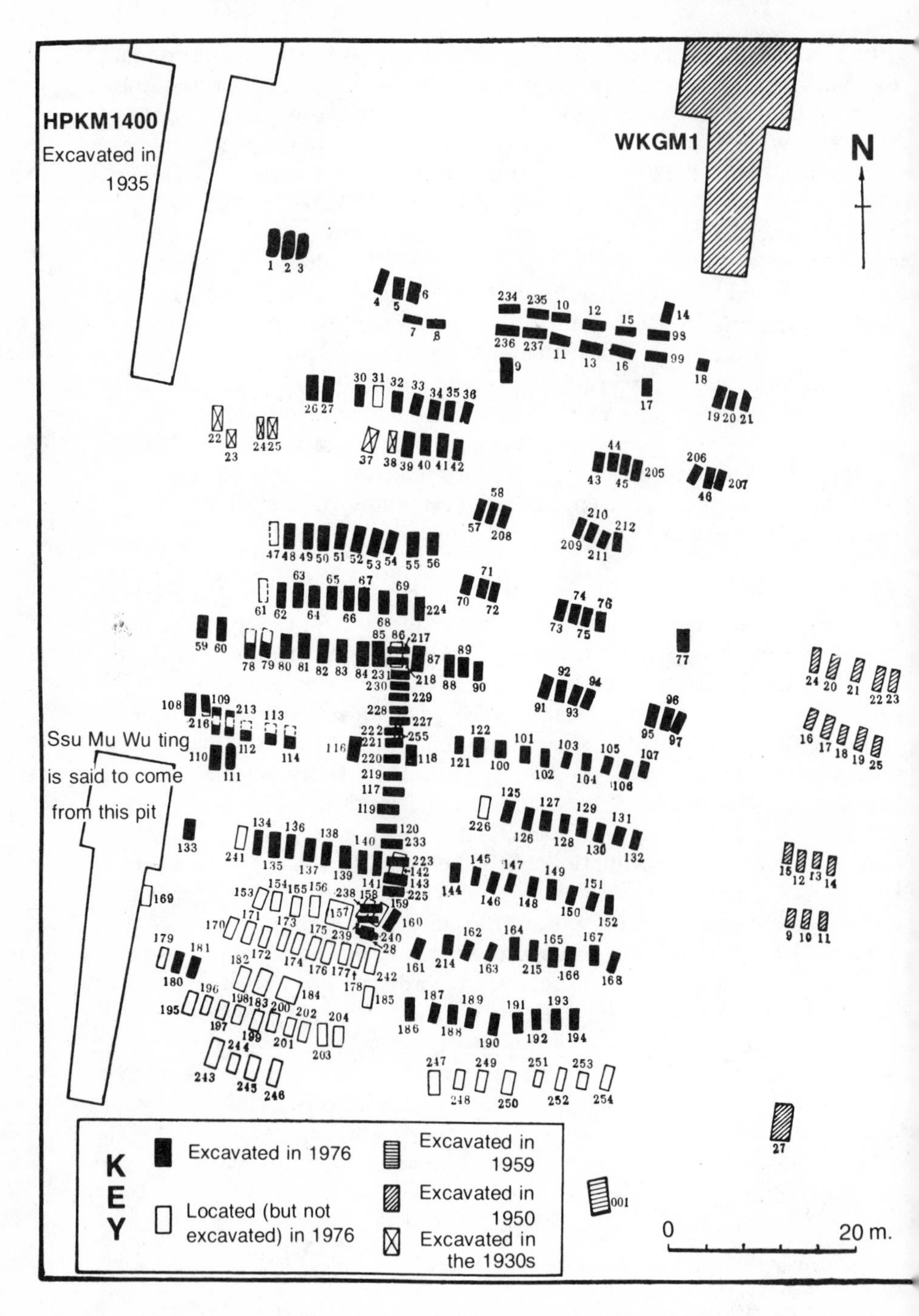

36. Small graves in the eastern section of Hsi-pei-kang excavated in 1969 and 1976 (after Yang Hsi-chang, and Yang Pao-ch'eng, "Ts'ung Shang tai chi-ssu k'eng k'an Shang tai nu-li she-hui ti jen sheng").

37. Examples of human skeleton layouts in the small graves at Hsi-pei-kang (after Yang Hsi-chang and Yang Pao-ch'eng, "Ts'ung Shang tai chi-ssu k'eng k'an Shang tai nu-li she-hui ti jen sheng").

1934–35 material, fifty-eight of the 131 single burials of complete skeletons were associated with pottery vessels, bronze vessels, weapons, implements, and musical instruments, and so forth, and many of the multiple burials with complete skeletons were also found with pottery, bronze vessels and weapons, and ornaments. But of the fifty-two burials with heads and bodies separated, only nine included grave goods, and these were more meager in quality and quantity; only three of the skulls-only graves had furnishings; and the bodies-only graves were furnished, if at all, with knife-ax-whetstone sets.[106] The same pattern is repeated in the 1976 data: of the 191 graves excavated, thirteen were furnished, mostly sparsely, and except for one the thirteen were all burials with complete skeletons.[107] It appears that among the human victims for rituals there were at least two classes of people, those who were buried whole and sometimes with grave goods, and those who were beheaded and buried without furnishings. There is another thing that deserves some note (but cannot yet be interpreted): of the twenty-two groups of 1976, one (M 26, M 32, M 33) has yielded skeletons more robust and taller than all the others.[108]

4. *OTHER SHANG SITES IN AN-YANG*

Archaeological sites within the An-yang area that have been excavated or investigated are distributed on both banks of the river Huan, to the northwest of An-yang city, in an area approximately 6 kilometers long and 4 kilometers deep, from Hou-kang in the east to north of Fan-chia-chuang in the west on the southern bank of the river, and on the northern bank from southeast of Ta-ssu-k'ung-ts'un in the east to T'ung-lo-chai (near Ch'iu-k'ou-ts'un) in the west. On the basis of a 1958–59 survey of the area, it was found that the Shang settlements in the area exhibited the following pattern: "On the whole, (Shang settlements) centered at the Yin palaces (near the present Hsiao-t'un village) on the southern bank of the Huan River, and surrounding the palace area were residential loci, handicraft workshops, and cemeteries. On the northern bank of the river the area north of Wu-kuan-ts'un and Hou-chia-chuang served as a center, having yielded the royal mausoleums of the Yin dynasty, noblemen's burials, and human sacrificial pits in the thousands,

106. *Ibid.*, 6–7.

107. *KK*, "An-yang Yin hsü nu-li chi-ssu k'eng ti fa-chüeh" 安陽殷墟奴隸祭祀坑的發掘, 26–27.

108. *Ibid.*, 26.

and outward from it were also found Yin dynasty settlements and cemeteries. They were most abundant in the area of Hsiao-t'un, as seen from underground deposits, and encircling this center were settlements of varying sizes. Although these settlements did not form a continuous block, their distribution was rather dense. It became somewhat sparser in areas farther away from the center."[109] After the discovery of the Fu Hao tomb in 1976, the view was presented that "in the early period of the Yin dynasty, the area of the palaces was not very large, and some of the royal tombs were placed near the palaces."[110]

Having described Hsiao-t'un and Hsi-pei-kang above, we now turn to the other Shang settlements that have been archaeologically investigated, beginning with the south bank sites, from east to west.

SOUTH BANK OF THE RIVER HUAN

1. Hou-kang, Kao-lou-chuang 高樓莊後岡. The village of Kao-lou-chuang lies between An-yang city and Hsiao-t'un; a low mound north of the village, called Hou-kang ("Mound in the Rear"), was found to be the center of the Shang remains, but they were also seen to the north and south of the mound, into the village itself. Major archaeological work took place here in 1931 (two seasons), 1933, 1934, 1958–60, 1971, and 1972. It was here, in 1931, that the famous Hou-kang stratigraphy, which shows the successive relationship of Yang-shao, Lung-shan, and Shang cultures for the first time, was disclosed. Insofar as Shang remains are concerned, they include inscribed oracle bones and a large-scale tomb with two ramps (north and south), a cross-shaped chamber, and human victims. This appears to be an area where nobility was present at the least.[111]

2. Hsüeh-chia-chuang Locus North 薛家莊北地. Minor excavation in 1957 resulted in ashy pits and burials. In some of the pits were found objects of daily use, some human skeletons without burial pits, and little if any mortuary goods. The burials contained some furnishings

109. *KK*, "1958–1959 nien Yin hsü fa-chüeh chien pao" 1958-1959年殷墟發掘簡報, 65.

110. *KKHP*, "An-yang Yin hsü wu-hao mu ti fa-chüeh" 安陽殷墟五號墓的發掘, 96.

111. Liang Ssu-yung 梁思永, "Hou-kang fa-chüeh hsiao chi" 後岡發掘小記, Shih Chang-ju 石璋如, "Ho-nan An-yang Hou-kang ti Yin mu" 河南安陽後岡的殷墓; Kuo Mo-jo 郭沫若, "An-yang yüan k'eng mu chung ting ming k'ao shih" 安陽圓坑墓中鼎銘考釋; *KK*, "1971 nien An-yang Hou-kang fa-chüeh chien pao" 1971年安陽後岡發掘簡報; *KK*, "1972 nien ch'un An-yang Hou-kang fa-chüeh chien pao" 1972年春安陽後岡發掘簡報.

but no human victims. This locus appears to have been a residential area for people of relatively lowly status.[112]

3. Hsüeh-chia-chuang Locus South 薛家莊南地. Minor excavations, at this locus also in 1957, disclosed bronze foundry and bone manufacture remains and burials with simple furnishings. This was apparently a workshop area.[113]

4. Miao-p'u Locus North 苗圃北地. The archaeological locus north of Miao-p'u ("Tree Nursery"), about one kilometer southeast of Hsiao-t'un, is an important and large (at least 10,000 square meters) one. The burials found here in recent years provide a type sequence for Shang ceramics, and in 1958–59 a large quantity of bronze foundry remains (crucible sherds, clay models, clay molds) as well as ground house floors and storage pits were brought to light.[114] This was undoubtedly another bronze foundry, possibly part of the same industrial precinct as the Hsüeh-chia-chuang Locus South only some 400 meters to the east. The ground house floors there suggest that ground houses were used not only by the royal family and the nobility but also by bronze smiths; similar associations occur at Shang sites in Cheng-chou also.

5. Hua-yüan-chuang Locus Northwest 花園莊西北地. It has been stated that many inscribed oracle bones were found at Hsiao-t'un Locus West, which leads one to ask just how far west the palace area at Hsiao-t'un extended. Remains from the Ssu-p'an-mo locus (see below), about one kilometer west of Hsiao-t'un, make it clear that that area was outside the palace precinct. In between Hsiao-t'un and Ssu-p'an-mo there are only two archaeological loci where excavations have taken place. The one in the north is the so-called "Thirty-seven Mou Land" (northwest of the Hua-yüan-chuang village), and the one in the south lies near Wang-yü-k'ou and Huo-chia-hsiao-chuang.

The Hua-yüan-chuang Locus Northwest was dug in 1950, but only a small quantity of remains ("potsherds, bone tools, stone objects, and oracle bones") were encountered,[115] pointing to a residential area of people other than royal and noble statuses.

6. Wang-yü-k'ou 王裕口 and Huo-chia-hsiao-chuang 霍家小

112. *KK*, "Ho-nan An-yang Hsüeh-chia-chuang Yin tai yi-chih mu-tsang ho T'ang mu fa-chüeh chien pao" 河南安陽薛家莊殷代遺址墓葬和唐墓發掘簡報.

113. Chao Hsia-kuang 趙霞光, "An-yang shih hsi chiao ti Yin tai wen-hua yi-chih" 安陽市西郊的殷代文化遺址, 31; Chou Tao 周到 and Liu Tung-ya 劉東亞, "Yi-chiu-wu-ch'i nien ch'iu An-yang Kao-lou-chuang Yin tai yi-chih fa-chüeh" 一九五七年秋安陽高樓莊殷代遺址發掘.

114. *KK*, "1958–1959 nien Yin hsü fa-chüeh chien pao" 1958-1959年殷墟發掘簡報, 67–69.

115. Kuo Pao-chün 郭寶鈞, "Yi-chiu-wu-ling nien ch'un Yin hsü fa-chüeh pao kao 一九五〇年春殷墟發掘報告, 58.

莊. Excavated in 1932, the locus, on flat land north of Wang-yü-k'ou, east of Huo-chia-hsiao-chuang, and west of Hua-yüan-chuang, yielded pit houses and burials with *hang-t'u* and some grave goods, and it seems to be a residential and burial area for commoners and lesser nobles.[116]

7. Ssu-p'an-mo 四盤磨. There were several archaeological finds near the village of Ssu-p'an-mo, but their spatial interrelationship has not been made clear, although digging took place there in 1931, 1933, and 1950. Burials with *hang-t'u* fills were encountered in 1931 and 1933, and ground house floors, inscribed oracle bones, and burials with fairly abundant grave goods as well as those with few or no grave goods.[117] Apparently here was a small center with noblemen's residences and a cemetery.

8. Pai-chia-fen 白家墳. Remains of living sites and burials were brought to light in this area in 1958–59, but detailed reports are still lacking. Apparently this is an important loci for Shang ceramic chronology.[118]

9. Mei-yüan-chuang 梅園莊. On the western margin of Yin hsü in An-yang, Mei-yan-chuang is a small site with few remains. But it is important because it is the type site with pottery similar to the Erh-li-kang lower stratum of Cheng-chou, thus predating the predynastic period of Hsiao-t'un.[119]

10. Hsiao-min-t'un Locus South 孝民屯南地. Three chariot pits were found in 1958–1959 and in 1972, providing invaluable data for Shang chariot reconstruction.[120]

11. Pei-hsin-chuang Locus South 北辛莊南地. Also excavated in 1958–59, this locus is best known for a bone workshop find: a ground house floor, a pit full of bone materials, and remains of bone materials, half-finished bone artifacts, and bone-working tools, within an area of over 200 square meters.[121]

12. Fan-chia-chuang Locus North 范家莊北地. Tested in 1935

116. Wu Chin-ting 吳金鼎, "Chai chi Hsiao-t'un yi hsi chih san ch'u hsiao fa-chüeh" 摘記小屯迤西之三處小發掘, 631–633.

117. Kuo Pao-chün 郭寶鈞, "Yi-chiu-wu-ling nien ch'un Yin hsü fa-chüeh pao-kao" 一九五〇年春殷墟發掘報告, 48–58; Li Chi 李濟, "An-yang tsui-chin fa-chüeh pao-kao chi liu tz'u kung-tso chih tsung ku-chi" 安陽最近發掘報告及六次工作之總估計, 568; Wu Chin-ting 吳金鼎, "Chai chi Hsiao-t'un yi hsi chih san ch'u hsiao fa-chüeh" 摘記小屯迤西之三處小發掘, 627–628.

118. *KK*, "1958–1959 nien Yin hsü fa-chüeh chien pao" 1958-1959年殷墟發掘簡報, 63; Yang Pao-ch'eng 楊寶成, personal communication.

119. *Ibid.*, 65.

120. *Ibid.*, 72–73; *KK*, "An-yang hsin fa-hsien ti Yin tai ch'e-ma k'eng" 安陽新發現的殷代車馬坑.

121. *KK*, "1958–1959 nien Yin hsü fa-chüeh chien pao" 1958-1959年殷墟發掘簡報, 69.

and excavated in 1958–59, this locus has yielded generally simpler remains, but also burials with bronzes.[122]

NORTH BANK OF THE RIVER HUAN

1. Ta-ssu-k'ung-ts'un Locus South 大司空村南地. This locus is actually situated on the east bank of the river, directly across the river from Hsiao-t'un Locus North, and it could be an exceedingly important area. Archaeological excavations took place here several times (in 1935, 1936, 1953–54, 1958, 1958–59, and 1962) but have been of relatively small scale, and reports on only a small portion of the remains have seen the light of print.[123] These include pits, ground house floors, chariot-and -horse burials, and human burials. The burials were sharply differentiated according to the shape of the pit, the use of the wooden chamber, and the nature and amount of grave goods. Two inscribed oracle bones were found in 1958–59. These point to a fair-sized settlement whose residents included nobility of considerable status.

2. Ssu-mien-pei 四面碑. Only very sketchily investigated in 1932, the conditions at this locus are not well understood. It is south of Hsiao-ssu-k'ung-ts'un 小司空村, directly across the river from Hsiao-t'un Locus North and could be of considerable significance.

3. Pa-t'ai 壩台 south of Wu-kuan-ts'un. This is in a small mound situated directly across the river from Ssu-p'an-mo. It has been claimed that it and Ssu-p'an-mo originally formed a single site, which was then cut in two by the river Huan. A small-scale excavation in 1934 resulted in the discovery of pits, burials, and oracle bones.[124]

4. Hou-chia-chuang Locus South 侯家莊南地. This locus was excavated once in 1934 following reports of inscribed oracle bones, uncovering pits, ground house floors, and burials with *hang-t'u* fill, as well as inscribed oracle bones.[125] This is the fifth archaeological locus in

122. *Ibid.*, 63.

123. *KK*, "1958–1959 nien Yin hsü fa-chüeh chien pao" 1958-1959年殷墟發掘簡報, 65, 66, 69, 73, 75: *KK*, "1962 nien An-yang Ta-ssu-k'ung ts'un fa-chüeh chien pao" 1962年安陽大司空村發掘簡報; *KK*, "Yi-chiu-wu-pa nien ch'un Ho-nan An-yang shih Ta-ssu-k'ung ts'un Yin tai mu-tsang fa-chüeh chien pao 一九五八年春河南安陽市大司空村殷代墓葬發掘簡報; Ma Te-chih 馬得志, Chou Yung-chen 周永珍, Chang Yun-p'eng 張雲鵬, "Yi-chiu-wu-san nien An-yang Ta-ssu-k'ung ts'un fa-chüeh pao-kao" 一九五三年安陽大司空村發掘報告; Shih Chang-ju 石璋如, "Yin hsü tsui-chin chih chung-yao fa-hsien fu lun Hsiao-t'un ti-ts'eng" 殷墟最近之重要發現附論小屯地層, 12, 75; "Hou chi" 後記.

124. Shih Chang-ju 石璋如, "Yin hsü tsui-chin chih chung-yao fa-hsien fu lun Hsiao-t'un ti-ts'eng" 殷墟最近之重要發現附論小屯地層, 75; Shih Chang-ju 石璋如, "Hsiao-t'un ti wen-hua ts'eng" 小屯的文化層.

125. Shih Chang-ju 石璋如, "Yin hsü tsui-chin chih chung-yao fa-hsien fu

the An-yang area that has yielded inscribed oracle bones. (The other four are Hsiao-t'un, Hou-kang, Ta-ssu-k'ung-ts'un, Ssu-p'an-mo.)

5. Kao-ching-t'ai-tzu 高井台子. Pits and simple remains were turned up here in 1932.[126]

6. T'ung-lo-chai 同樂寨. Minor excavations in 1934 disclosed burials with bronze vessels. Near the locus a large area of *hang-t'u*, possibly a cemetery, was located, but it has yet to be excavated.[127]

The above archaeological loci in both banks of the river constitute a web-like network made up of the following nodules: Hsiao-t'un as the royal palace-temple block with its service accessories, workshops, and (during some of the periods) huge graves; the royal cemetery at Hsi-pei-kang; residential hamlets, some of which had diversified social strata and others those of commoners, but most if not all equipped with their own burial grounds; and workshops or workshop quarters. These nodules were not spatially contiguous so as to form an urban area of dense houses and streets, but the whole network was the political and ceremonial center of the royal capital, and, in the context of the Shang state, the center of the entire state (fig. 38).

5. *ARCHAEOLOGY OF THE SHANG CAPITAL OUTSIDE AN-YANG*

If our discussion in the beginning of this chapter on the spatial extent of the Shang capital at Yin has been validly based, then the An-yang network constituted by the An-yang sites was only the core of the capital, which at a higher level of organization had other nodules constituting a larger network. If we take the Hsin-hsiang (in the south) to Hsing-t'ai (in the north) area as the area of the larger capital, it was then an area about 200 kilometers long from north to south, in the plains east of the T'ai-hang Mountains, which was drained by several small rivers (Ch'i 淇, Huan 洹, and Chang 漳,), which flowed into the river Wei 衛. An-yang was at the spatial center of this area, about 100 kilometers from each end of it, and archaeologically it was the command nucleus of the vast capital.

Outside An-yang, very little archaeology has been done within

---

lun Hsiao-t'un ti-ts'eng" 殷墟最近之重要發現附論小屯地層, 74; Tung Tso-pin 董作賓, "An-yang Hou-chia-chuang ch'u-t'u chih chia ku wen-tzu" 安陽侯家莊出土之甲骨文字.

126. Wu Chin-ting 吳金鼎, "Kao-ching-t'ai-tzu san chung t'ao yeh kai lun" 高井台子三種陶業概論.

127. Shih Chang-ju 石璋如, "Yin hsü tsui-chin chih chung-yao fa-hsien fu lun Hsiao-t'un ti ts'eng" 殷墟最近之重要發現附論小屯地層, 75.

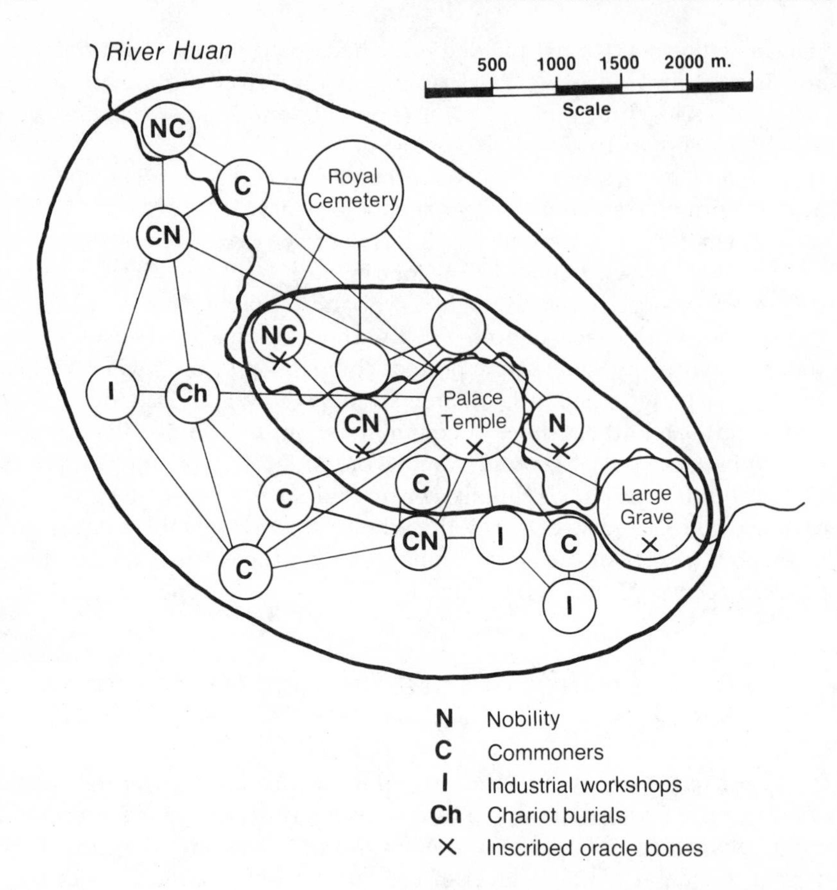

38. A structural model of the An-yang urban network during the Shang dynasty based on archaeological loci.

this larger capital area. One Shang site has been located 15 kilometers up the Huan River (Ta-cheng-chi 大正集) and another 15 kilometers downriver (Kuo-ts'un 郭村), both yielding some implements and pottery indicative of farming settlements of small size and early date (pre-Hsiao-t'un for Ta-cheng-chi and Period I or earlier for Kuo-ts'un), thus perhaps not even parts of the Shang dynastic capital.[128]

Ch'ao-ko 朝歌, south of An-yang, in the administrative county of T'ang-yin, is the location that many scholars place to the immediate east of Mu-yeh 牧野, the last battleground of the Chou conquest, and the

128. *KK*, "An-yang Huan ho liu-yü chi-ko yi-chih ti shih chüeh" 安陽洹河流域幾個遺址的試掘, 332, 333–335.

front line of the capital's unsuccessful defense.[129] Local folklore attributed three probably concentric stamped-earth enclosures to the Shang dynasty, but archaeological study showed them more likely to date from Eastern Chou. But abundant remains of both Hsiao-t'un and pre-Hsiao-t'un types have been found scattered in a wide area, indicative of extensive Shang occupation.[130]

Further to the south, Shang sites have been reported from Hui Hsien and Hsin-hsiang. In Hui Hsien, Shang remains have turned up at three loci: Hua-mu-ts'un 花木村 and Ch'u-ch'iu 褚丘, to the west of the town, and Liu-li-ko 琉璃閣, to the south.[131] Residential remains, mostly lithics and ceramics, were found at all three sites and appear to be of Cheng-chou's earlier phase. Burial sites occurred at Liu-li-ko only, including both early (pre-dynastic Hsiao-t'un) and late (dynastic Hsiao-t'un) phases. Some of the late tombs were of considerable size, equipped with waist-pits and accompanied by human sacrificial victims.[132] If this area was within the Shang capital, it would be a small center inhabited by members of the ruling class. In Hsin-hsiang, further to the south, a pottery kiln and three burials were excavated at Lu-wang-fen in 1958, yielding remains of both early and late phases.[133]

North of An-yang, Shang sites are first encountered at Hsia-p'an-wang[134] and Chieh-tuan-ying[135] in Tz'u Hsien, across the Chang river from An-yang, and Chien-kou-ts'un in Han-tan,[136] all in the southern end of Hopei Province. Remains from these sites (stone implements and pottery) suggest residential hamlets of both earlier and later periods within the Shang, although an elaborately made pottery wine container turned up at Hsia-p'an-wang, possibly from a tomb of some person of status. Further to the north in the district of Hsing-t'ai, southern Hopei,

129. Ch'ü Wan-li 屈萬里, *Shang shu chin chu chin shih* 尚書今註今釋, p. 70.

130. An Chin-huai 安金槐, "T'ang-yin Ch'ao-ko-chen fa-hsien Lung-shan ho Shang tai teng wen-hua yi-chih" 湯陰朝歌鎮發現龍山和商代等文化遺址.

131. *KK*, "Ho-nan Wei ho chih-hung kung-ch'eng chung ti k'ao-ku tiao-ch'a chien pao" 河南衛河滞洪工程中的考古調查簡報, *KK*, "Ho-nan Hui hsien Ch'u-ch'iu ch'u-t'u ti Shang tai t'ung-ch'i" 河南輝縣褚丘出土的商代銅器; Kuo Pao-chün 郭寶鈞 Hsia Nai 夏鼐, et. al., *Hui hsien fa-chüeh pao-kao* 輝縣發掘報告.

132. For the high instancy of dental disease and malnutrition of the sacrificial victims, see Mao Hsieh-chün 毛燮均 and Yen Yen 嚴誾, "An-yang Hui hsien Yin tai jen ya ti yen-chiu pao-kao" 安陽輝縣殷代人牙的研究報告.

133. *KKHP*, "Ho-nan Hsin-hsiang Lu-wang-fen Shang tai yi-chih fa-chüeh pao-kao" 河南新鄉潞王墳商代遺址發掘報告.

134. *KKHP*, "Tz'u hsien Hsia-p'an-wang yi-chih fa-chüeh pao-kao" 磁縣下潘汪遺址發掘報告, 98–99.

135. *KK*, "Tz'u hsien Chieh-tuan-ying fa-chüeh chien pao" 磁縣界段營發掘簡報, 360–363.

136. *KK*, "Ho-pei Han-tan Chien-kou ts'un ku yi-chih fa-chüeh chien pao" 河北邯鄲澗溝村古遺址發掘簡報, 201.

a large series of Shang sites has been located, revealing a small network of settlements on the An-yang model (albeit lacking the latter's aristocratic center). Remains are predominantly residential, including pit-houses, lithics, pottery, and a few bronzes (such as arrowheads, awls, adzes, and the like), and (uninscribed) oracle bones, but several pottery kilns have also turned up. As yet no burials have been found, and no ground house floors, inscriptions (except for potters' marks), bronze vessels, or other indicators of the ruling class. If this was within the capital area, it does not seem to have been more than a residential network of farmers and potters.[137]

6. *THE ROYAL CAPITAL IN THE WRITTEN RECORDS*

The archaeology of the royal capital described above has so far disclosed a network of sites of different sizes and magnitudes in an area about 200 kilometers long north to south, with the An-yang sites, constituting another network at a lower level of contrast, as its core. Outside An-yang, sites are as yet few and poorly known, but appear to represent farming villages. The An-yang core, however, marks an ancient civilization of great sophistication and distinctive character. The Hsiao-t'un locus has yielded blocks of ground houses, some on platforms, and some of two stories, arranged in a symmetrical plan, associated with a square platform and multiple gates, all oriented north-south.

But this was a civilization that flourished three millennia ago, and it was a capital city that was at least in part burned to the ground. The dry and heavily eroded North China loess was not particularly conducive to archaeological preservation, and Chinese farmers have turned the surface soil over and over for thousands of years. Antique thieves have, in addition, plundered the buried treasures for at least one thousand years. Under these conditions one can readily conceive that the archaeological picture is but a pale reflection of the life of a city in which the finest bronze vessels the world has ever seen, to mention only one example, were manufactured.

Written records add a little to the archaeological picture, but the few that exist touched upon only the kings and their doings. The oracle bone inscriptions often referred the king's ritual and other activities to

137. *WW*, "Hsing-t'ai shih fa-hsien Shang tai yi-chih" 邢台市發現商代遺址; *WW*, "Hsing-t'ai Shang tai yi-chih chung ti t'ao yao" 邢台商代遺址中的陶窯; T'ang Yün-ming 唐雲明, "Hsing-t'ai Nan-ta-kuo ts'un Shang tai yi-chih t'an-chüeh chien pao" 邢台南大郭村商代遺址探掘簡報; *WW*, "Hsing-t'ai Chia ts'un Shang tai yi-chih shih chüeh chien pao" 邢台賈村商代遺址試掘簡報; *KKHP*, "Hsing-t'ai Ts'ao-yen-chuang yi-chih fa-chüeh pao-kao" 邢台曹演莊遺址發掘報告.

the places within the palace where they took place—presumably somewhere in the ground houses at Locus North in Hsiao-t'un or its environs. There are many *men* 門—doors or gates: doors to the *tsung* 宗 (lineage) ritual chamber, door to the courtyard, the *yi* 乙 door, the *ting* 丁 door, the Southern Gate, the Three Gates, and so forth. There were *shih* 室 or chambers: T'ai shih 太室 or "Primary Chamber," and the four chambers in the four directions. There were *kung* 宫, or Officiating Halls. There were *chin* 寢, or sleeping rooms, presumably those of the royal family members. There was a *t'an* 壇, an earthen platform or altar. Then, most important, there were the various *tsung* or lineage halls, in which ancestral tablets were placed.[138]

How the Shang halls of worship and living were spatially arranged is not clear from the sketchy references to them in the oracle records. Ch'en Meng-chia speculated that the Shang lineage temples and sleeping rooms "were all like the (modern-day) *ssu-ho-yüan* 四合院 style of architecture (with houses on all four sides facing one another, enclosing a courtyard at the center), having rooms on east, west, south, and north. Sleeping rooms were called East Room and West Room. . . . The Southern Chamber and the Primary Chamber were lineage halls in the lineage temple, places for rituals. The Southern Chamber . . . should be in the south, south of the Primary Chamber, which backed to the north and faced the south."[139]

This idea of having four lineage halls all facing onto a central primate hall coincides with Wang Kuo-wei's reconstruction of the ancient Chinese sacred hall—a place for important rituals performed to ancestors and to deities, referred to as *shih shih* 世室 (*ta shih*) by the Hsia, *chung wu* 重屋 by the Shang, and *ming t'ang* 明堂 by the Chou, according to *K'ao kung chi* in *Chou li*.[140] Kao Ch'ü-hsün believes that Wang's reconstruction is probably essentially valid, and on that basis he compares the cross-shaped burial pit at Hsi-pei-kang to an underground sacred hall, but he does not believe that all palace and temple structures in Yin were necessarily of this shape.[141] None of the ground houses or their layouts could be strictly compared to this shape. Either the

138. Ch'en Meng-chia 陳夢家, *Yin hsü p'u-tz'u tsung shu* 殷墟卜辭綜述, pp. 468–482; Ch'en Pang-huai 陳邦懷, *Yin tai she-hui shih-liao cheng ts'un* 殷代社會史料徵存, pp. 14–21.

139. Ch'en Meng-chia 陳夢家, *Yin hsü p'u-tz'u tsung shu* 殷墟卜辭綜述, p. 481.

140. Wang Kuo-wei 王國維, "Ming-t'ang ch'in miao t'ung k'ao" 明堂寢廟通考.

141. "Yin tai ta mu ti mu shih chi ch'i han-yi chih t'ui-ts'e" 殷代大墓的墓室及其涵義之推測.

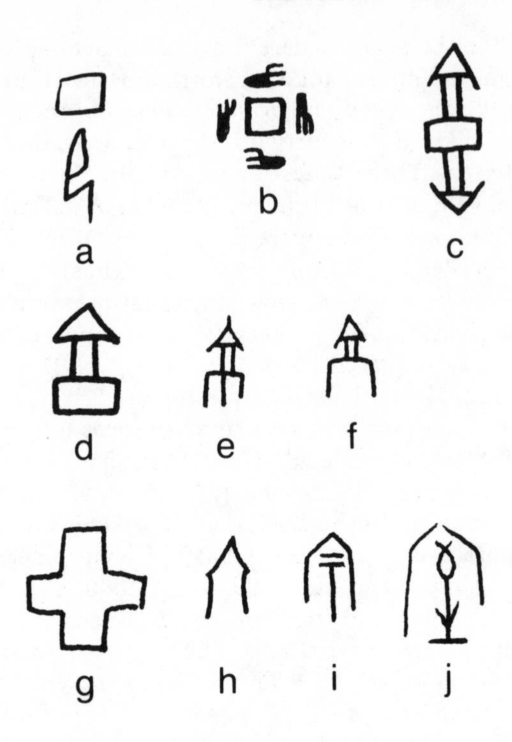

39. Shang characters indicative of contemporary architecture (all from *KKHCK, Chia ku wen pien*, except for *b*, from *KKHCK, Chin wen pien*).

reconstruction is more imaginary than realistic, or the real sacred halls of the Shang kings are still buried underground.

A few characters in the Shang oracle bone inscriptions are related to buildings and may contribute to our image of the Shang capital. The character for *yi* 邑 (settlement) (fig. 39 *a*) and for *wei* 衛 ("defense") (fig. 39 *b*) both show that the essence of a settlement was a walled enclosure. The Shang city at Cheng-chou had such an enclosure (see chapter 5), but no such a wall has been discovered in An-yang. Possibly a walled enclosure existed around the Hsiao-t'un center, and its remains have eluded the archaeologists' reach, but it is also possible that the last royal capital was so vast and its garrison forces so concentrated that a wall had not been necessary in this instance. The character for "city wall" (*hsiang* 享 = *yung* 墉, *c* in fig. 39) shows an enclosure with two or four gate towers, suggesting that such a wall was indeed the usual feature.

Several characters (*d, e, f*) show a platform on which a house with gabled roof was built. Shih Chang-ju's reconstructions of some of the Hsiao-t'un ground houses confirm the house shape in these characters, but the latter emphasize the prominent feature of the high platform. In textual references to many prominent buildings the word *t'ai* 台 ("platform") was invariably a part of the name, pointing in the same direction. Characters for ceremonial buildings (*g, h, i, j*) have two components: a cross-shape, which has just been mentioned, and a gabled roof as symbol for a ritual chamber.

2 Natural and Economic Resources

1. *LANDSCAPE AND CLIMATE OF NORTH CHINA DURING THE SECOND MILLENNIUM B.C.*

The royal capital, of which An-yang was the core, was situated in a plains area, at about 36° north latitude and 114° east longitude, that extended toward both the north and the south but was confined in the west by the T'ai-hang Mountains and in the east by the lower Yellow River alluvium, then probably a marshland if not in part submerged. The lower Yellow River changed course repeatedly during the historical period, but historical geographers generally believe that in the ancient historical period it flowed north, after merging with the river Yün 沇 (The upper course of the river Chi 濟) toward the Gulf of Chihli, taking in three west-to-east tributaries along the way: the Ch'ing, the Ch'i and the Chang (fig. 40).[1] The capital area was essentially the plains area that was drained by these three rivers before they joined with the Yellow River. Since the Yellow River appeared on the oracle bone inscriptions—as simply *ho* 河, "River"[2]—the North China plain must have been wide enough (from east to west) to accommodate it. Some geographers believe the Shang sites along the T'ai-hang were located right on the coast, most of the alluvial plains being still submerged.[3] But if the Yellow River had been flowing on the plains during the Shang period, the plains must have already long emerged. We believe that the Shang sites were not on the coast, but were separated from the coastal area, some distance away, by the Yellow River itself.

There is good reason to believe that the river plains where the royal capital was located were heavily vegetated and that the climate of the area was warmer and moister than at present. It was possible to

1. Li Tao-yüan 酈道元, *Shui ching chu* 水經注, pp. 79–103; Wang Shih-to 汪士鐸, *Shui ching chu t'u* 水經注圖, pp. 9–10.

2. Ch'en Meng-chia 陳夢家, "Ku wen-tzu chung chih Shang Chou chi-ssu" 古文字中之商周祭祀, 124–130.

3. Ting Su 丁驌, "Hua Pei ti-hsing shih yü Shang Yin ti li-shih" 華北地形史與商殷的歷史, 155–162.

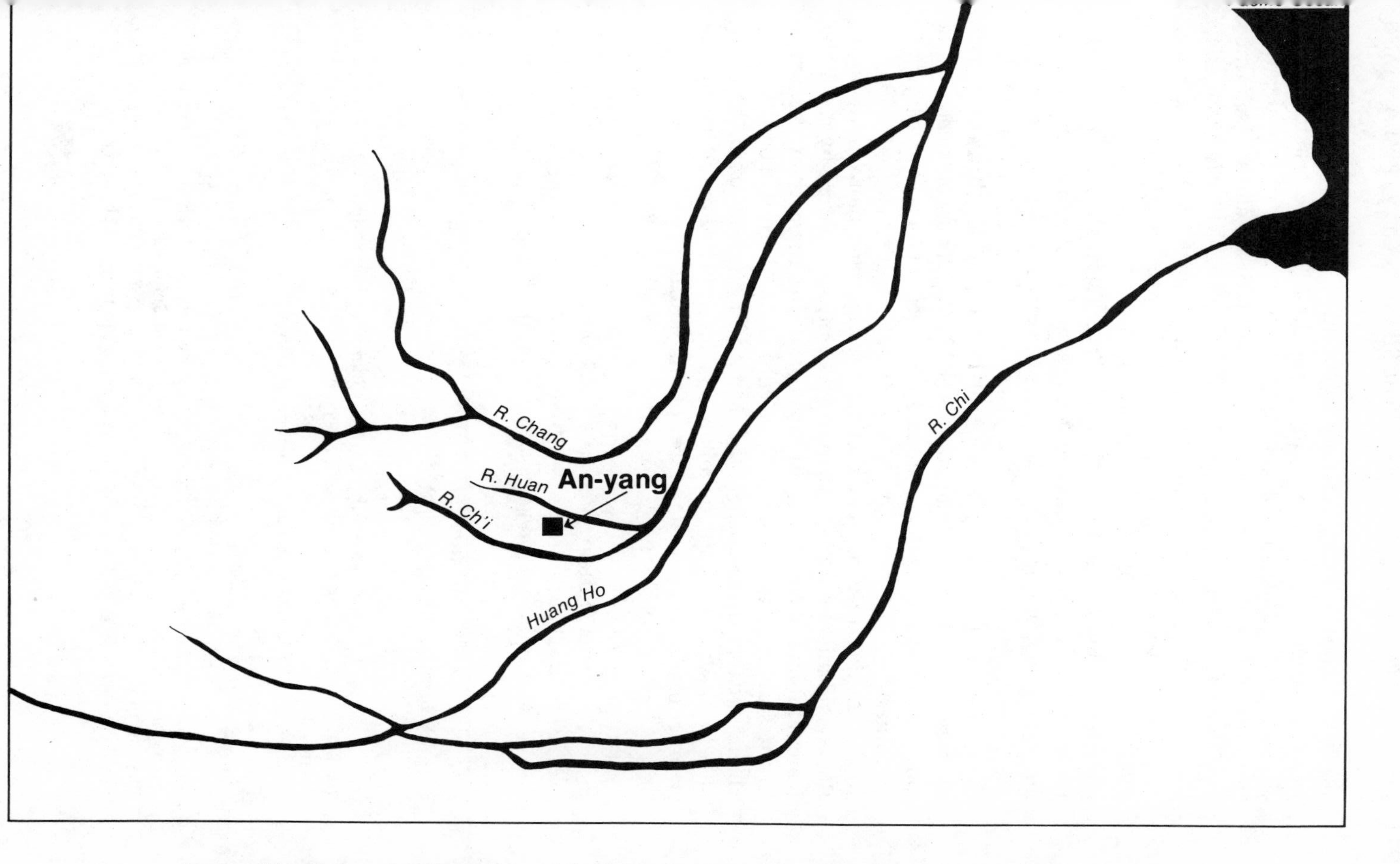

40. Possible palaeogeography of An-yang during ancient period (based on Wang Shih-to, *Shui-ching-chu t'u*).

reach that conclusion as early as 1959 on the basis of then available evidence in geomorphology, fauna, and flora.[4] In the last few years, palynological studies of Holocene deposits (especially of peat deposits) in southern Liaoning have disclosed a solidly based climatic sequence, as follows: *P'u-lan-tien period,* 10,300–8,000 B.P., *Early Ta-ku-shan period,* 8,000–5,000 B.P., *Late Ta-ku-shan period,* 5,000–2,500 B.P., and *Chuang-ho period,* 2,500 B.P. to present. After the close of the Pleistocene, there was a general trend toward climatic amelioration, and the optimum was reached during the Ta-ku-shan periods. "The Early Ta-ku-shan period has the warmest and most moist climate, with an annual temperature average of 13° C, which is 3–5° C higher than the present. . . . The Late Ta-ku-shan period . . . had a climate drier than the Early period, but it was still 2–4° C warmer than the present with an annual average temperature of 12° C."[5] This conclusion of the most recent studies is consistent with other studies done elsewhere in China.[6]

In the An-yang area, a climate warmer and more moist during the second millennium B.C. than the present is supported by the faunal material found at the Shang archaeological sites themselves. According to the studies of this material by Teilhard de Chardin, Young Chung-chien, and Liu Tung-sheng,[7] the mammalian remains from the Shang sites in An-yang indicate the following animals (listed in the table below in order of estimated total number of individuals):

Over 1,000
- water buffalo (*Bubalus mephistopheles*)
- boar (*Sus vittatus* var. *frontalis*)
- elaphure (*Elaphurus menziesianus*)

Over 100
- dog (*Canis familiaris*)
- pig (*Sus* cf. *scrofa*)

4. Chang Kwang-chih 張光直, "Chung-kuo hsin shih-ch'i shih-tai wen-hua tuan-tai" 中國新石器時代文化斷代; see also *The Archaeology of Ancient China,* chapter 1.

5. *SS,* "Liao-ning sheng nan-pu yi-wan nien lai tzu-jan huan-ching ti yen-pien" 遼寧省南部一萬年來自然環境的演變, 609.

6. Chu K'o-chen 竺可楨, "Chung-kuo chin wu-ch'ien nien lai ch'i-hou pien-ch'ien ti ch'u-pu yen-chiu" 中國近五千年來氣候變遷的初步研究, 15–18.

7. Teilhard de Chardin and Young, "On the Mammalian Remains from the Archaeological Site of Anyang;" C. C. Young (Yang Chung-chien), "Budorcao, a New Element in the Proto-historic Anyang Fauna of China"; Yang Chung-chien 楊鍾健 and Liu Tung-sheng 劉東生, "An-yang Yin hsü chih pu-ju tung-wu ch'ün pu yi" 安陽殷墟之哺乳動物羣補遺.

water deer (*Hydropotes inermis*)
sika deer (*Pseudaxis hotulorum*)
Shang sheep (*Ovis shangi*)
cattle (*Bos exiquus*)

Over 10

raccoon dog (*Canis* [*Nystereutes*] *procyonides*)
bear (*Ursus* sp.)
badger (*Meles leucurus*)
tiger (*Felis tigris*)
rat (*Epimys rattus*)
bamboo rat (*Rhizomys* cf. *troglotyles*)
rabbit (*Lepus* sp.)
horse (*Equus caballus*)

Under 10

fox (*Vulpes* cf. *vulgaris*)
Ussuri bear (*Ursus* cf. *japonicus*)
leopard (*Felis pardus*)
cat (*Felis* sp.)
whale (Cetacea indet.)
field rat (*Siphneus psiluras*)
tapir (*Tapirus* cf. *indicus*)
rhinoceros (*Rhinoceros* sp.)
goat (*Capra* sp.)
antelope (*Budocras taxicola*)
elephant (*Elephas indicus*)
monkey (*Macacus tchihliensis*)

Young and Liu, observing that this fauna certainly differs from the contemporary fauna of the An-yang area, suggested that the difference may be explained by the following alternatives: exhaustion by hunting, deforestation, artificial transportation, and climatic change, but they feel that the abundance of water buffalo indicates the indigenous nature of this animal and a warmer and more moist climate.[8] In recent years, water buffalo bones have been found extensively in Neolithic sites in the lower Yangtze that may be dated to the fifth millennium B.C. or earlier.[9] The abundance of water buffalo skeletons in An-yang suggests climatic conditions shared with the latter area. The elaphure,

8. Yang Chung-chien 楊鍾健 and Liu Tung-sheng 劉東生, *op. cit.*, 151.
9. *KKHP*, "Ho-mu-tu yi-chih tung chih wu yi-ts'un ti chien-ting yen-chiu" 河姆渡遺址動植物遺存的鑑定研究, 96 and 101.

attributed to a homeland in the Huai River valley in a recent study,[10] has long been regarded as an animal whose native habitat was flat marshy land.[11] The wild boar, the wild animal with the largest population, is also an inhabitant of the forest. This—that a warmer and, especially, more moist and heavily forested environment was the original habitat—is also true for the next most common wild animals: the water deer, the sika deer, and the bamboo rat. All three animals were identified at the Neolithic site at Pan-p'o, near Sian, Shensi. The zoologists who studied the bones concluded thus: "Today, the water deer and the bamboo rat are distributed in the Yangtze valley and south of the Yangtze . . . indicating that the climate in Sian was warmer and more moist at the time. Water deer live in marshland, and bamboo rats in bamboo groves. This suggests that there were marshes and bamboo groves in the Sian area. . . . Sika deer suggest that there were forested hills in the Pan-p'o area in the Neolithic period."[12]

A small number of fish and bird bones excavated from An-yang have been identified. Of the six kinds of fish, five (*Pelteobargrus fulvidraco, Cyprinus carpio, Mylopharyngodon, Ctenopharyngodon idellus,* and *Squaliobarbus curriculus*) are still common in the An-yang area, but the remaining type, the mullet (*Mugil* sp.), is only seen in coastal or estuarine waters and never reported from the interior.[13] This confirms the topographic discussion above, placing An-yang closer to the seacoast than it is now. Among the bird bones, other than possible chicken bones,[14] only three are known: The peacock (*Paco* cf. *muticus*), the cinereous vulture (*Aegypicus monachus*), and the silver pheasant (*Gennaeus* cf. *nycthermerus*).[15] Of these, the peacock and the silver pheasant are interesting. If the *muticus* identification is confirmed, then the bird in question is the green, or Javanese, peacock, which does not tolerate cold weather.[16] The modern silver pheasants are all found in Southeast China and mainland Southeast Asia[17] and the true silver

10. Ts'ao K'o-ch'ing 曹克清, "Shang-hai fu-chin ch'üan-hsin-shih ssu-pu-hsiang-lu ya-hua-shih ti fa-hsien yi-chi wo-kuo che-shu tung-wu ti ti-shih ti-li fen-pu" 上海附近全新世四不像鹿亞化石的發現以及我國這屬動物的地史地理分布.

11. J. G. Andersson, "Researches into the Prehistory of the Chinese," 38–40.

12. *KKHCK, Hsi-an Pan-p'o* 西安半坡, pp. 267–268.

13. Wu Hsien-wen 伍憲文, "Chi Yin hsü ch'u-t'u chih yü ku" 記殷墟出土之魚骨, 140.

14. Shih Chang-ju 石璋如, "Ho-nan An-yang Hsiao-t'un Yin mu chung ti tung-wu yi-hsieh" 河南安陽小屯殷墓中的動物遺骸, 12.

15. Personal communication from Raymond A. Paynter, Jr., Museum of Comparative Zoology, Harvard University, received 14 January 1960. His identification was made on bony specimens supplied by Li Chi.

16. N. G. Gee, L. I. Moffett, and G. D. Wilder, *A Tentative List of Chinese Birds*, p. 57; B. F. King and E. C. Dickinson, *A Field Guide to the Birds of South-East Asia*, p. 110.

17. Jean Delacour, *The Pheasants of the World*, pp. 139–155; Philip Wayre,

pheasant (*G. nycthermerus*) is found only in the forests of South China and Eastern Tonkin.[18]

The faunal data from An-yang are conclusive in showing that the area, a river plain, was heavily forested and near marshes, and somewhat warmer than the area today, a conclusion totally consistent with palynological studies elsewhere in China, both to the north and to the south.[19] This conclusion is further reinforced by written materials. Hu Hou-hsüan has pointed out that many placenames contained in the oracle records indicate or imply that the settlement was located on top of a hill or a mound,[20] a fact long pointed up by Meng Wen-t'ung on the basis of ancient texts.[21] The location of some settlements on high ground must mean that the low lands were wet or marshy, which would not be incongruent with the paleontological conclusions that have already been discussed.

The most direct evidence on the Shang climate may be in the oracle record itself. Hu Hou-hsüan listed the following as the metero-logical evidence that a warmer and moister climate prevailed: (a) There are records of rainfall all year round, including January through March, the winter months during which precipitation now takes the form of snow, and the rare records of snow refer to snow that fell mixed with rain or in the evenings. (b) Records of rain that fell continually for as long as more than ten days (eighteen days in one instance) appear to suggest that there were monsoons in the Shang period in the An-yang area. (c) Records of harvests indicate that two crops of both millet and rice were harvested annually in the An-yang area. (d) References to rice, elephant, and rhinoceros are seen in the oracle records. (e) Records of hunts referred to such animals as rhinoceros, elephant, tiger, elaphure, boar, wolf, and pheasant that again would indicate a warmer and more forested environment.[22]

A Guide to the Pheasants of the World, pp. 155–156.

18. Delacour, *op. cit.*, pp. 153–154; King and Dickinson, *op. cit.*, p. 105; Gee et al., *op. cit.*, pp. 52–53.

19. Ho Ping-ti, however, in several recent publications (*Huang-t'u yü Chung-kuo nung-yeh ti ch'i-yüan* 黄土與中國農業的起源; "The Loess and the Origin of Chinese Agriculture"; and *The Cradle of the East*), takes strong issue with this conclusion, maintaining that North China was steppe-like throughout its recent geohistory. Ho's use of the pollen data has been criticized by Richard J. Pearson and Ting Su, and the literary data he based his view upon are much too late for our purposes.

20. Hu Hou-hsüan 胡厚宣, "P'u-tz'u ti ming yü ku jen chü ch'iu shuo" 卜辭地名與古人居丘説.

21. Meng Wen-t'ung 蒙文通, "Ku-tai Ho-yü ch'i-hou yu ju chin Chiang-yü shuo" 古代河域氣候有如今江域説.

22. Hu Hou-hsüan 胡厚宣, "Ch'i-hou pien-ch'ien yü Yin tai ch'i-hou chih chien-t'ao" 氣候變遷與殷代氣候之檢討. See also Karl A. Wittfogel, "Meteorological Records from the Divination Inscriptions of Shang," and Tung Tso-pin 董作賓, "Tu

2. *WILD AND DOMESTIC ANIMALS*

The faunal list based on the archaeological data from An-yang given earlier shows the range of animals available to the capital's inhabitants. The wild animals, especially wild boar, elaphant, sika deer, and water deer, were dwellers of the forests and marshes near and to the east of An-yang, and some of them as well as other mammals such as the mountain goat and the antelope may have come from the T'ai-hang Mountains to the west. Many of these animals undoubtedly provided meat, skin, horn, and bone for the Shang, but hunting of them was also a major royal sport.[23]

To what extent wild animals were depended upon for food by the Shang is a debatable point. Insofar as the hunting records in the oracle bone inscriptions are concerned, hunting was more a sport than a subsistence activity, but the game that was hunted was presumably to be consumed.[24] From the hunting records, at least one thing was quite certain: the forests were densely inhabited. One such record, dated to King Wu Ting's reign, lists the following game:

> Divined on the day Wu-wu
> Ku made the inquiry:
> We are going to chase at "Ch'iu"; any capture?
> Hunting on this day, (we) actually capture:
> Tigers, one;
> Deer, forty;
> Foxes, one hundred and sixty-four;
> Hornless deer, one hundred and fifty-nine;
> and so forth.[25]

Hunts thus described were numerous; the greatest catch that was recorded was one of 348 elaphures.[26] Ch'en Meng-chia says that animals that appeared in hunting records more than five hundred times were elaphures, fox, water deer, and deer; those that appeared over one

Wei-t'e-fu Shang tai p'u-tz'u chung ti ch'i-hsiang chi-lu" 讀魏特夫商代卜辭中的氣象記錄, and Chang Ping-ch'üan 張秉權, "Shang tai p'u-tz'u chung ti ch'i-hsiang chi-lu chih shang-ch'üeh" 商代卜辭中的氣象紀錄之商榷.

23. Li Chi 李濟, "Hunting Records, Faunistic Remains, and Decorative Patterns from the Archaeological Site of An-yang."

24. Shima Kunio 島邦男, *Inkyo bokuji kenkyū* 殷墟卜辞研究, p. 503; Ch'en Meng-chia 陳夢家, *Yin hsü p'u-tz'u tsung shu* 殷墟卜辭綜述, p. 552.

25. Tung Tso-pin 董作賓, *Yin hsü wen-tzu Yi pien* 殷虛文字乙編 (Yi-2908). Translated in Li Chi, *The Beginnings of Chinese Civilization*, p. 23.

26. Shima Kunio 島邦男, *Inkyo bokuji kenkyū* 殷墟卜辞研究, p. 503.

hundred times were boar and wild cattle; and that tiger, a larger deer, and another animal as yet undeciphered appeared fewer than ten times.[27] The incidence of animals that appeared in the hunting records is thus largely in agreement with the faunal list prepared by zoologists from bone remains.

Domesticated and tamed animals were probably of much greater importance as sources of meat, skin, antler, and bone, and some of these were also of ritual significance. These include dog, cattle, water buffalo, sheep, horse, pig, and, in all probability, the elaphure, and they should be discussed separately. The elaphure was not domesticated in the same sense as the others, but elaphure herds are sometimes thought to have been fenced in to assure a steady supply, as a supplement to hunted animals.[28] The water buffalo, on the other hand, was a fully domesticated animal and a major source of shoulder blades for the diviners.[29]

Dogs, cattle, sheep, horses, pigs, and chickens were used for ritual purposes and found in burials.[30] Of these, all but the horse were identified also in garbage heaps and were, thus, consumed. The horse, however, was probably used exclusively to pull the chariot. It was probably not raised locally and had to be imported. Oracle records mentioned the "entry" of horses; Hu Hou-hsüan believes that they were imported from the northwest.[31]

It should be mentioned that domesticated animals were a highly significant resource in Shang life; the number of cattle used in rituals is truly amazing: 1,000 cattle in one ritual once, 500 once, 400 once, 300 thrice, 100 nine times, and so on, according to Hu Hou-hsüan's inventory of oracle records.[32] One gets an inkling from these numbers about the size of the herd. In fact, Wang Hai, a predynastic ancestor of the Shang, is credited in *Shih pen* with being the originator of cattle breeding, and Wang Kuo-wei characterized him as a true cultural hero who civilized the Shang people.[33] *Yi ching* mentions his death at the

27. Ch'en Meng-chia 陳夢家, *Yin hsü p'u-tz'u tsung shu* 殷墟卜辭綜述, pp. 555–556. Also see Huang Jan-wei 黃然偉, "Yin wang t'ien lieh k'ao (chung)" 殷王田獵考(中).

28. See Teilhard de Chardin and C. C. Young, "On the Mammalian Remains from the Archaeological Site of Anyang," 38.

29. Ch'en Meng-chia 陳夢家, *Yin hsü p'u-tz'u tsung shu* 殷墟卜辭綜述, p. 5.

30. Shih Chang-ju 石璋如, "Ho-nan An-yang Hsiao-t'un Yin mu chung ti tung-wu yi-hsieh" 河南安陽小屯殷墓中的動物遺骸.

31. "Wu Ting shih wu chung chi shih k'o tz'u k'ao" 武丁時五種記事刻辭考, 51.

32. "Yin tai p'u kuei chih lai-yüan" 殷代卜龜之來源, 5–6.

33. Wang Kuo-wei 王國維, "Yin p'u-tz'u chung so chien hsien kung hsien wang k'ao" 殷卜辭中所見先公先王考.

hands of the Yu Yi Shih, a northern tribe, probably as a result of a dispute over grazing grounds.[34]

3. *NATURAL AND CULTIVATED PLANTS*

Except for two pieces of wood,[35] no botanical samples have been subjected to scientific analysis, and our knowledge about the plant resources available to the Shang in An-yang is totally derived from the oracle bone inscriptions, supplemented by textual data on ancient plants in general.

At the present time the area of An-yang—and, in fact, most of eastern North China—is in the natural vegetation zone characterized by deciduous broad-leaved forests predominated by deciduous oaks.[36] However, in Shang times, given an annual temperature 2–4° C higher than the present, the An-yang area would easily move into the zone of mixed mesopytic forests of the Yangtze valley.[37] Significantly, the two pieces of Shang wood that have been identified are *Rehderodendron* sp. and *Melliodendron* sp., both members of the mixed mesophytic forest now growing in the upper Yangtze valley.[38] But we must await many additional botanical studies of the archaeological remains in the An-yang area before we are in a firm position to further characterize the native plant assemblage during the Shang period in An-yang.

The most direct reference to plants in the An-yang area is found in the *Shih ching*, the *Book of Songs*. Ho Ping-ti gathered together all botanical names in the *Shih ching* and concluded from a study of them that they show that "the ancient loess area indeed had the natural landscape of semi-arid steppes."[39] The primary evidence for this conclusion was the incidence of references to *Artemisia* in the *Shih ching*: "The single genus of *Artemisia*, with ten varietal names, leads all the plants recorded in this ancient work, arboreal and nonarboreal, by a

34. Ku Chieh-kang 顧頡剛, "Chou Yi kua yao tz'u chung ti ku-shih" 周易卦爻辭中的故事.

35. Ho T'ien-hsiang 何天相, "Chung-kuo chih ku mu (2)" 中國之古木(二), 274–275, 280–281.

36. C. W. Wang, *The Forests of China*, pp. 10–11.

37. According to Wang, *Ibid.*, p. 71 the mean annual temperature (MAT) in K'ai-feng, Honan, just south of An-yang, is 14.4° C. Add 2–4° to it and we will have an MAT of 16.4–18.4° C. The lower end corresponds to the present MAT of Hang-chou (p. 97) and the upper end would bring our area to the temperature range of southern Chekiang and northern Fukien (p. 131).

38. Wang, *op. cit.*, p. 226.

39. *Huang-t'u yü Chung-kuo nung-yeh ti ch'i-yüan* 黃土與中國農業的起源, p. 85.

wide margin. . . . [this] is an unmistakable indication that the loess area was a semi-arid steppe."[40]

Ho's heavy reliance on *Artemisia* in *Shih ching* to "prove" that ancient North China was "semi-arid" has been criticized by both Pearson[41] and William Ting;[42] Ting pointed out that references to *Artemisia*—or, for that mater, to any plant—are more useful for determining microclimates and soil than for generalizing about zonal climatic conditions. One can further point out that in Western Chou North China (a time period and area covered by the *Shih ching*) climatic conditions presumably varied from region to region, and that for this reason the poems in this work should first be analyzed on a regional basis.

After the Chou conquest of Chòu, the Shang capital, as mentioned before, was divided into three statelets: Pei, Yung, and Wei (*Han shu Ti-li-chih*). In the *Shih ching* are nineteen odes collected from Pei, ten from Yung, and ten from Wei. Whatever the true significance of *Artemisia* for the determination of climate, only a single reference to it is found in the thirty-nine odes from the An-yang area. The landscape that emerges from these odes is one with trees, forests, bamboo groves, and lots of water:[43]

> Look at that little bay of the Ch'i,
> Its green bamboo so delicately waving. [*Ch'i ao, Wei feng*]
>
> The Ch'i spreads its waves;
> Oars of juniper, boat of pine-wood. [*Chu kan, Wei feng*]
>
> Where the water of the river, deep and wide,
> Flows northward in strong course,
> In the fish-net's swish and swirl
> Sturgen, snout-fish leap and lash. [*Shuo jen, Wei feng*]
>
> Here we stop, here we stay,
> Here we lose horses
> And here find them again
> Down among the woods. [*Chi ku, Pei feng*]

The landscape these lines (incidentally) depict is surely no "semi-arid steppe"! Unfortunately, *Shih ching* has collected no folk songs

40. *The Cradle of the East*, p. 33.

41. Pearson, "Pollen Count in North China."

42. William Ting (Ting Su), "Chung-kuo ti-li min-tsu wen-wu yü ch'uan-shuo shih" 中國地理民族文物與傳說史, 86.

43. Translation by Arthur Waley, *The Book of Songs*. For the second line in *Ch'i ao*, Waley used the word "kitesfoot" (A kind of reed-like grass) to translate the original, *lü chu*, green bamboo. Here the original wording is restored.

such as these from the Shang people who lived in this area just centuries before these lines were written. In the oracle bone inscriptions, there are no landscape-depicting lines, although many characters have wood and grass compounds that possibly provide some data for study. Presumably these were among the characters that the Shang used to designate the plants from which they derived food, timber, fiber, and many materials for various crafts.

Li Hsiao-ting's *Chia-ku wen-tzu chi-shih* (''*Collected Interpretations of Oracle Bone Characters*'')[44] has collected 48 characters with the *mu* 木 (wood, tree) compound, including those identified with the following trees: apricot, willow, medlar (*Lysium chinensis*) and cypress. The same book includes 25 characters with the *ho* 禾 (cereal) compound.[45] Of these (and a few characters otherwise classified according to the *Shuo wen* compounds), Yü Hsing-wu singled out the following seven as of particular significance: *shu* (黍), *chi* (稷), *tao* (稻), *mai* (麥), *lai* (來), *ni* (秜) and *ho* (禾).[46] Since among these were the Shang's major crops, each deserves some detailed explanation and discussion.

SHU

The word *shu* appears in oracle bone records much more frequently than any other cereal: oracle bone specialists are agreed that this was the Shang's leading grain,[47] and most scholars of ancient Chinese agriculture are agreed, too, that *shu* referred to panic millet (*Panicum miliaceum*).[48] Shang archaeology has not yet yielded remains of panic millet (or any other millet) to confirm this, but in Neolithic archaeology there is only a single occurrence of this millet, and the circumstances of its occurrence were unclear[49], and all other millet finds have been identified as the foxtail millet (*Setaria italica*). This situation could have been the result of a major change of preferred cereals from the Neolithic to the Shang, or it could be an indication of inadequate archaeology.

44. Li Hsiao-ting 李孝定, *Chia ku wen-tzu chi shih* 甲骨文字集釋, pp. 1937–2047.

45. *Ibid.*, pp. 2349–2420.

46. Yü Hsing-wu 于省吾, ''Shang tai ti ku lei tso-wu'' 商代的穀類作物.

47. Chang Ping-ch'üan 張秉權, ''Yin tai ti nung-yeh yü ch'i-hsiang'' 殷代的農業與氣象, 303–304; Yü Hsing-wu, *Ibid.*, 88.

48. Yü Ching-jang 于景讓, ''Shu chi su liang yü kao-liang'' 黍稷粟粱與高粱; Te-tz'u Chang, ''The Origin and Early Cultures of the Cereal Grains and Food Legumes,'' 2. But Edward Schafer considers *shu* a glutinous variety of this millet; see his ''T'ang,'' in K. C. Chang, ed., *Food in Chinese Culture*, p. 88.

49. Carl W. Bishop, ''The Neolithic Age in Northern China,'' p. 395.

Both foxtail millet and panic millet are thought by many to have been domesticated in North China,[50] but Jack Harlan has pointed out that "both are found in a sprinkling of Neolithic village sites over Europe through the sixth millennium B.P. . . . *Panicum* has also been reported from Jemdet Nasr, Mesopotamia, at 5,000 B.P. and possibly Argissa, Greece, about 7,500 B.C."[51] He speculated that both millets may have been independently domesticated in several parts of Eurasia. But in any event there is no question, as of now, that *shu* was a native Northern Chinese cultigen and a major Shang staple.

CHI

The oracle bone character that Yü Hsing-wu interprets as *chi*, which is a common character for an ancient grain in the classical texts, is variously interpreted as other crops by other scholars,[52] and as a version of the character *shu* by Li Hsiao-ting in his Shang dictionary.[53] Since no other character in the Shang inscriptions is convincingly shown to be *chi*,[54] and since *chi* was a major grain, Yü's interpretation is thus highly appealing quite aside from its etymological and epigraphical merits.

But the botanical identity of *chi* is highly controversial. Half of the scholars identify it as *Panicum miliaceum* (glutinous or non-glutinous) and the other half as *Setaria italica*; "the nomenclatural confusions surrounding the two millets may never be resolved by available evidence and records."[55] But *Panicum* and *Setaria* have both been identified archaeologically. Yü Hsing-wu identified the characters *shu* and *chi* in oracle bone inscriptions (with *shu* occurring more than a hundred times and *chi* 40 times); and both *shu* and *chi* appear frequently in the *Shih ching* (*shu* occurring 19 times, *chi* 18 times, in 12 occurrences appearing together).[56] These parallelisms lead one to general agreement with the conclusion that *chi* was most likely *Setaria italica*, with *shu* being commonly agreed to be *Panicum miliaceum*.[57] During the Shang period,

50. Ho, *The Cradle of the East*; Te-tz'u Chang, "The Origin and Early Cultures of the Cereal Grains and Food Legumes."

51. "The Origins of Cereal Agriculture in the Old World," 379–380.

52. Yü Hsing-wu 于省吾, "Shang tai ti ku lei tso-wu" 商代的穀類作物, 92.

53. Li Hsiao-ting 李孝定, *Chia ku wen-tzu chi shih* 甲骨文字集釋, p. 2387.

54. *Ibid.*, p. 2351.

55. Te-tz'u Chang, "The Origin and Early Cultures of the Cereal Grains and Food Legumes," 28.

56. Ch'i Ssu-ho 齊思和, "Mao Shih ku ming k'ao" 毛詩穀名考, 268.

57. Tsou Shu-wen 鄒樹文, "Shih-ching shu chi pien" 詩經黍稷辨.

chi, although it appears in the oracle records less frequently, was in fact used more often than *shu* for ancestral rituals.[58]

TAO

The character depicting grains in a jar is commonly interpreted as *tao*,[59] the word for rice, although Yü Hsing-wu regards it as soybean[60] and Ch'en Meng-chia thinks it was a variety of millet.[61] According to Chang Ping-ch'üan, rice was of comparable importance with millet in the Shang oracles, since divinations about rice harvests often took place together with divinations about millet harvests.[62]

Rice (*Oryza sativa*) remains have been found in Honan from a Neolithic context,[63] and it is widely cultivated today in North China with improved irrigation. Given the North China climate during the Shang period that was characterized earlier, there should have been no environmental barrier to rice being planted in the Shang fields in the An-yang area and elsewhere within the Shang territory. Rice was probably first domesticated in South China or thereabout,[64] but its introduction into North China undoubtedly took place long before the Shang.

MAI

Wheat was used for rituals, but oracle bone inscriptions contain no certain references to wheat harvests (such as those to millet and rice harvests). Almost certainly an introduction from Western Asia,[65] wheat—also called *lai*, "the one that came," in oracle records—was unlikely an important crop in Shang fields. In oracle records the word *mai* is often preceded by the word *kao* or "to tell about," "to inform

58. Yü Hsing-wu 于省吾, "Shang tai ti ku lei tso-wu" 商代的穀類作物, 93; Chang Ping-ch'üan 張秉權, "Yin tai ti nung-yeh yü ch'i-hsiang" 殷代的農業與氣象, 303.

59. Li Hsiao-ting 李孝定, *Chia ku wen-tzu chi shih* 甲骨文字集釋, pp. 2355–2358; Chang Ping-ch'üan 張秉權, "Yin tai ti nung-yeh yü ch'i-hsiang" 殷代的農業與氣象, 304–306.

60. Yü Hsing-wu 于省吾, "Shang tai ti ku lei tso-wu" 商代的穀類作物, 95.

61. Ch'en Meng-chia 陳夢家, *Yin hsü p'u-tz'u tsung shu* 殷墟卜辭綜述, p. 257.

62. Chang Ping-ch'üan 張秉權, *op. cit.*, 305–306.

63. G. Edman and E. Söderberg, "Auffindung von Reis in einer Tonscherte ais einer etwa fünftausendjährigen Chinesischen Siedlung"; J. G. Andersson, "Prehistoric Sites in Honan."

64. Te-tz'u Chang, "The Origin, Evolution, Cultivation, Dissemination, and Diversification of Asian and African Rices."

65. Jack Harlan, "The Origins of Cereal Agriculture in the Old World."

about." Yü Hsing-wu's interpretation was: "The Shang king's border officials kept close watch over the *mai* harvest of neighboring tribes and sent intelligence reports to the Shang king. The king engaged in raids on the basis of such intelligence."[66]

NI

The word *ni*, interpreted as wild rice, occurs in oracle records only once,[67] but its meaning is unequivocal. The fact that wild rice was "harvested" near (possibly west of) An-yang is highly significant in the history of rice domestication in China.[68]

There are characters of and references to other cereals,[69] but as yet they are of less importance and their botanical identities are as yet unclear. One suspects that among the many food, fiber, and other economic plants and vegetables that are known to have been planted in North China since antiquity[70] most could be traced back to the Shang period. The one plant that is well documented, however, is the mulberry, the all-important food tree for the silkworm. Oracle records contained the characters for mulberry, silkworm, and silk, and archaeological remains from An-yang include silk-impressions on bronzes and on wood, the silkworm motif in bronze art, and jade sculptures of the silkworm.[71]

4. *ROCKS AND CLAYS*

Of the 444 stone implements and weapons from Yin hsü that have been studied by petrologists, 405, or about 91 percent, were made of eight rocks: slate (273, or 61.49 percent), diabase (37, or 8.33 percent), limestone (16, or 3.6 percent), quartzite (also 16), phylite (14, or 3.15

66. Yü Hsing-wu 于省吾, "Shang tai ti ku lei tso-wu" 商代的穀類作物, 97. Yü, however, interprets *mai* as barley, and regards another word, *lai*, to be wheat. Most other scholars regard *mai* and *lai* to be the same cereal, wheat.

67. Chang Ping-ch'üan 張秉權, "Yin tai ti nung-yeh yü ch'i-hsiang" 殷代的農業與氣象, 308.

68. See Ho Ping-ti 何炳棣, *Huang-t'u yü Chung-kuo nung-yeh ti ch'i-yüan* 黃土與中國農業的起源, pp. 140–160.

69. See Chang Ping-ch'üan 張秉權, *op. cit.*, 308–309.

70. Ch'i Ssu-ho 齊思和, "Mao Shih ku ming k'ao" 毛詩穀名考; Li Hui-lin, "The Origin of Cultivated Plants in Southeast Asia", and "The Vegetables of Ancient China."

71. Hu Hou-hsüan 胡厚宣, "Yin tai ti ts'an sang ho ssu-chih" 殷代的蠶桑和絲織; Wan Chia-pao 萬家保, "Ts'ung Hsi-yin ts'un ti ts'an-chien t'an tao Chung-kuo tsao-ch'i ti ssu-chih kung-yeh" 從西陰村的蠶繭談到中國早期的絲織工業; V. Sylvan, "Silk from the Yin Dynasty."

percent), sandstone (11, or 2.48 percent), and jade (7, or 1.58 percent). The sources of these rocks have not been scientifically determined, although Li Chi has stated that "generally speaking, some of the commonly used rocks, such as slate, limestone, and diabase, were probably produced in the neighborhood of An-yang."[72] We will leave the question of jade to the last section of the chapter.

Obviously different rocks were selected for different artifacts. Diabase and limestone were most often used for axes and adzes; the overwhelming majority of harvesting knives (95.88 percent or 243 pieces) was of slate; and most of the weapons were made of slate and jade.[73] On the other hand, the *ko* halberds found in tombs were made of marble, chalcedony, and jade, whereas those found in pit houses were made of limestone, quartzite, onyx, opal, chalcedony, and a fine, compact, silicified rock.[74]

Scientific analysis of the ceramics in Shang's An-yang has been barely started, but the results unmistakably point to very careful selection of clays for each ware and the possibility that all of them were not simply locally available mixtures. Li Chi distinguishes the pottery from An-yang into five major wares: white, black, gray, hard and/or glazed, and painted. The painted and the black wares belonged to the prehistoric cultural strata in An-yang, quite unrelated to the Shang, but a comparison of their chemical compositions with analysis of similar pottery elsewhere suggested to Li Chi that the painted pottery was probably locally made of local clays, but that the black pottery was the product of much more discriminating selection of clays. The Shang pottery, as represented by the gray, white, and glazed wares of Hsiao-t'un, represents a further advancement, according to Li Chi: "They indicate very high skills of clay selection and mixture. . . . The raw material for pottery making of the Painted Pottery period was derived from locally available sources. This condition had been altered by the Yin–Shang period."[75]

The glazed pottery of An-yang deserves closer attention. Similar pottery from Cheng-chou and from Chang-chia-p'o has been regarded as imported from South China, possibly from the lower Yangtze delta.[76]

72. Li Chi 李濟, "Yin hsü yu jen shih-ch'i t'u shuo" 殷虛有刄石器圖說, 524–525.

73. *Ibid.*, 525.

74. *Ibid.*, 534–535.

75. Li Chi 李濟, "Hsiao-t'un t'ao ch'i chih-liao chih hua-hsüeh fen-hsi" 小屯陶器質料之化學分析.

76. Chou Jen 周仁, Li Chia-chih 李家治, Cheng Yüng-fu 鄭永圃, "Chang-chia-p'o Hsi Chou chü-chu yi-chih t'ao-tz'u sui-p'ien ti yen-chiu" 張家坡西周居住遺址陶瓷碎片的研究.

The An-yang glazed ware is somewhat distinctive, and whether or not it was made locally cannot yet be determined.

5. *COPPER AND TIN*

Bronze making was a major industry during the Shang period—major in the sense, among others, of the quantity of ores that were smelted to meet the demand. As mentioned in the last chapter, the Fu Hao tomb excavated in 1976 shows that this single at most second-ranking member of the royal family was able to accumulate, in life and in death, more than 400 objects of bronze. These included more than 200 ritual vessels, the largest being a pair of square cauldrons, weighing 117.5 kilograms or 258.5 pounds each.[77] Where did they obtain their copper and tin ores?

There was a time when many scholars looked to the south as the source of both copper and tin for the Shang,[78] since North China has been regarded as being relatively poor in copper and tin deposits, whereas South China is known to be rich. But both Amano [79] and Shih[80] have argued, quite reasonably, that the Shang could have quarried in large or small mines that have been exhausted of ores and, therefore, that that historical records of ancient mines in North China must be consulted to see if such mines were available. Amano discovered that both copper and tin were amply available in the four provinces of North China: 6 copper mines and 6 tin mines in Honan, 2 copper and 2 tin in Shantung, 15 copper and 6 tin in Shansi, and 4 copper and 1 tin in Hopei. Shih identified 3 copper mines and 4 tin mines within 100 kilometers of An-yang, 6 copper and 3 tin within 200 kilometers, 11 copper and 4 tin within 300 kilometers, and 6 copper and 6 tin within 400 kilometers (fig. 41). Shih concluded:

> It was possible to transport [copper] from locations within 400 kilometers [of the capital], especially those between which there was frequent interaction, requiring from half a

77. *KKHP*, "An-yang Yin hsü wu-hao mu ti fa-chüeh" 安陽殷墟五號墓的發掘, 63.

78. Kuo Mo-jo 郭沫若, *Ch'ing-t'ung ch'i shih-tai* 青銅器時代; Chien Po-tsan 翦伯贊, "Chung-kuo shih kang" 中國史綱, vol. 1; Umehara Sueji 梅原末治, *Tōa Kōkogaku ronkō* 東亜考古学論考; Sekino Takeshi 関野雄, "Chūgoku seidōki bunka no ichi seikaku" 中国青銅器文化の一性格.

79. Amano Motonosuke 天野元之助, "Indai sangyō ni kansuru jakkan no mondai" 殷代産業に関する若干の問題, 231–237.

80. Shih Chang-ju 石璋如, "Yin tai ti chu t'ung kung-yi" 殷代的鑄銅工藝.

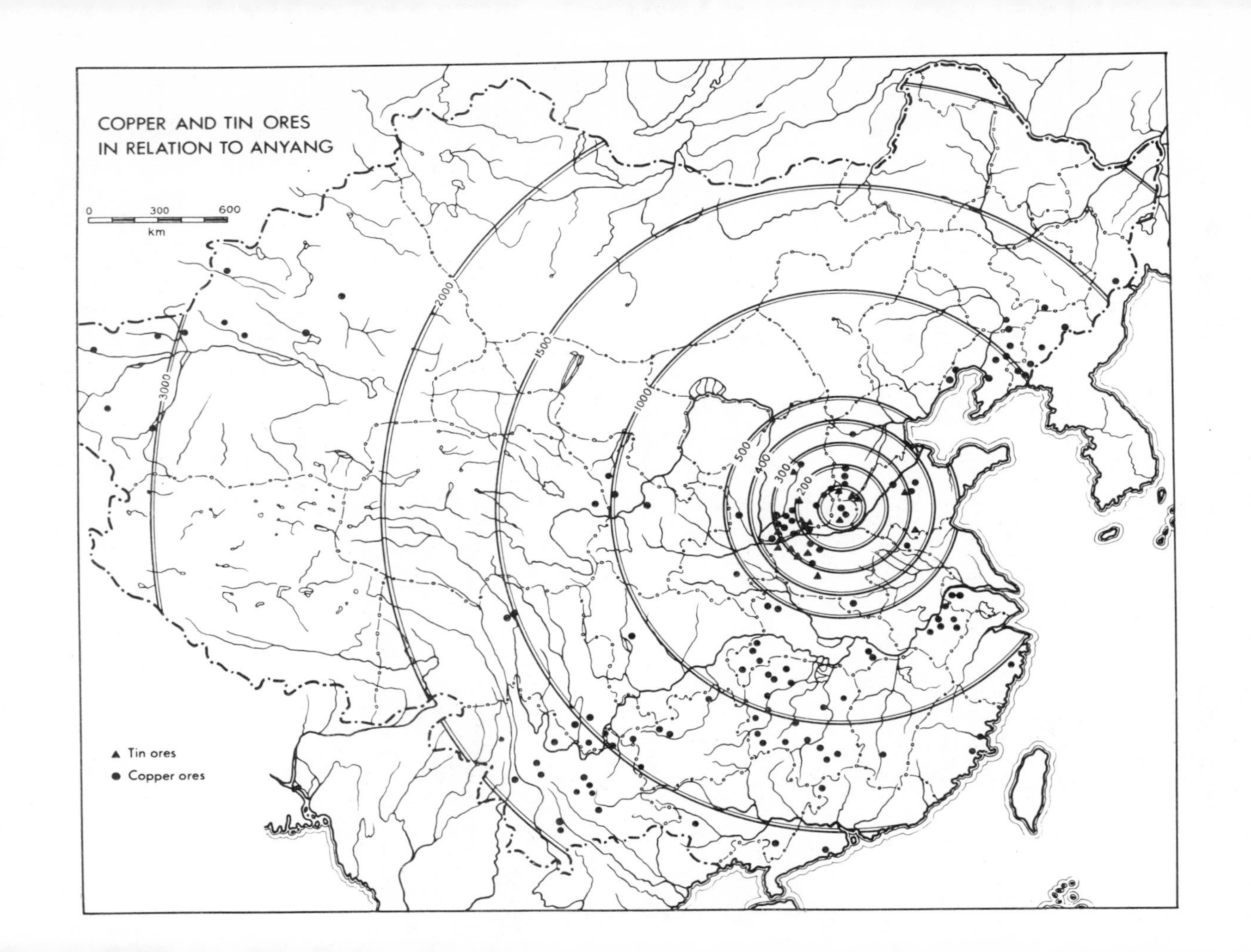

COPPER AND TIN ORES
IN RELATION TO ANYANG
0
300
600
km
3000
2000
1500
1000
500
400
300
200
▲ Tin ores
● Copper ores

> month to a month for a round trip. Ting Wen-chiang stated, in *An Outline of Mineral Industries in China*, that "copper ores were widely deposited in China and mining of them began early. But their history shows that the center of the copper mining industry was in Honan and Chekiang during the Han, in Shansi and Hopei during the T'ang, in Fukien and Kiangsi during the Sung, and in Szechwan and Yunnan during the Ming and the Ch'ing. No place flourished for more than three hundred years." If so, the Yin copper ores did not have to be looked for in the Yangtze valley, or even south of the Yellow River. The route from Chi-yüan to Yüan-ch'ü, to Chiang Hsien, to Wen-hsi, led to the Chung-t'iao Mountains, where copper deposits were rich.[81]

Shih further raised the interesting possibility that the alien state known as Kung Fang, which Hu Hou-hsüan has located in northern Shensi,[82] was a major supplier of copper ore for the Shang. Oracle bone inscriptions frequently record warring expeditions to Kung Fang, and, if Kung Fang was indeed a major copper-ore supplier, Shih wondered if these wars had anything to do with this particular important resource that the Shang must have regarded as being vital.[83] As for tin ores, south Shansi was also a major tin region.

Amano's and Shih's studies convincingly show that both copper and tin were available to the Shang miners, but they do not prove that they were actually mined by the Shang. For that we must have archaeological evidence from the mines or scientific evidence linking the ores found in An-yang to the mines. So far we have neither.

6. *PRECIOUS MATERIALS*

Of all the precious materials the Shang possessed, the cowrie shell (*Cypraea moneta* and *C. annulus*) must have had a special place. The word "precious," *pao* 寶, in oracle script as in modern script, features a cowrie, and many bronze inscriptions recorded gifts of so many strings of cowries. A string of cowries, possibly five or ten shells, was a basic monetary unit during the Shang.[84] In the Fu Hao tomb, almost 4,000 cowries were found;[85] she was indeed a very rich woman.

81. *Ibid.*, 102.
82. Hu Hou-hsüan 胡厚宣, "Kung fang k'ao" 舌方考.
83. Shih Chang-ju 石璋如, *op. cit.*, 102–103.
84. Kao Ch'ü-hsün 高去尋, "Yin li ti han pei wo pei" 殷禮的含貝握貝.
85. *KKHP*, "An-yang Yin hsü wu-hao mu ti fa-chüeh" 安陽殷墟五號墓的發掘, 62.

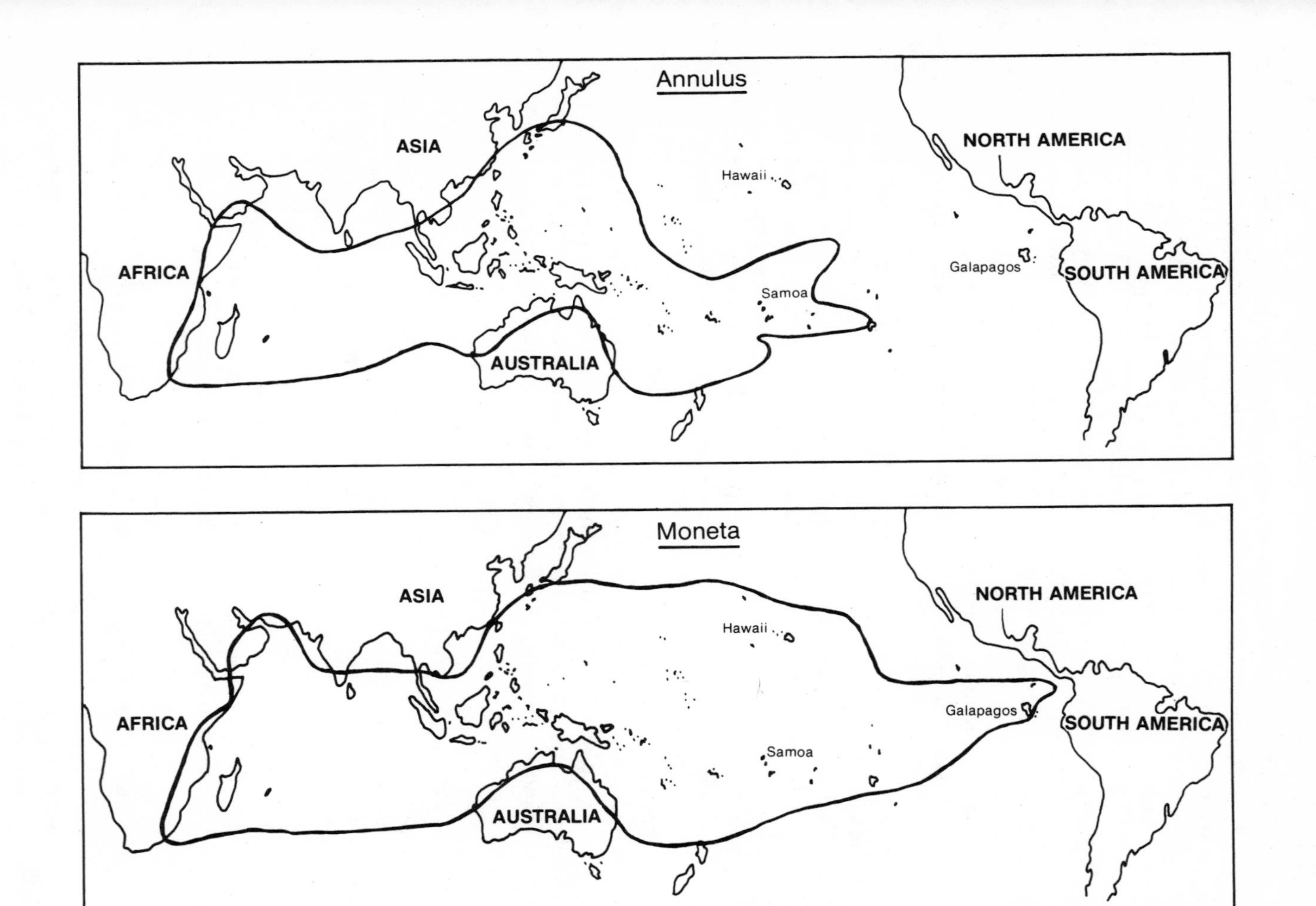
Annulus
ASIA
NORTH AMERICA
Hawaii
AFRICA
Galapagos
SOUTH AMERICA
Samoa
AUSTRALIA
Moneta
ASIA
NORTH AMERICA
Hawaii
AFRICA
Galapagos
SOUTH AMERICA
Samoa
AUSTRALIA

The value of the cowries was evidently derived in part from the distance they were transported to be imported to the capital. Both *C. moneta* and *C. annulus*, the two cowries most commonly used as money, are, like all cowries, marine molluscs; *C. annulus* may be found today on the eastern seacoast of China south of the Yangtze delta, but *C. moneta* is not seen on mainland Chinese coasts at all (fig. 42).[86] The oracle bone inscriptions contain little information on how the cowries were procured.

Another precious material of the Shang was the turtle shell that was used for divination, from which so many of our written records were derived. On the basis of actual records and educated estimates, Hu Hou-hsüan believed that at least a total of 160,000 pieces of turtle shells, both inscribed and uninscribed, had been unearthed from An-yang.[87] Using the rough figure of ten pieces per shell, he came up with the figure of 16,000 turtles. (Each turtle yielded two shells, a carapace and a plastron, but most inscribed pieces were plastrons, and so the figure 16,000 does not have to be significantly reduced to account for both shells.) The exact figure may be suspect, but one could not argue with the fact that a vast number of turtle shells were procured and used for divination. Where did these shells come from?

As stated previously, several species of turtles have been identified from the shells that have been excavated: *Ocadia sinensis, Chinemys reevesi, Mauremys mutica, Cuora* sp., and *Testudo emys. Chinemys reevesi* is seen in North China today, but all the others are found only in the Yangtze valley and further south.[88] This zoological fact is consistent with Hu Hou-hsüan's findings that in both ancient texts and in modern gazetteers turtles, of whatever kind, are recorded predominantly in Chinese provinces of the Yangtze valley and farther south, with only rare references to them in the northern provinces.[89]

Fortunately, in the oracle bone inscriptions there are ample records pertaining to those turtle shells that were imported. On some of the turtle shells (on the "bridges," the bones that connect the carapace with the plastron, at the tail-end of the plastrons, and on the margins of the carapaces) the Shang sometimes made records in the following format: "So-and-so *ju* 入 ('entered,' 'brought in') so many [shells]," meaning that a batch of X number of turtle shells was brought in from this or that person, tribe, or state. Hu Hou-hsüan in another of his significant statistical works[90] collected these entry records and made the following conclusions:

86. C. M. Burgess, *The Living Cowries*, pp. 341–344.
87. "Yin tai p'u kuei chih lai-yüan" 殷代卜龜之來源, 5.
88. C. H. Pope, *The Reptiles of China*, pp. 33–34, 45–47, 48–50, 54.
89. Hu Hou-hsüan 胡厚宣, "Yin tai p'u kuei chih lai-yüan" 殷代卜龜之來源.
90. "Wu Ting shih wu chung chi shih k'o tz'u k'ao" 武丁時五種記事刻辭考, 55.

> There are altogether 48 entries pertaining to turtle shells. Twenty of them are recorded as having been brought in by persons. . . . Four are by officials. . . . Eleven by states. . . . Thirteen names cannot be determined as to what they were. . . . Largely speaking, turtle shells were brought in either by officials of the Yin court or by people with close ties to the Yin king. Although the turtles were produced in the south, the turtle shells that were brought in did not have to originate in the south. Hua and Feng, for example, were states to the east of Yin, and Ch'üeh, Tien, and Ch'üan were states to the west. . . .
>
> The number of shells within each entered batch varied. Five hundred shells were in a batch once, 300-shell batches appeared twice, a batch of 250 once, 200 once, 150 once, 130 once, 120 twice, 100 twelve times, 50 six times. . . . The records yielded a total of 12,334 turtles.

Some of these states mentioned here will be discussed in a fuller context in our discussion on the Shang political order.

Jade, another common precious material of the Shang, offers an excellent material for scientific analysis for the determination of origins, but such analysis has not yet begun. What we call jade usually consists of two types of stone, nephrite and jadeite. "Nephrite is a calcium-magnesium silicate, a mineral of crypto-crystalline structure, while jadeite is a sodium-aluminum silicate belonging to the pyroxene group of minerals. The latter is an aggregate of small grains instead of short interlocked fibres and, consequently, it is the harder of the two."[91] Jade of both kinds constituted an important material for sculptures and ornamental and ceremonial objects, but it was also used occasionally for weapons found in burials.[92] From the tomb of Fu Hao alone, more than 590 jade carvings were brought to light, all made of varieties of nephrite.[93] No jade source is known in the An-yang area and its immediate vicinity, but Nan-yang 南陽, in southwestern Honan, about 375 kilometers away from An-yang, is a close source,[94] and Shensi (specifically, Lau-t'ien 藍田 and Feng-hsiang 鳳翔) is regarded as being

91. Cheng Te-k'un 鄭德坤, "The Carving of Jade in the Shang Period."

92. Li Chi 李濟, "Yen-chiu Chung-kuo ku yü wen-t'i ti hsin tzu-liao" 研究中國古玉問題的新資料, 179–182; "Yin hsü yu jen shih-ch'i t'u-shuo" 殷虛有刄石器圖說, 525–526, 534; Max Loehr, *Ancient Chinese Jades*.

93. *KKHP*, "An-yang Yin hsü wu-hao mu ti fa-chüeh" 安陽殷墟五號墓的發掘, 74.

94. *Ibid.*, 74. In summer of 1977 I visited the jade factory of Anyang city and found that Nan-yang jade is a major material that is being used.

an old source that has long been exhausted.[95] More remote sources that have been identified include southern Sinkiang,[96] Lake Baikal,[97] and Hsiu-yen 岫岩 in Liaoning.[98] Scientific analyses of jade objects will surely be able to provide specific data on sources, but these have not yet been undertaken.

Gold, the precious metal that was valued by many ancient civilizations of the world, was rare at Shang sites in An-yang. Fragments of thin sheets of gold, probably covers for some horse and chariot fittings or other ornaments, have turned up in the large tombs in Hou-kang (13 pieces)[99] and Hsi-pei-kang (77 pieces in seven tombs in the western section),[100] and small nuggets and sheets have been found in pit houses in Hsiao-t'un.[101] No large art objects are known to be made of gold. Yoshida pointed out that gold sources were long known in Shantung; the fact that Shantung was not always under the direct control of the Shang state may account for the rarity of gold in Shang metal inventory.[102] But other rare materials had been imported, and Shantung's ties with Shang must be said to be very close.[103] The rarity of gold can only be read in terms of Shang's own values.

95. B. Laufer, *Jade*, pp. 23–24; Chang Hung-chao 章鴻釗, *Shih ya* 石雅, pp. 130–134.

96. *KKHP*, "An-yang Yin hsü wu-hao mu ti fa-chüeh" 安陽殷墟五號墓的發掘, 74; Loehr, *Ancient Chinese Jades*, p. 5.

97. Loehr, *loc. cit.*

98. *KKHP*, "An-yang Yin hsü wu-hao mu ti fa-chüeh" 安陽殷墟五號墓的發掘, 74.

99. Shih Chang-ju 石璋如, "Ho-nan An-yang Hou-kang ti Yin mu" 河南安陽後岡的殷墓.

100. Liang Ssu-yung 梁思永 and Kao Ch'ü-hsün 高去尋, *Hou-chia-chuang Ti 1001, 1002, 1003, 1004, 1005, 1500, 1550 hao ta mu.*

101. Li Chi 李濟, "An-yang tsui-chin fa-chüeh pao-kao chi liu tz'u kung-tso chih tsung ku-chi" 安陽最近發掘報告及六次工作之總估計, 566; Shih Chang-ju 石璋如, "Ti ch'i tz'u Yin hsü fa-chüeh: E-ch'ü kung-tso pao-kao" 第七次殷墟發掘：E區工作報告, 726.

102. Yoshida Mitsukuni 吉田光邦, "Indai gijutsu shōki" 殷代技術小記, 175–178.

103. Yin Chih-yi 殷之彝, "Shan-tung Yi-tu Su-fu-t'un mu-ti ho 'Ya ch'ou' t'ung-ch'i" 山東益都蘇埠屯墓地和'亞醜'銅器.

3 The Shang Dynasty and Its Ruling Apparatus

The central focus of the Shang civilization as it manifests itself in the An-yang data is the king. The history of the Shang as recorded in *Shih chi* is in fact the history of its kings, and the oracle inscriptions recorded the kings' divinations almost exclusively. The Western Chou poem *Pei shan* proclaimed, "Everywhere under Heaven / Is no land that is not the king's / To the borders of all those lands / None but is the king's slave" (translated by Arthur Waley). What was true for the Chou was certainly true for the Shang as well. All the resources described in the preceding chapter were at the king's disposal, and he ruled through a complex and highly stratified governmental network. To understand how Shang society worked, we must first take a close look at the Shang kingship.

The Shang kingship may be characterized as an institution that had two major elements: first, it occupied the top of a vast state structure that served as the center of a centripetal economy and rested upon legitimate force and explicit law; second, it lay at the core of a vast kinship organization, based on actual and legendary blood relations and coupled with the state structure. In this chapter the latter characteristic will be discussed in detail. The next chapter will deal with the former—state—structure.

1. TSU 族 (*LINEAGE*) *AND* YI 邑 (*TOWN*)

The social structure of the royal capital was undoubtedly complex, but it was essentially a complex version of the structure of the fundamental social and political unit of the Shang, namely, the *yi* or town. A description of Shang social structure may well begin with a description of a simple, small Shang town.

A town the Shang called a *yi*, the character that consists of two elements: a square enclosure above and a kneeling person below. These elements signify the two essentials of a Shang town, a walled enclosure to mark its boundaries, and its resident people.[1] In oracle bone inscriptions we find many divinations about *tso yi* 作邑, "building of towns,"[2] which was a deliberate, planned event rather than a gradual, "natural" growth. Under specific circumstances, e.g., building a town in a frontier to open up new farm land,[3] the king would send a party out to physically build a town and fill it with people. *Shih ching* has several poems vividly describing the town-building activities of the Chou people, which give us some idea about similar activities of the Shang. Here is a description of T'ai Wang's building in Chou Yüan:

Of old Tan-fu the duke
At coming of day galloped his horses,
Going west along the river bank
Till he came to the foot of Mount Ch'i.
Where with the lady Chiang
He came to look for a home.

The plain of Chou was very fertile,
Its celery and sowthistle sweet as rice-cakes
"Here we will make a start; here take counsel,
Here notch our tortoise."
It says, "Stop," it says, "Halt.
Build houses here."

So he halted, so he stopped,
And left and right
He drew the boundaries of big plots and little,
He opened up the ground, he counted the acres
From west to east;
Everywhere he took his task in hand.

Then he summoned his Master of Works,
Then he summoned his Master of Lands
And made them build houses
Dead straight was the plumb-line,
The planks were lashed to hold the earth;
They made the Hall of Ancestors, very venerable.

1. Li Hsiao-ting 李孝定, *Chia-ku wen-tzu chi-shih* 甲骨文字集釋, p. 2165.

2. Shima Kunio 島邦男, *Inkyo bokuji sōrui* 殷墟卜辞綜類, p. 43, lists forty-four recorded items on town building.

3. See Chang Cheng-lang 張政烺, "P'u-tz'u p'ou t'ien chi ch'i hsiang-kuan chu wen-t'i" 卜辭裒田及其相關諸問題, 114.

They tilted in the earth with a rattling,
They pounded it with a dull thud,
They beat the walls with a loud clang,
They pared and chiselled them with a faint *p'ing, p'ing*;
The hundred cubits all rose;
The drummers could not hold out.

They raised the outer gate;
The outer gate soared high.
They raised the inner gate;
The inner gate was very strong.
They raised the great earth-mound,
Whence excursions of war might start.

And in the time that followed they did not abate their sacrifices,
Did not let fall their high renown;
The oak forests were laid low,
Roads were opened up.
The K'un tribes scampered away;
Oh, how they panted!

[Translated by Arthur Waley]

The following are segments of other poems describing various building activities.

The Ting-star is in the middle of the sky;
We begin to build the palace at Ch'u.
Orientating them by the rays of the sun
We set to work on the houses at Ch'u,
By the side of them planting hazels and chestnut-trees,
Catalpas, Pawlownias, lacquer-trees
That we may make the zitherns great and small.

[*Ting-chih-fang-chung, Yung feng*, translated by Waley]

To give continuance to foremothers and forefathers
We build a house, many hundred cubits of wall;
To south and west its doors.
Here shall we live, here rest,
Here laugh, here talk.

We bind the frames, creak, creak;
We hammer the mud, tap, tap,
That it may be a place where wind and rain cannot enter,
Nor birds and rats get in,
But where our lord may dwell.

[*Ssu-kan, Hsiao Ya*, translated by Waley]

A good example of a small Shang town with a mud enclosure and large houses for the lords is the P'an-lung-ch'eng ("Town of Curled Dragon") site in Huang-p'i, Hupei, discovered in 1963 and excavated in 1974. Here was a town wall of *hang-t'u* construction, 290 meters north-south and 260 meters east to west, in which was found a large palace consisting of a hall of four bays girded by a continuous corridor. On the four sides outside the corridor were forty-three large post holes originally holding wooden posts for supporting eaves. Many burials were found inside and outside the town wall, including a large grave with carved wooden chamber and three human sacrificial victims.[4]

Who were the people to inhabit the new town? It depended on the size and rank of the town, as *Shuo wen* made clear under the word *yi* ("According to the rules of the early kings, [they] varied in size according to their high status or low"). Oracle bone records indicate that many officials of the Shang court, as well as some princes and royal consorts, had their own walled towns outside the capital area, from which they presumably derived some of their own wealth.[5] From two passages in *Tso chuan*, we know that in Chou times when the king sent off a relative or official to build his own walled town, he would be granted, among other things:

1. The original name of his clan (*hsing* 姓)
2. The land
3. People in *tsu* units
4. A new name (*shih* 氏) designating his new polity
5. Ritual paraphernalia and regalia befitting his new political status and that of his town.

The last items, together with his ancestral tablets, he placed in a ritual chamber (*tsung* 宗) which symbolized his line of descent in relation to the ancestral trunk.[6]

4. See prolegomena note 198.

5. Hu Hou-hsüan 胡厚宣, *Yin tai feng-chien chih-tu k'ao*" 殷代封建制度考.

6. In the above summary I have presented a simple statement with regard to some very complex and basically controversial issues, including the definitions of *hsing, shih, tsung,* and *tsu*. Specialists of ancient China will realize the controversies involved as well as the fact that I have based the above on the simplest and most straightforward reading of two crucial paragraphs in *Tso chuan*:

Eighth Year of Yin Kung 隱公八年: "When the Son of Heaven would enoble the virtuous, he gives them surnames from their birth-places, he rewards them with territory, and the name of it becomes their *shih*" (translated by James Legge).

Fourth Year of Ting Kung 定公四年: "When King Wu had subdued Shang, King Ch'eng completed the establishment of the new dynasty, and those and appointed [the princes of] intelligent virtue, to act as bulwarks and screens to Chou. Hence it was that the duke of Chou gave his aid to the royal House for the adjustment of all the king-

How much of this Chou system of town building and people settling is applicable to Shang situations has been a topic of debate.[7]

---

dom, he being most dear and closely related to Chou. To the duke of Lu there were given —a grand chariot, a grand flag with dragons on it, the *huang*-stone of the sovereigns of Hsia, and the [great bow], Fan-jo of Feng-fu. [The heads of] six clans of the people of Yin—the T'iao, the Hsü, the Hsiao, the So, the Ch'ang-shao, and the Wei-shao, were ordered to lead the chiefs of their kindred, to collect their branches, the remoter as well as the near, to conduct the multitude of their connexions, and to repair with them to Chou, to receive the instructions and laws of the duke of Chou. They were then charged to perform duty in Lu, that thus the brilliant virtue of the duke of Chou might be made illustrious. Lands [also] were apportioned [to the duke of Lu] on an enlarged scale, with priests, superintendents of the ancestral temple, diviners, historiographers, all the appendages of State, the tablets of historical records, the various officers and the ordinary instruments of their offices. The people of Shang Yen were also attached; and a charge was given to Po Ch'in, and the old capital of Shao Kao was assigned as the center of his State.

"To K'ang Shu there were given a grand carriage, four flags—of various coloured silks, of red, of plain silk, and ornamented with feathers—and [the bell], Ta-lü, with seven clans of the people of Yin—the T'ao, the Shih, the Fan, the Ch'i, the Fan, the Chi, and the Chung-k'uei. The boundaries of his territory extended from Wu-fu southwards to the north of P'u-t'ien. He received a portion of the territory of Yu-yen, that he might discharge his duty to the king, and a portion of the lands belonging to the eastern capital of Hsiang-t'u, that he might be able the better to attend at the king's journeys to the east. Tan Chi delivered to him the land, and Mao Shu the people. The charge was given to him, as contained in the 'Announcement to K'ang,' and the old capital of Yin was assigned as the center of his State. Both in Wei and Lu they were to commence their government according to the principles of Shang, but their boundaries were defined according to the rules of Chou.

"To T'ang Shu there were given a grand carriage, the drum of Mi-hsü, the *Chüeh-kung* mail, the bell *Ku-hsien*, nine clans of the surname Huai, and give presidents over the different departments of office. The charge was given to him, as contained in the 'Announcement of T'ang,' and the old capital of Hsia was assigned as the center of his State. He was to commence his government according to the principles of Hsia, but his boundaries were defined by the rules of the Jung." (translated by James Legge; the transliterations of names have been changed to the Wade-Giles spellings).

In the above quotation the term *tsu* was translated as "clan" by Legge. It is evident that "lineage" is much more appropriate. Some of these features are confirmed in a Western Chou text on a *p'an* vessel found in 1976, in Fu-feng, Shensi. "[The inscription on Ch'iang 墻 *p'an*] states that his ancestor originally lived in the state of Wei 微 . . . Wu Wang ordered Chou Kung to give him land and have him live in Ch'i Chou . . . His son was the Yi ancestor of Ch'iang . . . Ch'iang's grandfather was Ya ancestor Tsu Hsin . . . He became separate from the ancestral temple and established his own new lineage, and he began to use the *shih* name of 'Yang ts'e 奉册,' according to his original office" (T'ang Lan 唐蘭, "Lüeh lun Hsi Chou Wei shih chia-tsu chiao-ts'ang t'ung-ch'i ch'ün ti chung-yao yi-yi" 略論西周微史家族窖藏銅器羣的重要意義, 19).

For other notable descriptions of the kinship organization of the royal houses, see Paul Wheatley, *The Pivot of the Four Quarters*, and Leon Vandermeersch, *Wangdao ou la voie royale*, tome 1, especially chapter 5 on the Shang clan.

7. Wang Kuo-wei 王國維, "Yin Chou chih-tu lun" 殷周制度論; Hu Hou-hsüan 胡厚宣, "Yin tai feng-chien chih-tu k'ao" 殷代封建制度考.

With the growing knowledge about Shang society in recent years, however, scholars are no longer reluctant to project most if not all of the essential features of the Chou system into the Shang period. The issues of clan name, land, and ritual paraphernalia and regalia are never any problem. Current knowledge about *tsu*, *shih*, and *tsung* leaves few doubts about their nature; the central issue concerns the *tsu*. It was the members of *tsu* groups who inhabited the towns; *tsu* were grouped into *tsung* in ritual contexts and into *shih* in terms of political status and political symbols. A male individual was known by the name of his town or his *shih*, but a female individual was usually known by the name of her clan.[8]

Some of these statements require further discussion. The oracle bone character for *tsu* has two elements, a flag above and an arrow below. Ting Shan's interpretation, that it originally signified a military unit,[9] is generally accepted.[10] In ancient China the association of flags with military units is well known,[11] and in oracle bone inscriptions *tsu* are shown to be action units in military campaigns.[12] Its size was probably a hundred strong on an average, the hundred adult men coming from a hundred households.[13] But military action was only one of the functions of the *tsu* (another function being reclaiming farmland),[14] and composition was apparently based on kinship. The definition of *tsu* by the *Pai hu t'ung* (A.D. 79) as a unit of kin "from great-grandfather to great-grandson" may not exactly apply to the *tsu* of the Shang era, but the same principles that defined a patrilineage of the Han period probably applied to the Shang patrilineages also. Ting Shan believes that Shang *tsu* and Shang *shih* were two sides of the same coin: *tsu* referred to the group's military-like organization, and *shih* was its symbol, while the group in question was "totemic" in

8. Cheng Ch'iao 鄭樵, *T'ung Chih* 通志 ("Shih tsu lüeh" 氏族略, "Shih tsu hsü" 氏族序,): "During the Three Dynasties and previously, *hsing* and *shih* were separated into two. Men were designated according to their *shih* and women according to their *hsing*. *Shih* was [used] to discriminate the noble from the lowly: the noble had *shih* but the lowly had no *shih*, only their personal names." See also Chang Ping-ch'üan 張秉權, "Chia-ku wen chung so-chien jen ti t'ung ming k'ao" 甲骨文中所見人地同名考.

9. Ting Shan 丁山, *Chia-ku wen so-chien shih-tsu chi ch'i chih-tu* 甲骨文所見氏族及其制度, p. 33.

10. Li Hsiao-ting 李孝定, *Chia-ku wen-tzu chi-shih* 甲骨文字集釋, pp. 2231–2233.

11. Hayashi Minao 林巳奈夫, "Chūgoku senshin jidai no hata" 中国先秦時代の旗.

12. Ch'en Meng-chia 陳夢家, *Yin hsü p'u-tz'u tsung shu* 殷墟卜辭綜述, p. 497: "Largely they were pertaining to military affairs."

13. Chang Cheng-lang 張政烺, "P'u-tz'u p'ou t'ien chi ch'i hsiang-kuan chu wen-t'i" 卜辭裒田及其相關諸問題, 110–11.

14. *Ibid.*, 111.

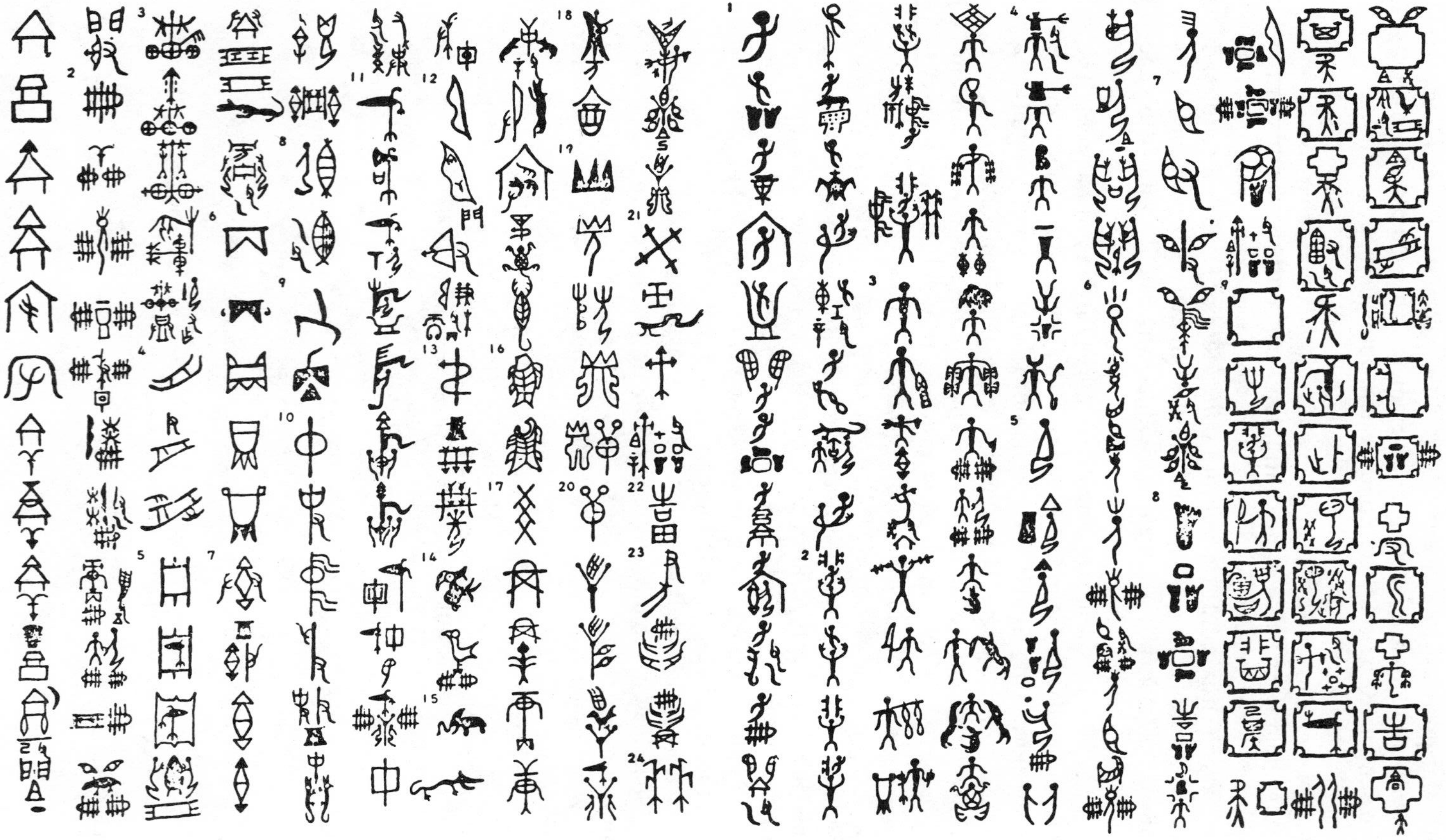

43. "Emblems" in Shang bronze inscriptions (after Shirakawa, *In no kiso shakai*).

nature. He believed that he was able to distinguish more than two hundred *tsu*.[15] The view that Shang society was based on discrete totemic clans called *tsu*, is also shared by Shirakawa Shizuka, who has undertaken substantial studies of a number of important *tsu* during the dynastic period of the Shang.[16]

The notion of totemic clans largely came from the great number of the so-called clan emblems in bronze and oracle bone inscriptions, many of which are pictographs derived from animal symbols (fig. 43). But as Hayashi Minao has convincingly shown, these animal-based symbols had several different derivations and, often found in clusters, they must represent groups of several levels, all of which cannot be totemic in the strict sense of the term.[17] In studying the formal characteristics and decorative motifs of Shang bronzes grouped according to their emblems, I have detected an appreciable tendency for bronzes with different emblems to behave somewhat differently with regard to the selection of decorative styles, which is possibly due to subcultural variations in different lineage groups.[18] Some of these lineages were obviously subdivisions of the same clans, while others represent different clans. The *tsu* groups that formed the social units of the people of a walled town, thus, varied in at least two ways: they belonged to different clans, and they represented differing political statuses.

2. *THE ROYAL LINEAGE IN AN-YANG*

The town-lineage organization outlined above is simple enough to comprehend easily, and it probably applied to a large number of small to medium-sized Shang towns. But the same principles applied to the royal capital; only here the variations were greater and the hierarchy was far more stratified. From oracle bone records, the ruling class at the top may be characterized, from the point of view of kinship grouping, as follows. The Tzu clan was the ruling clan, although not all of its members could be king. Within the Tzu clan, there was a *wang tsu* 王族, or royal lineage, from which kings were chosen, and *tzu tsu* 子族 or *to tzu tsu* 多子族, members of which often served as the king's

15. Ting Shan 丁山, *op. cit*.

16. Shirakawa Shizuka 白川靜, "In no kiso shakai" 殷の基礎社会; "In no ōzoku to seiji no keitai" 殷の王族と政治の形態; "Indai yūzoku kō" 殷代雄族考.

17. Hayashi Minao 林巳奈夫, "In Shū jidai no zushō kigō" 殷周時代の図象記号.

18. Chang Kwang-chih 張光直, "Shang Chou ch'ing-t'ung-ch'i ch'i-hsing chuang-shih hua-wen yü ming-wen tsung-ho yen-chiu ch'u-pu pao-kao" 商周青銅器器形裝飾花紋與銘文綜合研究初步報告.

loyal warriors. Some female members of the Tzu clan (presumably from the royal lineage) became the endogamous spouses of the kings. Female members of other clans are known to have been the exogamous spouses of the kings. Other members of other clans also shared the power to rule as the king's subordinates.[19]

We begin with *wang tsu*, "the royal lineage," a word that appears in oracles bone inscriptions often; Shima's concordance registers twenty instances. We do not know what were the perimeters of this group, nor all its functions. Kaizuka Shigeki ascribes to it a special group of diviners,[20] but as mentioned this is a controversial issue that is not likely to be resolved in Kaizuka's favor. But the lineage is unquestionably delineated at its core by the kings throughout the dynastic rule and their ritually recognized spouses. Earlier we discussed the genealogy of the kings as recorded in *Yin pen chi*. Studies of oracle bone inscriptions have confirmed that genealogy at many points, but modified it at others.

Named in oracle records are a number of remote ancestors of the Shang kings who were sacrificed to, but their relations are not systematically understood and seem to be more legendary (even mythical) than historical. Ch'en Meng-chia lists ten names that he considered more important than others: K'u 嚳, Wang Hai 王亥, T'u 土, Chi 季, Wang Heng 王恒, Yüeh 岳, Ho 河, Hsiung 兇, Yao 夭, and Yeh 戚.[21] The only one of these that can be compared with a counterpart in *Yin pen chi* is Wang Hai, corresponding to Chen in the latter text.[22] Wang Hai is a Shang figure of great importance according to both ancient texts and oracle records.[23] In the oracle records he is one of the three Shang ancestors (the other two being K'u and Ta Yi) who were given the title Kao Tsu 高祖, "High Ancestor",[24] and he is stated to be the father of Shang Chia, the king who initiated the schedule of rituals.[25] The oracle-inscription character for Wang Hai is often found associated with a sign

19. Hu Hou-hsüan 胡厚宣, "Yin tai hun-yin chia-tsu tsung-fa sheng-yü chih-tu k'ao" 殷代婚姻家族宗法生育制度考; Ting Shan 丁山, *Chia ku wen so-chien shih-tsu chi ch'i chih-tu* 甲骨文所見氏族及其制度; Shirakawa Shizuka 白川靜, "In no kiso shakai" 殷の基礎社会.

20. See chapter 1, p. 102.

21. Ch'en Meng-chia 陳夢家, *Yin hsü p'u-tz'u tsung shu* 殷墟卜辭綜述, pp. 338–345.

22. Wang Kuo-wei 王國維, "Yin p'u-tz'u chung so-chien hsien kung hsien wang k'ao" 殷卜辭中所見先公先王考.

23. Naitō Torajiro 内藤虎次郎, "Ōi" 王亥, "Zoku Ōi" 續王亥.

24. Hu Hou-hsüan 胡厚宣, "Chia-ku wen Shang tsu niao t'u-t'eng ti yi-chi" 甲骨文商族鳥圖騰的遺跡, 150–151.

25. Hu Hou-hsüan 胡厚宣, "Chia-ku wen so-chien Shang tsu niao t'u-t'eng ti hsin cheng-chü" 甲骨文所見商族鳥圖騰的新証據, 84.

of a bird, sometimes believed to be the totemic animal of the Shang people.[26] In the historical texts Wang Hai appears in *Shan hai ching* and *Yi* as a cultural hero having to do with the Shang's involvement with cattle.[27] Although his name does not contain a *kan*-sign, the oracle records show that the rituals performed to him were mostly performed on the *hsin* day, as were rituals performed to some of the other legendary ancestors in cases where records are available.[28]

The first Shang ancestor that the Shang kings enumerated in their ritual calendar was Shang Chia. After him, oracle records list Pao Yi, Pao Ping, Pao Ting, Shih Jen, and Shih Kuei in that order. *Yin pen chi* speaks of Pao Ting first, followed by Pao Yi and Pao Ping; this order is evidently in error. The oracle records also contain the names of Shih Jen's and Shih Kuei's spouses: P'i Keng and P'i Chia, respectively.

Then, beginning with Ta Yi, the dynasty's founder, the list of Shang kings (and their spouses) that scholars have reconstructed out of the oracle records is as follows:

1*	(1)	Ta Yi 大乙	= P'i Ping 妣丙
2	(0)	Ta Ting 大丁	= P'i Wu 妣戊
	(2)	P'u Ping 卜丙	
	[(3)	Chung Jen]†	
3	(4)	Ta Chia 大甲	= P'i Hsin 妣辛
4	[(5)	Wo Ting]	
	(6)	Ta Keng 大庚	= P'i Jen 妣壬
5	(7)	Hsiao Chia 小甲	
	(8)	Lü Chi 呂己	
	(9)	Ta Wu 大戊	= P'i Jen 妣壬
6	(10)	Chung Ting 仲丁	= P'i Chi 妣己, P'i Kuei 妣癸
	(11)	P'u Jen 卜壬	
7	(12)	Ch'ien Chia 戔甲	
	(13)	Tsu Yi 祖乙	= P'i Chi 妣己 (P'i Keng 妣庚)
8	(14)	Tsu Hsin 祖辛	= P'i Keng 妣庚, P'i Chia 妣甲

*First number designates generation; second number (in parentheses) designates order of ascension according to *Yin pen chi*.

†Names in brackets are according to *Yin pen chi*. They have not yet been identified in the oracle records.

26. Hu Hou-hsüan, see 24 and 25 above.

27. Ku Chieh-kang 顧頡剛, "Chou Yi kua yao tz'u chung ti ku-shih" 周易卦爻辭中的故事; Hu Hou-hsüan 胡厚宣, "Chia-ku wen Shang tsu niao t'u-t'eng ti yi-chi" 甲骨文商族鳥圖騰的遺跡.

28. Chang Kwang-chih 張光直, "T'an Wang Hai yü Yi Yin ti chi jih ping tsai lung Yin Shang wang-chih" 談王亥與伊尹的祭日並再論殷商王制.

9	(15)	Ch'iang Chia 羌甲	= P'i Keng 妣庚
10	(16)	Tsu Ting 祖丁	= P'i Keng 妣庚, P'i Hsin 妣辛, P'i Chi 妣己, P'i Kuei 妣癸
	(17)	Nan Keng 南庚	
11	(18)	Hu Chia 虎甲	
	(19)	P'an Keng 盤庚	
	(20)	Hsiao Hsin 小辛	
	(21)	Hsiao Yi 小乙	= P'i Keng 妣庚
12	(22)	Wu Ting 武丁	= P'i Hsin 妣辛, P'i Kuei 妣癸, P'i Wu 妣戊
13	(0)	Tsu Chi 祖己	
	(23)	Tsu Keng 祖庚	
	(24)	Tsu Chia 祖甲	= P'i Wu 妣戊
14	(25)	Fu Hsin 父辛	
	(26)	K'ang Ting 康丁	= P'i Hsin 妣辛
15	(27)	Wu Yi 武乙	= P'i Wu 妣戊
16	(28)	Wen Wu Ting 文武丁	= P'i Kuei 妣癸
17	(29)	Fu Yi 父乙	
18	(30)	[Ti Hsin]	

Comparing the above royal genealogy table with the one of *Yin pen chi* in the prolegomena, we see three major areas of difference. First, some of the names of kings are different. Two, some of the relationships of neighboring kings have changed. Three, the new genealogical table has names of some spouses. All three require some explanation.

First, the names of kings. Each consists of two parts. The second, and main, part is a *kan* character, one of the ten celestial signs, *chia, yi, ping, ting, wu, chi, keng, hsin, jen, kuei*. The first, less important, part consists of a character (and in one case two characters) meaning father, ancestor, great, middle, or small, or a character of unknown or uncertain meaning. This part, which quite possibly was used primarily to distinguish between kings with identical *kan* names, will be discussed presently. The *kan* character is the important part, and in many cases the kings' names are placed in the above genealogy in a certain position because the *kan* characters match the positions given in *Yin pen chi*. But why were the kings named after the day signs? In fact, this is a question of general significance, because both Shang and Early Chou bronze inscriptions show that *kan* characters were apparently employed for ancestral names outside the royal family as well.

I have discussed this issue of the significances of day-signs in names at length and in detail in previously published works,[29] which I will briefly summarize here. Formerly, the interpretation had been that Shang people were given posthumous names after death according to the day of the ten-day "week" on which they were born. Thus, it was held that King Shang Chia was given this posthumous temple name because he was born on a *chia* day, and Ta Yi (T'ang) was so called because he was born on a *yi* day.[30] After the discovery and study of oracle bone inscriptions, it was found that frequently a sacrifice to a deceased king was performed on the day with the same sign as the name of the king. Tung Tso-pin proposed that the names were temple names that were given to correspond to death, rather than birth, days,[31] but Ch'en Meng-chia believed that these day-signs were given in successive order according to generation, age, enthronement, and death.[32] All of these hypotheses are based on the principle that association of an individual with a day-sign was an accident—the accident of birth, death, or other life event.

The fact of the matter is that this association cannot have been based on such accidental associations. If it had been, the occurrence of the ten day-signs in a population would show a statistical randomness. But in fact it is anything but random. In a catalogue of inscribed bronzes, 1,295 inscriptions contain ancestral names with day-signs. The distribution of the ten day-signs in this small population is shown in fig. 44. The distributional pattern shown cannot be explained by an hypothesis that is based on random or accidental distributions. Of the ten day-signs, five are seen on 1,134 bronzes (86 percent of the total) and these five are the five even numbers. Is it likely that in this small population 86 percent of the people were born (or died) on the five even-numbered days?

The pattern of occurrence of the ten day-signs in the Shang royal genealogy again shows an unusual regularity. In the table below let us take the names of kings and their spouses in the genealogical order given above (whose difference with *Yen pen chi* will be commented on presently) and list only the *kan*-signs.

29. Chang Kwang-chih 張光直, *op. cit.*; "Shang wang miao-hao hsin k'ao" 商王廟號新考; K. C. Chang, "*T'ien Kan*: A Key to the History of the Shang."

30. *Pai hu t'ung* 白虎通 ("Hsing ming p'ien" 姓名篇): "The Yin people named their sons according to their birthdays." See Tung Tso-pin 董作賓, "Lun Shang jen yi shih jih wei ming" 論商人以十日爲名.

31. Tung Tso-pin 董作賓, *op. cit.*; see also his *Yin li p'u* 殷曆譜, and "Chia-ku wen tuan-tai yen-chiu li" 甲骨文斷代研究例.

32. "Shang wang ming hao k'ao" 商王名號考, and *Yin hsü p'u-tz'u tsung shu* 殷墟卜辭綜述.

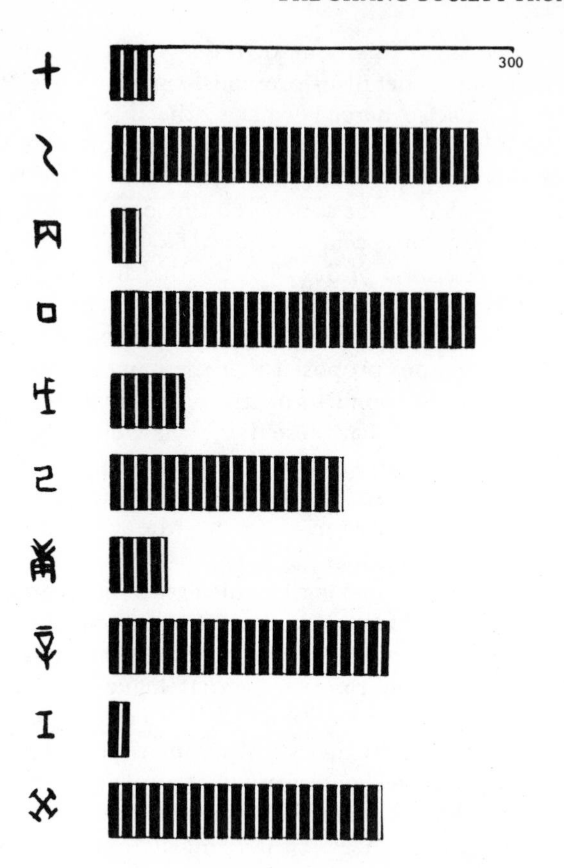

44. Frequency of occurrence of the ten celestial signs in 1295 bronze inscriptions.

Yi (= Ping)——Ting (= Wu)——Chia (= Hsin)——Keng (= Jen)——
Ting: Ping, Jen
Keng: Ting

Wu (= Jen)——Ting (= Chi, Kuei)——Yi (= Chi, Keng)——
Wu: Chia, Chi
Ting: Jen
Yi: Chia

Hsin (= Keng, Chia)——Chia (= Keng)——Ting (= Keng, Hsin, Chi, Kuei)——
Ting: Keng

Yi (= Keng)——Ting (= Hsin, Kuei, Wu)——Chia (= Wu)——
Yi: Chia, Keng, Hsin
Chia: Chi, Keng

Ting (= Hsin)——Yi (= Wu)——Ting (= Kuei)——Yi——Hsin
Hsin

This chart reveals two significant features in the distribution of the *kan*-signs. The first is the fact that some of the signs tend to cluster together either within the generation or across two generations among the kings. Thus, if we list the names of the kings of every other generation, we obtain two groups, listed below:

A	*B*
Yi	Ting
Chia	Ping
Wu	Jen
Chi	Keng
Keng	Hsin
Hsin	

Among these, *chia, yi, wu, chi* occur together, and so do *ping, ting* and *jen*. *Keng* and *hsin* could go with either group. *Kuei* does not occur among the names of the kings after Ta Yi. This peculiar phenomenon can in no way be explained under the birth-day (or death-day) hypothesis.

The second feature of a regular nature in the above genealogical order is that the ritually recognized spouses did not have the same day-signs as their husbands.[33] As mentioned above, the names of spouses were not available in *Yin pen chi* but have been worked out from the sacrificial records in the Shang oracle bone inscriptions. The Shang kings performed sacrifices to their mothers and female ancestors as well as to their male ancestors, and the oracle records are full of their names. Take King Wu Ting, for example. In his oracle records, the names of the following ancestresses occur: Chia, Yi, Ping, Ting, Wu, Chi, Keng, Jen, Kuei; and there are also the following *kan* signs among the names of his (classificatory) mothers: Chia, Ping, Ting, Wu, Chi, Keng, Hsin, Jen, Kuei.[34] But some of these female ancestors and mothers took on special status in the oracle records of kings Tsu Chia, Ti Yi, and Ti Hsin. During the reigns of these kings ancestors and ancestresses were sacrificed to according to a neatly organized ritual schedule, and when female ancestors are described as being sacrificed to they are usually described

33. Yang Shu-ta 楊樹達, "Shuo Yin hsien kung hsien wang yü ch'i p'i jih ming chih pu t'ung" 說殷先公先王與其妣日名之不同, in his *Nai-lin-ch'ing chia wen shuo* 耐林廎甲文說.

34. Ch'en Meng-chia, *Yin hsü p'u-tz'u tsung shu* 殷墟卜辭綜述, pp. 447–449.

as "the female-ancestor day-sign who was *ch'ou* 奭 of the male-ancestor [king] day-sign."[35] The word *ch'ou* has been interpreted in various ways, but scholars are agreed that it meant "spouse."[36] The spouse-names given above include only those that appeared in these circumstances,[37] since presumably only these female ancestors were afforded ritually recognized status. The observation that spouses did not have identical names to their mates applies only to this ritually recognized group. In many (but not all) cases the number of recognized spouses of an individual king is the same as the number of kings in the next generation.[38]

It is clear from the above that the naming of the Shang kings (and their spouses and subjects) was not based on such accidental events as the birth day, the death day, or the order of ascension. My hypothesis is that the royal lineages were organized into ten ritual units, named after the ten *kan*-signs (day-signs). Kings were selected from various units and were named posthumously according to their day-sign units, which also regulated the rituals performed to them. Details of this system will be discussed in the next section; it suffices to say here that as far as the names of the kings are concerned we have provided an explanation for the second part of these names, namely the day-signs.

The first parts of the kings' names, then, were discriminating words to identify an individual king and to distinguish him from all other royal relatives (including other kings) who had the same day-sign. Ta Yi's son could refer to him simply as Fu ("Father") Yi, and his son Ta Ting could be called Fu Ting by *his* son, Ta Chia. But by the time of Wu Ting, the first king who definitely had left oracle records, there were already three Yis—Ta Yi, Tsu Yi, and Hsiao Yi. It became necessary to distinguish them with discriminating words. These words include the following:

Shang: "Upper, above, first rank." This word is used exclusively for Shang Chia, the ancestor who initiated the ritual schedule of Tsu Chia.

Pao: "Ritual chamber, niche." Used only for the succeeding three ancestors, Yi, Ping, and Ting.

Shih: "Ritual tablet." For the succeeding two ancestors, Jen and Kuei.

35. *Ibid.*, pp. 380, 383.

36. Li Hsiao-ting 李孝定, *Chia-ku wen-tzu chi-shih* 甲骨文字集釋, pp. 1161–1195.

37. Except for P'i Wu of King Wu Yi, whose name came from a bronze inscription.

38. Tung Tso-pin 董作賓, *Chia ku hsüeh liu-shih nien* 甲骨學六十年, p. 78.

(The six ancestors designated by these three words represent the day-sign-designated ancestors before the founding of the dynasty under Ta Yi. Many scholars regard them as ritual symbols, rather than actual persons, that were used to represent the ancestors as a body).[39]

Ta: "Great." This designation is used five times, beginning with Ta Yi, the dynasty's founder. In all cases it is used in conjunction with a *kan*-sign when it appeared in the genealogy for the first time and only with a king who was in the main line of descent (see below): Ta Yi, Ta Ting, Ta Chia, Ta Keng, and Ta Wu.

Hsiao: "Small." It appears two or three times with a day-sign that was appearing in the genealogy for the second time.

Chung: "Middle." Used for the second ancestor when the same sign was used at least three times.

Tsu: "Ancestor." This ordinary designation was retained in the later stages of the genealogy since the earlier kings of the same signs were otherwise designated.

Others: Wai, Wo, Yüng (Lü), Ch'ien, Ch'iang, Nan, Hu, P'an, Wu, Lin, K'ang, and Wen Wu. Ch'en Meng-chia believed that some of these names were perhaps the kings' personal names during their lifetimes, while others were "honorific" or "complimentary" names applied in the same vein as similar posthumous titles conferred upon later-day emperors.[40] But Chang Ping-ch'üan speculated that "before Shang Chia, the names of the early lords and remote ancestors without *kan*-signs seem to be the names of their given lands, whereas after Shang Chia such names as Shih (Shih Jen, Shih Kuei), T'ang and Hsien (Ta Yi), Yung (Yung Chi), Ch'iang (Ch'iang Chia), Nan (Nan Keng), Hu (Hu Chia), Wu (Wu Ting, Wu Yi), K'ang (K'ang Ting), and Lin (Lin Hsin) may be the names of their given towns which they ruled [as nobles] before their enthronement [as kings]."[41]

The last suggestion, whether or not valid for explaining the kings' names, is important in pointing up the possibility that members of

39. *Ibid.*, p. 75.

40. Ch'en Meng-chia 陳夢家, *Yin hsü p'u-tz'u tsung shu* 殷墟卜辭綜述, p. 439.

41. Chang Ping-ch'üan 張秉權, "Chia-ku wen chung so-chien jen ti t'ung ming k'ao" 甲骨文中所見人地同名考.

the royal lineages were given their own *tsu* and ruled over their own *yi* outside the capital area in the fashion that has been described for the Shang ruling aristocracy as a whole.

Having disposed, for now, of the matter of kings' names, we can come back to compare the royal genealogy that has just been given with the *Yin pen chi* genealogy in regard to the question of the interrelationship of the various kings. The most important evidence concerning the genealogy in the oracle records consists of the following trunk-line (one king per generation) lists of kings:

1. "Shang Chia, ten; Pao Yi, three; Pao Ping, three; Pao Ting, three; Shih Jen, three; Shih Kuei, three; Ta Yi, ten; Ta Ting, ten; Ta Chia, ten; Ta Keng, seven; . . . Tsu Yi, ten. . . ."[42]
2. "Beginning with Shang Chia, Ta Yi, Ta Ting, Ta Chia, Ta Keng, Ta Wu, Chung Ting, Tsu Yi, Tsu Hsin, [to] Tsu Ting, ten tablets in total."[43]
3. "The King made the prognostication and said: [Inauspicious!]. Nan Keng bedevils. Tsu Ting [bedevils]. Great Shih Tsu Yi, Tsu Hsin, Ch'iang Chia [also] bedevil."[44]
4. "At the Five Tablets to tell: Ting, Tsu Yi, Tsu Ting, Ch'iang Chia, Tsu Hsin."[45]
5. "The King requests audience with: Tsu Yi, Tsu Ting, Tsu Chia, K'ang Tsu Ting, Wu Yi."[46]
6. "The King says, Use the Precious Vessel for Wen Wu Ting and Ti Yi on the meat stand" [translation tentative].[47]

From these, the following sequence can be collated: Shang Chia—Pao Yi—Pao Ping—Pao Ting—Shih Jen—Shih Kuei—Ta Yi—Ta Ting—Ta Chia—Ta Keng—Ta Wu—Chung Ting—Tsu Yi—Tsu Hsin—Ch'iang Chia—Tsu Ting—Hsiao Yi—Wu Ting—Tsu Chia—K'ang Ting—Wu Yi—Wen Wu Ting—Ti Yi—[Ti Hsin]. The oracle record sequence is largely in agreement with the *Yin pen chi* records and the latter's historicity thus has gained immense credibility.

There are, however, a few differences. First, the order of the

42. Kuo Mo-jo 郭沫若, *Yin ch'i ts'ui pien* 殷契萃編, no. 112.

43. Shang Ch'eng-tso 商承祚, *Yin ch'i yi ts'un* 殷契佚存, no. 986.

44. Chang Ping-ch'üan 張秉權, *Yin hsü wen-tzu Ping pien Chung erh* 殷墟文字丙編, 中二, no. 395, pp. 459–462.

45. Kuo Mo-jo 郭沫若, *Yin ch'i ts'ui pien* 殷契粹編, no. 250. Here the order of the given ancestors begins with the more recent.

46. Lo Chen-yü 羅振玉, *Yin hsü shu ch'i hou pien shang* 殷虛書契後編上 no. 20.5.

47. Tung Tso-pin 董作賓, "*Yin li p'u* hou chi" 殷曆譜後記, 199.

first four kings should be Chia, Yi, Ping, Ting; here *Yin pen chi* is in error. The only other major correction is to make Ch'iang Chia (the Wo Chia of *Yin pen chi*) the *son* of Tsu Hsin, instead of his brother, and the father of Tsu Ting. This change is amply justified by king lists 3 and 4 above, but oracle bone scholars do not accept this, mainly for two reasons: King list 2, above, has no Chiang Chia between Tsu Hsin and Tsu Ting, and Tsu Yi, Tsu Hsin's father, has two recognized spouses in the ritual calendar and, thus, should have had two enthroned sons instead of one.[48] None of these is conclusive proof. Here list 2 directly conflicts with lists 3 and 4; if 3 and 4 are valid, then there must be some explanation for 2. Actually, list 2 speaks of ten tablets and gives ten names; the order of these names cannot be reversed, but the names need not be inclusive. On another occasion "three tablets" are mentioned as a unit, but they are Ta Yi, Ta Chia, and Tsu Yi, who did not adjoin one another in three successive generations at all.[49] As to Tsu Yi having two recognized spouses, it is by no means an inviolate rule that the number of recognized spouses must be identical with the number of kings in the next generation. The number of kings in each generation is by no means always known.

As for the other kings not on the above trunk-line list, the above genealogy follows closely the general agreement among oracle bone scholars.[50] The only major departure from some oracle bone studies and from *Yin pen chi* is my placement of Ch'ien Chia (Ho T'an Chia) as son of Chung Ting and brother of Tsu Yi, rather than as brother of Chung Ting, as originally believed. Here I followed *Han shu* and my correction has been accepted by Hsü Chin-hsiung.[51]

3. *INTERNAL DIVISIONS OF THE ROYAL LINEAGE AND SUCCESSION RULES*

We have stated that we assume the *wang tsu*, or royal lineage, to have been a special group within the ruling Tzu clan, and that it

48. Hsü Chin-hsiung 許進雄, "Tui Chang Kuang-chih hsien-sheng ti 'Shang wang miao hao hsin k'ao' ti chi tien yi-chien" 對張光直先生的'商王廟號新考'的幾點意見, 130; Chang Ping-ch'üan 張秉權, *Yin hsü wen-tzu Ping pien* 殷虛文字丙編, pp. 459–462.

49. Shang Ch'eng-tso 商承祚, *Yin ch'i yi ts'un* 殷契佚存, no. 917.

50. The principal works are Ch'en Meng-chia 陳夢家, "Chia-ku tuan-tai hsüeh chia pien" 甲骨斷代學甲編; *Yin hsü p'u-tz'u tsung shu* 殷墟卜辭綜述, pp. 367–399; Wang Kuo-wei 王國維, "Yin p'u-tz'u chung so-chien hsien kung hsien wang k'ao" 殷卜辭中所見先公先王考, "Hsü k'ao" 續考; Kuo Mo-jo 郭沫若, *P'u-tz'u t'ung ts'uan* 卜辭通纂; Tung Tso-pin 董作賓, *Yin li p'u* 殷曆譜.

51. Hsü Chin-hsiung 許進雄, *op. cit.* (in note 48).

consisted of all kings, present and past, their official spouses, male members who were eligible to be heirs, and female members who were eligible to be the king's endogamous official spouses. The lineage must also include those present and past members who were not eligible to higher office but who were closely related (i.e., fathers, mothers, and siblings to those who were eligible). Until additional data become available to define *wang tsu* more adequately, we may use the above as a minimal definition, but even with this minimal definition we can already see that the lineage divided itself internally along inherent lines of division such as those determined by sex, generation, order of birth, and consanguinity and affinity.

Other internal divisions were institutional and structural in nature.

THE YI-TING SYSTEM AND THE OLD AND NEW SCHOOLS

It has been pointed out above that, according to their pattern of occurrence in the genealogical table, the *kan*-signs of the Shang kings clustered in two groups: A (Chia, Yi, Wu, Chi) and B (Ping, Ting, Jen), with Keng and Hsin going in either group. Kuei, the remaining sign, is placed, at least provisionally, in the B group. We have stated that because of this and other factors we must categorically reject the traditional view that the king's posthumous names represented their birthdays.

What alternative interpretation should be brought forth to account not only for the use of the *kan*-signs but also for their occurrence patterns? One can simply reach into ancient texts for another old explanation. In a T'ang annotation to *Shih chi*, a certain Chiao Chou 譙周 (c. A.D. 250) was quoted as having said in his book *Ku shih k'ao* 古史考 (no longer extant), that "[he was] named Chia because after death one is referred to by his tablet in the temple." How did one get assigned to a specific temple tablet after death? It would be reasonable to assume that, in the ancestral temple, tablets were arranged according to some internal structure of the kinship unit that formed the focus of the temple. One would assume, therefore, that the two groups of *kan*-signs that are shown in the royal genealogy represent two divisions within the royal lineage. Because the number of occurrences of these two signs is the greatest, and also because these two signs were not used by any of the recognized royal spouses (who will be discussed presently), I will refer to the two divisions as the Yi group and the Ting group.

There are several other facts that must now be presented and brought to bear on the Yi-Ting system to provide persuasive evidence for an interpretation. The first is the fact, already mentioned, that the kings' ritually recognized spouses did not have the same *kan*-signs as their husbands, the kings. In oracle bone inscriptions of the Wu Ting era, there are many names with the following format: Fu ("consort") + character with *nü* ("woman") element. Many scholars believe that these referred to the royal consorts who came from various clans, the second characters in their names being their clan names.[52] In view of the fact that among these Fu-X names was the name Fu Hao, or the Fu from the Tzu clan, Ting Shan had speculated that some of the royal marriages were endogamous.[53] The Fu Hao tomb, as described earlier, has yielded many bronze vessels inscribed with both the name Fu Hao and the title Ssu Mu Hsin (or Hou Hsin), leading to the justifiable conclusion that Fu Hao *was* the P'i Hsin that appeared in the oracle records as one of Wu Ting's three recognized spouses. In fact, the name Fu Hao must have been used to refer to all of the king's endogamous consorts and not just any single individual. Among Wu Ting's consorts of various names (i.e., from various clans), the name Fu Hao's has appeared the most often.[54] Possibly the name referred to at least three actual persons, those known posthumously as P'i Hsin, P'i Kuei, and P'i Wu. In other words, the kings' recognized spouses came from within the *wang tsu* or the royal lineage, but they came from tablet unit outside of the kings' own.

Another fact that has a strong bearing on the Yi-Ting system has to do with Yi Yin, the well-known prime minister who served under Ta Yi or T'ang. Textual records say that after T'ang's death Yi Yin was involved in a power struggle that in the end pitted him against Ta Chia, who according to some records was exiled by Yi Yin or, according to other records, had Yi Yin killed.[55] In the oracle records, Yi Yin has been found to have been worshipped during the reign of Wu Ting but not during Tsu Chia's reign. When he was worshipped, the ritual was as a rule performed on the *ting*-day.[56] These bits of information strongly point to the possibility that Yi Yin was the head of the Ting group at the time of the dynasty's founding and that as such he was the king's deputy chief when the kingship was in the hands of the head of the Yi group (Ta Yi in this case).

52. Hu Hou-hsüan 胡厚宣, "Yin tai hun-yin chia-tsu tsung-fa sheng-yü chih-tu k'ao" 殷代婚姻家族宗法生育制度考; Ting Shan 丁山, *Chia ku wen so-chien shih-tsu chi ch'i chih-tu* 甲骨文所見氏族及其制度.

53. Ting Shan 丁山, *op. cit.*, p. 56.

54. Wang Yü-hsin 王宇信, Chang Yung-shan 張永山, and Yang Sheng-nan 楊升南, "Shih lun Yin hsü wu-hao mu ti 'Fu Hao'" 試論殷墟五號墓的'婦好', 1.

55. Ch'en Meng-chia 陳夢家, "Chia-ku tuan-tai hsüeh chia pien" 甲骨斷代學甲編, 22–25.

56. Chang Kwang-chih 張光直, "T'an Wang Hai yü Yi Yin ti chi jih ping tsai lun Yin Shang wang-chih" 談王亥與伊尹的祭日並再論殷商王制, 115.

Other bits of information also bear upon the Yi-Ting system, although their significance is more corroborative than direct. In the oracle records are references to *Yi men* 乙門 ("Yi door" or "Yi gate") and *Ting men* 丁門, possibly referring to doors leading to the two halves of the temple.[57] Yi and Ting are also the two days on which many rituals were performed in the Western Chou period according to Western Chou bronze inscriptions.[58] In fact, as I have pointed out in an earlier work,[59] rituals performed to Chou ancestors of the *chao* 昭 generation were often performed on the *ting*-day, whereas those for ancestors of the *mu* 穆 generation were often given on the *yi*-day. One can be tempted to see strong resemblances between the Yi-Ting system of the Shang and the chao-mu system of the Chou.

In the above we have given the essential facts pertaining to a possible Yi-Ting system of internal division within the Shang royal lineage. How does one interpret them? Here ethnographical models can come to our aid. They tell us about some actual systems with components similar to those of the Shang and, thus, about possible ways in which we can realistically and reasonably piece together our disconnected facts.

In a general study of the rules of succession to high office, Jack Goody[60] distinguishes four types of dynastic institutions: the "royal descent group" of the Basuto, the southern Bantu generally, and of many other societies; the "dynasty" which constitutes the only significant descent unit in the society, as is the case among the Gonja, Lozi, Hausa, Nupe, and in some of the Mossi states; the "narrow lineal dynasty" of the Baganda in the nineteenth century, and more especially of the Ottoman Turks; and the "bilateral or familial dynasty" of the kind found in modern Europe (fig. 45).

Since the Shang kings belonged to no fewer than ten tablet units, and in view of the fact that in the royal genealogy the kingship shifts between tablet units, never continuing within a single unit, plainly the Shang system is not consistent with the characteristics of the stem or the familial dynasty systems. In the two other systems there is a very common practice that Goody has called the "circulating succession." This was found widely in Africa, Europe, Asia, and the Pacific, and although it had many variations its general underlying principles are not complex. In societies with such systems, kingship is confined to a ruling class, circulating within this class among its various sections or

57. Ch'en Meng-chia 陳夢家, *Yin hsü p'u-tz'u tsung shu* 殷墟卜辭綜述, p. 478.

58. Chang Kwang-chih 張光直, "Shang wang miao-hao hsin k'ao" 商王廟號新考, 93.

59. *Ibid.*

60. *Succession to High Office*, p. 26.

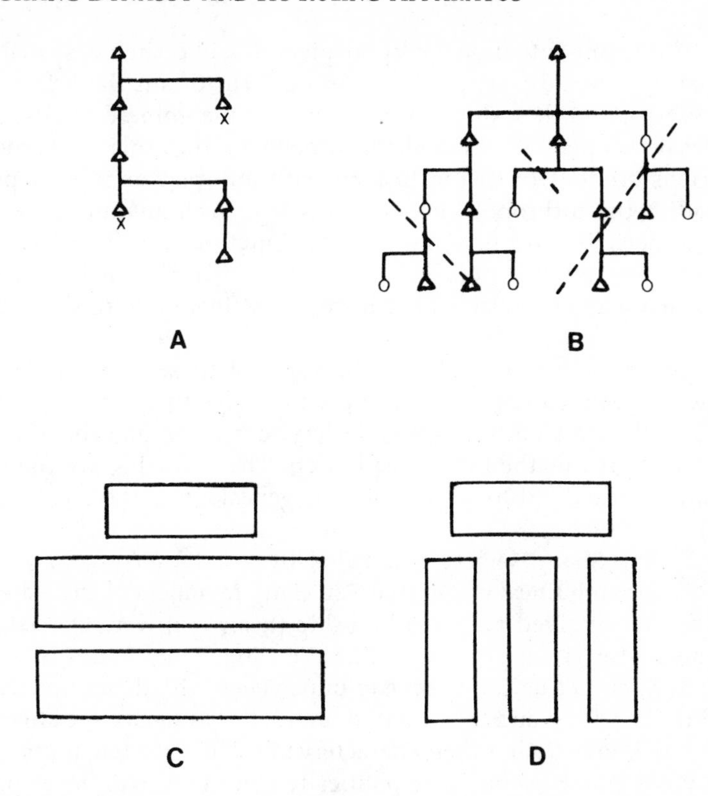

45. Four types of dynastic structure. *A*. Stem dynasty (agnatic succession over time). *B*. Familial dynasty (English pattern, exclusion of children of non-succeeding daughters and grandchildren of non-succeeding sons). *C*. Dynastic descent group. The short rectangle on top represents a hereditary dynasty, segmented in circulating systems, and the longer rectangles represent other estates. *D*. Royal descent group. Each rectangle represents a unilineal descent group (after Jack Goody, *Succession to High Office*, p. 27).

segments. These segments may be unrelated descent groups (the "royal descent group"), or they may be subdivisions of a single kin-based ruling unit ("the dynasty" or "the dynastic descent group"). In many cases there is a tendency toward dualistic grouping of these segments, with the throne being assumed by members of the two parties in turn in alternate generations. In the case of alternate succession among two or more lines, the high chiefs of the groups not currently in power often serve as assistant or secondary chiefs or prime ministers. Among these lines of royal descent there usually are elaborate marriage ties. When these lines constitute segments of a single dynasty, the dynasty is often endogamous.

The Shang situation looks suspiciously like such a system, in particular like the "dynastic descent group." Historians think forward, not backward, and they should remember that the Chinese agnatic stem dynasties developed out of the Shang system, not the other way around. The serious student of Shang history with an open mind will profit from reading the anthropological accounts of such circulating succession systems, especially those in Malaya[61] and in Futafuni of the Ellis Islands,[62] Fakaofo in the Union Group,[63] and in Rotuma[64] in the Pacific Islands, societies that may even claim some historical affiliation with the ancient Chinese.

Despite these illustrations, the value of these accounts is only heuristic. We must attempt to write a set of rules that can account for the empirical data from the Shang society, even though ethographical analogy may give us the initial inspiration. The following are the rules that I have worked out to account for the genealogy of the Shang kings (fig. 46).

1. The Shang society was ruled by a hereditary ruling class, of a single consanguineal origin (the Tzu clan). Members of the clan that were actively involved with the kingship (*wang tsu*) were classed into ten segments for ritual purposes: Chia, Yi, Ping, Ting, Wu, Chi, Keng, Hsin, Jen, Kuei. Let us call them *kan* units. These ritual *kan* units were also political entities, and they figured importantly in marriage alliances. We do not know their other characteristics, but the ten units were probably not equals. Some were politically more powerful, more populous, and/or more ritually prominent than others. Chia, Yi, and Ting were three such units.

2. The ten *kan* units were affiliated with one another to form two major divisions, A and B. Chia and Yi were undoubtedly fellow members of A, and Ting a member of B. These units were the most politically powerful. The other *kan* units aligned themselves similarly: Ping was a member of division B; Wu and Chi undoubtedly were units of A; and Jen and Kuei were perhaps B. Keng and Hsin were non-aligned, or perhaps formed a separate segment a level above or parallel to both A and B, although Hsin, at least, probably sided more often with B.

3. Succession did not follow automatic rules except for two: first, it could not stay within the same *kan* unit, and second, when the

61. J. M. Gullick, *Indigenous Political Systems of Western Malaya.*

62. Robert W. Williamson, *The Social and Political Systems of Central Polynesia,* vol. 1, pp. 378–379.

63. A. M. Hocart, "Chieftainship and the Sister's Son in the Pacific."

64. F. L. S. Bell, "A Functional Interpretation of Inheritance and Succession in Central Polynesia."

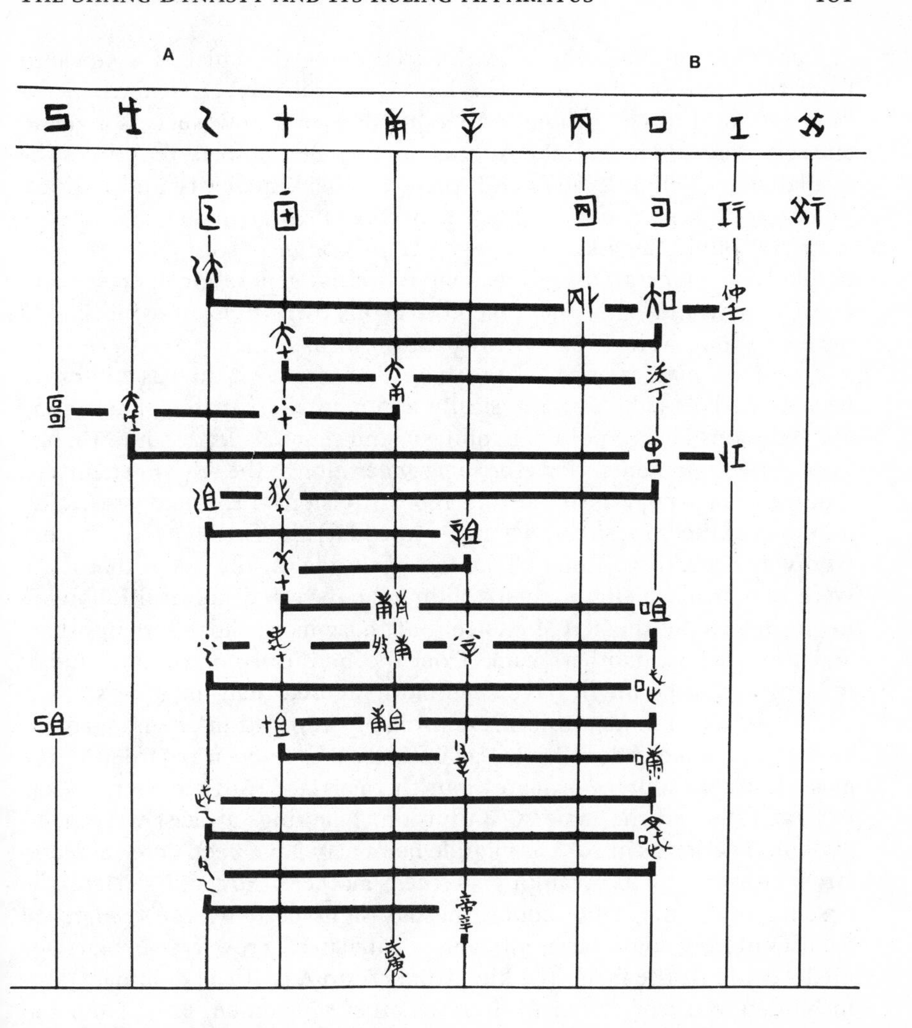

46. A hypothetical model of the ten ritual units (in two major divisions) in the royal house of the Shang dynasty and their circulating succession to kingship.

kingship stayed within division A or B, it had to be assumed by an heir from another *kan* unit from within the same generation as the former king, but if it went over to the other division it had to go to an heir of the next generation. To phrase this differently: when the kingship passed over to the next generation, it had to move to the opposite division. Keng and Hsin counted as either division, but the same cross-divisional and generational rules applied.

4. The king was assisted by a (formal or loosely informal) council

of important officials, the prime official being the chief of a *kan* unit from the opposite division. The heir was probably chosen when the king was still alive, although after his demise a new successor could emerge. The choice of the successor was determined by, first, the availability of eligible heirs and, then, by their capability and political following. There could be bloody or bloodless struggles. The prime minister could play a key role in the transition of power, and he would be likely to favor a cross-divisional and cross-generational succession, because it would enthrone a member of his own division, conceivably his own son or at least one of his younger affiliates.

5. A male member of the dynastic descent group was eligible to become an heir if he was physically and mentally capable of assuming the assiduous task of political, military, and religious leadership. He had to be of the right generation: the same generation as the reigning monarch if he (the monarch) was in the same A or B division, or the next generation if he was of the opposite division. He (the heir) also had to have a mother who was a member of one of the ten *kan* units. In the event that there were two or more eligible heirs, military power and political following might determine the actual choice, but those more capable than others and those whose mothers came from the politically or ritually higher ranking *kan* units might have been more favored than the others.

6. The ten *kan* units were probably engaged in an endogamous network of some order. Particular units may have been regarded as the most desirable sources of mates, but the marriage traffic does not seem to have followed the same A–B division. The kings at least were polygynous. The status of sons as eligible heirs may have been determined in large measure by the ranking of their mother's *kan* units. Here the absence of Yi and Ting among the day-signs used by the recognized spouses of king could be significant. A patrilateral cross-cousin marriage model could fit the facts: the king from group A (with Yi dominant) was forbidden to marry a woman from the other preëminent unit, Ting, and his son would inherit a smaller dose of political preëminence than the son of a cousin of his (the king's) generation in group B, who, possibly a son of the Ting unit, was allowed to marry a woman of the Yi group, who could also be his father's sister's daughter. The kingship would, thus, be potentially handed over from A to B in the next generation to an heir whose parents represented both Yi and Ting units. This, however, is only a possible model to explain the alternation of kingship between the two units but alternation of kingship does not depend on this explanation for its validity.

The above rules have been formulated to fit the facts. Although facts are few and are subject to varying interpretations, I am confident that the division of the royal lineage into two groups that alternated in holding the rulership must now be considered, if not fact, at least a better hypothesis than any other that is known to me. The only major point to bear in mind is that under such a system kings from neighboring generations were classificatory fathers and sons to each other but not blood fathers and blood sons. This is certainly allowed by the kin terminology of the Shang, even though it may appear strange to us. Since I first brought forth this hypothesis in 1963, there have been many reactions,[65] most of them negative. I should note that Paul Wheatley based his analysis of the Shang aristocracy[66] on this hypothesis, although in a later writing he has apparently shown some second thoughts.[67] This is no place to engage in polemics on this issue, but permit me to point out that none of my critics have been able to refute the facts and that none of them have proposed an alternative hypothesis to explain them. Oracle bone scholars have observed a studied silence on the subject, essentially ignoring the facts that I have presented. But these facts are at the heart of the Shang kingship, and they must be explained.

The Yi-Ting system, moreover, would provide an institutional explanation for another controversial hypothesis, namely, Tung Tso-pin's division of Shang ritual practices under the Shang kings from Wu Ting to Ti Hsin into two schools, the Old School (*Chiu p'ai* 舊派) and the New School (*Hsin p'ai* 新派). But actually, the controversy over this hypothesis centers only on whether or not these schools alternated cyclically. There is no question that Wu Ting's ritual practices underwent drastic changes under Tsu Chia. The question is whether the older practices, or at least very many of them, were revived under Wen Wu Ting. If the many oracle records Tung assigned into his Period IV (Wu Yi and Wen Wu Ting) should instead, as advocated by Ch'en Meng-chia and Kaizuka Shigeki (see chapter 1), be placed into the Wu Ting period as well,

65. Ting Su 丁驌, "Lun Yin wang p'i shih fa" 論殷王妣謚法; Ting Su 丁驌, "Tsai lun Shang wang p'i miao hao ti liang tsu shuo" 再論商王妣廟號的兩組說; Hsü Cho-yün 許倬雲, "Kuan-yü Shang wang miao-hao hsin k'ao yi wen ti chi-tien yi-chien" 關於商王廟號新考一文的幾點意見; Liu Pin-hsiung 劉斌雄, "Yin Shang wang-shih shih-fen-tsu chih shih lun" 殷商王室十分組制試論; Lin Heng-li 林衡立, "P'ing Chang Kwang-chih Shang wang miao hao hsin k'ao chung ti lun cheng fa" 評張光直商王廟號新考中的論証法; Hsü Chin-hsiung 許進雄, "Tui Chang Kwang-chih hsien-sheng 'Shang wang miao hao hsin k'ao' ti chi tien yi-chien" 對張光直先生的'商王廟號新考'的幾點意見; Yang Hsi-mei 楊希枚, "Lien ming chih yü p'u-tz'u Shang wang miao hao wen-t'i" 聯名制與卜辭商王廟號問題; Ch'en Ch'i-nan 陳其南, "Chung-kuo ku-tai chih ch'in-shu chih-tu—tsai lun Shang wang miao hao ti she-hui chieh-kou yi-yi" 中國古代之親屬制度—再論商王廟號的社會結構意義; Itō Michiharu 伊藤道治, *Kodai In Ōchō no nazo* 古代殷王朝のなぞ; Hayashi Minao 林巳奈夫, "In Shū jidai no zushō kigō" 殷周時代の図象記号.

66. *The Pivot of the Four Quarters*, pp. 52–61.

67. "Review of K. C. Chang, *Early Chinese Civilization*," 544.

then the change would be a linear one. If, however, one sides with Tung, as I do, in the periodization issue, then one faces a cyclical phenomenon of old-new-old-new alternation. But one need not adopt the Yi-Ting system to explain this, for it could simply be, as Tung conceived, a linear sequence of orthodoxy-renovation-revival-revival of renovation. The Yi-Ting system, however, would provide the basis for viewing the old and new schools as the contemporary subcultural variations of the B and A groups within the royal lineage.

According to Tung Tso-pin's chronology,[68] the length of the reigns of the nine Shang kings whose oracle records have been found at Hsiao-t'un are as listed in the table below.

Wu Ting	59 years
Tsu Keng	7 "
Tsu Chia	33 "
Lin Hsin	6 "
K'ang Ting	8 "
Wu Yi	4 "
Wen Wu Ting	13 "
Ti Yi	35 "
Ti Hsin	52 "

Tung believed that the ritual practices as shown by their oracle records underwent at least three changes from the Wu Ting norm: the first time under Tsu Chia, the second under Wen Wu Ting, and the third under Ti Yi. He used these four kings to represent the four periods of change and assigned the other kings to them according to available data.[69] Thus, the kings are broken down into the Old and the New Schools as follows:

Old School	*New School*
P'an Keng, Hsiao Hsin, Hsiao Yi	
Wu Ting (59 years)	
Tsu Keng (7 years)	
	Tsu Chia (33 years)
	Lin Hsin (6), K'ang Ting (8)
Wu Yi (4 years)	
Wen Wu Ting (13 years)	
	Ti Yi (35 years)
	Ti Hsin (52 years)

68. *Yin li p'u* 殷曆譜.

69. *Yin li p'u* 殷曆譜; *Yin hsü wẹn-tzu Yi pien hsü* 殷墟文字乙編序; "Yin tai li-chih ti hsin chiu liang p'ai" 殷代禮制的新舊兩派.

The major changes in ritual practices from Wu Ting to Tsu Chia may be illustrated by the following summary:

Wu Ting	Tsu Chia
1. Made offerings to early "legendary" ancestors such as K'uei, Wang Hai, Chi	1. Made no offerings to early ancestors before Shang Chia
2. Made offerings to natural deities (Yüeh or Mountain, Ho or River, and T'u or Earth, all of which are regarded by some as early ancestors)	2. Did not give offerings to natural deities
3. Made offerings to deceased major officials such as Yi Yin and Wu Hsien	3. Made no offerings to early officials
4. Performed rituals and made offerings to ancestral kings beginning with Shang Chia who were in the trunk line (*ta tsung* 大宗)*	4. Performed rituals and gave offerings to all ancestral kings both on the trunk line (*ta tsung* 大宗) and on the branches (*hsiao tsung* 小宗)*
5. Performed rituals and made offerings to spouses of *ta tsung* ancestral kings up to five generations previous	5. Performed rituals and made offerings to spouses of all *ta tsung* ancestral kings beginning with Shih Jen
6. Each ritual to an ancestor was performed as an ad hoc arrangement, involving divination to determine timing and amount of offering	6. Annual ritual schedule, in which rituals to individual ancestors were performed on fixed dates according to the day-signs in the ancestral names
7. Many kinds of rituals	7. Some rituals were the same, but other were new. The main rituals were five: 彡 ("drum music"), 翌 ("feather dance"), 祭 ("wine and

*For *ta tsung* and *hsiao tsung*, see below.

			meat"), 壹 ("millets") and 劦 ("Grand Harmony"). The five were performed successively, but overlappingly in part, and the completion of all five would take a year, or *ssu* 祀 ("ritual" or "ritual cycle").
8.	In lunar calendar, months were named one through twelve. In leap year, added thirteenth month at end of year.	8.	First lunar month was named *cheng yüeh* 正月 or First Month. Added intercalary month whenever it was due, resulting in two second months, third months, and so on. No thirteenth month
9.	The *kan-chih* or 60-day cycle was independent.	9.	The *kan-chih* cycle was tied to lunar months; a day-sign was referred to as being *within* (*tsai* 在) a certain lunar month.
10.	Used shells and bone to divine on following matters: rituals, battles, hunts, journeys, sacrifices, king's movements, well-being during the coming *hsün* (week), well-being during the coming evening, informing ancestors, misfortune, harvests, solar and lunar eclipses, births, dreams, illnesses, deaths, rains, requests for fair weather	10.	Divination largely confined to the first eight items at left only
11.	Unsystematic use of shells and shoulder blades for divinations on various items	11.	Use of same piece of shell or bone for the same kinds of divinations
12.	Details of some characters are distinctive. Example: King was 王	12.	Same characters are distinctively different in details. Example: King was 王

The above examples clearly illustrate that Tsu Chia was indeed an innovative king: he considerably simplified the ritual practices and rendered them more systematic and routinized. But many of his innovations were apparently demolished, and older practices revived, under Wen Wu Ting;[70] then after a relatively brief reign (thirteen years) Tsu Chia's changes were restored under Ti Yi.

As aforementioned, once we accept Tung Tso-pin's dating of the Period IV oracle records to Wen Wu Ting, there can be no getting away from accepting also the Wen Wu Ting "revival" of Wu Ting institutions. It is highly suggestive that the two kings (Wu Ting, Wen Wu Ting) who were mainly responsible for the Old School rituals were Ting-group kings, and the two (Tsu Chia, Ti Yi) responsible for the New School were Yi-group kings. It is almost inevitable for one to suspect that the so-called Old and New Schools were in fact Ting and and Yi subcultures. When Ting was king, the Ting subculture was recorded in the official ritual archives, but the Yi subculture was presumably practiced by the Yi group on their own in areas not involving the king and other royal activities. When Yi became king, the situation became reversed, although inevitably there was also some linear change from one reign to another.

It should, of course, be noted and emphasized that the kingship shifted six times between the divisions from the time of Wu Ting to the dynasty's end, but the ritual practices shifted only four times between the Old and the New Schools. Additional studies of K'ang Ting and, especially, Ti Hsin oracle records are needed.

In addition to the Old and New Schools of ritual practices, other subcultural dichotomies within the royal lineage may be noted. The "royal cemetery" at Hsi-pei-kang, as has been described, is divided into a western sector and an eastern sector. According to the rules of the Western Chou, ancestors of the *chao* generation were worshipped in temples on the "left" side, that is, the left side of the ultimate ancestor sitting on the north facing south, in other words, on the east. The *mu* generation ancestors, on the other hand, were placed in temples on the right, namely, on the west. It was stated earlier that in the Yi-Ting system of the Shang, Yi may be made to correspond to the Chou's *mu*, and Ting, to *chao*. Thus, Shang kings of the Yi group could be buried on the west side, whereas those of the Ting group on the east side. In the western sector, there are seven large graves, and four have been found so far in the eastern sector. Now, there happen to have been seven kings in the Yi group in An-yang (P'an Keng, Hsiao Hsin, Hsiao Yi, Tsu Keng, Tsu Chia, Wu Yi, Ti Yi), and four in the Ting group (Wu

70. See Tung Tso-pin 董作賓, . . . *Yi pien hsü* 乙編序, under his subtitle: "Wen Wu Ting revived the ancient institutions!" (p. 12).

Ting, Lin Hsin, K'ang Ting, and Wen Wu Ting). (The last king, Ti Hsin, has not been counted in these figures, since he was beheaded by the Chou and was not known to have been given a grand burial.) According to Kao Ch'ü-hsün,[71] the western sector has been extensively tested and he does not believe it will yield additional large graves; the western seven then, are the right figure for the seven Yi kings. But the eastern sector is still imperfectly explored, and there is strong likelihood of a fifth large grave that may have been the resting place for a royal spouse (perhaps Hou Wu, whose name was cast on a large bronze vessel known to have come from there).[72] Until the eastern sector is thoroughly investigated, we are not certain about the number of large graves contained there and about the latter's correspondence with the number of Ting-group kings. But the division of this cemetery into an eastern and a western part is a highly significant fact by itself, a fact which should be noted along with the layout of the house floors of Hsiao-t'un, also arranged in a symmetrical fashion with eastern and western parts.

THE TRUNK LINE AND THE BRANCH LINE KINGS

It doesn't matter whether the Shang dynasty kings were chosen from various tablet units within the royal lineage or whether, possibly, they were uncles and nephews between neighboring generations and grandfathers and grandsons every other generation. (The term *fu*, father, applied to all male relatives of the first ascending generation, and *mu*, mother, to all female relatives of that generation.) Once they were chosen kings, they were placed together head to tail in a sequence in the divination records and their diverse origins became obscure. Consequently, one is father to the next, and their true relationship remained hidden during the past three thousand years.

But a new pair of divisions emerged linearly in the oracle records, namely *Ta tsung* and *Hsiao tsung*. Another pair of words, *Ta shih* 大示 and *Hsiao shih* 小示, is considered their equivalents. The character *shih* 示 apparently signifies an ancestral tablet, and that for *tsung* 宗 the same tablet under a roof, signifies the chamber housing the tablet. Possibly in this context these were interchangeable words.[73] In the following lines from the oracle records we see that ancestral kings worshipped as *Ta tsung* or "the Grand Tablets" (or "in the Grand

71. "The Royal Cemetery of the Yin Dynasty at An-yang."

72. *KK*, "An-yang Yin hsü nu-li chi-ssu k'eng ti fa-chüeh" 安陽殷墟奴隸祭祀坑的發掘.

73. Chin Hsiang-heng 金祥恆, "P'u tz'u chung so-chien Yin Shang tsung-miao chi Yin chi k'ao" 卜辭中所見殷商宗廟及殷祭考.

Chamber'') were treated differently from those worshipped as *Hsiao tsung*, ''the Small Tablets'' (or ''in the Small Chamber''):

> On day Yi-Wei, inquired: To worship the thirteen [Grand] tablets beginning with Shang Chia, [using] cattle? [To worship] the small tablets, [using] sheep?[74]
>
> On day Yi-Mou, inquired: To pray for harvest with the six [Grand] tablets beginning [with Chia], using cattle? With small tablets using . . . sheep?[75]
>
> [For] Grand Tablets, use one head of cattle to perform the *mou* ritual? For Small Tablets, use sheep to perform it?[76]

There are somewhat differing interpretations of the categories *ta tsung* (*ta shih*) and *hsiao tsung* (*hsiao shih*).[77] On the basis of the ritual calendars of Tsu Chia, Ti Yi, and Ti Hsin, in which one king per generation was often given special place in certain rituals (see above), Hu Hou-hsüan's interpretation seems the most reasonable: *ta tsung* kings, whose spouses were the only ones recognized in the ritual calendar and whose sons were enthroned, represented the trunk line of the royal succession, whereas *hsiao tsung* kings were on branch lines since their sons did not succeed them on the throne. However, under the Yi-Ting system interpretation, the new king was son to none of the older kings of the previous generation, and the criteria for separating *ta tsung* kings and *hsiao tsung* kings must be different.

4. *OTHER MEMBERS OF THE RULING CLASS*

Members of the ruling class other than the royal lineage and its kings are the *fu*s (royal consorts), the *tzu*s (the princes) and the officials. All of them probably had specific duties in the capital, but at least many of them were granted titles to walled towns with agricultural land.

74. Lo Chen-yü 羅振玉, *Yin hsü shu ch'i hou pien* 殷墟書契後編, shang 28.8.

75. Tung Tso-pin 董作賓, *Yin hsü wen-tzu Chia pien* 殷虛文字甲編, Chia-712.

76. Shang Ch'eng-tso 商承祚, *Yin ch'i yi ts'un* 殷契佚存, no. 6.

77. Chin Hsiang-heng 金祥恆, ''P'u-tz'u chung so-chien Yin Shang tsung-miao chi Yin chi k'ao'' 卜辭中所見殷商宗廟及殷祭考, 315; Hu Hou-hsün 胡厚宣, ''Yin tai hun-yin chia-tsu tsung-fa sheng-yü chih-tu k'ao'' 殷代婚姻家族宗法生育制度考, 16; Ch'en Meng-chia 陳夢家, *Yin hsü p'u-tz'u tsung shu* 殷墟卜辭綜述, pp. 465–466, 473.

FU

In the oracle records of the Old School one frequently encounters names consisting of the character *fu* 婦 followed by a second character usually containing a "woman" element. Most oracle bone scholars follow Kuo Mo-jo[78] in regarding the word *fu* as "royal consort" and the second character as the name of the clan from which she originally came, although some are more inclined to see the second character as personal name.[79] Hu Hou-hsüan has identified sixty-four *fu* names.[80] The word *to fu* ("the multitude of *fus*") in oracle records[81] seems to indicate that the many *fus* constituted a category of persons in Shang language.

If the name of the *fu* indicates her clan origin, the *fu* names, then, provide useful data for the social sources of Shang women. They include, however, the name *hao*, which compounds the woman element with the name Tzu, Shang's own clan name. The royal lineage appears to have been, thus, both endogamous and exogamous.[82] As just suggested, these variations in marriage type were probably politically based.

The royal consorts were active and of high status. "They were ordered to perform sacrifices or to lead military campaigns. They came and went to perform chores for the king, being no different from the king's close officials."[83] The Fu Hao whose tomb was excavated in 1976 was surely a woman of very high distinction in view of the rich furnishings to which her grave was entitled. As we mentioned before, Fu Hao was a military leader, had her own walled town, performed rituals, and was the subject of Wu Ting's divinations concerning her illnesses, childbirths, and general well-being.[84]

TZU

Again in the oracle records of the Old School, a number of names—fifty-three by Hu Hou-hsüan's count[85]—consisted of two

78. "Ku chiu k'o tz'u chih yi k'ao-ch'a" 骨臼刻辭之一考察.

79. Ch'en Meng-chia 陳夢家, *Yin hsü p'u-tz'u tsung shu* 殷墟卜辭綜述, p. 493.

80. Hu Hou-hsüan 胡厚宣, "Yin tai hun-yin chia-tsu tsung-fa sheng-yü chih tu k'ao" 殷代婚姻家族宗法生育制度考, 8.

81. Shang Ch'eng-tso 商承祚, *Yin ch'i yi ts'un* 殷契佚存, no. 321.

82. Ting Shan 丁山, *Chia-ku wen so-chien shih-tsu chi ch'i chih-tu* 甲骨文所見氏族及其制度, pp. 55–56.

83. Hu Hou-hsüan 胡厚宣, "Yin tai feng-chien chih-tu k'ao" 殷代封建制度考, 4.

84. Wang Yü-hsin 王宇信, Chang Yung-shan 張永山, and Yang Sheng-nan 楊升南, "Shih lun Yin hsü wu-hao mu ti 'Fu Hao'" 試論殷墟五號墓的'婦好'.

85. Hu Hou-hsüan 胡厚宣, "Yin tai feng-chien chih-tu k'ao" 殷代封建制度考, 9.

parts, the first the character *tzu* and the second a character usually read as a personal name (which could of course have been derived from a town name). The oracle records also contain the phrases *to tzu* 多子 ("the multitude of *tzu*") and *to tzu tsu* 多子族 ("the *tsu* of the multitude of *tzu*" or "the multitude of *tzu tsu*"), and these are usually regarded as collective terms for the many names with *tzu* in them.[86]

Tung Tso-pin first regarded all these names with *tzu* in them as the names of Wu Ting's sons[87]—since if Wu Ting could have had sixty-four consorts he surely could have had fifty-three sons. Tung's interpretation is commonly followed, and Kaizuka goes so far as to regard the *tzu*s or princes as forming a politically and militarily powerful group with its own divining agents.[88] However, the only kinship criterion such a group could have been based on was generation, but in that case it is incompatible with the inherent definition of the word *tsu*. That all people with *tzu* names were sons of Wu Ting has also been questioned; Ting Shan believed that some *tzu*-named individuals could have been of Wu Ting's own generation since Tzu Yang, for one, is known to have been venerated together with Wu Ting's parents.[89]

As Kaizuka has pointed out, *tzu*-X names are seen frequently on bronzes functioning as emblems. Since Tzu was the name of the Shang ruling clan, it would be simplest to regard the *tzu*-X name as a subdivision of the Tzu clan, with the *tzu* character used here to distinguish it from all other *tsu*.[90] Since it has been recognized that the names of *tsu* or of lineages and clans, the names of the towns in which they settled, and those of their individual members were interchangeable,[91] this interpretation is not incompatible with the traditional interpretation of regarding *tzu*-X names in the oracle records as names of individual persons.

Tzu-X names are given in oracle records in connection with the performance of rituals, with hunting in the company of the king,

86. Hu Hou-hsün 胡厚宣, "Yin tai hun-yin chia-tsu tsung-fa sheng-yü chih-tu k'ao" 般代婚姻家族宗法生育制度考, 26–27; Ch'en Meng-chia 陳夢家, *Yin hsü p'u-tz'u tsung shu* 般墟卜辭綜述, p. 496; Kaizuka Shigeki 貝塚茂樹, *Chūgoku kodai shigaku no hakken* 中国古代史学の発展, pp. 291–292.

87. Tung Tso-pin 董作賓, "Chia-ku wen tuan-tai yen-chiu li" 甲骨文斷代研究例, "Wu teng chüeh tsai Yin Shang" 五等爵在般商.

88. Kaizuka Shigeki 貝塚茂樹, *Chūgoku kodai shigaku no hakken* 中国古代史学の発展.

89. Ting Shan 丁山, *Yin Shang shih-tsu fang-kuo chih* 般商氏族方國志, p. 75.

90. Chang Kwang-chih 張光直, "Shang Chou ch'ing-t'ung-ch'i ch'i-hsing chuang-shih hua-wen yü ming-wen tsung-ho yen-chiu ch'u-pu pao-kao" 商周青銅器器形裝飾花紋與銘文綜合研究初步報告, 269; Jao Tsung-yi 饒宗頤, *Yin tai chen p'u jen-wu t'ung k'ao* 般代貞卜人物通考, p. 1198.

91. Chang Ping-ch'üan 張秉權, "Chia-ku wen chung so-chien jen ti t'ung ming k'ao" 甲骨文中所見人地同名考.

and with war. Apparently these "princes," as in the case of the *fu*, performed significant functions in the royal court by virtue of their nepotistic advantages.

MAJOR COURT OFFICIALS

Ch'en Meng-chia stated that in the oracle records he recognized more than twenty titles of officials, which he grouped into three categories: ministers (*ch'en* 臣), generals, and archivists.[92] Many individual officials are well known in the textual and oracle records: Yi Yin, the prime minister under Ta Yi[93] and general (*mu*) 戠 or (*chih mu*) 沚戠 under Wu Ting[94] are examples. But the most important categories of officials insofar as our available data are concerned are the diviners, *p'u* 卜, and the inquirers, whose names proceeded the word *chen* 貞. Jao Tsung-yi enumerated the activities of as many as 117 diviners and inquirers in the oracle records.[95] Ch'en Meng-chia counted 120.[96] Since divination played a crucial role in the art of governance in the Shang period (see below), the diviners and inquirers must have been persons of considerable power, although the king himself was more often than not the one person who made the all-important prognostications.

Another important category of influential officials of the court, which Ch'en did not list among his officials, is the priest. In *Chün shih*, a *Shu ching* document, Chou Kung is quoted as listing the famous Shang ministers as follows: "T'ang . . . had with him Yi Yin, making his virtue like that of great Heaven; that T'ai Chia had the same Yi Yin; that T'ai Wu had Yi Chih and Ch'en Hu through whom his virtue was made to affect God, and Wu Hsien 巫咸 who regulated the royal house; that Tsu Yi had Wu Hsien 巫賢; and that Wu Ting had Kan P'an."[97] Wu [Priests] Hsien 咸 and Hsien 賢 are listed alongside the famous Yi Yin, and their importance in the royal court is evident. In the oracle records, the name Wu Hsien 戊咸 has been identified, its title part 戊

92. Ch'en Meng-chia 陳夢家, *Yin hsü p'u-tz'u tsung shu* 殷墟卜辭綜述, p. 503.

93. Chang Kwang-chih 張光直, "T'an Wang Hai yü Yi Yin ti chi jih ping tsai lun Yin Shang wang-chih" 談王亥與伊尹的祭日並再論殷商王制.

94. Chih Mu, see Hu Hou-hsüan 胡厚宣, "Yin tai feng-chien chih-tu k'ao" 殷代封建制度考, 8–13. But Shirakawa Shizuka 白川靜 believes that Chih Mu was a *ts'e* 册 officer, in charge of ritual affairs in the troops; see his "Sakusatsukō" 作册考.

95. Jao Tsung-yi 饒宗頤, *Yin tai chen p'u jen-wu t'ung k'ao* 殷代貞卜人物通考.

96. Ch'en Meng-chia 陳夢家, *Yin hsü p'u-tz'u tsung shu* 殷墟卜辭綜述, p. 202.

97. Based on Waltham, *Shu Ching*, p. 184.

believed to be an equivalent of the character *wu* 巫 for priest. Several other names also appear with the Wu 戊 title.[98]

LANDED LORDS

Most if not all of the court officials, including the king's consorts and princes, appear to have been granted title to land with income from harvests and walled towns for their *tsu* people.[99] Ting Shan saw these lords divided into two groups: those given land within or near the royal capital, and those given land and towns elsewhere in the state. Ting's groupings seem valid although his precise scheme of hierarchy within each group and his terminology are forced and unconvincing,[100] and will be discussed in detail in the next chapter. The lords whose land was within the outer limits of the capital were able to serve on the royal court as fulltime officials, but the lords whose land was outside the capital's limits—sometimes quite far away—presumably moved between their court jobs and their own towns under some kind of arrangement; however the details of such arrangement are not known.

Each of the lords represented his *tsu*, his walled town, and his land of whatever size, with the man himself, his *tsu*, and the town all known by the same name, but all such names found in oracle records and in bronze inscriptions were related to one another hierarchically and discriminately in accordance with their relationships. Ting Shan has recognized more than two hundred such names, but he is convinced that many more can be identified,[101] Chang Ping-ch'üan has singled out 173 cases where personal names were found to be identical with town names.[102] Among these names, some are particularly prominent; one may assume that these had bigger land, bigger and more towns, and greater population, and they had greater voice while in the court. One prominent example of such *tsu* is the Ch'üeh 雀, or the Sparrow lineage, studied by Hu Hou-hsüan,[103] Ting Shan,[104] and

98. Ch'en Meng-chia 陳夢家, *Yin hsü p'u-tz'u tsung shu* 殷墟卜辭綜述, p. 365; "Shang tai ti shen-hua yü wu-shu" 商代的神話與巫術, 537.

99. Hu Hou-hsüan 胡厚宣, "Yin tai feng-chien chih-tu k'ao" 殷代封建制度考.

100. Ting Shan 丁山, *Chia-ku wen so-chien shih-tsu chi ch'i chih-tu* 甲骨文所見氏族及其制度.

101. *Ibid.*, p. 32.

102. "Chia-ku wen chung so-chien jen ti t'ung ming k'ao" 甲骨文中所見人地同名考.

103. Hu Hou-hsüan 胡厚宣, "Yin tai feng-chien chih-tu k'ao" 殷代封建制度考, 13–17.

104. Ting Shan 丁山, *Chia-ku wen so-chien shih-tsu chi ch'i chih-tu* 甲骨文所見氏族及其制度, pp. 123–125.

Shirakawa.[105] The head of the Ch'üeh was considered to be a near relative; the king (Wu Ting) made frequent divinations about his well-being, his health, and his comings and goings; he was sometimes asked to go out on a hunt, perform rituals, or otherwise be of service to the king; his territory was often said to have been entered by the king or by some one from the capital; he was often recorded as having brought into the capital a certain number of turtle shells; he was recorded to be at war with a neighboring town. His territory is regarded as being in southern Shansi or in central Honan.

A more detailed discussion of the hierarchy of the landed lords will be given in the next chapter in connection with the political order of the Shang state.

5. *MILITARY FORCE*

Both externally and internally the Shang rulers had ample force at their command. Oracle records abound in mentions of military campaigns involving the use of three thousand, five thousand, or even thirteen thousand troops and the taking of prisoners of war, as many as thirty thousand at one time.[106] Within their own society, overwhelming garrison force must have been necessary for the imprisonment and sacrificial use of war captives in such large numbers: oracle records mention the sacrifice of as many as three hundred Ch'iang for a ritual of ancestral worship,[107] and archaeological finds show that as many as more than 600 human victims were put to death at Hsiao-t'un for the construction of a single house[108] and 164 were sacrificed at Hsi-pei-kang for the inside of a single tomb.[109] *Shu ching* records that on the eve of his conquest of Hsia, T'ang (Ta Yi) made a speech to his people explaining his actions, in which he admonished them thus about the coming battle:

> I pray you, assist me, the One Man, to carry out the punishment [of Hsia] appointed by Heaven. I will greatly reward

105. Shirakawa Shizuka 白川靜, "Indai yūzoku kō, sono ni, Jaku," 殷代雄族考，其二，雀.

106. Yang Shang-k'uei 楊尚奎, *Chung-kuo ku-tai she-hui yü ku-tai ssu-hsiang yen-chiu* 中國古代社會與古代思想研究, pp. 20–21; Ch'en Meng-chia 陳夢家, *Yin hsü p'u-tz'u tsung shu* 殷墟卜辭綜述, pp. 276–277.

107. Ch'en Meng-chia 陳夢家, *op. cit.*, pp. 279–280.

108. Shih Chang-ju 石璋如, *Pei-tsu mu-tsang* 北組墓葬; *Chung-tsu mu-tsang* 中組墓葬.

109. Liang Ssu-yüng 梁思永 and Kao Ch'ü-hsün 高去尋, *Hou-chia-chuang 1001-hao ta mu* 侯家莊1001號大墓.

> you. . . . If you do not obey the words I have spoken to you I will put your children to death with you. You will find no forgiveness.[110]

When P'an Keng spoke to cajole his people regarding the move of his capital to Yin, he gave this warning to those who disagreed: "From this time forward, attend respectfully to your business; have the duties of your offices regularly adjusted; bring your tongues under the rule of law lest punishment come upon you when repentance will be of no avail."[111]

Such were evidently not empty threats, for there is ample archaeological evidence that much of the physical punishment was actually carried out (see below). What was the implement of that force? What were the size and shape of the king's military force that he used both internally and externally? There has been no systematic study of these questions, but we know certain facts pertaining to them.

First, the Shang's basic social organization had a strong military aspect. As mentioned at the beginning of this chapter, the Shang's basic social unit, the *tsu*, is regarded by many scholars as a military unit.[112] In a small walled town, which was a defensive instrument as well as a living settlement, the *tsu* inhabiting it performed military functions as an integral part of its activities, and the *tsu* chief was a military leader. In the royal capital, this military aspect of the *tsu* simply was enlarged and stratified. The king was the town's (as well as the state's) military leader, and he was required to possess physical strength. Under him there were a number of *tsu*, including, as has just been mentioned, *tsu* groups headed and led by the king himself, by his consorts, and by his princes. All *tsu*, thus, were military as well as social-political units. In time of peace, order was maintained by a standing army, perhaps called *lü* 旅,[113] which included only a portion of the *tsu* members, but in case of necessity, which was probably quite frequent, a large or small part of the *tsu* members could be mobilized to be thrown into military campaigns. For example, a King Wu Ting period oracle record spoke of an expedition to the Ch'iang territory, involving a *lü* army ten thousand strong plus three thousand members of the *tsu* of the king's consort, Fu Hao.[114] If further help was needed,

110. Translated in Waltham, *Shu Ching*, p. 68.

111. *Ibid.*, p. 89.

112. Chin Hsiang-heng 金祥恆, "Ts'ung chia-ku p'u-tz'u yen-chiu Yin Shang chün-lü chung chih wang tsu san hang san shih" 從甲骨卜辭研究殷商軍旅中之王族三行三師.

113. Ch'en Meng-chia 陳夢家, *Yin hsü p'u-tz'u tsung shu* 殷墟卜辭綜述, p. 277.

114. *Ibid.*, p. 276.

soldiers and units were to be contributed by the various walled towns ruled by the *tsu* members of various clans in various parts of the state.[115] In fact, the *tsu* members of Fu Hao who participated in the above campaign were in all likelihood residents of her own walled town outside the capital.

But let us focus now upon the professional military only. First, in the oracle records there are various titles that seem to refer to military officials: Ch'en Meng-chia has listed the following: *ma* 馬 ("horse attendant"?), *ya* 亞 (a military title of considerable importance), *fu* 箙 ("archery commandant"?), *she* 射 ("archery commandant"?), and *wei* 衛 ("garrison commandant"?), *ch'üan* 犬 ("dog attendant"?), and *hsü* 戍 ("frontier commandant"?).[116] Their functions and duties are not at all clear; however, these titles clearly indicate that the Shang army was of considerable scale and complexity. But armies were also commanded by the king, by his consorts, by his princes, and by the "civilian" leaders of *tsu*.

According to the oracle records, Shang foot-soldiers and archers seem to have been organized into companies of one hundred soldiers each, with three companies forming a regiment, arranged as the left, middle, and right companies.[117] Such formations have not been archaeologically substantiated, but a series of sacrificial burials that apparently accompany house floor *yi*-7 at Hsiao-t'un has suggested to Shih Chang-ju that the Shang charioteers were organized as follows:[118]

1. Five chariots formed a squadron, and five squadrons formed a company.
2. Each chariot had three charioteers: the middle one was driver, carrying a whip; the one on the left was striker, carrying a *ko*-halberd; the one on the right was archer, carrying bow and arrows.

Most of the archaeological remains of weapons have been found in the chariot burials, although some human and animal burials have also yielded them. The following weapons seem to have formed a set: bow,

115. Hu Hou-hsüan 胡厚宣, "Yin tai feng-chien chih-tu k'ao" 殷代封建制度考, 30–31.

116. Ch'en Meng-chia 陳夢家, *Yin hsü p'u-tz'u tsung shu* 殷墟卜辭綜述, pp. 508–517.

117. *Ibid.*, p. 513.

118. "Hsiao-t'un C-ch'ü ti mu-tsang ch'ün" 小屯C區的墓葬羣; "Yin hsü fa-chüeh tui-yü Chung-kuo ku-tai wen-hua ti kung-hsien 殷墟發掘對於中國古代文化的貢獻.

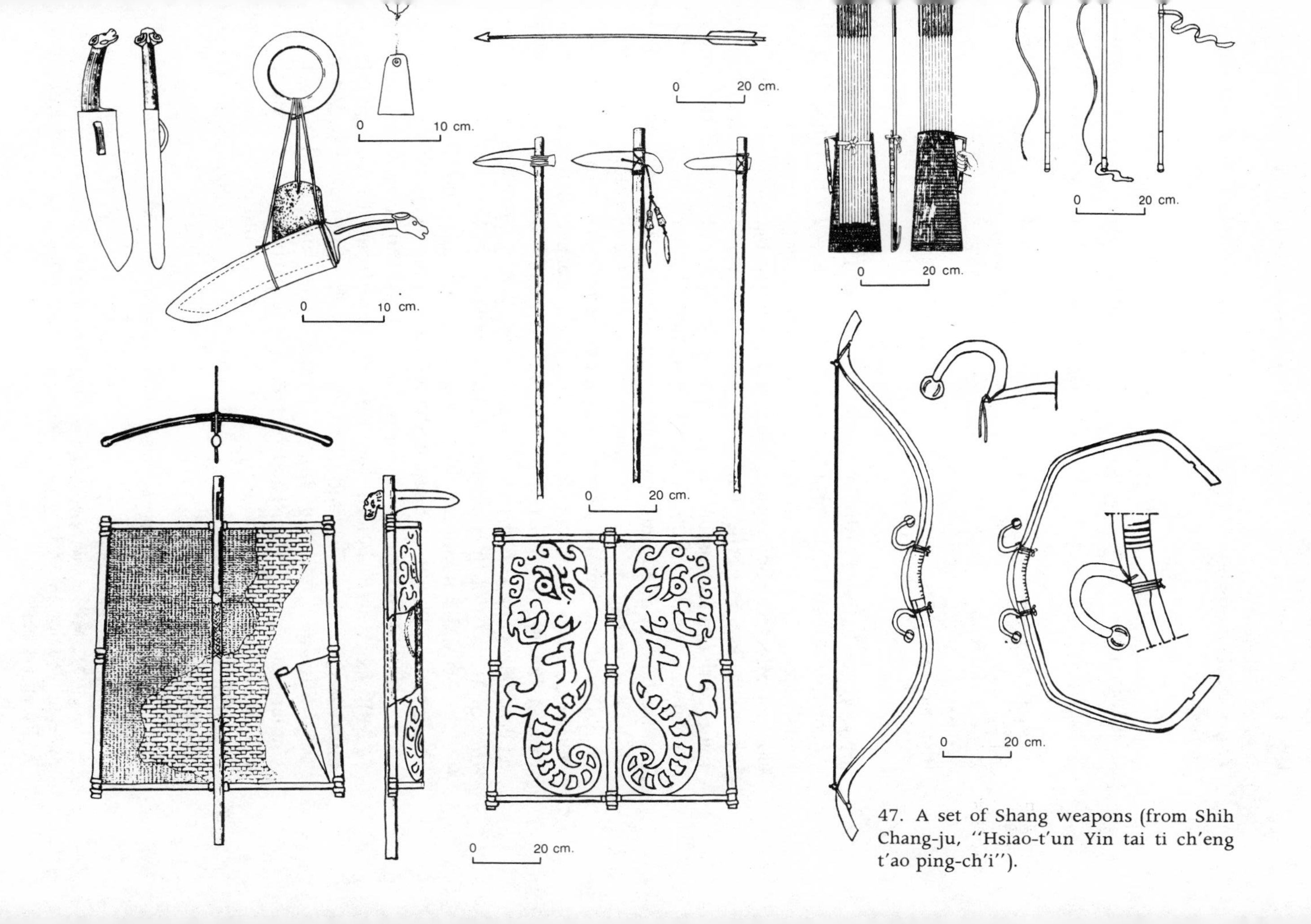

47. A set of Shang weapons (from Shih Chang-ju, "Hsiao-t'un Yin tai ti ch'eng t'ao ping-ch'i").

TABLE 2 Dimensions of Five Chariots from Yin-hsü (all figures are in cm)

	Wheel	*Axle*	*Body*	*Pole*	*Yoke*
M 40, Hsiao-t'un	—	290	80–85 high 120 wide	255	210
M 20 (1), Hsiao-t'un	—	290	88–94 high 115 wide	265	170
M 20 (2), Hsiao-t'un	—	270	66–74 high 115 wide	220	140
Ta-ssu-k'ung-ts'un	146 (18 spokes)	300	94 wide	280	—
Hsiao-min-t'un (1972)	133–144 (22 spokes)	306	74 high 129–133 wide	256	110

arrows, *ko*-halberd, shield, small knife, and sharpening stone.[119] According to Shih Chang-ju's reconstruction based on archaeological finds and epigraphical information, the Shang *bow* was a strong composite (reflective) bow about equal in length to a man's height, made of cattle sinews and horns. The Shang *arrow* was made of a head of stone, bone, antler, shell, or bronze and a wooden shaft about half the bow's length equipped with feathers. The Shang *ko*-halberd 戈 consisted of a bronze blade hafted onto a wooden shaft about 1.1 meters long. Shang *shields* were of two kinds: large ones for chariot use (longer than the *ko*-halberd) and small ones for foot soldiers (shorter than the *ko*-halberd), both made of a wooden frame and leather or basket surface painted on the outside with tiger patterns. The *small knife* of bronze was apparently a personal weapon worn in a sheath. The *sharpening stone* was, obviously, the counterpart of the modern soldier's oil can (fig. 47).

Any discussion of the Shang weaponry must not leave out the chariot itself. Remains of seven Shang chariots are available for detailed study and reconstruction—three from Hsiao-t'un (tombs M 20 and M 40) excavated before the war;[120] one from Ta-ssu-k'ung-ts'un excavated in 1953;[121] and three from Hsiao-min-t'un excavated in 1958–59[122] and 1973 (fig. 48).[123] The basic structures of all of them are similar: the chariot consisted of five major parts: wheels, axle, body mounted on the axle, pole, and yoke, and it was pulled by two horses (fig. 49). The dimensions of the five best preserved chariots are given in table 2.

119. Shih Chang-ju 石璋如, "Hsiao-t'un Yin tai ti ch'eng t'ao ping-ch'i" 小屯殷代的成套兵器.

120. Shih Chang-ju 石璋如, *Pei-tsu mu-tsang* 北組墓葬.

121. Ma Te-chih 馬得志, Chou Yung-chen 周永珍, Chang Yün-p'eng 張雲鵬. "Yi-chiu-wu-san nien An-yang Ta-ssu-k'ung-ts'un fa-chüeh pao-kao" 一九五三年安陽大司空村發掘報告.

48. Remains of a horse chariot found at Hsiao-min-t'un (after *KK*, "An-yang hsin fa-hsien ti Yin tai ch'e-ma k'eng").

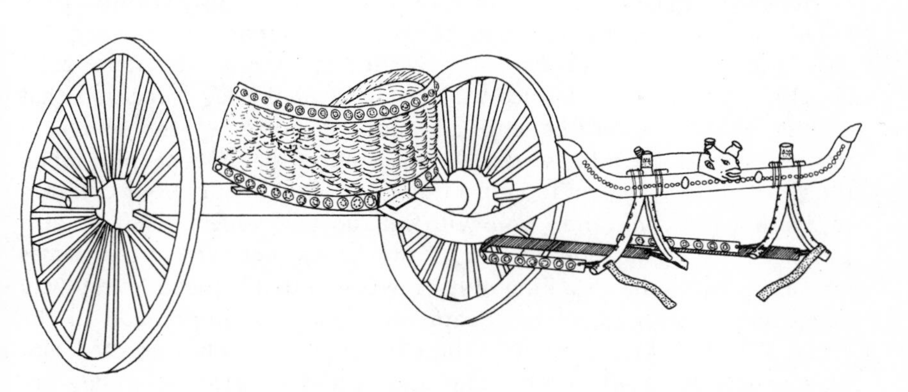

49. A reconstruction of the Shang chariot in M 20 (after Shih Chang-ju, *Pei tsu mu-tsang*, p. 28).

122. *KK*, "1958–1959 nien Yin hsü fa-chüeh chien pao" 1958-1959年殷墟發掘簡報.

123. *KK*, "An-yang hsin fa-hsien ti Yin tai ch'e-ma k'eng" 安陽新發現的殷代車馬坑.

Thus, these were roughly the same in size, except for M 20 (2), which was somewhat smaller. The wheels of the Hsiao-t'un samples, detachable by means of linchpins, had been removed before burial, but the other two chariots provided good data on them. The body, with openings mostly toward the rear, was made of wooden frame and possibly wickerwork and leather. The pole was bent so that the rear end went under the chassis but the frontal end was of appropriate height for the horses. Both chariot and horses were richly decorated with bronze and turquoise ornaments, and the chariot body was perhaps painted with animal designs.

6. *LAW*

Leopold Pospisil[124] sees in legal decisions four attributes whose coexistence defines law: authority, intention of universal application, *obligatio*, and sanction. Shang data on legal *decisions* are so rare as to be nonexistent, but each of the four attributes is manifest in available data in some fashion. But first let us consider the parties involved in such decisions. All we can see are the king and the authority he represented, on the one hand, and his subjects, on the other. His subjects were those of his people addressed in the *Shu ching* documents and those who bodily bore the consequences of his sanctions apparently because they failed, or were regarded as having failed, their part of the *obligatio*.

In *T'ang shih*, of *Shu ching*, we see the *obligatio* attribute most clearly, with *obligatio* defined as "that part of the legal decision that defines the rights of the entitled and the duties of the obligated parties".[125] On the king's part, he demanded that the people "obey the words I have spoken to you"; otherwise he "will put your children to death with you" and "you will find no forgiveness." But he also promised, by implication, that he, T'ang, would not commit the crimes he was accusing the Hsia king of having committed: "[he] in every way exhausts the strength of his people and exercises oppression in the cities." The Hsia king committed these crimes and must be punished, and "his people have all become idle and will not assist him. They are saying, 'When wilt thou, O sun, expire? We will all perish with thee!'" Thus, the *obligatio* equation was made up of promise of benevolent rule on the part of the king and the expectation of obedience on the part of his subjects. When the king, or his descendants, failed to keep

124. *The Ethnology of Law*.
125. *Ibid.*, p. 22.

his part of the bargain, he was fit to be overthrown—as he was at the end of the Shang dynasty—at least from the point of view of the Chou. (But does our present *T'ang shih* represent a Shang ideology or a Chou ideology, as it is commonly regarded as an Eastern Chou version of an older document? We cannot prove it either way, but the king's obligation toward his subordinate lords at least may be said to be documented in the oracle records about reports of alien intrusion of border regions.)

Obviously this reciprocal understanding was by no means a fair one between parties of equal status. For the punishment of a king one had to wait for cataclysmic events such as the rise and fall of dynasties, whereas the punishment for his subjects was immediate and clear cut. From Shang written characters some authors have concluded that the following physical penalties may have been imposed: mutilation of a leg, mutilation of the nose, mutilation of an ear, the piercing of an eye, castration, tattooing of face or forehead, and the use of shackles and irons (of wood?).[126] Unequivocal records of all of these punishments are available for the Chou, and their existence in the Shang period is entirely likely.

Other bits of data in the oracle records pertaining to legal decisions under the Shang dynasty are tantalizing but uncertain. Ch'en Pang-huai says that "five instances of Yin's legal procedures are found in the oracle records: (a) There was a litigation between two parties. A judge presided over it, and he was regarded as being fair. (b) The king asked a Small Official (*hsiao ch'en* 小臣) about an imprisonment matter. The Small Official, standing at the king's east, duly responded. (c) A criminal was tried by a judge and was sentenced to die, but the execution was stayed and the criminal was placed back into custody. (d) A criminal was sentenced to die, but he was pardoned by the king. (e) A criminal was sentenced to grind grains as punitive labor, and an official applied for exemption on his behalf."[127] In each case, however, Ch'en's reading of the relevant passage depends upon uncertain interpretation of one or two characters. A better understanding of the legal system of the Shang can only be achieved with the discovery of some texts with codified legal rules; after all, we find that, according to *To shih* in *Shu ching*, "[the] fathers of the Yin dynasty had their archives [*ts'e* 册] and statutes [*tien* 典]."[128] The oracle records were probably a part of the archives, but no trace of the Shang statutes has been found.

126. Shen Wen-cho 沈文倬, "Fu yü chi" 艮與耤; Hu Hou-hsüan 胡厚宣, "Yin tai ti yüeh hsing" 殷代的刖刑.

127. *Yin tai she-hui shih-liao cheng ts'un* 殷代社會史料徵存, p. 2.

128. Waltham, *Shu Ching*, p. 177.

7. *RITUALS*

Because the oracle records are religious and ritual in nature, Shang religions and rituals have been somewhat exhaustively studied,[129] but the role of rituals and their underlying religious concepts in the political culture of the Shang has been studied less.[130] The following quote from David N. Keightley, however, characterizes the situation briefly but well:

> Shang religion was inextricably involved in the genesis and legitimation of the Shang state. It was believed that Ti, the high god, conferred fruitful harvest and divine assistance in battle, that the king's ancestors were able to intercede with Ti, and that the king could communicate with his ancestors. Worship of the Shang ancestors, therefore, provided powerful psychological and ideological support for the political dominance of the Shang kings. The king's ability to determine through divination, and influence through prayer and sacrifice, the will of the ancestral spirits legitimized the concentration of political power in his person. All power emanated from the theocrat because he was the channel, "the one man," who could appeal for the ancestral blessings, or dissipate the ancestral curses, which affected the commonality. It was the king who made fruitful harvest and victories possible by the sacrifices he offered, the rituals he performed, and the divinations he made. If, as seems likely, the divinations involved some degree of magic making, of spell casting, the king's ability to actually create a good harvest or a victory by divining about it rendered him still more potent politically.[131]

129. Ch'en Meng-chia 陳夢家, "Ku wen-tzu chung chih Shang Chou chi-ssu" 古文字中之商周祭祀; "Shang tai ti shen-hua yü wu-shu" 商代的神話與巫術; Hu Hou-hsüan 胡厚宣, "Yin p'u-tz'u chung ti shang-ti ho wang-ti" 殷卜辭中的上帝和王帝; Itō Michiharu 伊藤道治, "Bokuji ni mieru sorei kannen ni tsuite" 卜辞に見える祖霊観念について; Itō Michiharu 伊藤道治, "Shūkyō men kara mita Indai no ni-san no mondai" 宗教面から見た殷代の二, 三の問題, Tsung-tung Chang, *Der Kult der Shang-Dynastie im Spiegel der Orakelinschriften: Eine paläographische Studie zur Religion im archaischen China.*

130. Paul Wheatley, *Pivot of the Four Quarters*; David Keightley, "The Religious Commitment: Shang Theology and the Genesis of Chinese Political Culture"; P'an Wu-su 潘武肅, "Religion and Chronology in Shang China"; Itō Michiharu 伊藤道治, "Shūkyō men kara mita Indai no ni-san no mondai" 宗教面から見た殷代の二三の問題, (also in his *Chūgoku kodai ōchō no keisei* 中国古代王朝の形成).

131. Keightley, *op. cit.*, 212–213.

Thus, in the act of governance, divination was basis of all other rituals as well as precedent for all other actions. As aforementioned, divinations served to inquire about as many as twenty different matters, which may be further grouped into four main categories:

1. Further ritual actions, such as sacrifices, requests for rain or for fair weather.
2. The king's fortune during a period of time (for instance, a *hsün*, an evening).
3. The potential outcome of contemplated action, such as a war expedition, hunt, movement, journey, etc.
4. Interpretation of the potential outcome of an independent event, such as a dream, natural calamity, birth, illness, or death.

Response to inquiries in all categories provided both basis and justification for the ensuing action on the part of the king. In some of the records there are the king's prognostication and then its subsequent verification. "The king made the prognosis and said, this will be so and thus," the record would faithfully put this down, and it surely would continue, "Indeed when the time came it was so and thus." There could be no question, then, that the ancestor spoke through the bones or the shells, and the king made the correct prognostication. The action he prescribed was, thus, surely the correct action to take. As P'an Keng said, "I have consulted the tortoise shell and obtained the reply: 'This is no place for us.' . . . If we do not follow the example of these old times, we shall be refusing to acknowledge that Heaven is making an end of our dynasty here."[132] That, of course, would not do.

Some of the contemplated action was additional ritual, which was to be performed only with ancestral consent. Under the Old School, both the time and the amount of offering must be approved by the ancestor himself who was to devour it. Even under the New School, although offerings were presented according to a neat schedule of rituals, inquiries about them were still routinely made on the eve of the beginning of every *hsün* week.[133]

132. Waltham, *Shu Ching*, p. 86.

133. Tung Tso-pin 董作賓, *Yin li p'u* 般曆譜; Shima Kunio 島邦男, *Inkyo bokuji kenkyū* 般墟卜辭研究; Hsü Chin-hsiung 許進雄, *Yin p'u-tz'u chung wu chung chi-ssu ti yen-chiu* 般卜辭中五種祭祀的研究; "Yin p'u-tz'u chung wu-chung chi-ssu yen-chiu ti hsin kuan-nien" 般卜辭中五種祭祀研究的新觀念; "Wu chung chi-ssu ti hsin kuan-nien yü Yin li ti t'an-t'ao" 五種祭祀的新觀念與般曆的探討.

8. *ROYAL SYMBOLS*

From the *Tso chuan* passages quoted at the beginning of this chapter we have seen that among the necessary properties granted by the Chou king to a noble in the establishment of a new town were ritual paraphernalia and symbolic regalia that included such items as chariots, flags, jades, feathered bows, bronze bells, and the drums. The *Shu ching* document *Mu shih* describes that on the battle field at Mu Yeh, just before his troops and followers went on the attack of Shang King Chòu, Chou Wu Wang "came to the open country of Mu in the borders of Shang and addressed his army. In his left hand he carried a battle-ax, yellow with gold, and in his right he held a white ensign which he waved." The battle-ax and the flag, as well as the other items listed above, were symbols of the authority of the kings of Shang just as much as the kings of Chou, but different colors surely characterized different states, as in *Li chi*:

> [The princes of Lu] had, as carriages, that of [Shun], the lord of Yü, furnished with bells; that of the sovereign of Hsia, with its carved front; the Great carriage (of wood), or that of Yin; and the carriage (adorned with jade), or that of Chou.
>
> They had, as flags or banners, that of (Shun), the lord of Yü; the yak's tail of the sovereign of Hsia; the great white flag of Yin; and the corresponding red one of Chou.
>
> They had the white horses of the sovereign of Hsia, with their black manes; the white horses of Yin, with their black heads; and the bay horses of Chou, with red manes.

And so on and so forth, so the Lu lords used all the trappings of the Four Dynasties to assert their own authority. It is important that these regalia and paraphernalia were not simply made fresh to order; they each carried a history of past associations with some authoritative regime so that present possession of them signified transfer of such authority and, thus, the legitimacy of the present rulers. Such concepts of transfer of authority and legitimacy of present possessors are best described in this passage of *Tso chuan* (Hsüan Kung, third year) about ritual bronzes as royal symbols:

> The viscount of Ch'u invaded the Jung of Lu-hun, and then went on as far as the Lo, where he reviewed his troops on the borders of Chou. When King Ting sent Wang-sun Man to

him with congratulations and presents, the viscount asked about the size and weight of the [bronze] *ting*-tripods.

Man replied: "[The strength of the state] depends on the [sovereigh's] virtue, and not on the tripods. In ancient times, when Hsia was distinguished for its virtue, the distant regions sent pictures of their [remarkable] objects in tripods. The nine pastors sent in the metal of their provinces, and the tripods were cast, with representations on them of those objects. All the objects were represented, and [instructions were given] for the preparations to be made in reference to them, so that the people might know the sprites and evil things. Thus, the people, when they went among the rivers, marshes, hills, and forests, did not meet with the injurious things, and the hill-sprites, monstrous things, and water-sprites, did not meet with them [to do them injury]. Hereby a harmony was secured between the high and the low, and all enjoyed the blessing of Heaven. When the virtue of Chieh was all-obscured, the tripods were transferred to Shang, for six hundred years. Chòu of Shang proved cruel and oppressive, and they were transferred to Chou. When the [ruler's] virtue is commendable and brilliant, the tripods, though they are small, would be heavy; when it gives place to its reverse, to darkness and disorder, though they are large, they would be light. Heaven blesses intelligent virtue; on that its favor rests. King Ch'eng fixed the tripods in Hsin-ju, and divined that the dynasty should extend through thirty reigns, over seven hundred years. Though the virtue of Chou is decayed, the decree of Heaven is not yet changed. The weight of the tripods may not yet be inquired about. [Translated by Legge.]

Although the above discourse took place in the Late Chou period, the principle it ascribes probably applied to the Shang as well, and we indeed read in *Yi Chou shu* about the sacking of the Shang capital at the time of the conquest and the removal of its "Nine Tripods" (*Chiu ting* 九鼎). This ultimate royal symbol of the Shang may simply refer to their most venerable sets of ritual bronzes, of which archaeological remains are, of course, abundant. We can enumerate the following as the Shang royal symbols that we can confidently substantiate with archaeological or epigraphical data:

1. Some of the more elaborate sets of ritual *bronzes*. Since ritual bronzes were precious objects used for the ancestral rites of the upper class, all bronzes were in some senses symbols of high status, but there

50. Human face lined by two tigers on the handle of a Shang bronze vessel (from the cardboard jacket of Itō Michiharu, *Zusetsu Chūgoku no rekishi,* vol. 1). (By permission of Kodansha International.)

51. *Ya*-shaped characters (From *KKHCK, Chin-wen pien*).

may be a hierarchy of ritual bronzes marked for levels with size, weight, shape, decoration, and inscriptions. The human face placed between two tiger jaws (fig. 50) that is found on the largest examples of *fang ting* 方鼎 is sometimes inscribed for the royal consorts, and it could be a symbol of the highest status.[134] The inscription *ya hsing* 亞形 (fig. 51) is variously interpreted as a royal symbol[135] or as an official title.[136]

2. *Flags* were apparently an important symbol of authority throughout the ancient period.[137] No archaeological remains can substantiate this, but oracle bone and bronze inscriptions show many characters with a flag compound (fig. 52). The *Li chi* says that Shang flags were white, but in view of the many tiger designs on Shang ceremonial paraphernalia of wood[138] and weapons,[139] a tiger very possibly also decorated the royal colors.

3. The *battle-ax* Chou Wu Wang was holding in his left hand as he addressed his troops could have been a crucial part of the Shang royal symbolism of authority as well, especially in view of its evident

134. David N. Keightley, "The Late Shang State: When, Where, and What?," p. 79.

135. See Kao Ch'ü-hsün 高去尋, "Yin tai ta-mu ti mu shih chi ch'i han-yi chih t'ui-ts'e" 殷代大墓的墓室及其涵義之推測.

136. Ch'en Meng-chia 陳夢家, *Yin hsü p'u-tz'u tsung shu* 殷墟卜辭綜述, pp. 510–511.

137. Hayashi Minao 林巳奈夫, "Chūgoku senshin jidai no hata" 中国先秦時代の旗.

138. Umehara Sueji 梅原末治, *Inbo hatsugen mokki in'ei zuroku* 殷墓発現木器印影図録.

139. Shih Chang-ju 石璋如, "Hsiao-t'un Yin tai ti ch'eng t'ao ping-ch'i" 小屯殷代的成套兵器.

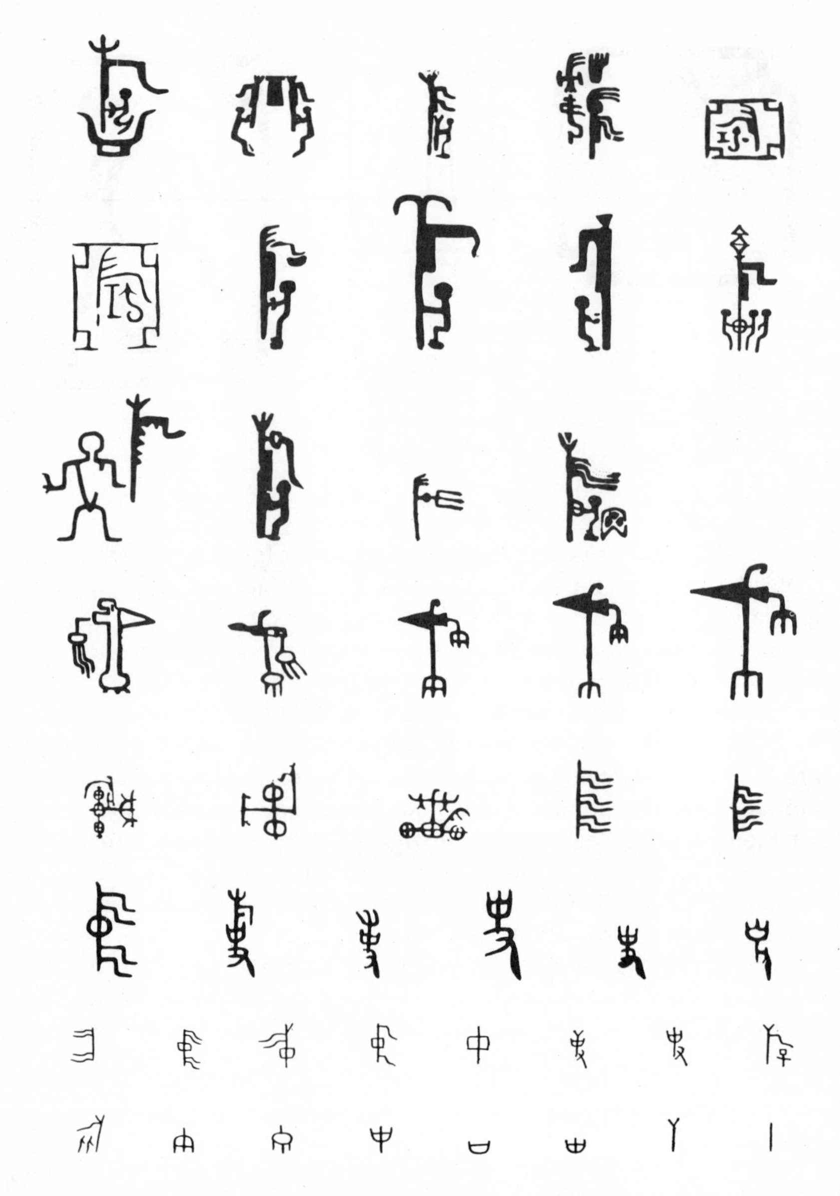

52. Flags in Shang characters (after Hayashi Minao, "Chūgoku senshin jidai no hata," 240).

implication of sanction. Lin Yün[140] suggested that the character for the word king itself was derived from a pictograph of an ax. Many large bronze axes with round holes are known in various collections, but the finds of two such axes, with animal faces on them, in a large grave at the Shang site of Su-fu-t'un, Yi-tu, in Shantung,[141] which were unearthed along the northern wall of the grave pit, are particularly noteworthy for their symbolic significance.

4. The whole *animal style* of decorative art, which was used extensively on bronze, wood, bone, and probably other materials, may also be looked at from a political perspective and be regarded as a symbolic art that, in combination with its underlying religious concepts, helped to provide the aura for those members of the Shang society who were vested with the authority to rule. The characteristic Shang art is, as universally observed, an animal art, featuring faces and bodily parts of animals of various sorts, but principally tigers, cattle, and birds. Tigers were wild beasts that were the prey in royal sports.[142] Cattle were the domestic animals associated in Shang lore with Wang Hai, and birds were also associated in inscriptions with the name Wang Hai.[143] And all animals figured importantly in Shang myths as messengers of communication with the ancestors, a role best symbolized by the use of shoulder blades and turtle shells for the king's communication with their departed ancestors.[144] The kind of animal art of the Shang, in short, is one which drew upon, and reflected, the life of members of the royal group as it involved the animal kingdom.

140. Lin Yün 林沄, "Shuo 'wang'" 說'王'.

141. *WW*, "Shan-tung Yi-tu Su-fu-t'un ti-yi-hao nu-li hsün-tsang mu" 山東益都蘇埠屯第一號奴隸殉葬墓.

142. Li Chi 李濟, "Hunting Records, Faunistic Remains, and Decorative Patterns from the Archaeological Site of An-yang."

143. Tung Tso-pin 董作賓, "Yin tai ti niao shu" 殷代的鳥書; Hu Hou-hsüan 胡厚宣, "Chia-ku wen Shang tsu niao t'u-t'eng ti yi-chi" 甲骨文商族鳥圖騰的遺迹, "Chia-ku wen so-chien Shang tsu niao t'u-t'eng ti hsin cheng-chü" 甲骨文中所見商族鳥圖騰的新証據.

144. Chang Kwang-chih 張光直, "Shang Chou shen-hua yü mei-shu chung so-chien jen yü tung-wu kuan-hsi chih yen-pien" 商周神話與美術中所見人與動物關係之演變.

4 Economy and the Political Order of the State

In the previous chapter we attempted to characterize the rulership of the Shang. Here we will endeavor to see how the rulers ruled, i.e., how they structured and maintained the units through which the economic resources flowed. These units will be discussed in relation to the Shang state, which we now set about to characterize.

1. *THE SHANG STATE NETWORK*

We stated earlier that walled towns were the principal ruling instruments in Shang China, and that they were the residential locales of unilateral kin groups with *tsu* as basic units. The Shang state can be characterized, simply, as the network of such towns that was under the Shang king's direct control. By "direct control" we mean that the Shang king was responsible for granting the title to the township and the land that supported the township to the lord who ruled it, and that for this act the king was entitled in return to the lord's services and grains. Such a network was vast—Tung Tso-pin says that he counted close to a thousand town names[1]—and its rule was hierarchical and its perimeters flexible. All of these will become clear as we proceed with our attempt to characterize the Shang state.

The first distinction that one must make in characterizing the Shang state structure is one between the capital (*nei fu* 內服) and the domain (*wai fu* 外服). When Chou Kung established K'ang Shu as ruler of Wei he is said to have described the condition of the Shang capital—the area in which Wei was located—to admonish him against indulgence in drinking, a vice that was prevalent in the Shang capital during the reign of its last king, as follows:

1. "P'u-tz'u chung ti Po yü Shang" 卜辭中的亳與商, p. 8.

> In the exterior domains [*wai fu*], the princes of the Hou, T'ien, Nan, and Wei states with their presiding chiefs, and in the interior domain [*nei fu*, i.e. capital] all the various officers, directors of the several departments, inferior officers and employees, heads of great houses, and the men of distinguished name living in retirement, all eschewed indulgence in spirits.[2]

The alleged indulgence in spirits aside, the division of the Shang domains into an interior and an exterior dimension is consistent with the level of attention the Shang are shown to have given to their subjects in the oracle records.

THE CAPITAL

The capital area, or the king's interior domain, was the area of the king's regular activities. It consisted of two interrelated but different regions: Shang and the current capital (in the An-yang area). A third sphere of regular royal activities was the royal hunting territory, but it may conceptually represent a bridge between the capital and the domain.

Shang. A crucial question in Shang history pertains to the fact that in the oracle bone records Shang was the name of an important town, but that the town named Shang has been shown not to have been the Shang's royal capital in the last 273 years of the dynasty's life. This question bears looking into.

Shang was a name both the Shang themselves and the Chou people used. The Shang poem *Hsüan niao* says, "Heaven bade the dark bird / To come down and bear the Shang," and the Chou poem *Pi kung* speaks of the Great King, "who lived on the southern slopes of Mount Ch'i/And began to trim the Shang" (translated by Arthur Waley). The word Shang appeared in the oracle bone inscriptions very frequently, always referring to a town, which was also called Ta yi Shang 大邑商 ("Great City Shang") or T'ien yi Shang 天邑商 ("Heaven City Shang"). Briefly at one time in the early years of oracle bone inscription scholarship the name was considered to refer to the Shang capital in An-yang,[3] but Tung Tso-pin showed, conclusively, that Shang was at a considerable distance from the current capital. This conclusion was based on the itinerary reconstructed by Tung of Ti Hsin's military

2. Waltham, *Shu Ching*, p. 155.

3. Lo Chen-yü 羅振玉, *Yin hsü shu ch'i k'ao shih* 殷虛書契考釋, Hsü 序 and Hsia 下 54; Wang Kuo-wei 王國維, "Shuo Shang" 說商; Hu Hou-hsüan 胡厚宣, "P'u-tz'u chung so-chien chih Yin tai nung-yeh" 卜辭中所見之殷代農業, 42.

campaign against Jen Fang 人方, an alien state east of Shang. On the basis of thirty-three pieces of inscribed shell and bone left during the tenth and eleventh year of Ti Hsin[4] in the course of the king's journey to the east to subdue Jen Fang, Tung Tso-pin reconstructed a detailed itinerary in which the king's movements were keyed to a number of town names, including the names Shang 商 and Po 亳. Selected segments of this reconstructed itinerary follow.[5]

Tenth Year		
Ninth Month	Day Chia-Wu	The king divined about the campaign to subdue Jen Fang together with Hou ("Marquis") Hsi, and received a favorable reply.[6]
Ninth Month (intercalary)	Day Kuei-Hai	King was at Ku (twenty-five kilometers southeast of Fan Hsien, Shantung).
Eleventh Month	Days Hsin-Ch'ou and Jen-Yin	*King was at Shang.*
	Days Kuei-Ch'ou and Chia-Yen	King was at Po.
Twelfth Month	Day Ping-Wu	King was at Huai. (Huai was located on the Huai River.)
Eleventh Year		
First and second Months	Days Yi-Ssu to Kuei-Yu	King was at Yu. (Yu was the fief of Marquis Hsi, located south of the river Huai.)
Fifth Month	Day Ping-Wu	*King was at* (*returned to*) *Shang.*
Sixth Month	Day Kuei-Yu	King was at Yün, a town on the Ho (the Yellow River.)

4. Li Hsüeh-ch'in 李學勤, in *Yin tai ti-li chien lun* 殷代地理簡論 believes that it was Ti Yi, rather than Ti Hsin, who carried out the Jen Fang campaign. His argument, however, is not persuasive.

5. Tung Tso-pin 董作賓, *Yin li p'u* 殷曆譜 ("Ti Hsin jih p'u" 帝辛日譜). See also Ting Su 丁驌, "Ch'ung ting Ti Hsin cheng Jen Fang jih p'u" 重訂帝辛正人方日譜.

6. This was based on an inscription published in Kuo Mo-jo 郭沫若, *P'u-tz'u t'ung ts'uan* 卜辭通纂, no. 592. In the same passage was the sentence, "kao yü Ta yi Shang" ("to inform [the ancestors] at Ta yi Shang"). Both Ch'en Meng-chia 陳夢家 (*Yin hsü p'u-tz'u tsung shu* 殷墟卜辭綜述, p. 301) and Li Hsüeh-ch'in 李學勤 (*Yin tai ti-li chien lun* 殷代地理簡論, p. 41) believed that the *kao* 告 took place at Ta yi Shang, which was, thus, the current capital and the beginning point of the campaign. Tung Tso-pin, however, interpreted this as being an additional objective of the campaign ("to subdue Jen Fang *and* to inform ancestors at Ta yi Shang") (see His *Yin li p'u* 殷曆譜, "Ti Hsin jih p'u" 帝辛日譜, p. 61). Tung's interpretation is followed here, since it is consistent with the general usage of the capital names.

The journey continued on into the seventh month, but by then the king and his party were probably quite close to home. This was a major campaign, lasting a whole year, but the important point here is that the king is shown to have been to Shang (the city) both on his way to Jen Fang and on his return. The decision to go east was made on day Chia-Wu of the ninth month of the tenth year. We do not have the starting date, but by day Kuei-Hai of the intercalary ninth month the king had reached southwestern Shantung, and only more than a month after that did he reach Shang. On his return, it also took him almost a month to move from Shang back to a town near the Yellow River, which was then on a course closer to An-yang than it is now. On the strength of the length of the journey alone, I am convinced that Tung's placement of Shang in Shang-ch'iu and of Po near Po Hsien is correct.

The importance of locating the city of Shang at a place near Shang-ch'iu (or, for that matter, at any other fixed location outside An-yang) lies in the fact that Shang provided the one immobile central place for the dynasty and the state called Shang, whose kings and their capitals have proved to be highly mobile. As we have seen before, there were several dynastic capitals after T'ang founded the Shang dynasty, moving around largely in the eastern half of Honan, but the city of Shang provided a fixed point for their state territory: "The Yin people used their ancestral capital, Great City Shang, as the center, referring to it as Chung Shang 中商 [Central Shang], and accordingly divided their land into four quarters, the Eastern Land, the Southern Land, the Western Land, and the Northern Land."[7] The city of Shang was probably the place where the Shang kings kept their most sacred ancestral temples, tablets, and regalia, and it figured importantly in certain rituals and in many military campaigns.[8]

The area of Shang-ch'iu and Po Hsien, which is intimately concerned with predynastic and early dynastic Shang history, may yet prove to be an important region in Shang archaeology. Unfortunately, because of the repeated changes of the course of the Yellow River, this region has been covered by many meters of silt from repeated floodings, and is within the archaeologically least known area of North China, from K'ai-feng to the Grand Canal.

"The Present Capital." If, as Tung Tso-pin maintained, the city named Shang was at a fixed location unchangeable throughout Shang history, then each of the royal capitals must have had its own name.

7. Tung Tso-pin 董作賓, *Yin li p'u* 殷曆譜 ("Ti Hsin jih p'u" 帝辛日譜, p. 62).

8. Ch'en Meng-chia 陳夢家, *Yin hsü p'u-tz'u tsung shu* 殷墟卜辭綜述, p. 257.

These names are supplied in ancient texts: Po, Hsiao (Ao), Hsiang, Hsing, Yen, and Yin. The name Po appears in the oracle inscriptions, as has just been mentioned, but so far the name Yin has not been identified in the oracle records;[9] in fact, in the oracle records we have not identified any specific name with which the Shang referred to this capital city of theirs for (as alleged in *Chu shu*) 273 years. The only word that was so used was *tzu yi* 茲邑 or "this town." *Tzu yi* was sometimes the object of concern in the oracle records in the event of a flooding of the river Huan, and it unquestionably referred to the city near the Huan River whose ruins are our principal archaeological record.[10] Possibly the name of the city still lies buried in the corpus of characters that are yet to be deciphered, but in any event it is significant that in the Shang conception their ancestral capital at Shang was the fixed point of their political and ritual universe, around which their other cities, including their royal capitals, orbited.

The current capital in the An-yang area is known largely from archaeological records, and I have described it in chapter 1.

The Area of the Royal Hunts. One of the royal activities most frequently referred to in the oracle bone inscriptions was the hunt; the most extreme estimate places oracle records regarding the hunt at about half of the total of divinations,[11] but other estimates are more conservative and, perhaps, more reliable.[12] However, there is hardly any question that the hunt was an important activity in which the king (especially some kings) engaged. Li Chi rightly pointed out that the large-scale hunts recorded in oracle bone inscriptions "were evidently confined to the royalty and the aristocratic class,"[13] but he surely underestimated the economic and symbolic importance of these hunts when he argued that "the game huntings mentioned in the ancient inscriptions were evidently pursued for pleasure and excitement rather than for economic necessities."[14] As we mentioned in chapter 2, the yield of these hunts were considerable, providing meat, skin, and bones and antlers for the kitchens and the workshops.

9. With regard to the name Yin in the oracle bone inscriptions, see Ch'en Meng-chia 陳夢家, *Ibid.*, p. 264.

10. Shima Kunio 島邦男, *Inkyo bokuji kenkyū* 殷墟卜辞研究, p. 360.

11. Chung Po-sheng 鍾柏生, *P'u-tz'u chung so chien Yin wang t'ien-yu ti ming k'ao—chien lun t'ien-yu ti-ming yen-chiu fang-fa* 卜辭中所見殷王田游地名考—兼論田游地名研究方法, 6.

12. Huang Jan-wei 黃然偉, "Yin wang t'ien lieh k'ao (shang)" 殷王田獵考(上) 1.

13. "Hunting Records, Faunistic Remains and Decorative Patterns from the Archaeological Site of Anyang," 12.

14. *Ibid.*

Because of the economic importance of the hunt, it is useful for us to find out what the territorial scope of the hunting trips made by the kings was. If the king was a provider of sorts, it is important to determine the territorial unit within which he served in that capacity. In the oracle bone records two kinds of data have been used for this determination: names of locations where the hunts took place, and the distance between points measured by time, i.e. the number of days it took the king and his hunting party to travel.[15] Unfortunately, neither of the two provides indisputable proof, and three drastically different conclusions have been drawn by different scholars:

1. Royal hunts were restricted largely to the capital area;[16]
2. Hunts were undertaken in restricted areas outside the capital, the most favored being the area of Ch'in-yang 沁陽 in central-western Honan[17] or near Shang-ch'iu in western Shantung;[18]
3. The royal hunting parties roamed throughout the Shang territory.[19]

It is difficult, if not impossible, to determine which, if any, of the above hypotheses is the most reliable, because the only two pillars on which to build a hypothesis are both of questionable firmness. The names of places are now hard to pin down, and the distance measured by time is subject to even greater uncertainties than that by space. I am, however, sufficiently confident of the essential continuity of many of the place-names from Shang to later historical periods that it seems prudent to combine hypotheses (b) and (c) into our working hypothesis. That is, the many placenames at or near which royal hunts took place were distributed throughout the Shang state, but a large number of them appear to be concentrated in the Ch'in-yang area. This working hypothesis will serve as an important consideration in exploring the resource flow patterns of the Shang state.

15. Chung Po-sheng 鍾柏生, *op. cit.*

16. Matsumaru Michio 松丸道雄, "Inkyo bokuji chū no denryōchi ni tsuite—Indai kokka kōzō kenkyū no tame ni" 殷墟卜辞中の田猟地について—殷代国家構造研究のために.

17. Li Hsüeh-ch'in 李學勤, *Yin tai ti-li chien lun* 殷代地理簡論; Ch'en Meng-chia 陳夢家, *Yin hsü p'u-tz'u tsung shu* 殷墟卜辭綜述; Wang Kuo-wei 王國維, "Yin hsü p'u tz'u chung so chien ti ming k'ao" 殷虛卜辭中所見地名考; Kuo Mo-jo 郭沫若, *P'u tz'u t'ung ts'uan* 卜辭通纂.

18. Tung Tso-pin 董作賓, *Yin li p'u* 殷曆譜.

19. Shima Kunio 島邦男, *Inkyo bokuji kenkyū* 殷墟卜辞研究; Hayashi Taisuke 林泰輔, *Shina jōdai no kenkyū* 支那上代の研究; Huang Jan-wei 黄然偉, "Yin wang t'ien lieh k'ao 殷王田獵考.

THE DOMAIN

By *the domain* we refer, conceptually, to the territorial unit within which the Shang king had direct access to economic resources. As the Chou poem *Pei shan* says, "Everywhere under Heaven / Is no land that is not the king's. / To the borders of all those lands / None but is the king's slave".[20] This was surely as applicable to Shang as it was to Chou, but we can visualize, in any event, a territorial unit in which the king was entitled to a share of all its produce and all its labor force. The entitlement was achieved in no small part by virtue of the king's status as the head of the grand lineage from which all the branch lineages were split, but it was certainly ensured through the king's military force and his control of near and remote walled towns by proxy through the lords he appointed to all corners of his kingdom. Therefore, in actual data, we recognize the Shang state from the An-yang data through the following criteria:

1. Harvest divinations. The oracle records show that the king was concerned about the harvests in his capital, at Shang, in all his domain (wo 我, or "among all of us"), and for each of his lords, and that he divined about them, but he was not shown to divine about the harvest of any of the *fang* 方.[21] The area of harvest divinations presumably coincided with the area in which the king had a direct economic interest.

2. The areas of the royal hunt. This, as has just been mentioned, indicates the area in which the king had direct access to some of its economic resources.

3. The area outlined on all sides by *fang*s. The word *fang* 方 in oracle bone inscriptions apparently referred to polities other than towns under Shang's control. The word for "settlement" was *yi* or a square enclosure, and it and *fang* were apparently two contrastive territorial units. As shown by Western Chou bronze inscriptions, the word for "garrison" had two different versions, one having foot soldiers guarding the accesses to a □ and the other having them guarding those to a 方,[22] suggesting that these were alternative concepts or units of successive levels. Thus, the Shang territory—quartered into the Eastern, Northern, Western, and Southern Lands, or the *ssu t'u* 四土—was outlined by the *ssu fang* 四方 or the Four *Fang*s.

4. The area occupied by the lords. By "the lords" I refer to men

20. Waley, *The Book of Songs*, p. 320.

21. Ch'en Meng-chia 陳夢家, *Yin hsü p'u-tz'u tsung shu* 殷墟卜辭綜述, p. 639.

22. *KK*, "Shan-hsi Ch'i-shan Ho-chia-ts'un Hsi Chou mu-tsang" 陝西岐山賀家村西周墓葬, 34.

(and some women) who (a) ruled over walled towns, presumably through entitlement by the king, (b) were known in the oracle records by the names of their towns, and (c) were, additionally, known by a title preceding their names such as *po* 伯, *t'ien* 田, or *hou* 侯. These subject lords were collectively known in the king's records as *to po yü to t'ien* 多伯與多田 ("the many *pos* and *t'iens*") or some such collective phraseology.[23] Shima Kunio, who accepts only *hou* and *po* as such titles, has counted 35 *hou* names and 40 *po* names.[24] In addition, as we have already mentioned, many *fu* and *tzu*, who figured actively in the royal court, also had their towns. Thus, the territory occupied by such lords as *tzu*, *fu*, *hou*, and *po* may be considered as the king's land. The king, however, had differing degrees of control over any particular piece of land within his territory, and his extent of control changed over time. Moreover, the various lords and their towns would be of varying importance in the overall hierarchy of towns within the whole state.

To take some measure of the king's degree of control over, or at least contact with, the various towns and of their varying importance, David Keightley has designed a formula to get at the "state score" of any place name—Shang's ally, dependency, or subordinate—by multiplying the known number of the occurrence of that name in Shima Kunio's *Concordance* by the number of times that inscriptions pertaining to it meet the thirty-nine criteria that he has formulated for this purpose.[25] Some examples:

Sovereignhty

1. The king order (*ling* 令) X.
2. A Shang state member orders X (Y orders X) or X orders Y.
3. The king calls upon or cries out for (*hu* 乎) X to act.
4. X assists the king's affairs (*ku wang shih* 固王事).
5. X leads or takes officers or men.

Territoriality

10. The king hunts, or inspects, or does some other activity at X.
11. The king goes to, from, enters into, returns to X.
12. The king sends men to X, or calls upon officers or men to go to X, or divines about Y going to X.

23. Tung Tso-pin 董作賓, "Wu teng chüeh tsai Yin Shang" 五等爵在殷商; Hu Hou-hsüan 胡厚宣, "Yin tai feng-chien chih-tu k'ao" 殷代封建制度考.

24. Shima Kunio 島邦男, *Inkyo bokuji kenkyū* 殷墟卜辭研究, pp. 427, 435.

25. "The Late Shang State: When, Where, and What?"

13. The king issues orders at X or orders the men of X to do something.
14. The king divines at X.
20. X combined with the title of *Hou* (or *Po*?), *Tzu, Fu, or* more lowly titles.
(21. The term A-*fang*, used of non-Shang groups. A negative criterion.)

Religion and kingship

22. The king offers sacrifices to or at X.
23. The king offers rituals, sacrifices, for X, or Tzu-X, etc.
24. X participates in a Shang ritual.
27. Royal concern about the health of X.
28. Incantations to ensure X's well-being.
29. X will receive harvest, rainfall.

Alliances and warfare

31. The king (or his officers) follows X, or X follows Y.
32. The king will destroy A at Y.
33. The king divines that X will perhaps lose *chung* or *jen*.

Exchange: Trade and Tribute

38. Income notations: X sent in shells and scapulas.
39. X will supply other goods.

As Keightley has pointed out in his preliminary but very illuminating study, these criteria are still in the process of being formulated and the meeting of single criteria may not mean anything. But the "state scores"—criteria met times number of occurrences—that can be worked out for specific names may carry considerable significance. The following Shang places have scored 200 or more in Keightley's preliminary study:

(Ch'a)	Scored 6480	Probable location:	Shansi
(Chih)	3312		Shansi
(Chou)	1648		Shensi
(Shang)	1529		Honan
(Yüeh)	1350		Shansi
(Wang)	1328		Honan
(Shun)	1144		Honan
(Yü)	1092		Hopei
(Kung)	845		Hopei
(Fu)	792		Shansi
(Sang)	696		Shantung
(Hui?)	459		Shantung

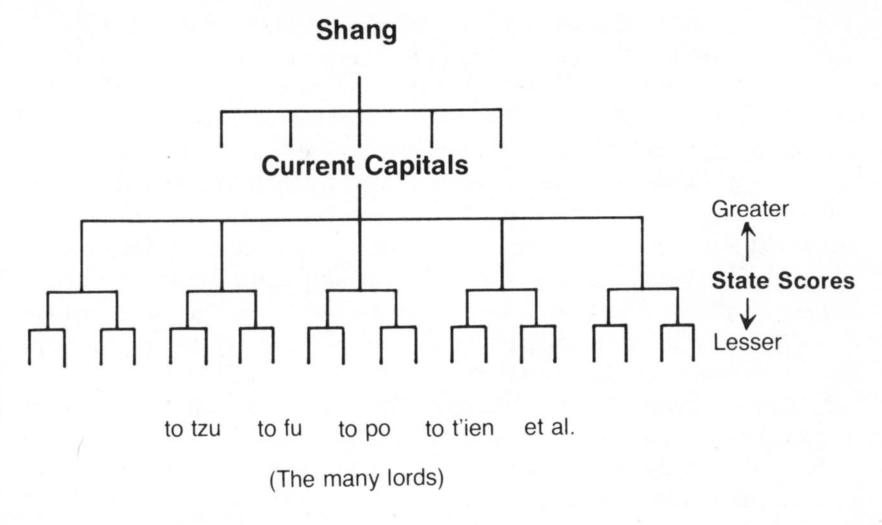

53. The hierarchy of the Shang state network.

䨻 (Pei)	406	Shansi
𢀛 (Shu)	384	Honan
𡧊 (Wu)	240	Honan
㐭 (Hsiang)	200	Shantung

Some of the above state scores may be questionable for our purposes of ranking the towns within the state. Shang, for example, should be eliminated, because it was Shang itself. Yü was often a *fang* and should not be counted as a state member of unshifting standing. But such studies point to the higher-ranking hierarchical position of some of the towns as compared with others, and these may have formed secondary centers around which other towns orbited. (The lateral actions of X-Y pairs tend to bear this out.)

THE STATE NETWORK AND TERRITORY

Taking all of the above into account, the structural network of the Shang state may be diagramed as in fig. 53. Our next job, now that we have a tentative structural framework, is to spread that framework over the Chinese landscape, and for this task we can only rely upon the painstaking task of textual historians and oracle bone specialists working together to identify, one single name by one single name, the Shang placenames with the earliest known names in the ancient texts.

The task we can accomplish from two directions. First, we try to plot the names of *hou*s and *po*s onto the territory of the Shang and, secondary, we try to plot the *fang*s or alien states on the peripheries of the state. The territory filled by the *hou* and *po* names and, at the same time, left blank by the *fang* plottings, constitutes the territorial spread of the Shang state during its various periods at An-yang.

For these operations we may rely upon Shima's scholarship. Figure 54 show the distribution of *hou*s and *po*s, which are recorded within the modern provinces of northern and central Honan, southwestern Shantung, southwestern Shansi, and central-eastern Shensi. Figure 55 shows the approximate locations of the various *fang*s, which are shown to be in northern Shansi and Shensi, central Hopei, and northern Kiangsu.[26] An overlap between the *hou* and *po* maps and the *fang* maps suggests that the Shang borders in the northwest in Shansi and in the southeast in the Huai River valley were unstable but that the base of the Shang state has always been northern and central Honan and southwestern Shantung.[27]

2. *FLOW OF RESOURCES WITHIN THE STATE*

The political framework outlined above becomes especially meaningful when viewed as the organization to regulate and facilitate the flow of produce, goods, and services—the economic resources—in a particular manner. In this section we will attempt to describe and reconstruct the Shang economy: the production of economic resources and the pattern and dynamics of their flow.

AGRICULTURAL PRODUCTION

In chapter 2 we named the crops that were planted by the Shang, but other components are needed to complete the production cycle: we also need human labor, in some organized manner, to apply a technology to the land to produce the crops. Let us now discuss these other components—land, technology, and organized labor—of Shang agricultural production.

There is no evidence that land was privately owned during any of the Shang period. On the contrary, in Shang divinations farming fields on the northwestern border that were reportedly being attacked by an alien state were referred to as *wo t'ien* 我田, "My fields" or "our

26. Shima Kunio 島邦男, *Ibid.*, pp. 423, 433, 441.

27. Cf. Li Hsüeh-ch'in 李學勤, *Yin tai ti-li chien lun* 殷代地理簡論. For discussion of the dynamic opposition between what was within the state and what was outside, see Lien-sheng Yang, "Historical Notes on the Chinese World Order."

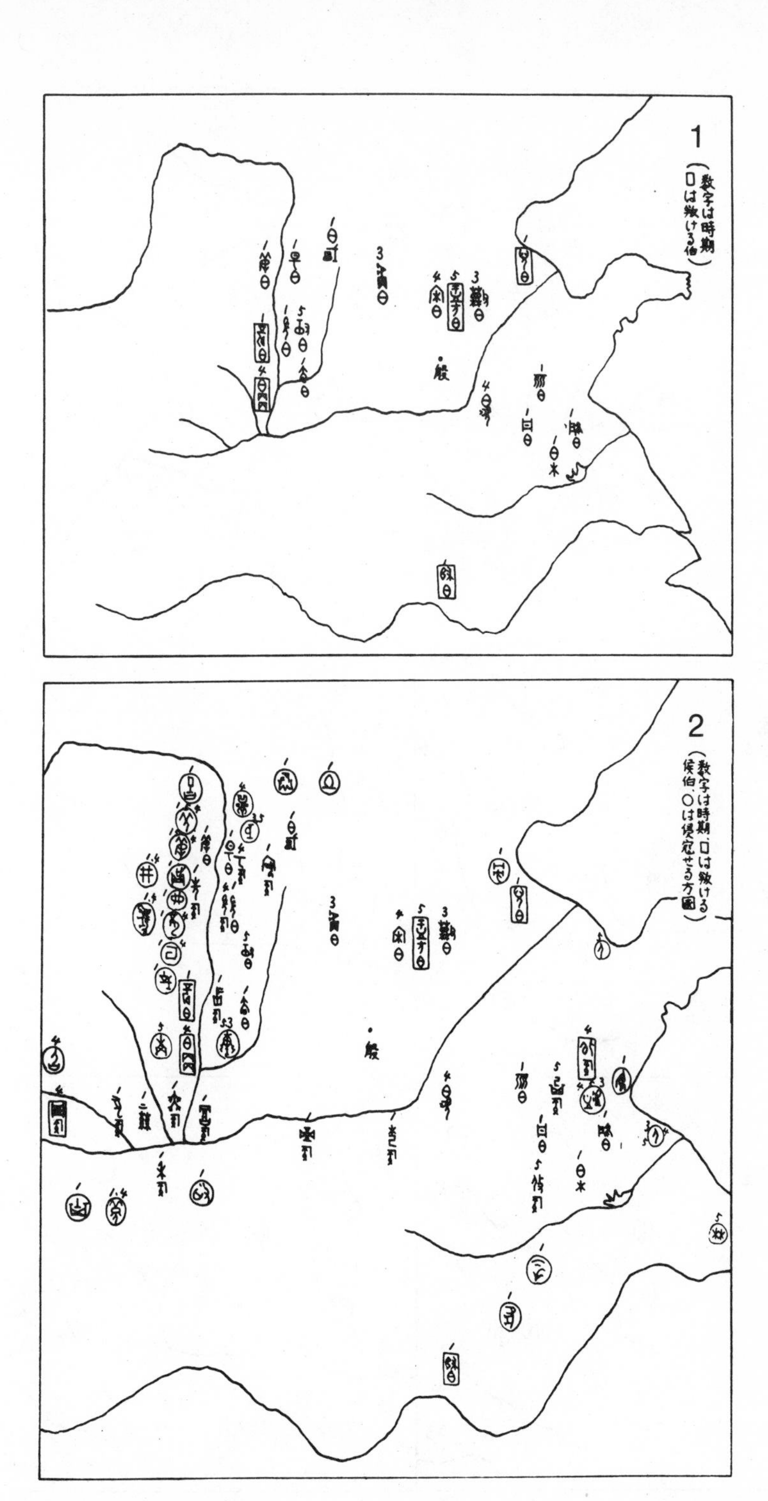

54. Distribution of Shang lords according to Shima Kunio (after his *Inkyo bokuji kenkyū*, p. 441). (1) Approximate locations of *po* lords. (2) Approximate locations of all lords and neighboring alien states (circled). (By permission of Kyuko Shoin.)

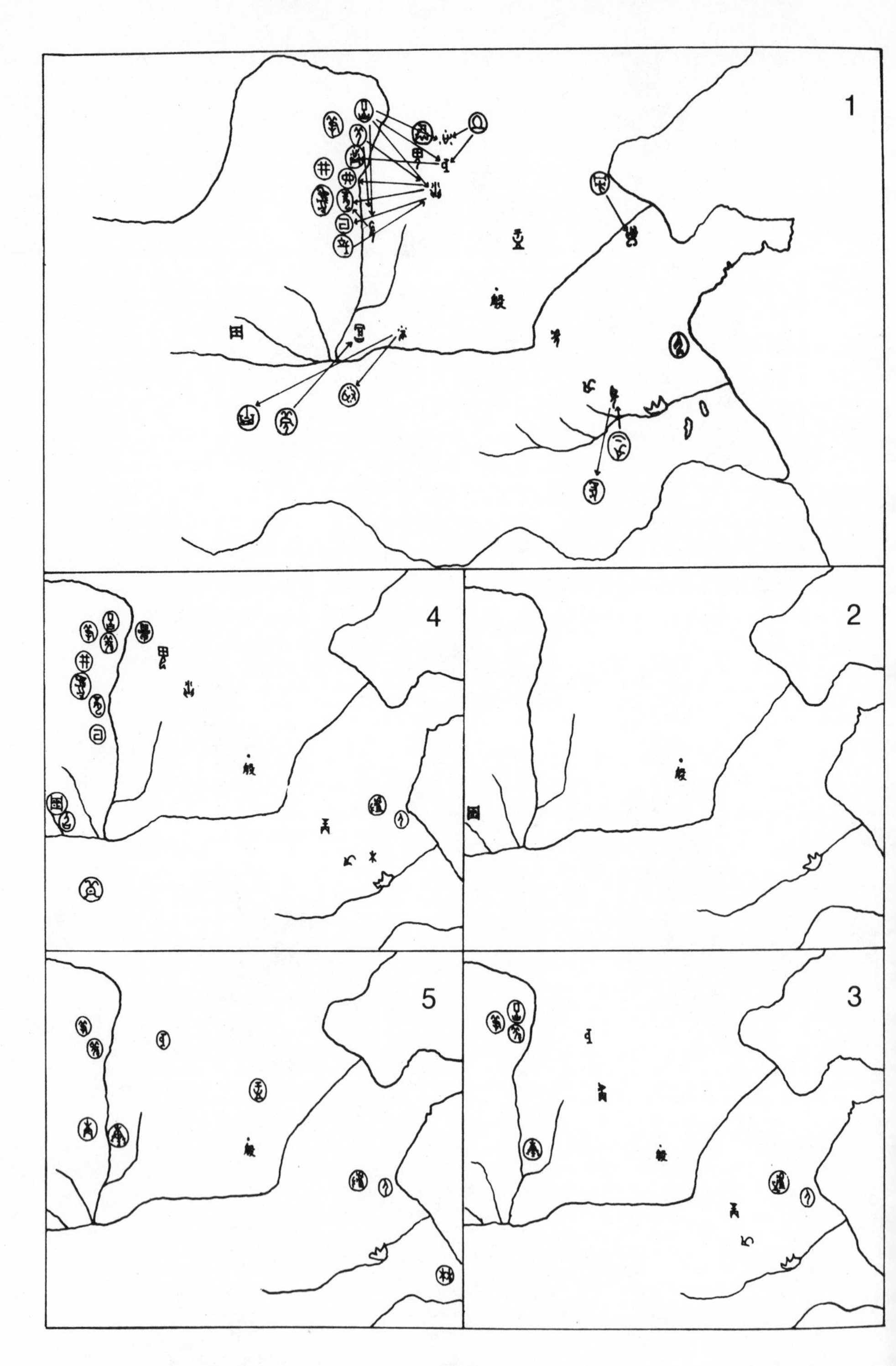

55. Distribution of Shang *fang*s during periods 1–5 according to Shima Kunio (after his *Inkyo bokuji kenkyū*, p. 423). (By permission of Kyuko Shoin.)

fields."[28] The character *wo* in oracle inscriptions was unquestionably a reference of self-address on the part of the state or of the king,[29] its shape (weapon with flag) suggesting its basis in military control. Such concepts on land were identical with those of the Western Chou described earlier: "Everywhere under Heaven / Is no land that is not the king's."

New land was cleared and opened for farming on the order of the king. In the oracle records the act of clearing new fields for cultivation was referred to by the word *p'ou*, written as [illegible] with several variations, all of which are comprised of an element of working hands and an element of earth.[30] According to Chang Cheng-lang's study, the *p'ou*-ing of new fields was undertaken primarily during the sixth month (the month of summer solstice) or the twelth month (the month of the winter solstice), times of the year that were suitable, according to a number of late Chou and Han texts, for barking the trees to kill them and ready them for burning the following year.[31] Barking was used, Chang maintains, because of the lacking of effective (e.g. metal) tree-felling implements. Whether or not this was the case, Shang implements that are attributable to uses in agriculture were probably manufactured of wood, stone, bone, and shell for the most part. Despite occasional claims to the contrary,[32] bronze was not an oft-used material for implements. Of the 332 bronze artifacts with working edges excavated from Yin hsü, 317 are weapons and only fifteen are classifiable as tools; the latter were all wood-working not farming implements.[33] On the other hand, huge quantities of slate knives were unearthed, and these—the so-called Hsiao-t'un stone knives—were reasonably regarded as harvesting knives or sickles.[34] In addition, stone axes and "spades" are believed to have

28. Lo Chen-yü 羅振玉, *Yin hsü shu ch'i ch'ing hua* 殷虛書契菁華. See Yü Hsing-wu 于省吾, "Ts'ung chia-ku wen k'an Shang tai she-hui hsing-chih" 從甲骨文看商代社會性質, 101–102.

29. Ch'en Meng-chia 陳夢家, *Yin hsü p'u-tz'u tsung shu* 殷墟卜辭綜述, p. 318.

30. Chang Cheng-lang 張政烺, "P'u-tz'u p'ou t'ien chi ch'i hsiang-kuan chu wen-t'i" 卜辭裒田及其相關諸問題; Yü Hsing-wu 于省吾, "Ts'ung chia-ku wen k'an Shang tai ti nung-t'ien k'en-chih" 從甲骨文看商代的農田墾殖.

31. Chang Cheng-lang 張政烺, *Ibid*. See also Shih Sheng-han 石聲漢, *Ch'i-min-yao-shu chin shih* 齊民要術今釋, p. 3.

32. Lu Mao-te 陸懋德, "Chung-kuo fa-hsien chih shang-ku t'ung li k'ao" 中國發現之上古銅犂考. Also the special exhibits on bronze agricultural implements of ancient China in the Shanghai Metropolitan Museum.

33. Li Chi 李濟, "Chi Hsiao-t'un ch'u-t'u chih ch'ing-t'ung ch'i Chung p'ien feng-jen ch'i" 記小屯出土之青銅器, 中篇, 鋒刄器.

34. Li Chi 李濟, "Yin hsü yu jen shih-ch'i t'u shuo" 殷虛有刄石器圖說, 616. There were altogether 3,600-plus of these knives at Hsiao-t'un alone; see p. 590 of above article.

56. *Lei* held by ancient sages as depicted in the stone art in the Wu family temple of Eastern Han (after Jung Keng, *Han Wu-liang tz'u hua-hsiang lu*). *Left:* Shen Nung Shih; *right*: Hsia Yü.

served agriculture-related uses, but the single most important agricultural implement of the Shang period may be a wooden tool that has largely eluded the archaeologist's spade thus far. This is the *lei* 耒 widely mentioned in ancient texts. Many oracle bone characters concerned with cultivation contain a component in the shape of a two-pronged digging stick, the same shape attributed to the *lei* in Han art (fig. 56), and it is likely that the basic Shang implement to turn over the soil for cultivation was such a digging stick.[35] Possibly it was a large and heavy affair that may have required not only one person holding it and pushing it into the soil but also a second person (or even a beast) to help to pull it (fig. 57).[36] Some scholars believe that plows were used by the Shang farmers,[37]

35. Hsü Chung-shu 徐中舒, "Lei ssu k'ao" 耒耜考; Sun Ch'ang-hsü 孫常敘, *Lei ssu ti ch'i-yüan chi ch'i fa-chan* 耒耜的起源及其發展.

36. Sun Ch'ang-hsü 孫常敘, *Ibid.*; Liu Hsien-chou 劉仙洲, *Chung-kuo ku-tai nung-yeh chi-hsieh fa-ming shih* 中國古代農業機械發明史, p. 8.

37. Hu Hou-hsüan 胡厚宣, "P'u-tz'u chung so-chien chih Yin tai nung-yeh" 卜辭中所見之殷代農業.

57. Possible interpretation of the term *ou keng* as an early form of the plow (after Liu Hsien-chou, *Chung-kuo ku-tai nung-yeh chi-hsieh fa-ming shih,* p. 8).

but the evidence that they give essentially concerns *lei* being pulled as well as pushed.

The fact that with the aid of such primitive tools (wooden *lei*, stone and shell sickles, and stone axes and spades) the Shang were able to produce enough food to build a great civilization is sufficient grounds for speculating that it was at the level of labor that the Shang agriculture received its greatest energy input, and the oracle bone records clearly bear this out. The following divination is a good example:

> The king ordered the *chung-jen* [衆人 "the multitude"] and said, *hsieh* [劦] the fields so that there will be good harvest! In the eleventh month.[38]

38. Lo Chen-yü 羅振玉, *Yin hsü shu ch'i hsü pien* 殷虛書契續編, no. 2.28.5.

Two words in this passage are noteworthy. The first is *hsieh* 劦, generally interpreted to mean "cultivate collectively,"[39] perhaps including the practice of pushing and pulling the *lei* in pairs, sometimes referred to as *ou* 耦 ("pair") *keng* 耕.[40] Such a practice strongly suggests agricultural production units of some size,[41] discipline, and supervision by the king and his government. Among the many *hsiao ch'en* 小臣 ("small officials") recorded in the oracle inscriptions are presumably those concerned with the task of supervising collective agricultural teams.[42]

Who were the principal members of these collective farming teams? *Chung-jen*, according to the above passage. *Chung-jen* or *chung* 衆[43] is generally read to mean "the multitude," but some scholars believe that the *chung*, working in collective units and under supervision, must be seen as the slave laborers of the Marxian slave society,[44] but most others, citing the Shang document *P'an keng*, in which the king not only announced his decision to move his capital but also tried to justify it to the *chung*, see them as free farmers who were members—lowly, to be sure—of the ruler's own groups.[45] Even given the latter view, the *chung* farmers need not have been "free" in any sense of that word. Chang Cheng-lang's interpretation probably sums it up best:

> "Chung jen" were farmers, and were the fighting men in wars. They . . . usually occupied a very lowly position, opposite the . . . nobility. They had no title to land . . . and they were securely tied up with agricultural collectives, controlled by the . . . rulers, were conscribed to become soldiers, paid tributes, and performed labor services. When they were

39. Yü Hsing-wu 于省吾, "Ts'ung chia-ku wen k'an Shang tai she-hui hsing-chih" 從甲骨文看商代社會性質, 102–103.

40. For *ou keng* 耦耕, see Wang Ning-sheng 汪寧生, "Ou keng hsin chieh" 耦耕新解; Wan Kuo-ting 萬國鼎, "Ou keng k'ao" 耦耕考; Ho Tzu-ch'üan 何兹全, "T'an ou keng" 談耦耕.

41. Chang Cheng-lang 張政烺, on good oracle bone and textual evidence, suggests 100–200 for clearing new fields; see his "P'u tz'u p'ou t'ien chi ch'i hsiang-kuan chu wen-t'i" 卜辭裒田及其相關諸問題, 112.

42. Hu Hou-hsüan 胡厚宣, "P'u-tz'u chung so-chien chih Yin tai nung-yeh" 卜辭中所見之殷代農業, 67; Shen Wen-cho 沈文倬, "Fu yü chi" 艮與耤, 338.

43. Ch'en Meng-chia's 陳夢家 division between *chung* 衆 and *chung-jen* 衆人 is not convincing; see his *Yin hsü p'u-tz'u tsung shu* 殷墟卜辭綜述, pp. 605–611, and Su Shih-cheng 束世澂, "Hsia tai ho Shang tai ti nu-li chih" 夏代和商代的奴隸制, 42.

44. Wang Yü-che 王玉哲, "Shih shu Yin tai ti nu-li chih-tu ho kuo-chia ti hsing-ch'eng" 試述殷代的奴隸制度和國家的形成.

45. Hu Hou-hsüan 胡厚宣, "P'u-tz'u chung so-chien chih Yin tai nung-yeh" 卜辭中所見之殷代農業, 71–72; Su Shih-cheng 束世澂, "Hsia tai ho Shang tai ti nu-li chih" 夏代和商代的奴隸制, 42; Yü Hsing-wu 于省吾, "Ts'ung chia-ku wen k'an Shang tai she-hui hsing-chih" 從甲骨文看商代社會性質, 114–115.

> soldiers they would become slaves when captured, and if they refused to become soldiers they and their families would instantly become slaves also. Their lives and their possessions were controlled by the king and the nobles, being in essence their tools and possessions.[46]

This statement, as translated, is firmly supportable with contemporary evidence. As we have seen in chapter 3, the basic Shang social unit was the *tsu*, and the *tsu*, by virtue of the incessant ramification of its member units, was the seed of social stratification within itself and among one another. Within each *tsu*, there were high and lowly members, and among the various *tsu* there were high and lowly *tsus*. *Chung-jen* were probably the lowly members of each *tsu*, especially of each lowly *tsu*, within the various clans within the Shang state. They were the direct participants in farming labor (oracle bone inscriptions give numerous instances); they were lectured to and threatened with death for disobedience (*P'an keng*); and their escape (*sang chung* 喪衆, or "the loss of *chung*") was a major topic of concern in the royal divinations.[47] Whether or not they fit the image of "slaves" in a slave society, and even though they obviously were not driven in leg irons to the fields to work, the *chung jen* were the mainstay of Shang agricultural labor and constitute a whole lowly economic class.

There is even credible evidence that this lowly laboring class was transfused with new members by means of war captives. In one inscription we read (fig. 58):

> Inquired: The king to order the many Ch'iang to clear new field?[48]

Here the key word Ch'iang is incomplete in the original piece, but the reading of *to Ch'iang* 多羌, "the Many Ch'iang," is credible, since the phrase was a common one.[49] Ch'iang, the people of Ch'iang Fang, a coun-

46. Chang Cheng-lang 張政烺, "P'u-tz'u p'ou t'ien chi ch'i hsiang-kuan chu wen-t'i" 卜辭裒田及其相關諸問題, 117.

47. Hu Hou-hsüan 胡厚宣, "P'u-tz'u chung so-chien chih Yin tai nung-yeh" 卜辭中所見之殷代農業, 71–72.

48. Kuo Mo-jo 郭沫若, *Yin ch'i ts'ui pien* 殷契粹編, no. 1222.

49. Chao Hsi-yüan 趙錫元, in his "Tui 'Shih shu Yin tai ti nu-li chih-tu ho kuo-chia ti hsing-ch'eng' yi wen ti yi-chien" 對'試述殷代的奴隸制度和國家的形成'一文的意見, reads the word as To Yang 多羊, the many members of the Sheep Tsu. Such a usage would be quite unusual. Li Hsüeh-ch'in 李學勤 (in *Yin tai ti-li chien lun* 殷代地理簡論, p. 80) claims that he inspected the original piece of the oracle bone and determined a totally different reading, which does not contain the word Ch'iang at all and has nothing to do with agricultural cultivation.

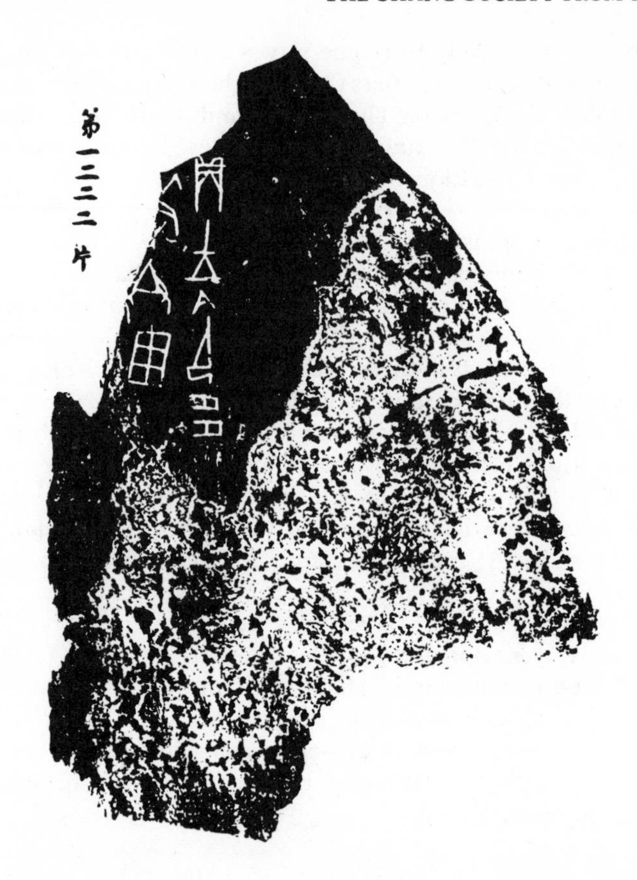

58. Rubbing of inscription in which the Ch'iang captives may be described as being ordered to cultivate new fields (after Kuo Mo-jo, *Yin ch'i ts'ui pien,* no. 1222).

try probably to the west of Shang, were the frequent source of war captives by the Shang (fig. 59), and these captives were frequent victims in Shang ancestral rites, used as offerings in the same order as cattle, sheep, and kids as the oracles related:

> Perform the *yu* ritual to Tsu Yi [and sacrifice] ten Ch'iang? Twenty Ch'iang? Thirty Ch'iang?[50]
>
> On the Chia-Wu day, divined. Inquired: The following day Yi-Wei, perform the *yu* ritual to Tsu Yi [and sacrifice] Ch'iang, fifteen persons? Perform the *mou* ritual [and use]

50. Fang Fa-lien 方法斂 (Frank H. Chalfant), *K'u Fang erh shih ts'ang chia-ku p'u-tz'u* 庫方二氏藏甲骨卜辭, no. 1535.

59. Clay figures of war captives (Collection of Academia Sinica. Photo from *Life*).

a kid? Perform the *yu* ritual and use one cow? In the fifth month.[51]

Divined. Inquired: [Perform ritual and sacrifice] Ch'iang, four hundred, to Tsu X . . . ?[52]

Lines such as these can go on for some pages. Hu Hou-hsüan has counted at least 7,426 Ch'iang individuals that had been contemplated for

51. Shang Ch'eng-tso 商承祚, *Yin ch'i yi ts'un* 殷契佚存, no. 154.

52. Hu Hou-hsüan 胡厚宣, *Chan-hou nan pei so chien chia-ku lu* 戰後南北所見甲骨錄, Shih 師 1.40; *Chia ku hsü ts'un* 甲骨續存 *shang* 上 295.

sacrifice in this manner in the divination records where numbers of Ch'iang considered for sacrifice were given.[53] The Ch'iang people were not the only ones used in this manner,[54] but they were the only "foreigners" favored for this purpose,[55] and one may reasonably assume that human sacrifice was one of the possible fates awaiting war captives of the Shang. The divination record cited above suggests that farm labor was another—undoubtedly a more welcome—fate. *To Ch'iang*, "the many Ch'iang," are also shown in the oracle records to have been participants in the royal hunt,[56] so that their joining in agricultural production with the *chung jen* should not be regarded as an unusual event despite the rarity of such records in the available data.

The above discussion should make clear that insofar as agricultural production and their roles in it are concerned, the various members of the Shang society are divisible into the strata shown in fig. 60.

PRODUCTION OF OTHER GOODS AND SERVICES

It is unquestionable that agriculture occupied the central place in Shang food production, and products probably included grains, vegetables, fruits, and nuts. Meat was provided in part by hunting and fishing, but in view of the huge numbers of domestic animals (mainly cattle and sheep) that were used for ritual sacrifices the major source of animal meat was probably domestic animals. From the shape of some of the characters having to do with domestic animals, it appears that cattle, sheep, and horses were kept in rectangular pens. No such pens have so far been identified in the archaeological remains of An-yang or elsewhere; we would be interested in their construction, size, and, especially, distribution within the settlements for evidence pertaining to herding patterns and association of herding with specific lineage groups.

Lineage (*tsu*) groups appear to have been occupational units engaging in the production of various industrial goods and in specialized services. We saw earlier that *Tso chuan* spoke of the gift of *tsu* of Shang people to the founding Chou lords; the names of these *tsu* are often

53. "Chung-kuo nu-li she-hui ti jen hsün ho jen chi" 中國奴隷社會的人殉和人祭, 57.

54. See Hu Hou-hsüan 胡厚宣, *op. cit.*, and Wang Ch'eng-chao 王承祒, "Shih lun Yin tai ti 'hsi,' 'ch'i,' 'fu' ti she-hui shen-fen" 試論殷代的'奚'、'妾'、'艮'的社會身份.

55. See Shirakawa Shizuka 白川靜, "Kyōzoku" 羌族考. Shima Kunio 島邦男 (in *Inkyo bokuji kenkyū* 殷墟卜辞研究) interprets the word Ch'iang as "feathered dance" and, thus, denies that they were sacrificed in rituals. His arguments are not supportable.

56. Shima Kunio 島邦男, *Inkyo bokuji sōrui* 殷墟卜辞綜類, p. 18.

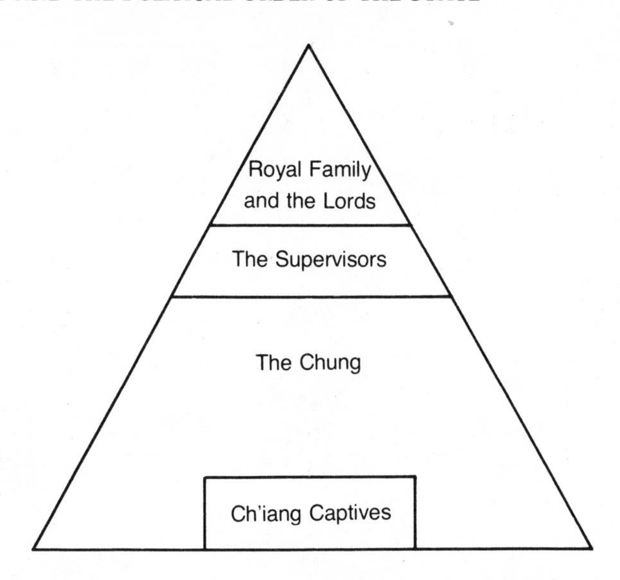

60. Shang economic classes in agricultural production.

occupation-related: T'ao 陶 (pottery); Shih 施 (flag); Ch'i 錡 (cooking pot); Ch'ang shuo 長勺 and Wei shuo 尾勺 (wine vessels); So 索 (cordage); Fan 繁 (horse plume); Fan 樊 (fence).[57] Since the many pictorial signs on Shang and early Chou bronzes are regarded as being clan and lineage emblems,[58] *tsu* names undoubtedly appear in these emblems and many of them may depict their specialized occupations. Of the probable emblems on bronzes included in the catalogue that my associates and I have compiled,[59] the ones shown in fig. 61 may be occupation-related.[60] These emblems are the obvious—though by no means unquestionable—ones, but many others are also possible. In view of the high level of technological sophistication of Shang industrial products, there were presumably such other professions as stone makers, wood-carvers, leathermakers, lacquerwaremakers, horse-fitting-manufacturers, cooks of various specialties, and other professions responsible for producing all other kinds of artifacts both found and recorded, and many if not all of these professions were probably the specialties of various lineages

57. Li Ya-nung 李亞農, *Yin tai she-hui sheng-huo* 殷代社會生活, p. 50.

58. Kuo Mo-jo 郭沫若, "Yin yi chung t'u-hsing wen-tzu chih yi chieh" 殷彝中圖形文字之一解.

59. *Shang Chou ch'ing-t'ung ch'i yü ming-wen ti tsung-ho yen-chiu* 商周青銅器與銘文的綜合研究.

60. For Ts'e, the interpretation of Shirakawa Shizuka 白川靜 is followed here; see his "Sakusatsu kō" 作冊考.

61. Emblems that may be related to professions.
a. animal herder; *b.* trader; *c.* carrier; *d.* food service; *e.* painter; *f.* archivist; *g.* herder; *h.* butcher; *i.* guardsmen; *j.* messenger; *k.* knife-maker; *l.* bowmaker; *m.* arrowmaker; *n.* quiver-maker; *o.* halberd-maker; *p.* shield-maker; *q.* bowman; *r.* halberder; *s.* executioner; *t.* flag-maker; *u.* chariot-maker; *v.* boat-maker; *w.* house-builder; *x.* *ting*-tripod-maker; *y.* *yen*-steamer-maker; *z.* *li*-tripod-maker; *aa.* *chüeh*-cup-maker; *bb.* wine-maker; *cc.* silk-maker; *dd.* woodsman; *ee.* orchard grower; *ff.* net-hunter (most from *KKHCK, Chin Wen Pien*).

and lineage-branches. One can assume that most—if not all—of these occupations were being practiced in the royal capital and that they were scarcer in the provinces. In chapter 1 we described the archaeological remains of some workshops in the An-yang area; it is only through such remains that we have access to some of the productive activities that were going on here and elsewhere:

Bronze making. As described in chapter 1, two major bronze workshops have been located in the An-yang area, one in the heart of Hsiao-t'un and the other in the Miao-p'u-pei-ti / Hsüeh-chia-chuang locus. At the latter site, remains of a ground house, approximately 8 by 4 meters and built on rammed earth foundations and with rammed earth walls, were found associated with clay molds and crucible fragments.[61] Since both ground houses and rammed earth architecture were often associated with people of higher status, one is tempted to infer that bronze smiths, or at least the higher-status ones among them, enjoyed perquisites reserved for the upper class. The inference is by no means unreasonable, considering that the Shang metallurgists were highly skilled craftsmen. In view of Noel Barnard's comprehensive studies of the Shang bronze metallurgy,[62] I refer to his works for the details of the technology and confine myself to a few observations. At the workshop sites almost no copper or tin ores were found in their original rocky conditions, suggesting that smelting was done at the mines. If some of the mines were within the Shang territory, we may expect to find remains of old mines and the workshops where the smelting was done, or perhaps some ores and/or smelted copper and tin were traded from outside the state. But, in any event, the procurement of the metal sources for the bronze alloys must have been a considerable part of the overall bronze-making activity that has not yet been even visible in the existing archaeological record. At the workshop sites in An-yang, clay was prepared to make models of ritual vessels and molds (single and double) for some weapons and implements. On the models the artisans would prepare the necessary decorative details and then make clay molds in sections (hence called section or piece molds). Then they would complete the decorative details on the inner surfaces of the molds, scrape off a layer of clay from the model surface, and put piece molds and the reduced models (now known as "cores") together (fig. 62), plant them on the ground, together with or separate from the single and double molds

61. *KK*, "1958–1959 nien Yin hsü fa-chüeh chien pao" 1958-1959年殷墟發掘簡報, 67.

62. Noel Barnard and Satō Tamotsu, *Metallurgical Remains of Ancient China*; Barnard, *Bronze Casting and Bronze Alloys in Ancient China*.

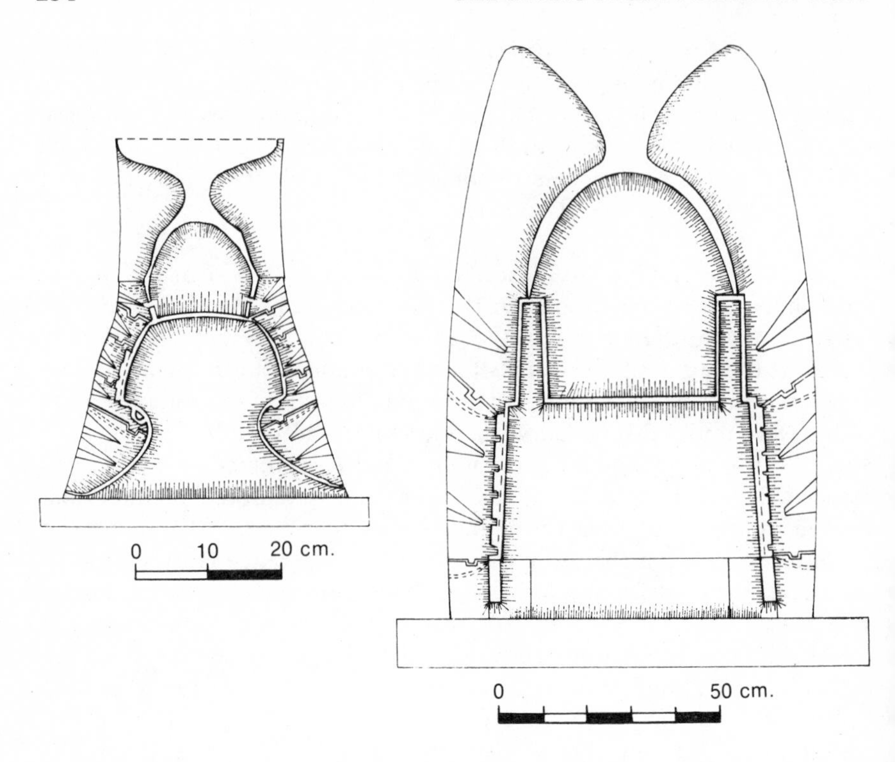

62. Clay molds for casting bronze vessels, Shang period. (after Shih Chang-ju, "Yin tai ti chu t'ung kung-yi," 113, 117).

properly installed, and then, on some auspicious day or moment,[63] pour the molten metal into the cavities to produce the vessels. The alloy was reasonably standardized (approximately 80–95 percent copper, 5–20 percent tin, and some lead and other metals), but the size of some of the ritual vessels (one bronze quatropod measured 180 by 110 centimeters and weighed 875 kilograms) would require such massive and precise efforts to make them that their manufacture must have been both masterful and collective.

Pottery Making. Although pottery workshops have been archaeologically located, details are not available for any of them and we are not clear about the living conditions of the potters. But pottery was the main item of the Yin hsü archaeological inventory, and there must

63. Yen Yün 燕耘, "Shang tai p'u-tz'u chung ti yeh-chu shih liao" 商代卜辭中的冶鑄史料, 299.

have been many centers of pottery supply even within An-yang itself. Furthermore, in view of the careful selection of clay for various wares (see chapter 2), the use of potter's wheel, the sophistication of their white pottery engraving, and the significant use of glaze, some pottery making in the Shang period in An-yang was extremely skillful.[64] The overwhelming majority of Shang pottery, however, was simple gray ware, paddle-impressed with cordage patterns. The pottery centers in An-yang were probably of many kinds, specializing in different wares, and these centers must have formed stratified relationships among themselves.

Stone and Jade Making. Many grades of skills and scales of operation were evident in the fashioning of artifacts from stone. Stone implements such as harvesting knives of slate were probably the specialty of workshops devoted to ordinary fare, but jade carvings and marble sculpture must have required large-scale operations and master craftsmen. Experienced workers at the Peking Jade Factory have concluded, after experimental investigation of some of the Shang jade carvings, that they required an extremely high level of workmanship and workshops of considerable size. Groove cutters and awls of bronze must have been used.[65] Remains of a house believed to be associated with a stone and jade workshop was found at Hsiao-t'un in 1975. It not only had rammed and plastered walls, the interior wall was even decorated with bichromic (black and red) murals. Inside the house was found a pit containing a dismembered skeleton, with a bronze vessel lid (inscribed), possibly the remains of a ritual event.[66] Such remains indicate considerable social status and may suggest that the family or lineage in charge of this workshop, or at least its chief, had a status similar to that of other crafts.

THE UPWARD AND CENTRIPETAL FLOW OF ECONOMIC RESOURCES

Where did the foodstuffs and the industrial products go after they had been produced at the villages and the workshops throughout the state? Compared with some of the other ancient civilizations (such as Sumerian) the Shang is singularly lacking in records of economic transaction. This is a significant feature in itself and will be further commented upon, but at this juncture it must be held responsible for

64. Li Chi 李濟, *Hsiao-t'un t'ao ch'i* 小屯陶器; "Yin hsü ch'u-t'u ti kung-yeh ch'eng-chi—san li" 殷墟出土的工業成績—三例.

65. *KK*, "Tui Shang tai cho yü kung-yi ti yi-hsieh ch'u-pu k'an-fa" 對商代琢玉工藝的一些初步看法.

66. *KK*, "1975 nien An-yang Yin hsü ti hsin fa-hsien" 1975年安陽殷墟的新發現.

our inability at this time to answer, directly and with full documentation, the simple and necessary question given above. But we can certainly try to provide an answer, although one which is based sometimes on inference and lacks detail in most respects.

From the perspective of An-yang (where the divination records were kept and from which the best archaeological evidence avails), the incoming traffic of economic resources of all sorts was heavy, consisting of grain, game and domestic animals, industrial products, and services. The outgoing flow was lighter, primarily consisting of royal gifts to provincial lords, maintenance of a military "umbrella," and ritual expressions of the king's wishes for their well-being.

First, the income. The most basic and important royal income was probably grain, principally millet. The divination records show that the king was concerned about the harvests of the four quarters (Eastern Land, Western Land, Northern Land, and Southern Land) of his kingdom, and he was concerned about the harvests in the lands of his consorts, his princes, and his lords, but not about the millet harvests of the alien states (*fang*). Such records allow the inference that the king had a share in the grain harvests throughout his state.[67] In addition, other goods were sent in by various lords within the state, and sometimes during the reign of Wu Ting these sources of income were recorded on the bridges of turtle shells or at the bottom of the sockets or along the flat edges of shoulder blades. From these we know that turtle shells, cattle shoulder blades, perhaps cowry shells, cattle, horses, elephants, war captives, Ch'iang captives, and so forth, were "entered by" (*ju* 入) or "came" (*lai* 來) from this or that lord name. On one bone hairpin found in Hsi-pei-kang is recorded that it was one of a pair sent in by Marquis Pei 㫄.[68] Gifts like these probably represent a tiny proportion of the many scarce goods sent in by the provinces to the capital.

But the king did not just sit in his capital to wait for the gifts and tributes to roll in from his lords; he sometimes went out personally to pick them up. The royal hunt that we mentioned was engaged in throughout his state and was probably a device of economic exploitation of the provinces on the king's part as well as a sport, and the gain was sometimes considerable. The king also made all sorts of journeys into the provinces, not to mention his military campaigns against his neighbors.[69] On these journeys undoubtedly the king and his large party

67. Hu Hou-hsüan 胡厚宣, "P'u-tz'u chung so-chien chih Yin tai nung-yeh" 卜辭中所見之殷代農業; Ch'en Meng-chia 陳夢家, *Yin hsü p'u-tz'u tsung shu* 殷墟卜辭綜述, pp. 313–316.

68. Hu Hou-hsüan 胡厚宣, "Wu Ting shih wu-chung chi-shih k'o-tz'u k'ao" 武丁時五種記事刻辭考.

69. Tung Tso-pin 董作賓, *Yin li p'u* 殷曆譜 (hsia 下, vol. 9, "Wu Ting jih p'u" 武丁日譜).

lived off his subjects in the areas they went through. There are divination records concerning the *ch'ü* 取 ("taking") of horses, cattle, and sheep; possibly some of the expropriations took place on these outings.[70] At the end of successful military operations captives in large or small numbers were brought back, contributing to the wealth of the capital.

In the outgo column, the only significant records pertain to royal gifts to the king's provincial lords. Such records were rare and occasional in the oracle inscriptions, but since a royal gift of cowries or bronze often led to the commemorative casting of ritual vessels, that event was sometimes recorded in bronze inscriptions. In the Shang-Chou bronze catalogue mentioned earlier, as many as fifty objects of supposedly Shang date bear inscriptions commemorating the royal gift-giving.[71] Obviously such gifts represent a "redistribution" of the state's wealth only at the top stratum of society.

In fact, our balance sheets, incomplete as they are, clearly show that the flow of wealth (grains, meat, goods, and services) was vastly uneven in favor of the upper stratum of Shang society and of the large towns of the settlement network (especially the largest of them all, the capital). The archaeological remains of the ground houses at Hsiao-t'un and the royal tombs at Hsi-pei-kang represent significant cumulations of Shang wealth at the top and center. An excellent illustration is provided by the inventory of the goods buried in Fu Hao's tomb:[72]

Wooden chamber and lacquered wooden coffin
16 sacrificial victims
6 sacrificial dogs
Almost 7,000 cowries
More than 200 bronze ritual vessels
5 large bells and 18 small bells of bronze
44 bronze implements (27 of them knives)
4 bronze mirrors
1 bronze spatula
130-plus bronze weapons
4 bronze tigers or tiger-heads
20-plus bronze artifacts of other descriptions
590-plus jade and jade-like objects
100-plus jade beads, discs, and pieces
20-plus opal beads

70. Ch'en Meng-chia 陳夢家, *Yin hsü p'u-tz'u tsung shu* 殷墟卜辭綜述, p. 318.

71. Chang Kwang-chih 張光直 et al., *Shang Chou ch'ing-t'ung-ch'i yü ming-wen ti tsung-ho yen-chiu* 商周青銅器與銘文的綜合研究.

72. *KKHP*, "An-yang Yin hsü wu-hao mu ti fa-chüeh" 安陽殷墟五號墓的發掘.

2 quartz crystal objects
70-plus stone sculptures and other stone objects
5 bone implements
20-plus bone arrowheads
490-plus bone hairpins
3 ivory carvings
4 pottery vessels and 3 clay whistles

In this one tomb were placed scarce goods gathered from both within and beyond the Shang state and manufactured by countless workers in countless workshops, probably both in An-yang and elsewhere in the state. She was indeed both at the center (An-yang) and near the top (royal consort of King Wu Ting) of the Shang society. Members of the opposite end of the social stratum, whose pit houses and graves were numerous in the archaeological remains but warranted only brief or even statistical accounts, obviously did not command any wealth of such proportions. Their life did not appear in the divination records, but some of the Western Chou poems in *Shih ching* described it closely enough:

K'am-K'am, you hew the t'an wood
You place it on the bank of the River;
The waters of the River are clear and wavy;
If you do not sow and do not reap,
How can you bring in three hundred yard-fulls of grain?
If you do not chase and do not hunt,
How can we see suspended badgers in your courtyard?
That nobleman,
Indeed he does not eat the food of idleness!

[*Fa-t'an*, translated by B. Karlgren]

Big rat, big rat,
Do not gobble our millet.
Three years we have slaved for you,
Yet you take no notice of us.
At last we are going to leave you
And go to that happy land;
Happy land, happy land,
Where we shall have our place.

[*Shuo shu*, translated by Arthur Waley]

In the seventh month the Fire ebbs;
In the ninth month I hand out the coats.
In the days of the First, sharp frosts;
In the days of the Second, keen winds.

Without coats, without serge,
How should they finish the year?
In the days of the Third they plough;
In the days of the Fourth out I step
With my wife and children,
Bringing hampers to the southern acre
Where the field-hands come to take good cheer.

"The spring days are drawing out;
They gather the white aster in crowds.
A girl's heart is sick and sad
Till with her lord she can go home."

In the seventh month the Fire ebbs;
In the eighth month they pluck the rushes,
In the silk-worm month they gather the mulberry-leaves,
Take that chopper and bill
To lop the far boughs and high,
Pull towards them the tender leaves.
In the seventh month the shrike cries;
In the eighth month they twist thread,
The black thread and the yellow:
"With my red dye so bright
I make a robe for my lord."

In the fourth month the milkwort is in spike,
In the fifth month the cicada cries.
In the eighth month the harvest is gathered,
In the tenth month the boughs fall.
In the days of the First we hunt the racoon,
And take those foxes and wild-cats
To make furs for our Lord.
In the days of the Second is the Great Meet;
Practice for deeds of war.
The one-year-old we keep;
The three-year-old we offer to our Lord.

In the fifth month the locust moves its leg,
In the sixth month the grasshopper shakes its wing,
In the seventh month, out in the wilds;
In the eighth month, in the farm,
In the ninth month, at the door.
In the tenth month the cricket goes under my bed.
I stop up every hole to smoke out the rats,
Plugging the windows, burying the doors:

"Come, wife and children,
The change of the year is at hand.
Come and live in this house."

[*Ch'i yüeh*, translated by Arthur Waley]

The life of the Western Chou farmers may not have been identical with that of the Shang, but the Shang farmers left no poems, and the comparison of these glimpses of the life of the Chou peasants with the Fu Hao tomb inventory serves well to illustrate the upward and centripetal resource flow that was common to both dynasties.

COMMUNICATION AND TRANSPORTATION

We have seen that the Shang state network consisted of hundreds of walled towns in hierarchical interrelationship, and that economic resources flowed among the towns in a basically upward and centripetal pattern. Tools were obviously required to effect or at least facilitate the flow, and they primarily involved communication and transportation among various units of the network and especially between the capital and the provinces.

I will first discuss transportation because there is very little data. The kind of industrial specialization and resource flow described above must take as a prerequisite an effective transportation network to move raw materials, grain and other foods, and industrial goods over great distances. Undoubtedly human caravans carrying ore, bags of grain, chunks of rock, clay, and other heavy or light loads must have been seen strewn along long stretches of roads linking the various settlements, but what did the Shang have other than human labor to carry on the vast transportation effort? Boats, undoubtedly, where rivers large and small were passable, as shown by the bronze and oracle bone characters of boat. Carts and carriages, pulled by men and other beasts (horses and cattle)? Beasts of burden (such as cattle) to help carry the loads on their backs? All of these are possible. Wheeled vehicles were of course known in the form of horse chariots, but transport vehicles have not been identified either in the archaeological remains or in the shapes of written characters. *Chiu kao* in *Shu ching* spoke of, "with your carts *and* oxen" or, rather, carts pulled by oxen? In either case cattle probably did play an important part in the formation of the Shang civilization, as shown by the prominence of Wang Hai in Shang rituals and by Wang Hai's legendary role as the originator of cattle breeding.[73]

73. Wang Kuo-wei 王國維, "Yin p'u-tz'u chung so-chien hsien kung hsien

We are not any too clear about the question of who managed the transportation of goods. Since some of the *tsu* were groups of professional traders and since cowries were used as currency of exchange, undoubtedly traders played an important role in Shang society; in fact, the Shang were such skillful traders that many of their descendants found careers in trading and to this day the word for merchant, *shang jen* 商人, is the same as the word for the Shang people. Unfortunately, we have no reliable information whatever on details of the Shang trade and traders.

Along with materials and goods, information, messages, and instructions must have also passed among the various settlements, and the communication of language, oral and written, must have been another prerequisite for the formation of the Shang state network. It is in this connection that a look at the origin of Chinese writing may prove useful—we may be helped in grasping a culture as a whole if we pay heed to the aspect of the culture that writing was first invented to record.

Although the bulk of the Shang writing is in the form of oracle records incised on turtle shells and cattle shoulder blades, the earliest forms of Chinese writing have been found on pottery. The first examples of inscribed pottery dating from early China came to light in the 1870s in Shantung and Hopei, especially in the area of Lin-tzu.[74] These artifacts proved to be made mostly in the states of Ch'i and Lu in the late Chou period, and their inscriptions pertain to the identity and the location of the potters. Inscribed pottery allegedly of late Chou date also but of a very different style was found through scientific excavations at the Ch'eng-tzu-yai site in Shantung in the late 1920s and early 1930s, where inscribed potsherds have also been reported from the prehistoric Lung-shan culture stratum.[75] At the same time, pottery with inscriptions was found at the Shang ruins in An-yang.[76] In the 1930s, pottery with similar marks had been found on the Kwangtung coast of southernmost China[77] and on the Hang-chou Bay in central China.[78] Thus, before the

---

wang k'ao'' 殷卜辭中所見先公先王考; ''Hsü k'ao'' 續考; Wu Ch'i-ch'ang 吳其昌, ''P'u-tz'u so-chien Yin hsien kung hsien wang san hsü k'ao'' 卜辭所見殷先公先王三續考; Ku Chieh-kang 顧頡剛, ''Chou Yi kua yao tz'u chung ti ku-shih'' 周易卦爻辭中的故事; Ch'en Meng-chia 陳夢家, ''Shang tai ti shen-hua yü wu-shu'' 商代的神話與巫術; Hu Hou-hsüan 胡厚宣, ''Chia-ku wen Shang tsu niao t'u-t'eng ti yi-chi'' 甲骨文商族鳥圖騰的遺跡; Naitō Torajiro 内藤虎次郎, ''Ōi'' 王亥, ''Zoku Ōi'' 續王亥.

74. First recorded in Wu Ta-cheng 吳大澂, *Shuo-wen ku chou pu* 說文古籀補 and Liu Eh 劉鶚, *T'ieh-yün ts'ang t'ao* 鐵雲藏匋.

75. Fu Ssu-nien 傅斯年, Li Chi 李濟, et al., *Ch'eng-tzu-yai* 城子崖.

76. Li Chi 李濟, *Hsiao-t'un t'ao ch'i* 小屯陶器.

77. D. J. Finn, ''Archaeological Finds on Lamma island near Hong Kong,''

war, pottery inscriptions already were well known archaeologically, not only from the earliest historical periods (the latter two of the Three Dynasties) but from prehistoric periods as well. But relatively little attention had been paid to these inscriptions. Those of the Shang were, of course, overwhelmed by the sheer quantity of oracle bone writings, and the few prehistoric pieces were too scanty, too scattered, and perhaps too simple to command much scholarly attention at the time.

In recent years, much scholarly attention has been devoted to these ancient Chinese pottery inscriptions. New archaeological discoveries since 1949 have not only brought to light pottery inscriptions at earlier historical sites in Cheng-chou[79] and Yen-shih[80] but have also yielded similar marks on pottery at the very early Neolithic site at Pan-p'o,[81] a site that can now be dated by radiocarbon to early fifth millennium B.C. Several historians and archaeologists have recently written about these early inscriptions, focusing their attention on the issue of the origin of Chinese writing.[82] Li Hsiao-ting concludes that the Pan-p'o pottery marks fully warrant the term "writing," and he dates the origin of the Chinese writing to the cultural period of this important site.[83] Pushing the theme further, Ho Ping-ti believes that some of the Pan-p'o marks were numerals and that they were "the earliest [numerals] ever created by man."[84]

This—the origin of Chinese writing and how China compares with the rest of the world from the perspective of their respective

part II; W. Schofield, "The Proto-historic Site of the Hong Kong Culture at Shek Pek, Lantau, Hong Kong"; R. Maglioni, *Archaelogical Discovery in Eastern Kwangtung*.

78. Ho T'ien-hsing 何天行, *Hang Hsien Liang-chu chen chih shih-ch'i yü hei-t'ao* 杭縣良渚鎮之石器與黑陶; Shih Hsin-keng 施昕更, *Liang-chu* 良渚.

79. An Chih-min 安志敏, "Yi-chiu-wu-erh nien ch'iu chi Cheng-chou Erh-li-kang fa-chüeh chi" 一九五二年秋季鄭州二里岡發掘記, 77; *KKHP*, "Cheng-chou Shang tai yi-chih ti fa-chüeh" 鄭州商代遺址的發掘, 83; *KKHCK*, *Cheng-chou Erh-li-kang* 鄭州二里岡, p. 17.

80. *KK*, "Ho-nan Yen-shih Erh-li-t'ou yi-chih fa-chüeh chien pao" 河南偃師二里頭遺址發掘簡報, 222.

81. *KKHCK*, *Hsi-an Pan-p'o* 西安半坡.

82. Li Hsiao-ting 李孝定, "Ts'ung chi chung shih-ch'ien ho yu-shih tsao-ch'i t'ao wen ti kuan-ch'a li-ts'e Chung-kuo wen-tzu ti ch'i-yüan" 從幾種史前和有史早期陶文的觀察蠡測中國文字的起源; Kuo Mo-jo 郭沫若, "Ku-tai wen-tzu chih pien-cheng ti fa-chan" 古代文字之辯證的發展; Cheng Te-k'un 鄭德坤, "Chung-kuo shang-ku shu ming ti yen-pien chi ch'i ying-yung" 中國上古數名的演變及其應用; Yü Hsing-wu 于省吾, "Kuan-yü ku wen-tzu yen-chiu ti jo-kan wen-t'i" 關於古文字研究的若干問題; Ho Ping-ti, *The Cradle of the East*, chapter 6.

83. Li Hsiao-ting 李孝定 *op. cit.*; Li Hsiao-ting 李孝定, "Chung-kuo wen-tzu ti yüan-shih ho yen-pien" 中國文字的原始和演變.

84. Ho Ping-ti, *The Cradle of the East*, p. 223.

histories of writing—is not a theme I wish to explore here. To me, even more significant issues pertaining to the ceramic inscriptions of ancient China concern their distinctive style and the place of such inscriptions within Chinese culture. But first let us enumerate the archaeological finds of prehistoric and Shang pottery inscriptions thus far:

Prehistoric

Pan-p'o-ts'un 半坡村, Sian, Shensi (Yang-shao culture)[85]
Wu-lou 五樓, Ch'in-tu-chen, Sian, Shensi (Yang-shao culture)[86]
Hsin-yeh-ts'un 莘野村, Ho-yang Hsien, Shensi (Yang-shao culture)[87]
Chiang-chai 姜寨, Lin-t'ung, Shensi (Yang-shao culture)[88]
Liu-wan 柳灣, Lo-tu, Chinghai (Ma-ch'ang culture)[89] (fig. 63)
Ling-yang-ho 陵陽河, Chü Hsien, Shantung (Ta-wen-k'ou culture)[90]
Ch'ien-chai 前寨, Chu-ch'eng, Shantung (Ta-wen-k'ou culture)[91]
Ch'eng-tzu-yai 城子崖, Lung-shan-chen, Shantung (Lung-shan culture)[92]
Sung-tse 崧澤, Ch'ing-p'u, Shanghai (Sung-tse culture)[93]
Liang-chu 良渚, Hang Hsien, Chekiang (Liang-chu culture)[94]
Feng-pi-t'ou 鳳鼻頭, Kao-hsiung, Taiwan (Feng-pi-t'ou culture)[95]
Pa-tzu-yüan 菝仔園 (Pat-ea-hui) and Pao-lou 寶樓 (Po-lao), Hai-feng, Kwangtung (Geometric pottery culture)[96]
Ta-wan 大灣, Lamma Island, Hong Kong (Geometric)[97]
Shek-pik 石壁, Lantau Island, Hong Kong (Geometric)[98]

85. *KKHCK, Hsi-an Pan-p'o* 西安半坡.

86. *KK*, "Feng Hao yi-tai k'ao-ku tiao-ch'a chien pao" 豐鎬一帶考古調查簡報, 29.

87. *KK*, "Huang-ho San-men-hsia shui-k'u k'ao-k'u tiao-ch'a chien pao" 黃河三門峽水庫考古調查簡報, pl. I, no. 2.

88. *WW*, "Lin-t'ung Chiang-chai hsin-shih-ch'i shih-tai yi-chih ti hsin fa-hsien" 臨潼姜寨新石器時代遺址的新發現, 82.

89. *KK*, "Ch'ing-hai Lo-tu Liu-wan yüan-shih she-hui mu-ti fan-ying ch'u ti chu-yao wen-t'i" 青海樂都柳灣原始社會墓地反映出的主要問題.

90. *KKHCK, Ta-wen-k'ou* 大汶口, p. 117.

91. *Ibid.*

92. Fu Ssu-nien 傅斯年, Li Chi 李濟, et al., *Ch'eng-tzu-yai* 城子崖.

93. *KKHP*, "Shang-hai shih Ch'ing-p'u hsien Sung-tse yi-chih ti shih chüeh" 上海市青浦縣崧澤遺址的試掘, 7.

94. Ho T'ien-hsing 何天行, *Hang hsien Liang-chu chen chih shih-ch'i yü hei-t'ao* 杭縣良渚鎮之石器與黑陶; Shih Hsin-keng 施昕更, *Liang-chu* 良渚.

95. Chang Kwang-chih 張光直 et al., *Fengpitou, Tapenkeng, and the Prehistory of Taiwan*, p. 100.

96. R. Maglioni, *Archaeological Discovery in Eastern Kwangtung.*

97. D. J. Finn, "Archaeological Finds on Lamma Island near Hong Kong, Part II."

98. W. Schofield, "The Proto-historic Site of the Hong Kong Culture at Shek Pik, Lantau, Hong Kong."

63. Pottery inscriptions at the Ma-ch'ang culture site at Liu-wan, Chinghai (after *KK*, "Ch'ing-hai Lo-tu Liu-wan yüan-shih she hui mu-ti fan-ying ch'u ti chu-yao wen-t'i," 376).

Early Historic

Erh-li-t'ou, Yen-shih, Honan[99]
Erh-li-kang, Cheng-chou, Honan[100]
Nan-kuan-wai, Cheng-chou, Honan[101]
Hsiao-t'un, An-yang, Honan[102]
T'ai-hsi-ts'un, Kao-ch'eng, Hopei[103]
Wu-ch'eng, Ch'ing-chiang, Kiangsi[104]

A detailed description or a full reproduction of the pottery inscriptions at all the above sites would be unnecessary here, since the question here has to do with the purposes for which the pottery marks

99. *KK*, "Ho-nan Yen-shih Erh-li-t'ou yi-chih fa-chüeh chien pao" 河南偃師二里頭遺址發掘簡報.

100. See note 79 above.

101. *KKHP* "Cheng-chou Nan-kuan-wai Shang tai yi-chih ti fa-chüeh" 鄭州南關外商代遺址的發掘, 83.

102. Li Chi 李濟, *Hsiao-t'un t'ao ch'i* 小屯陶器.

103. *WW*, "Kao-ch'eng T'ai-hsi Shang tai yi-chih fa-hsien ti t'ao-ch'i wen-tzu" 藁城台西商代遺址發現的陶器文字.

104. T'ang Lan 唐蘭, "Kuan-yü Chiang-hsi Wu-ch'eng wen-hua yi-chih yü wen-tzu ti ch'u-pu t'an-so" 關於江西吳城文化遺址與文字的初步探索.

were made. My opinion on this issue is that the overwhelming majority of the ceramic marks, both Shang and prehistoric, were markers and emblems of families, lineages, clans, or some divisions of one of these, and as such, attempts to match them with known characters and to translate them into meaningful sentences are unlikely to be productive in most cases. There are two considerations behind the above observation. The first concerns the purpose of these marks, and the second has to do with the status of the inscribers.

First, on the purpose for which these marks were incised. Several students of Chinese archaeology have expressed the belief that the marks that were incised *before* firing of the pottery were probably done to identify the workmanship of individual potteries, while those scratched on *after* firing were to identify possession rights of users. It is true that many Lin-tzu pottery inscriptions appear to be names of individual potters or potters' shops,[105] but these ceramics were produced during the late Chou period when potters and other craftsmen were fulltime specialists and tradesmen. Almost certainly the Yang-shao pottery was not manufactured by specialists; pottery making in the Pan-p'o village was likely a domestic activity of every household. There is evidence, at the Pan-p'o site, that particular pottery inscriptions tended to be concentrated in particular areas in the village:

> We have found that many similar signs occur in the same storage pits or in the same areas. For example, an analysis of the provenance data of the most common sign, the single vertical stroke, shows that most of the seventy-two pieces bearing this sign were found at six loci that basically adjoin one another in an area of just over a hundred square meters. In storage pit H341 we found two sherds with the same sign. All five Z-shaped signs clustered within two grid squares.[106]

Similar indications are seen at the Feng-pi-t'ou site in Taiwan, where sherds with incised X-signs cluster in a single area on the southern edge of the village.[107] This last phenomenon also suggests that the so-called numerals several scholars have read out of the prehistoric signs were probably nothing more than signs that happened to be identical in shape with some of the numerals of early historic China. The numerals 1, 2, 3, and 4 were simply characters with 1, 2, 3, or 4 short strokes, 5 is

105. Ku T'ing-lung 顧廷龍, *Ku t'ao wen yi lu* 古匋文舂錄, p. 8.
106. *KKHCK*, *Hsi-an Pan-p'o* 西安半坡, p. 198.
107. Chang Kwang-chih 張光直 et al., *Fengpitou, Tapenkeng, and the Prehistory of Taiwan*, pl. 54.

an X mark, and 7 simply a cross shape. These forms are common at many sites.[108] The other Chinese numerals, 6, 8, 9, are more arbitrarily designated in the numerals system, and they have not been found to occur in pottery inscriptions. As Li Chi has asked, with regard to the pottery inscriptions at Hsiao-t'un, "how is it that some numerals (7) are seen so frequently, others (1, 3, 4) are rare, and still others (2, 6, 8, 9) are not found at all?"[109] Since single or multiple strokes, crosses, and X's are signs commonly used in many cultures to identify and distinguish lots, these probably were simply meant to mark pottery vessels to indicate that they belonged to a certain lot, possibly in relation to some social divisions. Characters identifiable as names or emblems went a step further, identifying pottery vessels with specific, named groups, but in principle there is little difference between these and the others with lot marks. If this view proves valid, then it will account for most of Hsiao-t'un's pottery inscription classes. As for the "positional marks" of Hsiao-t'un, Tung Tso-pin had pointed out that the characters for "left," "middle," and "right" could also serve to designate persons.[110] And names of persons, as we have learned from oracle bone inscriptions, are often indistinguishable from names of social and political groups.[111]

This interpretation of some or most prehistoric and Shang pottery inscriptions—as markers or emblems of social groups using the pottery—is very much in agreement with the usage of many inscriptions on Shang bronzes. Elsewhere I have discussed the emblems of Shang bronzes in some detail,[112] and one of the findings was that many inscriptions consist of multiple characters designating social groups of various hierarchical levels.[113] The occasional cases of multiple characters in inscribed pottery could probably be explained, at least in some cases, in terms of the hierarchical strata of social groups.

According to this view, then, pottery inscriptions form a

108. They are, in fact, also found in a part of the world that could not have used the same Chinese numerals. My former Yale colleague, Professor Harvey Weiss, kindly showed me some dozen sherds with similar marks from Qabr Sheykheyn, a late Ubaid (c. 4000 B.C.) site in Khuzistan, southwestern Iran, excavated in 1971. Incised signs that could be identified as Chinese numerals 1, 2, 3, 20 (i.e., V), and 30 (V plus another arm), as well as a grass shape, were placed near the base of a large bowl type.

109. Li Chi 李濟, *Hsiao-t'un t'ao ch'i* 小屯陶器, p. 124.

110. *Ibid.*, p. 147.

111. Chang Ping-ch'üan 張秉權, "Chia-ku wen chung so-chien jen ti t'ung ming k'ao" 甲骨文中所見人地同名考.

112. Chang Kwang-chih 張光直, "Shang Chou ch'ing-t'ung-ch'i ch'i-hsing chuang-shih hua-wen yü ming-wen tsung-ho yen-chiu ch'u-pu pao-kao" 商周青銅器器形裝飾花紋與銘文綜合研究初步報告.

113. Chang Kwang-chih 張光直, "T'an Wang Hai yü Yi Yin ti chi jih ping tsai lun Yin Shang wang-chih" 談王亥與伊尹的祭日並再論殷商王制.

distinctive system of writing that should not be looked at in the same vein as the writings found on many other media, such as shells and bones, bamboo and wooden slips, and silk. This Lo Chen-yü had long ago noted: "The pottery script is a variant form of the archaic script, and, along with the seal and coin scripts, differs from the ordinary archaic inscriptions. Wu Ta-cheng had put the pottery inscriptions together with ancient ritual vessel inscriptions, but this actually is not quite appropriate. The pottery script contains many abbreviations and variations, and [palaeographic] explications should not be forced upon them."[114] Here I am not sure that Lo's criticism of Wu was entirely justified, since some of the bronze inscriptions—the emblems—perhaps belonged to the same system of writing as the pottery inscriptions, as implied in the discussion above. But his point about the pottery script being closer to the seal and coin scripts than to the regular archaic script is well taken.

The reason that late Chou pottery inscriptions resemble seal and coin inscriptions is probably that these were the writings of craftsmen and traders, people of different life station than archivists and historians who wrote with brush on silk and bamboo. Prehistoric and Shang potters did not necessarily have comparable status to Eastern Chou potters, but they were indeed closer to the common people than were the oracle and bronze scribes. As mentioned above, scholars have used the pottery inscriptions to discuss the great antiquity of Chinese writing. I see the significance of pottery inscriptions in the issue of the origin of Chinese writing also in this light: The invention of writing in China was more associated with social identification than with economic transaction, and it was initiated by the common potters rather than society's heroes and geniuses (such as a Ts'ang Chieh 倉頡). Obviously, Pan-p'o village was not a stratified, class society, and its writing served the mere common villagers instead of any specialists or rulers. This same village tradition of inscribing pottery continued into the Shang period, even though by then writings of a much more sophisticated order were used for other purposes by people of very different social status.[115] But the probable fact that Chinese writing had its roots in the marking of pottery for social identification, in marked contrast to the roots of Near Eastern writing in an accounting system,[116] may give us a

114. Lo Chen-yü 羅振玉, *Meng-an ts'ang t'ao* 夢庵藏匋 *hsü* 序.

115. Even in modern China, people of different social stations may use somewhat different writing systems. Examples are the so-called *su tzu* (vulgar characters) and the popular series of numerals (〡 〢 〣 〤 〥 〦 〧 〨 〩 十) that are not likely to be found in scholarly essays or government decrees.

116. Denise Schmandt-Besserat, "The Earliest Precursor of Writing."

strong hint of ancient Chinese priorities: Membership in one's kin group was the first thing that the first writing recorded, because it was key to ancient Chinese social order. Information that was essential to the working of the economic network that has been described was transmitted within the network of lineages. We cannot say that records of economic transactions were unnecessary under such a framework, but the fact is that available archaeological records of Shang writing—the only instruments of information transmittal that we can ever hope to find—consist of group identification marks (pottery marks and bronze emblems), divination records (oracle bone inscriptions), and records of gift exchanges (most of them long bronze inscriptions and the "tribute records" from Wu Ting's reign). Only the last kind of written records can be called economical, but even there their explicit purpose was possibly political. And the most important written records of all, the oracle records, are political in purpose: the king's ability to communicate with his ancestors and to successfully prognosticate future courses of action and events has been shown by David Keightley[117] to be an instrument of legitimation of his rule—and his economic powers.

3. *RELATIONS WITH OTHER STATES*

What do we know about Shang's contacts with neighboring states? Among the *to fang* 多方 ("the many alien states") during the period of the oracle records, the largest number was registered in Period 1 records: Shima Kunio counted thirty-three *fang* names for that period, whereas he identified two in Period 2, thirteen in Period 3, twenty-three in Period 4, and eight in Period 5.[118] Of these, the names Kung Fang and T'u Fang were mentioned most frequently: 486 occurrences for Kung Fang and 92 occurrences for T'u Fang. The next most mentioned state is Jen Fang, seen 28 times in Period 5 oracle records. But the importance of an alien state is not always indicated by the frequency of references to it in the oracle records. Let us look briefly at eight of the more important states and their probable locations according to oracle record scholars.

1. Kung Fang 𢀛方. Most scholars place Kung Fang in the far northwest, probably in northern Shensi or even farther north in the

117. "Legitimation in Shang China."
118. Shima Kunio 島邦男, *Inkyo bokuji kenkyū* 殷墟卜辭研究, pp. 384–385.

Ordos area.[119] Although interaction with Kung Fang was frequent during Wu Ting's reign, it was probably not a very powerful state; their raids involved small losses and evoked responses to a maximum of six thousand troops.[120] There were also times when Shang and Kung Fang were in such good terms that in the Shang oracle records we find that Shang inquired about Kung Fang carrying out errands for the king.[121] The name appeared infrequently after Period 1. According to Tung Tso-pin, the Kung Fang people were herders.[122]

2. T'u Fang 土方. Another important state during Period 1, T'u Fang was probably located in northern Shansi. Its name disappeared after Period 1, presumably because T'u Fang was extinguished by Wu Ting's conquests.[123]

3. Ch'iang Fang 羌方. This was a special country for the Shang, since it was the only country whose people were mentioned as sacrificial victims in the Shang ancestral rituals, and wars against it sometimes involved vast numbers of Shang troops—13,000 in one instance.[124] Unquestionably Ch'iang Fang was west of Shang, but its location has been variously placed in western Honan,[125] southernmost Shansi and adjacent areas in Shensi and Honan,[126] or northern Shensi to the south of Kung Fang.[127] *Shuo wen* explains the character *ch'iang* 羌 as sheep herders; the oracle bone character bears this out with its sheep-shaped upper element. Ch'iang was one of the states with which the Shang had a continuing relationship; the name appears in oracle records of Periods 1, 3, 4, and 5. Ch'iang was also among the states that joined with Chou in the final conquest of Shang (see *Mu shih*).

4. Chou Fang 周方. The name Chou Fang or Chou appeared in the records of Periods 1, 2, and 4, but its absence in Period 5 records is surely accidental, since it was the same Chou that became the Shang's nemesis and conqueror at the end of that period. Among all the *fang*s in the Shang oracle records, Chou was the only one with its own written history, although its predynastic period is not adequately documented

119. Kuo Mo-jo 郭沫若, *P'u-tz'u t'ung ts'uan* 卜辭通纂; Tung Tso-pin 董作賓, *Yin li p'u* 殷曆譜; Hu Hou-hsüan 胡厚宣, "Kung fang k'ao" 舌方考; Shima Kunio 島邦男, *Inkyo bokuji kenkyū* 殷墟卜辞研究, pp. 385–388; Ch'en Meng-chia 陳夢家, *Yin hsü p'u-tz'u tsung shu* 殷墟卜辭綜述, pp. 273–274.

120. Li Hsüeh-ch'in 李學勤, *Yin tai ti-li chien lun* 殷代地理簡論, p. 64.

121. Chang Ping-ch'üan 張秉權, *Yin hsü wen-tzu Ping pien* 殷墟文字丙編, *hsia erh* 下二, pp. 67–68.

122. Tung Tso-pin 董作賓, *Yin li p'u* 殷曆譜, "Wu Ting jih p'u" 武丁日譜, 38.

123. Shima Kunio 島邦男, *Inkyo bokuji kenkyū* 殷墟卜辞研究, pp. 388–389.

124. Ch'en Meng-chia 陳夢家, *Yin hsü p'u-tz'u tsung shu* 殷墟卜辭綜述.

125. Shirakawa Shizuka 白川靜, "Kyōzoku" 羌族考, 61.

126. Ch'en Meng-chia 陳夢家, *Yin hsü p'u-tz'u tsung shu* 殷墟卜辭綜述p.282.

127. Shima Kunio 島邦男, *Inkyo bokuji kenkyū* 殷墟卜辞研究, pp. 404–405.

and its earliest homeland is still a matter for speculation and debate. The center of activity for predynastic Chou has generally been placed in the Weishui valley of Shensi,[128] but Ch'ien Mu[129] believes that the Chou, before the time of T'ai Wang 太王 and Wang Chi 王季, lived in the Fen River valley of southern Shansi. The disagreement cannot yet be resolved,[130] but there is no question that the middle and lower Weishui valley near Ch'i-shan was the political center of Chou since T'ai Wang's reign. As the Lu ode, *Pi kung*, says,

> Descendant of Hou Chi
> Was the Great King
> Who lived on the southern slopes of Mount Ch'i
> And began to trim the Shang.
> [Translation by Arthur Waley]

The Chou's power is seen to have risen during the reign of T'ai Wang ("Great King," above) in the middle Weishui valley. It was during the reign of Chi Li 季歷, T'ai Wang's son, that the *Ku pen Chu shu chi nien* records major contacts and conflicts with the Shang beginning to take place:

> Thirty-fourth year of King Wu Yi: Chi Li, King of Chou, brought his homage.
>
> Fourth year of King Ta Ting [Wen Wu Ting]: Chi, King of Chou, was appointed a Mu shih 牧師 of Yin.
>
> King Wen Ting: The king had Chi Li killed.

Chi Li's son, Wen Wang 文王, was referred to in some texts as Hsi Po Ch'ang, or Ch'ang, the Western Po, and his son, Wu Wang, undertook the conquest of Shang in his eleventh year of reign. All of these bits of textual information are not clearly seen in the oracle records, although Shima[131] believes that the oracle records confirm Chou's location in the Ch'i-shan area. Late in 1977, according to a preliminary news report,[132] a batch of more than a hundred pieces of inscribed oracle records was discovered in a room in a "palace structure" found at Ching-tang Commune in Ch'i-shan Hsien, Shensi. These records are reported to date

128. E.g., Ting Shan 丁山, "Yu San-tai tu-yi lun ch'i min-tsu wen-hua" 由三代都邑論其民族文化; Ch'i Ssu-ho 齊思和, "Hsi Chou ti-li k'ao" 西周地理考.

129. Ch'ien Mu 錢穆, "Chou ch'u ti-li k'ao" 周初地理考.

130. Hsü Cho-yün 許倬雲, "Chou jen ti hsing-ch'i chi Chou wen-hua ti chi-ch'u" 周人的興起及周文化的基礎.

131. Shima Kunio 島邦男, *Inkyo bokuji kenkyū* 殷墟卜辞研究, p. 410.

132. Hsin-hua She news dispatch, November 1, 1977.

from Wen Wang's reign and contain information on Shang-Chou contacts, which will be discussed later.

5. Chao Fang. This was a notable *fang* during Wu Yi's reign in Period 4. Wu Yi's military moves toward Chao Fang were of considerable scale, involving the king himself as commander and members of the royal lineage as troops.[133] The state is also placed to the west of Shang, neighboring on Ch'iang Fang, perhaps in central Shensi.[134]

6. Yu Fang. This name has appeared only twice in the oracle records, both probably dating from the reign of King Wen Wu Ting in Period 4.[135] The texts in which this name appears makes it clear that Yu Fang was located beyond the Nan T'u, the Southern Land, of the Shang. Ch'en Meng-chia,[136] who pointed out that this was the only reference to the Southern Land in Wu Ting's records (to which he dated these pieces) in connection with hostilities, places Yu Fang in the Huai River valley south of Shang-ch'iu. But the Huai River valley was clearly associated more with Shang's Eastern Land than Shang's Southern Land, and Li Hsüeh-ch'in's idea of placing the state in Hupei, in the Han River valley, appears to be the more plausible.[137]

It was pointed out long ago that most of the alien invasions came from the north and northwest of the Shang,[138] but the Shang's southern flank was not without incident. The ode *Yin wu* in *Shih ching* describes Wu Ting's campaign deep into the Han River valley:

> Swiftly those warriors of Yin
> Rushed to the onslaught upon Ching and Ch'u,
> Entered deep into their fastnesses,
> Captured the hosts of Ching,
> Divided and ruled their places;
> Such was the work of T'ang's descendants.
>
> O you people of Ching and Ch'u,
> You must have your home in the southern parts.
> Long ago there was T'ang the Victorious;

133. Ch'en Meng-chia 陳夢家, *Yin hsü p'u-tz'u tsung-shu* 殷墟卜辭綜述, p. 287.

134. *Ibid.*, p. 287; Shima Kunio 島邦男, *op. cit.*, p. 404.

135. Tung Tso-pin 董作賓, *Yin hsü wen-tzu Chia pien* 殷虛文字甲編, Chia nos. 2902, 2907.

136. Ch'en Meng-chia 陳夢家, *Yin hsü p'u-tz'u tsung shu* 殷墟卜辭綜述, p. 289.

137. Chiang Hung 江鴻, "P'an-lung-ch'eng yü Shang ch'ao ti nan t'u" 盤龍城與商朝的南土, 45.

138. Kuo Mo-jo 郭沫若, *P'u-tz'u t'ung ts'uan* 卜辭通纂, no. 549; Ch'en Meng-chia 陳夢家, *Yin hsü p'u-tz'u tsung shu* 殷墟卜辭綜述, p. 267.

Of those Ti and Ch'iang
None dared not to make offering to him,
None dared not to acknowledge him their king,
Saying, "Shang for ever!"
[Translated by Arthur Waley]

The conqueror's haughtiness here was probably backed by his deeds, since the southern states were indeed mentioned only rarely. The Yu Fang divination was a rare occurrence, although there were a few other mentions that may have been relating to the south.[139] We will take up this question again in discussing the archaeological data in the Han River valley.

7. Jen Fang 人方. Jen Fang was mentioned in the oracle records throughout, but became exceedingly important toward the end of the Shang dynasty. Two major campaigns were undertaken against Jen Fang under the personal command of Ti Hsin, the first in the eighth year of his reign and the second in the tenth year. The latter we have mentioned before in connection with the location of Shang the city. It is generally agreed that these campaigns weakened the Shang's political strength and helped the Chou in their conquest.[140] The location of Jen Fang is also agreed by most scholars to have been the middle and lower Huai River valley, in the present provinces of Kiangsu and southern Shantung.

8. Yü Fang 盂方. This is the name of a major political unit not very far to the northeast of the An-yang area, probably in central Hopei.[141] It was an area where Shang kings often engaged in the royal hunts, and its ruler was probably considered a "lord." But in Period 5 there was apparently a rebellion, resulting in major military action on the part of Ti Hsin.[142]

The above eight *fang*s are only a small part of the total recorded,[143] but they suffice in outlining the approximate territorial expanse of the Shang state as follows: the northern half of Honan, the southern half of Hopei, western Shantung, northernmost Anhwei and northwestern Kiangsu. Around this area, Shang was encircled by T'u Fang in the

139. Chiang Hung 江鴻, *op. cit.*, pp. 42–46.

140. Shima Kunio 島邦男, *Inkyo bokuji kenkyū* 殷墟卜辞研究, p. 391; Ch'en Meng-chia 陳夢家, *Yin Hsü p'u-tz'u tsung shu* 殷墟卜辭綜述, p. 304.

141. Shima Kunio 島邦男, *op. cit.*, pp. 374–375.

142. Tung Tso-pin 董作賓, *Yin li p'u* 殷曆譜 (hsia 下 vol. 2, pp. 45–46); Ch'en Meng-chia 陳夢家, *Yin hsü p'u-tz'u tsung shu* 殷墟卜辭綜述, pp. 309–310.

143. For detailed studies see Shima Kunio 島邦男, *op. cit.*, pp. 384–424; Ch'en Meng-chia 陳夢家, *Yin hsü p'u-tz'u tsung shu* 殷墟卜辭綜述, pp. 269–310; Li Hsüeh-ch'in 李學勤, *Yin tai ti-li chien lun* 殷代地理簡論.

north (northern Shansi), Kung Fang in the northwest (northern Shensi), Ch'iang Fang, Chou Fang, and Chao Fang in the west in central Shensi and vicinity, Yu Fang in the south in the middle Han river valley, Jen Feng in the east in the Huai river valley and coastal Kiangsu and Shantung, and Yü Fang in the northeast in central Hopei.

The above territorial definition is not only approximate and highly speculative but also dynamic and flexible. Several points must be taken into account in evaluating the state-to-state relationship. First, states were political units but not cultural or ethnic units. Sometimes historians, in their enthusiasm to demarcate ancient China into various regional or local units, have unduly and without sufficient evidence exaggerated the cultural, ethnic, and linguistic differences among the political groups. Ting Shan, for example, characterized the Hsia, Shang, and Chou dynasties as the political manifestations of three separate ethnic groups,[144] and Wolfram Eberhard attributed to them not only cultural but also linguistic differences.[145] But obviously cultural classifications must be based on evidence of cultural—not political—differences. As we will discuss in the next chapters on the basis of archaeological evidence, the cultural classifications of the archaeological remains in the areas of the Shang period *fang*s did not coincide with their political affiliations.

Second, not only may the people in the various states have been culturally similar, they may even have been on occasion related in the most intimate sense. Members of different states may have become regular marriage partners; the possibility that the Chiang 姜 clan, a well-known marriage partner of the Chi clan, of the royal house of Chou, came from Ch'iang Fang of Shang has been remarked upon by Shirakawa.[146] In tracing the distribution of individual emblems in bronze inscriptions, one finds that it did not follow political borders. The *chü* emblem, for example, occurs in bronzes known to have been unearthed in an area that stretches from Ch'i-shan to Shantung and from Honan to Hunan.[147] The segmentation of the ancient Chinese lineages was apparently a process that was not confined within single states.

Even from that perspective alone, one can see that state boundaries were shifting at best and state-state relations were seldom permanently cast. There is even good data to show, at least on some occasions,

144. Ting Shan 丁山, "Yu San-tai tu-yi lun ch'i min-tsu wen-hua" 由三代都邑論其民族文化.

145. W. Eberhard, *Lokalkulturen im Alten China*.

146. "Kyōzoku kō" 羌族考.

147. Chang Kwang-chih 張光直, "Shang Chou ch'ing-t'ung-ch'i ch'i-hsing chuang-shih hua-wen yü ming-wen tsung-ho yen-chiu ch'u-pu pao-kao" 商周青銅器器形裝飾花紋與銘文綜合研究初步報告, 269.

the dynamics of territorial expansion of the Shang state by swallowing up chunks of land or even entire small states next to the Shang borders. The process, described in the following passage by Chang Cheng-lang, merits a full translation:

> In ancient China the area was vast and the social and economic development was uneven. During the Hsia and Shang periods there were still many backward areas where livelihoods of gathering, fishing and hunting, or herding remained. But then . . . the agricultural economy displayed its superiority, and gradually it acquired a leading status. In the Shang period, farming and hunting were actually two different activities, but they shared the practice of burning of hills and marshes, and eventually many hunting grounds turned into farming fields. Among the oracle inscriptions cited earlier are the following:
>
>> Day Kuei-( ) [divined], ( ) inquired: ( ) to order [name] to open up new [fields] in the land of Hsien Hou?
>>
>> . . . Today open up new field [in the land of] Hsien Hou?
>
> Hsien Hou 先侯 was a lord of the king, presumably having his own land with accepted borders, but then why it was necessary for the Shang king to send people in to open up new fields? Then, there is the following record:
>
>> Day Kuei-Chi divined. Pin inquired: To order Chung Jen ( ) to enter into Yang Fang to open up new field?
>
> . . . Yang Fang had their own state borders, which is why it says, above, "to enter into." That the Shang state would enter into the territory of another state to open up new fields is a bit curious but not incomprehensible. The ancient states had differing economies and uneven societal developments. When agricultural states had population increases and new field requirements, they could go out to look for uncultivated land and would turn neighboring hunting areas and grazing pastures into farming fields. This the ancients had a term for, *chi t'ien* 寄田 . . . . *Chi t'ien* meant to cultivate new land in another state. When they opened up new fields thus and came to cultivate them for a long time, the Shang people naturally would not

care to give them up, and the newly opened fields would, thus, turn into another part of the land of the Shang king. *Meng Tzu* ("T'eng Weng Kung hsia") described a part of the history of the Shang at the dynasty's founding, based on *Shang shu*: "When T'ang was in Po, . . . his territory adjoined the state of Ko. The Earl of Ko was a wilful man who neglected his sacrificial duties. T'ang sent someone to ask, 'why do you not offer sacrifice?' 'We have no suitable animals.' T'ang sent gifts of oxen and sheep to the Earl of Ko, but he used them for food and continued to neglect his sacrificial duties. T'ang once again sent someone to ask, 'Why do you not offer sacrifices?' 'We have no suitable grain.' T'ang sent the people of Po to help in the ploughing and also sent the aged and young with gifts of food. The Earl of Ko led his people out and waylaid those who were bringing wine, food, millet and rice, trying to take these things from them by force. Those who resisted were killed. A boy bearing millet and meat was killed and the food taken. . . . When an army was sent to punish Ko for killing the boy, the whole Empire said, 'This is not coveting the Empire but avenging common men and common women.'"[148]

Ko was a lord of the Hsia dynasty, an Eastern Yi state founded by the Ying clan. The people probably engaged in fishing and hunting but lacked cattle, sheep, millet, and rice, and they had different customs, manners, and religious beliefs from those of the Shang . . . T'ang sent the people from Po into Ko to cultivate land . . . The result was that T'ang absorbed Ko, using the killing of the boy as a mere excuse. The Yang Fang in the oracle records . . . was probably a herding country . . . Period 1 records mentioned "to enter into Yang Fang to open up new fields," and also that "Yang brought five [turtle shells]" . . . These indicate that at that time Shang and Yang Fang were perhaps unequal states but they lived in peace. Oracle records of Period 3 stated:

> This autumn, . . . Inform (   ) about the military operation against Yang?

. . . Period 4 records say:

> (   ), inquired: To order the many (officials) to open up new field in Yang?

148. Quotation from *Meng-tzu* translated by D. C. Lau, *Mencius*, pp. 109–110.

> This last record dates from Wu Yi's reign. Yang was no longer referred to as *fang*, perhaps by then already a part of the Shang state . . . To look at this as a whole: Shang's relation to Yang Fang was characterized, first, by clearing of new fields, and, then, by military operations, and, finally, by the annexation of Yang Fang as a part of the Shang territory.[149]

The process described above could also presumably have been reversed, and Shang could have lost territories to neighboring states or at least stock and grain to raiders from neighboring states where herding, for example, was the dominant subsistence mode. The following Wu Ting period inscriptions are well known:

> Day Kuei-Ssu, divined. K'o inquired: No ill fortune during the *hsün*? The king prognosticated and said: There will be bad fortune. There will be trouble that will be inflicted, arriving three times. Five days later on day Ting-Yu, trouble was indeed inflicted, from the west. Chih Mu stated that T'u Fang reached the eastern border region and inflicted casualties to two towns. Kung Fang also came to graze in our fields in the western border region[150] (fig. 64).
>
> . . . The king prognosticated and said: There will be bad fortune. There will be trouble that will be inflicted, arriving three times. Seven days later on day Chi-Ssu, trouble was indeed inflicted, from the west. Ch'ang Yu Chiao reported that Kung Fang came out to graze in our fields in Shih Lai, [causing casualities of] seventy-five people.[151]

Border clashes of this nature were probably one of the major reasons for wars between the states, and wars took place for other economic reasons. The oracle records referred often to information about wheat harvests, references that Yü Hsing-wu believes to be really intelligence reports in preparation for border raids by the Shang, who did not plant as much wheat as perhaps some of the neigboring states and had to rely on raids for some of their wheat needs.[152]

149. Chang Cheng-lang 張政烺, "P'u-tz'u p'ou t'ien chi ch'i hsiang-kuan chu wen-t'i" 卜辭裒田及其相關諸問題, 107–108. In my translation I have changed all mentions of Yin to Shang.

150. Lo Chen-yü 羅振玉, *Yin hsü shu ch'i ch'ing hua* 殷虛書契菁華, no. 2.

151. *Ibid.*

152. Yü Hsing-wu 于省吾, "Ts'ung chia-ku wen k'an Shang tai she-hui hsing-chih" 從甲骨文看商代社會性質, 104.

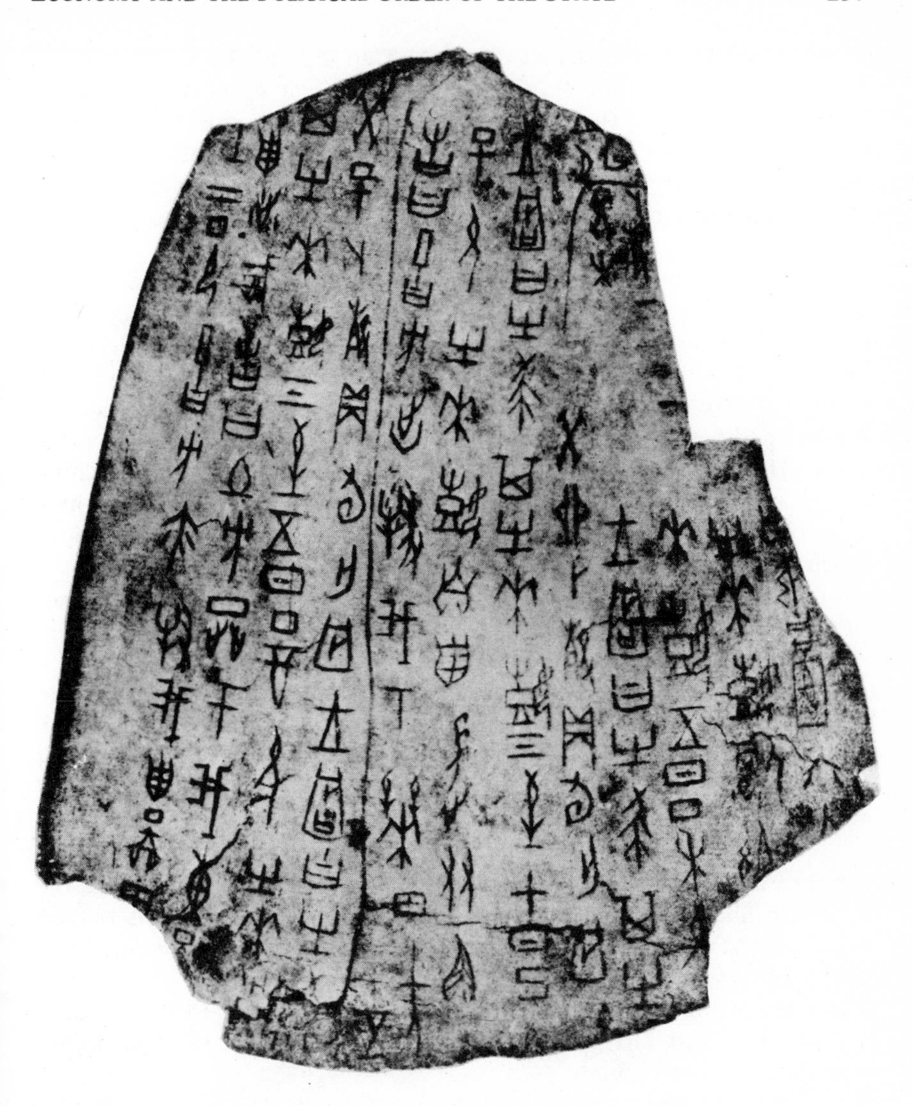

64. Rubbing of Shang inscriptions in which raids from T'u Fang and Kung Fang were recorded (after Lo Cheng-yü, *Yin hsü shu ch'i ch'ing-hua*, no. 2).

Economic considerations could also have lain behind many of the wars Shang fought in the northwest. In the above territorial definition we left out southern Shansi, and that is because the political groups in southern Shansi apparently oscillated the most often in their relationships with the Shang: Sometimes they seem to be alien states and at other times they appear to be among Shang's own subject lords. Ch'en Meng-chia listed Chou 周, T'ao 缶, Ch'üan 犬, Ch'uan 串, Kuo 郭, Hsün 𢎘, Chih 旨, Chih 沚, and Ch'üeh 雀 as the "southern Shansi states during the reign of Wu Ting,[153]" although Chou should actually have been located in Shensi and Ch'üeh is actually placed by him in western Honan. They were also "buffer" states between Shang and the more remote states such as Kung Fang, and Shang records show much concern about their conflicts with the other states. Southern Shansi, it must be noted, was an area of tremendous economic import. Among the twenty-eight known copper ore locations within a radius of 400 kilometers from An-yang listed by Shih Chang-ju, Noel Barnard, and Satō Tomatsu,[154] thirteen or almost half are in Shansi, mostly in the southern third of the province, and among seventeen tin ore locations six are in Shansi. Since southern Shansi is also the legendary birth place of the Hsia dynasty, the first full-fledged bronze civilization of China (see chapter 7), the rich copper and tin deposits of southern Shansi may have played a more prominent role in the rise of Bronze Age civilizations in China than has been generally recognized.

Southern Shansi has also been an important center of salt production. The salt marshes near Lu-ts'un 蘆村, in Hsieh Hsien in southern Shansi, are the only salt mines in the North China Nuclear Area next to Shensi and were the source of salt nearest to An-yang in the western direction, since no salt deposits (rock or brine) are known in Honan, Hopei, Anhwei, or Hupei, the provinces within easy reach of An-yang.[155] Even in recent years Hsieh Hsien salt provided much of the needs of Shensi in the west and Honan in the east.[156]

If southern Shansi was the principal source of the supplies of copper, tin, and salt for Shang, it would be small wonder that the southern Shansi states played such active roles in Shang's interaction with alien states in the northern and western directions. Ch'en Meng-chia's observation that the loyalties of the states to the west of the T'ai-hang Mountains (i.e., southern Shansi) were a key to the rise and fall of Chou and Shang in the late Shang period[157] could be highly significant in such a view.

Whatever the reason, one may state with fair confidence that

153. Ch'en Meng-chia 陳夢家, *Yin hsü p'u-tz'u tsung shu* 殷墟卜辭綜述, pp. 291–298.

154. Shih Chang-ju 石璋如, "Yin tai ti chu t'ung kung-yi" 殷代的鑄銅工藝; Noel Barnard and Satō Tomatsu, *Metallurgical Remains in Ancient China*.

155. Hu Hsiang-yün 胡翔雲, *Ch'üan kuo tsui chin yen ch'ang lu* 全國最近鹽場錄; Chang Hung-chao 章鴻釗, *Shih ya* 石雅, p. 185.

156. Huang Cho-hsün 黃著勳, *Chung-kuo k'uang-ch'an* 中國礦產, p. 11.

157. Ch'en Meng-chia 陳夢家, *Yin hsü p'u-tz'u tsung shu* 殷墟卜辭綜述, p. 312.

in the state-to-state dynamics, tension was the overriding factor, and war, though not a constant occurrence, was nevertheless a prominent feature in the divination records. Earlier we mentioned that captives were held as the result of wars or even that their capture was sometimes the incentive for war. Yü Hsing-wu believes that some records also related to the number of enemy casualties in battles: One casualty figure that was encountered was 2,656.[158] At the conclusion of a successful battle, enemy chiefs were often slain and their heads taken as trophies. Hu Hou-hsüan enumerated eleven human skull fragments with inscriptions that were found.[159] The same fate, of course, came upon Ti Hsin after his capital fell to the Chou troops.

Since alien states and the Shang's own subject lords were under some circumstances interchangeable entities, the state scores criteria suggested by Keightley for measuring intrastate cohesion could also be applied to state-to-state relations, at least for the periods in which wars were not prevailing. The king is known to have divined about alien states, as well about as his own lords, in connection with their "lack of ill fortune" (*wu huo* 無禍), their running the king's errands (*ku wang shih* 固王事), and their coming into Shang territory and Shang's entry into theirs.

158. "Ts'ung chia ku wen k'an Shang tai she-hui hsing-chih" 從甲骨文看商代社會性質, 111.

159. Hu Hou-hsüan 胡厚宣, "Chung-kuo nu-li she-hui ti jen hsün ho jen chi" 中國奴隸社會的人殉和人祭, 60, 63.

PART II SHANG HISTORY BEYOND AN-YANG

5 Cheng-chou

An-yang is so very important in Shang historiography because it not only has yielded an enormously rich archaeological site but also is the only Shang site with sufficient written data to help paint a picture of the world outside An-yang that was as large as the Shang's vision and contacts had reached. But what about that world as seen from its own remains? Shang archaeology in the last thirty years has begun to fill in our picture of that world with some real data, and the first major Shang site—and still the major Shang site—outside An-yang was brought to light at Cheng-chou in 1950.

1. *THE ERH-LI-KANG PHASE OF SHANG CIVILIZATION*

One hundred fifty kilometers south of An-yang and immediately south of the Yellow River, Cheng-chou is a bustling industrial city of more than a million and the capital of Honan province since 1954. The importance of the city in part reflects the importance of its location. North China is divided into western highlands and the eastern plains. The Yellow River flows out of the western loess highlands in northern Honan and has poured into the eastern plains along several different courses throughout history. Cheng-chou is located near the Yellow River's exit from the highlands, at the meeting place between the west and the east. It is also right at the intersection of two major railways of China criss-crossing the whole country, one from north to south (The Peking-Canton Railway) and the other from west to east (Lan-chou to Lien-yün).

The modern city, with an old walled enclosure about 1.5 kilometers east-west and 1 kilometer north-south at its center, is situated on a flat plain drained by three small rivers—the Chin-shui, Chia-lu, and Hsiung-erh rivers—that originate in the rugged hills to the west and southwest of the city that are the eastern termini of the Sung Shan mountains. The area of the remains of the Shang city here—remains first found in the autumn of 1950 at Erh-li-kang, a small mound one kilometer southeast of the old town—has been found to coincide almost exactly with the area of the present city site, which is considerably larger than the older walled town. Since the history of the archaeological excavations has already been summarized at the beginning of this volume, our description will be based on the Shang remains here as they are known to date, without recounting some of the problematical issues. But it is worth repeating that because of the fact that the Shang city here lies directly underneath the area of present-day occupation (and unlike An-yang where Shang remains lie beneath wheat and cotton fields), the archaeology here has been difficult and slow, and our knowledge of the Shang site is still fragmentary.

Remains of several cultural phases from prehistoric and early historic periods have been brought to light in Cheng-chou since 1950, but the one phase that concerns us now is characterized by the Erh-li-kang site—hence the name Erh-li-kang phase. First we describe the major characteristics of this cultural phase and state our reasons for calling it Shang. The Erh-li-kang phase is generally regarded as being earlier than the dynastic period in An-yang, and the reasons for thus categorizing it will also become clear in the following account.

1. The most abundant and characteristic remains of Shang of the Erh-li-kang phase are its gray pottery, of fine or gritty clay, hand-made but often molded and then wheel-finished, impressed with cord marks, and mostly used for utilitarian purposes. The most common or characteristic types are the *li*-tripod with long and pointed hollow legs, a large beaker with huge flared mouth, and a basin and a jar with round or flat base (fig. 65). There are also steamers with attached or detached top, *ting*-tripod, *chüeh*- and *chia*-tripods, *kuei*, *tou*, and other types.[1] All of the above types are similar to, and have been reasonably regarded as being the antecedents of, the gray pottery of dynastic period Hsiao-t'un. Pottery similar to Erh-li-kang phase pottery has been identified at Mei-yüan-chuang in the southeastern part of the An-yang area.

Other pottery wares included red ware, hard pottery, and glazed pottery. The hard pottery ware was often impressed with geometric patterns, similar to the so-called geometric pottery of the lower Yangtze and the southeastern coast.[2] The glaze was of a yellow-greenish color, applied on brown or gray ware with mat- or basket-impressions.[3]

1. *KKHCK*, *Cheng-chou Erh-li-kang* 鄭州二里岡, pp. 16–30; An Chih-min 安志敏, "Yi-chiu-wu-erh nien ch'iu chi Cheng-chou Erh-li-kang fa-chüeh chi" 一九五二年秋季鄭州二里岡發掘記.

2. *WW*, "Chiang-hsi ti-ch'ü t'ao-tz'u ch'i chi-ho-hsing p'ai yin wen-yang tsung shu" 江西地區陶瓷器幾何形拍印紋樣綜述.

3. Clarence Shangrow, "Early Chinese Ceramics and Kilns"; *KK*, "Cheng-chou shih Ming-kung-lu hsi ts'e ti liang tso Shang tai mu" 鄭州市銘功路西側的兩座商代墓, 503.

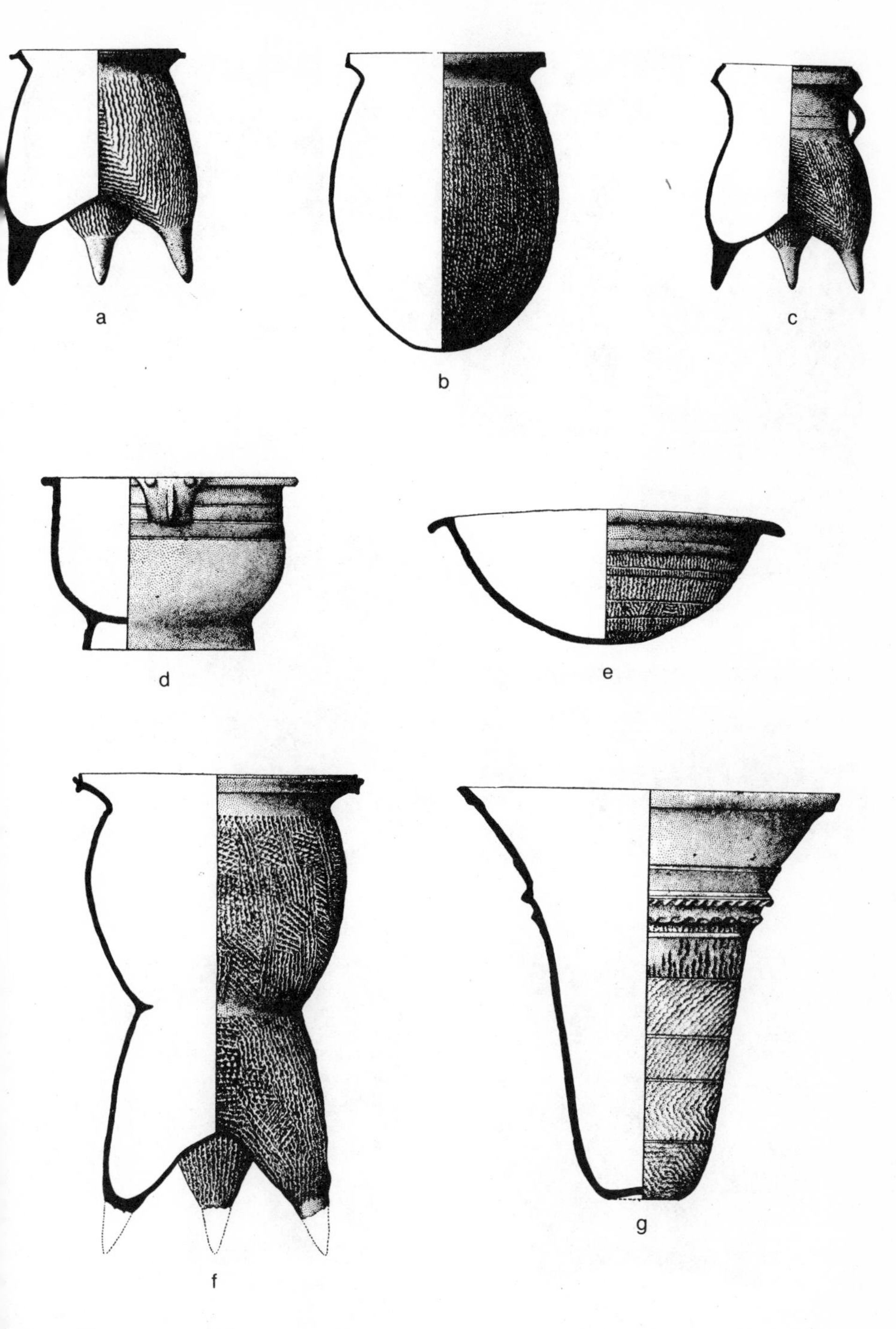

65. Major types of pottery of Erh-li-kang phase. *a. li; b. kuan; c. chia; d. kuei; e. p'en; f. hsien; g. tsun.*

66. Major types of bronze vessels from Erh-li-kang phase sites in Cheng-chou (after Committee of the Exhibition of Archaeological Finds in the People's Republic of China, *The Exhibition of Archaeological Finds in the People's Republic of China*).

These two kinds of pottery seem to be very rare but represent the high-quality pottery of the area. White pottery similar to that of An-yang has been mentioned in reports of findings,[4] but has not been fully described.

2. Stone and bone-antler industries in the Erh-li-kang phase feature tools and implements that are typologically similar to those of An-yang.

3. Bronze artifacts of the Erh-li-kang phase are highly characteristic (fig. 66). Although relatively few in number and found mostly in graves,[5] the ritual vessels were cast similarly to those of An-yang and attained similar forms. However, they are thinner and lighter, and their decorations, though in the same stylistic tradition characterized by animal motifs, are simpler. Decorations are for the most part confined to broad bands around the body, and the animal design is not separated from background spirals.[6] In the terminology of Max Loehr, styles I–III are found here, but styles IV and V are not. None of the vessels can unquestionably be described as being inscribed,[7] although emblems are seen on bronze weapons of this phase.

The Erh-li-kang bronzes are of tremendous interest in Shang scholarship for a number of reasons. In line with the scheme of stylistic evolution proposed by Max Loehr, these bronzes appear to be antecedent to Style IV and V pieces of dynastic An-yang; the similarity of the bronzes from four predynastic graves of Hsiao-t'un to the Erh-li-kang assemblage has been noted earlier, although the "predynastic" dating of the Hsiao-t'un bronzes in question was based almost totally on the typology of the bronzes. But there are other reasons for believing that Erh-li-kang was antecedent to Hsiao-t'un and Hsi-pei-kang, and thus the bronze vessels here provide a full-ranging assemblage of ritual bronzes believed to be ancestral to the An-yang bronzes, whose ancestry and early history of development had long been a puzzle in Chinese archaeology.[8] But though these bronzes may be ancestral they are not primitive, and as they fully attest to the existence of a social class of

4. An Chin-huai 安金槐, "Cheng-chou ti-ch'ü ti ku-tai yi-ts'un chieh-shao" 鄭州地區的古代遺存介紹, 19; "Shih lun Cheng-chou Shang tai ch'eng chih—Ao tu" 試論鄭州商代城址—隞都, 78.

5. *WW*, "Cheng-chou shih Pai-chia-chuang Shang tai mu-tsang fa-chüeh chien pao" 鄭州市白家莊商代墓葬發掘簡報; *KK*, "Cheng-chou shih Ming-kung-lu hsi ts'e ti liang tso Shang tai mu" 鄭州市銘功路西側的兩座商代墓; *WW*, "Cheng-chou hsin ch'u-t'u ti Shang tai ch'ien ch'i ta t'ung ting" 鄭州新出土的商代前期大銅鼎.

6. T'ang Lan 唐蘭, "Ts'ung Ho-nan Cheng-chou ch'u-t'u ti Shang tai ch'ien-ch'i ch'ing-t'ung-ch'i shuo ch'i" 從河南鄭州出土的商代前期青銅器說起, 6.

7. T'ang Lan 唐蘭, *loc. cit.* See here an emblem in the shape of a turtle.

8. A. C. Soper, "Early, Middle, and Late Shang: A Note."

high status in Cheng-chou, they are significant for the study of the political as well as artistic and technological history of the Shang.

4. The social complexity and stratification in the Erh-li-kang phase are indicated by more than bronze assemblages. The Shang site here is marked by a rammed-earth wall that extended almost seven kilometers to form a roughly square enclosure 1690–1870 meters long on each side. The *hang-t'u* technique of construction we have become quite familiar with through the house foundations and grave fillings in An-yang, but no Shang period earthen town wall has thus far been identified in the An-yang area. *Hang-t'u* town walls are a familiar feature on the northern Chinese landscape throughout Chinese history, and the Erh-li-kang wall was one of the earliest, although it is preceded by similar walls of the Lung-shan villages at Ch'eng-tzu-yai in Shantung[9] and at Hou-kang in An-yang, Honan,[10] and of an Erh-li-t'ou culture town site in Hsia Hsien, Shansi (see chapter 7).[11] The wall of Erh-li-kang Cheng-chou is of significance architecturally, but as an enormous piece of public works[12] and as a presumably defensive construction it is a sensitive indicator of the level of complexity of the society it enclosed.

In the northeastern part of the enclosure was an area of Erh-li-kang occupation characterized by large *hang-t'u* house foundations with large postholes in long rows, probably remains of a habitation area "palatial" in scope.[13] Greater details will be given in the next section, but we mention them here to further support the statement that Erh-li-kang Cheng-chou was a Shang town with sharp social stratification and probable political importance.

But how important was Erh-li-kang Cheng-chou in Shang times? Was it an important town, a provincial capital, or even a royal capital? In addition to the emblems on bronze artifacts aforementioned, there are two other kinds of writing that offer clues of its importance. One consists of potters' marks, mostly on the interior of the flaring rims of the large beakers,[14] and the other inscriptions on three pieces of bone (a rib,

9. Fu Ssu-nien 傅斯年, Li Chi 李濟, et al., *Ch'eng-tzu-yai* 城子崖.

10. Shih Chang-ju 石璋如, "Ho-nan An-yang Hou-kang ti Yin mu" 河南安陽後岡的殷墓.

11. Hu Hou-hsüan 胡厚宣, personal communication, 1978.

12. An Chin-huai 安金槐, "Shih lun Cheng-chou Shang tai ch'eng chih—Ao tu" 試論鄭州商代城址—隞都.

13. *WW*, "Cheng-chou Shang tai ch'eng chih shih chüeh chien pao" 鄭州商代城址試掘簡報, 25–27.

14. *KKHCK, Cheng-chou Erh-li-kang* 鄭州二里岡, p. 17; An Chih-min 安志敏, "Yi-chiu-wu-erh nien ch'iu chi Cheng-chou Erh-li-kang fa-chüeh chi" 一九五二年秋季鄭州二里岡發掘記, 77; *KKHP*, "Cheng-chou Nan-kuan-wai Shang tai yi-chih ti fa-chüeh" 鄭州南關外商代遺址的發掘, 83.

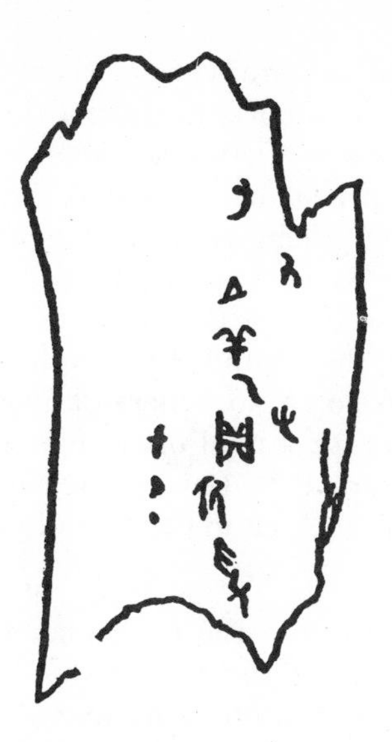

67. Inscription on a rib found at the site of Erh-li-kang, Cheng-chou (after *KKHCK, Cheng-chou Erh-li-kang,* p. 38).

a limb bone, and a small fragment).[15] Of the three inscribed bones, two had a single character each, but the rib has ten characters (fig. 67), including the words *chen* 貞 ("inquire"), *yang* 羊 ("sheep" or "Yang the state"), *shou* 受 ("to receive"), and *t'u* 土 ("earth").[16] Ch'en Meng-chia believed that the inscribed rib resulted from "practicing" to incise characters and that the characters appear to be "Late Yin" style.[17] Since the original is not available for examination and the published reproduction of the piece is not clear, we have to take Ch'en's word for it concerning its meaning (or lack of meaning, as Ch'en would have it) although one is tempted to suggest some possible meaning to it. As for its being late Yin, this statement is highly misleading. The inscribed rib was found at Erh-li-kang, although its exact stratigraphic position is unknown. Since Erh-li-kang has not yielded archaeological remains that postdated the Erh-li-kang phase, there is no reason not to regard the inscribed rib as an integral part of the Erh-li-kang culture, i.e., from the

15. Ch'en Meng-chia 陳夢家, *Yin hsü p'u-tz'u tsung shu* 殷墟卜辭綜述, p. 27.

16. *KKHCK, Cheng-chou Erh-li-kang* 鄭州二里岡, p. 38.

17. Ch'en Meng-chia 陳夢家, *Yin hsü p'u-tz'z tsung shu* 殷墟卜辭綜述. See also Li Hsüeh-ch'in 李學勤, "T'an An-yang Hsiao-t'un yi-wai ch'u-t'u ti yu tzu chia ku" 談安陽小屯以外出土的有字甲骨, 17.

period corresponding to the predynastic Shang of Hsiao-t'un. Both of these issues are extremely important, since if the bone in question is in fact of Erh-li-kang date and if its inscription consists of a divination record involving the official act of ritual inquiry—*chen*—then the chance that Erh-li-kang Cheng-chou was a royal capital would be strengthened.

As has been described at the beginning of this volume, according to textual accounts, the second royal capital of the Shang dynasty, after T'ang's Po, was Hsiao or Ao, where Chung Ting and Wai Jen had their royal headquarters for a total of twenty-six years, until King Ho T'an Chia moved the capital to Hsiang. According to T'ang Lan, the town of Hsiao or Ao was located in the area of Cheng-chou:

> According to Li Tao-yüan's commentary [sixth century, Northern Wei] of *Shui ching*, "Chi Shui" section: "the Chi River flows to the east of Mountain Ao. . . . In the mountains is a walled town, the site to which King Chung Ting had moved." This old Shang period town extant in the Northern Wei period was located in the general area of Cheng-chou. . . .
>
> Ao the Shang capital is stated in textual materials to be located in a hilly area. The earliest reference was made by Huang-fu Mi, who stated that "it is identified by some with the Ao Ts'ang [the Ao Granaries] in Honan." . . . The present city of Cheng-chou, historically speaking, may be identified with Kuan, to which Kuan Shu was enfeoffed at the beginning of Chou. . . . We may come to see that, although Ao, Chung Ting's capital, was named after Mountain Ao, it could nevertheless include in its area the site of Kuan to its east, just as the term Yin Hsü historically includes Ch'ao-kuo.[18]

T'ang Lan's inclusion of the Erh-li-kang town site into the area of the broadly defined Shang capital Ao is reasonable in light of the broad definition of royal capital we have made concerning the An-yang area, and any more specific and precise identification based on the fragmentary and somewhat conflicting textual data would be unproductive and unnecessary. Most recently, Tsou Heng proposed a most unconventional view, identifying the Shang town Cheng-chou with T'ang's Po, the

18. "Ts'ung Ho-nan Cheng-chou ch'u-t'u ti Shang tai ch'ien-ch'i ch'ing-t'ung-ch'i t'an ch'i" 從河南鄭州出土的商代前期青銅器談起, 7–8; See, for discussion on the Erh-li-kang site and its literary equivalent, An Chin-huai 安金槐, "Shih lun Cheng-chou Shang tai ch'eng chih—Ao tu" 試論鄭州商代城址—隞都, and Liu Ch'i-yi 劉啟益, "'Ao-tu' chih yi" '隞都' 質疑.

first Shang capital.[19] There have been absolutely no legends recorded in the Cheng-chou area concerning Shang's Po to support this view, and none of the many historical identifications of Po places it in the Cheng-chou area. The only thing going for this idea may be the fact that the Erh-li-kang phase town was not only large in size but was of considerable temporal duration. Ao was a royal capital for only twenty-six years, but Po served as the capital of nine kings for—according to Tung Tso-pin's chronology[20]—a period of 183 years.

Whether the Shang town of the Erh-li-kang phase was a royal capital and, if so, with which capital known in literary history it should be identified, are topics yet to be explored on the basis of additional evidence, especially textual evidence if it should become available. But on two points there does not appear to be much doubt. First, the town here was part of the Shang dynasty, and, second, its main occupation—Erh-li-kang phase—was earlier than An-yang.

The designation of an archaeological find as "Shang," once a seemingly simple undertaking that consisted of matching the new find with the An-yang type site, is becoming increasingly difficult and uncertain as the result of the extensive discoveries that are stretching the Shang stereotype both temporally and spatially. In the latter sense, the area that Shang-like remains have been found in—from Liaoning in the north to southern Hunan in the south and from Shensi in the west to the Pacific coast in the east—is well larger than any territory the Shang dynasty could possibly have directly ruled, even by the most generous estimates. The term Shang, thus, takes on a broadly defined meaning that denotes both a style of civilization and a time period. But in temporal terms, civilizational development in ancient China—at least during the *san tai* ("Three Dynasties") period—is shown to be characterized more by continuity than by discontinuity. This the Chou people had long recognized; to wit, their sayings: "The rituals [or the rules] of the Three Dynasties are one" (*Li chi*), and "the Yin inherited their rituals [or rules] from the Hsia, and what they took out or added on is known, and the Chou inherited their rituals [or rules] from the Yin, and what they took out or added on is known" (*Lun yü*). The Shang civilization extends upward into Hsia or downward into Chou, and the thresholds were merely political events while the evolution of culture and society was continuous. When we find a site somewhere in North China, often we can no longer identify it with Hsia, Shang, or Chou on the basis of cultural characteristics alone.

We will discuss this point at some length later on when we look

19. Tsou Heng 鄒衡, "Cheng-chou Shang ch'eng chi T'ang tu Po shuo" 鄭州商城即湯都亳說.

20. *Yin li p'u* 殷曆譜 part I, vol. 4.

at ancient China as a whole and try to delineate the archaeological markers of Hsia, Shang, and Chou. The Erh-li-kang phase is identifiable with Shang certainly in that context. But the most reliable criteria in this identification are temporal and spatial criteria. By this we mean that the Erh-li-kang phase in Cheng-chou was located at the heart of the traditional Shang domain, with archeological evidence supported by the folk tradition in this area concerning King Chung Ting's city of Ao. Chronologically, the Erh-li-kang phase may be placed within the early half of the traditional Shang dynastic period. One may note that textual and folkloristic traditions have been given much emphasis. This is inevitable when contemporary evidence is inconclusive but when an integrated approach—instead of a purely archaeological one—is pursued.

The chronology of the Erh-li-kang phase may be approached on several grounds. As of this writing, two radiocarbon dates are available from the town walls of Erh-li-kang Cheng-chou:[21]

ZK-177	3215 ± 90 B.P.	(calibrated to 1560 ± 160 B.C.)
ZK-178	3235 ± 90 B.P.	(calibrated to 1590 ± 160 B.C.)

Both dates fall within the first part of the Shang dynastic reign. Although we will not come back to the issue of the absolute chronology of Shang civilization until chapter 7, it is obvious that the chronological segment to which these radiocarbon dates belong is on the whole earlier than the dynastic period at Hsiao-t'un in An-yang.

The chronological precedency of the Erh-li-kang phase over the dynastic period in An-yang is supported in every key area relevant to dating. Stratigraphically, the Erh-li-kang phase lies below a later Shang phase in Cheng-chou, the People's Park phase, the typological equivalent of dynastic Hsiao-t'un.[22] In artifact typology, Erh-li-kang is situated between dynastic Hsiao-t'un, on the one hand, and Honan Lung-shan, on the other, particularly in connection with bronze vessels and pottery. Further exposition on this point would be superfluous.

2. *THE SHANG CITY AT CHENG-CHOU IN THE ERH-LI-KANG PHASE*

The Shang city at Cheng-chou was similar to that at An-yang in scope and conception. In an area of approximately twenty-five square

21. Hsia Nai 夏鼐, "T'an-14 ts'e-ting nien-tai ho Chung-kuo shih-ch'ien k'ao-ku hsüeh" 碳-14測定年代和中國史前考古學, 229.

22. *WW*, "Cheng-chou shih Yin Shang yi-chih ti-ts'eng kuan-hsi chieh-shao" 鄭州市殷商遺址地層關係介紹; Tsao Heng 鄒衡, "Shih lun Cheng-chou hsin fa-hsien ti Yin Shang wen-hua yi-chih" 試論鄭州新發現的殷商文化遺址.

kilometers drained by the Chin-shui 金水 and Hsiung-erh 熊兒 rivers, a number of Shang (Erh-li-kang phase) settlements formed a network that consisted of a large walled enclosure and a number of functionally specialized settlements around the enclosure (fig. 68). The area inside the walled enclosure has not been fully excavated because it coincides with the present Cheng-chou city, but it appears to be the equivalent of Hsiao-t'un and Hsi-pei-kang in the An-yang network.

THE WALLED ENCLOSURE

First discovered in 1955 and excavated in 1956–73, the earthen wall of the Shang town[23] has proved to be approximately seven kilometers long, forming a rough square shape with a crooked northern wall. The lengths of the four sides are: 1690 meters, north wall; 1700 meters, east and south walls; 1870 meters, west wall. Most of the wall is now buried under the present ground surface, although portions are still exposed. Eleven gaps have been located along the wall, at least some of them possibly being remains of the original gates.

The wall was built by the *hang-t'u* 夯土 method, namely, planks were erected on both sides of the wall, earth (*t'u*) was poured in to fill the space between the planks, and the earth was then tightly pounded (*hang*), layer by layer, with a heavy pounder. Most layers are 8–10 centimeters thick, but occasionally they are as thin as 3 centimeters or as thick as 20. On the upper surface of each layer (when the layer above is removed) are seen densely distributed round pits (2–4 centimeters in diameter and 1–2 centimeters deep) with round or pointed bottoms (fig. 69). The cross-section of the wall is trapezoidal. The layers in the middle were laid horizontally, while the layers at both ends recline outward. The middle layers (about 10.5 meters interior-exterior, pounded in between planks about 2.5–3.3 meters long, 0.15–0.3 meter wide) were the main body of the wall, built in sections about 3.8 meters long. The sloping layers of earth were pounded at the bases both inside and outside the wall to form reinforcements about 5 meters wide. On the upper surface of these reinforcing bases was laid a layer of gravel. The height of the walls is unknown; the tallest of the remaining sections is 9.10 meters from the base.

When the wall was first uncovered, the reporting was sketchy[24]

23. *WW*, "Cheng-chou Shang tai ch'eng-chih shih chüeh chien pao" 鄭州商代城址試掘簡報; An Chin-huai 安金槐, "Shih lun Cheng-chou Shang tai ch'eng chih—Ao tu" 試論鄭州商代城址—隞都; *WW*, "Cheng-chou Shang ch'eng yi-chih nei fa-hsien Shang tai hang-t'u t'ai-chi ho nu-li t'ou ku" 鄭州商城遺址內發現商代夯土台基和奴隸頭骨.

24. An Chin-huai 安金槐, *op. cit.*

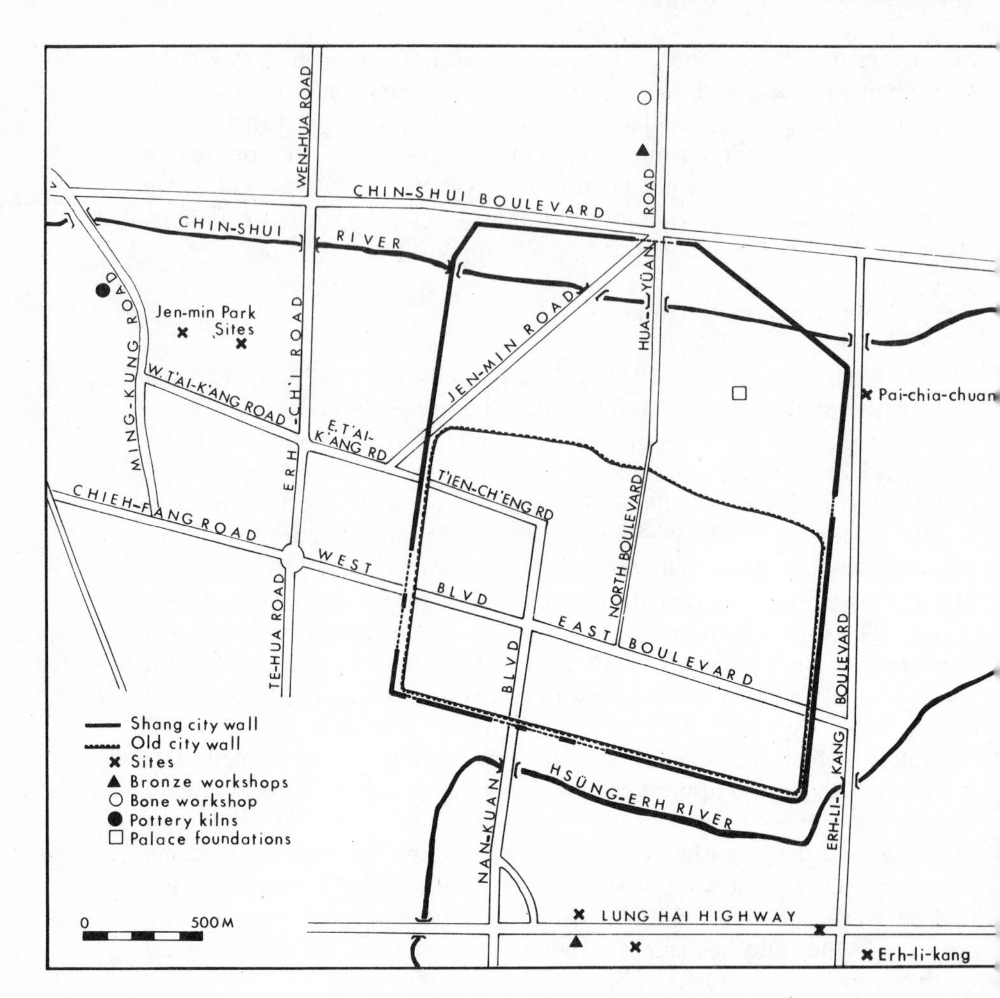

68. Archaeological sites of the Shang period in Cheng-chou.

and there were questions about the true date of the wall.[25] Later extensive explorations along the wall have shown that it was built on top of occupation layers of pre–Erh-li-kang phases (see below) but that it was intruded into by Erh-li-kang and later occupation features, burials, and

25. An Chin-min 安志敏, "Kuan-yü Cheng-chou 'Shang ch'eng' ti chi-ko wen-t'i" 關于鄭州'商城'的幾個問題, Liu Ch'i-yi 劉啓益, "'Ao tu' chih yi" '隞都'質疑.

69. Sections of the wall of the Shang town at Cheng-chou (photo by author, 1975).

70. Human skulls found in ditch in Shang palace in Cheng-chou (photo by author, 1975).

debris, showing that the wall was probably completed at the beginning of Erh-li-kang occupation.[26]

Within the walls have been found a variety of scattered finds. The most noteworthy are a cluster of *hang-t'u* house foundations in the northeastern region of the enclosure excavated in 1974. A large floor, 34 meters north-south by 10.2 meters east-west in remaining area, was built by the *hang-t'u* technique, and it had seven rows of posts in some arrangement. The floor was wrecked by a north-south ditch, in which were dumped various kinds of rubbish and many human skulls, some of which were sawed into halves (fig. 70). Most of the skulls appear to be those of young adult males. Possibly this whole area was a part of an architectural cluster of some political and ritual significance.

Other parts of the area inside the enclosure are known only through a number of test trenches. At the northeast and northwest corners of the walled-in area were found a number of house floors; some of the better-preserved ones are rectangular or square, paved with a layer of fine yellow clay or white limey clay, with some remaining wall bases. Some of them had a door on the south wall and a raised

26. *WW*, "Cheng-chou Shang tai ch'eng-chih shih chüeh chien pao" 鄭州商代城址試掘簡報, 23–24.

earthen altar against the center of the interior of the northern wall. Residential rubbish, including potsherds, stone implements, shell and bone implements, and oracle bones, was also found in scattered areas along and against the walls. Some kinds of rubbish was also found in storage pits. Also along the east, north, and west walls were located twenty-nine pit graves furnished with sets of pottery vessels, including wine vessels such as *chüeh-* and *chia*-tripods. At two spots in the northeast and northwest were brought to light pits containing dog skeletons; in the northeast eight such pits, in three rows, contained a large number of dogs—a minimum of six in one pit and a maximum of twenty-three in another. In one of the dog pits two human skeletons lay underneath the dog skeletons, and in another were small, thin pieces of gold.

These miscellaneous remains are insufficient for any clear understanding of the settlement pattern inside the walls, but clearly the conditions were quite complex. If there were "palatial" areas within the walls, there were also living quarters and graves of commoners and remains perhaps ritual in nature. A mixture of such complexity also occurs at Hsiao-t'un, so that no conclusion can yet be drawn, but obviously this walled-in area is where additional research must be concentrated.

AREA NORTH OF ENCLOSURE

Some two hundred meters north of the northern wall is an archaeological locality (known as Tzu-ching-shan North 紫荊山北) that seems to be associated with bronze metallurgy. In an area of 275 square meters were found four house floors, each separated from the next by about 10 meters. The houses were rectangular, with the long axis placed east-west. Each house was partitioned into two rooms, one or both having a door facing south and an earthen altar built against the northern wall facing the door. Both floor and altar were plastered with white limey clay. The floor was built 0.2–0.5 meter under the ground surface, and the walls were built of *hang-t'u* layers. On the floor of one of the houses and nearby on the outside were found conical pits with bronze-like deposits, 184 clay molds for bronze weapons and vessels, crucible fragments, and cores for bronze vessel legs. Associated pottery places the site during the Erh-li-kang phase.[27] The association of a bronze workshop with *hang-t'u* houses is significant and is similar to the situation in An-yang.

27. Liao Yung-min 廖永民, "Cheng-chou shih fa-hsien ti yi ch'u Shang tai chü-chu yü chu-tsao t'ung-ch'i yi-chih chien chieh" 鄭州市發現的一處商代居住與鑄造銅器遺址簡介.

One hundred meters further north was a Shang pit from which came to light, in addition to a few potsherds, a number of bone artifacts—sawed and polished bones as materials, bone debitage, half-finished objects, bone arrowheads, and bone hairpins. There were also polishing stones. The bones were those of cattle, deer, and humans. These finds evidently indicate a bone workshop nearby but further excavations are still awaited.[28]

AREA EAST OF ENCLOSURE

A short distance to the northeast of the walled town is the Pai-chia-chuang 白家莊 village, near which archaeological excavations were undertaken in 1954–55, resulting in findings both of residential remains and graves with bronze vessels. The residential remains consist of house floors and wall bases plastered with white limey clay, storage pits, a *hang-t'u* structure, a ditch, and rubbish heaps.[29] There were four graves, excavated on a small mound to the west of the village. Grave no. 2, a rectangular pit, has yielded five bronze vessels (*lei, chüeh, p'an, chia,* and *ting*), a jade, and an ivory vase. Grave no. 3, also a rectangular pit 2.9 by 1.17 meters and 2.13 meters deep, had an *erh-ts'eng-t'ai* ("second-level ledge") built of earth along the walls, and a "waist pit" at bottom center containing a dog skeleton. Two human skeletons were found, one inside a coffin within the pit chamber and the other, probably a sacrificial victim, on the western side of the second-level ledge. Nine bronze vessels (three *ting,* two *chia,* one *lei,* two *ku,* and one *chüeh*), two jades, an ivory comb, and a few other objects were found on the ledge, mostly at the southwestern corner. All of the bronzes are classifiable into Loehr's styles I and II.[30] Significantly, the construction of Grave no. 3 was in the same tradition as the An-yang graves, and these tombs suggest a burial area here for people of considerable social status.

Near the southeastern corner of the Shang town wall was another burial area near Yang-chuang 楊莊. No details are available.[31]

28. *KK,* "Cheng-chou shih ku yi-chih mu-tsang ti chung-yao fa-hsien" 鄭州市古遺址墓葬的重要發現, 18–19; *KKHP,* "Cheng-chou Shang tai yi-chih ti fa-chüeh" 鄭州商代遺址的發掘, 57–58.

29. *WW,* "Cheng-chou Pai-chia-chuang yi-chih fa-chüeh chien pao" 鄭州白家莊遺址發掘簡報.

30. *WW,* "Cheng-chou shih Pai-chia-chuang Shang tai mu-tsang fa-chüeh chien pao" 鄭州市白家莊商代墓葬發掘簡報.

31. *KK,* "Cheng-chou shih ku yi-chih mu-tsang ti chung-yao fa-hsien" 鄭州市古遺址墓葬的重要發現, 17.

AREA SOUTH OF ENCLOSURE

About 500 meters southeast of the South Gate (of the old Cheng-chou city), in 1954 was found a second bronze workshop in an area of approximately 1,050 square meters. In it there were three kinds of crucibles, including the large beaker with flared mouth; more than a thousand fragments of clay piece moulds for arrowheads, knives, adzes, and ritual vessels such as *li, chia* and *chüeh*; small bronze implements; remains of ashes and charcoal; and numerous fragments of vertigris.[32]

Further to the east, at the intersection of Lung-hai and Erh-li-kang (Ch'eng-tung) roads is a cluster of residental remains, including storage pits, rubbish heaps, potsherds, stone implements, oracle bones and turtle shells, small bronze implements, and other objects of daily use. In some of the rubbish deposits were human skeletons apparently buried there without grave pits or furnishings.[33]

Still further to the east, about a kilometer southeast of the southeastern corner of the old city wall, is Erh-li-kang itself, a hill about 1500 meters east-west, 600 meters north-south, and 5–10 meters above the surrounding level land. Evidently at this locality there was an important residential area, the remains including storage pits, rubbish heaps, burials in the rubbish area furnished with a few pottery vessels and, in one case, a stone halberd. The artifacts found in these remains are pottery, stones and bones, and small bronze artifacts, including a bronze awl believed to be a tool for grooving and hollowing oracle bones. A residential area of commoners is indicated by these finds, but it was also from here that the aforementioned inscribed rib was found.[34]

AREA WEST OF ENCLOSURE

Three hundred meters to the west of the west wall of the Shang town, two bronze square quatropods were found in 1974 buried side by side about 6 meters under the present ground surface. Each is just over 60 centimeters to a side; one is taller (100 centimeters) and heavier (86.4 kilograms) than the other (87 centimeters, 64.25 kilograms). Inside

32. *KKHP*, "Cheng-chou Shang tai yi-chih ti fa-chüeh" 鄭州商代遺址的發掘, 56–57.

33. *WW*, "Cheng-chou ti wu wen-wu ch'ü ti yi hsiao ch'ü fa-chüeh chien pao" 鄭州第五文物區第一小區發掘簡報, *KKHP*, "Cheng-chou Nan-kuan-wai Shang tai yi-chih ti fa-chüeh" 鄭州南關外商代遺址的發掘.

34. *KKHCK*, *Cheng-chou Erh-li-kang* 鄭州二里岡; An Chih-min 安志敏, "Yi-chiu-wu-erh nien ch'iu chi Cheng-chou Erh-li-kang fa-chüeh chi" 一九五二年秋季鄭州二里岡發掘記.

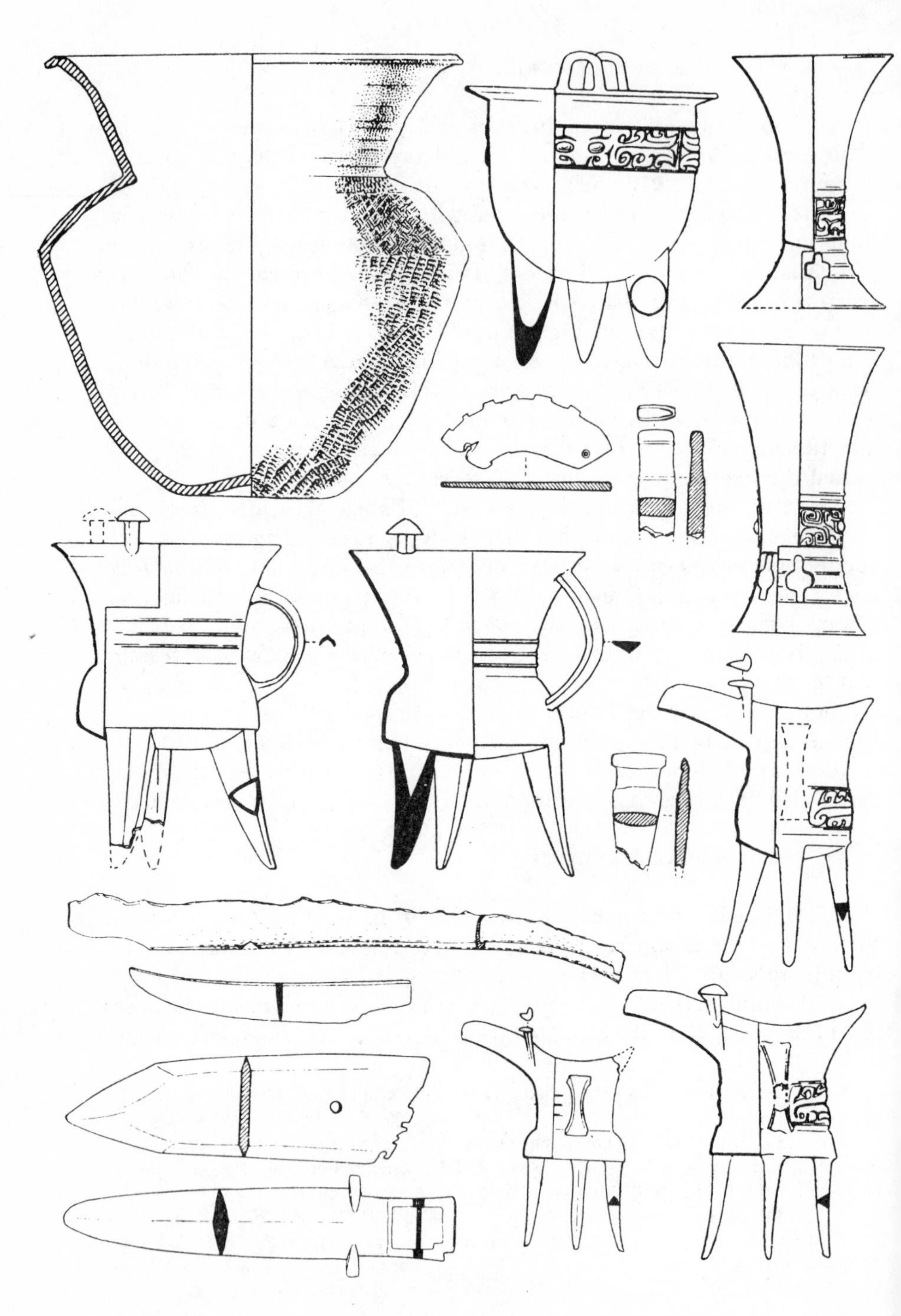

71. Bronze vessels from Shang grave west of Ming-kung-lu in Cheng-chou (after *KK*, "Cheng-chou shih Ming-kung-lu hsi ts'e ti liang tso Shang tai mu").

the small vessel was found a bronze *li*-tripod. The *li* had only string decorations, but both quatropods were decorated with characterizistic Style I patterns.[35] The excavators spoke of a possible human burial or hoarding, but these bronzes could also be the remains of an important ritual.

Further west, just under a kilometer from the west wall of the Shang town, is the important Shang cemetery at the People's Park locus. Most of the burials here, however, are dated to a period after the Erh-li-kang phase, corresponding to the dynastic strata at Hsiao-t'un,[36] but the cemetery was apparently first used back in the Erh-li-kang phase. One pit grave reported from this earlier period has yielded a glazed pottery beaker, a bronze *chüeh*-vessel, a bronze knife, a jade object, and other artifacts.[37]

Further to the west, to the west of Ming-kung 銘功 Road, is a large archaeological locus of the Erh-li-kang phase that has yielded dwelling remains, storage pits, graves with bronze vessels (fig. 71), and a pottery workshop. Just to the north was a group of house floors covered with white limey plaster. The largest one was 16.2 meters east-west and 7.6 meters north-south. Associated with the floors were storage pits and graves. Some of the graves had waist pits with dog skeletons and grave furnishings including pottery, a few jades, and a bronze vessel, and one grave (with a waist pit) contained a pottery jar in which cremated bones were placed. (This is the only cremation recorded for a Shang burial, and the possibility that the jar was intrusive into a Shang grave cannot be ruled out).[38]

South of the largest house floor in an area 1250 meters square was a cluster of pottery kilns. These were round excavations with an opening for fuel and another, covered by a grill, for the placement of pottery to be fired. In the many pits nearby were unfired pottery, misfired pottery, paddles, and impressing paddles. Nearby white plastered floors appear to be associated with some of the kilns.[39]

35. *WW*, "Cheng-chou hsin ch'u-t'u ti Shang tai ch'ien-ch'i ta t'ung ting" 鄭州新出土的商代前期大銅鼎.

36. An Chih-min 安志敏, "Cheng-chou shih Jen-min kung-yüan fu-chin ti Yin tai yi-ts'un" 鄭州市人民公園附近的殷代遺存.

37. *WW*, "Cheng-chou shih Jen-min kung-yüan ti erh-shih-wu hao Shang tai mu-tsang ch'ing-li chien-pao" 鄭州市人民公園第二十五號商代墓葬清理簡報.

38. *WW*, "Cheng-chou shih Ming-kung-lu hsi ts'e fa-hsien Shang tai chih t'ao kung-ch'ang fang-chi teng yi-chih" 鄭州市銘功路西側發現商代製陶工場房基等遺址, 64; Ma Ch'üan 馬全, "Cheng-chou shih Ming-kung-lu hsi ts'e ti Shang tai yi-ts'un" 鄭州市銘功路西側的商代遺存.

39. *WW*, "Cheng-chou shih Ming-kung-lu hsi ts'e fa-hsien Shang tai chih t'ao kung-ch'ang fang-chi teng yi-chih" 鄭州市銘功路西側發現商代製陶工場房基等遺址, 64; *WW*, "Cheng-chou fa-hsien ti Shang tai chih t'ao yi-chi" 鄭州發現的商代製陶遺跡; *KKHP*, "Cheng-chou Shang tai yi-chih ti fa-chüeh" 鄭州商代遺址的發掘, 57.

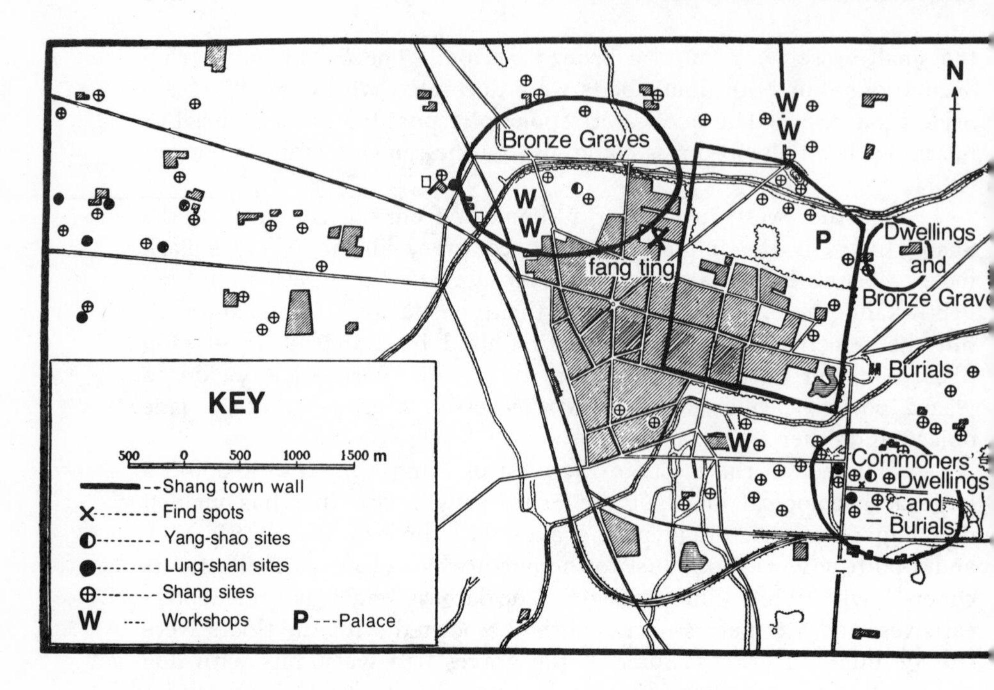

72. A structural model of the Shang urban network in Cheng-chou.

A few meters to the south of the kilns was another burial area, excavated in 1965. Five graves were opened, but only two better furnished ones have been reported.[40] Both were pit graves, not equipped with *erh-ts'eng-t'ai*, and were furnished with bronze vessels, bronze weapons, jades, glazed pottery beakers, bone objects, and shell beads, and were apparently the tombs of people with social status comparable to the Pai-chia-chuang bronze graves.

SUMMARY

The remains described above[41] represent quite a small portion of the total material that is apparently available, and even the material

40. *KK*, "Cheng-chou shih Ming-kung-lu hsi ts'e ti liang-tso Shang tai mu" 鄭州市銘功路西側的兩座商代墓.

41. Cf. *KKHP*, "Cheng-chou Shang tai yi-chih ti fa-chüeh" 鄭州商代遺址的發掘; Hsia Nai, "Workshop of China's Oldest Civilization"; An Chin-huai 安金槐, "Shih lun Cheng-chou Shang tai ch'eng chih—Ao tu" 試論鄭州商代城址—隞都; *WW*, "Cheng-chou Shang tai ch'eng-chih shih chüeh chien pao" 鄭州商代城址試掘簡報 *WW*, "Cheng-chou Shang tai yi-chih" 鄭州商代遺址.

that is available has resulted mainly from salvage work. From these sketchy data a picture of the city of the Erh-li-kang phase emerges which repeats in the main the pattern that we have observed in An-yang on the basis of more abundant, better-excavated, and better-reported data. Again one sees not only a highly stratified and specialized society but also a settlement pattern in which differences in social strata and profession were spatially expressed. At the heart was an enclosure in which were probably seated the rulers of the town, together with support personnel. Workshops of various kinds were found scattered in all directions outside the wall, some of them associated with ground houses with or without *hang-t'u* floors and walls, possibly indicating—as in the An-yang case—that some craftsmen were appended to the upper, rather than the lower, class. In the northern suburbs graves of considerable sophistication, with *erh-ts'eng-t'ai*, waist-pits, human sacrificial victims, dogs, and ritual bronze vessels, have been found together with the dwelling quarters of their nobleman masters, whereas dwellings of commoners and their burials in trash pits have been identified widely in the southern suburbs (fig. 72).

These patterns of the Shang settlement are merely what we have been able to put together on the basis of still-sketchy data. We await, with interest, additional information from future research, especially in the area inside the earthen enclosure and its southwestern suburbs.

3. *ERH-LI-KANG PHASE IN ANCIENT NORTHERN HONAN CULTURAL STRATIGRAPHY*

Here a brief attempt will be made to place the Erh-li-kang phase, together with the later An-yang phase of the dynastic period, into the general context of the cultural chronology of northern Honan. A more detailed discussion of the issues involved here cannot be made until we have presented the Shang archaeological data from other areas of China, and until we have dealt with a number of general problems concerning the ancient Chinese history and archaeology.

The northern Honan ancient cultural stratigraphy is summarized in table 3. A fuller explanation of the table will be made later in this volume, but preliminary comments may be desirable at this juncture.

Palaeolithic and Mesolithic cultures (1, 2). The northern part of Honan had been occupied by man since the Upper Palaeolithic period at the latest, as shown by the stone assemblages from the cave of Hsiao-nan-hai 小南海 southwest of An-yang[42] and from the sand dunes near

42. An Chih-min 安志敏, "Ho-nan An-yang Hsiao-nan-hai chiu-shih-ch'i shih-tai tung-hsüeh tui-chi ti shih chüeh" 河南安陽小南海舊石器時代洞穴堆積的試掘.

TABLE 3 Northern Honan Cultural Stratigraphy

Cultures	*Phases*	*Type Sites*	*Calibrated C-14 Dates* (B.C.)
9. Shang	Dynastic An-yang	An-yang	1210 ± 160
			1280 ± 150
8. Shang	Erh-li-kang	Cheng-chou	1560 ± 160
			1590 ± 160
7. Hsia	Lo-ta-miao	Lo-ta-miao, Cheng-chou	1470 ± 190
6. Lung-shan		Hou-kang, An-yang	2340 ± 140
5. Yang-shao	Ta-ssu-k'ung-ts'un	Ta-ssu-k'ung-ts'un, An-yang;	3070 ± 190
			3130 ± 190
		Ta-ho-ts'un, Cheng-chou	3425 ± 130
			3685 ± 125
4. Yang-shao	Hou-kang	Hou-kang, An-yang	4185 ± 200
			4390 ± 140
3. Early Neolithic		P'ei-li-kang, Hsin-cheng	5935 ± 480 (uncalibrated)
2. Mesolithic		Ling-ching, Hsü-ch'ang	
1. Palaeolithic		Hsiao-nan-hai, An-yang	10760 ± 220

Ling-ching 靈井, in Hsü-ch'ang, south of Cheng-chou.[43] Both are characterized by flake and microflake implements and date to near the border between Pleistocene and Holocene, although Hsiao-nan-hai is considered earlier on faunal grounds. These assemblages represent the continuing population and culture of the Central Plains, and it was among these people that the transition to an agricultural life took place, a process yet to be fully documented by archaeological material.

Early Neolithic (3). One of the very few sites that can truly be called Early Neolithic in North China is the P'ei-li-kang 裴李崗 site near Hsin-cheng, south of Cheng-chou, discovered and excavated in early 1977. There are polished stone implements here, including "spades," sickle-like objects, and milling stones, suggesting the use of cereal grasses. There is pottery—red, coarse, mostly plain, occasionally comb-impressed or rocker-stamped—in the form of jugs, jars, bowls, and *ting*-tripods.[44] There is no stratigraphic evidence at the site for the culture's great antiquity, but one carbon-14 date of 7885 ± 480 B.P. (based on half-life of 5730 ± 40) has been determined. Another

43. Chou Kuo-hsing 周國興, "Ho-nan Hsü-ch'ang Ling-ching ti shih-ch'i shih-tai yi-ts'un" 河南許昌靈井的石器時代遺存.

44. *KK*, "Ho-nan Hsin-cheng P'ei-li-kang hsin-shih-ch'i shih-tai yi-chih" 河南新鄭裴李岡新石器時代遺址.

site that has yielded similar pottery has been reported from Tz'u-shan 磁山 in Wu-an in southern Hopei, and there two carbon dates of similar antiquity (7355 ± 100 and 7330 ± 105 B.P.)[45] corroborate the Early Neolithic status of cultural assemblages of this kind. At the Tz'u-shan site were remains of carbonized cereals and also bones of such possibly domesticated animals as pigs, dogs, cattle, and sheep. From further studies of this newly discovered culture one may reasonably expect growing knowledge about the beginning of food production in North China, and northern Honan seems to be definitely within the broad area in which this crucial process took place.

Yang-shao culture (4, 5). By the time of the well-known Yang-shao culture with painted pottery (5000–3000 B.C.),[46] the northern Honan area was well-populated. The earliest known manifestation of this culture appears to be the Hou-kang site in An-yang,[47] but by the fourth millennium B.C. it had become widespread. In the An-yang area the Yang-shao phase at Ta-ssu-k'ung-ts'un is the best known,[48] and in the Cheng-chou area two well-excavated sites are those near Lin-shan-chai 林山砦 [49] and Ta-ho-ts'un 大河村.[50]

Lung-shan culture (6). By the period of the Lung-shan culture, approximately the third millennium B.C., the population in the northern Honan area became dense, as indicated by the large number of Lung-shan culture sites here. A number of the Shang localities discussed above in both An-yang and Cheng-chou had a pre-Shang cultural stratum characterized by gray and black pottery of Lung-shan forms. In terms of pottery, stone and bone artifacts, the use of shoulder blades for oracles, and overall cultural complexity, Lung-shan culture provided the base from which Shang and similar early historical cultures sprang.

45. *KK*, "Ho-pei Tz'u-shan hsin-shih-ch'i yi-chih shih chüeh" 河北磁山新石器遺址試掘.

46. Dates according to Hsia Nai 夏鼐, "T'an-14 ts'e-ting nien-tai ho Chung-kuo shih-ch'ien k'ao-ku hsüeh 碳-14測定年代和中國史前考古學, 222; Chang Kwang-chih 張光直, "Chung-kuo k'ao-ku-hsüeh shang ti fang-she-hsing t'an-su nien-tai chi ch'i yi-yi" 中國考古學上的放射性碳素年代及其意義, 38.

47. *KK*, "1971 nien An-yang Hou-kang fa-chüeh chien pao" 1971年安陽後岡發掘簡報; *KK*, "1972 nien ch'un An-yang Hou-kang fa-chüeh chien pao" 1972年春安陽後岡發掘簡報.

48. *KK*, "1958–1959 nien Yin hsü fa-chüeh chien pao" 1958-1959年殷墟發掘簡報.

49. Mao Pao-liang 毛寶亮, "Cheng-chou hsi chiao Yang-shao wen-hua yi-chih fa-chüeh chien pao" 鄭州西郊仰韶文化遺址發掘簡報; Chao Ch'ing-yün 趙青雲, "1957 nien Cheng-chou hsi chiao fa-chüeh chi yao" 1957年鄭州西郊發掘紀要; An Chin-huai 安金槐, "Cheng-chou ti-ch'ü ti ku-tai yi-ts'un chieh-shao" 鄭州地區的古代遺存介紹, 16.

50. *KK*, "Cheng-chou Ta-ho-ts'un Yang-shao wen-hua ti fang chi yi-chih" 鄭州大河村仰韶文化的房基遺址.

More detailed discussion of this issue will be deferred until the final chapter.

Hsia civilization (7). This is a cultural phase that is seen sandwiched between the Lung-shan culture and the Shang civilization of the Erh-li-kang phase, both stratigraphically and typologically. On the basis of the three sites that have been used as the type-sites of this culture—Lo-ta-miao 洛達廟,[51] Shang-chieh 上街,[52] and the lower stratum of Nan-kuan-wai 南關外[53]—one may note that this culture has the following outstanding characteristics: The pottery is most typically impressed with clear and deep cord marks, similar to the Lung-shan, and check-impressions are also frequent, again a Lung-shan feature; *ting*-tripods are seen rather often, and one or two forms of jars are distinctive; a pottery basin with grooved interior is characteristic, sometimes called a "squeezer" or "shredder"; oracle bones of shoulder blades were seldom prepared before they were torched, and turtle shells were extremely rare to nonexistent. All these features place this phase—Lo-ta-miao phase in the literature—at an earlier position than the Erh-li-kang phase (although the single C-14 date from the Lo-ta-miao site is later than the Erh-li-kang dates), but at the same time its affinity with the latter is unmistakable. For these reasons it has long been considered Early Shang, a phase that has been archaeologically extended westward to the Lo-yang area, where it is identified with the cultural phase represented by the Erh-li-t'ou site. Thus, beginning in the 1960s the term "Early Shang phase" (typified by Erh-li-t'ou and Lo-ta-miao) has been used to describe the initial phase of the development of the Shang civilization.[54]

The picture is beginning to change in the late 1970s. The term Early Shang (Erh-li-t'ou or Lo-ta-miao phase) is being closely reexamined with a view to identifying it, instead, with the historical Hsia civilization. Detailed discussion of the issue will be presented in the final chapter, but let me anticipate that by simply stating that the northern Honan area at the end of the Lung-shan culture was within the eastern part of the domain of the Hsia civilization with its center of activities further

51. *WW*, "Cheng-chou Lo-ta-miao Shang tai yi-chih shih chüeh chien pao" 鄭州洛達廟商代遺址試掘簡報.

52. *KK*, "Cheng-chou Shang-chieh Shang tai yi-chih ti fa-chüeh" 鄭州上街商代遺址的發掘; *KK*, "Ho-nan Cheng-chou Shang-chieh Shang tai yi-chih fa-chüeh pao-kao" 河南鄭州上街商代遺址發掘報告.

53. *KK*, "Cheng-chou Nan-kuan-wai Shang tai yi-chih fa-chüeh chien pao" 鄭州南關外商代遺址發掘簡報; *KKHP*, "Cheng-chou Nan-kuan-wai Shang tai yi-chih ti fa-chüeh" 鄭州南關外商代遺址的發掘.

54. See Kwang-chih Chang, *The Archaeology of Ancient China*, pp. 269–271.

west in the Lo River valley and also in the lower Fen River valley of Shansi.

Shang (8). The change from the Lo-ta-miao phase to the Erh-li-kang phase, then, involved a major political upheaval, although there was essential cultural continuity. The northern Honan area saw the arrival of new rulers—the Shang—in the new phase, best exemplified by the Shang city in Cheng-chou, but also manifest in the archaeological assemblages of similar style and date such as Mei-yüan-chuang (lower stratum) and predynastic Hsiao-t'un[55] in the An-yang area; Liu-li-ko and Ch'u-ch'iu in Hui Hsien;[56] Lu-wang-fen in Hsin-hsiang;[57] and Ch'ao-ko in T'ang-yin.[58] Insofar as the greater capital area of late Shang is concerned, the whole area was in fact inhabited by Shang people in the Erh-li-kang phase, since remains dated to it have also been found to occur in Tz'u Hsien,[59] Han-tan,[60] and Hsing-t'ai.[61]

Shang (9). Finally, for the dynastic An-yang phase, the same sites in northern Honan continued to be inhabited, but the center of activities had been shifted from Cheng-chou to An-yang. At An-yang, as we have seen in chapter 1, the passage from predynastic to dynastic periods transformed the area from a relatively small cluster of villages, with perhaps a few members of the upper class whose graves have been brought to light at Hsiao-t'un (but possibly a small administrative center even then), into a bustling city. On the other hand, activities in Cheng-chou subsided drastically in the next local phase, the People's Park phase, which is generally considered to correspond to dynastic Hsiao-t'un. The only archaeological loci where remains of this late phase have significantly occurred are the People's Park just under a kilometer from the (presumably then-abandoned) Shang town wall[62] and the Ko-la-wang

55. *KK*, "1958–1959 nien Yin hsü fa-chüeh chien pao" 1958-1959年殷墟發掘簡報, 65, 73.

56. Kuo Pao-chün, Hsia Nai, et al., *Hui Hsien fa-chüeh pao-kao* 輝縣發掘報告.

57. *KKHP*, "Ho-nan Hsin-hsiang Lu-wang-fen Shang tai yi-chih fa-chüeh pao-kao" 河南新鄉潞王墳商代遺址發掘報告.

58. An Chin-huai 安金槐, "T'ang-yin Ch'ao-ko-chen fa-hsien Lung-shan ho Shang tai teng wen-hua yi-chih" 湯陰朝歌鎮發現龍山和商代等文化遺址.

59. *KK*, "Tz'u hsien Chieh-tuan-ying fa-chüeh chien pao" 磁縣界段營發掘簡報; *KKHP*, "Tz'u hsien Hsia-p'an-wang yi-chih fa-chüeh pao-kao" 磁縣下潘汪遺址發掘報告.

60. *KK*, "1957 nien Han-tan fa-chüeh chien pao" 1957年邯鄲發掘簡報; *KK*, "Ho-pei Han-tan Chien-kou-ts'un ku yi-chih fa-chüeh chien pao" 河北邯鄲澗溝村古遺址發掘簡報.

61. *KKHP*, "Hsing-t'ai Ts'ao-yen-chuang yi-chih fa-chüeh pao-kao" 邢台曹演莊遺址發掘報告.

62. An Chih-min 安志敏, "Cheng-chou shih Jen-min kung-yuan fu-chin ti Yin tai yi-ts'un" 鄭州市人民公園附近的殷代遺存.

site 6.5 kilometers west of the wall.[63] The People's Park cemetery has tombs with human sacrificial victims and bronze vessels, suggesting that the place remained under the care of the lords. Whether the Shang city here was Po or Ao, the royal dynasty did not move directly to An-yang, so that insofar as the capitals are concerned a gap remains between the two cities, although in terms of cultural phases the gap is not a glaring one.

63. *KKHP*, "Cheng-chou Ko-la-wang-ts'un yi-chih fa-chüeh pao-kao" 鄭州旭旮王村遺址發掘報告.

6 Shang Archaeology outside An-yang and Cheng-chou

In this chapter we present currently available archaeological evidence of the cultures in North China and immediately adjacent areas that were contemporary with An-yang and Cheng-chou, i.e., that may be dated to the six hundred years approximately from 1700 to 1100 B.C.[1] Archaeologists always classify the cultures and the remains they discover, and in presenting their discoveries in the archaeological literature they present them as "Shang sites" or local cultures or something in between. It is neither possible nor necessary to declassify the archaeological cultures and do our own classifications from scratch below. However, we take all current nomenclature as provisional and, in presenting the following material, perform the necessary reassessments and evaluations as we proceed.

The contemporary adjacent cultures will be described in two sections: those believed to be contemporary with Erh-li-kang (Cheng-chou) and those believed to be contemporary with the dynastic period in Hsiao-t'un (An-yang). Contemporaneity is in most—if not all—cases determined on the basis of pottery and/or bronze typology, supplemented in rare cases by inscriptions, radiocarbon dates, and other data that may be useful and available. The northern Honan area, briefly covered at the end of the last chapter, will be omitted here.

1. *MAJOR SITES OF THE ERH-LI-KANG PHASE*

In the last major synthesis of Shang archaeology published in 1962, the following general definition of the phase of Shang civilization characterized by Erh-li-kang was given as follows:

> The Early Shang culture was recognized in 1952 with the excavation of Erh-li-kang in Cheng-chou. Subsequently,

1. For discussion on absolute chronology, see chapter 7, section 1.

> remains of the same culture have been found in many localities in Honan, including Yin hsü of An-yang, and at Han-tan in Hopei. . . . The Early Shang characteristics are manifested in pottery as follows: the walls are relatively thin, the decorative patterns are mainly fine cord marks, but they also include *t'ao-t'ieh* and thundercloud patterns similar to those on bronze vessels as well as various stamped patterns; the vessel types include *li*-tripod, *hsien*-tripod, *tou*, jar, urn, beaker with large flared mouth, and the *chia*-tripod rarely seen in late Shang; the tripods, in particular, are conspicuously different from late Shang types, exhibiting such modes as thin and tall legs with pointed ends and overted or inverted rims. The bronze vessels are characterized by: predominantly flat base, thin walls, relatively coarse and sparse decorative patterns.[2]

The above characterization can now be significantly enriched and expanded, with sixteen additional years of discoveries, although the basic elements in ceramics and bronze vessels enumerated above have not changed (see beginning of last chapter). Archaeological sites where remains fit the above characterization have been uncovered and reported from an area that extended from central Shantung in the east to Shansi or even, possibly, central-eastern Shensi in the west, from Peking in the north to the middle Yangtze in the south. Assemblages that are found throughout this area are referred to as Shang in an archaeological-classificatory sense. Since virtually no contemporary historical records are available from this period, we can only speculate as to the size of the territory of political control.

NORTH

It has been shown that remains of Erh-li-kang type occur throughout the region that was to become the Shang capital in the dynasty's final centuries, in Tz'u Hsien, Han-tan, and Hsing-t'ai. Further north, an important Shang site was found near T'ai-hsi-ts'un 台西村, west of Kao-ch'eng, near Shih-chia-chuang, and excavated in 1965,[3] 1972,[4] and 1973.[5] The bulk of the remains can definitely be

2. *KKHCK, Hsin Chung-kuo ti k'ao-ku shou-hu* 新中國的考古收穫, pp. 45–46.

3. *KK*, "Ho-pei Kao-ch'eng hsien Shang tai yi-chih ho mu-tsang ti tiao-ch'a" 河北藁城縣商代遺址和墓葬的調查.

4. *KK*, "Ho-pei Kao-ch'eng T'ai-hsi-ts'un ti Shang tai yi-chih" 河北藁城台西村的商代遺址.

5. *WW*, "Ho-pei Kao-ch'eng hsien T'ai-hsi-ts'un Shang tai yi-chih 1973

dated to the period of Shang civilization prior to dynastic Hsiao-t'un, using the Fu Hao tomb to mark the culture of the King Wu Ting period, but they are apparently later than the classical Erh-li-kang phase and should perhaps be assigned to a late subphase of Erh-li-kang.

The T'ai-hsi-ts'un site is located in an area about one tenth of a square kilometer in size, centering on three earthen platforms, called West Mound, South Mound, and North Mound. Each was rectangular, 100 by 60–80 meters, and 6–7 meters high. Most of the remains were recovered in the eastern, western, and southern parts and nearby areas of the North Mound, and include house floors, a well, and graves. The house floors (eleven of them having been uncovered) were above ground (except for one semi-subterranean) and lined with walls built of *hang-t'u* in the lower parts and unfired clay bricks in the upper portions. They consisted of one, two, or three adjoining rooms. The largest house, of three rooms, was 14.2 meters long north-south and 4–4.35 meters wide east-west. Post holes and stone and potsherd post bases indicate large and sophisticated timber structures. Around the house, near the doors, underneath the floor, and below the post bases were buried animals and humans (including beheaded adult men and young girls), apparently victims of sacrificial rituals. The house has been called a nobleman's residence, compared to the palatial buildings and their associated burials at Hsiao-t'un. Near one of the houses was a round well (ca. 3 meters across), almost 6 meters deep. At the bottom was a wooden framework, within which were found many pottery jars, probably fallen into the well when they were dropped down at the end of a rope to scoop up water.

At least fifty-eight burials were brought to light in the area of the West Mound. All of them rectangular pit graves about 2 by 1 meters, they were divided into two groups: Five of the graves were larger than the rest and have yielded sacrificial victims, bronze ritual vessels and/or weapons, and/or other furnishings including oracle bones, gold, jade, bone, and stone objects and lacquerware. The sacrificial victims were mostly one to a grave, bound, and placed on the second-level ledge. The rest of the graves were poor in grave furnishings: one or two pottery vessels and, occasionally, a bronze halberd or arrowhead or two. Most of the bodies were buried prone, singly, in a coffin, over a waist-

nien ti chung-yao fa-hsien" 河北藁城縣台西村商代遺址1973年的重要發現; *WW*, "Kao-ch'eng T'ai-hsi Shang tai yi-chih fa-hsien ti t'ao-ch'i wen-tzu" 藁城台西商代遺址發現的陶器文字; Keng Chien-t'ing 耿鑒庭 and Liu Liang 劉亮, "Kao-ch'eng Shang tai yi-chih chung ch'u-t'u ti t'ao jen ho yü-li jen" 藁城商代遺址中出土的桃仁和郁李仁; Ho-pei sheng Po-wu-kuan 河北省博物館 et al., *Kao-ch'eng T'ai-hsi Shang tai yi-chih* 藁城台西商代遺址.

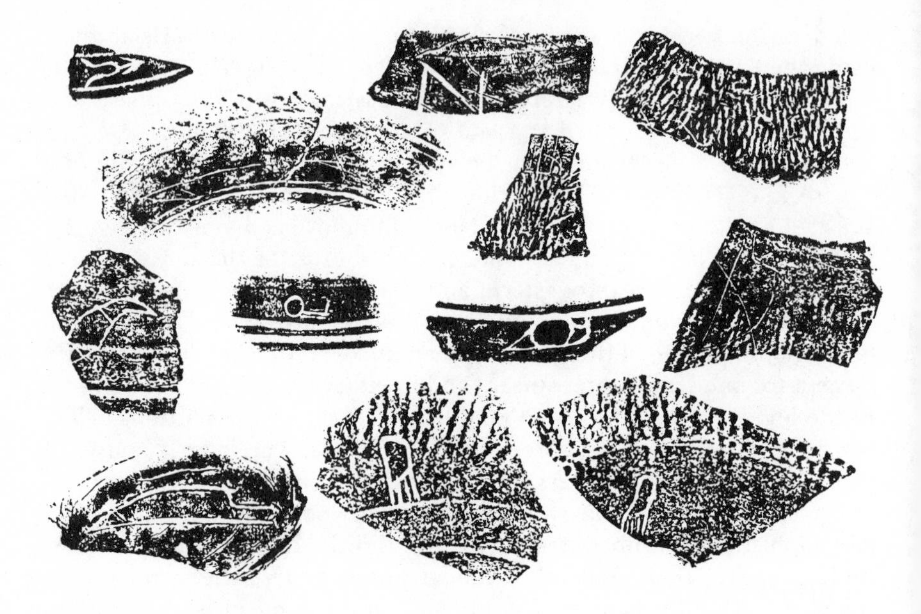

73. Pottery inscriptions from the Shang site in Kao-ch'eng (after *WW*, "Kao-ch'eng T'ai-hsi Shang tai yi-chih fa-hsien ti t'ao-ch'i wen-tzu," 50).

pit. In two cases, there were two bodies placed in the same coffin, in one of them two men and the other a man and a woman, but one of the two men and the woman appear to be sacrificial victims buried with their masters. However, the fact that rich and poor were placed together in the same cemetery and among one another significantly suggests that they were members of the same lineage and that lineages were highly stratified, conclusions that are in complete accord with what we have described about the Shang lineage organization from oracle bone inscriptions and ancient texts.

From the residential and burial remains at the T'ai-hsi-ts'un site a number of interesting and important finds may be mentioned. More than thirty pits of at least three kinds of peaches and prunes (*Prunus persica*, *P. tomentosa*, and *P. japonica*) were found, possibly collected for medicinal use. Twelve potsherds were inscribed with what seem to be written characters (fig. 73), again likely lineage emblems. A small number of "white pottery" sherds and many pieces of hard, glazed, hardware pottery have been reported. A bronze ax with an iron blade from the site was the center of some heated debate concerning iron casting under the Shang, but the final word is that the iron

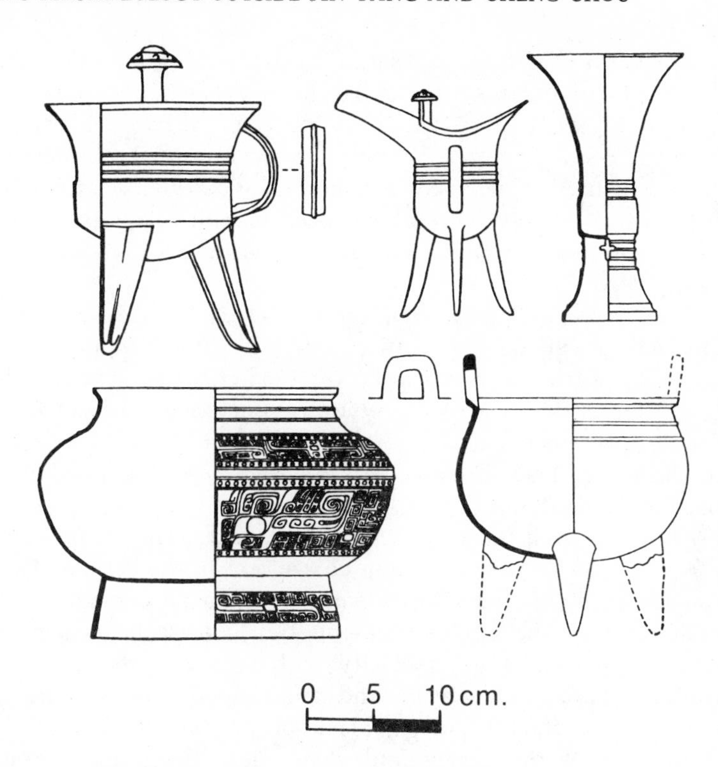

74. Bronze vessels from the Shang site in Kao-ch'eng (after *KK*, "Ho-pei Kao-ch'eng hsien Shang tai yi-chih ho mu-tsang ti tiao-ch'a").

used was meteoritic.[6] Finally, a number of bronze ritual vessels have been found (fig. 74). Some of the *chüeh-* and *chia-*tripods, with round bottoms and solidly constructed bodies and appendages, are similar to dynastic Hsiao-t'un samples, but the decorative patterns of animal motifs that have been published are classifiable as Loehr's styles II and III, and no style IV and V pieces have been reported. Although it is likely, according to the vessel types, that the site contains a dynastic Hsiao-t'un phase, we must also conclude, on the basis of available data, that the initial occupations corresponded in time to the predynastic Hsiao-t'un phase, i.e., Erh-li-kang. However, typologically speaking, T'ai-hsi-ts'un (early occupations) and pre-dynastic Hsiao-t'un are both classifiable into a late subphase of Erh-li-kang.

6. T'ang Yün-ming 唐雲明, "Kao-ch'eng T'ai-hsi Shang tai t'ieh jen t'ung yüeh wen-t'i ti t'an-t'ao" 藁城台西商代鐵刃銅鉞問題的探討; Li Chung 李衆, "Kuan-yü Kao-ch'eng Shang tai t'ung yüeh t'ieh jen ti fen-hsi" 關於藁城商代銅鉞鐵刃的分析.

Further north, in the eastern suburbs of Peking, another archaeological site of comparable nature has been excavated at Liu-chia-ho 劉家河, in P'ing-ku Hsien. It was a pit grave, and it has yielded sixteen ritual bronze vessels, another bronze ax with iron blade, bronze horse and chariot fittings, some gold ornaments (two armlets, an earring, a hairpin, and small sheets), several jade objects, nine turquois beads, and impressions of hemp fabrics. The bronze vessels are clearly of late Erh-li-kang types.[7]

The Peking area may be on the borderline between what can be characterized as Shang civilization and the contemporary culture directly to its north, namely, the Lower Hsia-chia-tien 夏家店 culture, at least insofar as the Erh-li-kang phase is concerned. The Lower Hsia-chia-tien culture, named after its type site at Hsia-chia-tien, near Ch'ih-feng in the upper Liao River valley, where a typical assemblage of it was discovered in 1959–60 in a lower stratum,[8] is known to center in the Ch'eng-te basin in the Luan River valley, extending as far south as T'ang-shan and as far west as Chang-chia-k'ou.[9] In the Peking–Tientsin area, Lower Hsia-chia-tien sites have proved to be common.[10] In its artifact inventory, the Lower Hsia-chia-tien culture bears significant resemblance to the Shang, especially with regard to its cord-marked gray pottery characterized by *li-* and *hsien*-tripods. But sufficient differences in its artifact typology—lack of bronze ritual vessels and pottery tripods of the *chüeh-* and *chia*-types, distinctive decorative modes such as the lug handle on *li-* and *hsien*-tripods and appliquéd ridge with pressings, a significant percentage of red pottery in the total of ceramic ware and a distinctive lithic assemblage including microlithic implements—seem to warrant the use of a cultural designation separate from the Shang.

The Lower Hsia-chia-tien, though perhaps not part of Shang proper, deserves our close attention for future yieldings, especially in relation to its Shang connection. The three radiocarbon dates that are now available for this culture—2410 ± 140 B.C., 1890 ± 130 B.C. and 1690 ± 160 B.C.[11] make it, at least in part, quite a bit earlier than the

7. *WW*, "Pei-ching shih P'ing-ku hsien fa-hsien Shang tai mu-tsang" 北京市平谷縣發現商代墓葬.

8. *KKHP*, "Ch'ih-feng Yao-wang-miao Hsia-chia-tien yi-chih shih chüeh pao-kao" 赤峯藥王廟夏家店遺址試掘報告.

9. Cheng Shao-tsung 鄭紹宗, "Yu kuan Ho-pei Ch'ang-ch'eng ch'ü-yü yüan-shih wen-hua lei-hsing ti t'ao-lun" 有關河北長城區域原始文化類型的討論, 664.

10. *KK*, "Ho-pei Ta-ch'ang Hui-tsu tzu-chih-hsien Ta-t'o-t'ou yi-chih shih chüeh chien pao" 河北大廠回族自治縣大坨頭遺址試掘簡報; *KK*, "Pei-ching Liu-li-ho Hsia-chia-tien hsia ts'eng wen-hua mu-tsang" 北京琉璃河夏家店下層文化墓葬.

11. The first two dates from Hsia Nai 夏鼐; see his "T'an-14 ts'e-ting nien-tai ho Chung-kuo shih-ch'ien k'ao-ku-hsüeh" 碳-14測定年代和中國史前考古學, 231; the

Erh-li-kang phase of Shang civilization. It also makes the copper artifacts from sites of the Hsia-chia-tien culture[12] among the earliest metal objects in Chinese archaeology. Moreover, the earliest archaeological find of oracle bones (of deer and possibly sheep shoulder blades) has occurred in the area of the upper Liao River, but it came from a previous cultural stratum dated to ca. 3350 B.C.[13] What Shang civilization owed to the Lower Hsia-chia-tien culture, as well as what is passed on to it, constitutes an important topic in the study of the Shang origins, to which we will return later.

EAST

The eastern part of Honan and its adjacent areas, in which the Great City Shang in the oracle bone inscriptions was located (see chapter 4), ought to be an important area of Earlier Shang archaeology. This was recognized as soon as the Yin hsü excavations began. As Li Ching-tan 李景聃, one of the earliest participants in the Yin hsü excavations, put it:

> In eastern Honan in the region adjoining Kiangsu and Shangtung is a county called Shang-ch'iu. Its name alone is sufficient to attract our attention. This region was on the old course of the Yellow River and could very possibly be the beginning place of the Shang dynasty. . . . Therefore, the ancestry of Yin hsü could be located in the Shang-ch'iu area. Because of these considerations, as part of their deliberations about the work assignment in the second half of 1936 for the Society for the Study of Honan Antiquities, Messrs. Fu [Ssu-nien], Li [Chi], Liang [Ssu-yung], Tung [Tso-pin], and Kuo [Pao-

third date from *KK*, "Fang-she-hsing t'an-su ts'e-ting nien-tai pao-kao (wu)" 放射性碳素測定年代報告(五), 285.

12. *Hsia-chia-tien* 夏家店, *lower stratum*: *KKHP*, "Ch'ih-feng Yao-wang-miao Hsia-chia-tien yi-chih shih chüeh pao-kao" 赤峯藥王廟夏家店遺址試掘報告, 127; *Ning-ch'eng* 寧城 *Hsiao-yü-shu-lin-tzu* 小榆樹林子: Cheng Shao-tsung 鄭紹宗, "Yu kuan Ho-pei Ch'ang-ch'eng ch'ü-yü yüan-shih wen-hua lei-hsing ti t'ao-lun" 有關河北長城區域原始文化類型的討論, 666;
T'ang-shan 唐山 *Ta-ch'eng-shan* 大城山: *KKHP*, "Ho-pei T'ang-shan shih Ta-ch'eng-shan yi-chih fa-chüeh pao-kao" 河北唐山市大城山遺址發掘報告;
Liao-ning Chao-wu-ta-meng Ao-han ch'i Ta-tien-tzu kung-she 遼寧昭烏達盟敖漢旗大甸子公社: *KK*, "Ao-han ch'i Ta-tien-tzu yi-chih" 敖漢旗大甸子遺址, 99.

13. *KK*, "Nei Meng-ku Pa-lin-tso-ch'i Fu-ho-kou-men yi-chih fa-chüeh chien pao" 内蒙古巴林左旗富河溝門遺址發掘簡報. For its dating, see Hsia Nai 夏鼐, "T'an-14 ts'e-ting nien-tai ho Chung-kuo shih-ch'ien k'ao-ku-hsüeh" 碳-14測定年代和中國史前考古學, 231.

> chün] decided to undertake an investigation of the Shang-ch'iu area in eastern Honan.[14]

Thereupon Li Ching-tan, together with Han Wei-chou and Meng Ch'ang-lu, embarked upon an investigative journey that lasted just over a month. The result was disappointing: a few Lung-shan sites were found on some higher mounds, but no Shang sites were identified. This area is a difficult one for field research, since it has been repeatedly flooded and its vast plains are covered with a thick layer of silt. According to Li Ching-tan, during the seven hundred and thirty years from 971 to 1699, there is record here of seventeen major deluges from collapsed dikes of the Yellow River. "Usually the ground surface has about 2.5 meters of silt, underneath which is a layer of yellow sand. . . . No wonder that even Han sherds are not visible, let alone prehistoric sites!"[15]

Forty years later, at the instigation of the Loyang Field Team of the Institute of Archaeology, Academia Sinica, an investigative party was organized in 1976 and began their work in the Shang-ch'iu area "in order to understand the pertinent issues of the late primitive society period and the cultures of Hsia and Shang periods".[16] The same difficulty was encountered and prehistoric remains were sometimes seen buried seven or eight meters under the ground surface.[17] A late Lung-shan site located on a higher mound was excavated,[18] but no other finds have so far been reported. The existence of Early Shang remains in this area, however, is tantalizingly suggested by a *chüeh*-tripod with thin walls and a flat base, and generally clumsy-looking, in the collection of the Tientsin Museum, said to have come from the Shang-ch'iu area.[19]

Farther to the east, the whole province of Shantung is said to be highly productive of Shang sites, but the only Erh-li-kang find consists of some bronze vessels found in 1970 at Ta-hsin-chuang 大辛莊, near Chi-nan, in central Shantung.[20] Similar finds had also been made as early as 1935, together with bronze weapons and bone and stone arti-

14. "Yü tung Shang-ch'iu Yung-ch'eng tiao-ch'a chi Tsao-lü-t'ai Hei-ku-tui Ts'ao-ch'iao san ch'u hsiao fa-chüeh" 豫東商邱永城調查及造律台黑孤堆曹橋三處小發掘, 84.

15. *Ibid.*, p. 88.

16. *KK*, "1977 nien Ho-nan Yung-ch'eng Wang-yu-fang yi-chih fa-chüeh kai-k'uang" 1977年河南永城王油坊遺址發掘概況.

17. Hsia Nai 夏鼐, personal communication, 1977.

18. Same as note 16.

19. *WW*, "T'ien-chin shih hsin shou-chi ti Shang Chou ch'ing-t'ung-ch'i" 天津市新收集的商周青銅器, 33.

20. Ch'i Wen-t'ao 齊文濤, "Kai shu chin nien lai Shan-tung ch'u-t'u ti Shang Chou ch'ing-t'ung-ch'i" 概述近年來山東出土的商周青銅器.

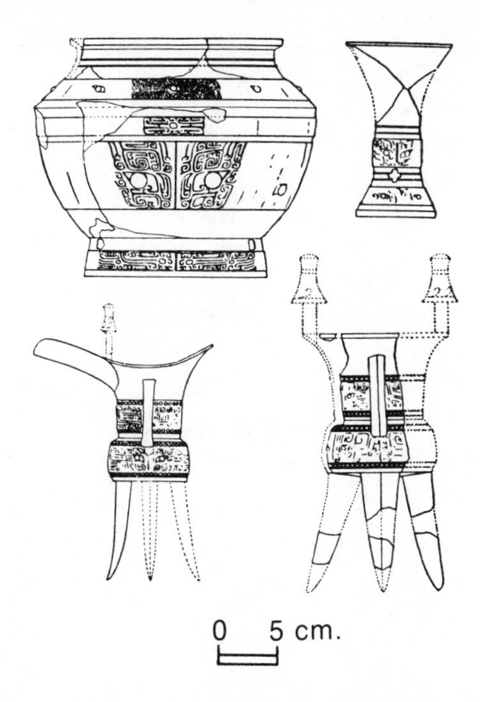

75. Bronze vessels from the Shang site in Chia-shan (after *WW*, "An-hui Chia-shan hsien Po-kang-yin-ho ch'u-t'u ti ssu-chien Shang tai t'ung-ch'i").

facts.[21] The typology and decoration of the vessels suggest a late Erh-li-kang affiliation, similar to the Kao-ch'eng assemblage.

SOUTH

In the south, a group of four bronze vessels (fig. 75) was found in Chia-shan in northeastern Anhwei at the heart of the Huai River valley, which exhibited typological and decorative features of a late Erh-li-kang subphase (corresponding to all of the late Erh-li-kang assemblages described above).[22] But two recent finds in the Yangtze River valley are much better known and more remarkable. These are the Shang-period sites at P'an-lung-ch'eng 盤龍城 (the "Coiling Dragon Town") and Wu-ch'eng 吳城 (the "Wu Town").

21. F. S. Drake, "Shang Dynasty Find at Ta-hsin-chuang, Shantung"; "Ta-hsin-chuang Again."

22. *WW*, "An-hui Chia-shan hsien Po-kang-yin-ho ch'u-t'u ti ssu chien Shang tai t'ung ch'i" 安徽嘉山縣泊崗引河出土的四件商代銅器.

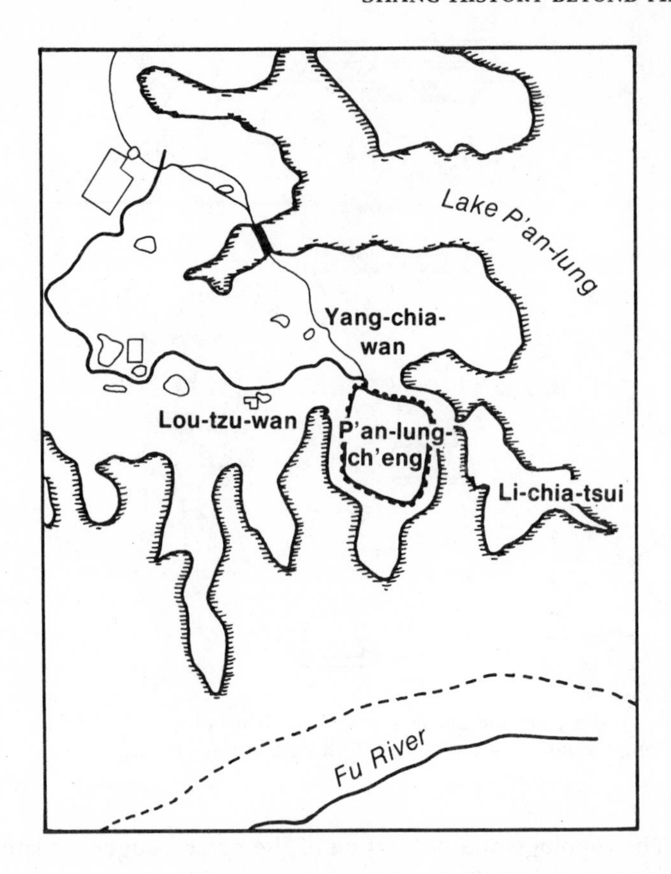

76. The Shang sites at P'an-lung-ch'eng (after *WW*, "P'an-lung-ch'eng yi-chiu-ch'i-ssu nien tu t'ien-yeh k'ao-ku chi yao," fig. 1).

P'an-lung-ch'eng is a walled enclosure, 290 meters north-south and 260 meters east-west, located near the Nieh-k'ou 聶口 village in Huang-p'i county of Hupei, just over five kilometers north of the city of Wu-han. South of the enclosure is a small tributary of the Yangtze, the Fu River, and to its north is a series of low hills. To its east is a small lake, P'an-lung Lake, which during high water-level seasons would extend along the low grounds south of the enclosure all the way to its west. Shang remains, first discovered in 1954,[23] are scattered within and around the enclosure in an area on the hills about 1.1 kilometers east-west and 1 kilometer north-south. Excavations here took place in

23. Lan Wei 藍蔚, "Hu-pei Huang-p'i hsien P'an-t'u-ch'eng fa-hsien ku ch'eng yi-chih chi shih-ch'i teng" 湖北黃陂縣盤土城發現古城遺址及石器等.

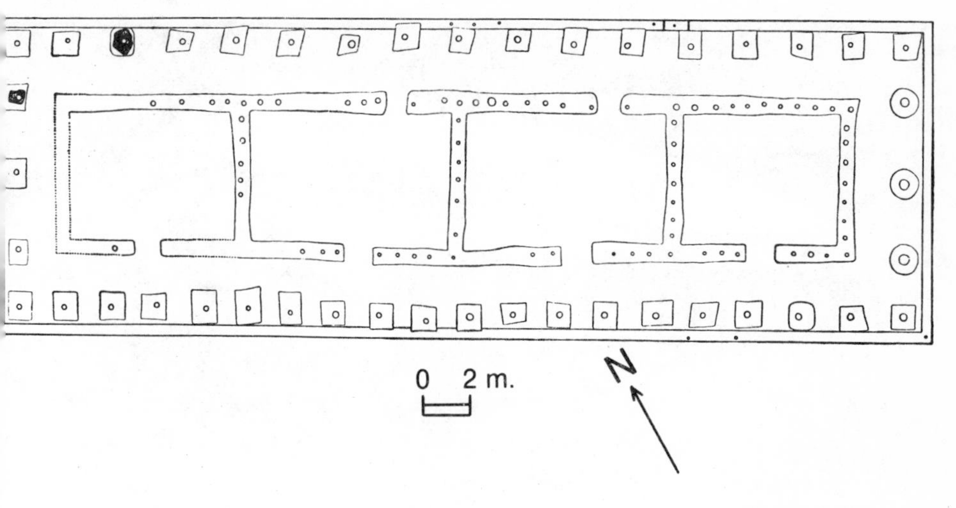

77. House floor F-1 at the Shang site at P'an-lung-ch'eng (after *WW*, "P'an-lung-ch'eng yi-chiu-ch'i-ssu nien tu t'ien-yeh k'ao-ku chi yao," 9).

the 1950s[24] and 1960s,[25] but it was not until 1974 that a digging of large enough scale to reveal the site's remarkable importance was undertaken.[26]

The Shang site here, as it has been disclosed so far, consists of the P'an-lung-ch'eng enclosure at the center and three burial areas to its west (Lou-tzu-wan 樓子灣), north (Yang-chia-wan 楊家灣), and east (Li-chia-tsui 李家嘴) (fig. 76).

The earthen enclosure was oriented 20° north-northeast and was built of *hang-t'u* layers about eight to ten centimeters thick. Only the basal portions are now standing, and a moat ten meters wide may have surrounded the whole wall. The northeastern portion is the area of highest ground within the enclosure, and the southwestern part the lowest. It appears that a huge *hang-t'u* foundation, 60 meters wide east-west and at least 10 meters long north-south, was built, its northern edge only about 10 meters from the northern wall of the town. On top

24. Kuo Ping-lien 郭氷廉, "Hu-pei Huang-p'i Yang-chia-wan ti ku yi-chih tiao-ch'a" 湖北黃陂楊家灣的古遺址調查.

25. Kuo Te-wei 郭德維 and Ch'en Hsien-yi 陳賢一, "Hu-pei Huang-p'i P'an-lung-ch'eng Shang tai yi-chih ho mu-tsang" 湖北黃陂盤龍城商代遺址和墓葬, 420–421; *WW*, "Yi-chiu-liu-san nien Hu-pei Huang-p'i P'an-lung-ch'eng Shang tai yi-chih ti fa-chüeh" 一九六三年湖北黃陂盤龍城商代遺址的發掘.

26. *WW*, "P'an-lung-ch'eng yi-chiu-ch'i-ssu nien tu t'ien-yeh k'ao-ku chi-yao" 盤龍城一九七四年度田野考古紀要.

78. A reconstruction of the house on house floor F-1 at the Shang site at P'an-lung-ch'eng (after Yang Hung-hsün, "Ts'ung P'an-lung-ch'eng Shang tai kung-tien yi-chih . . . .").

of the foundation, large rectangular houses ("palaces") were then built one alongside the next, parallel to the northern wall. Three such houses have been uncovered to date, but only the first from the north has been fully excavated (fig. 77). It consisted of a hall (34 by 6 meters) of four bays girded by a continuous corridor. On the four sides outside the corridor were forty-three large post holes originally holding wooden posts for supporting eaves. This whole house was built on a rectangular platform (40 meters east-west, 12 meters north-south) raised about 20 centimeters from the large *hang-t'u* foundation (fig. 78). The overall plan and probable function of these houses will not be known until the entire site has been excavated and reported, but evidently it corresponded to Hsiao-t'un of An-yang and the "palace area" (also in the northeastern portion of a walled enclosure) of Cheng-chou.

Of the three excavated outlying areas with burials, the Yang-chia-wan site is the most impoverished ("small pit graves furnished with a few pottery vessels or sometimes a single bronze vessel, probably a burial ground for the 'commoner freemen'").[27] From the Lou-tzu-wan locus excavated in 1963 came residential remains and five burials. The graves were pits with waist-pits and second-level ledges, each equipped with a few bronze ritual vessels, bronze weapons and implements,

27. *Ibid.*, 11.

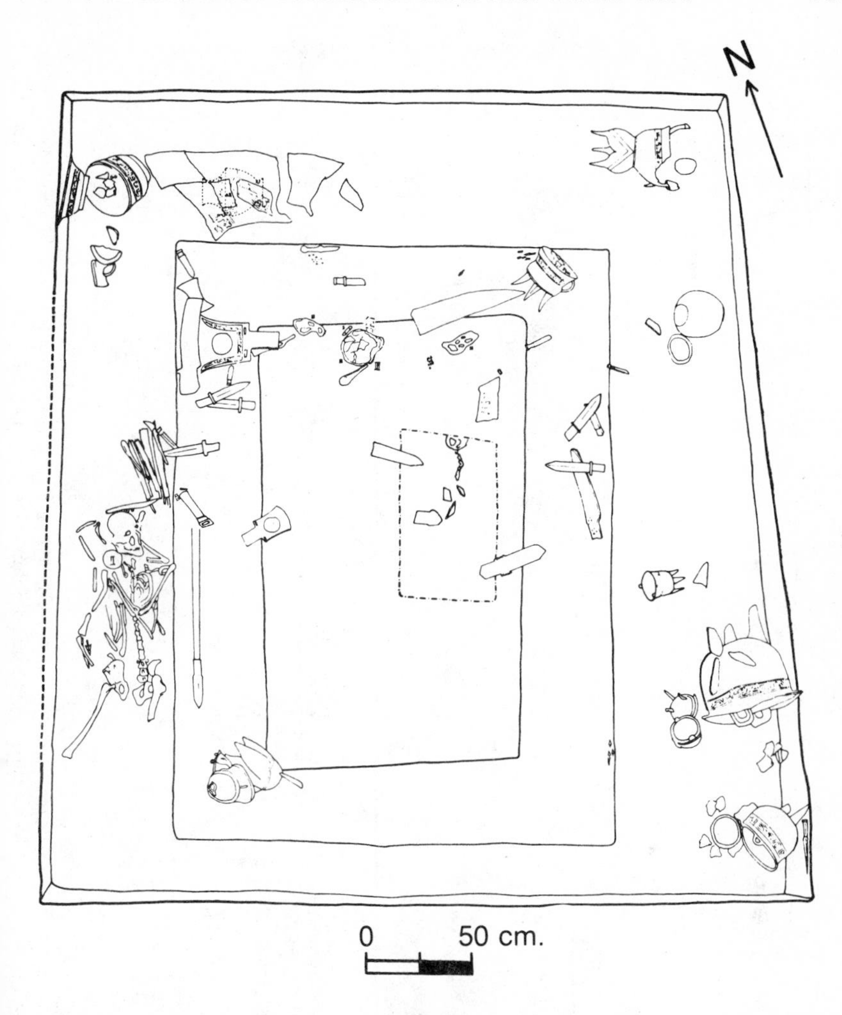

79. Shang grave M 2 at Li-chia-tsui, P'an-lung-ch'eng (after *WW*, "P'an-lung-ch'eng yi-chiu-ch'i-ssu nien tu t'ien-yeh k'ao-ku chi yao," 12).

jades, and/or pottery vessels (some glazed).[28] The richest burials, however, have been found at the Li-chia-tsui locus, where four graves have been reported so far. They were pit graves with wooden chambers and coffins. The chamber, in two layers, was elaborately carved and painted on the exterior, and waist-pits again occur at the bottom. Bronzes, jades,

28. *WW*, "Yi-chiu-liu-san nien Hu-pei Huang-p'i P'an-lung-ch'eng Shang tai yi-chih ti fa-chüeh" 一九六三年湖北黃陂盤龍城商代遺址的發掘.

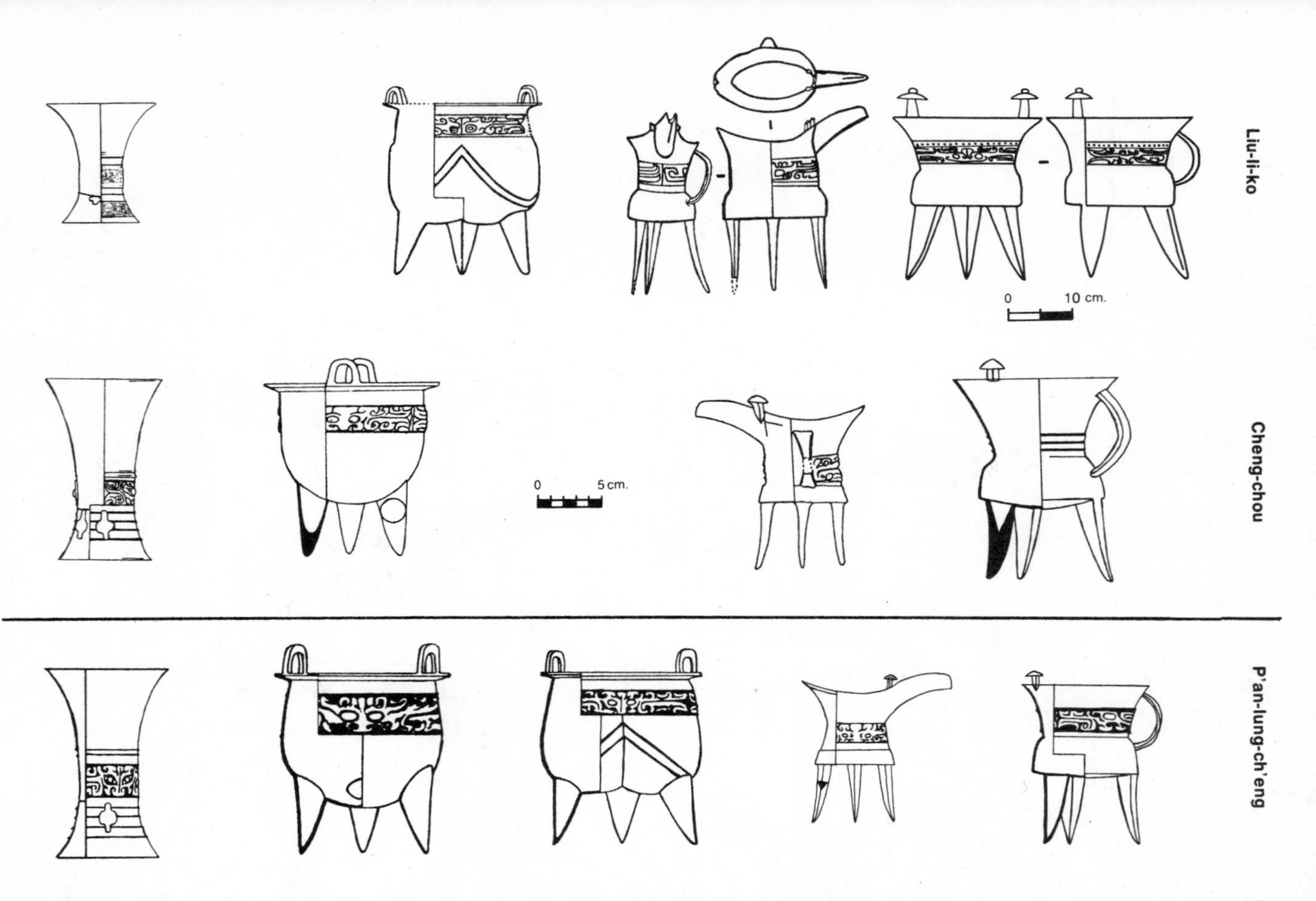

80. P'an-lung-ch'eng bronze vessels (*lower row*) compared with similar types from Liu-li-ko, Hui Hsien (*upper row*) and Cheng-chou (*middle row*) (P'an-lung-ch'eng types from *WW*, "Yi-chiu-liu-san nien Hu-pei Huang-p'i P'an-lung-ch'eng Shang tai yi-chih ti fa-chüeh," and *WW*, "P'an-lung-ch'eng Shang tai Erh-li-kang ch'i ti ch'ing-t'ung-ch'i"; Hui Hsien types from Kuo Pao-chün, Hsia Nai, et al., *Hui Hsien fa-chüeh pao-kao*; Cheng-chou

wooden objects, and pottery vessels constituted the furnishings of the graves. Twenty-two ritual vessels were found in Grave no. 1, and sixty-three bronze vessels, weapons and implements in no. 2. The latter also had three sacrificial victims, apparently placed on top of the burial chamber (fig. 79).

Altogether 159 bronze artifacts have been recovered from the P'an-lung-ch'eng site, including 18 implements, 51 weapons, 1 horse mask, and 68 ritual vessels.[29] They are in general thin and fragile. The four samples that have been analyzed contain respectively the following percentages of *copper*: 81.82, 88.68, 71.59, 70.76; *tin*: 8.41, 5.54, 3.92, 6.16; and *lead*: 6.78, 1.38, 24.45, and 21.76. From various parts of the site were found crucible fragments, copper ore, charcoal, and burned clay, suggesting that bronzes were not only locally cast but also locally smelted. The vessels were judged to be cast by the piece mold technique, although no piece molds have been reported. The two kinds of alloys produced bronzes of different colors: the alloy with the low lead content was greenish, and that with high lead was grayish. Insofar as the typology and decorative designs are concerned, the P'an-lung-ch'eng bronzes are virtually identical with the bronzes of Cheng-chou and Hui Hsien (fig. 80, 81).

Unquestionably, the P'an-lung-ch'eng site is of exceeding importance in Shang archaeology.[30] As the excavators pointed out, P'an-lung-ch'eng was almost an exact duplica of Cheng-chou, five hundred kilometers away. They had identical town wall construction techniques, palace construction techniques, burial customs, and bronze, jade and pottery technologies.[31] We might add that the pattern of settlement of P'an-lung-ch'eng is, again, a condensed copy of Cheng-chou, with a walled enclosure, a palace area inside at the northeastern corner, and residential and burial areas outside. But P'an-lung-ch'eng was much smaller, and its smallness brings the city's internal order into even sharper focus. The hierarchy of burials is clearly etched out by the three groups of graves. The large bronze ax reminds one of the royal symbols in An-yang (fig. 82). And the relative abundance of bronze implements is also noteworthy.

The Yangtze River, which is virtually on the southern doorstep of the P'an-lung-ch'eng site, may be looked at—on the basis of current evidence—as the southern boundary of the Shang civilization of the

29. *WW*, "P'an-lung-ch'eng Shang tai Erh-li-kang ch'i ti ch'ing-t'ung-ch'i" 盤龍城商代二里岡期的青銅器.

30. See an excellent summary and comments by Robert W. Bagley, "P'an-lung-ch'eng: A Shang City in Hupei."

31. *WW*, "P'an-lung-ch'eng yi-chiu-ch'i-ssu nien tu t'ien-yeh k'ao-ku chi yao" 盤龍城一九七四年度田野考古紀要, 14–15.

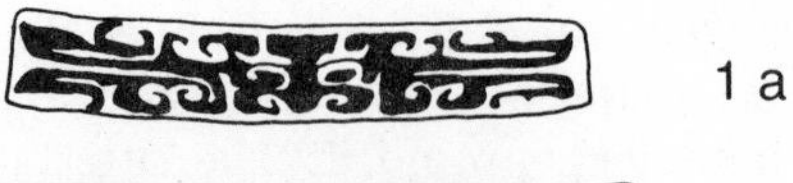

81. P'an-lung-ch'eng bronze decorative motifs (*1b–6b*) compared with similar motifs from Hui Hsien (*2a, 3a, 6a*) and Cheng-chou (*1a, 4a, 5a*) (sources same as in fig. 80).

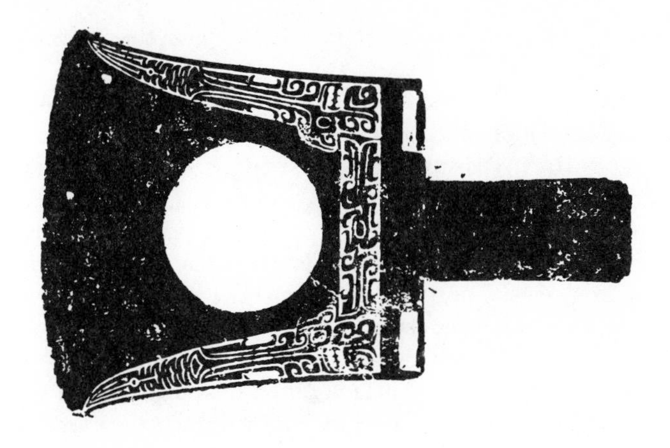

82. Large bronze ax found at the Shang site in P'an-lung-ch'eng (after *WW*, "P'an-lung-ch'eng Shang tai Erh-li-kang ch'i ti ch'ing-t'ung-ch'i," 33).

Erh-li-kang phase, strictly defined. South of the Yangtze the cultures contemporary with the Erh-li-kang Shang are not yet well known, but enough is known in Kiangsi for us to recognize a culture—or a series of cultures—with distinctive features, although there was in it also unmistakable evidence of very close ties with the Shang. This—a local culture with unmistakable ties with the Shang—is well illustrated by the Shang-period site near Wu-ch'eng, in the district of Ch'ing-chiang, Kiangsi. Here, in 1973, in an area almost 4 kilometers square were found scattered remains indicative of a Shang date and an intensive occupation. Excavations in 1973 and 1974 within and near an old earthen enclosure (Wu-ch'eng) at the center of the site disclosed a house floor, forty-eight storage pits, thirteen burials, and a pottery kiln. Among the more than five hundred individual artifacts that have been recovered were bronze weapons (*ko*-halberd, knife) and implements (ax); stone molds for weapons (knife, arrowhead) and implements (ax, adz, chisel); a bronze *chia*-tripod from one of the graves; stone implements (ax, stepped adz, chisel, knife, sickle), and weapons (*ko*-halberd, spearhead); pottery implements (knife, spindle-whorl, sinker, pottery anvil); and pottery. Among the pottery vessels the most common types are *li*-tripods, jars, *hsien*-steamers, *tou*, beakers with flared mouths, bowls, and the feet of tripods that are presumed to be *chia* and *chüeh*.[32] A number of pottery vessels and stone molds were carved with signs. Some artifacts bear multiple characters, one having as many as twelve. The characters show

32. *WW*, "Chiang-hsi Ch'ing-chiang Wu-ch'eng Shang tai yi-chih fa-chüeh chien pao" 江西清江吳城商代遺址發掘簡報.

some basic resemblance to Shang writing, but they cannot yet be deciphered.[33]

At the Wu-ch'eng site one can readily recognize many artifacts that resemble the Shang civilization of both Erh-li-kang and later phases. Some of the pottery vessels such as *li*-tripods, *tou*, and beakers recall similar types in the north. The single bronze vessel—flat-based *chia*—is the usual Erh-li-kang type. A few of the written characters are similar.[34] On the other hand, the site is distinctive in a number of local features: animal-mask motif on a vessel lid (collected on the ground) that was composed of thundercloud patterns; the extensive use of bands of small circles for pottery decoration; the wide use of the pottery knife; very extensive use of hard and glazed pottery; and the use of stone molds for bronze casting.[35] To these one may add the use of a writing system that had important differences from the contemporary writing of North China. In fact, the extensive use of hard (sometimes glazed) pottery with stamped geometric designs—similar to the stamped pottery in Cheng-chou, where it may be an intrusive element from the south—places the Wu-ch'eng site easily into a local cultural context, for the Neolithic culture characterized by geometric hard pottery has long been recognized as a southeastern coastal product[36] and, specifically, a native Kiangsi specialty.[37] It appears likely that this native culture and the Shang civilization sustained close and continued interaction across the Yangtze, and a number of cultural elements changed hands. From the south the glazed and the geometric pottery went north, and from the north certain pottery types and bronze ritual vessel types went south.[38]

WEST

The western extension of Shang civilization of the Erh-li-kang phase is the least known. The area of Honan west of Cheng-chou was the territory of the Erh-li-t'ou phase, heretofore believed to be Early

33. T'ang Lan 唐蘭, "Kuan-yü Chiang-hsi Wu-ch'eng wen-hua yi-chih yü wen-tzu ti ch'u-pu t'an-so" 關于江西吳城遺址與文字的初步探索.

34. But the reading of the Shang king name Shang Chia in one of the pottery pieces is not convincing; see Chao Feng 趙峯, "Ch'ing-chiang t'ao-wen chi ch'i so fan-ying ti Yin tai nung-yeh ho chi-ssu" 清江陶文及其所反映的殷代農業和祭祀.

35. *WW*, "Chiang-hsi Ch'ing-chiang Wu-ch'eng Shang tai yi-chih fa-chüeh chien pao" 江西清江吳城商代遺址發掘簡報, 58–59.

36. Tseng Chao-yüeh 曾昭燏 and Yin Huan-chang 尹煥章, "Ku-tai Chiang-su li-shih shang ti liang-ko wen-t'i" 古代江蘇歷史上的兩個問題, 15–16.

37. *WW*, "Chiang-hsi ti-ch'ü t'ao-tz'u-ch'i chi-ho-hsing p'ai-yin wen-yang tsung-shu" 江西地區陶瓷器幾何形拍印紋樣綜述.

38. For additional finds of bronze vessels of Erh-li-kang type, see *WW*, "Chin nien Chiang-hsi ch'u-t'u ti Shang tai ch'ing-t'ung-ch'i" 近年江西出土的商代青銅器.

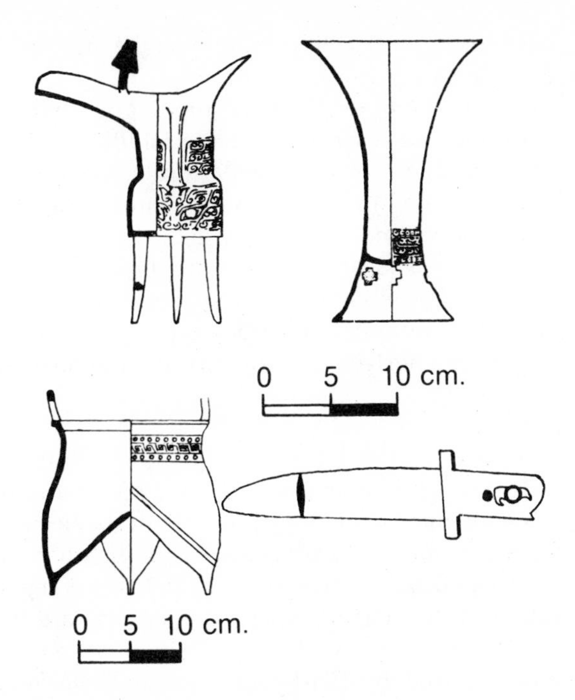

83. Bronze vessels from the Shang site at Ching-tang, Ch'i-shan (after *WW*, "Shan-hsi sheng Ch'i-shan hsien fa-hsien Shang tai t'ung-ch'i").

Shang but now increasingly regarded as Hsia. It will be discussed in detail later. Shang remains of the Erh-li-kang phase have not been clearly reported in this whole area. There are indications that Erh-li-kang-type remains have occurred in the T'ai-yüan area of central Shansi[39] and in Hsia Hsien in southern Shansi,[40] but details of these finds are not yet available. A group of pottery artifacts found in Fu-feng, deep in the Wei River valley in Shensi, contains pieces (of *li*, *tou*, and jar types) that are believed to resemble the Kao-ch'eng types and to data from predynastic Hsiao-t'an,[41] but this classification is by no means conclusive. But a group of bronze ritual vessels (fig. 83) found at Ching-tang 京當 village

39. *WW*, "Shan-hsi sheng shih nien lai ti wen-wu k'ao-ku hsin shou-hu" 山西省十年來的文物考古新收穫, 2.

40. A recent report of radiocarbon dates contains samples from Hsia Hsien that were labelled as Erh-li-kang type; see *WW*, "T'an-shih-ssu nien-tai ts'e-ting pao-kao, hsü yi" 碳十四年代測定報告, 續一.

41. *WW*, "Fu-feng Pai-chia-yao shui-k'u ch'u-t'u ti Shang Chou wen-hua" 扶風白家窰水庫出土的商周文化.

in Ch'i-shan, also in the Wei valley, convincingly indicates Shang cultural presence of the Late Erh-li-kang subphase.[42]

Further west, the outer limits of the Shang civilization of the Erh-li-kang phase did not reach beyond the middle Wei River valley. In the upper Wei and the T'ao River valleys of eastern Kansu the Ch'i-chia 齊家 culture prevailed in the end of the third millennium and the early centuries of the second millennium B.C., and after that the area was occupied by several local cultures with bronzes. These cultures have been well described elsewhere,[43] but it may be worth repeating here that the Ch'i-chia culture used copper implements and oracle bones at a slightly earlier time horizon than the Erh-li-kang Shang culture.

SUMMARY

Currently available archaeological evidence indicates that the Shang civilization of the Erh-li-kang phase is divisible into two subphases: Erh-li-kang proper and Late Erh-li-kang. (Erh-li-kang at Cheng-chou is usually divided into Lower and Upper Erh-li-kang strata. Both are here considered Erh-li-kang proper). The criteria are based on the typology and decorative styles of bronze ritual vessels. Erh-li-kang bronzes are characterized by flat-based *chia-* and *chüeh*-tripods with cylindrical bodies that do not form two parts and by decorative designs that are mostly styles I and II in the Loehr classification. Late Erh-li-kang bronzes include *chia-* and *chüeh*-tripods that may be slightly convex of base and may have a body divided into an upper and a lower part, and also more decorative patterns of Loehr's style III.

Erh-li-kang proper sites have a restricted area of distribution: Cheng-chou and Hui Hsien in the north and P'an-lung-ch'eng in the south, and if the Tientsin Museum *chüeh* did in fact come from Shang-ch'iu, then eastern Honan also. Late Erh-li-kang sites are found in a much wider area: Peking in the north, central Shantung in the east, the Huai River valley in the southeast, and the middle Wei River valley in the west. Beyond the Shang, the Lower Hsia-chia-tien culture fronted the Shang in the north, the geometric pottery culture neighbored the Shang across the Yangtze in the south, and in the west the Ch'i-chia and its descendant cultures existed side by side with the Shang in the upper Wei River valley. Within the Shang civilizational sphere thus outlined (fig. 84), there is much more Shang archaeology in the eastern parts than in the western. Both the Lower Hsia-chia-tien and the Ch'i-chia cultures

42. *WW*, "Shan-hsi sheng Ch'i-shan hsien fa-hsien Shang tai t'ung-ch'i" 陝西省岐山縣發現商代銅器

43. K. C. Chang, *The Archaeology of Ancient China*, pp. 195–199, 397–409.

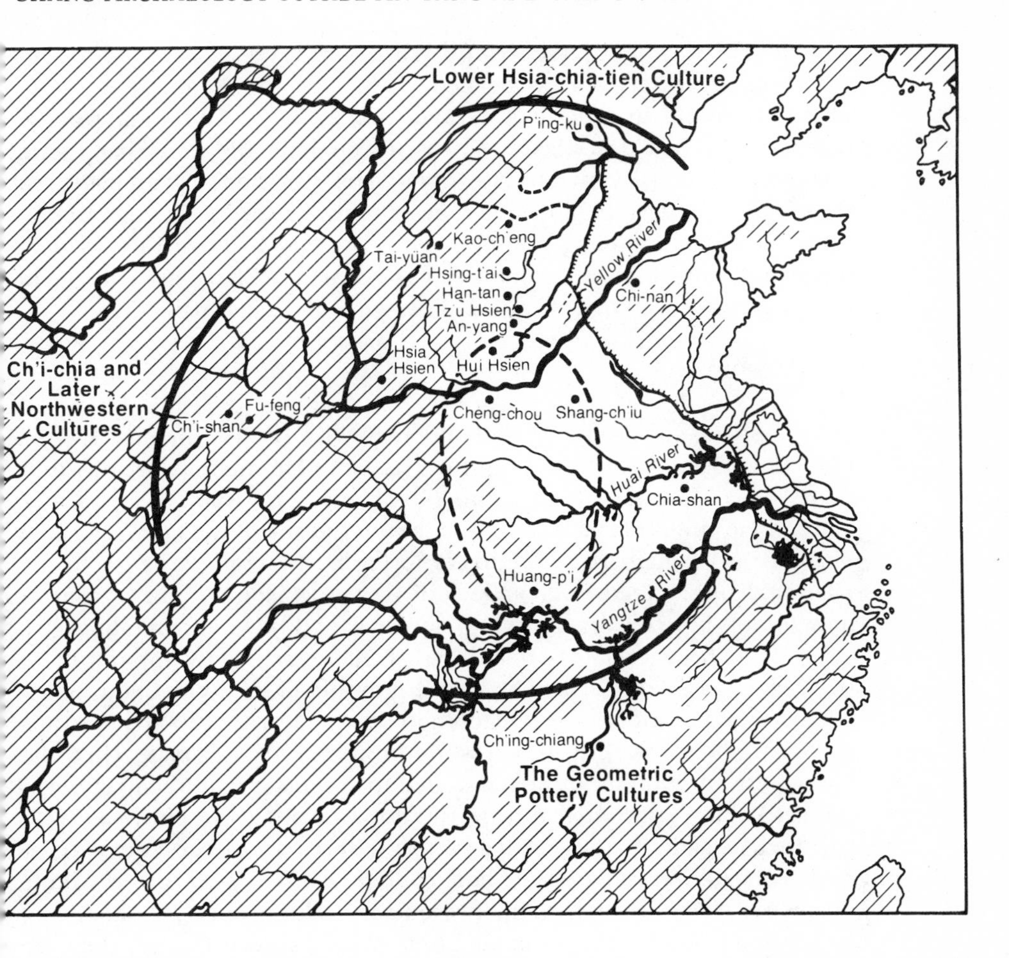

84. Distribution of Erh-li-kang phase sites (broken oval indicates approximate area of Erh-li-kang phase; the three solid arcs indicate approximate area of late Erh-li-kang sites; hatched areas represent highlands above 200 m.).

used copper implements, and the early use of copper or bronze in the south has always been regarded as a possibility.

2. *MAJOR SITES OF THE DYNASTIC AN-YANG PHASE*

As we stated before, we use the typological and decorative style of the bronzes in the Fu Hao tomb at Hsiao-t'un to mark the beginning of the dynastic period of the Shang civilization in An-yang. Looking beyond the greater capital area (of which An-yang was core), we find that bronze vessels and associated pottery of the dynastic An-yang phase are found in roughly the same area as in the Erh-li-kang phase that we have just described, and that throughout the area Shang sites increased in density in all directions. The situation in the southern frontier, however, is not quite as straightforward; the interaction between dynastic Shang and the south appears to have increased in tempo and intensity, but there is as yet a dearth of Shang settlements in the current archaeological record. This we will discuss presently.

NORTH

Shang sites roughly contemporary with Hsiao-t'un and Hsi-pei-kang have been identified along the T'ai-hang Mountains northward in Tz'u Hsien, Han-tan, Hsing-t'ai, Kao-ch'eng, Ling-shou,[44] and Ch'ü-yang.[45] Pao-ting, further north, was the alleged site of the famous "three Shang dynasty halberds".[46] Further to the north, from Peking[47] to the Luan and upper Liao river valleys of western Liaoning[48] have come a number of bronze vessels with emblems of known Shang lineages. These have been variously dated, but the consensus now appears to be that these were left during the very beginning of Western Chou, when northern Hopei and western Liaoning were the territory of the Marquis of Yen.[49] Since Late Erh-li-kang-style bronzes had already reached the Peking area, it would not be farfetched to speculate that Shang civilization in Peking continued during the dynastic An-yang phase as well, and that it made further inroads into the territory of the Lower Hsia-chia-tien culture. After the Chou conquest, Wu Wang placed Duke Chao in Pei Yen (North Yen), presumably taking over an old Shang territory and its Shang lineages. These bronzes, even though they are datable to the early part of Western Chou, are useful for indicating the Shang occupation in this area as well.

44. *KK*, "Ho-pei Ling-shou hsien Pei-chai-ts'un Shang tai yi-chih tiao-ch'a" 河北靈壽縣北宅村商代遺址調查.

45. An Chih-min 安志敏, "Ho-pei Ch'ü-yang tiao-ch'a chi" 河北曲陽調查記.

46. Lo Chen-yü 羅振玉, *Meng-wei-ts'ao-t'ang chi chin t'u* 夢郼草堂吉金圖, vol. 2, pp. 1–3.

47. *KK*, "Pei-ching fu-chin fa-hsien ti Hsi Chou nu-li hsün tsang mu" 北京附近發現的西周奴隸殉葬墓.

48. *WW*, "Je-ho Ling-yüan hsien Hai-tao-ying-tzu-ts'un fa-hsien ti ku-tai ch'ing-t'ung-ch'i" 熱河凌源縣海島營子村發現的古代青銅器; *KK*, "Liao-ning K'o-tso hsien Pei-tung-ts'un fa-hsien Yin tai ch'ing-t'ung-ch'i" 遼寧喀左縣北洞村發現殷代青銅器; *KK*, "Liao-ning K'o-tso hsien Pei-tung-ts'un ch'u-t'u ti Yin Chou ch'ing-t'ung-ch'i" 遼寧喀左縣北洞村出土的殷周青銅器.

49. Yen Wan 晏琬, "Pei-ching Liao-ning ch'u-t'u t'ung-ch'i yü Chou ch'u ti Yen" 北京遼寧出土銅器與周初的燕.

EAST

Bronze and pottery vessels of the types found at dynastic An-yang have long been known throughout Shantung,[50] but the most important archaeological find in the province must be said to be the large graves at Su-fu-t'un 蘇埠屯, in Yi-tu, in central Shantung, only about 70 kilometers from the sea. These graves have long been known for their bronze vessels; a group freshly plundered (in 1931) had been studied by Ch'i Yen-p'ei in 1936.[51] But it was not until 1965–66 that four of such large graves were excavated; only one has been reported on.[52] This, however, was a most impressive large grave (fig. 85): its pit was 15 meters long north-south, 10.7 meters wide east-west; it had four ramps, the southern one, 26 meters long, being the longest and the only ramp to reach the bottom of the pit, whereas the other ramps led only to the top of the second-level ledge. At the center of the grave was a cross-shaped wooden chamber, in which the coffin was originally placed over a waist-pit containing a sacrificial dog and a human victim. Elsewhere forty-seven other human victims and five other dogs were buried. A number of bronze vessels and weapons and jades were the grave furnishings, but most had long ago been plundered away. Almost four thousand cowrie shells were still left inside the chamber. On the strength of the size and shape, the number of human victims, and the discovery of two bronze axes, the excavators characterized this largest grave outside An-yang as one of a Shang lord, perhaps the king of the state of Po-ku 薄姑, a state allied with the Shang.[53]

SOUTH

In the Huai River valley, which as we saw has yielded good evidence of Shang occupation in the Erh-li-kang phase, there have been a number of late Shang sites that have been reported on, but the only site of any notable scale is the residential-plus-burial site at Ch'iu-wan

50. F. S. Drake, "Shang Dynasty Site at Li-ch'eng Wang-she-jen-chuang, Shantung"; *WW*, "Shan-tung Ch'ang-ch'ing ch'u-t'u ti ch'ing-t'ung-ch'i" 山東長清出土的青銅器; *WW*, "Shan-tung Ts'ang-shan hsien ch'u-t'u ch'ing-t'ung-ch'i" 山東蒼山縣出土青銅器; Ch'i Wen-t'ao 齊文濤, "Kai shu chin-nien lai Shan-tung ch'u-t'u ti Shang Chou ch'ing-t'ung-ch'i" 概述近年來山東出土的商周青銅器; *WW*, "Shan-tung Tsou hsien yu fa-hsien Shang tai t'ung-ch'i" 山東鄒縣又發現商代銅器; *KK*, "Shan-tung Hui-min hsien fa-hsien Shang tai ch'ing-t'ung-ch'i" 山東惠民縣發現商代青銅器.

51. Ch'i Yen-p'ei 祁延霈, "Shan-tung Yi-tu Su-fu-t'un ch'u-t'u t'ung-ch'i tiao-ch'a chi" 山東益都蘇埠屯出土銅器調查記.

52. *WW*, "Shan-tung Yi-tu Su-fu-t'un ti-yi-hao nu-li hsün-tsang mu" 山東益都蘇埠屯第一號奴隷殉葬墓.

53. Yin Chih-yi 殷之彝, "Shan-tung Yi-tu Su-fu-t'un mu-ti ho 'Ya Ch'ou' t'ung-ch'i" 山東益都蘇埠屯墓地和'亞醜'銅器.

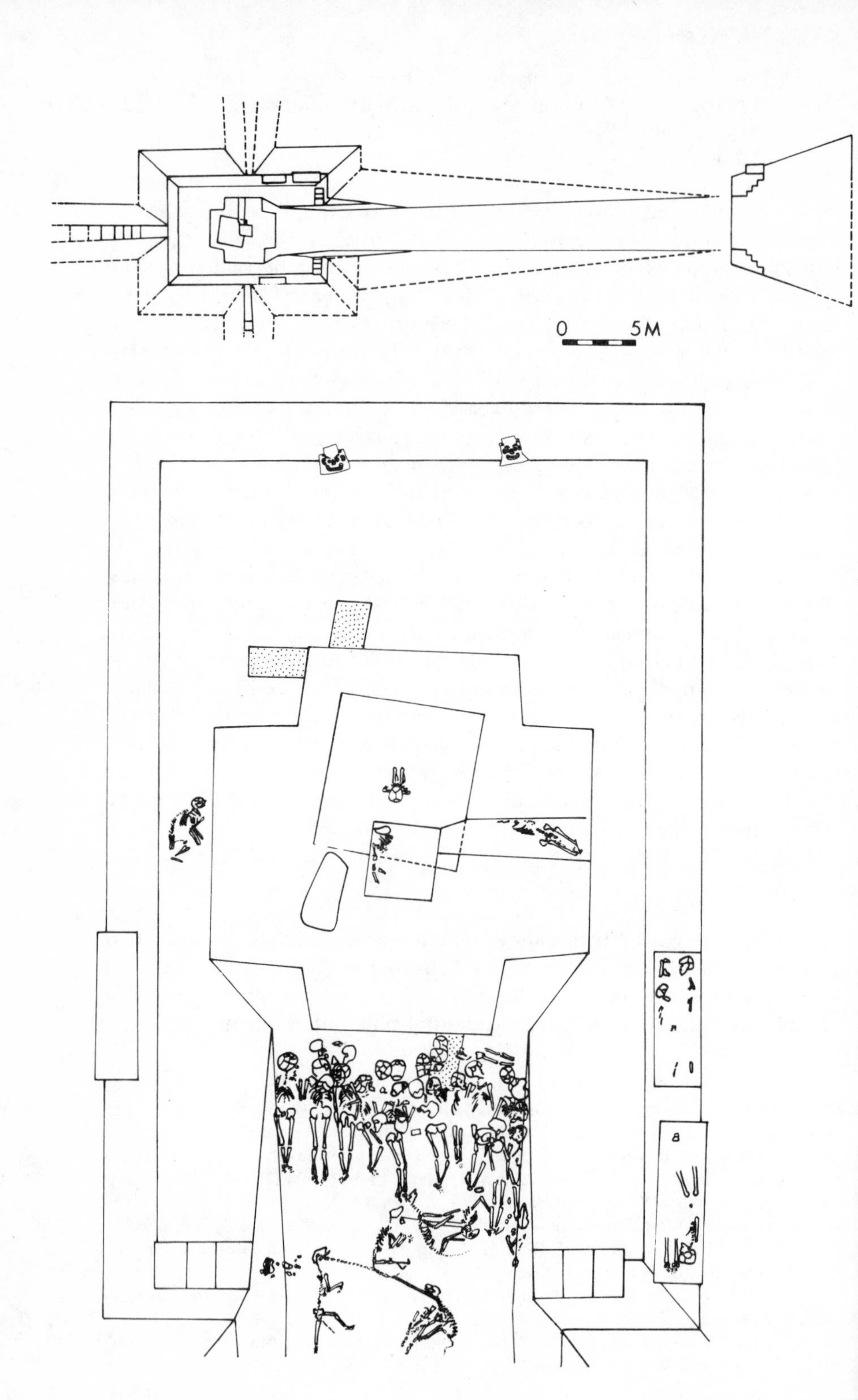

85. Shang tomb at Su-fu-t'un, Yi-tu, Shantung (after *WW*, "Shan-tung Yi-tu Su-fu-t'un ti-yi-hao nu-li hsün-tsang mu").

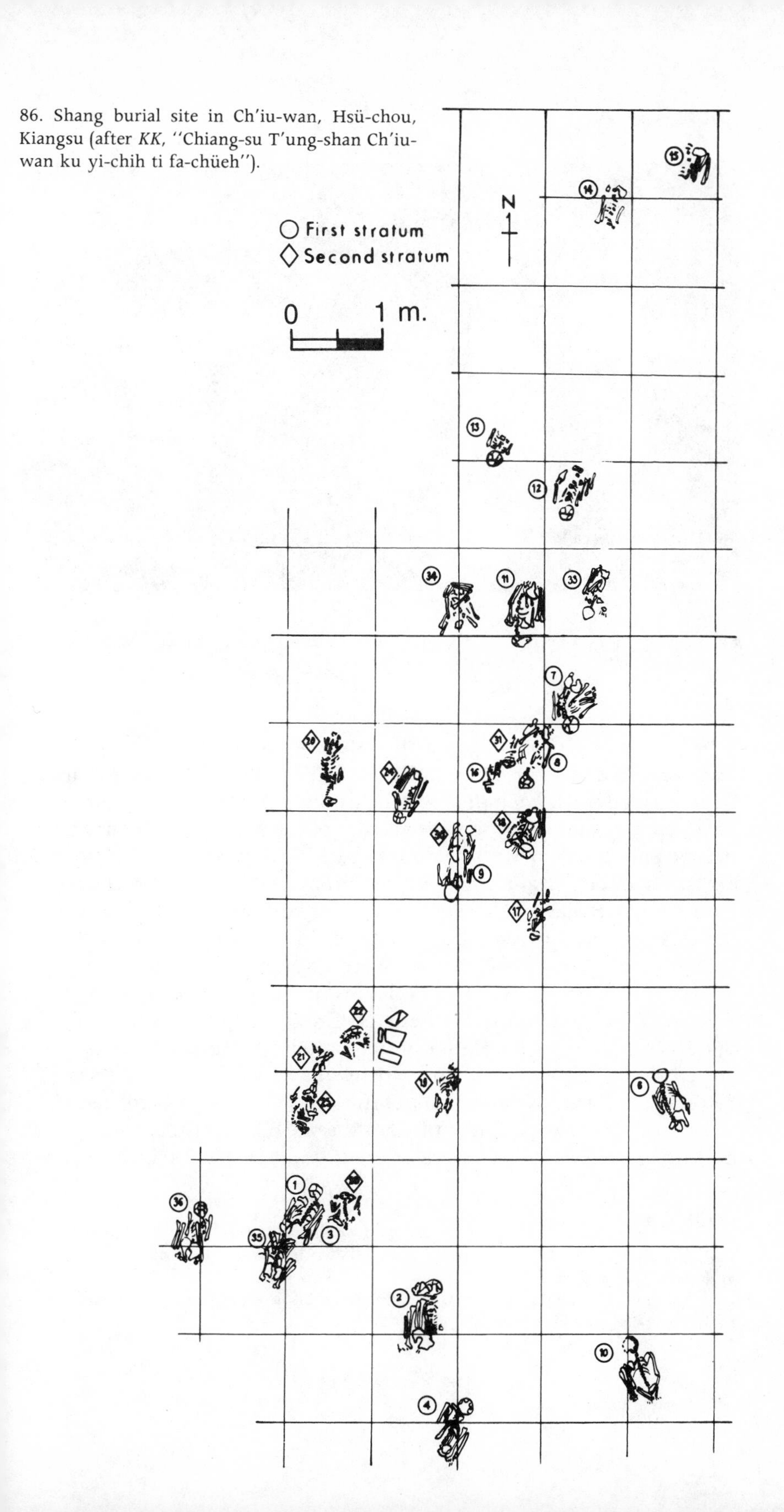

86. Shang burial site in Ch'iu-wan, Hsü-chou, Kiangsu (after *KK*, "Chiang-su T'ung-shan Ch'iu-wan ku yi-chih ti fa-chüeh").

87. Erected rocks at center of Shang burial site in Ch'iu-wan (after *KK*, "Chiang-su T'ung-shan Ch'iu-wan ku yi-chih ti fa-chüeh").

丘灣, north of Hsü-chou in northwestern Kiangsu, discovered in 1959 and excavated in 1959, 1960, and 1965.[54] From the residential area living floors (paved with *hang-t'u*), post holes, hearths, and storage pits were uncovered, yielding stone implements, pottery, a bronze knife, and a bronze chisel. The pottery includes characteristic late Yin hsü types in the site's upper stratum and earlier types underneath. Oracle bones, both shoulder blades and turtle shells, were found, and some contain hollows produced by chiseling. South of the dwelling region, within an area of about 75 square meters, were twenty human skeletons, two human skulls, and twelve dog skeletons (fig. 86). Four large rocks were erected at the center of the burial area (fig. 87), and the human and dog burials appeared to be placed around them. All of the humans were buried facing down, with knees bent and most with their arms tied behind their backs. No grave pits, coffins, or grave goods were identified. This burial area has been identified as the site of a *she*-ritual 社, in which human and dog sacrifices were offered,[55] and the area which included

54. *KK*, "1959 nien tung Hsü-chou ti-ch'ü k'ao-ku tiao-ch'a" 1959年冬徐州地區考古調查, 25; *KK*, "Chiang-su T'ung-shan Ch'iu-wan ku yi-chih ti fa-chüeh" 江蘇銅山丘灣古遺址的調查.

55. Yü Wei-ch'ao 俞偉超, "T'ung-shan Ch'iu-wan Shang tai she ssu yi-chi ti t'ui-ting" 銅山丘灣商代社祀遺迹的推定.

Hsü-chou is considered to be the location of the state of Ta-p'eng 大彭 or P'eng, a state that was alternatively an ally and an enemy of the Shang, according to both traditional texts and oracle records.[56]

To the south of Hsü-chou, the more southern parts of the Huai River valley and the Yangtze valley give only beginning hints of some late Shang settlement sites.[57] However, quite a number of bronze ritual vessels has been reported from this region, vessels typologically classified as late Shang but associated with little or no information on provenance. These include at least thirteen bronze vessels from Fu-nan, Anhwei;[58] at least two vessels from Fei-hsi, Anhwei;[59] a large bronze drum in Ch'ung-yang, southern Hupei;[60] at least ten bronze vessels (including the famous *fang ting* with human faces) from Ning-hsiang, Hunan;[61] an elephant *tsun* from Li-ling, Hunan;[62] at least one bronze vessel from Ch'ang-ning, Hunan;[63] a bronze *hsien* from Tu-ch'ang, Kiangsi;[64] and three bronze vessels and some weapons from P'eng Hsien, Szechwan.[65] These vessels undoubtedly indicate that late Shang civilization was a conspicuous presence throughout the middle Yangtze River valley, but that details of occupation can only be regarded as

56. Wang Yü-hsin 王宇信 and Ch'en Shao-ti 陳紹棣, "Kuan-yü Chiang-su T'ung-shan Ch'iu-wan Shang tai chi-ssu yi-chih" 關于江蘇銅山丘灣商代祭祀遺址.

57. Chou Shih-jung 周世榮, "Hu-nan Shih-men hsien Tsao-shih fa-hsien Shang Yin yi-chih" 湖南石門縣皂市發現商殷遺址; *KK*, "An-hui Han-shan hsien Sun-chia-kang Shang tai yi-chih tiao-ch'a yü shih chüeh" 安徽含山縣孫家崗商代遺址調查與試掘.

58. Ko Chieh-p'ing 葛介屏, "An-hui Fu-nan fa-hsien Yin Shang shih-tai ti ch'ing-t'ung-ch'i" 安徽阜南發現殷商時期的青銅器; Shih Chih-lien 石志廉, "T'an-t'an lung hu tsun ti chi-ko wen-t'i" 談談龍虎尊的幾個問題.

59. Foreign Language Press, *Historic Relics Unearthed in New China*, no. 40; Committee of the Exhibition of Archaeological Finds in the People's Republic of China, *The Exhibition of Archaeological Finds in the People's Republic of China*, no. 90.

60. *WW*, "Hu-pei Ch'ung-yang ch'u-t'u yi-chien t'ung ku" 湖北崇陽出土一件銅鼓.

61. Kao Chih-hsi 高至喜, "Shang tai jen mien fang ting" 商代人面方鼎; Kao Chih-hsi 高至喜, "Hu-nan Ning-hsiang Huang-ts'ai fa-hsien Shang tai t'ung-ch'i ho yi-chih" 湖南寧鄉黃材發現商代銅器和遺址.

62. Hsiung Ch'uan-hsin 熊傳新, "Hu-nan Li-ling fa-hsien Shang tai t'ung hsiang tsun" 湖南醴陵發現商代銅象尊.

63. Committee of the Exhibition of Archaeological Finds in the People's Republic of China, *op. cit.*, no. 91.

64. T'ang Ch'ang-p'u 唐昌朴, "Chiang-hsi Tu-ch'ang ch'u-t'u Shang tai t'ung-ch'i" 江西都昌出土商代銅器; *WW*, "Chin nien Chiang-hsi ch'u-t'u ti Shang tai ch'ing-t'ung-ch'i" 近年江西出土的商代青銅器, 60.

65. Wang Chia-yu 王家祐, "Chi Ssu-ch'uan P'eng hsien Chu-wa-chieh ch'u-t'u ti t'ung-ch'i" 記四川彭縣竹瓦街出土的銅器; Hsü Chung-shu 徐中舒, "Ssu-ch'uan P'eng hsien Meng-yang-chen ch'u-t'u ti Yin tai erh chih" 四川彭縣濛陽鎮出土的殷代二觶.

being unknown for lack of archaeological sites of settlements, cemeteries, or bronze workshops where such bronzes were produced. One sees vessel types and decorative styles similar to, or even identical with, their An-yang counterparts, but at the same time there are distinctively southern features. Virginia Kane sees in the Fu-nan bronzes, for example, a mixture of both early and late features on the An-yang scale, "[betraying] the hand of a regional artist familiar perhaps with early and later examples of this vessel-type [*tsun*] but not aware of the correct combination of all of its elements and therefore oblivious to the inconsistencies in his designs."[66] She also sees the Hunan bronzes to be "based on imported An-yang prototypes, but also at times of fearlessly inventive design."[67] Her conclusion, with which one can largely agree, was that these Anhwei and Hunan bronze vessels of the late Shang period included products of local bronze industries and that, although they were based on An-yang prototypes, they incorporated designs original in the south.

WEST

Archaeological data in the west from cultures contemporaneous with the dynastic period in An-yang consist mainly of material from two groups of very important sites. The first group of data includes a number of bronze vessel and weapon assemblages (some found in a burial context) in central and northwestern parts of Shansi and in an adjoining region in Shensi.[68] Many of the artifacts bear emblems that have appeared on bronzes closer to the An-yang area. The second comprises the newly excavated "palaces" of western Chou (from before the conquest) at

66. "The Independent Bronze Industries in the South of China Contemporary with the Shang and Western Chou Dynasties," 80.

67. *Ibid.*, 85.

68. *WW*, "Shan-hsi Shih-lou hsien Erh-lang-p'o ch'u-t'u Shang Chou t'ung-ch'i" 山西石樓縣二郎坡出土商周銅器; *WW*, "Shih-lou hsien fa-hsien ku-tai t'ung-ch'i" 石樓縣發現古代銅器; Hsieh Ch'ing-shan 謝青山 and Yang Shao-shun 楊紹舜, "Shan-hsi Lü-liang hsien Shih-lou chen yu fa-hsien t'ung-ch'i" 山西呂梁縣石樓鎮又發現銅器; Kuo Yung 郭勇, "Shih-lou Hou-lan-chia-kou fa-hsien Shang tai ch'ing-t'ung-ch'i chien pao" 石樓後蘭家溝發現商代青銅器簡報; *KK*, "Shan-hsi Shih-lou Yi-tieh fa-hsien Shang tai t'ung-ch'i" 山西石樓義牒發現商代銅器; *WW*, "Shan-hsi Shih-lou Yi-tieh Hui-p'ing fa-hsien Shang tai ping-ch'i" 山西石樓義牒會坪發現商代兵器; *WW*, "Shan-hsi Shih-lou hsin cheng-chi tao ti chi-chien Shang tai ch'ing-t'ung-ch'i" 山西石樓新徵集到的幾件商代青銅器; Shen Chen-chung 沈振中, "Hsin hsien Lien-ssu-kou ch'u-t'u ti ch'ing-t'ung-ch'i" 忻縣連寺溝出土的青銅器; Wu Chen-lu 吳振彔, "Pao-te hsien hsin fa-hsien ti Yin tai ch'ing-t'ung-ch'i" 保德縣新發現的殷代青銅器; *WW*, "Shan-hsi Sui-te Yen-t'ou-ts'un fa-hsien yi-p'i chiao-ts'ang Shang tai t'ung-ch'i" 陝西綏德墕頭村發現一批窖藏商代銅器.

Ching-tang village in Ch'i-shan, central Shensi. Although scientific reports of the latter are not yet available, the preliminary news dispatch contained information important enough to warrant a full translation:

> Chou Yüan 周原 [The Plains of the Chou] is situated in the western portions of Kuan Chung in Shensi, between Ch'i Mountain in the north and the Wei River in the south, and is [generally regarded as being] the original homeland of the Chou dynasty. The Chou Yüan archaeological district coincides with the capital area of the Chou when they were in the Chou Yüan (including the present Fa-men village and Huang-tui village in Fu-feng Hsien and the Ching-tang village in Ch'i-shan Hsien). A group of oracle bones was recovered from a storage area in a house on the western side of the First Group of the Palace-Temple Compound at Feng-ch'u 鳳雛 in the Ching-tang village.
>
> This valuable lot of oracle bones numbered more than fifteen thousand pieces, including more than 14,800 pieces of turtle shells and more than 120 pieces of shoulder blades. A part of the oracle turtle shells has been cleaned and studied, and among these 127 pieces were found to be inscribed. A preliminary study has recognized divination records pertaining to ritual offerings, rituals to inform ancestors, comings and goings, hunting, war, harvest, and other items. One inscribed turtle shell piece recorded the ritual performed by Chou Wen Wang for Shang Ti Yi. Another piece mentioned the Shang king's visit in Shensi. Other pieces mentioned "a hunt by the king of Yin," "offerings to Wen Wu Ti Yi" 文武帝乙, "Ch'eng T'ang" 成湯, "T'ai Chia" 太甲, and the "Po of Chou Fang." These inscriptions positively established that these buildings were dated to Chou Wen Wang, and they indicate that Western Chou was a subordinate state of the Shang before the Wu Wang conquest.[69]

This find has confirmed the information about the Chou available from both ancient texts and from the oracle bone inscriptions from An-yang (see chapter 4). We await the scientific publication of this extremely important discovery with keen interest.[70]

69. Hsin Hua She dispatch from Sian; see *Mei-chou Hua-ch'iao Jih-pao* 美洲華僑日報, New York City, 1 November 1977.

70. In a recent batch of radiocarbon dates published by the Carbon-14 Laboratory of Peking University (*WW*, "T'an-shih-ssu ts'e-ting nien-tai pao-kao, hsü yi" 碳十四測定年代報告, 續一), there are three new dates on samples from Feng-ch'u 鳳

3. *GENERAL DISCUSSION*

Virtually the whole of the archaeological material described and discussed in this and the previous chapters has been made available since 1950. Up to 1950, the Shang civilization was perceived only in its An-yang form, which is now known to be its last stages. New material brought to light in the last twenty-eight years, both in An-yang and elsewhere, has not only given us a good sequence of cultural development that led to the An-yang form but also a larger picture of the civilization and its contemporaries. But the picture is far from complete. One of the most important lessons we should have learned from the new archaeological work in China in the last three decades is, I believe, the old adage that facts are stranger than fiction. Many of our previous hypotheses concerning Shang development have crumbled in the face of new data. What is wrong with "dataism" (prolegomena, section 5) is never data per se. Dataism means data for data's sake, but data is surely not unimportant for historical understanding.

With the above as a cautionary note, let us see where we stand with regard to Shang archaeology and its contribution to Shang historiography. In this volume we recognize mainly two stages of Shang civilizational development: Erh-li-kang and dynastic An-yang. There are a good many sites that appear to be earlier than the dynastic period in An-yang but later than the classical Erh-li-kang site (divisable itself into lower and upper subphases) in Cheng-chou. These we classify as the late Erh-li-kang subphase so as to make clear that they are earlier than dynastic An-yang, using the Fu Hao tomb as the marker of the beginning of the latter phase. Thus, the following relative chronology is arrived at:

Dynastic An-yang (type site: dynastic An-yang)
Late Erh-li-kang (predynastic Shang, An-yang)
Erh-li-kang (Erh-li-kang, Cheng-chou)

The known distribution of these three phases and subphases is as

---

雛, Ching-tang 京當 village, Ch'i-shan 岐山. These are (based on 5730 ± 40 half-life):

BK 77011	1080 ± 90 B.C.	calibrated to 1210 ± 150
BK 76018	1040 ± 90 B.C.	1180 ± 150
BK 77012	890 ± 110 B.C.	1000 ± 170

The calibration was achieved according to the tables of P. E. Damon, C. W. Ferguson, A. Long, and E. I. Wallick, "Dendrochronologic Calibration of the Radiocarbon Time Scale."

follows: Erh-li-kang Shang is now known only in central Honan and northern Hupei (and presumably the intervening region) and possibly eastern Honan. By late Erh-li-kang time Shang civilization had reached its approximate maximum area: from Peking in the north to the Huai River and lower Hanshui in the south, and from Shantung in the east to possibly Shansi and eastern Shensi in the west. The culture contemporary to it to the north was the Lower Hsia-chia-tien culture, to the south was the culture with Geometric Stamped Pottery, and to the west was Ch'i-chia culture and its descendants. The core of the civilization filled approximately the same space in its dynastic An-yang phase, but in the north it made slight inroads into the Lower Hsia-chia-tien territory, in the south it brought about a large number of local Shang styles south of the Yangtze, and in the west it expanded significantly in the area of central and northwestern Shansi (fig. 88).

Since this distributional picture is based on data that have been gathered during a period of less than thirty years, in assessing its significance we should be well advised to stress what is rather than what is not. The first significant result of recent studies is the delineation of the areal expanse of the Shang civilization in two or all three of its phases and subphases. This offers powerful support to the classification of Erh-li-kang as Shang, since the classification of dynastic An-yang as Shang is unquestionable. The second point is that the Shang underwent considerable expansion in a later stage, but that that expansion was highlighted by greater density of sites and intensity of interaction rather than absolute areal enlargement.

Thirdly, comparing this areal scope of archaeological sites bearing a Shang label (as against archaeological assemblages on which a different cultural label must be conferred, such as Hsia-chia-tien, Geometric, and Ch'i-chia) with the areal distribution of states and Shang lords discussed in chapter 4, we find that most if not all the allied or antagonistic political units mentioned in the oracle records from An-yang are confined within the sphere of archaeological Shang civilization. If we transpose the archaeological spatial delineation onto the state maps prepared by Shima Kunio, we find that those states in the An-yang oracle records that are not within the areal scope of the archaeological Shang civilization are rather the exception than the rule. It appears that the Shang state interacted with people—in friendship or in war—only, or at least primarily, at their own developmental levels. This apparent fact carries some interesting implications, to which we will return in the next chapter.

Fourthly, some interesting comparisons can be made between the Shang sites of the Erh-li-kang phase and those of the dynastic An-yang phase. In the earlier phase Shang civilization had a sure

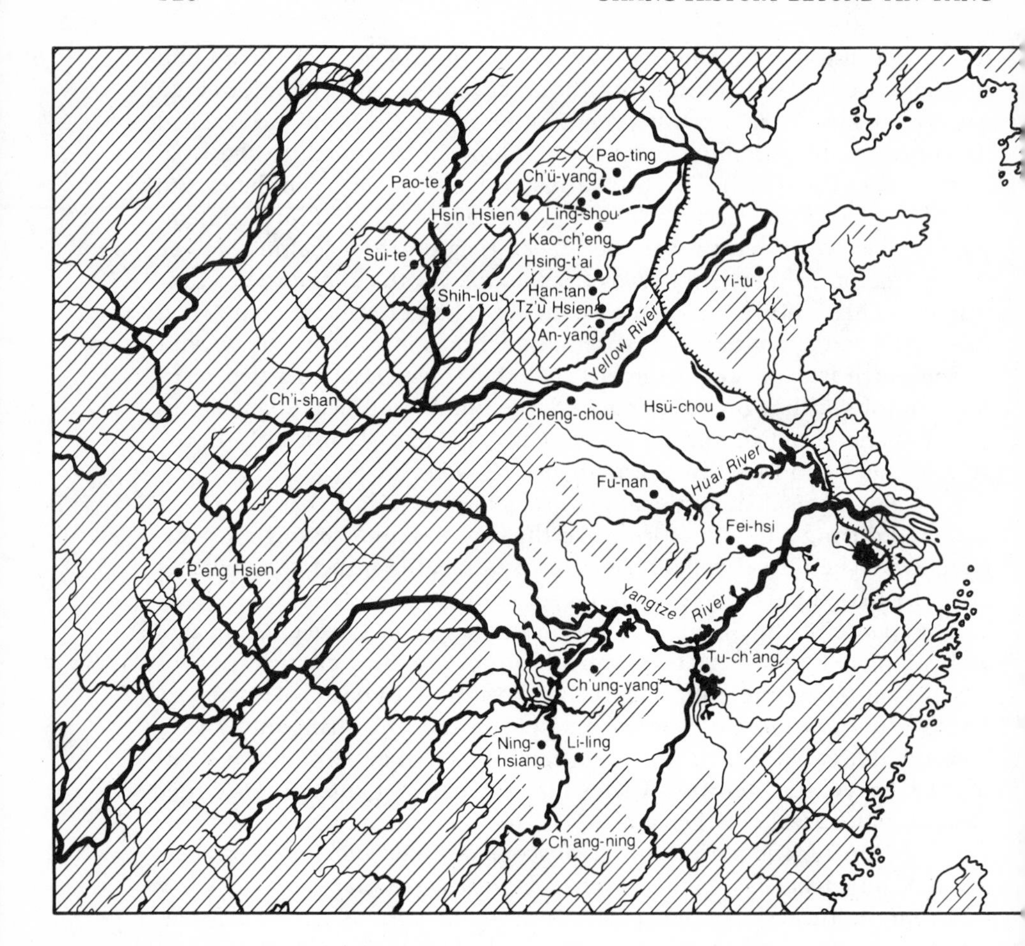

88. Distribution of archaeological sites of the dynastic An-yang phase (the hatched areas represent highlands above 200 m.).

presence in the Yangtze valley in the P'an-lung-ch'eng site, where the culture was a virtual carbon copy of Cheng-chou. In the later phase, there was more of Shang south of the Yangtze but there the Shang was of a more creative variety, and in the meantime the Shang made significant inroads into northern Shansi. Robert Bagley sees "the rise of [the] local centers" as an event that coincided "with the decline of direct Shang authority. In the south this decline is evidently reflected in the virtual abandonment of P'an-lung-ch'eng at about the same time that the capital was removed to the north, from Chengchou to Anyang. Numerous references in oracle bone inscriptions of the Wu Ting period to that king's campaigns in the Han River valley of Hupei show that the area was no longer a secure possession of the Anyang kings, and there is so far at least correspondingly little archaeological evidence of Anyang period sites in Hupei." Thus, he suggests that "an early expansion of dynastic power stimulated the rise of regional bronze-using societies, these in turn forcing a retrenchment of the dynasty around the beginning of the Anyang period."[71]

Attractive as this hypothesis may appear, the postulated retrenchment is based on the current lack of An-yang period sites in Hupei, and we may be well advised to have alternative hypotheses prepared in the eventuality of new archaeological finds. One alternative view may see the rise of the local styles south of Yangtze as evidence of increasing or increased interaction with cultures with regionally varied substrata in the south, thus accounting for both the greater quantity of Shang bronzes and the greater diversity of their styles. Another alternative hypothesis may see some outlying Shang settlements as colonists with special missions. The abandonment of P'an-lung-ch'eng coincided in time not only with the removal of the Shang capital from Cheng-chou to An-yang (after short intermediate stays elsewhere) but also with the opening of southern Shansi, another great copper and tin source, with a salt marsh as well. The rarity in the oracle inscriptions of war records from the southern front during the Wu Ting period and the apparent use of the south as a major source of precious goods (see chapter 4) suggest that the Shang's relations with the south were rather secure. Therefore, these alternative explanations demand our closest attention as Shang archaeology proceeds. They even hint at some possible explanations for the removal of the capital itself from a more southerly location to a more northerly location in An-yang.

71. "P'an-lung-ch'eng: A Shang City in Hupei," 212.

7 General Issues Concerning the Shang Civilization

Up to now we have presented a history of Shang culture and society based upon the evidence at An-yang and elsewhere. In this final chapter we will discuss the remaining issues of the Shang as a whole—the data for an absolute chronology of their development and their physical anthropology and language—and then the whole matter of their origins.

1. *EVIDENCE FOR AN ABSOLUTE CHRONOLOGY*

It was made clear in the prolegomena that textual sources are not sufficient to provide a firm absolute chronology of Chinese history prior to 841 B.C. The archaeological—including epigraphical—evidence from several directions provides a basis for relative dating of styles, assemblages, and institutional changes. Table 4 summarizes some of the major dated segments. At this time, this is where we should perhaps leave it, since scientific data are not as yet precise enough to enable us to resolve the uncertainties found in the texts. But let us review them just to see where we stand.

Two categories of scientific data relate to the absolute chronology of the Shang civilization. The first consists of radiocarbon dates at Shang sites, and the second refers to the records of lunar and solar eclipses in the oracle bone inscriptions.

Only five radiocarbon dates are available from Shang sites: two of them from Erh-li-kang Cheng-chou, one from a late Erh-li-kang site, and two from dynastic An-yang.[1] These are as follows (calibrated according to tree-ring dates):

1. See appendix for details of the dates.

TABLE 4 Relative Chronology of the Shang Civilization

Archaeological Phases	*Kings' Reigns*	*Tung I*	*Tung II*	*Pottery*	*Bronze Style*
	Ti Hsin				
	Ti Yi	5	New	Yin Hsü 4	
	Wen Wu Ting	4	Old		
	Wu Yi				
Dynastic	K'ang Ting			Yin Hsü 3	IV, V
	Lin Hsin	3			
An-yang	Tsu Chia	2	New	Yin Hsü 2	
	Tsu Keng				
	Wu Ting	1	Old		
	P'an Keng—Hsiao Yi			Yin Hsü 1	
Late Erh-li-kang					I, II, III
Erh-li-kang				Upper Erh-li-kang	I, II, III (rare)
				Lower Erh-li-kang	

Erh-li-kang		
Cheng-chou (ZK-178)	1590 ± 160	B.C.
Cheng-chou (ZK-177)	1560 ± 160	
Late Erh-li-kang		
Kao-ch'eng (BK-75007)	1500 ± 170	
Dynastic An-yang		
Hsiao-t'un (ZK-86)	1280 ± 150	
Wu-kuan-ts'un tomb (ZK-5)	1210 ± 160	

The An-yang dates are too few to be of any decisive value, but the three Erh-li-kang dates are highly significant. They are internally consistent and they cluster between 1500 and 1600 B.C., and none can be later than 1330 B.C. Since the latest Kao-ch'eng date is near the end of the period of Shang before P'an Keng's move to An-yang, 1300 B.C. looks like a probable latest limit for the establishment of An-yang as the last capital of the dynasty. If Cheng-chou was indeed Ao, then the founding of the dynasty under T'ang should be considerably earlier than the earliest of the Erh-li-kang sites. In other words, the segment of Shang history from Chung Ting (who moved the capital to Ao) to P'an Keng cannot—according to the very small number of radiocarbon dates—be later than 1300–1600 and could be significantly earlier, which would bring the founding of the dynasty by T'ang—nine reigns earlier—to before 1700 B.C.

For the period from P'an Keng to Ti Hsin, only two dates are currently available. They may tend to support the "longer" chronology of Tung Tso-pin more than the "shorter" chronology of Ch'en Meng-chia, as observed by Noel Barnard,[2] but more dates are obviously needed before any convincing direction is pointed at. On the other hand, in the oracle bone inscriptions dated (by the relative chronological method) to King Wu Ting's reign, there are no fewer than five references to lunar eclipses. They are as follows:

1. *Day Jen-Shen (9) Lunar Eclipse*
   Hsün. Jen-Shen, evening-night, the moon had eclipse.[3]
2. *Day Kuei-Wei (20) Lunar Eclipse*
   [On day Kuei-Wei] (divined). Cheng inquired: The ensuing day Chia-Shen gives sun? That evening-night, the moon eclipsed. [On day] Chia ( ), it didn't rain.[4]
3. *Day Yi-Yu (22) Lunar Eclipse*
   [On day] Kuei-Wei, divined. Cheng inquired: No ill fortune in the ensuing *hsün*? Three days later, on evening-night of Yi-Yu, the moon eclipsed—[so it was] heard. In the eighth moon.[5]
4. *Day Chia-Wu (31) Lunar Eclipse*
   (On day [Chi-] Ch'ou, divined. Pin inquired: The ensuing Yi [-Wei] offer wine and millet to Tsu Yi? [The king] made the prognostication and stated: "There will be misfortune: [There will not] be rain." Six days later, in the evening-night of day [Chia-] Wu, the moon eclipsed.[6]
5. *Day Keng-Shen (57) Lunar Eclipse*
   [Day] Kuei-Ch'ou, divined. Inquired: No ill fortune in the ensuing *hsün*? The king made the prognostication and said, "There will be misfortune." Seven days later, Chi-Wei, *yin*. Keng-Shen, the moon eclipsed.

2. *The First Radiocarbon Dates from China*, p. 30.

3. Wang Hsiang 王襄, *Fu-shih Yin ch'i cheng wen* 簠室殷契徵文, no. 2.

4. Chang Ping-ch'üan 張秉權, "P'u-tz'u kuei-wei yüeh-shih ti hsin cheng-chü" 卜辭癸未月食的新証據.

5. Tung Tso-pin 董作賓, "P'u-tz'u chung pa yüeh yi-yu yüeh-shih k'ao" 卜辭中八月乙酉月食考; Yen Yi-p'ing 嚴一萍, "Pa-yüeh yi-yu yüeh-shih fu chia ti p'in-ho yü k'ao-cheng ti ching-kuo" 八月乙酉月食腹甲的拚合與考証的經過.

6. Tung Tso-pin 董作賓, *Yin hsü wen-tzu Yi pien* 殷虛文字乙編, no. 3317.

Day Kuei-Hai, divined. Inquired: No ill fortune in the ensuing *hsün*?

Day Kuei-Yu, divined. Inquired: No ill fortune in the ensuing *hsün*?

Day Kuei-Wei, divined. Cheng inquired: No ill fortune in the ensuing *hsün*? The king made the prognostication and stated, "There will be misfortune." Three days later, day Yi-Yu, evening-night, *yin*. Day Ping-Wu, indeed came, entered into the teeth.

The thirteenth month.[7]

The last item is subject to differing interpretations with regard to the day of the eclipse because of different interpretations of the word *yin* 垔. Tung Tso-pin understood it to mean the performance of a ceremony; he put a period following it, which makes the day-sign before the phrase "the moon eclipsed," namely, Keng-Shen, the day of the eclipse.[8] Homer Dubs, however, interprets it to mean "continuing into," which, together with his belief that the Shang day began and ended at midnight (the "Roman" day), would make the eclipse take place on the day Chi-Wei (Day 56), continuing into day Keng-Shen (Day 57).[9] Tung, of course, believed that the Shang day was "Babylonian," i.e., beginning and ending at daybreak.[10] On the basis of consistency of usage as well as a recent palaeographic study of the word *yin*,[11] I am inclined toward the Babylonian interpretation, namely, that each day-sign covered the period of a day from daybreak to sundown and a night from sundown to daybreak. But let us not take sides for the time being and look at the evidence both ways to see if it makes a difference.

The five lunar eclipse records contain the following "hard" information: lunar eclipses were seen (and heard about) by the Shang in An-yang on the following five days:

9—Jen-Shen
20—Kuei-Wei

7. Fang Fa-lien 方法歛, *K'u Fang erh shih ts'ang chia-ku p'u-tz'u* 庫方二氏藏甲骨卜辭, no. 1595. See also Fang Fa-lien 方法歛, *Chin-chang so ts'ang chia-ku p'u tz'u* 金璋所藏甲骨卜辭, no. 594.

8. "Yin tai yüeh-shih k'ao" 殷代月食考, 140–142.

9. "The date of the Shang Period"; "The Date of the Shang Period—A Postscript."

10. "On the Method of Recording the 'Day' in the Yin Dynasty."

11. Lung Yü-ch'un 龍宇純, "Shih chia ku wen 'yin' tzu chien chieh hsi tsun" 釋甲骨文𡆥字兼解犧尊.

22—Yi-Yu (This day was in the eighth moon)
31—Chia-Wu
56—Chi-Wei
or (This day was in the thirteenth moon)
57—Keng-Shen

Since lunar eclipses that were visible in the An-yang area during the second half of the second millennium B.C. are astronomical events that can be scientifically calculated, our job is to match the above five lunar eclipses against the days and months in which eclipses did in fact occur. Such occurrences that were visible in North China between 1500 and 1000 B.C. can in fact be found in a "canon" provided by astronomers, such as the one first worked out by Homer Dubs and later expanded and corrected by Liu Pao-lin.[12]

But before we undertake to check our list above against Liu's canon, two or three assumptions must be stated. First, we assume that the use of the *kan-chih* cyclical signs has been continuous since the days of the Shang, an assumption that is necessary if we are to give every *kan-chih* day a Julian calendrical value. Second, we assume that the Shang system of tying lunar months to the solar year is similar to the Julian calendar so that the eighth moon in the oracle record corresponded to July, August, or September, and that the thirteenth (intercalary) moon corresponded to perhaps November, December, or January.[13]

Assuming the above to be true, and assuming, further, that the records were themselves accurate, we may now proceed to look for the five lunar records in Liu's canon. All five must be within a period of approximately 59 years (Wu Ting's traditional length of reign). In the following are two tables, the first (table 5) recording the years and months of all lunar eclipses that, according to the canon, occurred on the twelve-hour dark period following the cyclical day in question, and the second (table 6) the same information for the second half of the night preceding the day in question and the first half of the night following the day in question. For example, under Day 9 in the first (Babylonian) table (table 5) we put down all eclipses that occurred in the evening of Day 9 in the canon and all those that occurred in the early morning hours (midnight to daybreak) of Day 10 in the canon. But in the second (Roman) table (table 6), we list all occurrences under

12. Homer H. Dubs, "A Canon of Lunar Eclipses for Anyang and China, -1400 to -1000"; Liu Pao-lin 劉寶林, "Kung-yüan ch'ien 1500 nien chih Kung-yüan ch'ien 1000 nien yüeh-shih piao" 公元前1500年至公元前1000年月食表.

13. Tung Tso-pin 董作賓, *Yin li p'u* 殷曆譜.

TABLE 5 Years B.C. of the Occurrence of Five Shang Lunar Eclipses according to the Babylonian Day (Daybreak to Daybreak)

Day 9	*Day 20*	*Day 22* (*8th moon*)	*Day 31*	*Day 57* (*13th moon*)
–1379.8				
	–1376.12			
				–1356.5
				–1310.11
–1281.11				
		–1278.9		
	–1277.2			
				–1263.5
				–1258.8
	–1231.8			
			–1228.12	
		–1226.5		
				–1217.11
				–1211.2
	–1200.7			
			–1197.11	
–1188.10				
	–1184.2			
–1182.1		–1180.11		
	–1179.5			

TABLE 6 Years B.C. of the Occurrence of the Five Shang Lunar Eclipses According to the Roman Day (Midnight to Midnight)

Day 9	*Day 20*	*Day 22* (*8th moon*)	*Day 31*	*Day 56–57* (*13th moon*)
	–1376.12			
			–1367.6	
–1358.6				
		–1345.10		
	–1324.8			
			–1321.12	
–1306.3				
		–1303.1		
	–1231.8			
	–1226.11	–1226.5		
		–1205.4		
	–1200.7			
			–1197.11	
				–1191.12
–1188.10				
	–1184.2			
		–1180.11		
	–1179.5			

Day 9 in Liu's table, which was counted from midnight (after Day 8) to midnight (before day 9).

Looking at these tables carefully, we find we are unable to match the five eclipse records with the canon and at the same time fulfill *all* requirements. Take the Babylonian table, the one we prefer. Under Day 22 the only year with the right month is −1278. Under Day 57, two years have the right months: −1310 and −1217. There is no way to obtain a cluster of five years to cover all five eclipses with the right months that does not span a period very much longer than Wu Ting's 59 years. The cluster that includes −1310 and −1228 spans 82 years, and one that includes −1278 and −1217 must begin in −1281 or end in −1188 and would again be too long. In the second, the Roman, table, the only possible year under Days 56–57 is −1191, which must serve as our starting point. Again we are unable to find a cluster of five years to take care of everything. In fact, under Day 22 there is not a single year when an eclipse occurred during the right month.

Unless Liu's table contains some error, which only an astronomer can judge, we are forced into the conclusion that one or more of our assumptions is wrong. But which? The removal of any of several assumptions will result in more than a single possible cluster. For example, if we are free to ignore the months, then several possibilities would present themselves, and our headache would then be how to choose. Several scholars have chosen one or another possibility, but because they had to ignore one or another line of evidence none of their choices can be said to be scientifically perfect.[14]

Before additional evidence comes to light to help us eliminate the noises from the system of lunar eclipse records, I would like to suggest tentatively that the "thirteenth moon" in the Day 57 eclipse record be ignored, if for no other reason than its being in a long record. With this piece of puzzle removed from the Babylonian table, we can then obtain a cluster of five eclipse years that meet all other conditions that either begin with −1281 and end with −1228 (for a span of 53 years) or begin with −1226 and end with −1188 (for a span of 38 years). Above we stated that on the strength of radiocarbon evidence the removal of the Shang capital to An-yang cannot have been later than 1300 B.C. In that event, the −1281 lunar eclipse must have occurred quite early during Wu Ting's reign, which suggests that

14. Tung Tso-pin 董作賓, "Yin tai yüeh-shih k'ao" 殷代月食考. Homer H. Dubs, "The date of the Shang period"; "The Date of the Shang Period—A Postscript"; Ch'en Meng-chia 陳夢家, *Yin hsü p'u-tz'u tsung shu* 殷墟卜辭綜述; Chou Fa-kao 周法高, "Certain Dates of the Shang Period"; Chou Fa-kao, "On the Dating of a Lunar Eclipse in the Shang Period"; P'an Wu-su 潘武肅, "The Dates of Wu Ting's Reign."

Wu Ting's reign may not have been as early as 1339–1281 B.C. as Tung Tso-pin suggested, but it cannot be nearly as late as 1238–1180 as Ch'en Meng-chia believed.

This tentative placement of the Wu Ting lunar eclipses into an earlier time period is supported by the oracle bone inscription data on solar eclipses. According to Chang P'ei-yü of the Purple Mountain Observatory in Nanking, oracle records from Period 4 refer to solar eclipses that took place on the following six dates: Keng-Ch'en, Jen-Tzu, Kuei-yu, Hsin-Chi, Wu-Shen, and Yi-Chi. The only cluster of six solar eclipses that fell on those six dates consists of those that took place in 1198, 1177, 1176, 1172, and twice (on 7 May and 31 October) in 1161 B.C.[15] If Period 4 contains the time segment 1161–1198 B.C., then the Wu Ting reign, five generations earlier, could easily be pushed back to the first part of the thirteenth century B.C., and the removal of the capital to An-yang easily before 1300 B.C.

For the purpose of this volume, on the basis of all lines of evidence at our disposal, the following round figures may be used for the absolute chronology of the Shang history:

Founding of dynasty by T'ang	Earlier than	1700 B.C.
Removal of capital to An-yang	" "	1300 B.C.
Fall of the dynasty	ca.	1100 B.C.

2. *LANGUAGE AND PHYSIQUE*

On the language of the Shang little need be said in regard to its classification other than that the language of the oracle bone inscriptions was the earliest known form of Chinese. As Dobson has clearly stated, "Archaic Chinese is the precursor of later forms of Chinese and . . . descends from the language used by the diviners of the Shang Dynasty, which is preserved today in the enquiries and responses engraved on bone and shell."[16] Since the pottery script of the Shang, as we have seen in chapter 4, is of the same writing system as the oracular script, the earliest known Chinese language was apparently spoken by members of both upper and lower classes. And as the Shang class system was characterized more by intra-lineage and inter-lineage differentiation than by conqueror-conquerred stratification in any ethnic sense, there is no evidence that the Shang civilization was linguistically diverse in terms of familial classification.

15. Chang P'ei-yü 張培瑜, "Chia-ku-wen jih yüeh shih chi-shih ti cheng-li yen-chiu" 甲骨文日月食紀事的整理研究.

16. W. A. C. H. Dobson, *Early Archaic Chinese*, p. 1.

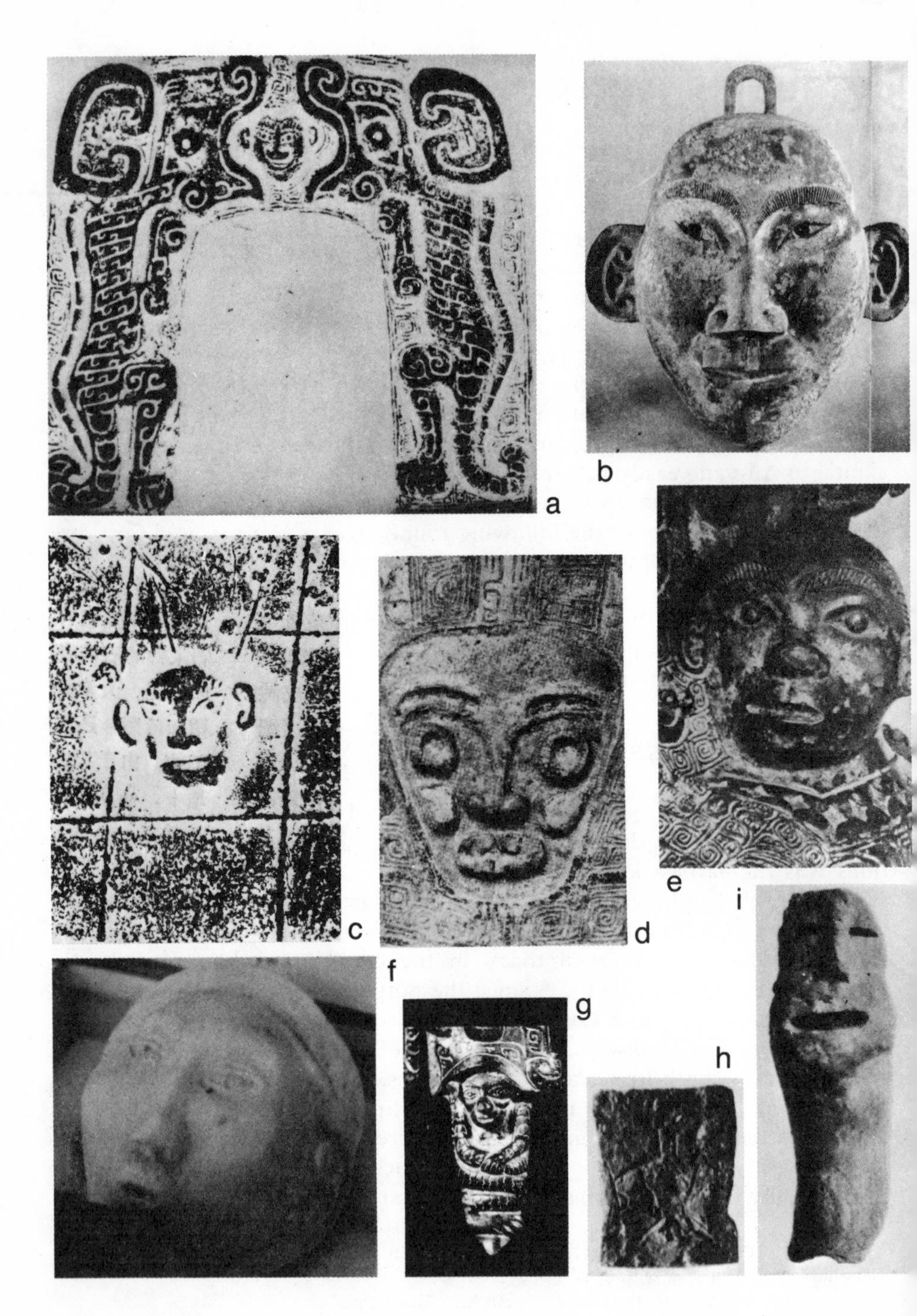

89. Human faces in Shang art (after K. C. Chang, *The Archaeology of Ancient China,* fig. 133).

On the physical morphology of the people of the Shang, there are two kinds of data. One consists of art objects in which human faces appear. Figure 89 gives a sampling of some of these faces, which show high malar bones and clear evidence of the Mongolian fold at the inner corner of the eyes. These objects range from a bronze mask, which may be more representative of the ruler than the commoners, to a small clay human head, which may be closer to the commoner than to the ruler. We are, thus, given a sampling of faces from different strata of society.

The other kind of data, on the other hand, pertains solely to the societal stratum or strata that provided the human victims for burial and ancestral offering rituals. Our evidence includes the skeletons and skulls recovered from the large graves and the ritual pits in Hsi-pei-kang, An-yang, and a much smaller number of skeletal remains from the Shang tombs at Liu-li-ko, Hui Hsien. All of them may be said to have been human sacrificial victims and none were the upper-class masters of the graves, since all of the large graves had been plundered previous to modern research and the centers of the burial chambers invariably disturbed.

According to Li Chi, "the skeletal materials collected from fifteen seasons of An-yang excavations amount to several thousands. . . . The Institute of History and Philology created a special section and invited a biometrician, Dr. Woo Ting-liang 吳定良, trained in the biometric laboratory of Dr. Karl Pearson in London, to take charge of the scientific investigation of this valuable collection. But the Japanese invasion and the war . . . interrupted the program . . . [and] the materials were greatly depleted."[17] Finally, in Taiwan, Yang Hsi-mei 楊希枚, a trained biologist, was given the task of studying and publishing the depleted collection—by final count, a collection of only 410 skulls, most (398) from Hsi-pei-kang and the rest (12) from Hsiao-t'un and Hou-chia-hsiao-chuang. Most if not all of these skulls came from skull burials and were unassociated with the skeletons from which they had been forcibly detached.[18] A number of publications have already resulted from the studies by Yang Hsi-mei and his colleagues.[19] Several American

17. *Anyang*, p. 255.

18. Yang Hsi-mei 楊希枚, "Ho-nan An-yang Yin hsü mu-tsang chung jen-t'i ku-ko ti cheng-li ho yen-chiu" 河南安陽殷墟墓葬中人體骨骼的整理和研究, 235.

19. Yang Hsi-mei, *Ibid.*; Yang Hsi-mei, "A Preliminary Report of Human Crania Excavated from Hou-chia-chuang and Other Shang Dynasty Sites at An-yang, Honan, North China"; Li Chi, "Notes on Some Metrical Characters of Calvaria of the Shang Dynasty Excavated from Houchiachuang, Anyang"; Hsü Tse-min 許澤民, "Yin hsü Hsi-pei-kang tsu t'ou-ku yü hsien-tai T'ai-wan Hai-nan hsi-lieh t'ou-ku ti lu-ting-chien-ku ti yen-chiu" 殷墟西北崗組頭骨與現代台灣海南系列頭骨的顱頂間骨的研

anthropologists have taken measurements on portions of the same collection. Among them to my knowledge are C. S. Coon, W. W. Howells, Loring Brace, and Christy Turner, but systematic reports of their research results have been sketchy and sporadic.[20]

Although, unsurprisingly, there is no disagreement among the researchers that the An-yang sample represents a Mongoloid population, there are some significant disagreements with regard to two issues: just how different were the Shang from the Neolithic Chinese, who were also Mongoloid, and just how homogeneous or heterogeneous were the Shang people among themselves.

On the matter of comparing the Shang population with the Neolithic skulls, Li Chi, in looking over some metric characters of calvaria of both the Shang and the Neolithic samples published by Davidson Black, detected considerable difference between the two, and he hinted at the possibility that "such significant changes are due to an infusion of a broader headed element accompanying the establishment of the imperial power of the Shang in North China."[21] On the other hand, William W. Howells, taking into account a number of more recently excavated Neolithic populations from archaeological sites in China, has concluded otherwise:

> I have noted that, in such mean measurements as can be compared the An-yang series does not appear to differ from the Neolithic samples in a discernible way, and Davidson Black long ago reached the opinion that there was no essential difference between Neolithic and modern Chinese, from evidence then available.[22]

Howells then goes on to ask a new question: Were the An-yang people (largely sacrificial victims) of composite or mixed origin? Li Chi found the range of variation of the cephalic index of the Hou-chia-chuang male population to be "a possible indication . . . of the non-homogeneity of the Hou-chia-chuang collection."[23] C. S. Coon believed that he saw in this population a mixture of Northern European and one or more

究; Lin Ch'un-yü 林純玉, "Ho-nan An-yang Yin hsü t'ou-ku nao-jung-liang ti yen-chiu" 河南安陽殷墟頭骨腦容量的研究; Tsang Chen-hua 臧振華, "An-yang Yin hsü t'ou-ku ch'i-hsing men-ch'ih ti yen-chiu" 安陽殷墟頭骨箕形門齒的研究.

20. C. Turner, "Dental Evidence on the Origins of the Ainu and Japanese"; W. W. Howells, "Origin of the Chinese Peoples: Interpretations of the Recent Evidence"; C. S. Coon, "An Anthropogeographic Excursion around the World."

21. Li Chi, *op. cit.*, 555.

22. Howells, *op. cit.*, 15.

23. Li Chi, *op. cit.*, 558.

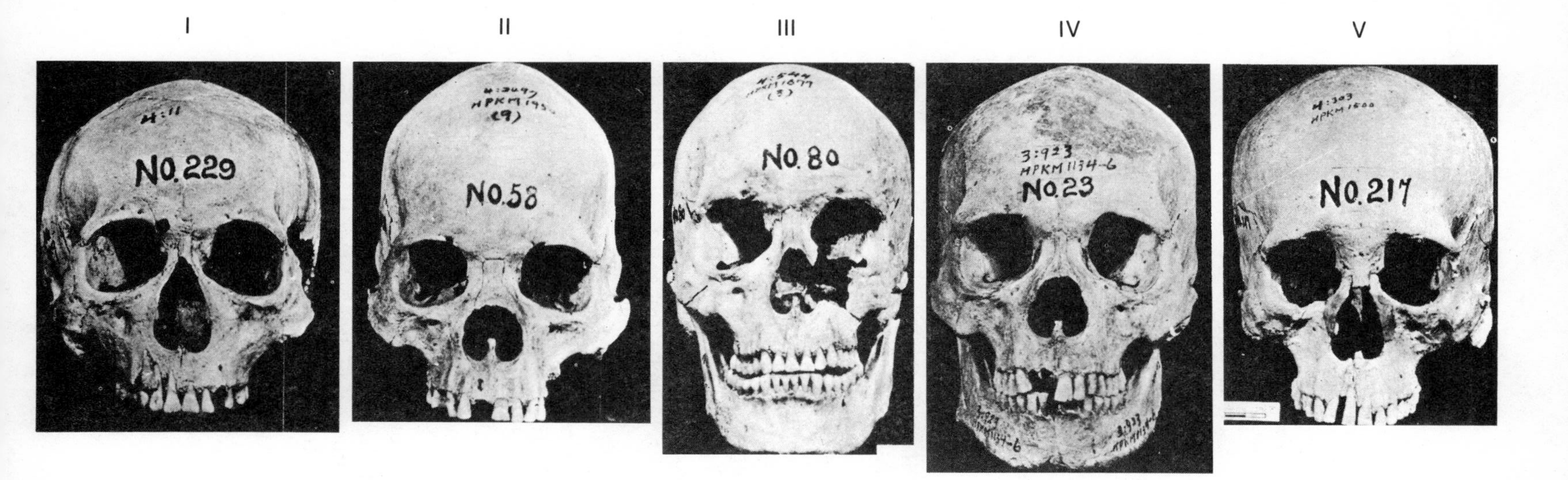

90. The five groups of Shang skulls according to Yang Hsi-mei (after his "Honan An-yang Yin hsü mu-tsang chung jen-t'i ku-ko ti cheng-li ho yen-chiu").

Mongoloid types.[24] In his *The Living Races of Man,* Coon observed as follows:

> At least two of the female skulls of this collection have Caucasoid traits in the eyesockets and nasal skeleton. A few others are brachycephalic and exaggeratedly Mongoloid, like the skulls of modern Buriats. The rest are of the usual northern Chinese type, with a mesocephalic braincase and moderately long, flattish face.[25]

Carrying this view of a heterogeneous Hou-chia-chuang population a step further, Yang Hsi-mei subdivided the population, according to what he refers to as "the whole morphological structure" of the skulls, into no fewer than five subgroups (fig. 90):

Subgroup I—The Classical Mongoloid type
Subgroup II—The Oceanic Negroid type
Subgroup III—The Caucasoid type
Subgroup IV—The Eskimoid type
Subgroup V—An unnamed type[26]

Of the Hou-chia-chuang skulls, Yang selected 70 as type specimens of the two Mongoloid subgroups (I and IV), 40 as type specimens of the Negroid subgroup (II), only 2 as type specimens of the Caucasoid subgroup (III), and as many as 50 as the unclassifiable fifth subgroup.

With this conclusion, Howells again takes sharp issue. Using discriminant analysis Howells finds that in all cranial features the An-yang group most resembles modern Chinese on Hainan island and Japanese from Hokkaido and Ryukyu, but not Europeans, American Indians or Polynesians. He further takes four type-specimens from Yang's subgroups II, III, IV, and V and undertakes to classify them by the discriminants, finding that "two of the four type specimens were placed with the An-yang series and two with the Hainan; in each case the second most likely classification was the other of these series."[27] He concludes that, although these type specimens do superficially and in specific features resemble this or that comparative specimen from other populations, "when multivariate methods are used, which take account of total conformation, it is evident that the 'types' do not stand the objective test of their apparent discreteness."

24. C. S. Coon, *op. cit.*
25. P. 133.
26. Yang Hsi-mei 楊希枚, see note 18 above.
27. Howells, *op. cit.*, 21.

To some extent the different views represent a terminological disagreement. There can be no question that there is a considerable range of variation within the Hou-chia-chuang population; the question concerns whether the range is normal here and is not so great as to indicate a mixture of racially divergent groups. Other studies tend to emphasize the generally Mongoloid character of the population. Hsü Tse-min finds that 26 of the 376 whole Hou-chia-chuang skulls (6.91%) have clear evidence of the Inca bone, a percentage that compares favorably with the figure for modern southern Chinese (5.7%).[28] In a comparative study of the cranial capacity of the Hou-chia-chuang skulls, Lin Ch'un-yü professes to see a confirmation of Yang's subgroups I and III, but not of his subgroups II and IV.[29] Finally, Tsang Chen-hua "examined the shovel-shaped incisors of each subgroup separately," finding that in all subgroups the frequency of occurrence of such incisors was "very high" (fig. 91). His conclusion: "As far as the frequency of shovel-shaped incisors is concerned, the racial affiliation of all five subgroups belongs basically to the Mongoloid."[30] Tsang's findings have duplicated similar results obtained on skulls found in An-yang and Hui Hsien in 1950–53: shovel-shaped incisors were identified on 80–90% of all cases.[31] All in all, we tend to agree with Howells that "at the moment the safest hypothesis seems to be that the population of China in this northern region has been constant in physique, or at least in cranial form, and also surprisingly homogeneous, since the Neolithic."[32]

3. *EARLY SHANG, HSIA, AND THE QUESTION OF THE SHANG'S ORIGINS*

The origin of the Shang civilization is the ultimate question in the minds of many, both those who have a scholarly interest in early China and those who are simply fascinated by Shang art or by some other aspect of Shang civilization. And since the origin of the Shang is in good part the origin of Chinese civilization, there is sound reason to regard the issue of the Shang's origins as being of more than narrow significance. But the word "origin" encompasses a number of complex

28. Hsu Tse-min 許澤民, *op. cit.*
29. Lin Ch'un-yü 林純玉, *op. cit.*, 48.
30. Tsang Chen-hua 臧振華, *op. cit.*, 82.
31. Mao Hsieh-chün 毛燮均 and Yen Yen 嚴誾, "An-yang Hui hsien Yin tai jen-ya ti yen-chiu pao-kao" 安陽輝縣殷代人牙的研究報告, 85.
32. Howells, *op. cit.*, 22.

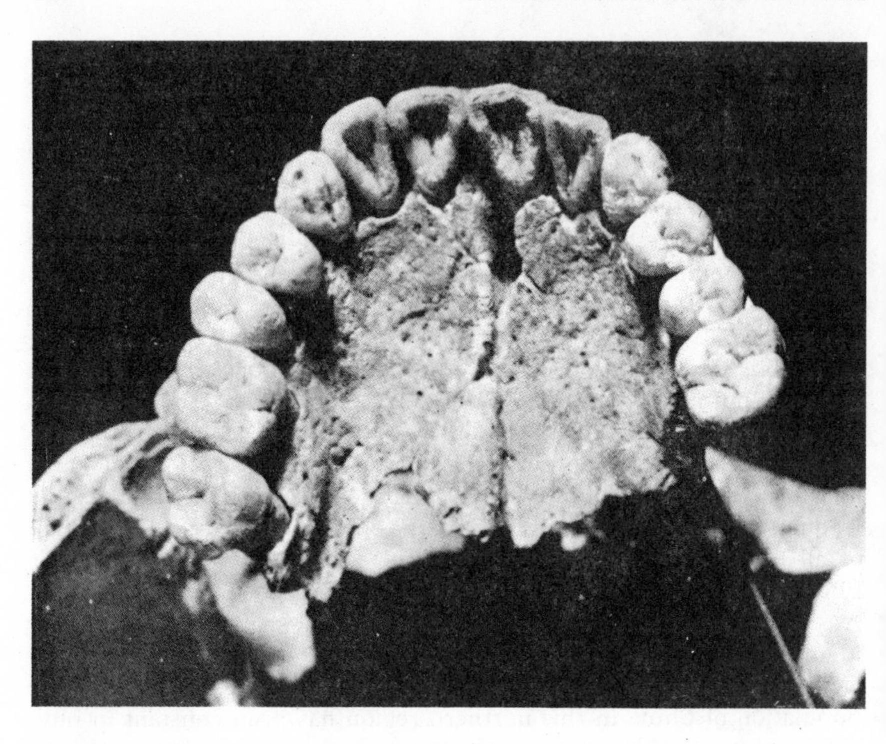

91. Shovel-shaped incisors on a Shang skull (after Tsang Chen-hua, "An-yang Yin hsü t'ou-ku chi-hsing men-ch'ih ti yen-chiu").

and interrelated issues. Under the rubric of the Shang origins are at least the following questions: Where did the Shang people come from—were they indigenous to the area of their activity or did they come from somewhere else? Was there a conquest involved, resulting in a stratification of aristocratic interlopers on top of the natives? Was the complex, stratified Shang society the result of a conquest or was it the end product of a long or short process of societal evolution? In any event, what was the history of the Shang development in terms of the archaeological record—both in the individual histories of development of the hallmarks of civilization, such as writing, the state, urbanism, great art, and so forth, and the interrelationship of these individual developmental processes? Finally, what "caused" the Shang civilization to develop, and to develop the way it did?

Clearly, we are not in a position to provide a simple and clear answer to questions such as whether the Shang was monogenetic or polygenetic, indigenous or imported, or partly indigenous and partly imported. We can, however, attempt to take a careful look at the archaeological antecedents of the Shang—both its Erh-li-kang and An-yang phases—and see what clear points can now be made and what directions further inquiries could be guided toward. In making this brief review, we shall not go over the issues in a historical perspective or retrace our efforts to study the Shang's origins in recent historiography, where one sees many claims being made and then superceded by new archaeological discoveries and epigraphical researches. Rather, we shall look at the issues from today's perspective, in the context of today's data.

The first thing that we are in a position to clearly state in any study of the Shang origins is that the Shang came in at the end (in point of time, in the eighteenth century B.C.) of a long history of cultural and social development. The cultural sequence in the northern Honan area has been briefly summarized in chapter 5. When our view is expanded to the whole of the Yellow River valley, and even beyond, to look for the larger context in which Shang appeared, we find that the same sequence holds, but that the situation becomes somewhat more complicated.[33]

1. *Early Neolithic Beginnings*. The earliest cultural remains in North China in which there is evidence of pottery and, possibly, of agriculture consist of those found in scattered sites. At some of those sites they were found stratigraphically below layers of the next, the Yang-shao culture, and are characterized by coarse and gritty pottery impressed with cord marks, comb marks, or rocker-stamped designs, without painting. Known sites of this period—some dated by carbon-14 to the eighth millennium B.C.—are found in the west (Shensi and northwestern Honan) and in the east (Hsin-cheng in Honan and Wu-an in Hopei) of North China. Those in the west, so far unpublished, are featured by cord-marked pottery, and those in the east, better reported, are characterized by combed pottery. These sites are as yet inadequately known, but they provide the first evidence for the crucial transition from the Palaeolithic hunting-fishing-collecting way of life to farming, and the pottery assemblage at these sites includes types and modes that were characteristic of the Yang-shao culture (e.g., *ting*-tripods and cord-marked pottery).

2. *Yang-shao Culture and Its Contemporary in Shantung*. Yang-shao culture, named after its type site at Yang-shao-ts'un, in Mien-

33. See K. C. Chang, *The Archaeology of Ancient China* and his "The Continuing Quest for China's Origins."

ch'ih Hsien, western Honan, excavated in 1921, is the first and best known culture in China of full-fledged village farmers. Firmly dated by radiocarbon to between the late sixth millennium and the beginning of the third millennium B.C., Yang-shao is the culture of millet farmers and pig breeders who manufactured red pottery impressed with cord-marks or painted with a wide variety of animal and geometric motifs. Farming villages, inhabited by members of clans and lineages, were evidently the basic social unit; there is no evidence for political groups larger than the village, nor evidence of war or social stratification.

The currently known Yang-shao sites were found in a large area of North China, but essentially confined to the western highland portions along large and small river valleys. They occur in the Wei River valley in Shensi, extending westward into eastern Kansu and Tsinghai and eastward along the Yellow River valley to Shansi and western Honan, and northward into Hopei along the eastern slopes of the T'ai-hang Mountains and the adjacent plains and south into the upper Han River valley.

East of the Yang-shao territory, at the heart of Shantung peninsula are sites with archaeological remains referred to as the Ch'ing-lien-kang 青蓮崗 culture. At that time much of the plains area between central Honan and central Shantung may have been marshy and partly submarged, and T'ai-shan mountain and its adjacent highlands may have formed an island off the North China coast. The Ch'ing-lien-kang sites were seen along the edges of this island area, in Shantung and northern Kiangsu, in what is now a part of the Huai River plains. Very few sites of this culture have been found, and even fewer are dug. We know that its pottery was red and sometimes painted or incised with parallel lines, and that its types include bowls and *ting*-tripods. At the same time, to the south of this area was an early center of farming culture characterized by rice, and some scholars have grouped the Shantung Ch'ing-lien-kang sites with these southern sites and refer to them all as the Ch'ing-lien-kang culture. This classification could be premature. The Shantung pottery resembles the Yang-shao pottery, especially the pottery of the northern Honan phase, in important ways, and we have not yet been informed of the people's subsistence system and whether the centerpiece of that system was millet, as in Yang-shao, or rice, as in the contemporary culture to the south. The likelihood is strong that the Shantung Ch'ing-lien-kang was basically an offshoot of the Yang-shao.

3. *The Lungshanoid Cultures*. From about 3000 B.C. to the end of the third millennium the cultures that are generally classified as Lungshanoid may be grouped as follows:

Honan: Miao-ti-kou II culture—Honan Lung-shan culture
Shantung: Ta-wen-k'ou culture—Shantung Lung-shan culture

Whatever was the origin of the Ch'ing-lien-kang culture in Shantung and northern Kiangsu, the Lungshanoid developments in Honan and Shantung clearly followed separate paths. The Honan development was characterized by *li-* and *chia*-tripods and jars of gray ware with cord-marked impressions, whereas the Shantung line was typified by *ting*-tripods and bowls on high pedestal stands (many with holes along the whole circumference) of gray and red ware without impressed cord marks. Nevertheless, in terms of societal development, the Lungshanoid cultures both inland and along the coast exhibit similar trends of transformation. On the Honan side, the clay phalli found at several sites of the Honan Lung-shan culture[34] are good evidence of the worship of male ancestors, and the practice of scapulimancy is suggestive of the religious beliefs and the political structure of the time. Wheel-made pottery points to highly specialized handicrafts.[35] In the fall of 1957, members of the Han-tan Archaeological Excavation Team of the Archaeology Program of Peking University brought to light a house foundation and two dry wells at a Lung-shan culture site at Chien-kou-ts'un, in Han-tan, southern Hopei. "Within the house foundation were found four human skulls with signs of blows and scalpings, apparently indicating that these victims were scalped after having been killed. . . . The water wells were first abandoned and then in them were buried five layers of human skeletons, including both males and females and both old and young individuals, some having been decapitated and some showing postures of struggling. From these one postulates that some of the dead were murdered or were buried alive."[36] This burial is probable evidence of inter-village warfare, indicating that by the time of Honan Lung-shan culture the northern Chinese society had reached a stage of "penal code internally and armed forces externally" (*Shang chün sh'us* characterization of Huang Ti's society). The earthen wall that has been found encircling the Lung-shan culture site at Hou-kang, An-yang,[37] points in the same direction.

34. J. G. Andersson, "Researches into the Prehistory of the Chinese," pl. 30: 1; J. G. Andersson, "Prehistoric Sites in Honan," pl. 31: 3.

35. *KKHCK, Miao-ti-kou yü San-li-ch'iao* 廟底溝與三里橋, p. 92.

36. *KK*, "1957 nien Han-tan fa-chüeh chien pao" 1957年邯鄲發掘簡報, 531–532.

37. Shih Chang-ju 石璋如, "Ho-nan An-yang Hou-kang ti Yin mu" 河南安陽後岡的殷墓.

Similar development is seen on the Shantung side. As regards the background of the society, several essays published in the last few years agree on the following points: Ta-wen-k'ou society consisted of rich and poor components (according to the amount and the nature of the furnishings of individual graves); there was specialization in the ceramic industry (wheeled pottery); and marriages were probably monogamous (graves with man-woman pairs).[38] By Shantung Lung-shan times, additional new cultural elements—scapulimancy, more and better wheel-made pottery, rammed earthen village walls, and metal objects—indicate an even higher level of societal development.

At this point, it may be stated with confidence that the Lung-shan cultures of both Honan and Shantung provided the necessary foundation on which the Shang civilization could eventually be built. It is also clear, however, that the Lung-shan cultures did not move immediately into the Shang. There were both continuities and innovations in the course of change from Lung-shan to Shang.

The Lung-shan–Shang Continuities are essentially cultural elements at the "popular" level. The most characteristic Shang pottery, the gray *li*-tripod with cord-marks, is also a Honan Lung-shan hallmark. Other Shang pottery vessel forms of the corded gray ware—the kind that was used by the commoners for utilitarian purposes—can also be traced to the Lung-shan cultures, mostly Honan but also sometimes Shantung. The Shang lithic, bone, and shell inventory, consisting basically of production implements used by the ordinary villagers, is again a Lung-shan carryover. The only stone item that distinguished the Shang from their Neolithic predecessors is the slate sickle, which was found in far greater numbers at Shang sites than at Lung-shan sites. This indicates the Shang's greater productivity rather than a new technology. Shang houses, with their semi-subterranean floors, sometimes plastered with limey clay, and their timber structure and wattle-and-daub walling, again carried on a Lung-shan tradition, and their *hang-t'u* construction technique was foreshadowed by the Lung-shan village enclosures. In food, the Shang's basic crop, millet, and basic fiber plant, hemp, were again of Neolithic heritage. One may say with

38. Wei Ch'in 魏勤, "Ts'ung Ta-wen-k'ou wen-hua mu-tsang k'an ssu-yu-chih ti ch'i-yüan" 從大汶口文化墓葬看私有制的起源; Tan Ta 單達 and Shih Ping 史兵, "Ts'ung Ta-wen-k'ou wen-hua yi-ts'un k'an wo-kuo ku-tai ssu-yu-chih ti jun-yü ho meng-ya" 從大汶口文化遺存看我國古代私有制的孕育和萌芽; Yü Chung-hang 于中航, "Ta-wen-k'ou wen-hua ho yüan-shih she-hui ti chieh-t'i" 大汶口文化和原始社會的解體; Lu Po 魯波, "Ts'ung Ta-wen-k'ou wen-hua k'an wo-kuo ssu-yu-chih ti ch'i-yüan" 從大汶口文化看我國私有制的起源; T'ang Lan 唐蘭, "Ts'ung Ta-wen-k'ou wen-hua ti t'ao-ch'i wen-tzu k'an wo-kuo tsui-tsao wen-hua ti nien-tai" 從大汶口文化的陶器文字看我國最早文化的年代.

confidence that as far as the Shang farmer was concerned, his life in its material essentials was not much changed from that of his Lung-shan ancestors; the changes that he was subjected to were economic and political in nature.

The Shang Innovations pertained mainly to the life of the upper class. In his lectures on *The Beginnings of Chinese Civilization,* Li Chi listed the following cultural traits as being what distinguished the Shang from their Neolithic forebears:

1. New development's of ceramic industry
2. Employment of bronze to cast tools, weapons, and sacrificial vessels
3. The presence of a highly developed writing system
4. Chamber burials and human sacrifices
5. Use of chariots
6. Advanced stone carvings[39]

The new developments in pottery here refer to the white and glazed potteries, again rare and presumably highly valuable items of material goods whose creation was for the exclusive use of the members of the upper class. In a sense, then, to seek the origins of the Shang is to seek the origins of the ruling group of the dynasty. Where did they come from? How did they amass the characteristic High Culture items that not only symbolized their rule but probably also enabled it?

The An-yang and the Erh-li-kang phases of the Shang represent two successive stages of the civilization but not its initial phase. Pushing the history of the civilization back one step further, beyond the earliest archaeologically known Shang culture, we come across the Erh-li-t'ou type of culture that seems to be placed, ideally, between the Lung-shan and the Erh-li-kang:

Dynastic An-yang
Erh-li-kang
→ Erh-li-t'ou
Honan Lung-shan
Miao-ti-kou II
Yang-shao

Erh-li-t'ou is the name of a village near Yen-shih, east of Lo-yang, in western Honan, where the type site for this new culture was found in

39. P. 15.

1959.[40] But the culture was first identified at Lo-ta-miao, in Cheng-chou, in 1956.[41] Characterized by archaeological finds from Shang-chieh 上街 (Cheng-chou); Tung-kan-kou 東乾溝 (Lo-yang), and Ch'i-li-p'u 七里鋪 (Shan Hsien), as well as Lo-ta-miao and Erh-li-t'ou, this new culture

> not only contained many characteristic features of the Early Shang [Erh-li-kang phase] but also posessed some elements of the Honan Lung-shan culture. For example, in its pottery decorations the most abundant patterns are the fine cord-marks, followed by basket-marks and accompanied by check and appliqued designs. Pottery vessel types include *ting*-tripod, jar, basin, urn, bowl on pedestal, *chüeh*-tripod, and beaker with short collar and flare mouth. *Ting* is the most typical vessel of this culture and is found very widely; usually it is made up of a round-based jar or basin as body and attached with flat or prismatic feet. Some of the *ting* are encircled with appliqued patterns. The basin type is also characteristic: deep body, round base, two flat handles attached horizontally below the rim. The production implements are mainly stones and bones, shells being very few. Also noteworthy are the rare finds of bronze knives. In addition, there are also oracle bones with burn marks only.[42]

Clearly this new type of culture, with its cord-marked gray pottery, served to link the Honan Lung-shan and the Erh-li-kang Shang, and it soon began to be referred to as Early Shang, with Erh-li-kang relegated to Middle Shang and An-yang as Late Shang.

In 1959, Hsü Ping-ch'ang 徐炳昶 and others of the Institute of Archaeology, Academia Sinica, set out on a journey to western Honan and southern Shansi to look for the remains of the Hsia civilization, which in ancient Chinese legendary history preceded the Shang. The area was chosen because, "as indicated by the fewer than thirty references to the Hsia dynasty capital cities retained in *Tso chuan*, *Kuo yü*, and *Ku pen Chu shu chi nien*, . . . two areas are particularly noteworthy [in any effort to look for the activity region of the Hsia]: the first is the Lo-yang plain and its neighboring area in central Honan, especially the area of Teng-feng and Yü Hsien in the upper Ying River valley.

40. Hsü Hsün-sheng 徐旭生, "1959 nien Yü hsi tiao-ch'a 'Hsia hsü' ti ch'u-pu pao-kao" 1959年豫西調查'夏墟'的初步報告.

41. *WW*, "Cheng-chou Lo-ta-miao Shang tai yi-chih shih chüeh chien pao" 鄭州洛達廟商代遺址試掘簡報.

42. *KKHCK*, *Hsin Chung-kuo ti k'ao-ku shou-hu* 新中國的考古收穫, p. 44.

The second is the area of the lower Fen River valley in southwestern Shansi (approximately south of Mount Ho).''[43] Erh-li-t'ou, 9 kilometers west of Yen-shih, on the southern bank of the Lo River, was one of the sites found by Hsü and his colleagues on this trip. However, because ''remains here are similar in nature to the remains of Lo-ta-miao of Cheng-chou and Tung-kan-kou of Lo-yang, [they] are probably Early Shang.''[44] Hsü then proceeded to identify the Erh-li-t'ou site with Po, T'ang's capital:

> The identification of Yen-shih as the capital of T'ang of Shang was probably made for the first time by Pan Ku in his commentary under Yen-shih Hsien, Ho-nan chün, in the chapter ''Ti li chih'' of *Han shu*: ''Shih-hsiang, Yin T'ang's capital.'' . . . Prior to this trip Hsü Hsün-sheng [Hsü Ping-ch'ang] was rather skeptical of the West Po hypothesis, but he could not completely ignore it because it was an old view from people of the Han dynasty. Because *Yen-shih chih* (compiled in the Ch'ien-lung period) contains clear information about its exact location, we thought we might on this trip check into its validity. Now we have seen this site, which is huge, although we did not attempt to delineate its borders. If what the natives told us (as to its vast area) turns out to be true, then it must have been a major city, with a good chance of being the capital city of T'ang of Shang.[45]

This tentative identification became strengthened with each new investigation of the site. In the 1965 report we find the observation that ''the possibility is great that the Erh-li-t'ou site was the capital city of T'ang of Shang, Hsi Po''.[46] In the 1974 report of the remains of a palatial structure[47] and the 1975 report of the excavations of sections 3 and 8 of the Erh-li-t'ou site,[48] the authors stated their further belief that new archaeological data have strengthened the case for the identification of Erh-li-t'ou with Po, T'ang's capital.

What in fact these new Erh-li-t'ou excavations have strengthened is the identification of it with a major historical town, but there has

43. Hsü Hsün-sheng 徐旭生, *op. cit.*, 594.

44. *Ibid.*, 598.

45. *Ibid.*, 598–600.

46. *KK*, ''Ho-nan Yen-shih Erh-li-t'ou yi-chih fa-chüeh chien pao'' 河南偃師二里頭遺址發掘簡報, 224.

47. *KK*. ''Ho-nan Yen-shih Erh-li-t'ou tsao Shang kung-tien yi-chih fa-chüeh chien pao'' 河南偃師二里頭早商宮殿遺址發掘簡報, 248.

48. *KK*, ''Ho-nan Yen-shih Erh-li-t'ou yi-chih san pa ch'ü fa-chüeh chien pao'' 河南偃師二里頭遺址三、八區發掘簡報, 308.

been no additional support for the town being Po. Rather, new archaeological developments in the 1970s have cast serious doubt on the Po identification but, instead, opened up the question of the Hsia civilization from two directions:

One, the judgment as to the Erh-li-t'ou culture being part of Hsia or being Early Shang must ultimately be based on the fundamental evidence of time and space. In space, the Erh-li-t'ou culture is seen "in Yen shih, at Hui-tsui as well as Erh-li-t'ou; in Lo-yang, at Tung-kan-kou; in Kung Hsien, at Shao-ch'ai; in Cheng-chou, at Lo-ta-miao; in Hsing-yang at Shang-chieh; in Shan Hsien, at Ch'i-li-p'u; and in dozens of other sites. In southern Shansi are also sites similar to those in western Honan. . . . Noteworthy is the fact that the area of the geographical distribution of the Erh-li-t'ou culture is precisely the area of the activities of the Hsia people as given in texts—the areas outlined by the Yi 伊, the Lo 洛, the Yellow 河, and the Chi 濟 rivers."[49]

As regards time, five samples from the Erh-li-t'ou site have been reported:[50]

ZK-31–1	Erh-li-t'ou "Early Shang"	2390 ± 190 B.C.
ZK-212	Erh-li-t'ou I	1910 ± 160 B.C.
ZK-285	Erh-li-t'ou I	1880 ± 150 B.C.
ZK-286	Erh-li-t'ou IV	1620 ± 150 B.C.
ZK-257	Erh-li-t'ou III	1430 ± 160 B.C.

The two Erh-li-t'ou I samples cluster together well and give a range of 1730–2030 B.C., falling within the Hsia period and beyond the Shang completely. Erh-li-t'ou III represents the site's peak of cultural development, having yielded a "palace" foundation, four bronze vessels of the *chüeh* type, and jades. The single sample from this stratum has yielded a chronological range of 1270–1590 B.C. But the fourth sample, from Erh-li-t'ou IV, has yielded an earlier date and could fall within very late Hsia. Either sample could be wrong. But the four strata of Erh-li-t'ou represent a continuous development, with level III marking its peak. Chen-hsün 斟鄩, capital of Hsia during the reign of its final king, Chieh, is identified by many highly respected advocates with the environs of Lo-yang.[51] A view to identify Erh-li-t'ou I and II with Hsia and Erh-li-

49. T'ung Chu-ch'en 佟柱臣, "Ts'ung Erh-li-t'ou lei-hsing wen-hua shih t'an Chung-kuo ti kuo-chia ch'i-yüan wen-t'i" 從二里頭類型文化試談中國的國家起源問題, 29.

50. See appendix for details.

51. See the modern synthesis in Chao T'ieh-han 趙鉄寒, *Ku shih k'ao shu* 古史考述.

t'ou III and IV with Hsia's terminal capital site would be consistent with the history of the Erh-li-t'ou site itself. In short, recent work at the Erh-li-t'ou culture sites tends to strengthen the view that regards the culture not as Early Shang but as Hsia.[52]

Two, the growing knowledge in the 1970s about the Ta-wen-k'ou 大汶口 culture is forcing a reappraisal of the Shang's eastern connection, always the favorite connection in the legendary history of the Shang. In a paper in which I examined the Early Shang and Hsia issue in the light of these new discoveries, I listed the following cultural traits and complexes as having been shared by Shang and the coastal Lung-shanoid cultures (but not by Shang and Honan Lung-shan):[53]

1. Very rich grave-furnishings
2. Wooden burial chambers and second-level ledges
3. Use of turtle shells
4. Some ceramic types and modes, including white pottery
5. Bone spatulas, bone carvings, turquois inlays; and certain decorative art designs.

I refer to my earlier work for detailed description and discussion of these shared features. Most of these items, as I pointed out, "had to do with religion, ritual life, and art of the ruling class."[54] The nature of these cultural traits seems to imply that the rulers of the Shang dynasty could have been a political group, and a conqueror, from the east. This implication certainly does no violence to the legendary accounts of the beginnings of the Shang dynasty in the east. Modern-day ancient historians are agreed that the early capitals of the Shang dynasty were located in the eastern part of Honan and western Shantung and that the territory under the control of their predynastic ancestors reached the sea. (See the prolegomena.) They are also agreed that the legend of the birth of the Tzu clan founder by a black bird associates the Shang

52. This has also been strengthened by recent work done elsewhere in southern Shansi and western Honan. At the Ts'o-li site, Erh-li-t'ou layers have been radiocarbon-dated to 2010 ± 220 B.C. (calibrated). (See *KK*, "Lo-yang Ts'o-li yi-chih shih chüeh chien pao" 洛陽矬李遺址試掘簡報. At the Tung-hsia-feng 東下馮 site in Hsia Hsien, Shansi, a walled town site was found which may be dated to the Erh-li-t'ou phase. The report of the excavations, however, has not been published; a large number of C-14 dates are available without stratigraphic information (in *WW*, "T'an-shih-ssu nien-tai ts'e-ting pao-kao, hsü yi" 碳十四年代測定報告, 續一, and see appendix). See also Yin Wei-chang 殷瑋璋, "Erh-li-t'ou wen-hua t'an t'ao" 二里頭文化探討, and *KK*, "1975 nien Yü hsi k'ao-ku tiao-ch'a" 1975年豫西考古調查.

53. Chang Kwang-chih 張光直, "Yin Shang wen-ming ch'i-yüan yen-chiu shang ti yi-ko kuan-chien wen-t'i" 殷商文明起源研究上的一個關鍵問題.

54. *Ibid.*, 165.

unmistakably with the ancient inhabitants of eastern coastal China.[55] It is noteworthy that in oracle bone inscriptions the name Wang Hai, one of the Shang predynastic ancestors, is often decorated with a bird symbol.[56] Wang Hai, we may recall, is recorded in ancient texts as having had a violent encounter with an alien group, Yu Yi Shih, in central Hopei, west of the Gulf of Chih-li and south of the Hsia-chia-tien culture territory. The Lower Hsia-chia-tien culture, as we mentioned earlier, was one of the earliest metal-using cultures neighboring on the Shang, and it may be possible to seek the earliest beginning of one of the Shang's most important innovation—bronze casting—in the direction of the east coast.

It is as yet impossible to trace the history, step by step, of each of the dynastic innovations Li Chi has listed, but we must speculate at least that their arrival in the Middle and Late Shang was not an unprecedented, sudden event and that the Hsia–Early Shang interval would be a very likely period in which to look for the earliest beginnings of at least a few of these innovations.[57] Such speculations would very simply explain the fact that Middle and Late Shang cultures contained elements attributable to both Honan Lung-shan and Shantung Lung-shan cultures. In short, the predynastic period of early lords and early kings of Shang history probably overlaps at least in part with the prehistoric cultures of the eastern coastal areas of North China; an Early Shang period in Shang archaeology must be postulated for the final stages of the predynastic Shang period and the early centuries of the dynastic period; and we can place this Early Shang in the area of easternmost Honan, western Shantung, and northwestern Anhwei. "This area is a part of the famous Yellow River flooding region throughout Chinese history, and it had been on the old course of the Yellow River itself. Ancient remains in this area must be buried deep under the silt deposited here during many centuries. For this reason alone, in the archaeology of North China this area—east of K'ai-feng and west of the Great Canal—has been the most barren area in yield of cultural remains. I believe if a real Early Shang culture can be found in this area in the future, it will bear some fundamental similarities with the Hsia culture of the

55. Fu Ssu-nien 傅斯年, "Yi Hsia tung hsi shuo" 夷夏東西說; Ch'en Meng-chia 陳夢家, "Shang tai ti shen-hua yü wu-shu" 商代的神話與巫術, 494–497; Yü Hsing-wu 于省吾, "Lüeh-lun t'u-t'eng yü tsung-chiao ch'i-yüan ho Hsia Shang t'u-t'eng" 略論圖騰與宗教起源和夏商圖騰.

56. Hu Hou-hsüan 胡厚宣, "Chia-ku wen Shang tsu niao t'u-t'eng ti yi-chi" 甲骨文商族鳥圖騰的遺跡; Hu Hou-hsüan, "Chia-ku wen so-chien Shang tsu niao t'u-t'eng ti hsin cheng-chü" 甲骨文所見商族鳥圖騰的新證據.

57. See Ho Ping-ti, *The Cradle of the East*, for useful discussion on some of the technologies in question.

Erh-li-t'ou type, on the one hand, and constitute an intermediate phase between the Ta-wen-k'ou and Lung-shan culture and the later phases of the Shang civilization, on the other hand. The later Shang civilization may thus be said to result from an intermixture of both eastern and western cultures."[58]

The above discussion leads to the following alignment of the ancient cultures in North China:

Dynastic An-yang: Late Shang
Erh-li-kang, Cheng-chou: Middle Shang
Hsia ———————— (Early Shang)
Honan Lung-shan – Shantung Lung-shan
Miao-ti-kou II – Ta-wen-k'ou
Yang-shao – Ch'ing-lien-kang
Early Neolithic

This realignment of the ancient cultures of North China, especially in regard to the interrelationship of Hsia and Early Shang, brings forth a new understanding of the interrelationship of the Three Dynasties in ancient Chinese history. Since the overall Three Dynasties context is important in placing the Shang development in proper perspective, it will be useful to expand this discussion to this larger issue.

The Three Dynasties (*san tai* 三代) period of Hsia, Shang, and Chou evidently was a crucial period in the ancient history of China: written records began in this period, the polities that eventually coalesced to form what we know as China first formed then, and the foundations for many customs and institutions found throughout Chinese history were laid down during this interval. Ever since the beginning of scientific archaeology in China in the early decades of this century, many scholars have been expecting to see important contributions made by archaeology to the history of the Three Dynasties period. With the important archaeological discoveries of the last decade, such contributions are at hand.

I believe we are now at a stage where we can recognize some of the new directions in which Three Dynasties studies will be going. One of the issues worthy of pursuit that one sees emerging in the currently available data pertains to the formation of states in ancient China. It is now evident that two elements that have formed the cornerstone of our understanding of the Three Dynasties history are due for a basic overhaul. These are an emphasis on the vertical, successional relation-

58. Chang Kwang-chih 張光直, *op. cit.* (in note 53 above), 168–169.

ship of the Three Dynasties, and the view of the Three Dynasties sequence of development as an island of civilization in the middle of a sea of barbarous contemporaries. Rethinking both old data and new data resulting from recent archaeology has led me to conclude that these two views constitute important barriers to a true understanding of the ancient history of China. I am convinced that the concept of the horizontal interrelationship of the three dynasties is key to the formation process of the ancient Chinese states. To make this concept clear and to place current and future archaeological data into a proper context, I conclude this section with a discussion of evidence of the nature of the Three Dynasties' interrelationship as seen in the ancient texts.

The *san tai* was a concept that appeared as early as late Chou (*Mencius*, "T'eng Wen Kung, shang": "The San Tai shared it"). Since the emergence of modern historiography in China, many scholars have engaged in discussing the nature of the interrelationship of the Three Dynasties, but most have centered on their cultural similarities and differences and on the resultant issue of the ethnic classification of their peoples. What I emphasize here is, instead, the political interrelationship of Hsia, Shang, and Chou, as three parallel, or at least overlapping, polities. Cultural classification and political classification are not necessarily identical, and both classifications may be considered. A view of the Three Dynasties that is consistent with current facts would be as follows: Hsia, Shang, and Chou were subcultures of a common—ancient Chinese—culture, but more particularly they were political groups in opposition to one another. Their horizontal, rather than sequential, interrelationship, is key to understanding their development, and it is, thus, key to understanding the process of formation of ancient Chinese states.[59]

CHRONOLOGY

From the point of view of their relative political eminence, the three dynasties succeeded one another: the Shang dynasty began when T'ang "overthrew" Hsia, and the Chou dynasty began when Wu Wang "conquered" Shang. The durations of these first two dynasties are, according to *Ku pen Chu shu chi nien*, as follows: "[The Hsia dynasty], from Yü to Chieh had seventeen kings . . . and lasted 471 years," and "[The Shang dynasty], from T'ang's subjugation of Hsia to Shou [Ti Hsin] had twenty-nine kings and lasted 496 years." The Chou dynasty began with Wu Wang's conquest of King Chòu, an event that has tradi-

59. See also Noel Barnard, "Review of Chou Hung-hsiang, *Shang-Yin ti-wang pen-chi*," 488–489.

tionally been placed at 1122 B.C.,[60] and ended with Ch'in's subjugation of the royal city in 256 B.C., totalling thirty-seven kings and 867 years. Altogether, the three dynasties lasted more than eighteen hundred years. It must be noted, however, that Hsia, Shang, and Chou were not merely three chronological segments, for Shang was a powerful political entity prior to its subjugation of Hsia, and Chou, too, was a powerful political entity prior to its subjugation of Shang. In other words, Hsia and Shang were two chronologically parallel—or at least overlapping—political groups, and so were Shang and Chou.

For how long during the approximately five hundred years of the Hsia dynasty did Shang exist as a significant political entity? According to myths and legends of late Chou and early Han (e.g., those recorded in *Shih pen* and *Ti hsi*), Yü, the founding father of the Hsia dynasty, descended from Tuan Hsü, a descendant of the Yellow Emperor, and Hsieh, the founding father of the ruling clan of the Shang dynasty, descended from Ti K'u, another descendant of the Yellow Emperor. *Shih chi* records that the primogenitors of three dynasties, Yü, Hsieh, and Hou Chi, served on the royal courts of Ti Yao and Ti Shun. From these accounts, Hsia and Shang, at least, were two political groups with parallel existences beginning with the Yellow Emperor. On the basis of more reliable data, however, one can say only that the Shang were able to claim a history of their own of considerable glory prior to their conquest of Hsia, a history known as that of the period of *hsien kung* 先公 and *hsien wang* 先王 or predynastic lords and predynastic kings. Fourteen of such lords and kings were recorded by *Shih chi* and other later texts. Ch'en Meng-chia contended that "perhaps the fourteen kings of Hsia were the same fourteen [predynastic] kings of Shang, and that the so-called T'ang Wu Revolution was in fact only a struggle for power among kinsmen."[61] However, it is doubtful that Hsia kings were indeed predynastic Shang kings, especially in view of the new archaeological picture that we have painted, but Ch'en's contention suggests the possibility that the Shang political group coexisted with the Hsia dynasty throughout the latter's reign. Because of the extreme scarcity of Hsia texts, data on direct contact between Hsia and Shang, however, do not become available until the period of Hsia's King Chieh and Shang's King T'ang. Nevertheless, according to Fu Ssu-nien, throughout their dynastic reign the Hsia were in constant conflict with eastern states that were Shang's allies.

60. See beginning part of this chapter for Shang dates and the prolegomena for discussion on the Chou conquest date.

61. Ch'en Meng-chia 陳夢家, "Shang tai ti shen-hua yü wu-shu" 商代的神話與巫術, 491.

> Prior to Shang and Western Chou, or during Shang and Western Chou periods, more than a single ethnic group was living in the area that is now Shantung, eastern Honan, northern Kiangsu, the northeastern corner of Anhwei, and perhaps the Gulf of Chihli coast of Hopei, and, across the gulf, the two sides of Liaotung peninsula and Korea. Those that one can find in textual records included such tribal units as Ta Hao 大皞, Shao Hao 少皞, Yu Chi 有濟, and Hsü Fang 徐方, and such clan names as Feng 風, Ying 盈, and Yen 偃; all of them were referred to as Yi 夷 . . . . The major events during the Hsia dynasty were conflicts with these Yi groups.[62]

The Shang, in Fu's belief, "were not Yi themselves, but they at times dominated the Yi peoples, and they adopted the Yi's culture and were supported by the Yi's people in their conquest and subjugation of the Hsia. The conquest can, thus, be said to be a Yi's triumph over Hsia."[63] In the context of the opposition between Yi and Hsia, Shang was evidently one of the Yi states, and it maintained a certain political status during the whole period of Hsia rule.

Concerning Chou's overlap with Shang during the latter period of Shang rule (approximately five hundred years) there are more and better data due to the more abundant textual material pertaining to Shang than to Hsia. These data have been discussed earlier in chapter 4 in connection with Chou Fang.

To conclude: both new and old textual data indicate considerable temporal overlap between Hsia and Shang as political powers and between Shang and Chou as well. This evidence is beginning to be substantiated by the radiocarbon dates (fig. 92). In other words, Shang was among the states that existed during the period when Hsia was given supremacy in Chou texts, and Chou was among the states during the period when Shang was given such supremacy. To state it from the other direction, Ch'i, the state that was the direct descendant of Hsia, was among the states during both Shang and Chou dynasties, and the state of Sung, Shang's postdynastic successor, was among the states during the Chou dynasty. The interrelationship of the Three Dynasties, thus, was not only one of sequential succession; it was also characterized by their parallel existence as contemporary states. In the context of North China as a whole, the latter must be viewed as the primary relationship, and the dynastic succession sequence may be regarded as marking the relative power changes of the three states.

62. Fu Ssu-nien 傅斯年, "Yi Hsia tung hsi shuo" 夷夏東西說, 1112.
63. *Ibid.*, 1117.

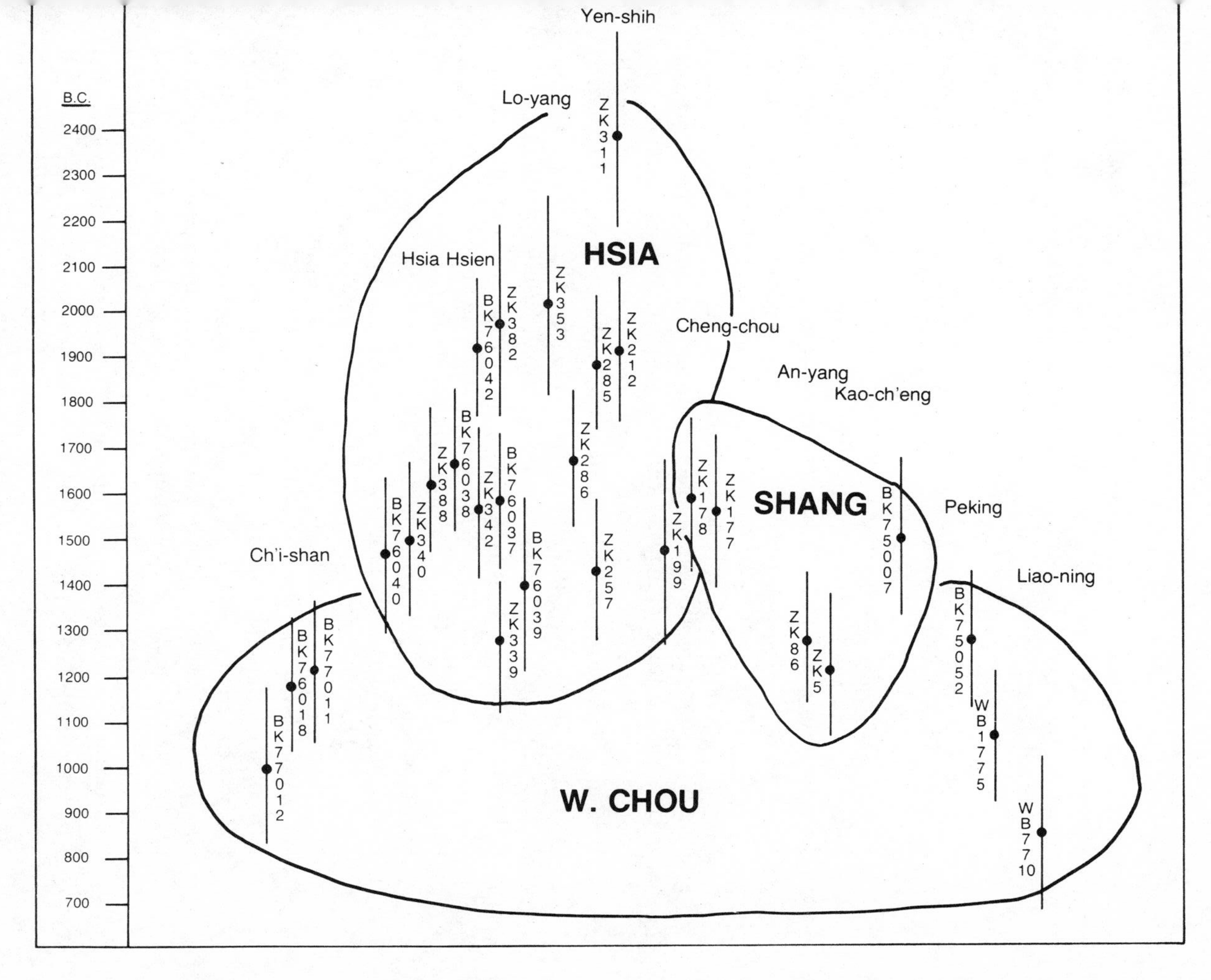

92. Radiocarbon dates from the Three Dynasties (for sources see appendix).

AREAS

The geographic centers of the reigning activities of the Three Dynasties, as plotted according to the locations of their capital cities, are generally agreed to being as follows: Chou was in the west, Hsia in the middle, and Shang in the east. This has been discussed in detail in the present volume and can be regarded as having been long established.

CULTURE AND SOCIETY

The Hsia, Shang, and Chou shared the same culture and only differed from one another in matters of detail—such is the general agreement of scholars according to both old and new written records. In *Li chi* ("Li ch'i"), it is stated that "the regulations of the Three Dynasties are the same, and all the people followed them." Confucius was quoted as saying, in *The Confucian Analects* ("Wei cheng"), that "the Yin Dynasty followed the regulations of the Hsia: wherein it took from or added to them may be known; the Chou Dynasty followed the regulations of the Yin: wherein it took from or added to them may be known." Some ancient historians have stressed these "takings or addings," maintaining that the Hsia, Shang, and Chou were three different ethnic groups. Ting Shan, for example, basing his views on the differences in ritual practices among the Three Dynasties as recorded in *The Confucian Analects, Mencius, Chou li* ("K'ao kung chi"), and *Li chi*, concludes that the Hsia's culture was native to the Central Plain, the Shang was a northeastern people affiliated with the Yen Po and the Shan Jung, and the Chou was a northwestern people related to Jung and Ti.[64] This view stresses the differences of detail. But "peoples" are classificatory categories based upon language and culture characteristics. We do not know the details of the Hsia people's language, but on the basis of the extant data on the Hsia we have no reason to speculate that it is any different from the language of the Shang or of the Chou. As to cultural classifications, they are often classifications of degree. To what extent cultures must differ for separate ethnic groups to be recognized is often a subjective judgment made to serve a specific purpose. As pointed out by Yen Yi-p'ing,[65] the sacred trees used for the earth ritual were indeed different among the Three Dynasties—pine for the Hsia,

64. Ting Shan 丁山, "Yu san-tai tu-yi lun ch'i min-tsu wen-hua" 由三代都邑論其民族文化.

65. Yen Yi-p'ing 嚴一萍, "Hsia Shang Chou wen-hua yi t'ung k'ao" 夏商周文化異同考, 394. See also Noel Barnard, "Review of Chou Hung-hsiang, *Shang-Yin ti-wang pen-chi*," for a clear discussion on the horizontal interrelationship of the Three Dynasties.

cypress for the Shang, and chestnut for the Chou—but all three performed such rituals and used sacred trees. Yen's conclusion, basing itself on broad similarities of culture rather than differences of detail, is that Hsia, Shang, and Chou were variations of the same cultural tradition.

In social organization and level of societal development, the Hsia, Shang, and Chou shared a very important feature, namely lineages in walled towns serving as the ruling instrument. The Hsia was a dynasty of the Ssu clan, the Shang, the Tzu clan, and the Chou, the Chi clan. All were similarly ruled by dynastic groups within clans, although the rulers of the three dynasties came from different clans. There were also some fundamental similarities in the royal succession rules; this topic I have discussed in detail in chapter 3. I have been able to show elsewhere[66] that the Shang system of royal succession was basically identical with the so-called *chao-mu* system of the Western Chou. The latter had by Eastern Chou times all but disappeared as the result of fundamental changes in the Chou society, and its details are no longer clear in extant Eastern Chou texts. Its nature can now be better understood because of our new understanding of the comparable system of the Shang. The Hsia system of succession to kingship is now not clear, but the Hsia also used the ten celestial stems for posthumous names,[67] and we have good reason to believe that the Hsia system resembles the Shang system in important details.[68] The Hsia, therefore, very possibly also had a *chao-mu* system.

Not only was it probable that the three dynasties had the same system of kingship; at least both Shang and Chou had the institution of enfeoffing royal lineage members, an institution that cannot be discussed separately from the early history of walled towns in ancient China.[69] All three dynasties built walled towns. *Shih pen* credits Kun, Yü's father, with the first building of walled towns, suggesting the importance of this institution in Hsia history. Shang's towns we have

66. Chang Kwang-chih 張光直, "Shang wang miao-hao hsin k'ao" 商王廟號新考; Chang Kwang-chih, "T'an Wang Hai yü Yi Yin ti chi jih ping tsai lun Yin Shang wang-chih" 談王亥與伊尹的祭日並再論殷商王制.

67. Yang Chün-shih 楊君實, "K'ang keng yü Hsia hui" 康庚與夏諱.

68. Chang Kwang-chih 張光直, "T'an Wang Hai yü Yi Yin ti chi jih ping tsai lun Yin Shang wang chih" 談王亥與伊尹的祭日並再論殷商王制. Sun Tso-yün 孫作雲, in his recently published study, "Ts'ung '*T'ien Wen*' k'an Hsia ch'u chien kuo shih" 從'天問'看夏初建國史 pointed out that, according to *T'ien Wen*, Yü, the founder of the Hsia dynasty, had an endogamous marriage with his wife, T'u Shan Shih, and that both after his death and after the death of his son the throne was the object of fierce competition among several lines. The situation could be easily explained in the light of our hypothesis of royal succession rules we have postulated for the Shang.

69. Kwang-chih Chang, *Early Chinese Civilization: Anthropological Perspectives*, pp. 68–71.

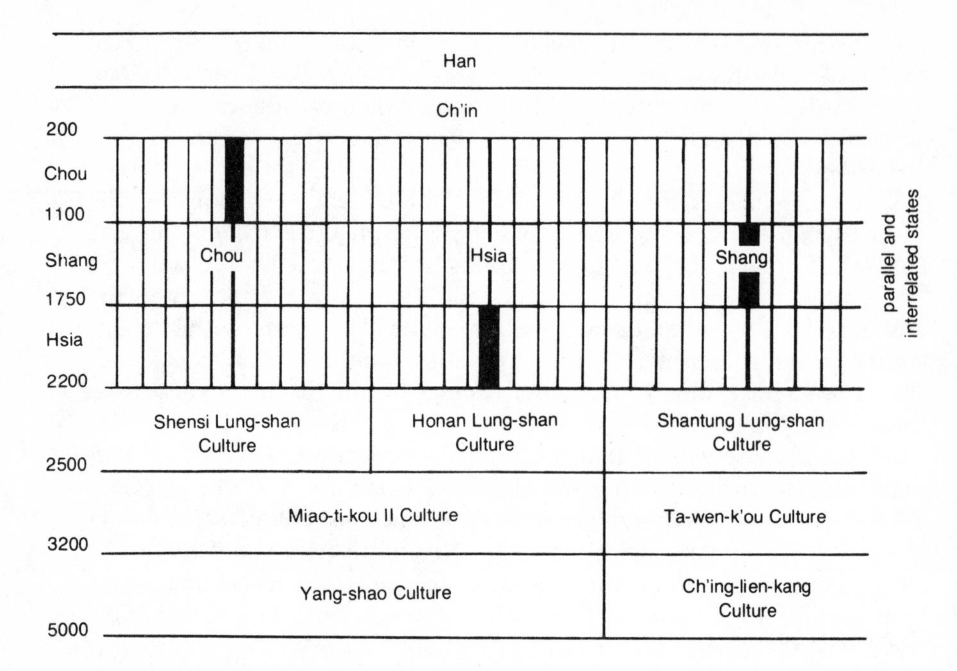

93. The parallel development model of the Three Dynasties civilizations.

discussed in detail. The Chou's town-building activities are vividly described in the *Shih ching* (e.g., "Mien"). All these point to a common level of societal development.

The above discussion should make it clear that the "insular model" of ancient Chinese civilizational development that up to now has dominated our thinking about ancient China—a model in which the Three Dynasties are seen in sequential order as an islands of civilization encircled by barbarous cultures—is inadequate. Instead, contemporary Three Dynasties archaeology points to a model characterized by parallel and interrelated development for the origins of Chinese civilization, one which sees a number of civilized states throughout a large area of North and Central China, and which sees their formation as being parallel, interrelated, and interactive. The terms Hsia dynasty, Shang dynasty, and Chou dynasty each have at least two different meanings. First, each term refers to a time period, namely, approximately 2200–1750 B.C. for Hsia, approximately 1750–1100 B.C. for Shang, and approximately 1100–220 B.C. for Chou. Second, it refers to a dynastic reign: namely, during the Hsia dynasty the rulers of the Hsia state were believed by late Chou and subsequent historians to have been given supreme status by a number of states during the Hsia period; during the Shang dynasty the Shang state's royal house was afforded that status; and during the Chou dynasty the Chou kings were believed to have reigned supreme. But, at the same time, Hsia, Shang, and Chou were three polities or states, and their interrelationship is a parallel one: the three states (and their ritual equivalents) were probably all in existence during all three dynasties, although their relative political power had shifted. Figure 93 makes clear the relationships among these various terms.

This parallel interrelationship of the three dynasties as seen in traditional texts is consistent with the world order as reconstructed from the oracle bone records and with the archaeological picture. As we have seen in chapter 6, the ancient Chinese civilization as established by archaeology has an areal scope approximating the interaction sphere of Shang and its contemporary states shown in the oracle records. The records disclose a vast number of interacting polities whose contending or subordinate status relative to the Shang state was a dynamic one. Chou, for example, appeared in the oracle records throughout as a parallel state, although its subordinate status relative to Shang is both presumable and established. Hsia, of course, does not appear in the oracle records of the Shang during the final stage of its rule, but Ch'i, Hsia's descendant state, does appear as a domain of a lord.[70]

70. Shima Kunio 島邦男, *Inkyo bokuji kenkyū* 殷墟卜辞研究, pp. 427–428.

Epilogue: Shang in the Ancient World

Scholars of the ancient world used to be in the habit of generalizing about universal issues solely on the basis of the history of the Western civilization, but they seldom do that now. For this we are indebted to New World prehistorians who have, in the past century, demonstrated that in the Western Hemisphere man achieved civilized status independent of any essential assist from Western civilization and, therefore, that in the study of universal patterns more than a single component of humanity must be examined individually. Thus, in a well-known and highly regarded study of the evolution of urban society, Robert McC. Adams selected an Old World and a New World example of early states as the major bases for comparison, in order "to minimize the possibility that similarities reflect genetic interconnection, that is, the operation of cultural diffusion, rather than independently occurring (and therefore presumably 'lawful,' cause-and-effect) regularities."[1]

In what way, then, can an individual examination of the earliest Chinese component of civilized humanity contribute to a study of universal patterns? In selecting Mesopotamia as his single Old World example for comparative study, Adams explains that he does so in part because one can be more sure of the pristine status of the ancient Mesopotamian civilization than with the civilizations "in Egypt, the Indus valley, and China." Adams listed two reasons why China was not used as his Old World example: the lateness of her first civilizations (relative to Mesopotamia) and the consequent prolonged exposure to a variety of direct and indirect influences from civilizations farther west, and the incompleteness of the archaeological record during the course of the urban revolution.[2]

No knowledgeable and fair-minded student of the ancient world would disagree with Adams on the choice of Mesopotamia and Mexico as his prime bases for comparative study. He should not, at the same time, be satisfied with these, or any, pair of ancient civilizations as the sole bases for generalizations that are meant to have world-wide

1. *The Evolution of Urban Society*, p. 20.
2. *Ibid.*, pp. 21–22.

applicability. It should be useful—indeed, vital—to constantly take stock of the current archaeological record of each of the important components of the ancient world and to see if the information from these areas offers additional grounds for reinforcing or modifying our working generalizations.

Shang was not the only civilized group of ancient China, not even the earliest. But as we have just seen it played a vital role in the formation of the early Chinese civilization, and it was the only one thus far on which we have adequate textual information about its own world order. And, since Adams wrote his book, Chinese archaeologists have gone a long way in enriching the record of the Shang. It may be useful, both to students of ancient China and to students of the ancient world, to examine some aspects of the Shang society and Shang civilization that may have wider implications.

1. *THE QUESTION OF "PRISTINENESS"*

There was a time when Chinese history could be pushed back no further than the Three Dynasties, which were preceded by a blank filled with mere myths and legends. It was not unreasonable, albeit premature, for Western scholars to turn to the Near East for Chinese precedents, where modern historiography and archaeology began much earlier and earlier civilizations had long been known.[3]

That era, an era of a prehistoric void, has long passed. A long sequence of cultural development has now firmly been established in North China beginning with Early Neolithic transformation and eventually leading up to the emergence of ranked and stratified societies and a literate civilization. To be sure, there are gaps in this sequence, and we await further details of that development from future archaeological evidence, but enough is now at hand for most writers on Chinese prehistory,[4] world prehistory,[5] and cultural evolution[6] to accept as a basic premise that Chinese civilization was an "indigenous" development.

But what exactly does the word "indigenous" mean? Because

3. See K. C. Chang, "The Origin of Chinese Civilization: A Review," for the various views.

4. K. C. Chang, *The Archaeology of Ancient China*; T. K. Cheng, "The Beginning of Chinese Civilization"; M. Sullivan, *The Arts of China*; L. Sickman and A. Soper, *The Art and Architecture of China*.

5. G. Daniel, *The First Civilizations;* B. Fagan, *People of the Earth*.

6. M. H. Fried, *The Evolution of Political Society*; Elman Service, *Origin of the State and Civilization*.

of our current preoccupation with cultural ecological premises many anthropologists and anthropologically oriented prehistorians tend to emphasize the local or regional ecosystems and to take the view that, whatever the outside stimuli, all local and regional developments must have an ecosystemic base and are, therefore, indigenous in that sense. Even at the cultural level, "political and economic development in the recipient culture had to reach a critical level before the integration of foreign institutions became possible or desirable."[7] Many scholars with such a view have tended to dismiss diffusion as an important factor of cultural and social dynamics. But diffusion should not be dismissed so easily. Cultural and social systems respond to many stimuli, including outside stimuli, in ways that that may result in systemic change. "The adopted institutions [may become] important catalysts in promoting further development of the social system. They also [may introduce] customs, practices, and a view of the world that were not of local origin or likely to have been paralleled at all closely by indigenous developments."[8]

Since it is a fact that Chinese civilization came into being at a later date than a few other civilizations elsewhere, it is entirely possible that the near antecedents of the Chinese civilization were exposed to stimuli from these other civilizations. Such exposure is best demonstrated by the presence of cultivated wheat as a food crop in the Shang civilization, since the history of domestication of wheat is well documented for the Near East.[9] The question, then, could be this: Would Chinese civilization have come about without such outside stimuli? Questions such as this are unanswerable, but obviously we must examine the history of each item of material culture and institution that may be shared by China and the Near East (or any other area) and try to determine its possibly catalyst role in the Chinese development. In his *The Cradle of the East,* Ho Ping-ti attempted such an examination, concluding that "the full inventory of cultural imports into ancient China is not only meager in quantity, but qualitatively and chronologically such as to have had no bearing whatever either on the beginnings of any of the major Chinese cultural elements or on the birth of China as a whole."[10]

Ho's case was built on a weighty foundation, but we can hardly hope that we have been delivered the final word on the matter. William H. McNeill, who wrote a foreword for Ho's book, was so impressed

7. Bruce G. Trigger, *Time and Traditions: Essays in Archaeological Interpretation,* p. 227.

8. *Ibid.,* p. 227.

9. Charles A. Reed, "A Model for the Origin of Agriculture in the Near East."

10. p. 362.

by the force of Ho's argument that he said he found it "hard to imagine what kind of evidence could upset or seriously modify the general conclusion of this work."[11] In a critical review of the same work, David Keightley rose to the challenge and enumerated several imagined lines of evidence that he felt could seriously upset Ho's thesis.[12] I don't wish to style myself a referee, but I must say that, although Ho's thesis is not the final word, we must accept—as I know Keightley does—Ho's general conclusions *until* future evidence of a convincing nature comes to light to contradict them.

But the real question at this juncture is not whether or not the Chinese development was indigenous—the preponderance of current evidence affirms that it was. Our question is, does the issue of the Chinese pristineness matter a good deal insofar as using the Chinese evidence for the study of universal patterns is concerned? To this, McNeill's answer was apparently quite affirmative: "[The indigenous view] requires Westerners to abandon their older opinion that all mankind followed essentially the same paths to civilization—a view, incidentally, enshrined in Marxian teachings about the universal stages of social development from primitive communism to capitalist exploitation, and beyond."[13]

Universal patterns and separate paths are not mutually exclusive. It is true that there was a single pristine atomic explosion, in 1945, in the United States, and all subsequent explosions in Great Britain, the USSR, France, China, and India were derivative. In all cases the thread of knowledge could be traced directly back to Los Alamos. But in every case the industrial milieu and technological procedures had to be repeated before an explosion could occur. Once an advance in knowledge or technology occurred anywhere in the world, it began to form the nucleus of a radiating web, and all subsequent occurrences become suspect. The extent of their indebtedness to this initial occurrence, however, must be studied in each case and until a thorough study has been made and a case proven one can only *assume* that a later occurrence was pristine or that it was not. But whether or not such conclusions or assumptions make a difference in our interpretive task is probably something that depends on the nature of that task. If we are to enumerate exhaustively the sources of stimuli that are believed to have caused a systemic change, then the history of each item of material culture and institution must be completely known before we can complete our assignment. But if we are to see, given such stimuli as they existed or

11. *Ibid.*, p. xiv.
12. "Ho Ping-ti and the Origin of Chinese Civilization," 411.
13. Ho Ping-ti, *The Cradle of the East*, p. xv.

occured, patterns of internal or induced changes, or factors that determined the shape and direction of such changes, or a number of other phenomena and the causes behind them, then the pristine or secondary status of the civilization, or that of any of its parts, becomes essentially irrelevant.

2. *SHANG'S POSITION IN EVOLUTIONARY SCHEMES*

From a social evolutionary perspective, the formation process of the ancient Chinese civilization underwent the following significant steps:

1. Level of Village Societies. Yang-shao and Ch'ing-lien-kang cultures. Individual villages were the primary social unit politically and economically.

2. Level of Intervillage Aggregates. At this level villages had developed political, economic, and military bonds of such natures that we find the following phenomena in the archaeological record: the beginning of internal differentiation into poor and rich groups; evidence of internal and/or external violence; specialized handicrafts (such as pottery); existence of religious specialists probably in the exclusive service of the chiefly class. Under these conditions, intervillage leagues of a more or less permanent nature must have formed, administered by full time rulers. Into this level we classify the Shensi, Honan, and Shantung Lung-shan cultures; the Ta-wen-k'ou culture of the east coast may have reached this level of development, but we are not certain yet of the classificatory status of the Miao-ti-kou II culture in the interior.

3. Level of the State Societies. This is the period of the Three Dynasties in ancient Chinese history; archaeologically we refer to the Erh-li-t'ou culture and its contemporaries, the Shang civilization, and the Chou civilization. At this level, settlements formed complex and permanent networks (often stratified into several levels). The fulltime rulerships of such networks became the monopoly of individual clans or lineages, and rulers were assisted by a relatively permanent control and administrative mechanism, including the mechanism to oppress with force, both internally and externally.

The earliest archaeological culture that we can attribute to this level is the Erh-li-t'ou culture of northwestern Honan, whose identification with the Hsia has been discussed above. Among the Hsia's contemporary states Shang was surely a most important one; it is believed that the Shang's earlier segments will be found in the general area of eastern Honan, western Shantung, and northernmost Anhwei. From

Middle Shang onwards, many Shang sites have been uncovered throughout North and Central China. People at these sites evidently lived under more than a single state, but of the many contemporary states within the area of distribution of Shang remains the state of Shang was apparently the most powerful. We do not know exactly what the word "reigned" entailed exactly in terms of the hierarchical relations Shang had with the other states during the Shang "dynasty." The reigning status undoubtedly involved political and ceremonial supremacy; there was probably a kind of tributary network, but how much real economic (aside from ceremonial and symbolic) significance this network had is unclear. The essential features of such networks have been discussed in chapter 4. After Wu Wang's conquest, the reigning status shifted to Chou. After Chou the contending states were replaced by a higher form of state society, namely, the centralized bureaucratic government of the Ch'in and Han empires.

Thus formulated, the above evolutionary sequence of ancient Chinese societies provides scholars of comparative social evolution with important new data and even makes its own unique contribution. In the last decade or so American anthropologists have shown an increasing interest in theories of social evolution, and a number of archaeologists have attempted to apply some of these theories to archaeological sequences in various regions of the world, focusing their attention, particularly, on the question of the origin of the state. In such discussions relatively few have utilized contemporary Chinese data, and, on the other hand, Chinese ancient historical issues have rarely been processed from a general, comparative perspective other than Marxian platitudes. It might be useful to see to what extent our current thinking about Three Dynasties archaeology can be related to social evolutionary schemes and to the issue of state origins.

The most widely adopted evolutionary scheme in contemporary American archaeology is that of Elman Service,[14] whose four "levels of integration," namely, band, tribe, chiefdom, and state, are widely used. We list in table 7 the Chinese stages in relation to this scheme and to the Marxian periodization scheme universally adopted in China. Although the Chinese archaeological sequence still has important gaps, its segmentation in accordance with the Service scheme is relatively clear, at least in my opinion. There has been some controversy with regard to the classification of the Three Dynasties into the chiefdom level or into the state level. The distinction between these two levels is conceptually clear, but some of the diagnostic features that separate

14. *Primitive Social Organization*; *Origins of the State and Civilization: The Process of Cultural Evolution*.

TABLE 7 Archaeological Cultures and Evolutionary Stages in China

<table>
<tr><th>Archaeological Cultures</th><th>Service</th><th>Marxian</th></tr>
<tr><td>Palaeolithic</td><td rowspan="2">Band</td><td rowspan="4">Primitive</td></tr>
<tr><td>Mesolithic</td></tr>
<tr><td>Yang-shao</td><td>Tribe</td></tr>
<tr><td>Lung-shan</td><td>Chiefdom</td></tr>
<tr><td>Three Dynasties (to Spring—Autumn)</td><td rowspan="2">State</td><td>Slave</td></tr>
<tr><td>Late Chou, Ch'in, Han</td><td>Feudal (beginning)</td></tr>
</table>

the two are quantitative in nature and often difficult to recognize in real data. According to Sanders and Price,[15] the major characteristic of the chiefdom is that its political ranking is tied in with its kinship system, whereas the state level is primarily characterized by legitimatized force. This distinction is further, more clearly, elaborated by Kent V. Flannery:

> The state is a type of very strong, unusually highly centralized government, with a professional ruling class, largely divorced from the bonds of kinship which characterize simpler societies. It is highly stratified and extremely diversified internally, with residential patterns often based on occupational specialization rather than blood or affinal relationship. The state attempts to maintain a monopoly of force, and is characterized by true law; almost any crime may be considered a crime against the state, in which case punishment is meted out by the state according to codified procedures, rather than being the responsibility of the offended party or his kin, as in simpler societies. While individual citizens must forego violence, the state can wage war; it can also draft soldiers, levy taxes, and exact tributes.[16]

In this view, a state society must possess two prerequisite features: replacement of blood bonds by territorial bonds in state organization, and legitimatized force. Applying these criteria to Shang, we find that the first is not applicable but the second is. Was the Shang a state society?

15. William T. Sanders and Barbara J. Price, *Mesoamerica.*
16. "The Cultural Evolution of Civilizations," 403–404.

In discussing the transition from chiefdom to state levels in Mesoamerica, Sanders suggested using architecture as an archaeological criterion: Rulers of chiefdoms could use forced labor to build temples and tombs, but only rulers of states could force the construction of their residential palaces.[17] Here the problem lies in the definition of the palace in terms of its magnitude. Shang palaces, temples, and tombs were all indeed impressive structures, but in architectural scale and permanency the Shang palaces are certainly inferior to the imperial palaces of Ch'in, Han, and later dynasties. Is Shang a chiefdom then, and not a state? But it would be absurd to decide so, for Shang fits the definition of the state with regard to its legitimate force, its hierarchical ruling structure, and its social classes. In short, the Shang data pose some definitional problems in regard to its classification as chiefdom or as state. There can be two ways to resolve them. One is to regard Shang as an aberration or an exception to the rule. As an example of this approach, Jonathan Friedman refers to those ancient states in which the distribution of political power was based on blood relationship as the "Asiatic state."[18] The second approach would be to include the ancient Chinese data in the data base for any general definition of the state, namely, to reassess the interrelationship of blood and territorial bonds in a state definition. The importance of the archaeology of the Three Dynasties period in a general theory of social evolution is, of course, explicit only under the latter approach.

3. *THE QUESTION OF STATE ORIGINS, CIVILIZATION, AND URBANISM*

State, civilization, and city are not only concurrent in their initial occurrence but also, in all likelihood, interrelated in the causes for their occurrence. But anthropologists seem determined to tackle them separately according to academic fashion. The 1950s were the decade of the cities, beginning with Gordon Childe's famous treatise on "The Urban Revolution"[19] and concluding with the conferences that resulted in *City Invinsible*[20] and *Courses Toward Urban Life*.[21] Civilization has been

17. William T. Sanders, "Chiefdom to State: Political Evolution at Kaminaljuyu, Guatemala," 109.

18. "Tribes, States, and Transformations," 195. For other recent discussion of the Asiatic state, see Centre d'Études et de Recherches marxistes, *Sur le mode de production Asiatique*; Perry Anderson, *Lineages of the Absolute State*.

19. 1950.

20. Carl H. Kraeling and Robert McC. Adams, eds.

21. Robert J. Braidwood and Gordon R. Willey, eds.

a perennial theme, but the decade of the 1960s saw more than its share of monumental tomes with that theme, from *The Dawn of Civilization*[22] to *The First Civilizations*.[23] The current decade, the 1970s, is the state's turn, if the mushrooming crop of books and articles on "state origins" or "state formations" is any indication.[24] The last fad, that of the origins of the state, one finds even in China,[25] although it probably was not the result of diffusion from America!

These concepts could best be looked at together and as part of overall evolutionary issues. One begins by looking for the essential societal features behind what we call civilizations in the first place.

What is a civilization? There are many definitions of the term, and many of them are very refined and sophisticated. But to most of us, at least to most of the reading public, civilization is a style, a quality, that is most characteristically represented by such objects of material culture in the archaeological record as monumental architecture and religious art. To put it bluntly, these are objects that are remote from daily use or from subsistence needs, or objects that are wasteful from a utilitarian point of view. When we see an ancient society willing and able to devote considerable wealth for seemingly useless tasks, we would admire its people and call them civilized. The more wasteful they are, the greater their civilization looms in our eyes.

Looked at this way, it is obvious that civilization is possible only with an abundant surplus of wealth within the society that produced it. It must be noted, however, that no surplus can come about naturally with advanced technology, because the subsistence threshold is always arbitrarily defined. A surplus is a man-made portion of wealth, arbitrarily imposed upon the society as a result of the reshuffling of its resources and its wealth. Such a reshuffling concentrates society's wealth in the hands of a small segment of the society, giving them both the capability and the necessity to create the wasteful hallmarks of the so-called civilizations. Such resource reshuffling is enabled by at least three sets of societal dichotomies or societal opposites. I would refer to civilization, as archaeologically recognized, as the cultural manifestation of these contrastive pairs of societal opposites: class-class, urban-nonurban, and state-state. In other words, economic stratification,

22. Stuart Piggott, ed.

23. Glyn Daniel.

24. Robert L. Carneiro, "A Theory of the Origin of the State"; Elman R. Service, *Origins of the State and Civilization*; R. Cohen and E. R. Service, eds., *Origins of the State*.

25. See, for example, T'ung Chu-ch'en 佟柱臣, "Ts'ung Erh-li-t'ou lei-hsing wen-hua shih t'an Chung-kuo ti kuo-chia ch'i-yüan wen-t'i 從二里頭類型文化試談中國的國家起源問題.

urbanization, and interstate relations are three of civilization's necessary societal determinants.

Truistic explanations suffice. Economic stratification enables the concentration of resources within the state, and urbanization is the mechanism whereby the state accomplishes that concentration within regional economic universes. Then interstate interaction in the form of warfare and trade makes possible a higher degree of flow of both resources and information which further widens the systemic sphere of the economy and facilitates the concentration of resources within the state. All of these have been shown to be working principles in Shang society. Current studies permit the generalization that the Shang society was sharply stratified into economic classes, that it is one in which there were highly sophisticated regional economic networks, and, more importantly, it was one of a number of contemporary polities of comparable complexity. Its archaeology is characterized by the hallmarks of what we regard as civilization.

We can further generalize from this to produce what I will immodestly call laws of ancient civilizational development. First, early civilizations came about only with a political situation in which more than a single state is involved. At least two states must be involved, more likely in excess of two. There can be no civilization in a single state surrounded by barbarians. As Henry Wright has pointed out, "[Complex chiefdoms] may exist on favored islands, but they do not seem to develop into states until they are drawn into a larger system. Our concern is with networks of chiefdoms regulated by warfare and alliance" and "[states], like chiefdoms, usually exist in networks of states. Among simpler states these networks seem to be regulated by competition and alliance, as was briefly noted for chiefdoms."[26]

In the Chinese situation, as we have noted, the various states—Hsia, Shang, and Chou, and others—occupied different territories in North and Central China, each characterized by certain distinctive resources. It has been further noted that the Shang-period oracle records suggest that the Shang's principal interactions were with other states of comparable civilizational level. The economic interacting relationship among three—or more—states of comparable levels of development would enable a degree of circulation of raw material and products North and Central China-wide that would not have been possible within single states or between a state and more primitive societies. Such circulation of goods would provide favorable conditions for the concentration of wealth and for the production of surpluses within each of the interacting states. In addition, threat of external violence

26. Henry Wright, "Recent Research on the Origin of the State," 382, 385.

would tend to promote internal integration, or at least such claims have been a favorite political technique throughout human history. As Trigger put it, "the truism that provides the point of departure for most of Service's recent arguments about the nature of early civilizations is the observation that no state can be held together by force alone. For a regime to survive, a majority of its subjects must remain convinced that there is no reasonable chance of seeing it replaced by a regime that might better serve their interests."[27] The competition among the states and any national consciousness that may be formed within each of the states in the course of long centuries and millennia must have been one of the major stabilizing factors within each of the states.

The second law-like statement one can make is that the more uneven or inequitable the resource reshuffling within the state, the greater the hallmarks of civilization that will be produced. And vice versa. This principle affords us the ability to predict the degree of economic stratification and complexity of regional economic system on the basis of the manifestations of civilization of that society. The higher that degree is in the archaeological manifestation we encounter, the more wastefully sophisticated or the less utilitarian it is from the point of view of subsistence needs. One look at King Tut's tomb, for example, without knowing anything about ancient Egypt, and we can predict that we are seeing an extremely stratified society, with an efficiently run and regionally differentiated economic universe and with fierce interstate or interpolity competition. There is no question that it is great art, but neither is there any question that it was purchased at extreme human cost. What is a rise of civilization and what is its fall? These value-charged words represent an evaluative judgment that has been made of the society's apex. I wonder if, in passing judgment over a civilization's rise and fall we should not, instead, take into account the meaning of these concepts in terms of lives away from the top and in terms of a society's evolutionary course. As often as not, a civilization's fall marks a society's progress. In John E. Pfeiffer's words, "one man's decadence . . . may be another man's renaissance. Less effort was being spent on the care and feeding of elites and more on the rest of the population, on such things as wider distribution of wealth and higher standards of living."[28]

27. Bruce G. Trigger, "Inequality and Communication in Early Civilizations," 36.

28. *The Emergence of Society*, p. 470.

Postscript

Since the construction of the Shang civilization presented in the preceding pages has been based to a large extent on recent archaeological data and epigraphical studies, one assumes that it is subject to change with new data and new studies. New material that has become available since the manuscript of the book was completed near the end of 1978 does not yet necessitate any change of our view, but a few additions should be noted.

At An-yang, new excavations in the western section of the Yin hsü that took place from 1969 to 1977 have been reported (*KKHP* 1979 [1], 27–146). These excavations, which brought to light 1,003 Shang dynasty tombs and 5 horse-and-chariot burials, involved a 300,000 square meter area outlined by Pai-chia-fen, Mei-yüan-chuang, Pei-hsin-chuang, and Hsiao-min-t'un. The tombs, of various degrees of elaborateness in terms of construction and furnishings, clustered into eight groups, "each distinguished by its own grave orientation, burial mode, and pottery assemblage." The excavators believe that each cluster represents the burial area of a discrete lineage (or *tsu*). It should be noted that grave furnishings varied greatly within each cluster, pointing to the stratified nature of the lineages within themselves. This adds to our discussion on *tsu* and their internal stratification in chapter 3.

A tomb with wooden chamber, sacrificial human victims, and ritual bronzes with decorative designs similar to those of M 333 of Hsiao-t'un (p. 82) is reported from north of Wu-kuan-ts'un, i.e., in the Hsi-pei-kang cemetery area (*KK* 1979 [3], 223–226). This indicates that the predynastic occupation of An-yang (chapter 1) had extended to the northern bank of the Huan River.

A newly reported stratified site at Hsia-ch'i-yuan in Tz'u Hsien, at the southern end of Hopei (well within our Royal Capital area; see chapter 1), is said to contain no fewer than four strata of cultural deposits, namely, from bottom to top, Erh-li-t'ou culture, Early Shang, Middle Shang, and Late Shang (*KKHP* 1979 [2], 185–214). The Erh-li-t'ou culture, represented solely by pottery, makes its first appearance in Hopei. The "Early Shang," compared by the reporters of the site with the Shang remains at Chien-kou in Han-tan, is again represented by pottery which is "typologically earlier" than the Erh-li-kang pottery of Cheng-chou. Whether this suffices to indicate an Early Shang focus within the widely distributed Erh-li-kang phase is as yet too early to tell.

In this connection, some newly reported radiocarbon dates are of interest. An unusually large new batch of radiocarbon dates reported by the Radiocarbon Laboratory of the Institute of Archaeology (*KK* 1979 [1], 89–94) contains the following samples from the Three Dynasties (the last figure calibrated according to Damon, Ferguson, Long, and Wallick, 1974).

Lab No.	*Civilization*	*Site*	*C-14 Date* ($\frac{1}{2}$*-life* = *5570*)	*Calibrated Years* B.C.
ZK-531	Erh-li-t'ou	Tung-hsia-feng, Hsia Hsien	3685 ± 100	2200 ± 165
ZK-435	"	"	3515 ± 150	1975 ± 200
ZK-436	"	"	3425 ± 100	1845 ± 110
ZK-486	Shang	Meng-chuang 孟庄, Che-ch'eng 柘城, Honan	3185 ± 80	1530 ± 95
ZK-487	"	"	3370 ± 90	1780 ± 100
ZK-488	"	"	3365 ± 90	1780 ± 100
ZK-446	Wu-ch'eng	Wu-ch'eng, Ch'ing-chiang, Kiangsi	3380 ± 150	1780 ± 155
ZK-447	"	"	3250 ± 150	1625 ± 105
ZK-480	Lower Hsia-chia-tien	Ta-tien-tzu, Ao-han Banner, Liaoning	3320 ± 85	1720 ± 95
ZK-530–1	Western Chou	Chang-chia-p'o, Feng-hsi, Ch'ang-an, Shensi	2660 ± 85	875 ± 100

The Tung-hsia-feng and Feng-hsi dates are consistent with their Hsia and Western Chou status, but all the other dates come out somewhat earlier than expected. Both Wu-ch'eng in the south and Ta-tien-tzu in the north, thought to be contemporary with Erh-li-kang, appear to be two hundred or so years earlier instead. The Meng-chuang site has not been reported; its early date and its location (in eastern Honan, near Po Hsien, the area of the earliest Shang dynastic locus) could be significant. All this makes it all too plain that the early historiography of the Shang civilization is still in a most fluid state. I hope my readers will watch with me for future developments with keen anticipation and openness of mind.

June 30, 1979

Appendix Radiocarbon Dates of Hsia, Shang, and Western Chou Archaeological Finds

Lab Number	*Site*	*Location*	*C-14 Years* B.P. *(Based on 5730)*	*C-14 Years* B.P. *(Based on 5570)*	*Years* B.C.*
ZK-86	An-yang	Hsiao-t'un Shang	3065 ± 90	2978 ± 90	1280 ± 150
ZK-5	"	Royal tomb, Wu-kuan-ts'un	3035 ± 100	2949 ± 100	1210 ± 160
ZK-178	Cheng-chou	Shang town wall	3330 ± 95	3235 ± 90	1590 ± 160
ZK-177	"	"	3310 ± 95	3215 ± 90	1560 ± 160
BK-75007	Kao-ch'eng	Shang	3250 ± 100	3155 ± 100	1500 ± 170
ZK-199	Lo-ta-miao, Cheng-chou	Erh-li-t'ou Culture Stratum	3230 ± 130	3140 ± 130	1470 ± 190
ZK-253	Ts'o-li, Lo-yang	"	3645 ± 130	3545 ± 130	2010 ± 220
ZK-31–1	Erh-li-t'ou, Yen-shih	"	3955 ± 115	3845 ± 115	2390 ± 190
ZK-212	"	"	3570 ± 95	3470 ± 95	1910 ± 160
ZK-285	"	"	3555 ± 80	3455 ± 80	1880 ± 150
ZK-286	"	Erh-li-t'ou IV Stratum	3340 ± 85	3245 ± 85	1620 ± 150
ZK-257	"	Erh-li-t'ou III Stratum	3195 ± 90	3105 ± 90	1430 ± 160
ZK-382	Tung-hsia-feng Hsia Hsien	76SW26 T501 (4B)	3635 ± 115	3535 ± 115	1980 ± 210
BK-76042	"	"	3580 ± 80	(3470 ± 80)	1910 ± 150
BK-76038	"	74SW26 T21 (3A)	3370 ± 90	(3270 ± 90)	1660 ± 160
ZK-388	"	76SW26 T501 (4B)	3360 ± 90	3265 ± 90	1620 ± 160
BK-76037	"	74SW26 H12	3320 ± 80	(3220 ± 80)	1590 ± 150
ZK-342	"	75SW26H1 (Early)	3305 ± 110	3210 ± 110	1560 ± 170

Lab Number	Site	Location	*C-14 Years* B.P. *(Based on 5730)*	*C-14 Years* B.P. *(Based on 5570)*	*Years* B.C.*
ZK-340	"	74SW26: 4B (Late)	3260 ± 110	3170 ± 110	1500 ± 170
BK-76040	"	74SW26 H105 (2)	3230 ± 100	(3130 ± 100)	1470 ± 170
BK-76039	"	74SW26 H9	3170 ± 140	(3075 ± 140)	1400 ± 190
ZK-339	"	74SW26 H15 (Middle)	3080 ± 105	2990 ± 105	1280 ± 170
BK-77011	Feng-ch'u, Ching-tang, Ch'i-shan	W. Chou	3030 ± 90	(2940 ± 90)	1210 ± 150
BK-76018	"	"	2990 ± 90	(2900 ± 90)	1180 ± 150
BK-77012	"	"	2840 ± 110	(2755 ± 110)	1000 ± 170
BK-75052	Pai-fu-lung-shan, Ch'ang-p'ing, Peking	"	3070 ± 90	2980 ± 90	1280 ± 150
WB-77–5	"	"	2895 ± 100	(2810 ± 100)	1060 ± 160
WB-77–10	Lung-wan, Wei-ying-tzu, Ch'ao-yang, Liaoning	"	2725 ± 100	(2640 ± 100)	850 ± 160

Based on the following sources:
Hsia Nai, "T'an-14 ts'e-ting nien-tai ho Chung-kuo shih-ch'ien k'ao-ku hsüeh."
KK, "Fang-she-hsing t'an-su ts'e-ting nien-tai pao-kao (wu)."
WW, "T'an-shih-ssu nien-tai ts'e-ting pao-kao, hsü yi."
WW, "Yeh-t'i shan-li-fa t'an-shih-ssu nien-tai ts'e-ting."

*Calibrated according to the tables in P. E. Damon, C. W. Ferguson, A. Long, and E. I. Wallick, "Dendrochronological Calibration of the Radiocarbon Time Scale."

Bibliography

General Readings on the Shang

Chao Lin 趙林. *Shang shih tai ting kao* 商史待定稿. (A preface to this as yet unpublished monograph, with a full table of contents, is seen in *Jen yü She-hui* 人與社會 1 [3] 1973, 101–103.)

Cheng Te-k'un 鄭德坤. *Shang China*. Cambridge: Heffer, 1960.

Itō Michiharu 伊藤道治. *Kodai In Ochō no nazo* 古代殷王朝のなぞ. Tokyo: Kadokawa shoden, 1967.

Kaizuka Shigeki 貝塚茂樹. *Kodai In daigoku* 古代殷帝国. Tokyo: Misuzu shobo, 1967.

Li Chi 李濟. *Anyang*. Seattle: University of Washington Press, 1977.

Peking University, Department of History. *Shang Chou k'ao-ku* 商周考古. Peking, 1979.

Shirakawa Shizuka 白川静. *Kōkotsubun no sekai—Kodai In Ochō no kōzo* 甲骨文の世界—古代殷王朝の構造. Tokyo: Heibansha, 1972.

Umehara Sueji 梅原末治. *Inshō* 殷墟. Tokyo: Asahishinbunsha, 1964.

Yang Chien-fang 楊建芳. *An-yang Yin hsü* 安陽殷墟. Peking: Chung-hua Shu-chü, 1965.

References Cited

Ackerman, Phyllis. *Ritual Bronzes of Ancient China*. New York: Dryden Press, 1945.

Adams, Robert McC. *The Evolution of Urban Society*. Chicago and New York: Aldine-Atherton, 1966.

Akatsuka Kiyoshi 赤塚忠. *(Kōhon) In kinbun kōshaku* (稿本)殷金文考釋. Tokyo, 1959.

Amano Motonosuke 天野元之助. "Indai sangyō no kansuru jakkan no mondai" 殷代産業の関する若干の問題. *Tōhōgakuhō (Kyotō)* 23 (1953): 231–258.

An Chih-min 安志敏. "Cheng-chou shih Jen-min kung-yüan fu-chin ti Yin tai yi-ts'un" 鄭州市人民公園附近的殷代遺存. *Wen-wu* 文物 1954 (6): 32–37.

———. "Ho-nan An-yang Hsiao-nan-hai chiu-shih-ch'i shih-tai tung-hsüeh tui-chi ti shih chüeh" 河南安陽小南海舊石器時代洞穴堆積的試掘. *K'ao-ku Hsüeh-pao* 考古學報 1965 (1): 1–27.

———. "Ho-pei Ch'ü-yang tiao-ch'a chi" 河北曲陽調查記. *K'ao-ku T'ung-hsün* 考古通訊 1955 (1): 39–44.

———. "Kuan-yü Cheng-chou 'Shang ch'eng' ti chi-ko wen-t'i 關於鄭州'商城'的幾個問題. *K'ao-ku* 考古 1961 (8): 448–450.

———. "Yi-chiu-wu-erh nien ch'iu chi Cheng-chou Erh-li-kang fa-chüeh chi" 一九五二年秋季鄭州二里岡發掘記. *K'ao-ku Hsüeh-pao* 考古學報 8 (1954): 65–107.

An Chin-huai 安金槐. "Cheng-chou ti-ch'ü ti ku-tai yi-ts'un chieh-shao" 鄭州地區的古代遺存介紹. *Wen-wu* 1957 (8): 16–20.

———. "Shih lun Cheng-chou Shang tai ch'eng chih—Ao tu" 試論鄭州商代城址—隞都. *Wen-wu* 1961 (4/5): 73–80.

———. "T'ang-yin Ch'ao-ko-chen fa-hsien Lung-shan ho Shang tai teng wen-hua yi-chih" 湯陰朝歌鎮發現龍山和商代等文化遺址. *Wen-wu* 1957 (5): 86.

Anderson, Perry. *Lineages of the Absolute State*. London: NLB, 1974.

Andersson, J. G. "Prehistoric Sites in Honan." *Bulletin of the Museum of Far Eastern Antiquities* 19 (1947).

———. "Researches into the Prehistory of the Chinese." *Bulletin of the Museum of Far Eastern Antiquities* 15 (1943).

Bagley, Robert W. "P'an-lung-ch'eng: A Shang City in Hupei." *Artibus Asiae* 39 (1977): 165–219.

Barnard, Noel. *Bronze Casting and Bronze Alloys in Ancient China*. Monumenta Serica Monograph 14, Tokyo, 1961.

———. "Chou China: A Review of the Third Volume of Cheng Te-k'un's *Archaeology in China*." *Monumenta Serica* 24 (1965): 307–459.

———. *The First Radiocarbon Dates from China*, new and enlarged. Monographs on Far Eastern History, 8. Canberra: Australian National University, 1975.

———. "Review of Chou Hung-hsiang, *Shang-Yin ti-wang pen-chi*." *Monumenta Serica* 19 (1960): 486–515.

———, and Satō Tamotsu. *Metallurgical Remains of Ancient China*. Tokyo: Nichiosha, 1975.

Bell, F. L. S. "A Functional Interpretation of Inheritance and Succession in Central Polynesia." *Oceania* 3 (1932): 167–206.

Bishop, Carl W. "The Neolithic Age in Northern China." *Antiquity* 7, no. 28 (1933): 389–404.

Braidwood, Robert J., and Gordon R. Willey, eds. *Courses toward Urban Life*. Chicago: Aldine, 1962.

Brew, John O. "Archaeology of Alkali Ridge, Southeastern Utah." *Papers of the Peabody Museum, Harvard University*, 21 (1946).

Burgess, C. M. *The Living Cowries*. New York: A. S. Barnes & Co., 1970.

Carneiro, Robert L. "A Theory of the Origin of the State." *Science* 169 (1970): 733–738.

Centre d'Études et de Recherches marxistes. *Sur la mode de production Asiatique*. Paris: Editions Sociales, 1969.

Chalfant, Frank H. (see also Fang Fa-lien). *Chin-chang so ts'ang chia-ku p'u-tz'u* 金璋所藏甲骨卜辭 [*The Hopkins collection of inscribed aracle bones*]. New York: The Chalfant Publication Fund, 1939.

———, and R. S. Britton. *Chia-ku p'u-tz'u ch'i chi* 甲骨卜辭七集 [Seven collections of inscribed oracle bone]. New York: The Chalfant Publication

Fund, 1938.
Chang Cheng-lang 張政烺. "P'u-tz'u p'ou t'ien chi ch'i hsiang-kuan chu wen-t'i" 卜辭裒田及其相關諸問題. *K'ao-ku Hsüeh-pao* 1973 (1): 93–118.
Chang Ching-hsien 張景賢. *Chung-kuo nu-li she-hui* 中國奴隸社會. Peking: Chung-hua, 1974.
Chang Hung-chao 章鴻釗. *Shih ya* 石雅 [Lapidarium sinicum]. *Ti-chih Chuan-pao* 地質專報, series 2, no. 2, 1917.
Chang Kuang-yüan 張光遠. "Hsi-Chou chung ch'i Mao kung ting" 西周重器毛公鼎. *Ku-kung Chi K'an* 故宮季刊 7, no. 2 (1973): 1–69. (An English abridgment of this article, by John Marney, appears in *Monumenta Serica*, 31 [1974/75]: 446–474).
Chang Kwang-chih 張光直. *The Archaeology of Ancient China*. 3d ed. New Haven and London: Yale University Press, 1977.
———. "Chung-kuo hsin shih-ch'i shih-tai wen-hua tuan-tai" 中國新石器時代文化斷代, *Bulletin of the Institute of History and Philology, Academia Sinica*, 30 (1959): 259–309.
———. "Chung-kuo k'ao-ku-hsüeh shang ti fang-she-hsing t'an-su nien-tai chi ch'i yi-yi" 中國考古學上的放射性碳素年代及其意義. *Bulletin of the Department of Archaeology and Anthropology*, National Taiwan University, 37/38 (1975): 29–43.
———. "The Continuing Quest for China's Origins." *Archaeology* 30 (1977): 116–123, 186–193.
———. *Early Chinese Civilization: Anthropological Perspectives*. Cambridge: Harvard University Press, 1976.
———. "Food and Food Vessels in Ancient China." *Transactions of the New York Academy of Sciences*, ser. II, 35 (1973): 495–520.
———. "The Origin of Chinese Civilization: A review." *Journal of the American Oriental Society* 98 (1978): 85–91.
———. "Shang Chou ch'ing-t'ung-ch'i ch'i-hsing chuang-shih hua-wen yü ming-wen tsung-ho yen-chiu ch'u-pu pao-kao" 商周青銅器器形裝飾花紋與銘文綜合研究初步報告. *Bulletin of the Institute of Ethnology, Academia Sinica* 30 (1970): 239–315.
———. "Shang Chou shen-hua yü mei-shu chung so-chien jen yü tung-wu kuan-hsi chih yen-pien 商周神話與美術中所見人與動物關係之演變." *Bulletin of the Institute of Ethnology, Academia Sinica* 16 (1963): 115–146.
———. "Shang wang miao-hao hsin k'ao" 商王廟號新考. *Bulletin of the Institute of Ethnology, Academia Sinica*, 15 (1963): 65–94.
———. "Some Dualistic Phenomena in Shang Society." *Journal of Asian Studies* 24 (1964): 45–61.
———. "T'an Wang Hai yü Yi Yin ti chi jih ping tsai lun Yin Shang wang-chih" 談王亥與伊尹的祭日並再論殷商王制. *Bulletin of the Institute of Ethnology, Academia Sinica*, 35 (1973): 111–127.
———. "*T'ien Kan*: A Key to the History of the Shang." In *Studies in Early Civilization* pp. 13–42, ed. by David Roy and T. H. Tsien. Hong Kong: Chinese University of Hong Kong, 1978.
———. "Ts'ung Hsia Shang Chou san-tai k'ao-ku lun san-tai kuan-hsi yü Chung-kuo ku-tai kuo-chia ti hsing-ch'eng" 從夏商周三代考古論三代關係與中國

古代國家的形成. In *Papers Presented to Mr. Ch'ü Wan-li on His Seventieth Birthday*, pp. 287–306. Taipei: Lien-ching Publishing Co., 1978.

———. "Yin hsü fa-chüeh wu-shih nien" 殷墟發掘五十年. In *Chung-yang Yen-chiu Yüan Wu-shih Chou Nien Chi-nien Lun-wen Chi* 中央研究院五十週年紀念論文集, pp. 291–311. Taipei: Academia Sinica, 1978.

———. "Yin Shang wen-ming ch'i-yüan yen-chiu shang ti yi-ko kuan-chien wen-t'i" 殷商文明起源研究上的一個關鍵問題. *Papers Presented to Mr. Shen Kang-po on His Eightieth Birthday*, pp. 151–169. Taipei: Lien-ching, 1976.

———, et al. *Fengpitou, Tapenkeng, and the Prehistory of Taiwan*. Yale University Publications in Anthropology, no. 73, New Haven: Department of Anthropology, Yale University, 1969.

———. et al. *Shang Chou ch'ing-t'ung-ch'i yü ming-wen ti tsung-ho yen-chiu* 商周青銅器與銘文的綜合研究. Monographs of the Institute of History and Philology, Academia Sinica, 62. Taipei: Academia Sinica, 1972.

Chang, P'ei-yü 張培瑜. "Chia-ku-wen jih yüeh shih chi-shih ti cheng-li yen-chiu" 甲骨文日月食紀事的整理研究. *Acta Astronomica Sinica* 天文學報 16 (1975): 210–224.

Chang Ping-ch'üan 張秉權. "Chia-ku wen chung so-chien jen ti t'ung ming k'ao" 甲骨文中所見人地同名考. In *Papers Presented to Mr. Li Chi on His Seventieth Birthday*, pp. 687–774. Taipei: The Tsinghua Journal, 1967.

———. "Chia-ku wen ti fa-hsien yü ku p'u hsi-kuan ti k'ao-cheng" 甲骨文的發現與骨卜習慣的考證. *Bulletin of the Institute of History and Philology, Academia Sinica*, 37 (1967): 827–879.

———. "Lun ch'eng t'ao p'u-tz'u" 論成套卜辭. In *Papers Presented to Mr. Tung Tso-pin on His Sixty-fifth Birthday*, pp. 389–401. Taipei: Institute of History and Philology, Academia Sinica, 1960.

———. "P'u kuei fu chia ti hsü shu" 卜龜腹甲的序數. *Bulletin of the Institute of History and Philology*, Academia Sinica, 28 (1956): 229–272.

———. "P'u-tz'u kuei-wei yüeh-shih ti hsin cheng-chü" 卜辭癸未月食的新證據. *Annals of the Academia Sinica* 3 (1956): 239–250.

———. "Shang tai p'u-tz'u chung ti ch'i-hsiang chi-lu chih shang-ch'üeh" 商代卜辭中的氣象紀錄之商榷. *Hsüeh-shu Chi-k'an* 學術季刊 6, no. 2, (1957): 74–98.

———. "Yin hsü p'u kuei chih p'u chao chi ch'i yu-kuan wen-t'i" 殷墟卜龜之卜兆及其有關問題. *Annals of the Academia Sinica* 1 (1954): 231–245.

———. *Yin hsü wen-tzu Ping pien* 殷虛文字丙編. Taipei: Institute of History and Philology, Academia Sinica, 1957–72.

———. "Yin tai ti nung-yeh yü ch'i-hsiang" 殷代的農業與氣象. *Bulletin of the Institute of History and Philology, Academia Sinica*, 42 (1970): 267–336.

Chang Te-tz'u. "The Origin and Early Cultures of the Cereal Grains and Food Legumes." Manuscript, 1978.

———. "The Origin, Evolution, Cultivation, Dissemination, and Diversification of Asian and African Rices." *Euphytica* 25 (1976): 425–441.

Chang Tsung-tung. *Der Kult der Shang-Dynastie im Spiegel der Orakelinschriften: Eine paläographische Studie zur Religion im archaischen China*. Wiesbaden: Otto Harrassowitz, 1971.

Chang Yü-che 張鈺哲. "Ha-lei hui-hsing kuei-tao yen-pien ti ch'ü-shih ho t'a ti ku-tai li-shih'' 哈雷慧星軌道演變的趨勢和它的古代歷史. *T'ien-wen Hsüeh-pao* 天文學報 19 (1978): 109–118.

Chao Ch'ing-yün 趙青雲. ''1957 nien Cheng-chou hsi chiao fa-chüeh chi yao'' 1957年鄭州西郊發掘紀要. *K'ao-ku T'ung-hsün* 1958 (9): 54–57.

Chao Ch'üan-ku 趙全嘏. ''Ho-nan chi ko hsin-shih-ch'i shih-tai yi-chih'' 河南幾個新石器時代遺址. *Hsin Shih-hsüeh T'ung-hsün* 新史學通訊 1, no. 1 (1951): 16.

Chao Feng 趙峯. ''Ch'ing-chiang t'ao-wen chi ch'i so fan-ying ti Yin tai nung-yeh ho chi-ssu'' 清江陶文及其所反映的殷代農業和祭祀. *K'ao-ku* 1976 (4): 221–228.

Chao Hsi-yüan 趙錫元. ''Tui 'Shih shu Yin tai ti nu-li chih-tu ho kuo-chia ti hsing-ch'eng' yi wen ti yi-chien'' 對'試述殷代的奴隸制度和國家的形成'一文的意見. *Li-shih Yen-chiu* 歷史研究 1959 (10): 70–80.

Chao Hsia-kuang 趙霞光. ''An-yang shih hsi chiao ti Yin tai wen-hua yi-chih'' 安陽市西郊的殷代文化遺址. *Wen-wu* 1958 (12): 31.

Chao P'ei-hsin 趙佩馨. ''An-yang Hou-kang yüan-hsing k'eng hsing-chih ti t'ao-lun'' 安陽後岡圓形坑性質的討論. *K'ao-ku* 1960 (6): 31–36.

Chao T'ieh-han 趙鉄寒. *Ku shih k'ao shu* 古史考述. Taipei: Cheng-chung, 1965.

Ch'en Ch'i-nan 陳其南. ''Chung-kuo ku-tai chih ch'in-shu chih-tu—tsai lun Shang wang miao hao ti she-hui chieh-kou yi-yi'' 中國古代之親屬制度—再論商王廟號的社會結構意義. *Bulletin of the Institute of Ethnology*, Academia Sinica, 35 (1973): 129–144.

Ch'en Meng-chia 陳夢家. ''Chia-ku tuan-tai hsüeh chia pien'' 甲骨斷代學甲編. *Yen-ching Hsüeh-pao* 燕京學報 40 (1951): 1–63.

———. ''Chia-ku tuan-tai yü k'eng-wei—Chia-ku tuan-tai hsüeh ting p'ien'' 甲骨斷代與坑位—甲骨斷代學丁篇. *Chung-kuo K'ao-ku Hsüeh-pao* 中國考古學報 5 (1951): 177–224.

———. *Hai-wai Chung-kuo t'ung-ch'i t'u lu* 海外中國銅器圖錄. Peiping: National Peiping Library, 1946.

———. *Hsi Chou nien-tai k'ao* 西周年代考. Shanghai: Commercial Press, 1945.

———. ''Ku wen-tzu chung chih Shang Chou chi-ssu'' 古文字中之商周祭祀. *Yen-ching Hsüeh-pao* 19 (1936): 91–155.

———. ''Shang tai ti shen-hua yü wu-shu'' 商代的神話與巫術. *Yen-ching Hsüeh-pao* 20 (1936): 486–576.

———. ''Shang wang miao-hao k'ao—Chia-ku tuan-tai hsüeh yi p'ien'' 商王廟號考—甲骨斷代學乙篇. *K'ao-ku Hsüeh-pao* 8 (1954): 1–48.

———. ''Shang wang ming hao k'ao'' 商王名號考. *Yen-ching Hsüeh-pao* 27 (1940): 115–142.

———. *Yin hsü p'u-tz'u tsung shu* 殷墟卜辭綜述. Peking: Science Press, 1956.

Ch'en Pang-huai 陳邦懷. *Yin tai she-hui shih-liao cheng ts'un* 殷代社會史料徵存. Tientsin: Jenmin Press, 1959.

Ch'eng Fa-jen 程發軔. *Ch'un-ch'iu Tso-shih-chuan ti ming t'u k'ao* 春秋左氏傳地名圖考. Taipei: Kuang-wen, 1967.

Cheng Shao-tsung 鄭紹宗. ''Yu kuan Ho-pei Ch'ang-ch'eng ch'ü-yü yüan-shih wen-hua lei-hsing ti t'ao-lun'' 有關河北長城區域原始文化類型的討論. *K'ao-ku* 1962 (12): 658–671.

Cheng Te-k'un 鄭德坤. ''Animal Styles in Prehistoric and Shang China.''

Bulletin of the Museum of Far Eastern Antiquities 35 (1963): 129–139.

———. "The Beginning of Chinese Civilization." *Antiquity* 47 (1973): 197–209.

———. "The Carving of Jade in the Shang Period." *Transactions of the Oriental Ceramic Society* 29 (1957): 13–30.

———. "Chung-kuo shang-ku shu ming ti yen-pien chi ch'i ying-yung" 中國上古數名的演變及其應用. *Bulletin of the Chinese University of Hong Kong* 1 (1973): 37–58.

Chi Fo-t'o 姬佛陀 and Wang Kuo-wei 王國維. *Chien-shou-t'ang so ts'ang Yin hsü wen-tzu* 戩壽堂所藏殷虛文字. Shanghai: Ts'ang-sheng-ming-chih Tahsüeh 倉聖明智大學, 1917.

Ch'i Ssu-ho 齊思和. "Hsi Chou ti-li k'ao" 西周地理考. *Yen-ching Hsüeh-pao* 燕京學報 30 (1946): 63–106.

———. "Mao Shih ku ming k'ao" 毛詩穀名考. *Yen-ching Hsüeh-pao* 36 (1949): 263–311.

Ch'i Wen-t'ao 齊文濤. "Kai shu chin-nien lai Shan-tung ch'u-t'u ti Shang Chou ch'ing-t'ung-ch'i" 概述近年來山東出土的商周青銅器. *Wen-wu* 1972 (5): 3–5.

Ch'i Yen-p'ei 祁延霈. "Shan-tung Yi-tu Su-fu-t'un ch'u-t'u t'ung-ch'i tiao-ch'a chi" 山東益都蘇埠屯出土銅器調查記. *Chung-kuo K'ao-ku Hsüeh-pao* 2 (1947): 167–177.

Chiang Hung 江鴻. "P'an-lung-ch'eng yü Shang ch'ao ti nan t'u" 盤龍城與商朝的南土. *Wen-wu* 1976 (2): 42–46.

Ch'ien Mu 錢穆. "Chou ch'u ti-li k'ao" 周初地理考. *Yen-ching Hsüeh-pao* 10 (1931): 1955–2008.

Chien Po-tsan 翦伯贊. *Chung-kuo shih kang* 中國史綱. Shanghai: San-lien, 1950.

Childe, V. Gordon. "The Urban Revolution." *Town Planning Review* 21, no. 1 (1950): 3–17.

Chin Hsiang-heng 金祥恆. "Lun chen-jen Fu ti fen ch'i wen-t'i" 論貞人扶的分期問題. In *Papers in Memory of Mr. Tung Tso-pin on the Fourteenth Anniversary of His Death*, pp. 89–101. Taipei: Yi-wen, 1978.

———. "P'u-tz'u chung so-chien Yin Shang tsung-miao chi Yin chi k'ao" 卜辭中所見殷商宗廟及殷祭考. *Ta-lu Tsa-chih* 大陸雜誌. 20 (1960): 249–253, 278–283, 312–318.

———. "Ts'ung chia-ku p'u-tz'u yen-chiu Yin Shang chün-lü chung chih wang tsu san hang san shih" 從甲骨卜辭研究殷商軍旅中之王族三行三師. *Chung-kuo Wen-tzu* 中國文字 52 (1974): 1–26.

Chin Te-chien 金德建. *Ssu-ma Ch'ien so chien shu k'ao* 司馬遷所見書考. Shanghai: Jen-min, 1963.

Chin Tsu-t'ung 金祖同. *Yin ch'i yi chu* 殷契遺珠. Peking: K'ung-te 孔德 Library, 1939.

Chou Fa-kao 周法高. "Certain Dates of the Shang Period." *Harvard Journal of Asiatic Studies* 23 (1960/61): 108–113.

———. "Hsi Chou nien tai k'ao" 西周年代考. *Journal of the Institute of Chinese Studies of the Chinese University of Hong Kong* 4 (1971): 173–205.

———. "On the Dating of a Lunar Eclipse in the Shang Period." *Harvard*

Journal of Asiatic Studies 25 (1964/65): 243–245.
———. ed. *San tai chi chin wen ts'un chu lu piao* 三代吉金文存箸錄表. Taipei: San-min, 1977.
———. et al. *Chin wen ku lin* 金文詁林. Hong Kong: The Chinese University of Hong Kong, 1974.
Chou Hung-hsiang 周鴻翔. "Computer Matching of Oracle Bone Fragments," *Archaeology* 26 (1973): 176–181.
———. *P'u-tz'u tui chen shu li* 卜辭對貞述例. Hong Kong: Wan-yu Shu-chü, 1969.
———. *Shang Yin ti wang pen chi* 商殷帝王本紀. Hong Kong: (privately printed), 1958.
———. "Yin tai k'o tzu tao ti t'ui-ts'e" 殷代刻字刀的推測. *Lien-ho Shu-yüan Hsüeh-pao* 聯合書院學報 6 (1967/68): 9–44.
Chou Jen 周仁, Li Chia-chih 李家治, and Cheng Yüng-fu 鄭永圃. "Chang-chia-p'o Hsi Chou chü-chu yi-chih t'ao-tz'u sui-p'ien ti yen-chiu" 張家坡西周居住遺址陶瓷碎片的研究. *K'ao-ku* 1960 (9): 48–52.
Chou Kuo-hsing 周國興. "Ho-nan Hsü-ch'ang Ling-ching ti shih-ch'i shih-tai yi-ts'un" 河南許昌靈井的石器時代遺存. *K'ao-ku* 1974 (2): 91–98.
Chou Shih-jung 周世榮. "Hu-nan Shih-men hsien Tsao-shih fa-hsien Shang Yin yi-chih" 湖南石門縣皂市發現商殷遺址. *K'ao-ku* 1962 (3): 144–146.
Chou Tao 周到, and Liu Tung-ya 劉東亞. "Yi-chiu-wu-ch'i nien ch'iu An-yang Kao-lou-chuang Yin tai yi-chih fa-chüeh" 一九五七年秋安陽高樓莊殷代遺址發掘. *K'ao-ku* 1967 (4): 213–216.
Chu K'o-chen 竺可楨. "Chung-kuo chin wu-ch'ien nien lai ch'i-hou pien-ch'ien ti ch'u-pu yen-chiu" 中國近五千年來氣候變遷的初步研究. *K'ao-ku Hsüeh-pao* 1972 (1): 15–38.
Ch'ü Wan-li 屈萬里. *Shang Shu chin chu chin shih* 尚書今註今釋. Taipei: The Commercial Press, 1972.
———. "*Shih-chi Yin pen chi* chi ch'i-t'a chi-lu chung so tsai Yin-Shang shih-tai ti shih shih" 史記殷本紀及其他紀錄中所載殷商時代的史事. *Bulletin of the College of Arts*, National Taiwan University, 14 (1965): 87–118.
———. "Shih fa lan-shang yü Yin tai lun 謚法濫觴於殷代論. *Bulletin of the Institute of History and Philology*, Academia Sinica, 13 (1948): 219–226.
———. *Yin hsü wen-tzu Chia pien k'ao shih* 殷虛文字甲編考釋. Taipei: Institute of History and Philology, Academia Sinica, 1961.
Chung Po-sheng 鍾柏生. *p'u-tz'u chung so-chien Yin wang t'ien-yu ti-ming k'ao—chien lun t'ien-yu ti-ming yen-chiu fang-fa* 卜辭中所見殷王田游地名考—兼論田游地名研究方法. Taipei: (privately printed), 1972.
Cohen, Ronald, and E. R. Service, eds. *Origins of the State: The Anthropology of Political Evolution*. Philadelphia: Institute for the Study of Human Issues, 1978.
Committee of the Exhibition of Archaeological Finds in the People's Republic of China. *The Exhibition of Archaeological Finds in the People's Republic of China*. Washington, D. C. 1975.
Coon, C. S. "An Anthropogeographic Excursion around the World." *Human Biology* 30 (1958): 29–42.
———. *The Living Races of Man*. New York: A. A. Knopf, 1964.

CR. "Best-preserved Yin Dynasty Tomb." *China Reconstructs* 1977 (10): 38–39.

Damon, P. E., C. W. Ferguson, A. Long, and E. I. Wallick. "Dendrochronologic Calibration of the Radiocarbon Time Scale." *American Antiquity* 39 (1974): 350–366.

Daniel, Glyn. *The First Civilizations*. New York: Crowell, 1968.

Delacour, Jean. *The Pheasants of the World*. London: Country Life, 1951.

Dobson, W. A. C. H. *Early Archaic Chinese*. Toronto: University of Toronto Press, 1962.

Drake, F. S. "Shang Dynasty Find at Ta-hsin-chuang, Shantung." *China Journal* 31 (1939): 77–80.

———. "Shang dynasty site at Li-ch'eng Wang-she-jen-chuang, Shantung." *China Journal* 31 (1939): 118–120.

———. "Ta-hsin-chuang Again." *China Journal* 33 (1940): 8–10.

Dubs, Homer H. "A Canon of Lunar Eclipses for Anyang and China, -1400 to -1000." *Harvard Journal of Asiatic Studies* 10 (1947): 162–178.

———. "The Date of the Shang Period." *T'oung Pao* 40 (1950): 322–335.

———. "The Date of the Shang Period—A Postscript." *T'oung Pao* 42 (1953): 101–105.

Eberhard, Wolfram. *Lokalkulturen im alten China*. I, London: Brill; II, Peking: Catholic University, 1942.

Edman, G., and E. Söderberg. "Auffindung von Reis in einer Tonscherte aus einer etwa fünftausendjährigen Chinesischen Siedlung." *Bull. Geo. Soc. China* 8 (1929): 363–368.

Eggan, Fred. "Social Anthropology and the Method of Controlled Comparison." *American Anthropologist* 56 (1954): 743–763.

Elisseeff, Vadime. *Bronzes archaiques Chinois au Musée Gernuschi*, vol. 1. Paris: L'Asiatheque, 1977.

———. "Possibilites du scalogramme dans l'étude des bronzes Chinois archaiques." *Methématiques et Sciences humaines* 11 (1965).

Fagan, Brian. *People of the Earth*. Boston: Little, Brown & Co., 1977.

Fairbank, Wilma. "Piece-Mold Craftsmanship and Shang Bronze Design." *Archives of the Chinese Art Society of America* 16 (1962): 8–15.

Fang Fa-lien 方法斂 [Frank H. Chalfant]. *K'u Fang erh shih ts'ang chia-ku p'u-tz'u* 庫方二氏藏甲骨卜辭. Shanghai: The Commercial Press, 1935.

Finn, D. J. "Archaeological Finds on Lamma Island near Hong Kong, Part II." *The Hong Kong Naturalist* 4, no. 1 (1933): 60–63.

Flannery, Kent V. "The Cultural Evolution of Civilizations." *Annual Review of Ecology and Systematics* 3 (1972): 399–426.

Ford, C. S. "On the Analysis of Behavior for Cross-Cultural Comparisons." In *Cross-Cultural Approaches*, C. S. Ford, ed., pp. 3–4. New Haven: Human Relations Area Files, 1967.

Foreign Language Press. *Historic Relics Unearthed in New China*. Peking: Foreign Language Press, 1972.

Fried, M. H. *The Evolution of Political Society*. New York: Random House, 1967.

Friedman, Jonathan. "Tribes, States, and Transformations." In: *Marxist Analysis and Social Anthropology*, M. Block, ed. London: Malaby Press, 1975,

pp. 161–202.
Fu Ssu-nien 傅斯年. "Li-shih Yü-yen Yen-chiu So kung-tso chih chih-ch'ü" 歷史語言研究所工作之旨趣. *Bulletin of the Institute of History and Philology,* Academia Sinica, 1, no. 1 (1928): 3–10.
———. "Yi Hsia tung hsi shuo" 夷夏東西說. *Papers Presented to Mr. Ts'ao Yüan P'ei on His Sixty-fifth Birthday,* pp. 1093–1134. Nanking: The Institute of History and Philology, Academia Sinica, 1935.
———. Li Chi 李濟, et al. *Ch'eng-tzu-yai* 城子崖. Nanking: The Institute of History and Philology, Academia Sinica, 1934.
Gee, N. G., L. I. Moffett, and G. D. Wilder. *A Tentative List of Chinese Birds.* Peking: The Peking Society of Natural History, 1926.
Gettens, R. J. *The Freer Chinese Bronzes: II, Technical Studies.* Washington, D. C.: Freer Gallery of Art, 1969.
Goody, Jack. *Succession to High Office.* Cambridge, Eng.: Cambridge University Press, 1966.
Gullick, J. M. *Indigenous Political Systems of Western Malaya.* L. S. E. Monographs on Social Anthropology 17. London, 1958.
Hansford, S. H. "A Visit to An-yang." *Transactions of the Oriental Ceramic Society* 24 (1951): 11–22.
Harlan, Jack. "The Origins of Cereal Agriculture in the Old World." In *Origins of Agriculture,* C. A. Reed, ed., pp. 357–383. The Hague: Mouton, 1977.
Hayashi Minao 林巳奈夫. "Chūgoku senshin jidai no hata" 中国先秦時代の旗. *Shirin* 史林 49 (1966): 234–262.
———. "In Shū jidai no zushō kigō" 殷周時代の図象記号. *Tōhōgakuhō (Kyoto)* 東方学報(京都) 39 (1968): 1–117.
———. "In Shū seidō iki no meishō to yōto" 殷周青銅彝器の名称と用途. *Tōhōgakuhō (Kyoto)* 34 (1964): 199–297.
Hayashi Taisuke 林泰輔. *Kikō jūkotsu moji* 亀甲獸骨文字. Shōshūemonkai, 1917.
———. *Shina jōdai no kenkyū* 支那上代の研究. N. p., 1927.
Ho Ping-ti 何炳棣. "Chou ch'u nien-tai p'ing yi" 周初年代平議. *Journal of the Chinese University of Hong Kong* 1 (1973): 17–35.
———. *The Cradle of the East.* Hong Kong: The Chinese University of Hong Kong and the University of Chicago Press, 1975.
———. *Huang-t'u yü Chung-kuo nung-yeh ti ch'i-yüan* 黃土與中國農業的起源. Hong Kong: The Chinese University, 1969.
———. The Loess and the Origin of Chinese Agriculture." *American Historical Review* 75 (1969): 1–36.
Ho T'ien-hsiang 何天相. "Chung-kuo chih ku mu (2)" 中國之古木(二) *Chung-kuo K'ao-ku Hsüeh-pao* 5 (1951): 247–293.
Ho T'ien-hsing 何天行. *Hang Hsien Liang-chu chen chih shih-ch'i yü hei-t'ao* 杭縣良渚鎮之石器與黑陶. Shanghai: Wu Yüeh shih-ti yen-chiu-hui 吳越史地研究會, 1937.
Ho Tzu-ch'üan 何茲全. "T'an ou keng" 談耦耕. *Chung-hua wen-shih lun ts'ung* 中華文史論叢 3 (1963): 101–109.
Hocart, A. M. "Chieftainship and the Sister's son in the Pacific." *American Anthropologist* 17 (1915): 631–646.

Ho-pei sheng Po-wu-kuan 河北省博物館 et al. *kao-ch'eng T'ai-hsi Shang tai yi-chih* 藁城台西商代遺址. Peking: Wen-wu, 1977.

Howells, William W. "Origin of the Chinese Peoples: Interpretations of the Recent Evidence." Manuscript, 1978.

Hsia Nai 夏鼐. "Ho-nan Ch'eng-kao Kuang-wu ch'ü k'ao-ku chi lüeh" 河南成皋廣武區考古紀略. *K'o-hsüeh T'ung-pao* 科學通報 2, no. 7 (1951): 724–729.

———. "T'an-14 ts'e-ting nien-tai ho Chung-kuo shih-ch'ien k'ao-ku hsüeh" 碳-14測定年代和中國史前考古學. *K'ao-ku* 1977 (4): 217–232.

———. "Workshop of China's Oldest Civilization." *China Reconstructs* 1957 (2), 18–21.

Hsiao Nan 肖楠. "An-yang Hsiao-t'un nan-ti fa-hsien ti 'Shih tsu p'u chia'—chien lun 'Shih tsu p'u tz'u ti shih-tai chi ch'i hsiang-kuan wen-t'i" 安陽小屯南地發現的'自組卜甲'—兼論'自組卜辭'的時代及其相關問題. *K'ao-ku* 1976 (4): 234–241.

Hsieh Ch'ing-shan 謝青山 and Yang Shao-shun 楊紹舜. "Shan-hsi Lü-liang hsien Shih-lou chen yu fa-hsien t'ung-ch'i" 山西呂梁縣石樓鎮又發現銅器. *Wen-wu* 1960 (7): 51–52.

Hsiung Ch'uan-hsin 熊傳新. "Hu-nan Li-ling fa-hsien Shang tai t'ung hsiang tsun" 湖南醴陵發現商代銅象尊. *Wen-wu* 1976 (7): 49–50.

Hsü Chin-hsiung 許進雄. *The Menzies Collection of Shang Dynasty Oracle Bones*, Vol. I. Toronto: The Royal Ontario Museum, 1972.

———. *P'u ku shang ti tsao tsuan hsing-t'ai* 卜骨上的鑿鑽形態. Taipei: Yi-wen, 1973.

———. "Tui Chang Kwang-chih hsien-sheng ti 'Shang wang miao hao hsin k'ao' ti chi tien yi-chien" 對張光直先生的'商王廟號新考'的幾點意見. *Bulletin of the Institute of Ethnology* 19 (1965): 121–135.

———. "Wu chung chi-ssu ti hsin kuan-nien yü Yin li ti t'an-t'ao" 五種祭祀的新觀念與殷曆的探討. *Chung-kuo Wen-tzu* 中國文字. 41 (1971): 11 pp.

———. *Yin p'u-tz'u chung wu chung chi-ssu ti yen-chiu* 殷卜辭中五種祭祀的研究. Taipei: Wen Shih Ts'ung K'an No. 26, College of Arts, National Taiwan University, 1968.

———. "Yin p'u-tz'u chung wu chung chi-ssu yen-chiu ti hsin kuan-nien" 殷卜辭中五種祭祀研究的新觀念. *Chung-kuo Wen-tzu* 35 (1970): 12 pp.

Hsü Cho-yün 許倬雲. "Chou jen ti hsing-ch'i chi Chou wen-hua ti chi-ch'u" 周人的興起及周文化的基礎. *Bulletin of the Institute of History and Philology*, Academia Sinica, 38 (1968): 435–458.

———. "Kuan-yü Shang wang miao-hao hsin k'ao yi wen ti chi-tien yi-chien" 關于商王廟號新考一文的幾點意見. *Bulletin of the Institute of Ethnology*, Academia Sinica, 19 (1965): 81–87.

Hsü Chung-shu 徐中舒. "Lei ssu k'ao" 耒耜考. *Bulletin of the Institute of History and Philology*, Academia Sinica, 2 (1930): 11–59.

———. "Ssu-ch'uan P'eng hsien Meng-yang-chen ch'u-t'u ti Yin tai erh chih" 四川彭縣濛陽鎮出土的殷代二觶. *Wen-wu* 1962 (6): 15–18.

Hsü Hsün-sheng 徐旭生. "1959 nien Yü hsi tiao-ch'a 'Hsia hsü' ti ch'u-pu pao-kao" 1959年豫西調查'夏墟'的初步報告. *K'ao-ku* 1959 (11): 592–600.

Hsü Tse-min 許澤民. "Yin hsü Hsi-pei-kang tsu t'ou-ku yü hsien-tai T'ai-wan

Hai-nan hsi-lieh t'ou-ku ti lu-ting-chien-ku ti yen-chiu" 殷墟西北崗組頭骨與現代台灣海南系列頭骨的顱頂間骨的研究. *Bulletin of the Institute of History and Philology*, Academia Sinica, 36 (1966): 703–739.

Hu Hou-hsüan 胡厚宣. *Chan-hou Ching Chin hsin huo chia ku chi* 戰後京津新獲甲骨集. Shanghai: Ch'ün-yi 羣益 Press, 1949.

———. *Chan-hou nan pei so chien chia-ku lu* 戰後南北所見甲骨錄. Peking: Lai-hsün-ko 來薰閣, 1951.

———. *Chan-hou Ning Hu hsin huo chia-ku chi* 戰後寧滬新獲甲骨集. Peking: Lai-hsün-ko, 1951.

———. *Chan-hou P'ing Chin hsin huo chia-ku chi* 戰後平津新獲甲骨集. Ch'eng-tu: Ch'i-lu University, 1946.

———. "Ch'i-hou pien-ch'ien yü Yin tai ch'i-hou chih chien-t'ao" 氣候變遷與殷代氣候之檢討. In *Chia ku hsüeh Shang shih lun ts'ung* 甲骨學商史論叢, vol. 2. Ch'eng-tu: Ch'i-lu University, 1945.

———. *Chia ku hsü ts'un* 甲骨續存. Shanghai: Ch'ün-lien 羣聯 Press, 1955.

———. *Chia ku liu lu* 甲骨六錄. Ch'eng-tu: Ch'i-lu University, 1945.

———. "Chia-ku wen Shang tsu niao t'u-t'eng ti yi-chi" 甲骨文商族鳥圖騰的遺跡. In *Li-shih Lun-ts'ung* 歷史論叢, vol. 1, pp. 131–159. Peking: Chung-hua, 1964.

———. "Chia-ku wen so-chien Shang tsu niao t'u-t'eng ti hsin cheng-chü" 甲骨文所見商族鳥圖騰的新証據. *Wen-wu* 1977 (2): 84–87.

———. "Chung-kuo nu-li she-hui ti jen hsün ho jen chi hsia p'ien" 中國奴隸社會的人殉和人祭，下篇. *Wen-wu* 1974 (8): 56–67.

———. "Kung fang k'ao" 舌方考. In *Chia ku hsüeh Shang shih lun ts'ung*, vol. 1. Ch'eng-tu: Ch'i-lu University, 1944.

———. "P'u-tz'u chung so chien chih Yin tai nung-yeh" 卜辭中所見之殷代農業. In *Chia ku hsüeh Shang shih lun ts'ung*, vol. 2. Cheng-tu: Chi-lu University, 1945.

———. "P'u-tz'u ti ming yü ku jen chü ch'iu shuo" 卜辭地名與古人居丘説. In *Chia-ku hsüeh Shang shih lun ts'ung*, vol. 1. 1944.

———. "Wu Ting shih wu-chung chi-shih k'o-tz'u k'ao" 武丁時五種記事刻辭考. In *Chia ku hsüeh Shang shih lun ts'ung* vol. 1. 1944.

———. *Yin hsü fa-chüeh* 殷墟發掘. Shanghai: Hsüeh-hsi Sheng-huo 學習生活 Press, 1955.

———. "Yin p'u-tz'u chung ti shang-ti ho wang-ti" 殷卜辭中的上帝和王帝. *Li-shih Yen-chiu* 歷史研究 1959 (9): 23–50; 1959 (10): 89–110.

———. "Yin tai feng-chien chih-tu k'ao" 殷代封建制度考. In *Chia ku hsüeh Shang shih lun ts'ung* vol. 1. 1944.

———. "Yin tai hun-yin chia-tsu tsung-fa sheng-yü chih-tu k'ao" 殷代婚姻家族宗法生育制度考. In *Chia ku hsüeh Shang shih lun ts'ung*, vol. 1. 1944.

———. "Yin tai p'u kuei chih lai-yüan" 殷代卜龜之來源. In *Chia ku hsüeh Shang shih lun ts'ung*, vol. 1. 1944.

———. "Yin tai ti ts'an sang ho ssu-chih" 殷代的蠶桑和絲織. *Wen-wu* 1972 (1): 2–7.

———. "Yin tai ti yüeh hsing" 殷代的刖刑. *K'ao-ku* 1973 (2): 108–117.

Hu Hsiang-yün 胡翔雲. *Ch'üan kuo tsui chin yen ch'ang lu* 全國最近鹽場錄. Peking: Ch'iu-chih Hsüeh-she 求志學社, 1915.

Huang Cho-hsün 黄著勳. *Chung-kuo K'uang-ch'an* 中國礦產. Shanghai: The Commercial Press, 1930.

Huang Jan-wei 黄然偉. "Yin wang t'ien lieh k'ao" 殷王田獵考, *Chung-kuo Wen-tzu* 14 (1964): 21 pp.; 15 (1964), 25–46; 16 (1965): 47–70.

Ikeda Suetoshi 池田末利. "Shima shi *Inkyo bokuji kenkyū* o yomu" 島氏殷墟卜辞研究を読む. *Kōtotsugaku* 甲骨学 7 (1959): 12–27.

Itō Michiharu 伊藤道治. "Bokuji ni mieru sorei kannen ni tsuite" 卜辞に見える祖霊観念について. *Tōhōgakuhō* (*Kyotō*) 26 (1956): 1–35.

———. *Chūgoku kodai ōchō no keisei* 中国古代王朝の形成. Tokyo: Sobunsha, 1975.

———. *Kodai In ōchō no nazo* 古代殷王朝のなぞ. Tokyo: Kadokawa Shoten, 1967.

———. "Shūkyō men kara mita Indai no ni-san no mondai" 宗教面から見た殷代の二、三問題. *Tōyōshi kenkyū* 東洋史研究 20 (1961): 36–58.

———. *Zusetsu Chūgoku no rekishi* 図説中国の歴史. Tokyo: Kodansha, 1976.

Jao Tsung-yi 饒宗頤. *Yin tai chen p'u jen-wu t'ung k'ao* 殷代貞卜人物通考. The Hong Kong University Press, 1959.

JH. "Yin hsü k'ao-ku ti hsin fa-hsien" 殷墟考古的新發現. *Jen-min Hua-pao* 人民畫報 1978 (1): 26–29.

Jung, Keng 容庚. *Han Wu-liang tz'u hua-hsiang lu* 漢武梁祠畫像錄. Peiping: K'ao-ku Hsüeh-she, 1936.

———. *Shang Chou yi-ch'i t'ung k'ao* 商周彝器通考. Yen-ching Journal of Chinese Studies Monographs 17. Peking: Harvard-Yenching Institute, 1941.

———. *Wu-ying-tien yi-ch'i t'u-lu* 武英殿彝器圖錄. Peiping: Harvard-Yenching Institute, Yenching University, 1934.

———, and Ch'ü Jun-min 瞿潤緡. *Yin ch'i p'u-tz'u* 殷契卜辭. Peiping: Harvard-Yenching Institute, 1933.

Kaizuka Shigeki 貝塚茂樹. *Chūgoku kodai shigaku no hakken* 中国古代史学の発展. Tokyo: Kōbundō, 1946.

———. *Kyotō Daigaku Jinbun Kagaku Kenkyūjo shozō kōkotsu moji* 京都大学人文科学研究所所蔵甲骨文字. Kyoto: Kyoto University, Institute of Humanistic Sciences, 1960.

———, and Itō Michiharu 伊藤道治. "Kōkotsubun dandaihō no saikentō—Tōshi no Bunbutei jidai bokuji o chūshin to shite" 甲骨文断代法の再検討—董氏の文武丁時代卜辞を中心として. *Tōhōgakuhō* (*Kyoto*) 23 (1953): 1–78.

Kane, Virginia. "The Chronological Significance of the Inscribed Ancestor Dedication in the Bronze Vessels." *Artibus Asiae* 35 (1973): 335–370.

———. "The Independent Bronze Industries in the South of China Contemporary with the Shang and Western Chou Dynasties." *Archives of Asian Art* 28 (1974/75): 77–107.

———. "A Re-examination of An-yang Archaeology." *Ars Orientalis* 10 (1975): pp. 93–110.

Kao Chih-hsi 高至喜. "Hu-nan Ning-hsiang Huang-ts'ai fa-hsien Shang tai t'ung-ch'i ho yi-chih" 湖南寧鄉黄材發現商代銅器和遺址. *K'ao-ku* 1963 (12): 646–648.

———. "Shang tai jen mien fang ting" 商代人面方鼎. *Wen-wu* 1960 (10): 57–58.

Kao Ch'ü-hsün 高去尋. "The Royal Cemetery of the Yin Dynasty at An-yang," *Bulletin of the Department of Archaeology and Anthropology*, National Taiwan University, 13/14 (1959): 1–9.

———. "Yin li ti han pei wo pei" 殷禮的含貝握貝. *Annals of the Academia Sinica* 1 (1954): 373–401.

———. "Yin tai ta-mu ti mu shih chi ch'i han-yi chih t'ui-ts'e" 殷代大墓的木室及其涵義之推測. *Bulletin of the Institute of History and Philology*, Academia Sinica, 39 (1969): 175–188.

Karlgren, Bernhard. *The Book of Odes*. Stockholm: The Museum of Far Eastern Antiquities, 1974.

———. "The Exhibition of Early Chinese Bronzes." *Bulletin of the Museum of Far Eastern Antiquities* 6 (1934): 81–136.

———. "New Studies on Chinese Bronzes." *Bulletin of the Museum of Far Eastern Antiquities* 9 (1937): 1–117.

———. "Some Characteristics of the Yin Art." *Bulletin of the Museum of Far Eastern Antiquities* 34 (1962): 1–28.

———. "Some weapons and tools of the Yin dynasty." *Bulletin of the Museum of Far Eastern Antiquities* 17 (1945): 114–121.

———. "Yin and Chou in Chinese Bronzes." *Bulletin of the Museum of Far Eastern Antiquities* 8 (1936).

Keightley, David N. "Ho Ping-ti and the Origin of Chinese Civilization." *Harvard Journal of Asiatic Studies* 37 (1977): 381–411.

———. "The Late Shang State: When, Where, and What?" Manuscript, 1978.

———. "Legitimation in Shang China." Manuscript, 1975.

———. "The Religious Commitment: Shang Theology and the Genesis of Chinese Political Culture." *History of Religions* 17 (1978), pp. 211–225.

———. "Shih Chen: A New Hypothesis about the Nature of Shang Divination." Manuscript, 1972.

———. *Sources of Shang History*. Berkeley and Los Angeles: University of California Press, 1978.

Keng Chien-t'ing 耿鑒庭 and Liu Liang 劉亮. "Kao-ch'eng Shang tai yi-chih chung ch'u-t'u ti t'ao jen ho yü-li jen" 藁城商代遺址中出土的桃仁和郁李仁. *Wen-wu* 1974 (8): 54–55.

King, B. F., and E. C. Dickinson. *A Field Guide to the Birds of South-East Asia*. Boston: Houghton-Mifflin, 1975.

KK (*K'ao-ku*.) "An-hui Han-shan Hsien Sun-chia-kang Shang tai yi-chih tiao-ch'a yü shih chüeh" 安徽含山縣孫家崗商代遺址調查與試掘. *K'ao-ku* 1977 (3): 166–168.

———. "An-yang hsin fa-hsien ti Yin tai ch'e-ma k'eng" 安陽新發現的殷代車馬坑. *K'ao-ku* 1972 (4): 24–28.

———. "An-yang Huan ho liu-yü chi-ko yi-chih ti shih chüeh" 安陽洹河流域幾個遺址的試掘. *K'ao-ku* 1965 (7): 326–338.

———. "An-yang Yin hsü nu-li chi-ssu k'eng ti fa-chüeh" 安陽殷墟奴隸祭祀坑的發掘. *K'ao-ku* 1977 (1): 20–36.

———. "An-yang Yin hsü wu-hao mu tso-t'an chi-yao" 安陽殷墟五號墓座談紀要. *K'ao-ku* 1977 (5): 341–350.

———. "An-yang Yin tai chi-ssu k'eng jen ku ti hsing-pieh nien-ling chien-

ting" 安陽殷代祭祀坑人骨的性別年齡鑒定. *K'ao-ku* 1977 (3): 210–214.
———. "Ao-han ch'i Ta-tien-tzu yi-chih 1974 nien shih chüeh chien pao" 敖漢旗大甸子遺址1974年試掘簡報. *K'ao-ku T'ung-hsün* 1958 (2): 6–9.
———. "Cheng-chou Nan-kuan-wai Shang tai yi-chih fa-chüeh chien pao" 鄭州南關外商代遺址發掘簡報. *K'ao-ku T'ung-hsün* 1958 (2): 6–9.
———. "Cheng-chou Shang-chieh Shang tai yi-chih ti fa-chüeh" 鄭州上街商代遺址的發掘. *K'ao-ku* 1960 (6): 11–12.
———. "Cheng-chou shih ku yi-chih mu-tsang ti chung-yao fa-hsien" 鄭州市古遺址墓葬的重要發現. *K'ao-ku T'ung-hsün* 1955 (3): 16–19.
———. "Cheng-chou shih Ming-kung-lu hsi ts'e ti liang tso Shang tai mu" 鄭州市銘功路西側的兩座商代墓. *K'ao-ku* 1965 (10): 500–506.
———. "Cheng-chou Ta-ho-ts'un Yang-shao wen-hua ti fang chi yi-chih" 鄭州大河村仰韶文化的房基遺址. *K'ao-ku* 1973 (6): 330–336.
———. "Chi-nan Ta-hsin-chuang yi-chih shih chüeh chien pao" 濟南大辛莊遺址試掘簡報. *K'ao-ku* 1959 (4): 185–187.
———. "Chiang-su T'ung-shan Ch'iu-wan ku yi-chih ti fa-chüeh" 江蘇銅山丘灣古遺址的發掘. *K'ao-ku* 1973 (2): 71–79.
———. "Ch'ing-hai Lo-tu Liu-wan yüan-shih she-hui mu-ti fan-ying ch'u ti chu-yao wen-t'i" 青海樂都柳灣原始社會墓地反映出的主要問題 *K'ao-ku* 1976 (6): 365–377.
———. "Fang-she-hsing t'an-su ts'e-ting nien-tai pao-kao (wu)" 放射性碳素測定年代報告(五). *K'ao-ku* 1978 (4): 280–287.
———. "Feng Hao yi-tai k'ao-ku tiao-ch'a chien pao" 豐鎬一帶考古調查簡報 *K'ao-ku T'ung-hsün* 1955 (1): 28–31.
———. "Ho-nan An-yang Hsüeh-chia-chuang Yin tai yi-chih mu-tsang ho T'ang mu fa-chüeh chien pao" 河南安陽薛家莊殷代遺址墓葬和唐墓發掘簡報. *K'ao-ku T'ung-hsün* 1958 (8): 22–26.
———. "Ho-nan Cheng-chou Shang-chieh Shang tai yi-chih fa-chüeh pao-kao" 河南鄭州上街商代遺址發掘報告. *K'ao-ku* 1960 (1): 1–7.
———. "Ho-nan Hsin-cheng P'ei-li-kang hsin-shih-ch'i shih-tai yi-chih" 河南新鄭裴李崗新石器時代遺址. *K'ao-ku* 1978 (2): 73–79.
———. "Ho-nan Hui hsien Ch'u-ch'iu ch'u-t'u ti Shang tai t'ung-ch'i" 河南輝縣褚丘出土的商代銅器. *K'ao-ku* 1965 (5): 255.
———. "Ho-nan Lin-ju Mei-shan yi-chih tiao-ch'a yü shih chüeh" 河南臨汝煤山遺址調查與試掘. *K'ao-ku* 1975 (5): 285–294.
———. "Ho-nan Meng hsien Chien-hsi yi-chih fa-chüeh" 河南孟縣澗溪遺址發掘. *K'ao-ku* 1961 (1): 33–39.
———. "Ho-nan Mien-ch'ih Lu-ssu Shang tai yi-chih shih chüeh chien pao" 河南澠池鹿寺商代遺址試掘簡報. *K'ao-ku* 1964 (9): 435–440.
———. "Ho-nan Nan-yang shih Shih-li-miao fa-hsien Shang tai yi-chih" 河南南陽市十里廟發現商代遺址 *K'ao-ku* 1959 (7), 370.
———. "Ho-nan Wei ho chih-hung kung-ch'eng chung ti k'ao-ku tiao-ch'a chien pao" 河南衛河滯洪工程中的考古調查簡報. *K'ao-ku T'ung-hsün* 1957 (2): 32–35.
———. "Ho-nan Yen-ling Fu-kou Shang-shui chi ch'u ku wen-hua yi-chih ti tiao-ch'a" 河南鄢陵扶溝商水幾處古文化遺址的調查. *K'ao-ku* 1965 (2): 94–96.

———. "Ho-nan Yen-shih Erh-li-t'ou tsao Shang kung-tien yi-chih fa-chüeh chien pao" 河南偃師二里頭早商宮殿遺址發掘簡報. *K'ao-ku* 1974 (4): 234–248.

———. "Ho-nan Yen-shih Erh-li-t'ou yi-chih fa-chüeh chien pao" 河南偃師二里頭遺址發掘簡報. *K'ao-ku* 1965 (5): 215–224.

———. "Ho-nan Yen-shih Erh-li-t'ou yi-chih san pa ch'ü fa-chüeh chien pao" 河南偃師二里頭遺址三、八區發掘簡報. *K'ao-ku* 1975 (5): 302–309.

———. "Ho-pei Han-tan Chien-kou ts'un ku yi-chih fa-chüeh chien pao" 河北邯鄲澗溝村古遺址發掘簡報. *K'ao-ku* 1961 (4): 197–202.

———. "Ho-pei Hsing-t'ai Tung-hsien-hsien ts'un Shang tai yi-chih tiao-ch'a" 河北邢台東先賢村商代遺址調查. *K'ao-ku* 1959 (2): 108–109.

———. "Ho-pei Kao-ch'eng hsien Shang tai yi-chih ho mu-tsang ti tiao-ch'a" 河北藁城縣商代遺址和墓葬的調查. *K'ao-ku* 1973 (1): 25–29.

———. "Ho-pei Kao-ch'eng T'ai-hsi ts'un ti Shang tai yi-chih" 河北藁城台西村的商代遺址. *K'ao-ku* 1973 (5): 266–271.

———. "Ho-pei Ling-shou hsien Pei-chai-ts'un Shang tai yi-chih tiao-ch'a" 河北靈壽縣北宅村商代遺址調查. *K'ao-ku* 1966 (2): 107–108.

———. "Ho-pei Ta-ch'ang Hui-tsu tzu-chih-hsien Ta-t'o-t'ou yi-chih shih chüeh chien pao" 河北大廠回族自治縣大坨頭遺址試掘簡報 *K'ao-ku* 1966 (1): 8–13.

———. "Ho-pei Tz'u-shan hsin-shih-ch'i yi-chih shih chüeh" 河北磁山新石器遺址試掘. *K'ao-ku* 1977 (6): 361–372.

———. "Hu-pei Huang-p'i K'uang-shan shui-k'u kung-ti fa-hsien liao ch'ing-t'ung-ch'i" 湖北黃陂礦山水庫工地發現了青銅器. *K'ao-ku T'ung-hsün* 1958 (9): 72–73.

———. "Huang-ho San-men-hsia shui-k'u k'ao-ku tiao-ch'a chien pao" 黃河三門峽水庫考古調查簡報. *K'ao-ku T'ung-hsün* 1956 (5): 1–11.

———. "Liao-ning K'o-tso hsien Pei-tung ts'un ch'u-t'u ti Yin Chou ch'ing-t'ung-ch'i" 遼寧喀左縣北洞村出土的殷周青銅器. *K'ao-ku* 1974 (6): 364–372.

———. "Liao-ning K'o-tso hsien Pei-tung ts'un fa-hsien Yin tai ch'ing-t'ung-ch'i" 遼寧喀左縣北洞村發現殷代青銅器. *K'ao-ku* 1973 (4): 225–226.

———. "Lo-yang Ts'o-li yi-chih shih chüeh chien pao" 洛陽矬李遺址試掘簡報 *K'ao-ku* 1978 (1): 5–17.

———. "Nei-meng-ku Pa-lin-tso-ch'i Fu-ho-kou-men yi-chih fa-chüeh chien pao" 內蒙古巴林左旗富河溝門遺址發掘簡報. *K'ao-ku* 1964 (1): 1–5.

———. "Pei-ching fu-chin fa-hsien ti Hsi Chou nu-li hsün tsang mu" 北京附近發現的西周奴隸殉葬墓. *K'ao-ku* 1974 (5): 309–321.

———. "Pei-ching Liu-li-ho Hsia-chia-tien hsia ts'eng wen-hua mu-tsang" 北京琉璃河夏家店下層文化墓葬. *K'ao-ku* 1976 (1): 59–60.

———. "Shan-hsi Ch'i-shan Ho-chia-ts'un Hsi Chou mu-tsang" 陝西岐山賀家村西周墓葬. *K'ao-ku* 1976 (1): 31–38.

———. "Shan-hsi Shih-lou Yi-tieh fa-hsien Shang tai t'ung-ch'i" 山西石樓義牒發現商代銅器. *K'ao-ku* 1972 (4): 29–30.

———. "Shan-tung Hui-min hsien fa-hsien Shang tai ch'ing-t'ung-ch'i" 山東惠民縣發現商代青銅器. *K'ao-ku* 1974 (3): 203.

———. "Shan-tung P'ing-yin hsien Chu-chia-ch'iao Yin tai yi-chih" 山東平陰

縣朱家橋殷代遺址. *K'ao-ku* 1961 (2): 86–93.
———. "Tui Shang tai cho yü kung-yi ti yi-hsieh ch'u-pu k'an-fa" 對商代琢玉工藝的一些初步看法. *K'ao-ku* 1976 (4): 229–233.
———. "Tz'u hsien Chieh-tuan-ying fa-chüeh chien pao" 磁縣界段營發掘簡報. *K'ao-ku* 1974 (6): 356–363.
———. "Yi-chiu-wu-ssu nien ch'iu-chi Lo-yang hsi chiao fa-chüeh chien pao" 一九五四年秋季洛陽西郊發掘簡報. *K'ao-ku T'ung-hsün* 1955 (5): 25–33.
———. "1957 nien Han-tan fa-chüeh chien pao" 1957年邯鄲發掘簡報. *K'ao-ku* 1959 (10): 531–536.
———. "1958 nien Lo-yang Tung-kan-kou yi-chih fa-chüeh chien pao" 1958年洛陽東乾溝遺址發掘簡報. *K'ao-ku* 1959 (10): 537–540.
———. "Yi-chiu-wu-pa nien ch'un Ho-nan An-yang shih Ta-ssu-k'ung ts'un Yin tai mu-tsang fa-chüeh chien pao" 一九五八年春河南安陽市大司空村殷代墓葬發掘簡報. *K'ao-ku T'ung-hsün* 1958 (10): 51–62.
———. "1958–1959 nien Yin hsü fa-chüeh chien pao" 1958-1959年殷墟發掘簡報. *K'ao-ku* 1961 (2): 63–76.
———. "1959 nien Hsu-chou ti-ch'ü k'ao-ku tiao-ch'a" 1959年徐州地區考古調查. *K'ao-ku* 1960 (3): 25–29.
———. "1962 nien An-yang Ta-ssu-k'ung ts'un fa-chüeh chien pao" 1962年安陽大司空村發掘簡報. *K'ao-ku* 1964 (8): 380–384.
———. "1971 nien An-yang Hou-kang fa-chüeh chien pao" 1971年安陽後岡發掘簡報. *K'ao-ku* 1972 (3): 14–25.
———. "1972 nien ch'un An-yang Hou-kang fa-chüeh chien pao" 1972年春安陽後岡發掘簡報. *K'ao-ku* 1972 (5): 8–19.
———. "1973 nien An-yang Hsiao-t'un nan-ti fa-chüeh chien pao" 1973年安陽小屯南地發掘簡報. *K'ao-ku* 1975 (1): 27–46.
———. "1975 nien An-yang Yin hsü ti hsin fa-hsien" 1975年安陽殷墟的新發現. *K'ao-ku* 1976 (4): 264–272.
———. "1975 nien Yü hsi k'ao-ku tiao-ch'a" 1975年豫西考古調查. *K'ao-ku* 1978 (1): 23–34.
———. "1977 nien Ho-nan Yüng-ch'eng Wang-yu-fang yi-chih fa-chüeh kai k'uang" 1977年河南永城王油坊遺址發掘概況. *K'ao-ku* 1978 (1): 35–40.
———. "Yin hsü k'ao-ku fa-chüeh ti yu yi chung-yao shou-hu—Hsiao-t'un fa-hsien yi-tso pao-ts'un wan-cheng ti Yin tai wang-shih mu-tsang" 殷墟考古發掘的又一重要收穫—小屯發現一座保存完整的殷代王室墓葬. *K'ao-ku* 1977 (3): 151–153.
KKHCK (*K'ao-ku-hsüeh Chuan K'an* 考古學專刊.) *Cheng-chou Erh-li-kang* 鄭州二里岡. Peking: Science Press, 1959.
———. *Chia ku wen pien* 甲骨文編. Peking: Chung-hua, 1965.
———. *Chin wen pien* 金文編. Peking: Science Press, 1959.
———. *Hsi-an Pan-p'o* 西安半坡. Peking: Wen-wu Press, 1963.
———. *Hsin Chung-kuo ti k'ao-ku shou-hu* 新中國的考古收穫. Peking: Wen-wu Press, 1962.
———. *Miao-ti-kou yü San-li-ch'iao* 廟底溝與三里橋. Peking: Science Press, 1959.
———. *Ta-wen-k'ou* 大汶口. Peking: Science Press, 1974.
KKHP (*K'ao-ku Hsüeh-pao* 考古學報.) "An-yang Yin hsü wu-hao mu li fa-

chüeh" 安陽殷墟五號墓的發掘. *K'ao-ku Hsüeh-pao* 1977 (2): 57–98.
———. "Cheng-chou Ko-la-wang-ts'un yi-chih fa-chüeh pao-kao" 鄭州旭旮王村遺址發掘報告. *K'ao-ku Hsüeh-pao* 1958 (3): 41–62.
———. "Cheng-chou Nan-kuan-wai Shang tai yi-chih ti fa-chüeh" 鄭州南關外商代遺址的發掘. *K'ao-ku Hsüeh-pao* 1973 (1): 65–91.
———. "Cheng-chou Shang tai yi-chih ti fa-chüeh" 鄭州商代遺址的發掘. *K'ao-ku Hsüeh-pao* 1957 (1): 53–73.
———. "Ch'ih-feng Yao-wang-miao Hsia-chia-tien yi-chih shih chüeh pao-kao" 赤峯葯王廟夏家店遺址試掘報告. *K'ao-ku Hsüeh-pao* 1974 (1): 111–144.
———. "Ho-mu-tu yi-chih tung chih wu yi-ts'un ti chien-ting yen-chiu" 河姆渡遺址動植物遺存的鑒定研究. *K'ao-ku Hsüeh-pao* 1978 (1): 95–106.
———. "Ho-nan Hsin-hsiang Lu-wang-fen Shang tai yi-chih fa-chüeh pao-kao" 河南新鄉潞王墳商代遺址發掘報告. *K'ao-ku Hsüeh-pao* 1960 (1): 51–60.
———. "Ho-nan Shan Hsien Ch'i-li-p'u Shang tai yi-chih ti fa-chüeh" 河南陝縣七里舖商代遺址的發掘. *K'ao-ku Hsüeh-pao* 1960 (1): 25–47.
———. "Ho-pei T'ang-shan-shih Ta-ch'eng-shan yi-chih fa-chüeh pao-kao" 河北唐山市大城山遺址發掘報告. *K'ao-ku Hsüeh-pao* 1959 (3): 17–34.
———. "Hsing-t'ai Ts'ao-yen-chuang yi-chih fa-chüeh pao-kao" 邢台曹演莊遺址發掘報告. *K'ao-ku Hsüeh-pao* 1958 (4): 43–50.
———. "Hsü-chou Kao-huang-miao yi-chih ch'ing-li pao-kao" 徐州高皇廟遺址清理報告. *K'ao-ku Hsüeh-pao* 1958 (4): 7–17.
———. "Lo-yang Chien pin ku wen-hua yi-chih chi Han mu" 洛陽澗濱古文化遺址及漢墓. *K'ao-ku Hsüeh-pao* 1956 (1): 11–28.
———. "Shang-hai shih Ch'ing-p'u hsien Sung-tse yi-chih ti shih chüeh" 上海市青浦縣崧澤遺址的試掘. *K'ao-ku Hsüeh-pao* 1962 (2): 1–28.
———. "Tz'u hsien Hsia-p'an-wang yi-chih fa-chüeh pao-kao" 磁縣下潘汪遺址發掘報告. *K'ao-ku Hsüeh-pao* 1975 (1): 73–115.
———. "1955 nien ch'iu An-yang Hsiao-t'un Yin hsü ti fa-chüeh" 1955年秋安陽小屯殷墟的發掘. *K'ao-ku Hsüeh-pao* 1958 (3): 63–72.
Ko Chieh-p'ing 葛介屏. "An-hui Fu-nan fa-hsien Yin Shang shih-tai ti ch'ing-t'ung-ch'i" 安徽阜南發現殷商時代的青銅器. *Wen-wu* 1959 (1): inside cover.
Kraeling, Carl H., and Robert McC. Adams, eds. *City Invincible*. Chicago: University of Chicago Press, 1960.
Ku Chieh-kang 顧頡剛. "Chou Yi kua yao tz'u chung ti ku-shih" 周易卦爻辭中的故事. *Yen-ching Hsüeh-pao* 6 (1930): 971–975.
———. *Ku shih pien* 古史辨, no. 1. Peking: P'u-she, 1926.
Ku T'ing-lung 顧廷龍. *Ku t'ao wen yi lu* 古陶文舂錄. Peiping: Kuo-li Pei-p'ing Yen-chiu-yüan Shih-hsüeh Yen-chiu-hui Wen-tzu Shih-liao Ts'ung-pien chih yi 國立北平研究院史學研究會文字史料叢編之一, 1936.
Kuo Jo-yü 郭若愚. *Yin ch'i shih tuo* 殷契拾掇. Peking: Lai-hsün-ko, 1951.
Kuo Jo-yü 郭若愚 et al. *Yin hsü wen-tzu chui-ho* 殷虛文字綴合. Peking: Science Press, 1955.
Kuo Mo-jo 郭沫若. "An-yang hsin ch'u-t'u chih niu chia-ku chi ch'i k'o tz'u" 安陽新出土之牛胛骨及其刻辭. *K'ao-ku* 1972 (2): 2–7.
———. "An-yang yüan k'eng mu chung ting ming k'ao-shih" 安陽圓坑墓中鼎銘考釋. *K'ao-ku Hsüeh-pao* 1960 (1): 1–5.

———. *Ch'ing-t'ung ch'i shih-tai* 青銅器時代. Ch'ung-ch'ing: Wen-chih, 1945.
———. *Chung-kuo ku-tai she-hui yen-chiu* 中國古代社會研究. Shanghai: Hsin-hsin, 1929.
———. "Ku chiu k'o tz'u chih yi k'ao-ch'a" 骨臼刻辭之一考察. In *Ku-tai ming k'o hui k'ao hsü pien* 古代銘刻彙考續編. Tokyo: Bunkyudō, 1934.
———. "Ku-tai wen-tzu chih pien-cheng ti fa-chan" 古代文字之辯證的發展. *K'ao-ku* 1972 (3): 2–13.
———. *Nu-li-chih shih-tai* 奴隸制時代. Peking: Jen-min, 1972.
———. *P'u-tz'u t'ung ts'uan* 卜辭通纂. Tokyo, 1933.
———. *Yin ch'i ts'ui pien* 殷契粹編. Tokyo: Bunkyūdo, 1937.
———. "Yin yi chung t'u-hsing wen-tzu chih yi chieh" 殷彝中圖形文字之一解. In *Yin Chou ch'ing-t'ung-ch'i ming-wen yen-chiu* 殷周青銅器銘文研究, vol. 1. Shanghai: Ta-tung, 1931.
Kuo Pao-chün 郭寶鈞. "B-ch'ü fa-chüeh chi chih yi" B-區發掘記之一. *An-yang fa-chüeh pao-kao* 安陽發掘報告 4 (1933): 579–596.
———. "B-chü fa-chüeh chi chih erh" B-區發掘記之二. *An-yang fa-chüeh pao-kao* 4 (1933): 597–608.
———. "Yi-chiu-wu-ling nien ch'un Yin hsü fa-chüeh pao-kao" 一九五〇年春殷墟發掘報告. *K'ao-ku Hsüeh-pao* 5 (1951): pp. 1–61.
———, Hsia Nai 夏鼐, et al. *Hui hsien fa-chüeh pao-kao* 輝縣發掘報告. Peking: Science Press, 1956.
———, and Lin Shou-chin 林壽晋. "1952 nien ch'iu-chi Lo-yang tung chiao fa-chüeh pao-kao" 1952年秋季洛陽東郊發掘報告. *K'ao-ku Hsüeh-pao* 9 (1955): 91–116.
Kuo Ping-lien 郭氷廉. "Hu-pei Huang-p'i Yang-chia-wan ti ku yi-chih tiao-ch'a" 湖北黃陂楊家灣的古遺址調查. *K'ao-ku T'ung-hsün* 1958 (1): 56–58.
Kuo Te-wei 郭德維 and Ch'en Hsien-yi 陳賢一. "Hu-pei Huang-p'i hsien P'an-lung-ch'eng Shang tai yi-chih ho mu-tsang" 湖北黃陂縣盤龍城商代遺址和墓葬. *K'ao-ku* 1964 (8): 420–421.
Kuo Yung 郭勇. "Shih-lou Hou-lan-chia-kou fa-hsien Shang tai ch'ing-t'ung-ch'i chien pao" 石樓後蘭家溝發現商代青銅器簡報. *Wen-wu* 1962 (4/5): 33–35.
Lan Wei 藍蔚. "Hu-pei Huang-p'i hsien P'an-t'u-ch'eng fa-hsien ku ch'eng yi-chih chi shih-ch'i teng" 湖北黃陂縣盤土城發現古城遺址及石器等. *Wen-wu* 1955 (4): 118–119.
Lao Kan 勞榦. "Chou ch'u nien-tai wen-t'i yü yüeh hsiang wen-t'i ti hsin k'an fa" 周初年代問題與月相問題的新看法. *Journal of the Institute of Chinese Culture*, Chinese University of Hong Kong, 7 (1974): 1–24.
Lau, D. C. *Mencius*. London: Penguin Books, 1970.
Laufer, B. *Jade*. Field Museum of Natural History Publication 154 (Anthropology Series 10). Chicago: Field Museum of Natural History, 1912.
Lefeuvre, J. A. "Les inscriptions des Shang sur carapaces de tortue et sur os." *T'oung Pao* 61 (1975): 1–82.
Legge, James. *The Ch'un Ts'ew, with the Tso Chuen*, vol. 5 of *The Chinese Classics*. Oxford: Clarendon Press, 1872.
———. *Confucian Analects*, vol. 1 of *The Chinese Classics*. Oxford: Clarendon Press, 1893.

Lei Hai-tsung 雷海宗. "Yin Chou nien-tai k'ao" 殷周年代考. *Wen Shih Chi K'an* 文史季刊 2, no. 1 (1931): 1–14.

Li Chi 李濟. "An-yang fa-chüeh yü Chung-kuo ku shih wen-t'i" 安陽發掘與中國古史問題. *Bulletin of the Institute of History and Philology*, Academia Sinica, 40 (1969): 913–944.

———. "An-yang tsui-chin fa-chüeh pao-kao chi liu tz'u kung-tso chih tsung ku-chi" 安陽最近發掘報告及六次工作之總估計. *An-yang fa-chüeh pao-kao* 4 (1933): 559–578.

———. *Anyang: A Chronicle of the Discovery, Excavation, and Reconstruction of the Ancient Capital of the Shang Dynasty*. Seattle: University of Washington Press, 1977.

———. *The Beginnings of the Chinese Civilization*. Seattle: University of Washington Press, 1957.

———. "Chi Hsiao-t'un ch'u-t'u chih ch'ing-t'ung ch'i" 記小屯出土之青銅器. *Chung-kuo K'ao-ku Hsüeh-pao* 3 (1948): 1–93.

———. "Chi Hsiao-t'un ch'u-t'u chih ch'ing-t'ung-ch'i chung p'ien" 記小屯出土之青銅器, 中篇 *Chung-kuo K'ao-ku Hsüeh-pao* 4 (1949): 1–70.

———. "Fu shen tsang" 俯身葬. *An-yang fa-chüeh pao-kao* 3 (1930): 447–480.

———. *Hsiao-t'un t'ao-ch'i*. (See *Yin-hsü ch'i-wu chia pien* . . . below.)

———. "Hsiao-t'un t'ao-ch'i chih-liao chih hua-hsüeh fen-hsi" 小屯陶器質料之化學分析. In *T'ai-ta Fu ku hsiao-chang Ssu-nien hsien-sheng chi-nien lun-wen chi* 台大傅故校長斯年先生紀念論文集, pp. 123–138, Taipei: National Taiwan University, 1952.

———. "Hsiao-t'un ti-mien hsia ch'ing-hsing fen-hsi ch'u-pu" 小屯地面下情形分析初步. *An-yang fa-chüeh pao-kao* 1 (1929): 37–48.

———. "Hsiao-t'un yü Yang-shao" 小屯與仰韶. *An-yang fa-chüeh pao-kao* 2 (1930): 337–347.

———. "Hunting Records, Faunistic Remains, and Decorative Patterns from the Archaeological Site of Anyang." *Bulletin of the Department of Archaeology and Anthropology*, National Taiwan University, 9/10 (1957): 10–20.

———. "Min-kuo shih-pa nien ch'iu-chi fa-chüeh Yin hsü chih ching-kuo chi ch'i chung-yao fa-hsien" 民國十八年秋季發掘殷虛之經過及其重要發現. *An-yang fa-chüeh pao-kao* 2 (1930): 218–252.

———. "Notes on Some Metrical Characters of Calvaria of the Shang Dynasty Excavated from Houchiachuang, Anyang." *Annals of the Academia Sinica* 1 (1954): 549–558.

———. "Pien hou yü" 編後語. *An-yang fa-chüeh pao-kao* 4 (1944): 732–733.

———. "Pien hsing pa lei chi ch'i wen-shih chih yen-pien" 笄形八類及其文飾之演變. *Bulletin of the Institute of History and Philology* Academia Sinica, 30 (1959): 1–69.

———. "Studies of the Hsiao-t'un Pottery: Yin and Pre-Yin." *Annals of the Academia Sinica* 2 (1955): 103–117.

———. "Yen-chiu Chung-kuo ku yü wen-t'i ti hsin tzu-liao" 研究中國古玉問題的新資料. *Bulletin of the Institute of History and Philology*, Academia Sinica, 13 (1948): 179–182.

———. *Yin hsü ch'i-wu chia pien T'ao-ch'i shang p'ien* 殷虛器物甲編陶器上篇. Taipei: Institute of History and Philology, Academia Sinica, 1956. (Abbreviated in notes as *Hsiao-t'un T'ao-ch'i*.)

———. "Yin hsü ch'u-t'u ch'ing-t'ung li-ch'i chih tsung chien-t'ao" 殷虛出土青銅禮器之總檢討. *Bulletin of the Institute of History and Philology*, Academia Sinica, 47 (1976): 783–811.

———. "Yin hsü ch'u-t'u ti kung-yeh ch'eng-chi—san li" 殷虛出土的工業成績—三例. *Bulletin of the College of Arts*, National Taiwan University, 25 (1976): 1–64.

———. "Yin hsü ch'u-t'u t'ung-ch'i wu chung chi ch'i hsiang-kuan chih wen-t'i" 殷虛出土銅器五種及其相關之問題. In *Papers Presented to Mr. Ts'ai Yuan P'ei on His Sixty-fifth Birthday*, pp. 73–104. Nanking: Institute of History and Philology, Academia Sinica, 1933.

———. "Yin hsü pai t'ao fa-chan chih ch'eng-hsü" 殷虛白陶發展之程序. *Bulletin of the Institute of History and Philology* Academia Sinica, 28 (1957): 853–882.

———. "Yin hsü yu jen shih-ch'i t'u shuo" 殷虛有刄石器圖説. *Bulletin of the Institute of History and Philology*, Academia Sinica, 23 (1951): 523–615.

———. "Yin Shang t'ao-ch'i ch'u-lun" 殷商陶器初論. *An-yang fa-chüeh pao-kao* 1 (1929): 49–58.

———. "Yu pien hsing yen-pien so k'an-chien ti Hsiao-t'un yi-chih yü Hou-chia-chuang mu-tsang chih shih-tai kuan-hsi" 由笄形演變所看見的小屯遺址與侯家莊墓葬之時代關係. *Bulletin of the Institute of History and Philology*, Academia Sinica, 29 (1958): 809–816.

———. "Yü pei ch'u-t'u ch'ing-t'ung kou-ping fen-lei t'u-chieh" 豫北出土青銅句兵分類圖解. *Bulletin of the Institute of History and Philology*, Academia Sinica, 22 (1950): 1–18.

Li Ching-tan 李景聃. "Yü tung Shang-ch'iu Yung-ch'eng tiao-ch'a chi Tsao-lü-t'ai Hei-ku-tui Ts'ao-ch'iao san ch'u hsiao fa-chüeh" 豫東商邱永城調查及造律台黑孤堆曹橋三處小發掘. *Chung-kuo K'ao-ku Hsüeh-pao* 2 (1947): 83–120.

Li Chung 李衆. "Kuan-yü Kao-ch'eng Shang tai t'ung yüeh t'ieh jen ti fen-hsi" 關於藁城商代銅鉞鐵刄的分析. *K'ao-ku Hsüeh-pao* 1976 (2): 17–34.

Li Hsiao-ting 李孝定. *Chia-ku wen-tzu chi-shih* 甲骨文字集釋. Institute of History and Philology, Academia Sinica, Monographs 50. Taipei: Institute of History and Philology, Academia Sinica, 1965.

———. "Chung-kuo wen-tzu ti yüan-shih ho yen-pien shang p'ien" 中國文字的原始和演變,上篇. *Bulletin of the Institute of History and Philology*, Academia Sinica, 45 (1974): 343–370.

———. "Ts'ung chi chung shih-ch'ien ho yu-shih tsao-ch'i t'ao wen ti kuan-ch'a li-ts'e Chung-kuo wen-tzu ti ch'i yüan" 從幾種史前和有史早期陶文的觀察蠡測中國文字的起源. *Nan-yang Ta-hsüeh Hsüeh-pao* 南洋大學學報 3 (1969): 1–28.

Li Hsüeh-ch'in 李學勤. "P'ing Ch'en Meng-chia *Yin hsü p'u-tz'u tsung shu*" 評陳夢家殷墟卜辭綜述. *K'ao-ku Hsüeh-pao* 1957 (1): 119–129.

———. "T'an An-yang Hsiao-t'un yi-wai ch'u-t'u ti yu tzu chia ku" 談安陽小屯以外出土的有字甲骨. *Wen-wu* 1956 (11): 16–17.

———. *Yin tai ti-li chien lun* 殷代地理簡論. Peking: Science Press, 1959.

Li Hui-lin 李惠林. "The Origin of Cultivated Plants in Southeast Asia." *Eco-*

nomic Botany 24 (1970): 3–19.
———. "The Vegetables of Ancient China." *Economic Botany* 23 (1969): 253–260.
Li Tao-yüan 酈道元. *Shui ching chu* 水經注. Shanghai: Commercial Press, 1933.
Li Ya-nung 李亞農. *Yin tai she-hui sheng-huo* 殷代社會生活. Shanghai: Jen-min, 1955.
Liang Ssu-yung 梁思永. "Hou-kang fa-chüeh hsiao chi" 後岡發掘小記. *An-yang fa-chüeh pao-kao* 4 (1933): 609–626.
———. "Hsiao-t'un Lung-shan yü Yang-shao" 小屯龍山與仰韶. In *Papers Presented to Mr. Ts'ai Yüan P'ei on His sixty-fifth Birthday* pp. 555–567. 1935.
Liang Ssu-yung 梁思永 and Kao Ch'ü-hsün 高去尋. *Hou-chia-chuang 1001-hao ta mu* 侯家莊1001號大墓. Taipei: Institute of History and Philology, Academia Sinica, 1962.
———. *Hou-chia-chuang 1002-hao ta mu* 侯家莊1002號大墓. 1965.
———. *Hou-chia-chuang 1003-hao ta mu* 侯家莊1003號大墓. 1967.
———. *Hou-chia-chuang 1217-hao ta mu* 侯家莊1217號大墓. 1968.
———. *Hou-chia-chuang 1004-hao ta mu* 侯家莊1004號大墓. 1970.
———. *Hou-chia-chuang 1500-hao ta mu* 侯家莊1500號大墓. 1974.
———. *Hou-chia-chuang 1550-hao ta mu* 侯家莊1550號大墓. 1976.
Liao Yung-min 廖永民. "Cheng-chou shih fa-hsien ti yi ch'u Shang tai chü-chu yü chu-tsao t'ung-ch'i yi-chih chien chieh" 鄭州市發現的一處商代居住與鑄造銅器遺址簡介. *Wen-wu* 1957 (6): 73–74.
Lin Ch'un-yü 林純玉. "Ho-nan An-yang Yin hsü t'ou-ku nao-jung-liang ti yen-chiu" 河南安陽殷墟頭骨腦容量的研究. *Bulletin of the Department of Archaeology and Anthropology*, National Taiwan University, 33/34 (1973): 39–58.
Lin Heng-li 林衡立. "P'ing Chang Kwang-chih Shang wang miao hao hsin k'ao chung ti lun cheng fa" 評張光直商王廟號新考中的論証法. *Bulletin of the Institute of Ethnology*, Academia Sinica, 19 (1965): 115–119.
Lin Yün 林澐. "Shuo 'wang'" 説'王'. *K'ao-ku* 1965 (6): 311–312.
Liu Eh 劉鶚. *T'ieh-yün ts'ang kuei* 鐵雲藏龜. Peking (?): Pao-ts'an shou-ch'üeh chai, 1903.
———. *T'ieh-yün ts'ang t'ao* 鐵雲藏匋. Pao-ts'an shou-ch'üeh chai, 1904.
Liu Ch'i-yi 劉啟益. "'Ao tu' chih yi" '敖都' 質疑. *Wen-wu* 1961 (10): 39–40.
Liu Pao-lin 劉寶林. "Kung-yüan ch'ien 1500 nien chih Kung-yüan ch'ien 1000 nien yüeh-shih piao" 公元前1500年至公元前1000年月食表. *Studia Astronomica Sinica* 天文集刊 1 (1978): 43–60.
Liu Hsien-chou 劉仙洲. *Chung-kuo ku-tai nung-yeh chi-hsieh fa-ming shih* 中國古代農業機械發明史. Peking: Science Press, 1963.
Liu Pin-hsiung 劉斌雄. "Yin Shang wang-shih shih-fen-tsu chih shih lun" 殷商王室十分組制試論. *Bulletin of the Institute of Ethnology*, Academia Sinica, 19 (1965): 89–114.
Lo Chen-yü 羅振玉. *Meng-an ts'ang t'ao* 夢庵藏陶. N.p., 1922.
———. *Meng-wei-ts'ao-t'ang chi chin t'u* 夢郼草堂吉金圖. N.p., 1917.
———. *Yin hsü shu ch'i ch'ien pien* 殷虛書契前編. N.p., 1913
———. *Yin hsü shu ch'i ch'ing hua* 殷虛書契菁華. N.p., 1914.
———. *Yin hsü shu ch'i hou pien* 殷虛書契後編. N.p., 1916.
———. *Yin hsü shu ch'i hsü pien* 殷虛書契續編. N.p., 1933.

———. *Yin hsü shu ch'i k'ao shih* 殷虛書契考釋. N.p., 1915.

Loehr, Max. *Ancient Chinese Jades*. Cambridge: Fogg Art Museum, 1975.

———. "The Bronze Styles of the An-yang Period (1300–1028 B.C.)." *Archives of the Chinese Art Society of America* 7 (1953): 42–53.

———. *Ritual Vessels of Bronze Age China*. New York: The Asia Society, 1968.

Lu Mao-te 陸懋德. "Chung-kuo fa-hsien chih shang-ku t'ung li k'ao" 中國發現之上古銅犂考. *Yen-ching Hsüeh-pao* 37 (1949): 11–26.

Lu P'o 魯波. "Ts'ung Ta-wen-k'ou wen-hua k'an wo-kuo ssu-yu-chih ti ch'i-yüan" 從大汶口文化看我國私有制的起源. *Wen-wu* 1976 (7): 74–81.

Lung Yü-ch'un 龍宇純. "Shih chia-ku wen *yin* tzu chien chieh hsi tsun" 釋甲骨文㞢字兼解犧尊. In *Papers Presented to Mr. Shen Kang-po on His Eightieth Birthday*, pp. 1–15. Taipei: Lien-ching, 1976.

Ma Ch'üan 馬全. "Cheng-chou shih Ming-kung-lu hsi ts'e ti Shang tai yi-ts'un" 鄭州市銘功路西側的商代遺存. *Wen-wu* 1956 (10): 50–51.

Ma Te-chih 馬得志, Chou Yung-chen 周永珍, and Chang Yün-p'eng 張雲鵬. "Yi-chiu-wu-san nien An-yang Ta-ssu-k'ung-ts'un fa-chüeh pao-kao" 一九五三年安陽大司空村發掘報告. *K'ao-ku Hsüeh-pao* 9 (1955): 25–90.

Maglioni, R. *Archaeological Discovery in Eastern Kwangtung*. Hong Kong Archaeological Society, Journal Monograph 2. Hong Kong: Hong Kong Archaelogical Society, 1975 (reprint).

Mao Hsieh-chün 毛燮均 and Yen Yen 嚴誾. "An-yang Hui hsien Yin tai jen-ya ti yen-chiu pao-kao" 安陽輝縣殷代人牙的研究報告. *Ku Chi-chui Tung-wu yü Ku Jen-lei* 古脊椎動物與古人類 1 (1959): 81–85.

Mao Pao-liang 毛寶亮. "Cheng-chou hsi-chiao Yang-shao wen-hua yi-chih fa-chüeh chien pao" 鄭州西郊仰韶文化遺址發掘簡報. *K'ao-ku T'ung-hsün* 1958 (2): 1–5.

Matsumaru Michio 松丸道雄. *In Shū kokka no kōzō* 殷周国家の構造. Iwanami Kōzo sekaishi 岩波講座世界史, vol. 4. Tokyo: Iwanami Kōzo, 1970.

———. "Inkyo bokuji chū no denryōchi ni tsuite—Indai kokka kōzō kenkyū no tame ni" 殷墟卜辞中の田猟地について—殷代国家構造研究のために. *Tōyō Bunka Kenkyūjo Kiyō* 東洋文化研究所紀要 31, no. 1 (1963): 1–163.

Mēng Wen-t'ung 蒙文通. "Ku-tai Ho-yü ch'i-hou yu ju chin Chiang-yü shuo" 古代河域氣候有如今江域説. *Yü kung* 禹貢 1 (1934): 14–15.

Menzies, James (see Ming Yi-shih).

Ming Yi-shih 明義士 [James Menzies]. *Yin hsü p'u-tz'u* 殷墟卜辭. Shanghai Pieh-fa Yang-hang, 1917.

Miyazaki Ichisada 宮崎市定. "Chūgoku jōdai no toshi kokka to sono bochi—Shōyū wa doko ni attaka" 中国上代の都市国家とその墓地—商邑は何処にあったか. *Tōyōshi Kenkyū* 東洋史研究 28 (1970): 265–282.

———. "Hoi" 補遺. *Tōyōshi Kenkyū* 29 (1970): 147–152.

Nadel, S. F. "Witchcraft in Four African Societies: An Essay in Comparison." *American Anthropologist* 54 (1952): 18–29.

Naitō Torajiro 内藤虎次郎. "Ōi" 王亥 and "Zoku Ōi" 續王亥. *Geibun* 藝文 1916–21. (Reprinted in Naitō Konan Zenshū 内藤湖南全集, vol. 7, pp. 469–500. Tokyo: Tsukuma Shobō, 1970.)

P'an Wu-su 潘武肅. "The Dates of Wu Ting's Reign," manuscript.

———. "Religion and Chronology in Shang China: The Scheduled Ancestor

Worship Rituals and the Chronology of the Late Shang Period." Ph. D. diss., University of Pennsylvania, 1976.

Pearson, Richard J. "Pollen Counts in North China," *Antiquity* 48 (1974): 276–278.

Pelliot, Paul. "The Royal Tombs of An-yang." In *Independence, Convergence and Borrowing*, Harvard University Tercentenary Publication, pp. 265–272. Cambridge: Harvard University Press, 1937.

———. "The Royal Tombs of An-yang." In *Studies in Chinese Art and Some Indian Influences*. London: India Society, 1938.

Pfeiffer, John E. *The Emergence of Society*. New York: McGraw-Hill, 1977.

Piggott, Stuart, ed. *The Dawn of Civilization*. New York: McGraw-Hill, 1961.

Pope, C. H. *The Reptiles of China*. Natural History of Central Asia, Vol. 10. New York: American Museum of Natural History, 1935.

Pospisil, Leopold. *The Ethnology of Law*. Addison-Wesley module in anthropology, no. 12. Readings Mass.: Addison-Wesley, 1972.

Ralph, E. K., H. N. Michael, and M. C. Han. "Radiocarbon Dates and Reality." *MASCA Newsletter* 9, no. 1 (1973).

Reed, Charles A. "A Model for the Origin of Agriculture in the Near East." In *Origins of Agriculture*, C. A. Reed, ed., pp. 543–567. The Hague: Mouton, 1977.

Rouse, Irving. *Prehistory in Haiti: A Study in Method*. Yale University Publications in Anthropology, no. 21. New Haven: Department of Anthropology, Yale University, 1939.

Sanders, William T. "Chiefdom to State: Political Evolution at Kaminaljuyu, Guatemala." In *Reconstructing Complex Societies*, C. B. Moore, ed. Supplement to the Bulletin of the American School of Oriental Research, no. 20. Cambridge, Mass.: American School of Oriental Research, 1974.

———, and Barbara J. Price. *Mesoamerica*. New York: Random House, 1968.

Schafer, Edward. "T'ang," In *Food in Chinese Culture*, K. C. Chang, ed., pp. 85–140. New Haven and London: Yale University Press, 1977.

Schmandt-Besserat, Denise. "The Earliest Precursor of Writing." *Scientific American* 238 no. 6, (1978): 50–59.

Schofield, W. "The Proto-historic Site of the Hong Kong Culture at Shek Pik, Lantau, Hong Kong." *Proceedings of the Third Congress of the Prehistorians of the Far East*, pp. 236–284. Singapore, 1938.

Sekino Takeshi 関野雄. "*Chūgoku seidōki bunka no ichi seikaku*" 中国青銅器文化の一性格. *Tōhōgaku* 東方学 2 (1951): 88–96.

Service, Elman. *Origins of the State and Civilization*. New York: Norton, 1974.

———. *Primitive Social Organization: An Evolutionary Perspective*. New York: Random House, 1962.

Shang Ch'eng-tso 商承祚. *Yin ch'i yi ts'un* 殷契佚存. Nanking: Chin-ling Ta-hsüeh Chung-kuo wen-hua yen-chiu so ts'ung-k'an chia chung 金陵大學中國文化研究所叢刋甲種, 1933.

Shangrow, Clarence. "Early Chinese Ceramics and Kilns." *Archaeology* 30 (1977): 382–393.

Shapiro, Harry. *Peking Man*. New York: Simon and Schuster, 1974.

Shen Chen-chung 沈振中. "Hsin hsien Lien-ssu-kou ch'u-t'u ti ch'ing-t'ung-ch'i'' 忻縣連寺溝出土的青銅器. *Wen-wu* 1972 (4): 67–68.

Shen Wen-cho 沈文倬. ''Fu yü chi'' 艮與耤. *K'ao-ku* 1977 (5): 335–338.

Shih Chang-ju 石璋如. *Chung-tsu mu-tsang* 中組墓葬. Taipei: Institute of History and Philolgy, Academia Sinica, 1971.

———. ''Ho-nan An-yang Hou-kang ti Yin mu'' 河南安陽後岡的殷墓. *Bulletin of the Institute of History and Philology*. Academia Sinica, 13 (1947): 21–48.

———. ''Ho-nan An-yang Hsiao-t'un Yin mu chung ti tung-wu yi-hsieh'' 河南安陽小屯殷墓中的動物遺骸. *Bulletin of the College of Arts*, National Taiwan University, 5 (1953): 1–14.

———. ''Hsiao-t'un C-ch'ü ti mu-tsang ch'ün'' 小屯C區的墓葬羣. *Bulletin of the Institute of History and Philology*, Academia Sinica, 23 (1951): 447–487.

———. ''Hsiao-t'un ti wen-hua ts'eng'' 小屯的文化層. *Liu-t'ung Pieh-lu* 六同别錄, vol. 1. Li-chuang: Institute of History and Philology, Academia Sinica, 1945. 42 pp.

———. ''Hsiao-t'un Yin tai Ping tsu chi-chih chi ch'i yu-kuan hsien-hsiang 小屯殷代丙組基址及其有關現象. In *Papers Presented to Mr. Tung Tso-pin on His Sixty-fifth Birthday*, pp. 781–802. Taipei, Institute of History and Philology, Academia Sinica, 1961.

———. ''Hsiao-t'un Yin tai ti ch'eng t'ao ping-ch'i'' 小屯殷代的成套兵器. *Bulletin of the Institute of History and Philology*, Academia Sinica, 22 (1950): 19–84.

———. ''Hsiao-t'un Yin tai ti chien-chu yi-chi'' 小屯殷代的建築遺蹟. *Bulletin of the Institute of History and Philology*, Academia Sinica, 26 (1955): 131–188.

———. *K'ao-ku nien piao* 考古年表. Institute of History and Philology, Academia Sinica, Monograph 35, 1952.

———. *Nan tsu mu-tsang* 南組墓葬. Institute of History and Philology, Academia Sinica, 1973.

———. *Pei tsu mu-tsang* 北組墓葬. Institute of History and Philology, Academia Sinica, 1970.

———. ''Ti ch'i tz'u Yin hsü fa-chüeh: E-ch'ü kung-tso pao-kao'' 第七次殷墟發掘：E區工作報告. *An-yang fa-chüeh pao-kao* 4 (1933): 709–728.

———. *Yi ch'ü chi-chih shang hsia ti mu-tsang* 乙區基址上下的墓葬. Institute of History and Philology, Academia Sinica, 1976.

———. *Yin hsü chien-chu yi-ts'un* 殷虛建築遺存. Institute of History and Philology, Academia Sinica, 1959.

———. ''Yin hsü fa-chüeh tui-yü Chung-kuo ku-tai wen-hua ti kung-hsien'' 殷虛發掘對於中國古代文化的貢獻. *Hsüeh-shu chi-k'an* 學術季刊 2 no. 4 (1953): 1–16.

———. ''Yin hsü tsui-chin chih chung-yao fa-hsien fu lun Hsiao-t'un ti-ts'eng'' 殷墟最近之重要發現附論小屯地層. *Chung-kuo K'ao-ku Hsüeh-pao* 2 (1947): 1–81.

———. ''Yin hsü tsui-chin chih chung-yao fa-hsien fu lun Hsiao-t'un ti-ts'eng hou chi'' 殷墟最近之重要發現附論小屯地層後記. *Chung-kuo K'ao-ku Hsüeh-pao* 4 (1949): 291–302.

———. ''Yin tai ti chu t'ung kung-yi'' 殷代的鑄銅工藝. *Bulletin of the Institute of History and Philology*, Academia Sinica, 26 (1955): 95–129.

———. ''Yin tai ti hang-t'u pan-chu yü yi-pan chien-chu'' 殷代的夯土版築與

一般建築. *Bulletin of the Institute of History and Philology*, Academia Sinica, 41 (1969): 127–168.

———. "Yin tai ti-shang chien-chu fu-yüan chih yi li" 殷代地上建築復原之一例. *Annals of the Academia Sinica*, 1 (1954): 267–280.

———. "Yin tai ti-shang chien-chu fu-yüan ti ti-erh li" 殷代地上建築復原的第二例. *Bulletin of the Institute of Ethnology*, Academia Sinica, 29 (1970): 321–341.

———. "Yin tai ti-shang chien-chu fu-yüan ti ti-san li" 殷代地上建築復原的第三例. *Bulletin of the Department of Archaeology and Anthropology*, National Taiwan University, 39/40 (1976): 140–157.

Shih Chih-lien 石志廉. "T'an-t'an lung hu tsun ti chi-ko wen-t'i" 談談龍虎尊的幾個問題. *Wen-wu* 1972 (11): 64–66.

Shih Hsin-keng 施昕更. *Liang-chu—Hang-hsien ti-erh ch'ü hei-t'ao wen-hua yi-chih ch'u-pu pao-kao* 良渚—杭縣第二區黑陶文化遺址初步報告. Hangchou: Hsi-hu Museum, 1938.

Shih Hsing 史星. *Nu-li she-hui* 奴隸社會. Shanghai: Jen-min Press, 1973.

Shih Sheng-han 石聲漢. *Ch'i-min-yao-shu chin shih* 齊民要術今釋. Peking: Science Press, 1957.

Shima Kunio 島邦男. *Inkyo bokuji kenkyū* 殷墟卜辞研究. Tokyo: Kyūko Shoin, 1958.

———. *Inkyo bokuji sōrui* 殷墟卜辞綜類. 2nd rev. ed. Tokyo: Kyūko Shoin, 1971.

Shirakawa Shizuka 白川静. "*In no kiso shakai*" 殷の基礎社会. In *Ritsumeikan sōritsu gojishūnen kinen ronbun shū Bungaku hen* 立命館創立五十週年紀念論文集文学篇, pp. 260–296. Kyoto: Ritsumeikan, 1951.

———. "In no ōzoku to seiji no keitai" 殷の王族と政治の形態. *Kodaigaku* 古代学 3 (1954): 19–44.

———. "Indai yūzoku kō, sono ni, Jaku" 殷代雄族考,其二,雀. *Kōkotsu Kinbungaku Ronsō* 甲骨金文学論叢 6 (1957): 1–62.

———. "Kyōzoku kō" 羌族考. *Kōkotsu Kinbungaku Ronsō* 9 (1958).

———. "Sakusatsu kō" 作册考. *Kōkotsu Kinbungaku Ronsō* 2 (1955).

Sickman, L., and A. Soper. *The Art and Architecture of China*. Penguin Books, 1971.

Smith, Bradley, and Wan-go Weng. *China, a History in Art*. New York: Harper and Row, 1972.

Soper, A. C. "Early, Middle, and Late Shang: A Note." *Artibus Asiae* 28 (1966): 5–38.

Spencer, Bruce. "Archaic Chinese Bronzes: A Statistical Study of Motif Co-occurrence." Manuscript.

SS (*Scientia Sinica*.) "Liao-ning sheng nan-pu yi-wan nien lai tzu-jan huan-ching chih yen-pien" 遼寧省南部一萬年來自然環境之演變. *Chung-kuo K'o-hsüeh* 中國科學 1977 (6): 603–614.

Su Shih-cheng 束世澂. "Hsia tai ho Shang tai ti nu-li chih" 夏代和商代的奴隸制. *Li-shih Yen-chiu* 1956 (1): 31–61.

Sullivan, Michael. *The Arts of China*, rev. ed. Berkeley and Los Angeles: University of California Press, 1977.

Sun Ch'ang-hsü 孫常敍. *Lei ssu ti ch'i-yüan chi ch'i fa-chan* 耒耜的起源及其發

展. Shanghai: Jen-min Press, 1959.

Sun Hai-p'o 孫海波. *Ch'eng-chai Yin hsü wen-tzu* 誠齋殷虛文字. Peking: Hsiu-wen-t'ang, 1940.

———. *Chia ku wen lu* 甲骨文錄. K'ai Feng: Ho-nan T'ung-chih Kuan 河南通志館, 1937.

Sun Tso-yün 孫作雲. "Ts'ung 'T'ien-wen' k'an Hsia ch'u chien kuo shih" 從'天問'看夏初建國史. *Shih-hsüeh* 史學 116, *Kuang-ming Jih-pao* 光明日報, 29 August 1978.

Sylvan, V. "Silk from the Yin Dynasty." *Bulletin of the Museum of Far Eastern Antiquities* 9 (1937): 119–126.

Tan Ta 單達 and Shih Ping 史兵. "Ts'ung Ta-wen-k'ou wen-hua yi-ts'un k'an wo-kuo ku-tai ssu-yu-chih ti jun-yü ho meng-ya" 從大汶口文化遺存看我國古代私有制的孕育和萌芽. *Wen-wu* 1976 (4): 84–88.

T'ang Ch'ang-p'u 唐昌朴. "Chiang-hsi Tu-ch'ang ch'u-t'u Shang tai t'ung-ch'i" 江西都昌出土商代銅器. *K'ao-ku* 1976 (4): 273.

T'ang Lan 唐蘭. "Kuan-yü Chiang-hsi Wu-ch'eng wen-hua yi-chih yü wen-tzu ti ch'u-pu t'an-so" 關于江西吳城文化遺址與文字的初步探索. *Wen-wu* 1975 (7): 72–76.

———. "Lüeh lun Hsi Chou Wei shih chia-tsu chiao-ts'ang t'ung-ch'i ch'ün ti chung-yao yi-yi" 略論西周微史家族窖藏銅器羣的重要意義. *Wen-wu* 1978 (3): 19–24.

———. "Ts'ung Ho-nan Cheng-chou ch'u-t'u ti Shang tai ch'ien-ch'i ch'ing-t'ung-ch'i t'an ch'i" 從河南鄭州出土的商代前期青銅器談起. *Wen-wu* 1973 (7): 5–14.

———. "Ts'ung Ta-wen-k'ou wen-hua ti t'ao-ch'i wen-tzu k'an wo-kuo tsui-tsao wen-hua ti nien-tai" 從大汶口文化的陶器文字看我國最早文化的年代. *Shih-hsüeh*, in *Kuang-ming Jih-pao* 14 July 1977.

T'ang Yün-ming 唐雲明. "Hsing-t'ai Nan-ta-kuo ts'un Shang tai yi-chih t'an-chüeh chien pao" 邢台南大郭村商代遺址探掘簡報. *Wen-wu* 1957 (3): 61–63.

———. "Kao-ch'eng T'ai-hsi Shang tai t'ieh jen t'ung yüeh wen-t'i ti t'an-t'ao" 藁城台西商代鉄刃銅鉞問題的探討. *Wen-wu* 1975 (3): 57–59.

Teilhard de Chardin, Pierre, and C. C. Young. *On the Mammalian Remains from the Archaeological Site of An-yang. Palaeontologia Sinica* C, vol. 12, fasc. 1. Peking, 1936.

Ting Shan 丁山. *Chia-ku wen so-chien shih-tsu chi ch'i chih-tu* 甲骨文所見氏族及其制度. Peking: Science Press, 1956.

———. *Yin Shang shih-tsu fang-kuo chih* 殷商氏族方國志. Peking: Science Press, 1956.

———. "Yu san-tai tu-yi lun ch'i min-tsu wen-hua" 由三代都邑論其民族文化. *Bulletin of the Institute of History and Philology*, Academia Sinica, 5 (1935): 89–129.

Ting Su 丁驌. "Chung-kuo ti-li min-tzu wen-wu yü ch'uan-shuo shih" 中國地理民族文物與傳說史. *Bulletin of the Institute of Ethnology*, Academia Sinica, 29 (1970): 43–98.

———. "Ch'ung ting Ti Hsin cheng Jen Fang jih p'u" 重訂帝辛正人方日譜. In *Tung Tso-pin Hsien-sheng shih-shih shih-ssu chou-nien chi-nien k'an* 董作賓

先生逝世十四週年紀念刊, pp. 16–35. Taipei: Yi-wen, 1978.
———. "Hua Pei ti-hsing shih yü Shang Yin ti li-shih" 華北地形史與商殷的歷史. *Bulletin of the Institute of Ethnology*, Academia Sinica, 20 (1965): 155–162.
———. "Lun Yin wang p'i shih fa" 論殷王妣謚法. *Bulletin of the Institute of Ethnology*, Academia Sinica, 19 (1965): 71–79.
———. "Sui tsai Ch'un-huo yü Wu Wang fa Chòu" 歲在鶉火與武王伐紂. *Hua-hsüeh Yüeh-k'an* 華學月刊 71 (1977): 36–46.
———. "Tsai lun Shang wang p'i miao hao ti liang tsu shuo" 再論商王妣廟號的兩組說. *Bulletin of the Institute of Ethnology*, Academia Sinica, 21 (1966): 41–79.
Trigger, Bruce G. "Inequality and Communication in Early Civilizations. *Anthropologica* n.s. 17 (1976): 27–52.
———. *Time and Traditions: Essays in Archaeological Interpretation*. New York: Columbia University Press, 1978.
Ts'ai Feng-shu 蔡鳳書. "Chi-nan Ta-hsin-chuang Shang tai yi-chih ti tiao-ch'a" 濟南大辛莊商代遺址的調查. *K'ao-ku* 1973 (5): 272–275.
Tsang Chen-hua 臧振華. "An-yang Yin hsü t'ou-ku ch'i-hsing men-ch'ih ti yen-chiu" 安陽殷墟頭骨箕形門齒的研究. *Bulletin of the Department of Archaeology and Anthropology*, National Taiwan University, 35/36 (1974): 69–82.
Ts'ao K'o-ch'ing 曹克清. "Shang-hai fu-chin ch'üan-hsin-shih ssu-pu-hsiang-lu ya-hua-shih ti fa-hsien yi-chi wo-guo che shu tung-wu ti ti-shih ti-li fen-pu" 上海附近全新世四不像鹿亞化石的發現以及我國這屬動物的地史地理分布. *Vetebrata Palasiatica* 13 (1975): 48–57.
Tseng Chao-yüeh 曾昭燏 and Yin Huan-chang 尹煥章. "Ku-tai Chiang-su li-shih shang ti liang-ko wen-t'i" 古代江蘇歷史上的兩個問題. In *Chiang-su-sheng ch'u-t'u wen-wu hsüan-chi* 江蘇省出土文物選集. Peking: Wen-wu Press, 1963.
Tsou Heng 鄒衡. "Cheng-chou Shang ch'eng chi T'ang tu Po shuo" 鄭州商城即湯都亳說. *Wen-wu* 1978 (2): 69–71.
———. "Shih lun Cheng-chou hsin fa-hsien ti Yin Shang wen-hua yi-chih" 試論鄭州新發現的殷商文化遺址. *K'ao-ku Hsüeh-pao* 1956 (3): 77–103.
———. "Shih lun Yin hsü wen-hua fen-ch'i" 試論殷墟文化分期. *Pei-ching Ta-hsüeh Jen-wen Hsüeh-pao* 北京大學人文學報 1964 (4): 37–58; 1964 (5): 63–90.
Tsou Shu-wen 鄒樹文. "Shih-ching shu chi pien" 詩經黍稷辨. *Nung-shih Yen-chiu Chi-k'an* 農史研究集刊 2 (1960): 18–34.
T'ung En-cheng 童恩正, Chang Sheng-k'ai 張陞楷, and Ch'en Ching-ch'un 陳景春. "Kuan-yü shih-yung tien-tzu chi-suan-chi chui-ho Shang tai p'u chia sui-p'ien ti ch'u-pu pao-kao" 關于使用電子計算機綴合商代卜甲碎片的初步報告. *K'ao-ku* 1977 (3): 205–209.
T'ung Chu-ch'en 佟柱臣. "Ts'ung Erh-li-t'ou lei-hsing wen-hua shih t'an Chung-kuo ti kuo-chia ch'i-yüan wen-t'i" 從二里頭類型文化試談中國的國家起源問題. *Wen-wu* 1975 (6): 29–33.
Tung Tso-pin 董作賓. "An-yang Hou-chia-chuang ch'u-t'u chih chia ku wen-tzu 安陽侯家莊出土之甲骨文字. *T'ien-yeh k'ao-ku pao-kao* 田野考古報告

1 (1936): 91–165.

———. (Yen Yi-p'ing 嚴一萍, ed.) *Chia ku hsüeh liu-shih nien* 甲骨學六十年. Taipei: Yi-wen, 1965.

———. "Chia ku nien piao" 甲骨年表. *Bulletin of the Institute of History and Philology,* Academia Sinca, 2 (1930): 241–260. (Revised and enlarged edition, prepared by Hu Hou-hsüan 胡厚宣, published in 1937).

———. "Chia-ku wen tuan-tai yen-chiu li" 甲骨文斷代研究例. In *Papers Presented to Mr. Ts'ai Yüan-p'ei on His Sixty-fifth Birthday* pp. 323–424. 1933.

———. "Lun Shang jen yi shih jih wei ming" 論商人以十日爲名. *Ta-lu Tsa-chih* 2, no. 3 (1951): 6–10.

———. "Min-kuo shih-ch'i nien shih yüeh shih chüeh An-yang Hsiao-t'un pao-kao shu" 民國十七年十月試掘安陽小屯報告書. *An-yang fa-chüeh pao-kao* 1 (1929): 3–36.

———. "On the Method of Recording the 'Day' in the Yin Dynasty." *Annals of the Academia Sinica* 2 (1955): 51–58.

———. "P'u-tz'u chung pa yüeh yi-yu yüeh shih k'ao" 卜辭中八月乙酉月食考. *Ta-lu Tsa-chih T'e-k'an* 大陸雜誌特刊 1 (1952): 281–294.

———. "P'u-tz'u chung ti Po yü Shang" 卜辭中的亳與商. *Ta-lu Tsa-chih* 6 (1953): 8–12.

———. "Ta kuei ssu pan k'ao shih" 大龜四版考釋. *An-yang fa-chüeh pao-kao* 3 (1931): 423–441.

———. "Tu Wei-t'e-fu Shang tai p'u-tz'u chung ti ch'i-hsiang chi-lu" 讀魏特夫商代卜辭中的氣象紀錄. *Hua-hsi Ta-hsüeh Chung-huo Wen-hua Yen-chiu So Chi K'an* 華西大學中國文化研究所集刊 3 (1943): 81–88.

———. "Wu teng chüeh tsai Yin Shang" 五等爵在殷商. *Bulletin of the Institute of History and Philology,* Academia Sinica, 6 (1936): 413–430.

———. "Wu Wang fa Chòu nien yüeh jih chin k'ao" 武王伐紂年月日今考. *Bulletin of the College of Arts,* National Taiwan University, 3 (1951): 177–212.

———. *Yin hsü wen-tzu Chia pien* 殷虛文字甲編. Nanking: Institute of History and Philology, Academia Sinica, 1948.

———. *Yin hsü wen-tzu Yi pien* 殷虛文字乙編. Nanking: Institute of History and Philology, Academia Sinica, 1948–49.

———. *Yin hsü wen-tzu Yi pien hsü* 殷虛文字乙編序. Nanking: Institute of History and Philology, Academia Sinica, 1948.

———. *Yin li p'u* 殷曆譜. Li-chuang: Institute of History and Philology, Academia Sinica, 1945.

———. "*Yin li p'u* hou chi" 殷曆譜後記. *Bulletin of the Institute of History and Philology,* Academia Sinica, 13 (1948): 183–207.

———. "Yin tai li-chih ti hsin chiu liang p'ai" 殷代禮制的新舊兩派. *Ta-lu Tsa-chih* 6 (1953): 69–74.

———. "Yin tai ti niao shu" 殷代的鳥書. *Ta-lu Tsa-chih* 6 (1953): 345–347.

———. "Yin tai yüeh-shih k'ao" 殷代月食考. *Bulletin of the Institute of History and Philology,* Academia Sinica, 22 (1950): 139–160.

Turner, Christie. "Dental Evidence on the Origins of the Ainu and Japanese." *Science* 193 (1976): 911–913.

Umehara Sueji 梅原末治. *Inbo hatsugen mokki in'ei zuroku* 殷墓発現木器印影図録. Kyoto: Benridō, 1959.

———. *Kanan Anyō ihō* 河南安陽遺宝. Kyoto: Kobayashi, 1940.
———. *Kodōki keitai no kōkogakuteki kenkyū* 古銅器形態の考古学的研究. Kyoto: Tōhō Bunka Kenkyūjo, 1940.
———. *Tōa kōkogaku ronkō* 東亜考古学論考. Kyoto: Hoshino Shoten, 1944.
Vandermeersch, Leon. *Wangdao ou la voie Royale,* vol. 1. Publications de l'École Française d'Extrême-Orient, vol. 63. Paris: l'École Française d'Extrême-Orient, 1977.
Waley, Arthur, trans. *The Book of Songs.* New York: Grove Press, 1960, Evergreen edition.
Waltham, Clae. *Shu Ching* (a modernized edition of the translation by James Legge). Chicago: Henry Regnery Co., 1971.
Wan Chia-pao 萬家保. "Ts'ung Hsi-yin ts'un ti ts'an-chien t'an tao Chung-kuo tsao-ch'i ti ssu-chih kung-yeh" 從西陰村的蠶繭談到中國早期的絲織工業. *Ku-kung Chi-k'an* 故宮季刊 11, no. 3 (1977): 1–17.
Wan Kuo-ting 萬國鼎. "Ou-keng k'ao" 耦耕考. In *Nung-shih Yen-chiu Chi-k'an* 農史研究集刊, pp. 75–81. Peking: Science Press, 1959.
Wang, C. W. *The Forests of China.* Maria Moors Cabot Foundation Publications, no. 5. Cambridge, Mass.: Botanical Museum, Harvard University, 1961.
Wang Ch'eng-chao 王承祒. "Shih lun Yin tai ti 'hsi' 'ch'ieh' 'fu' ti she-hui shen-fen" 試論殷代的'奚'、'妾'、'及'的社會身份. *Pei-ching Ta-hsüeh Hsüeh-pao Jen-wen K'o-hsüeh* 北京大學學報人文科學 1955 (1): 111–118.
Wang Chia-yu 王家祐. "Chi Ssu-ch'uan P'eng hsien Chu-wa-chieh ch'u-t'u ti t'ung-ch'i" 記四川彭縣竹瓦街出土的銅器. *Wen-wu* 1961 (11): 28–31.
Wang Hsiang 王襄. *Fu shih Yin ch'i cheng wen* 簠室殷契徵文. Tientsin: Tientsin Museum, 1925.
Wang Hsiang 王湘. "An-hui Shou hsien shih-ch'ien yi-chih tiao-ch'a pao-kao" 安徽壽縣史前遺址調查報告. *Chung-kuo K'ao-ku Hsüeh-pao* 2 (1947): 179–250.
Wang Kuo-wei 王國維. "Ming-t'ang ch'in miao t'ung k'ao" 明堂寢廟通考. In *Kuan-t'ang chi lin* 觀堂集林, vol. 3, pp. 123–144. N. p. 1921. (1959 Peking, Chung-hua Shu-tien edition).
———. "Shuo Po" 說亳, In *Kuan-t'ang chi lin,* vol. 12, 1921.
———. "Shuo Shang" 說商, In *Kuan-t'ang chi lin,* vol. 12, 1921.
———. "Shuo tzu Hsieh chih Ch'eng T'ang pa ch'ien" 說自契至成湯八遷. In *Kuan-t'ang chi lin,* vol. 12, 1921.
———. "Tsu mou fu mou hsiung mou" 祖某父某兄某. In *Kuan-t'ang chi lin,* vol. 9, 1921.
———. "Yin Chou chih-tu lun" 殷周制度論. In *Kuan-t'ang chi lin,* vol. 10, 1921.
———. "Yin hsü p'u-tz'u chung so chien ti ming k'ao" 殷墟卜辭中所見地名考. *Hsüeh-t'ang Ts'ung-k'o* 雪堂叢刻, vol. 11. 1915.
———. "Yin p'u-tz'u chung so chien hsien kung hsien wang k'ao" 殷卜辭中所見先公先王考, and "hsü k'ao" 續考. In *Kuan-t'ang chi lin,* vol. 9, 1921.
Wang Ning-sheng 汪寧生. "Ou keng hsin chieh" 耦耕新解. *Wen-wu* 1977 (4): 74–78.
Wang Pao-te 王保德. "Wu Wang fa Chòu tu yü Meng-chin ti nien-tai k'ao" 武王伐紂渡于孟津的年代考. *Chung-yüan Wen-hsien* 中原文獻 6, no. 2

(1974): 12–17.

Wang Shih-to 汪士鐸. *Shui-ching-chu t'u* 水經注圖. Ch'ang-sha, 1861.

Wang Yü-che 王玉哲. "Shih shu Yin tai ti nu-li chih-tu ho kuo-chia ti hsing-ch'eng" 試述殷代的奴隸制度和國家的形成. *Li-shih Chiao-hsüeh* 歷史教學 1958 (9).

Wang Yü-hsin 王宇信, Chang Yung-shan 張永山, and Yang Sheng-nan 楊升南. "Shih lun Yin hsü wu-hao mu ti 'Fu Hao'" 試論殷墟五號墓的'婦好'. *K'ao-ku Hsüeh-pao* 1977 (2): 1–22.

Wang Yü-hsin 王宇信, and Ch'en Shao-ti 陳紹棣. "Kuan-yü Chiang-su T'ung-shan Ch'iu-wan Shang tai chi-ssu yi-chih" 關于江蘇銅山丘灣商代祭祀遺址. *Wen-wu* 1973 (12): 55–58.

Waterbury, Florance. *Early Chinese Symbols and Literature: Vestiges and Speculations*. New York: E. Weyhe, 1942.

Wayre, Philip. *A Guide to the Pheasants of the World*. London: Country Life, 1969.

Wei Ch'in 魏勤. "Ts'ung Ta-wen-k'ou wen-hua mu-tsang k'an ssu-yu-chih ti ch'i-yüan" 從大汶口文化墓葬看私有制的起源. *K'ao-ku* 1975 (5): 264–270.

Wheatley, Paul. *The Pivot of the Four Quarters*. Chicago: Aldine, 1972.

———. "Review of K. C. Chang, *Early Chinese Civilization*." *Journal of Asian Studies* 36 (1977): 543–545.

Williamson, Robert W. *The Social and Political Systems of Central Polynesia*. Cambridge, Eng.: Cambridge University Press, 1924.

Wittfogel, Karl A. "Meterological Records from the Divination Inscriptions of Shang." *Geographical Review* 30 (1940): 110–131.

Wright, Henry. "Recent Research on the Origin of the State." *Annual Review of Anthropology* 6 (1977): 379–397.

Wu Chen-lu 吳振彔. "Pao-te hsien hsin fa-hsien ti Yin tai ch'ing-t'ung-ch'i" 保德縣新發現的殷代青銅器. *Wen-wu* 1972 (4): 62–64.

Wu Ch'i-ch'ang 吳其昌. "P'u-tz'u so-chien Yin hsien kung hsien wang san hsü k'ao" 卜辭所見殷先公先王三續考. *Yen-ching Hsüeh-pao* 14 (1933): 1–58.

Wu Chin-ting 吳金鼎. "Chai chi Hsiao-t'un yi hsi chih san ch'u hsiao fa-chüeh" 摘記小屯迤西之三處小發掘. *An-yang fa-chüeh pao-kao* 4 (1933): 627–633.

———. "Kao-ching-t'ai-tzu san chung t'ao yeh kai lun" 高井台子三種陶業概論. *T'ien-yeh k'ao-ku pao-kao* 1 (1936): 201–211.

Wu Hsien-wen 伍獻文. "Chi Yin hsü ch'u-t'u chih yü ku" 記殷墟出土之魚骨. *Chung-kuo K'ao-ku Hsüeh-pao* 4 (1949): 139–143.

Wu Ta-cheng 吳大澂. *Shuo-wen ku chou pu* 說文古籀補. N. p., 1885.

WW (*Wen-wu*). "An-hui Chia-shan hsien Po-kang-yin-ho ch'u-t'u ti ssu-chien Shang tai t'ung-ch'i" 安徽嘉山縣泊崗引河出土的四件商代銅器. *Wen-wu* 1965 (7): 23–25.

———. "Cheng-chou fa-hsien ti Shang tai chih t'ao yi-chi" 鄭州發現的商代製陶遺跡. *Wen-wu* 1955 (9): 64–66.

———. "Cheng-chou hsin ch'u-t'u ti Shang tai ch'ien-ch'i ta t'ung ting" 鄭州新出土的商代前期大銅鼎. *Wen-wu* 1975 (6): 64–68.

———. "Cheng-chou Lo-ta-miao Shang tai yi-chih shih chüeh chien pao" 鄭州洛達廟商代遺址試掘簡報. *Wen-wu* 1957 (10): 48–51.

———. "Cheng-chou Pai-chia-chuang Yi-chih fa-chüeh chien pao" 鄭州白家

莊遺址發掘簡報. *Wen-wu* 1956 (4): 3–5.
———. "Cheng-chou Shang ch'eng yi-chih nei fa-hsien Shang tai hang-t'u t'ai-chi ho nu-li t'ou ku" 鄭州商城遺址内發現商代夯土台基和奴隸頭骨. *Wen-wu* 1974 (9): 1–2.
———. "Cheng-chou Shang tai ch'eng-chih shih chüeh chien pao" 鄭州商代城址試掘簡報. *Wen-wu* 1977 (1): 21–31.
———. "Cheng-chou Shang tai yi-chih" 鄭州商代遺址. *Wen-wu* 1975 (5): 91–92.
———. "Cheng-chou shih Jen-min kung-yüan ti erh-shih-wu hao Shang tai mu-tsang ch'ing-li chien pao" 鄭州市人民公園第二十五號商代墓葬清理簡報. *Wen-wu* 1954 (12): 25–27.
———. "Cheng-chou shih Ming-kung-lu hsi ts'e fa-hsien Shang tai chih t'ao kung-ch'ang fang-chi teng yi-chih" 鄭州市銘功路西側發現商代製陶工場房基等遺址. *Wen-wu* 1956 (1): 64.
———. "Cheng-chou shih Pai-chia-chuang Shang tai mu-tsang fa-chüeh chien pao" 鄭州市白家莊商代墓葬發掘簡報. *Wen-wu* 1955 (10): 24–42.
———. "Cheng-chou shih Yin Shang yi-chih ti-ts'eng kuan-hsi chieh-shao" 鄭州市殷商遺址地層關係介紹. *Wen-wu* 1954 (12): 86–93.
———. "Cheng-chou ti wu wen-wu ch'ü ti yi hsiao ch'ü fa-chüeh chien pao" 鄭州第五文物區第一小區發掘簡報. *Wen-wu* 1956 (5): 33–40.
———. "Chi-nan Ta-hsin-chuang Shang tai yi-chih k'an-ch'a chi yao" 濟南大辛莊商代遺址勘查紀要. *Wen-wu* 1959 (11): 8–9.
———. "Chiang-hsi Ch'ing-chiang Wu-ch'eng Shang tai yi-chih fa-chüeh chien pao" 江西清江吳城商代遺址發掘簡報. *Wen-wu* 1975 (7): 51–71.
———. "Chiang-hsi ti-ch'ü t'ao-tz'u-ch'i chi-ho-hsing p'ai-yin wen-yang tsung shu" 江西地區陶瓷器幾何形拍印紋樣綜述. *Wen-wu* 1977 (9): 40–57.
———. "Chieh-shao chi chien ts'ung fei-t'ung chung chien hsüan ch'u-lai ti chung-yao wen-wu" 介紹幾件從廢銅中檢選出來的重要文物. *Wen-wu* 1960 (3): 75.
———. "Chin nien Chiang-hsi ch'u-t'u ti Shang tai ch'ing-t'ung-ch'i" 近年江西出土的商代青銅器. *Wen-wu* 1977 (9): 58–63.
———. "Fu-feng Pai-chia-yao shui-k'u ch'u-t'u ti Shang Chou wen-hua" 扶風白家窰水庫出土的商周文化. *Wen-wu* 1977 (12): 84–86.
———. "Ho-nan Hsi-ch'uan Hsia-wang-kang yi-chih ti shih chüeh" 河南淅川下王崗遺址的試掘. *Wen-wu* 1972 (10): 13–14.
———. "Ho-pei Kao-ch'eng hsien T'ai-hsi ts'un Shang tai yi-chih 1973 nien ti chung-yao fa-hsien" 河北藁城縣台西村商代遺址1973年的重要發現. *Wen-wu* 1974 (8): 42–49.
———. "Hsing-t'ai Chia ts'un Shang tai yi-chih shih chüeh chien pao" 邢台賈村商代遺址試掘簡報. *Wen-wu* 1958 (10): 29–31.
———. "Hsing-t'ai Shang tai yi-chih chung ti t'ao yao" 邢台商代遺址中的陶窰. *Wen-wu* 1956 (12): 53–54.
———. "Hsing-t'ai shih fa-hsien Shang tai yi-chih" 邢台市發現商代遺址. *Wen-wu* 1956 (9): 70.
———. "Hsing-t'ai Yin-kuo ts'un Shang tai yi-chih chi Chan-kuo mu-tsang shih chüeh chien pao" 邢台尹郭村商代遺址及戰國墓葬試掘簡報. *Wen-wu* 1960 (4): 42–45.

———. "Hu-pei Ch'ung-yang ch'u-t'u yi-chien t'ung ku" 湖北崇陽出土一件銅鼓. *Wen-wu* 1978 (4): 94.
——— "Je-ho Ling-yüan hsien Hai-tao-ying-tzu-ts'ung fa-hsien ti ku-tai ch'ing-t'ung-ch'i" 熱河凌源縣海島營子村發現的古代青銅器. *Wen-wu* 1955 (8): 16–27.
———. "Kao-ch'eng T'ai-hsi Shang tai yi-chih fa-hsien ti t'ao-ch'i wen-tzu" 藁城台西商代遺址發現的陶器文字. *Wen-wu* 1974 (8): 50–53.
———. "Lin-t'ung Chiang-chai hsin-shih-ch'i shih-tai yi-chih ti hsin fa-hsien" 臨潼姜寨新石器時代遺址的新發現. *Wen-wu* 1975 (8): 82–83.
———. "P'an-lung-ch'eng Shang tai Erh-li-kang ch'i ti ch'ing-t'ung-ch'i" 盤龍城商代二里岡期的青銅器. *Wen-wu* 1976 (2): 26–41.
———. "P'an-lung-ch'eng yi-chiu-ch'i-ssu nien tu t'ien-yeh k'ao-ku chi yao" 盤龍城一九七四年度田野考古紀要. *Wen-wu* 1976 (2): 5–15.
———. "Pei-ching shih P'ing-ku hsien fa-hsien Shang tai mu-tsang" 北京市平谷縣發現商代墓葬. *Wen-wu* 1977 (11): 1–8.
———. "Shan-hsi sheng Ch'i-shan hsien fa-hsien Shang tai t'ung-ch'i" 陝西省岐山縣發現商代銅器. *Wen-wu* 1977 (12): 86–87.
———. "Shan-hsi sheng shih nien lai ti wen-wu k'ao-ku hsin shou-hu" 山西省十年來的文物考古新收穫. *Wen-wu* 1972 (4): 1–4.
———. "Shan-hsi Shih-lou hsien Erh-lang-p'o ch'u-t'u Shang Chou ch'ing-t'ung-ch'i" 山西石樓縣二郎坡出土商周青銅器. *Wen-wu* 1958 (1): 36.
———. "Shan-hsi Shih-lou hsin cheng-chi tao ti chi-chien Shang tai ch'ing-t'ung-ch'i" 山西石樓新徵集到的幾件商代青銅器. *Wen-wu* 1976 (2): 94.
———. "Shan-hsi Shih-lou Yi-tieh Hui-p'ing fa-hsien Shang tai ping-ch'i" 山西石樓義牒會坪發現商代兵器. *Wen-wu* 1974 (2): 69.
———. "Shan-hsi Sui-te Yen-t'ou-ts'un fa-hsien yi-p'i chiao-ts'ang Shang tai t'ung-ch'i" 陝西綏德墕頭村發現一批窖藏商代銅器. *Wen-wu* 1975 (2) 82–83.
———. "Shan-tung Ch'ang-ch'ing ch'u-t'u ti ch'ing-t'ung-ch'i" 山東長清出土的青銅器. *Wen-wu* 1964 (4): 41–47.
———. "Shan-tung Ts'ang-shan hsien ch'u-t'u ch'ing-t'ung-ch'i" 山東蒼山縣出土青銅器. *Wen-wu* 1965 (7): 27–30.
———. "Shan-tung Tsou hsien yu fa-hsien Shang tai t'ung-ch'i" 山東鄒縣又發現商代銅器. *Wen-wu* 1974 (1): 77.
———. "Shan-tung Yi-tu Su-fu-t'un ti-yi-hao nu-li hsün-tsang mu" 山東益都蘇埠屯第一號奴隸殉葬墓. *Wen-wu* 1972 (8): 17–30.
———. "Shih-lou hsien fa-hsien ku-tai t'ung-ch'i" 石樓縣發現古代銅器. *Wen-wu* 1959 (3): 71–72.
———. "T'an-shih-ssu nien-tai ts'e-ting pao-kao, hsü-yi" 碳十四年代測定報告, 續一. *Wen-wu* 1978 (5): 75–76.
———. "T'ien-chin shih hsin shou-chi ti Shang Chou ch'ing-t'ung-ch'i" 天津市新收集的商周青銅器. *Wen-wu* 1964 (9): 33.
———. "Wen Hsien ch'u-t'u ti Shang tai t'ung-ch'i" 溫縣出土的商代銅器. *Wen-wu* 1975 (2): 88–91.
———. "Yeh-t'i shan-li-fa t'an-shih-ssu nien-tai ts'e-ting" 液體閃爍法碳十四年代測定. *Wen-wu* 1978 (5): 70–74.
———. "Yi-chiu-liu-san nien Hu-pei Huang-p'i P'an-lung-ch'eng Shang tai

yi-chih ti fa-chüeh" 一九六三年湖北黃陂盤龍城商代遺址的發掘. *Wen-wu* 1976 (1): 49–55.

———. "Yi nien lai Cheng-chou shih ti wen-wu tiao-ch'a fa-chüeh kung-tso" 一年來鄭州市的文物調查發掘工作. *Wen-wu* 1954 (4): 35–39.

Yang Chün-shih 楊君實. "K'ang keng yü Hsia hui" 康庚與夏諱. *Ta-lu Tsa-chih* 20, no. 3 (1960): 83–88.

Yang Chung-chien (see Young, C.C.).

Yang Hsi-chang 楊錫璋 and Yang Pao-ch'eng 楊寶成. "Ts'ung Shang tai chi-ssu k'eng k'an Shang tai nu-li she-hui ti jen sheng" 從商代祭祀坑看商代奴隸社會的人牲. *K'ao-ku* 1977 (1): 13–19.

Yang Hsi-mei 楊希枚. "Ho-nan An-yang Yin hsü mu-tsang chung jen-t'i ku-ko ti cheng-li ho yen-chiu" 河南安陽殷墟墓葬中人體骨骼的整理和研究. *Bulletin of the Institute of History and Philology*, Academia Sinica, 42 (1970): 231–265.

———. "Lien ming chih yü p'u-tz'u Shang wang miao hao wen-t'i" 聯名制與卜辭商王廟號問題. *Bulletin of the Institute of Ethnology*, Academia Sinica, 21 (1966): 17–39.

———. "A Preliminary Report of Human Crania Excavated from Hou-chia-chuang and Other Shang Dynasty Sites at An-yang, Honan, North China." *Annual Bulletin of the China Council for East Asian Studies* 5 (1966): 1–13.

Yang Hung-hsün 楊鴻勛. "Ts'ung P'an-lung-ch'eng Shang tai kung-tien yi-chih t'an Chung-kuo kung-t'ing chien-chu fa-chan ti chi ko wen-t'i" 從盤龍城商代宮殿遺址談中國宮廷建築發展的幾個問題. *Wen-wu* 1976 (2): 16–25.

Yang Lien-sheng 楊聯陞. "Historical Notes on the Chinese World Order." In *The Chinese World Order*, J. K. Fairbank, ed., pp. 20–23. Cambridge, Mass.: Harvard University Press, 1968.

Yang Shang-k'uei 楊尚奎. *Chung-kuo ku-tai she-hui yü ku-tai ssu-hsiang yen-chiu* 中國古代社會與古代思想研究. Shanghai: Jenmin Press, 1962.

Yang Shu-ta 楊樹達. *Chi-wei-chü tu-shu chi* 積微居讀書記. Peking: Chung-hua Shu-chü, 1962.

———. *Nai-lin-ch'ing chia wen shuo* 耐林廎甲文説. Shanghai: Ch'ün-lien Press, 1954.

Yen Wan 晏琬. "Pei-ching Liao-ning ch'u-t'u t'ung-ch'i yü Chou ch'u ti Yen" 北京遼寧出土銅器與周初的燕. *K'ao-ku* 1975 (5): 274–279.

Yen Yi-p'ing 嚴一萍. *Chia ku hsüeh* 甲骨學. Taipei: Yi-wen, 1978.

———. "Chia-ku wen tuan-tai yen-chiu hsin li" 甲骨文斷代研究新例. In *Papers Presented to Mr. Tung Tso-pin on His Sixty-fifth Birthday*, pp. 483–549. Institute of History and Philology, Academia Sinica, 1961.

———. "Hsia Shang Chou wen-hua yi t'ung k'ao" 夏商周文化異同考. *Ta-lu Tsa-chih T'e-k'an* 1 (1952): 387–421.

———. "Pa yüeh yi-yu yüeh-shih fu chia ti p'in-ho yü k'ao-cheng ti ching-kuo" 八月乙酉月食腹甲的拼合與考証的經過. *Ta-lu Tsa-chih* 9, no. 1, (1954): 17–21.

Yen Yün 燕耘. "Shang tai p'u-tz'u chung ti yeh chu shih liao" 商代卜辭中的冶鑄史料. *K'ao-ku* 1973 (5): 299.

Yin Chih-yi 殷之彝. "Shan-tung Yi-tu Su-fu-t'un mu-ti ho 'Ya Ch'ou' t'ung-ch'i'' 山東益都蘇埠屯墓地和'亞醜'銅器. *K'ao-ku Hsüeh-pao* 1977 (2): 23–33.

Yin Wei-chang 殷瑋璋. ''Erh-li-t'ou wen-hua t'an t'ao'' 二里頭文化探討. *K'ao-ku* 1978 (1): 1–4.

Yoshida Mitsukuni 吉田光邦. ''Indai gijutsu shōki'' 殷代技術小記. *Tōhōgakuhō (Kyoto)* 23 (1953): 175–178.

Young, C. C. 楊鍾健 [Yang Chung-chien]. ''Budorcao, a New Element in the Proto-historic An-yang Fauna of China.'' *American Journal of Science* 246 (1948): 157–164.

——— and Liu Tung-sheng 劉東生. ''An-yang Yin hsü chih pu-ju tung-wu ch'ün pu yi'' 安陽殷墟之哺乳動物羣補遺. *Chung-kuo K'ao-ku Hsüeh-pao* 4 (1949): 145–153.

Yü Ching-jang 于景讓. ''Shu chi su liang yü kao-liang'' 黍稷粟粱與高粱. *Ta-lu Tsa-chih* 13 (1956): 67–76, 115–120.

Yü Chung-hang 于中航. ''Ta-wen-k'ou wen-hua ho yüan-shih she-hui ti chieh-t'i'' 大汶口文化和原始社會的解體. *Wen-wu* 1976 (5): 64–73.

Yü Hsing-wu 于省吾. ''Kuan-yü ku wen-tzu yen-chiu ti jo-kan wen-t'i'' 關於古文字研究的若干問題. *Wen-wu* 1973 (2): 32–35.

———. ''Lüeh lun t'u-t'eng yü tsung-chiao ch'i-yüan ho Hsia Shang t'u-t'eng'' 略論圖騰與宗教起源和夏商圖騰. *Li-shih Yen-chiu* 1959 (10): 60–69.

———. ''Shang tai ti ku lei tso-wu'' 商代的穀類作物. *Tung-pei Jen-min Ta-hsüeh Jen-wen K'o-hsüeh Hsüeh-pao* 東北人民大學人文科學學報 1957 (1): 81–107.

———. ''Ts'ung chia-ku wen k'an Shang tai she-hui hsing-chih'' 從甲骨文看商代社會性質. *Tung-pei Jen-min Ta-hsüeh Jen-wen K'o-hsüeh Hsüeh-pao* 1957 (2/3): 97–136.

———. ''Ts'ung chia-ku wen k'an Shang tai ti nung-t'ien k'en-chih'' 從甲骨文看商代的農田墾殖. *K'ao-ku* 1972 (4): 40–41, 45.

Yü Wei-ch'ao 俞偉超. ''T'ung-shan Ch'iu-wan Shang tai she ssu yi-chi ti t'ui-ting'' 銅山丘灣商代社祀遺迹的推定. *K'ao-ku* 1973 (5): 296–298.

Index